Richard Doddridge Blackmore

The Maid of Sker

Richard Doddridge Blackmore

The Maid of Sker

ISBN/EAN: 9783337138936

Printed in Europe, USA, Canada, Australia, Japan

Cover: Foto ©ninafisch / pixelio.de

More available books at **www.hansebooks.com**

THE MAID OF SKER.

BY

R. D. BLACKMORE,

AUTHOR OF
'LORNA DOONE,' 'CLARA VAUGHAN,' AND 'CRADOCK NOWELL.'

Ἔῤῥε, θεοῖσίν τ' ἐχθρὲ, καὶ ἀνθρωποισιν ἄπιστε,
Ψυχρῳ ὃς ἐν κόλπῳ ποίκιλον ἔχες ὄφιν.

NEW EDITION,

WITH A FRONTISPIECE.

WILLIAM BLACKWOOD AND SONS
EDINBURGH AND LONDON
MDCCCXCIII

CONTENTS

CHAP.		PAGE
I.	FISHERMAN DAVY A FISH OUT OF WATER,	1
II.	HUNGER DRIVES HIM A-FISHING,	3
III.	THE FISH ARE AS HUNGRY AS HE IS,	7
IV.	HE LANDS AN UNEXPECTED FISH,	12
V.	A LITTLE ORPHAN MERMAID,	15
VI.	FINDS A HOME OF SOME SORT,	21
VII.	BOAT *VERSUS* BARDIE,	27
VIII.	CHILDREN WILL BE CHILDREN,	32
IX.	SAND-HILLS TURNED TO SAND-HOLES,	38
X.	UNDER THE ROCK,	44
XI.	A WRECKER WRECKED,	49
XII.	HOW TO SELL FISH,	57
XIII.	THE CORONER AND THE CORONET,	64
XIV.	IN ACCORDANCE WITH THE EVIDENCE,	70
XV.	A VERDICT ON THE JURY,	76
XVI.	TRUTH LIES SOMETIMES IN A WELL,	81
XVII.	FOR A LITTLE CHANGE OF AIR,	89
XVIII.	PUBLIC APPROBATION,	97
XIX.	A CRAFT BEYOND THE LAW,	106
XX.	CONFIDENTIAL INTERCOURSE,	112
XXI.	CROSS-EXAMINATION,	119
XXII.	ANOTHER DISAPPOINTMENT,	125
XXIII.	INTO GOOD SOCIETY,	131
XXIV.	SOUND INVESTMENTS,	137
XXV.	A LONG GOOD-BYE,	145
XXVI.	BRAUNTON BURROWS,	151
XXVII.	A FINE SPECTACLE,	158
XXVIII.	SOMETHING ABOUT HIM,	164
XXIX.	A VISIT TO A PARSON.	171
XXX.	ON DUTY,	182
XXXI.	TWO LOVERS,	189

XXXII.	AMONG THE SAVAGES,	194
XXXIII.	IN A STATE OF NATURE,	203
XXXIV.	WAITING AND LEARNING,	212
XXXV.	THE POLITE FERRYMAN,	220
XXXVI.	UNDER FAIRER AUSPICES,	227
XXXVII.	TWO POOR CHILDREN,	234
XXXVIII.	A FINE OLD GENTLEMAN,	241
XXXIX.	NOTICE TO QUIT,	250
XL.	FORCIBLE EJECTMENT,	257
XLI.	THE RIGHT MAN IN THE RIGHT PLACE,	267
XLII.	THE LITTLE MAID AND THE MIDSHIPMAN,	276
XLIII.	A FINE PRICE FOR BARDIE,	283
XLIV.	PROVIDES FOR EDUCATION,	292
XLV.	INTRODUCES A REAL HERO,	298
XLVI.	AFTER SEVEN YEARS,	305
XLVII.	MISCHIEF IN A HOUSEHOLD,	312
XLVIII.	A BREATHLESS DISINTERMENT,	320
XLIX.	ONE WHO HAS INTERRED HIMSELF,	327
L.	A BRAVE MAN RUNS AWAY,	334
LI.	TRIPLE EDUCATION,	341
LII.	GREAT MARCH OF INTELLECT,	347
LIII.	BEATING UP FOR THE NAVY,	356
LIV.	TAMING OF THE SAVAGES,	368
LV.	UPON FOREIGN SERVICE,	374
LVI.	EXILES OF SOCIETY,	380
LVII.	MANY WEAK MOMENTS,	387
LVIII.	MORE HASTE, LESS SPEED,	398
LIX.	IN A ROCKY BOWER,	403
LX.	NELSON AND THE NILE,	411
LXI.	A SAVAGE DEED,	415
LXII.	A RASH YOUNG CAPTAIN,	421
LXIII.	POLLY AT HOME,	430
LXIV	SUSAN QUITE ACQUITS HERSELF,	438
LXV	SO DOES POOR OLD DAVY,	447
LXVI.	THE MAID AT LAST IS "DENTIFIED,"	453
LXVII.	DOG EATS DOG,	458
LXVIII.	THE OLD PITCHER AT THE WELL AGAIN,	465

THE MAID OF SKER.

CHAPTER I.

FISHERMAN DAVY A FISH OUT OF WATER.

I AM but an ancient fisherman upon the coast of Glamorganshire, with work enough of my own to do, and trouble enough of my own to heed, in getting my poor living. Yet no peace there is for me among my friends and neighbours, unless I will set to and try—as they bid me twice a-day perhaps—whether I cannot tell the rights of a curious adventure which it pleased Providence should happen, off and on, amidst us, now for a good many years, and with many ins and outs to it. They assure me, also, that all good people who can read and write for ten, or it may be twenty, miles around the place I live in, will buy my book—if I can make it—at a higher price, perhaps, per lb., than they would give me even for sewin, which are the very best fish I catch: and hence provision may be found for the old age and infirmities, now gaining upon me, every time I try to go out fishing.

In this encouragement and prospect I have little faith, knowing how much more people care about what they eat than what they read. Nevertheless I will hope for the best, especially as my evenings now are very long and wearisome; and I was counted a hopeful scholar, fifty years agone perhaps, in our village school here—not to mention the Royal Navy; and most of all, because a very wealthy gentleman, whose name will appear in this story, has promised to pay all expenses, and £50 down (if I do it well), and to leave me the profit, if any.

Notwithstanding this, the work of writing must be very dull

to me, after all the change of scene, and the open air and sea, and the many sprees ashore, and the noble fights with Frenchmen, and the power of oaths that made me jump so in his Majesty's navy. God save the King, and Queen, and members of the Royal Family, be they as many as they will—and they seem, in faith, to be manifold. But His power is equal to it all, if they will but try to meet Him.

However, not to enter upon any view of politics—all of which are far beyond the cleverest hand at a bait among us—I am inditing of a thing very plain and simple, when you come to understand it; yet containing a little strangeness, and some wonder, here and there, and apt to move good people's grief at the wrongs we do one another. Great part of it fell under mine own eyes, for a period of a score of years, or something thereabout. My memory still is pretty good; but if I contradict myself, or seem to sweep beyond my reach, or in any way to meddle with things which I had better have let alone, as a humble man and a Christian, I pray you to lay the main fault thereof on the badness of the times, and the rest upon human nature. For I have been a roving man, and may have gathered much of evil from contact with my fellow-men, although by origin meant for good. In this I take some blame to myself; for if I had polished my virtue well, the evil could not have stuck to it. Nevertheless, I am, on the whole, pretty well satisfied with myself; hoping to be of such quality as the Lord prefers to those perfect creatures with whom He has no trouble at all, and therefore no enjoyment.

But sometimes, taking up a book, I am pestered with a troop of doubts; not only about my want of skill, and language, and experience, but chiefly because I never have been a man of consummate innocence, excellence, and high wisdom, such as all these writers are, if we go by their own opinions.

Now, when I plead among my neighbours, at the mouth of the old well, all the above, my sad shortcomings, and my own strong sense of them (which perhaps is somewhat over-strong), they only pat me on the back, and smile at one another, and make a sort of coughing noise, according to my bashfulness. And then if I look pleased (which for my life I cannot help doing), they wink, as it were, at one another, and speak up like this:—

"Now, Davy, you know better. You think yourself at least as good as any one of us, Davy, and likely far above us all. Therefore, Davy the fisherman, out with all you have to say, without any French palaver. You have a way of telling things so that we can see them."

With this, and with that, and most of all with hinting about a Frenchman, they put me on my mettle, so that I sit upon the side-stones of the old-well gallery (which are something like the companion-rail of a fore-and-after), and gather them around me, with the householders put foremost, according to their income, and the children listening between their legs; and thus I begin, but never end, the tale I now begin to you, and perhaps shall never end it.

CHAPTER II.

HUNGER DRIVES HIM A-FISHING.

In the summer of the year 1782, I, David Llewellyn, of Newton-Nottage, fisherman and old sailor, was in great distress and trouble, more than I like to tell you. My dear wife (a faithful partner for eight-and-twenty years, in spite of a very quick temper) was lately gone to a better world; and I missed her tongue and her sharp look-out at almost every corner. Also my son (as fine a seaman as ever went aloft), after helping Lord Rodney to his great victory over Grass the Frenchman, had been lost in a prize-ship called the Tonner, of 54 guns and 500 Crappos, which sank with all hands on her way home to Spithead, under Admiral Graves. His young wife (who had been sent to us to see to, with his blessing) no sooner heard of this sad affair as in the Gazette reported, and his pay that week stopped on her, but she fell into untimely travail, and was dead ere morning. So I buried my wife and daughter-in-law, and lost all chance to bury my son, between two Bridgend market-days.

Now this is not very much, of course, compared with the troubles some people have. But I had not been used to this matter, except in case of a messmate; and so I was greatly broken down, and found my eyes so weak of a morning, that I would not be seen out of doors, almost.

The only one now to keep a stir or sound of life in my little cottage, which faces to the churchyard, was my orphan grandchild "Bunny," daughter of my son just drowned, and his only child that we knew of. Bunny was a rare strong lass, five years old about then, I think; a stout and hearty-feeding child, able to chew every bit of her victuals, and mounting a fine rosy colour, and eyes as black as Archangel pitch.

One day, when I was moping there, all abroad about my bearings, and no better than water-ballasted, the while I looked at my wife's new broom, now carrying cobweb try-sails, this little Bunny came up to me as if she had a boarding-pike, and sprang into the netting hammocks of the best black coat I wore.

"Grand-da!" she said, and looked to know in what way I would look at her; "Grand-da, I must have sumkin more to eat."

"Something more to eat!" I cried, almost with some astonishment, well as I knew her appetite; for the child had eaten a barley-loaf, and two pig's feet, and a dog-fish.

"Yes, more; more bexfass, grand-da." And though she had not the words to tell, she put her hands in a way that showed me she ought to have more solid food. I could not help looking sadly at her, proud as I was of her appetite. But, recovering in a minute or two, I put a good face upon it.

"My dear, and you shall have more," I said; "only take your feet out of my pocket. Little heart have I for fishing, God knows; but a-fishing I will go this day, if mother Jones will see to you."

For I could not leave her alone quite yet, although she was a brave little maid, and no fire now was burning. But within a child's trot from my door, and down toward the sandhills, was that famous ancient well of which I spoke just now, dedicate to St John the Baptist, where they used to scourge themselves. The village church stood here, they say, before the inroad of the sand; and the water was counted holy. How that may be, I do not know; but the well is very handy. It has a little grey round tower of stone domed over the heart of it, to which a covered way goes down, with shallow steps irregular. If it were not for this plan, the sand would whelm the whole of it over; even as it has overwhelmed all the departure of the spring, and the cottages once surrounding it. Down these steps the children go, each with a little brown pitcher, holding hands and groping at the sides, as they begin to feel darker. And what with the sand beneath their feet, and the narrowing of the roof above, and the shadows moving round them, and the doubt where the water begins or ends (which nobody knows at any time), it is much but what some little maid tumbles in, and the rest have to pull her out again.

For this well has puzzled all the country, and all the men of great learning, being as full of contrariety as a maiden courted. It comes and goes, in a manner, against the coming and going of the sea, which is only half a mile from it; and twice in a day it is many feet deep, and again not as many inches. And the water is so crystal-clear, that down in the dark it is like a dream. Some people say that John the Baptist had nothing to do with the making of it, because it was made before his time by the ancient family of De Sandford, who once owned all the manors here. In this, however, I place no faith, having read my Bible to better purpose than to believe that John Baptist was the sort of man to claim anything, least of all any water, unless he came honestly by it.

In either case, it is very pretty to see the children round the entrance on a summer afternoon, when they are sent for water. They are all a little afraid of it, partly because of its maker's name, and his having his head on a charger, and partly on account of its curious ways, and the sand coming out of its "nostrils" when first it begins to flow.

That day with which I begin my story, Mrs Jones was good enough to take charge of little Bunny; and after getting ready to start, I set the thong of our latch inside, so that none but neighbours who knew the trick could enter our little cottage (or rather "mine" I should say now); and thus with conger-rod, and prawn-net, and a long pole for the bass, and a junk of pressed tobacco, and a lump of barley-bread, and a maybird stuffed with onions (just to refine the fishiness), away I set for a long-shore day, upon as dainty a summer morn as ever shone out of the heavens.

"Fisherman Davy" (as they call me all around our parts) was fifty and two years of age, I believe, that very same July, and with all my heart I wish that he were as young this very day. For I never have found such call to enter into the affairs of another world, as to forget my business here, or press upon Providence impatiently for a more heavenly state of things. People may call me worldly-minded for cherishing such a view of this earth; and perhaps it is not right of me. However, I can put up with it, and be in no unkindly haste to say "good-bye" to my neighbours. For, to my mind, such a state of seeking, as many amongst us do even boast of, is, unless in a bad cough or a perilous calenture, a certain proof of curiosity displeasing to our Maker, and I might even say of fickleness degrading to a true Briton.

The sun came down upon my head, so that I thought of bygone days, when I served under Captain Howe, or Sir Edward Hawke, and used to stroll away upon leave, with half a hundred Jacks ashore, at Naples, or in Bermudas, or wherever the luck might happen. Now, however, was no time for me to think of strolling, because I could no longer live at the expense of the Government, which is the highest luck of all, and full of noble dignity. Things were come to such a push that I must either work or starve; and could I but recall the past, I would stroll less in the days gone by. A pension of one and eightpence farthing for the weeks I was alive (being in right of a heavy wound in capture of the Bellona, Frenchman of two-and-thirty guns, by his Majesty's frigate Vesta, under Captain Hood) was all I had to hold on by, in support of myself and Bunny, except the slippery fish that come and go as Providence orders them. She had sailed from Martinique, when luckily we fell in with her; and I never shall forget the fun, and the five hours at close quarters. We could see the powder on the other fellows' faces while they were training their guns at us, and we showed them, with a slap, our noses, which they never contrived to hit. She carried heavier metal than ours, and had sixty more men to work it, and therefore we were obliged at last to capture her by boarding. I, like a fool, was the first that leaped into her mizen-chains, without looking before me, as ought to have been. The Frenchmen came too fast upon me, and gave me more than I bargained for.

Thus it happened that I fell off, in the very prime of life and strength, from an able-bodied seaman and captain of the foretop to a sort of lurcher along shore, and a man who must get his own living with nets and rods and suchlike. For that very beautiful fight took place in the year 1759, before I was thirty years old, and before his present most gracious Majesty came to the throne of England. And inasmuch as a villanous Frenchman made at me with a cutlash, and a power of blue oaths (taking a nasty advantage of me, while I was yet entangled), and thumped in three of my ribs before a kind Providence enabled me to relieve him of his head at a blow—I was discharged, when we came to Spithead, with an excellent character in a silk bag, and a considerable tightness of breathing, and leave to beg my way home again.

Now I had not the smallest meaning to enter into any of these particulars about myself, especially as my story must be all about other people—beautiful maidens, and fine young men, and several of the prime gentry. But as I have written it, so let it stay; because, perhaps, after all, it is well that people should have some little knowledge of the man they have to deal with, and learn that his character and position are a long way above all attempt at deceit.

To come back once again, if you please, to that very hot day of July 1782—whence I mean to depart no more until I have fully done with it—both from the state of the moon, I knew, and from the neap when my wife went off, that the top of the spring was likely to be in the dusk of that same evening. At first I had thought of going down straight below us to Newton Bay, and peddling over the Black Rocks towards the Ogmore river, some two miles to the east of us. But the bright sun gave me more enterprise; and remembering how the tide would ebb, also how low my pocket was, I felt myself bound in honour to Bunny to make a real push for it, and thoroughly search the conger-holes and the lobster-ledges, which are the best on all our coast, round about Pool Tavan, and down below the old house at Sker.

CHAPTER III.

THE FISH ARE AS HUNGRY AS HE IS.

To fish at Sker had always been a matter of some risk and conflict; inasmuch as Evan Thomas, who lived in the ancient house there, and kept the rabbit-warren, never could be brought to know that the sea did not belong to him. He had a grant from the manor, he said, and the shore was part of the manor; and whosoever came hankering there was a poacher, a thief, and a robber. With these hard words, and harder blows, he kept off most of the neighbourhood; but I always felt that the lurch of the tide was no more than the heeling of a ship, and therefore that any one free of the sea, was free of the ebb and flow of it.

So when he began to reproach me once, I allowed him to swear himself thoroughly out, and then, in a steadfast manner, said, "Black Evan, the shore is not mine or yours. Stand you here and keep it, and I will never come again;" for in three hours' time there would be a fathom of water where we stood. And when he caught me again, I answered, "Evan Black, if you catch me inland, meddling with any of your land-goods, coneys, or hares, or partridges, give me a leathering like a man, and I must put up with it; but dare you touch me on this shore, which belongs to our lord the King, all the way under high-water mark, and by the rod of the Red Sea I will show you the law of it."

He looked at me and the pole I bore, and, heavy and strong man as he was, he thought it wiser to speak me fair. "Well, well, Dyo, dear," he said in Welsh, having scarce any English, "you have served the King, Dyo, and are bound to know what is right and wrong; only let me know, good man, if you see any other rogues fishing here."

This I promised him freely enough, because, of course, I had no objection to his forbidding other people, and especially one vile Scotchman. Yet being a man of no liberality, he never could see even me fish there without following and abusing me, and most of all after a market-day.

That tide I had the rarest sport that ever you did see. Scarcely a conger-hole I tried without the landlord being at home, and biting savagely at the iron, which came (like a rate) upon him; whereupon I had him by the jaw, as the tax-collector has us. Scarcely a lobster-shelf I felt, tickling as I do under the weeds, but what a grand old soldier came to the portcullis of his stronghold, and nabbed the neat-hide up my fingers, and stuck thereto till I hauled him out "nolus-woluss," as we say; and there he showed his purple nippers, and his great long whiskers, and then his sides, hooped like a cask, till his knuckled legs fought with the air, and the lobes of his tail were quivering. It was fine to see these fellows, worth at least a shilling, and to pop them into my basket, where they clawed at one another. Glorious luck I had, in truth, and began to forget my troubles, and the long way home again to a lonely cottage, and my fear that little Bunny was passing a sorry day of it. She should have a new pair of boots, and mother Jones a good Sunday dinner; and as for myself, I would think, perhaps, about half a glass of fine old rum (to remind me of the navy), and a pipe of the short cut Bristol tobacco—but that must depend upon circumstances.

Now circumstances had so much manners (contrary to their

custom) that they contrived to keep themselves continually in my favour. Not only did I fetch up and pile a noble heap of oysters and mussels just at the lowest of the ebb, but after that, when the tide was flowing, and my work grew brisker—as it took me by the calves, and my feet were not cut by the mussels more than I could walk upon—suddenly I found a thing beating all experience both of the past and future.

This was, that the heat of the weather, and the soft south wind prevailing, had filled the deep salt-water pools among the rocks of Pool Tavan, and as far as Ffynnon wen, with the finest prawns ever seen or dreamed of; and also had peopled the shallow pools higher up the beach with shoals of silver mullet-fry—small indeed, and as quick as lightning, but well worth a little trouble to catch, being as fine eating as any lady in the land could long for.

And here for a moment I stood in some doubt, whether first to be down on the prawns or the mullet; but soon I remembered the tide would come first into the pools that held the prawns. Now it did not take me very long to fill a great Holland bag with these noble fellows, rustling their whiskers, and rasping their long saws at one another. Four gallons I found, and a little over, when I came to measure them; and sixteen shillings I made of them, besides a good many which Bunny ate raw.

Neither was my luck over yet, for being now in great heart and good feather, what did I do but fall very briskly upon the grey mullet in the pools: and fast as they scoured away down the shallows, fluting the surface with lines of light, and huddling the ripples all up in a curve, as they swung themselves round on their tails with a sweep, when they could swim no further—nevertheless it was all in vain, for I blocked them in with a mole of kelp, weighted with heavy pebbles, and then baled them out at my pleasure.

Now the afternoon was wearing away, and the flood making strongly up channel by the time I came back from Ffynnon wen—whither the mullet had led me—to my headquarters opposite Sker farmhouse, at the basin of Pool Tavan. This pool is made by a ring of rocks sloping inward from the sea, and is dry altogether for two hours' ebb and two hours' flow of a good spring-tide, except so much as a little land-spring, sliding down the slippery sea-weed, may have power to keep it moist.

A wonderful place here is for wild-fowl, the very choicest of all I know, both when the sluice of the tide runs out and when it comes swelling back again; for as the water ebbs away with a sulky wash in the hollow places, and the sand runs down in little crannies, and the bladder-weeds hang trickling, and the limpets close their valves, and the beautiful jelly-flowers look no better than chilblains,—all this void and glistening basin is at once alive with birds.

First the scapie runs and chatters, and the turn-stone pries about with his head laid sideways in a most sagacious manner, and the sanderlings glide in file, and the greenshanks separately. Then the shy curlews over the point warily come, and leave one to watch; while the brave little mallard teal, with his green triangles glistening, stands on one foot in the fresh-water runnel, and shakes with his quacks of enjoyment.

Again, at the freshening of the flood, when the round pool fills with sea (pouring in through the gate of rock), and the waves push merrily onward, then a mighty stir arises, and a different race of birds—those which love a swimming dinner—swoop upon Pool Tavan. Here is the giant grey gull, breasting (like a cherub in church) before he dowses down his head, and here the elegant kittywake, and the sullen cormorant in the shadow swimming; and the swiftest of swift wings, the silver-grey sea-swallow, dips like a butterfly and is gone; while from slumber out at sea, or on the pool of Kenfig, in a long wedge, cleaves the air the whistling flight of wild-ducks.

Standing upright for a moment, with their red toes on the water, and their strong wings flapping, in they souse with one accord and a strenuous delight. Then ensues a mighty quacking of unanimous content, a courteous nodding of quick heads, and a sluicing and a shovelling of water over shoulder-blades, in all the glorious revelry of insatiable washing.

Recovering thence, they dress themselves in a sober-minded manner, paddling very quietly, proudly puffing out their breasts, arching their necks, and preening themselves, titivating (as we call it) with their bills in and out the down, and shoulders up to run the wet off; then turning their heads, as if on a swivel, they fettle their backs and their scapular plume. Then, being as clean as clean can be, they begin to think of their dinners, and with stretched necks down they dive to catch some luscious morsel, and all you can see is a little sharp tail and a pair of red feet kicking.

Bless all their innocent souls, how often I longed to have a good shot at them, and might have killed eight or ten at a time with a long gun heavily loaded! But all these birds knew, as well as I did, that I had no gun with me; and although they kept at a tidy distance, yet they let me look at them, which I did with great peace of mind all the time I was eating my supper. The day had been too busy till now to stop for any feeding; but now there would be twenty minutes or so ere the bass came into Pool Tavan, for these like a depth of water.

So after consuming my bread and maybird, and having a good drink from the spring, I happened to look at my great flag-basket, now ready to burst with congers and lobsters and mullet, and spider-crabs for Bunny (who could manage any quantity), also with other good saleable fish; and I could not help saying to myself, " Come, after all now, Davy Llewellyn, you are not gone so far as to want a low Scotchman to show you the place where the fish live." And with that I lit a pipe.

What with the hard work, and the heat, and the gentle plash of wavelets, and the calmness of the sunset, and the power of red onions, what did I do but fall asleep as snugly as if I had been on watch in one of his Majesty's ships of the line after a heavy gale of wind? And when I woke up again, behold, the shadows of the rocks were over me, and the sea was saluting the calves of my legs, which up to that mark were naked; and but for my instinct in putting my basket up on a rock behind me, all my noble catch of fish must have gone to the locker of Davy Jones.

At this my conscience smote me hard, as if I were getting old too soon; and with one or two of the short strong words which I had learned in the navy, where the chaplain himself stirred us up with them, up I roused and rigged my pole for a good bout at the bass. At the butt of the ash was a bar of square oak, figged in with a screw-bolt, and roven round this was my line of good hemp, twisted evenly, so that if any fish came who could master me, and pull me off the rocks almost, I could indulge him with some slack by unreeving a fathom of line. At the end of the pole was a strong loop-knot, through which ran the line, bearing two large hooks, with the eyes of their shanks lashed tightly with cobbler's ends upon whipcord. The points of the hooks were fetched up with a file, and the barbs well backened, and the whole dressed over with whale-oil. Then upon one hook I fixed a soft crab, and on the other a cuttle-fish. There were lug-worms also in my pot, but they would do better after dark, when a tumbling cod might be on the feed.

Good-luck and bad-luck has been my lot ever since I can remember; sometimes a long spell of one, wing and wing, as you might say, and then a long leg of the other. But never in all my born days did I have such a spell of luck in the fishing way as on that blessed 10th of July 1782.

What to do with it all now became a puzzle, for I could not carry it home all at once; and as to leaving a bit behind, or refusing to catch a single fish that wanted to be caught, neither of these was a possible thing to a true-born fisherman.

At last things came to such a pitch that it was difficult not to believe that all must be the crowd and motion of a very pleasant dream. Here was the magic ring of the pool, shaped by a dance of sea-fairies, and the fading light shed doubtfully upon the haze of the quivering sea, and the silver water lifting like a mirror on a hinge, while the black rocks seemed to nod to it; and here was I pulling out big fishes almost faster than I cast in.

CHAPTER IV.

HE LANDS AN UNEXPECTED FISH.

Now, as the rising sea came sliding over the coronet of rocks, as well as through the main entrance—for even the brim of the pool is covered at high water—I beheld a glorious sight, stored in my remembrance of the southern regions, but not often seen at home. The day had been very hot and brilliant, with a light air from the south; and at sunset a haze arose, and hung as if it were an awning over the tranquil sea. First, a gauze of golden colour, as the western light came through, and then a tissue shot with red, and now a veil of silvery softness, as the summer moon grew bright.

Then the quiet waves began—as their plaited lines rolled onward into frills of whiteness—in the very curl and fall, to glisten with a flitting light. Presently, as each puny breaker overshone the one in front, not the crest and comb alone, but the slope behind it, and the crossing flaws inshore, gleamed with hovering radiance and soft flashes vanishing; till, in the deepening of the dusk, each advancing crest was sparkling with a mane of fire, every breaking wavelet glittered like a shaken seam of gold. Thence the shower of beads and lustres lapsed into a sliding tier, moving up the sands with light, or among the pebbles breaking into a cataract of gems.

Being an ancient salt, of course I was not dismayed by this show of phosphorus, nor even much astonished, but rather pleased to watch the brightness, as it brought back to my mind thoughts of beautiful sunburnt damsels whom I had led along the shore of the lovely Mediterranean. Yet our stupid landsmen, far and wide, were panic-struck; and hundreds fell upon their knees, expecting the last trump to sound. All I said to myself was this: "No wonder I had such sport to-day; change of weather soon, I doubt, and perhaps a thunderstorm."

As I gazed at all this beauty, trying not to go astray with wonder and with weariness, there, in the gateway of black rock, with the offing dark behind her, and the glittering waves upon their golden shoulders bearing her—sudden as an apparition came a smoothly-gliding boat. Beaded all athwart the bows and down the bends with drops of light, holding stem well up in air, and the forefoot shedding gold, she came as strait toward this poor and unconverted Davy as if an angel held the tiller, with an admiral in the stern-sheets.

Hereupon such terror seized me, after the wonders of the day, that my pole fell downright into the water (of which a big fish wronged me so as to slip the hook and be off again), and it was no more than the turn of a hair but what I had run away head over heels. For the day had been so miraculous, beginning with starvation, and going on with so much heat and hard work and enjoyment, and such a draught of fishes, that a poor body's wits were gone with it; and therefore I doubt not it must have been an especial decree of Providence that in turning round to run away I saw my big fish-basket.

To carry this over the rocks at a run was entirely impossible (although I was still pretty good in my legs), but to run away without it was a great deal more impossible for a man who had caught the fish himself; and beside the fish in the basket, there must have been more than two hundredweight of bass that would not go into it. Three hundred and a half in all was what I set it down at, taking no heed of prawns and lobsters; and with any luck in selling, it must turn two guineas.

Hence, perhaps, it came to pass (as much as from downright bravery, of which sometimes I have some little) that I felt myself bound to creep back again, under the shade of a cold wet rock, just to know what that boat was up to.

A finer floatage I never saw, and her lines were purely ele-gaunt, and she rode above the water without so much as parting it. Then, in spite of all my fear, I could not help admiring; and it struck me hotly at the heart, "Oh, if she is but a real boat, what a craft for my business!" And with that I dropped all fear. For I had not been able, for many years, to carry on my fishing as skill and knowledge warranted, only because I could not afford to buy a genuine boat of my own, and hitherto had never won the chance without the money.

As yet I could see no soul on board. No one was rowing, that was certain, neither any sign of a sail to give her steerage-way. However, she kept her course so true that surely there must be some hand invisible at the tiller. This conclusion flurried me again, very undesirably; and I set my right foot in such a manner as to be off in a twinkling of anything unholy.

But God has care of the little souls which nobody else takes heed of; and so He ordained that the boat should heel, and then yaw across the middle of the pool; but for which black rocks alone would have been her welcome.

At once my heart came back to me; for I saw at once, as an old sailor pretty well up in shipwrecks, that the boat was no more than a derelict; and feeling that here was my chance of chances, worth perhaps ten times my catch of fish, I set myself in earnest to the catching of that boat.

Therefore I took up my pole again, and finding that the brace of fish whom I had been over-scared to land had got away during my slackness, I spread the hooks, and cast them both, with the slugs of lead upon them, and half a fathom of spare line ready, as far as ever my arms would throw.

The flight of the hooks was beyond my sight, for the phosphorus spread confusion; but I heard most clearly the thump, thump of the two leaden bobs—the heavy and the light one—upon hollow planking. Upon this I struck as I would at a fish, and the hooks got hold (or at any rate one of them), and I felt the light boat following faster as she began to get way on the haul; and so I drew her gently toward me, being still in some misgiving, although resolved to go through with it.

But, bless my heart, when the light boat glided buoyantly up to my very feet, and the moon shone over the starboard gunwale, and without much drawback I gazed at it—behold! the little craft was laden with a freight of pure innocence! All for captain, crew, and cargo, was a little helpless child. In the stern-sheets, fast asleep, with the baby face towards me, lay a little child in white. Something told me that it was not dead, or even ailing ; only adrift upon the world, and not at all aware of it. Quite an atom of a thing, taking God's will anyhow ; cast, no doubt, according to the rocking of the boat, only with one tiny arm put up to keep the sun away, before it fell asleep.

Being taken quite aback with pity, sorrow, and some anger (which must have been of instinct), I laid hold of the bows of the skiff, and drew her up a narrow channel, where the landspring found its way. The lift of a round wave helped her on, and the bladder-weed saved any chafing. A brand-new painter (by the feel) it was that I caught hold of ; but instead of a hitch at the end, it had a clean sharp cut across it. Having made it fast with my fishing-pole jammed hard into a crevice of rock, I stepped on board rather gingerly, and, seating myself on the forward thwart, gazed from a respectful distance at the little stranger.

The light of the moon was clear and strong, and the phosphorus of the sea less dazing as the night grew deeper, therefore I could see pretty well ; and I took a fresh plug of tobacco before any further meddling. For the child was fast asleep ; and, according to my experience, they are always best in that way.

CHAPTER V.

A LITTLE ORPHAN MERMAID.

By the clear moonlight I saw a very wee maiden, all in white, having neither cloak nor shawl, nor any other soft appliance to protect or comfort her, but lying with her little back upon the aftmost planking, with one arm bent (as I said before), and the other drooping at her side, as if the baby-hand had been at work to ease her crying ; and then, when tears were tired out, had dropped in sleep or numb despair.

My feelings were so moved by this, as I became quite sure at last that here was a little mortal, that the tears came to mine own eyes too, she looked so purely pitiful. "The Lord in heaven have mercy on the little dear!" I cried, without another thought about it ; and then I went and sat close by, so that she lay between my feet.

However, she would not awake, in spite of my whistling

gradually, and singing a little song to her, and playing with her curls of hair; therefore, as nothing can last for ever, and the tide was rising fast, I was forced to give the little lady, not what you would call a kick so much as a very gentle movement of the muscles of the foot.

She opened her eyes at this, and yawned, but was much inclined to shut them again; till I (having to get home that night) could make no further allowance for her, as having no home to go to; and upon this I got over all misgivings about the dirtiness of my jacket, and did what I had feared to do, by reason of great respect for her; that is to say, I put both hands very carefully under her, and lifted her like a delicate fish, and set her crosswise on my lap, and felt as if I understood her; and she could not have weighed more than twenty pounds, according to my heft of fish.

Having been touched with trouble lately, I was drawn out of all experience now (for my nature is not over-soft) towards this little thing, so cast, in a dream almost, upon me. I thought of her mother, well drowned, no doubt, and the father who must have petted her, and of the many times to come when none would care to comfort her. And though a child is but a child, somehow I took to that child. Therefore I became most anxious as to her state of body, and handled her little mites of feet, and her fingers, and all her outworks; because I was not sure at all that the manner of her yawning might be nothing more or less than a going out of this world almost. For think, if you can see it so, how everything was against her. To be adrift without any food, or any one to tend her, many hours, or days perhaps, with a red-hot sun or cold stars overhead, and the greedy sea beneath her!

However, there she was alive, and warm, and limp, to the best of my judgment, sad though I was to confess to myself that I knew more of bass than of babies. For it had always so pleased God that I happened to be away at sea when He thought fit to send them; therefore my legs went abroad with fear of dandling this one, that now was come, in a way to disgrace a seaman; for if she should happen to get into irons, I never could get her out again.

Upon that matter, at any rate, I need not have concerned myself, for the child was so trim and well ballasted, also ribbed so stiff and sound, that any tack I set her on she would stick to it, and start no rope; and knowing that this was not altogether the manner of usual babies (who yaw about, and no steerage-way), I felt encouraged, and capable almost of a woman's business. Therefore I gave her a little tickle; and verily she began to laugh, or perhaps I should say by rights to smile, in a gentle and superior way—for she always was superior. And a funnier creature never lived, neither one that could cry so distressfully.

"Wake up, wake up, my deary," said I, "and don't you be afraid of me. A fine little girl I've got at home, about twice the size that you be, and goes by the name of 'Bunny.'"

"Bunny!" she said; and I was surprised, not being up to her qualities, that she could speak so clearly. Then it struck me that if she could talk like that I might as well know more about her. So I began, very craftily, with the thing all children are proud about, and are generally sure to be up to.

"Pretty little soul," I said, "how old do you call yourself?"

At this she gathered up her forehead, not being used to the way I put it, while she was trying to think it out.

"How old are you, deary?" said I, trying hard to suck up my lips and chirp, as I had seen the nurses do.

"I'se two, I'se two," she answered, looking with some astonishment; "didn't 'a know that? Hot's 'a name?"

This proof of her high standing and knowledge of the world took me for the moment a good deal off my legs, until I remembered seeing it put as a thing all must give in to, that the rising generation was beyond our understanding. So I answered, very humbly, "Deary, my name is 'old Davy.' Baby, kiss old Davy."

"I 'ill," she answered, briskly. "Old Davy, I likes 'a. I'll be a good gal, I 'ill."

"A good girl! To be sure you will. Bless my heart, I never saw such a girl." And I kissed her three or four times over, until she began to smell my plug, and Bunny was nobody in my eyes. "But what's your own name, deary, now you know old Davy's name?"

"I'se Bardie. Didn't 'a know that?"

"To be sure I did;" for a little fib was needful from the way she looked at me, and the biggest one ever told would have been a charity under the circumstances.

"Pease, old Davy, I'se aye hungry," she went on ere I was right again, "and I 'ants a dink o' yater."

"What a fool I am!" cried I. "Of course you do, you darling. What an atomy you are to talk! Stop here a moment."

Setting her on the seat by herself (like a stupid, as I was, for she might have tumbled overboard), I jumped out of the boat to fetch her water from the spring-head, as well as the relics of my food from the corner of the fish-basket. And truly vexed was I with myself for devouring of my dinner so. But no sooner was I gone, than feeling so left alone again after so much desertion, what did the little thing do but spring like a perfect grasshopper, and, slipping under the after-thwart, set off in the bravest toddle for the very bow of the boat, in fear of losing sight of me? Unluckily, the boat just happened to lift upon a bit of a wave, and, not having won her sea-legs yet in spite of that long cruise, down came poor Bardie with a thump, which hurt me more than her, I think.

Knowing what Bunny would have done, I expected a fearful roar, and back I ran to lift her up. But even before I could interfere, she was up again and all alive, with both her arms stretched out to show, and her face set hard to defy herself.

"I 'ont ky, I 'ont, I tell 'a. 'Ee see if I does now, and ma say hot a good gal I is."

"Where did you knock yourself, little wonder? Let old Davy make it well. Show old Davy the poor sore place."

"Nare it is. Gardy là! nare poor Bardie knock herself."

And she held up her short white smock, and showed me the bend of her delicate round knee as simply and kindly as could be.

"I 'ont ky; no, I 'ont," she went on, with her pretty lips screwed up. "Little brother ky, 'e know; but Bardie a gate big gal, savvy voo? Bardie too big enough to ky."

However, all this greatness vanished when a drop of blood came oozing from the long black bruise, and still more when I tried to express my deep compassion. The sense of bad-luck was too strong for the courage of even two years' growth, and little Bardie proved herself of just the right age for crying. I had observed how clear and bright and musical her voice was for such a tiny creature; and now the sound of her great woe, and scene of her poor helpless plight, was enough to move the rocks into a sense of pity for her.

However, while she had her cry out (as the tide would never wait), I took the liberty of stowing all my fish and fishing-tackle on board of that handy little boat, which I began to admire and long for more and more every time I jumped from the rock into her foresheets. And finding how tight and crank she was, and full of spring at every step and with a pair of good ash sculls, and, most of all, discovering the snuggest of snug lockers, my conscience (always a foremost feature) showed me in the strongest light that it would be a deeply ungracious, ungrateful, and even sinful thing, if I failed to thank an over-wise and overruling Providence for sending me this useful gift in so express a manner.

And taking this pious and humble view of the night's occurrence, I soon perceived a special fitness in the time of its ordering. For it happened to be the very night when Evan Thomas was out of the way, as I had been told at Nottage, and the steward of the manor safe to be as drunk as a fiddler at Bridgend; and it was not more than a few months since that envious Scotchman, Sandy Macraw (a scurvy limb of the coast-guards, who lived by poaching on my born rights), had set himself up with a boat, forsooth, on purpose to rogue me and rob me the better. No doubt he had stolen it somewhere, for he first appeared at night with it; and now here was a boat, in all honesty mine, which would travel two feet for each one of his tub!

By the time I had finished these grateful reflections, and resolved to contribute any unsold crabs to the Dissenting minister's salary (in recognition of the hand of Providence, and what he had taught me concerning it no longer ago than last Sabbath-day, when he said that the Lord would make up to me for the loss of my poor wife, though never dreaming, I must confess, of anything half so good as a boat), and by the time that I had moored this special mercy snugly, and hidden the oars, so that no vile wrecker could make off with her feloniously, that dear little child was grown quiet again, being unable to cry any more, and now beginning to watch my doings as much as I could wish, or more.

She never seemed tired of watching me, having slept out all her sleep for the moment; and as I piled up fish on fish, and they came sliding, slippery, she came shyly, eyeing them with a desire to see each one, pushing her mites of fingers out, and then drawing back in a hurry as their bellies shone in the moonlight. Some of the congers could wriggle still, and they made her scream when they did it; but the lobsters were her chief delight, being all alive and kicking. She came and touched them reverently, and ready to run if they took it amiss; and then she stroked their whiskers, crying, "Pitty, pitty! jolly, jolly!" till one great fellow, who knew no better, would have nipped her wrist asunder if I had not ricked his claw.

"Now, deary," said I, as I drew her away, "you have brought poor old Davy a beautiful boat, and the least that he can do for you is to get you a good supper." For since her tumble the little soul had seemed neither hungry nor thirsty.

"Pease, old Davy," she answered, "I 'ants to go to mama and papa, and ickle bother and Susan."

"The devil you do!" thought I, in a whistle, not seeing my way to a fib as yet.

"Does 'ee know mama and papa, and ickle bother, old Davy?"

"To be sure I do, my deary—better than I know you, almost."

"'Et me go to them, 'et me go to them. Hot ma say about my poor leggy peggy?"

This was more than I could tell; believing her mother to be, no doubt, some thirty fathoms under water, and her father and little brother in about the same predicament.

"Come along, my little dear, and I'll take you to your mother." This was what I said, not being ready, as yet, with a corker.

"I'se yeady, old Davy," she answered; "I'se kite yeady. 'Hen 'll 'e be yeady? Peshy voo."

"Ready and steady: word of command! march!" said I, looking up at the moon, to try to help me out of it. But the only thing that I could find to help me in this trouble was to push about and stir, and keep her looking at me. She was never tired of looking at things with life or motion in them; and this I found the special business of her nature afterwards.

Now, being sure of my boat, I began to think what to do with Bardie. And many foolish ideas came, but I saw no way to a wise one, or at least I thought so then, and unhappily looked to prudence more than to gracious Providence, for which I have often grieved bitterly, ever since it turned out who Bardie was.

For the present, however (though strongly smitten with her manners, appearance, and state of shipwreck, as well as impressed with a general sense of her being meant for good-luck to me), I could not see my way to take her to my home and support her. Many and many times over I said to myself, in my doubt and uneasiness, and perhaps more times than need have been if my conscience had joined me, that it was no good to be a fool, to give way (as a woman might do) to the sudden affair of the moment, and a hot-hearted mode of regarding it.

And the harder I worked at the stowing of fish, the clearer my duty appeared to me.

So by the time that all was ready for starting with this boat of mine, the sea being all the while as pretty as a pond by candle-light, it was settled in my mind what to do with Bardie. She must go to the old Sker-house. And having taken a special liking (through the goodness of my nature and the late distress upon me) to this little helpless thing, most sincerely I prayed to God that all might be ordered for the best; as indeed it always is, if we leave it to Him.

Nevertheless I ought never to have left it to Him, as every one now acknowledges. But how could I tell?

By this time she began to be overcome with circumstances, as might happen naturally to a child but two years old, after long exposure without any food or management. Scared, and strange, and tired out, she fell down anyhow in the boat, and lay like a log, and frightened me. Many men would have cared no more, but, taking the baby for dead, have dropped her into the grave of the waters. I, however, have always been of a very different stamp from these; and all the wars, and discipline, and doctrine I have encountered, never could imbue me with the cruelty of my betters. Therefore I was shocked at thinking that the little dear was dead.

CHAPTER VI.

FINDS A HOME OF SOME SORT.

However, it was high time now, if we had any hope at all of getting into Sker-house that night, to be up and moving. For though Evan Thomas might be late, Moxy, his wife, would be early; and the door would open to none but the master after the boys were gone to bed. For the house is very lonely; and people no longer innocent as they used to be in that neighbourhood.

I found the child quite warm and nice, though overwhelmed with weight of sleep; and setting her crosswise on my shoulders, whence she slid down into my bosom, over the rocks I picked my way, by the light of the full clear moon, towards the old Sker-Grange, which stands a little back from the ridge of beach, and on the edge of the sand-hills.

This always was, and always must be, a very sad and lonesome place, close to a desolate waste of sand, and the continual roaring of the sea upon black rocks. A great grey house, with many chimneys, many gables, and many windows, yet not a neighbour to look out on, not a tree to feed its chimneys, scarce a firelight in its gables in the very depth of winter. Of course, it is said to be haunted; and though I believe not altogether in any stories of that kind—despite some very strange things indeed which I have beheld at sea—at any rate, I would rather not hear any yarns on that matter just before bedtime in that house; and most people would agree with me, unless I am much mistaken.

For the whole neighbourhood—if so you may call it, where there are no neighbours—is a very queer one—stormy, wild, and desolate, with little more than rocks and sand and sea to make one's choice among. As to the sea, not only dull, and void it is of any haven, or of proper traffic, but as dangerous as need be, even in good weather, being full of draughts and currents, with a tide like a mill-race, suffering also the ups and downs which must be where the Atlantic Ocean jostles with blind narrowings: it offers, moreover, a special peril (a treacherous and a shifty one) in the shape of some horrible quicksands, known as the "Sker-Weathers:" these at the will of storm and current change about from place to place, but are, for the most part, some two miles from shore, and from two to four miles long, according to circumstances; sometimes almost bare at half-tide, and sometimes covered at low water. If any ship falls into them, the bravest skipper that ever stood upon a quarter-deck can do no more than pipe to prayers, though one or two craft have escaped when the tide was rising rapidly.

As for the shore, it is no better (when once you get beyond the rocks) than a stretch of sandhills, with a breadth of flaggy marsh behind them all the way to the mouth of Neath river, some three leagues to the westward. Eastward, the scene is fairer inland, but the coast itself more rugged and steep, and scarcely more inhabited, having no house nearer than Rhwychyns, which is only a small farm, nearly two miles from Sker-Grange, and a mile from any other house. And if you strike inland from Sker—that is to say, to the northward—there is nothing to see but sand, warren, and furze, and great fields marked with rubble, even as far as Kenfig.

Looking at that vast lonely house, there were two things I never could make out. The first was, who could ever have been mad enough to build it there?—for it must have cost a mint of money, being all of quarried and carried stone, and with no rich farm to require it. And the second thing was still worse a puzzle : how could any one ever live there?

As to the first point, the story is, that the house was built by abbots of Neath, when owners of Sker-manor, adding to it, very likely, as they followed one another; and then it was used as their manor-court, and for purposes more important, as a place of refection, being near good fisheries, and especially Kenfig Pool, stocked with all fresh-water fish, and every kind of wild-fowl.

But upon the other question all that I can say is this: I have knocked about the world a good bit, and have suffered many trials, by the which I am, no doubt, chastened and highly rectified ; nevertheless, I would rather end my life among the tombstones, if only allowed three farthings' worth of tobacco every day, than live with all those abbots' luxuries in that old grey house.

However, there were no abbots now, nor any sort of luxury, only a rough unpleasant farmer, a kind but slovenly wife of his, and five great lads, notorious for pleasing no one except themselves; also a boy of a different order, as you soon shall see.

Thinking of all this, I looked with tenderness at the little dear, fallen back so fast asleep, innocent, and trustful, with her head upon my shoulder, and her breathing in my beard. Turning away at view of the house, I brought the moonlight on her face, and this appeared so pure, and calm, and fit for better company, that a pain went to my heart, as in Welsh we speak of it.

Because she was so fast asleep, and that alone is something holy in a very little child ; so much it seems to be the shadow of the death itself, in their pausing fluttering lives, in their want of wit for dreaming, and their fitness for a world of which they must know more than this ; also to a man who feels the loss of much believing, and what grievous gain it is to make doubt of everything, such a simple trust in Him, than whom we find no better father, such a confidence of safety at the very outset seems a happy art unknown, and tempts him back to ignorance. Well aware what years must bring, from all the ill they have brought to us, we cannot watch this simple sort without a sadness on our side, a pity, and a longing, as for something lost and gone.

In the scoop between two sand-hills such a power of moonlight fell upon the face of this baby, that it only wanted the accident of her lifting bright eyes to me to make me cast away all prudence, and even the dread of Bunny. But a man at my time of life must really look to the main chance first, and scout all romantic visions; and another face means another mouth, however pretty it may be. Moreover, I had no wife now, nor woman to look after us; and what can even a man-child do, without their apparatus? While on the other hand I knew that (however dreary Sker might be) there was one motherly heart inside it. Therefore it came to pass that soon the shadow of that dark house fell upon the little one in my arms, while with a rotten piece of timber, which was lying handy, I thumped and thumped at the old oak door, but nobody came to answer me; nobody even seemed to hear, though every knock went further and further into the emptiness of the place.

But just as I had made up my mind to lift the latch, and to walk in freely, as I would have done in most other houses, but stood upon scruple with Evan Thomas, I heard a slow step in the distance, and Moxy Thomas appeared at last—a kindly-hearted and pleasant woman, but apt to be low-spirited (as was natural for Evan's wife), and not very much of a manager. And yet it seems hard to blame her there, when I come to think of it, for most of the women are but so. round about our neighbourhood—sanding up of room and passage, and forming patterns on the floor every other Saturday, and yet the roof all frayed with cobwebs, and the corners such as, in the navy, we should have been rope-ended for.

By means of nature, Moxy was shaped for a thoroughly good and lively woman; and such no doubt she would have been, if she had had the luck to marry me, as at one time was our signification. God, however, ordered things in a different manner, and no doubt He was considering what might be most for my benefit. Nevertheless, in the ancient days, when I was a fine young tar on leave, and all Sunday-school set caps at me (perhaps I was two-and-twenty then), the only girl I would allow to sit on the crossing of my legs, upon a well-dusted tombstone, and suck the things I carried for them (all being fond of peppermint), was this little Moxy Stradling, of good Newton family, and twelve years old at that time. She made me swear on the blade of my knife never to have any one but her; and really I looked forward to it as almost beyond a joke; and her father had some money.

"Who's there at this time of night?" cried Moxy Thomas, sharply, and in Welsh of course, although she had some English; "pull the latch, if you be honest. Evan Black is in the house."

By the tone of her voice I knew that this last was a fib of fright, and glad I was to know it so. Much the better chance was left me of disposing Bardie somewhere, where she might be comfortable.

Soon as Mrs Thomas saw us by the light of a home-made dip, she scarcely stopped to stare before she wanted the child out of my arms, and was ready to devour it, guessing that it came from sea, and talking all the while, full gallop, as women find the way to do. I was expecting fifty questions, and, no doubt, she asked them, yet seemed to answer them all herself, and be vexed with me for talking, yet to want me to go on.

"Moxy, now be quick," I said; "this little thing from out the sea——"

"Quick is it? Quick indeed! Much quick you are, old Dyo!" she replied in English. "The darling dear, the pretty love!" for the child had spread its hands to her, being taken with a woman's dress. "Give her to me, clumsy Davy. Is it that way you do carry her?"

"Old Davy tarry me aye nicely, I tell 'a. Old Davy good and kind; and I 'ont have him called kumsy."

So spake up my two-year-old, astonishing me (as she always has done) by her wonderful cleverness, and surprising Moxy Thomas that such clear good words should come from so small a creature.

"My goodness me! you little vixen! wherever did you come from? Bring her in yourself, then, Dyo, if she thinks so much of you. Let me feel her. Not wet she is. Wherever did you get her? Put her on this little stool, and let her warm them mites of feet till I go for bread and butter."

Although the weather was so hot, a fire of coal and driftwood was burning in the great chimney-place, for cooking of black Evan's supper; because he was an outrageous man to eat, whenever he was drunk, which (as a doctor told me once) shows the finest of all constitutions.

But truly there was nothing else of life, or cheer, or comfort, in the great sad stony room. A floor of stone, six gloomy doorways, and a black-beamed ceiling—no wonder that my little darling cowered back into my arms, and put both hands before her eyes.

"No, no, no!" she said. "Bardie doesn't 'ike it. When mama come, she be very angy with 'a, old Davy."

I felt myself bound to do exactly as Mrs Thomas ordered me, and so I carried Miss Finical to the three-legged stool of firwood which had been pointed out to me; and having a crick in my back for a moment after bearing her so far, down I set her upon her own legs, which, although so neat and pretty, were uncommonly steadfast. To my astonishment, off she started (before I could fetch myself to think) over the rough stone flags of the hall, trotting on her toes entirely, for the very life of her. Before I could guess what she was up to, she had pounced upon an old kitchen-towel, newly washed, but full of splinters, hanging on a three-legged horse, and back she ran in triumph with it—for none could say that she toddled—and with a want of breath, and yet a vigour that made up for it, began to rub with all her power, as well as a highly skilful turn, the top of that blessed three-legged stool, and some way down the sides of it.

"What's the matter, my dear?" I asked, almost losing my mind at this, after all her other wonders.

"Dirt," she replied; "degustin' dirt!" never stopping to look up at me.

"What odds for a little dirt, when a little soul is hungry?"

"Bardie a boofley kean gal, and this 'tool degustin' cochong!" was all the reply she vouchsafed me; but I saw that she thought less of me. However, I was glad enough that Moxy did not hear her, for Mrs Thomas had no unreasonable ill-will towards dirt, but rather liked it in its place; and with her its place was everywhere. But I, being used to see every cranny searched and scoured with holystone, blest, moreover, when ashore, with a wife like Amphitrite (who used to come aboard of us), could thoroughly enter into the cleanliness of this Bardie, and thought more of her accordingly.

While this little trot was working, in the purest ignorance of father and of mother, yet perhaps in her tiny mind hoping to have pleased them both, back came Mrs Thomas, bringing all the best she had of comfort and of cheer for us, although not much to speak of.

I took a little hollands hot, on purpose to oblige her, because she had no rum; and the little baby had some milk and rabbit-gravy, being set up in a blanket, and made the most we could make of her. And she ate a truly beautiful supper, sitting gravely on the stool, and putting both hands to her mouth in fear of losing anything. All the boys were gone to bed after a long day's rabbiting, and Evan Black still on the spree; so that I was very pleasant (knowing my boat to be quite safe) toward my ancient sweetheart. And we got upon the old times so much, in a pleasing, innocent, teasing way, that but for fear of that vile black Evan we might have forgotten poor Bardie.

CHAPTER VII.

BOAT *VERSUS* BARDIE.

GLAD as I was, for the poor child's sake, that Black Evan happened to be from home, I had perhaps some reason also to rejoice on my own account. For if anything of any kind could ever be foretold about that most uncertain fellow's conduct, it was that when in his cups he would fight—with cause, if he could find any; otherwise, without it.

And in the present case, perhaps, was some little cause for fighting; touching (as he no doubt would think) not only his marital but manorial rights of plunder. Of course, between Moxy and myself all was purely harmless, each being thankful to have no more than a pleasant eye for the other; and of course, in really serious ways, I had done no harm to him; that boat never being his, except by downright piracy. Nevertheless few men there are who look at things from what I may call a large and open standing-place; and Evan might even go so far as to think that I did him a double wrong, in taking that which was his, the boat, and leaving that which should have been mine—to wit, the little maiden—as a helpless burden upon his hands, without so much as a change of clothes; and all this after a great day's sport among his rocks, without his permission!

Feeling how hopeless it would be to reason these matters out with him, especially as he was sure to be drunk, I was glad enough to say "Good-night" to my new young pet, now fast asleep, and to slip off quietly to sea with my little frigate and its freight, indulging also my natural pride at being, for the first time in my life, a legitimate shipowner and independent deep-sea fisherman. By this time the tide was turned, of course, and running strong against me as I laid her head for Newton Bay by the light of the full moon; and proud I was, without mistake, to find how fast I could send my little crank barky against the current, having being a fine oarsman in my day, and always stroke of the captain's gig.

But as one who was well acquainted with the great dearth of honesty (not in our own parish only, but for many miles around), I could not see my way to the public ownership of this boat, without a deal of trouble and vexation. Happening so that I did not buy it, being thoroughly void of money (which was too notorious, especially after two funerals conducted to everybody's satisfaction), big rogues would declare at once, judging me by themselves, perhaps, that I had been and stolen it. And likely enough, to the back of this, they would lay me half-a-dozen murders and a wholesale piracy.

Now I have by nature the very strongest affection for truth that can be reconciled with a good man's love of reason. But sometimes it happens so that we must do violence to ourselves for the sake of our fellow-creatures. If these, upon occasion offered, are only too sure to turn away and reject the truth with a strong disgust, surely it is dead against the high and pure duty we owe them, to saddle them with such a heavy and deep responsibility. And to take still loftier views of the charity and kindness needful towards our fellow-beings—when they hanker for a thing, as they do nearly always for a lie, and have set their hearts upon it, how selfish it must be, and inhuman, not to let them have it! Otherwise, like a female in a delicate condition, to what extent of injury may we not expose them? Now sailors have a way of telling great facts of imagination in the most straightforward and simple manner, being so convinced themselves that they care not a rope's end who besides is convinced, and who is not. And to make other people believe, the way is not to want them to do it; only the man must himself believe, and be above all reasoning.

And I was beginning to believe more and more as I went on, and the importance of it grew clearer, all about that ill-fated ship of which I had been thinking ever since the boat came in. Twelve years ago, as nearly as need be, and in the height of summer—namely, on the 3d of June 1770—a large ship called the 'Planter's Welvard,' bound from Surinam to the Port of Amsterdam, had been lost and swallowed up near this very dangerous place. Three poor children of the planter (whose name was J. S. Jackert), on their way home to be educated, had floated ashore, or at least their bodies, and are now in Newton churchyard. The same must have been the fate of Bardie but for the accident of that boat. And though she was not a Dutchman's child, so far as one could guess, from her wonderful power of English, and no sign of Dutch build about her, she might very well have been in a Dutch ship with her father and mother, and little brother and Susan, in the best cabin. It was well known among us that Dutch vessels lay generally northward of their true course, and from the likeness of the soundings often came up the Bristol instead of the English Channel; and that this mistake (which the set of the stream would increase) generally proved fatal to them in the absence of any lighthouse.

That some ship or other had been lost, was to my mind out of all dispute, although the weather had been so lovely; but why it must have been a Dutch rather than an English ship, and why I need so very plainly have seen the whole of it myself (as by this time I began to believe that I had done), is almost more than I can tell, except that I hoped it might be so, as giving me more thorough warrant in the possession of my prize. This boat, moreover, seemed to be of foreign build, so far as I could judge of it by moonlight: but of that hereafter.

The wonder is that I could judge of anything at all, I think, after the long and hard day's work, for a man not so young as he used to be. And rocks are most confusing things to be among for a length of time, and away from one's fellow-creatures, and nothing substantial on the stomach. They do so darken and jag and quiver, and hang over heavily as a man wanders under them, with never a man to speak to; and then the sands have such a way of shaking, and of shivering, and changing colour beneath the foot, and shining in and out with patterns coming all astray to you! When to these contrary vagaries you begin to add the loose unprincipled curve of waves, and the up and down of light around you, and to and fro of sea-breezes, and startling noise of sea-fowl, and a world of other confusions, with roar of the deep confounding them—it becomes a bitter point to judge a man of what he saw, and what he thinks he must have seen.

It is beneath me to go on with what might seem excuses. Enough that I felt myself in the right; and what more can any man do, if you please, however perfect he may be? Therefore I stowed away my boat (well earned both by mind and body) snugly enough to defy, for the present, even the sharp eyes of Sandy Macraw, under Newton Point, where no one ever went but myself. Some of my fish I put to freshen in a solid mass of bladder-weed, and some I took home for the morning, and a stroke of business after church. And if any man in the world deserved a downright piece of good rest that night, with weary limbs and soft conscience, you will own it was Davy Llewellyn.

Sunday morning I lay abed, with Bunny tugging very hard to get me up for breakfast, until it was almost eight o'clock, and my grandchild in a bitter strait of hunger for the things she smelled. After satisfying her, and scoring at the "Jolly Sailors" three fine bass against my shot, what did I do but go to church with all my topmost togs on? And that not from respect alone for the parson, who was a customer, nor even that Colonel Lougher of Candleston Court might see me, and feel inclined to discharge me as an exemplary Churchman (when next brought up before him). These things weighed with me a little, it is useless to deny; but my main desire was that the parish should see me there, and know that I was not abroad on a long-shore expedition, but was ready to hold up my head on a Sunday with the best of them, as I always had done.

At one time, while I ate my breakfast, I had some idea perhaps that it would be more pious almost, and create a stronger belief in me, as well as ease my own penitence with more relief of groaning, if I were to appear in the chapel of the Primitive Christians, after certain fish were gutted. But partly the fear of their singing noise (unsuitable to my head that morning after the Hollands at Sker house), and partly my sense that after all it was but forecastle work there, while the church was quarter-deck, and most of all the circumstance that no magistrate ever went there, led me, on the whole, to give the preference to the old concern, supported so bravely by royalty. Accordingly to church I went, and did a tidy stroke of business, both before and after service, in the way of lobsters.

We made a beautiful dinner that day, Bunny and I, and mother Jones, who was good enough to join us; and after slipping down to see how my boat lay for the tide, and finding her as right as could be, it came into my head that haply it would be a nice attention, as well as ease my mind upon some things that were running in it, if only I could pluck up spirit to defy the heat of the day, and challenge my own weariness by walking over to Sker-Manor. For of course the whole of

Monday, and perhaps of Tuesday too, and even some part of Wednesday (with people not too particular), must be occupied in selling my great catch of Saturday: so I resolved to go and see how the little visitor was getting on, and to talk with her. For though, in her weariness and wandering of the night before, she did not seem to remember much, as was natural at her tender age, who could tell what might have come to her memory by this time, especially as she was so clever? And it might be a somewhat awkward thing if the adventures which I felt really must have befallen her should happen to be contradicted by her own remembrance: for all I wanted was the truth; and if her truths contradicted mine, why, mine must be squared off to meet them; for great is truth, and shall prevail.

I thought it as well to take Bunny with me, for children have a remarkable knack of talking to one another, which they will not use to grown people; also the walk across the sands is an excellent thing for young legs, we say, being apt to crack the skin a little, and so enabling them to grow. A strong and hearty child was Bunny, fit to be rated A.B., almost, as behoved a fine sailor's daughter. And as proud as you could wish to see, and never willing to give in; so I promised myself some little sport in watching our Bunny's weariness, as the sand grew deeper, and yet her pride to the last declaring that I should not carry her.

But here I reckoned quite amiss, for the power of the heat was such—being the very hottest day I ever knew out of the tropics, and the great ridge of sandhills shutting us off from any sight of the water—that my little grandchild scarcely plodded a mile ere I had to carry her. And this was such a heavy job among the deep dry mounds of sand, that for a time I repented much of the over-caution which had stopped me from using my beautiful new boat at once, to paddle down with the ebb to Sker, and come home gently afterwards with the flow of the tide towards evening. Nevertheless, as matters proved, it was wiser to risk the broiling.

This heat was not of the sun alone (such as we get any summer's day, and such as we had yesterday), but thickened heat from the clouds themselves, shedding it down like a burning-glass, and weltering all over us. It was, though I scarcely knew it then, the summing-up and crowning period of whole weeks of heat and drought, and indeed of the hottest summer known for at least a generation. And in the hollows of yellow sand, without a breath of air to stir, or a drop of moisture, or a firm place for the foot, but a red and fiery haze to go through, it was all a man could do to keep himself from staggering.

Hence it was close upon three o'clock, by the place the sun was in, when Bunny and I came in sight of Sker-house, and hoped to find some water there. Beer, of course, I would rather have; but never was there a chance of that within reach of Evan Thomas. And I tried to think this all the better; for half a gallon would not have gone any distance with me, after ploughing so long through sand, with the heavy weight of Bunny, upon a day like that. Only I hoped that my dear little grandchild might find something fit for her, and such as to set her up again; for never before had I seen her, high and strong as her spirit was, so overcome by the power and pressure of the air above us. She lay in my arms almost as helpless as little Bardie, three years younger, had lain the night before; and knowing how children will go off without a man's expecting it, I was very uneasy, though aware of her constitution. So in the heat I chirped and whistled, though ready to drop myself almost; and coming in sight of the house, I tried my best to set her up again, finding half of her clothes gone down her back, and a great part of her fat legs somehow sinking into her Sunday shoes.

CHAPTER VIII.

CHILDREN WILL BE CHILDREN.

THE "boys of Sker," as we always called those rough fellows over at Newton, were rabbiting in the warren; according to their usual practice, on a Sunday afternoon. A loose unseemly lot of lads, from fifteen up to two-and-twenty years of age, perhaps, and very little to choose between them as to work and character. All, however, were known to be first-rate hands at any kind of sporting, or of poaching, or of any roving pleasure.

Watkin, the sixth and youngest boy, was of a different nature. His brothers always cast him off, and treated him with a high contempt, yet never could despise him. In their rough way, they could hardly help a sulky sort of love for him

The seventh and last child had been a girl—a sweet little creature as could be seen, and taking after Watkin. But she had something on her throat from six months up to six years old; and when she died, some three months back, people who had been in the house said that her mother would sooner have lost all the boys put together, if you left Watkin out of them. How that was I cannot say, and prefer to avoid those subjects. But I know that poor black Evan swore no oath worth speaking of for one great market and two small ones, but seemed brought down to sit by himself, drinking quietly all day long.

When we came to the ancient hall (or kitchen, as now they called it), for a moment I was vexed—expecting more of a rush, perhaps, than I was entitled to. Knowing how much that young child owed me for her preservation, and feeling how fond I was of her, what did I look for but wild delight at seeing "old Davy" back again? However, it seems, she had taken up with another and forgotten me.

Watkin, the youngest boy of Sker, was an innocent good little fellow, about twelve years old at that time. Bardie had found this out already; as quickly as she found out my goodness, even by the moonlight. She had taken the lead upon Watkin, and was laying down the law to him, upon a question of deep importance, about the manner of dancing. I could dance a hornpipe with anybody, and forward I came to listen.

"No, no, no! I tell 'a. 'E mustn't do like that, Yatkin. 'E must go yound and yound like this; and 'e must hold 'a cothes out, same as I does. Gardy là! 'E must hold 'a cothes out all the time, 'e must."

The little atom, all the time she delivered these injunctions, was holding out her tiny frock in the daintiest manner, and tripping sideways here and there, and turning round quite upon tiptoe, with her childish figure poised, and her chin thrown forward; and then she would give a good hard jump, but all to the tune of the brass jew's-harp which the boy was playing for his very life. And all the while she was doing this, the amount of energy and expression in her face was wonderful. You would have thought there was nothing else in all the world that required doing with such zeal and abandonment. Presently the boy stopped for a moment, and she came and took the knee of his trousers, and put it to her pretty lips with the most ardent gratitude.

"She must be a foreigner," said I to myself: "no British

child could dance like that, and talk so; and no British child ever shows gratitude."

As they had not espied us yet, where we stood in the passage-corner, I drew Bunny backward, and found her all of a tremble with eagerness to go and help.

"More pay," said little missy, with a coaxing look; "more pay, Yatkin!"

"No, no. You must say 'more play, please, Watkin.'"

"See voo pay, Yatkin; I 'ants—more pay!" The funny thing laughed at herself while saying it, as if with some comic inner sense of her own insatiability in the matter of play.

"But how do you expect me to play the music," asked Watkin, very reasonably, "if I am to hold my clothes out all the time?"

"Can't 'a?" she replied, looking up at him with the deepest disappointment; "can't 'a pay and dance too, Yatkin? I thought 'a could do anything. I 'ants to go to my dear mama and papa and ickle bother."

Here she began to set up a very lamentable cry, and Watkin in vain tried to comfort her, till, hearing us, she broke from him.

"Nare's my dear mama, nare's my dear mama coming!" she exclaimed, as she trotted full speed to the door. "Mama! mama! here I is. And 'e mustn't scold poor Susan."

It is out of my power to describe how her little flushed countenance fell when she saw only me and Bunny. She drew back suddenly, with the brightness fading out of her eager eyes, and the tears that were in them began to roll, and her bits of hands went up to her forehead, as if she had lost herself, and the corners of her mouth came down; and then with a sob she turned away, and with quivering shoulders hid herself. I scarcely knew what to do for the best; but our Bunny was very good to her, even better than could have been hoped, although she came of a kindly race. Without standing upon ceremony, as many children would have done, up she ran to the motherless stranger, and, kneeling down on the floor, contrived to make her turn and look at her. Then Bunny pulled out her new handkerchief, of which she was proud, I can tell you, being the first she had ever owned, made from the soundest corner of mother Jones's old window-blind, and only allowed with a Sunday frock; and although she had too much respect for this to wet it with anything herself, she never for a moment grudged to wipe poor Bardie's eyes with it. Nay, she even permitted her—which was much more for a child to do—to take it into her own two hands and rub away at her eyes with it.

Gradually she coaxed her out of the cupboard of her refuge, and sitting in some posture known to none but women children, without a stool to help her, she got the little one on her lap, and stroked at her, and murmured to her, as if she had found a favourite doll in the depth of trouble. Upon the whole, I was so pleased that I vowed to myself I would give my Bunny the very brightest halfpenny I should earn upon the morrow.

Meanwhile, the baby of higher birth—as a glance was enough to show her—began to relax and come down a little, both from her dignity and her woe. She looked at Bunny with a gleam of humour, to which her wet eyes gave effect.

"'E call that a ponkey-hankerchy? Does 'a call that a ponkey-hankerchy?"

Bunny was so overpowered by this, after all that she had done, and at the air of pity wherewith her proud ornament was flung on the floor, that she could only look at me as if I had cheated her about it. And truly I had seen no need to tell her about mother Jones and her blind. Then these little ones got up, having sense of a natural discordance of rank between them, and Bunny no longer wiped the eyes of Bardie, nor Bardie wept in the arms of Bunny. They put their little hands behind them, and stood apart to think a bit, and watched each other shyly. To see them move their mouths and fingers, and peep from the corners of their eyes, was as good as almost any play without a hornpipe in it. It made no difference, however. Very soon they came to settle it between them. The low-born Bunny looked down upon Bardie for being so much smaller, and the high-born Bardie looked down upon Bunny for being so much coarser. But neither was able to tell the other at all what her opinion was; and so, without any further trouble, they became very excellent playmates.

Doing my best to make them friends, I seized the little stranger, and gave her several good tosses-up, as well as tickles between them; and this was more than she could resist, being, as her nature shows, thoroughly fond of any kind of pleasure and amusement. She laughed, and she flung out her arms, and every time she made such jumps as to go up like a feather. Pretty soon I saw, however, that this had gone on too long for Bunny. She put her poor handkerchief out of sight, and then some fingers into her mouth, and she looked as black as a dog in a kennel. But Bardie showed good-nature now, for she ran up to Bunny and took her hand and led her to me, and said very nicely, "Give this ickle gal some, old Davy. She haven't had no pay at all. Oh, hot boofley buckens oo's got! Jolly, jolly! Keel song grand!"

This admiration of my buttons—which truly were very handsome, being on my regulation-coat, and as good as gilt almost, with "Minotaur" (a kind of grampus, as they say) done round them—this appreciation of the navy made me more and more perceive what a dear child was come ashore to us, and that we ought to look alive to make something out of her. If she had any friends remaining (and they could scarcely have all been drowned), being, as she clearly was, of a high and therefore rich family, it might be worth ten times as much as even my boat had been to me, to keep her safe and restore her in a fat state when demanded. With that I made up my mind to take her home with me that very night, especially as Bunny seemed to have set up a wonderful fancy to her. But man sees single, God sees double, as our saying is, and her bits of French made me afraid that she might after all be a beggar.

"Now go and play, like two little dears, and remember whose day it is," I said to them both, for I felt the duty of keeping my grandchild up to the mark on all religious questions; "and be sure you don't go near the well, nor out of sight of the house at all, nor pull the tails of the chickens out, nor throw stones at the piggy-wiggy," for I knew what Bunny's tricks were. "And now, Watty, my boy, come and talk to me, and perhaps I will give you a juneating apple from my own tree under the Clevice."

Although the heat was tremendous now (even inside those three-feet walls), the little things did as I bade them. And I made the most of this occasion to have a talk with Watkin, who told me everything he knew. His mother had not been down since dinner, which they always got anyhow; because his father, who had been poorly for some days, and feverish, and forced to lie in bed a little, came to the top of the stairs, and called, requiring some attendance. What this meant I knew as well as if I had seen black Evan there, parched with thirst and with great eyes rolling after helpless drunkenness, and roaring, with his night-clothes on, for a quart of fresh-drawn ale.

But about the shipwrecked child Watty knew scarce anything. He had found her in his bed that morning—Moxy, no doubt, having been hard pushed (with her husband in that state) what to do. And knowing how kind young Watty was, she had quartered the baby upon him. But Watkin, though gifted with pretty good English (or " Sassenach," as we call it) beyond all the rest of his family, could not follow the little creature in her manner of talking; which indeed, as I found thereafter, nobody in the parish could do except myself, and an Englishwoman whose word was not worth taking.

"Indeed and indeed then, Mr Llewellyn," he went on in English, having an evident desire to improve himself by discourse with me, "I did try, and I did try; and my mother, she try too. Times and times, for sure we tried. But no use was the whole of it. She only shakes her head, and thinks with all her might, as you may say. And then she says, 'No! I'se not hot you says. I'se two years old, and I'se Bardie. And my papa he be very angy if 'e goes on so with me. My mama yoves me, and I yove her, and papa, and ickle bother, and everybody. But not the naughty bad man, I doesn't.' That isn't true English now, I don't think; is it then, Mr Llewellyn?"

"Certainly not," I answered, seeing that my character for good English was at stake.

"And mother say she know well enough the baby must be a foreigner. On her dress it is to show it. No name, as the Christians put, but marks without any meaning. And of clothes so few upon her till mother go to the old cupboard. Rich people mother do say they must be; but dead by this time, she make no doubt."

"Boy," I replied, "your mother, I fear, is right in that particular. To me it is a subject of anxiety and sorrow. And I know perhaps more about it than any one else can pretend to do."

The boy looked at me with wonder and eagerness about it. But I gave him a look, as much as to say, "Ask no more at present." However, he was so full of her that he could not keep from talking.

"We asked who the naughty bad man was, but she was afraid at that, and went all round the room with her eyes, and hid under mother's apron. And dreadful she cried at breakfast about her mama and her own spoon. To my heart I feel the pain when she does cry; I know I do. And then of a sudden she is laughing, and no reason for it! I never did see such a baby before. Do you think so, Mr Llewellyn?"

CHAPTER IX.

SAND-HILLS TURNED TO SAND-HOLES.

WHILE I was talking thus with the boy, and expecting his mother every minute (with hope of a little refreshment when the farmer should have dropped off into his usual Sunday sleep), a very strange thing began more and more to force itself on my attention. I have said that the hall of this desolate house was large and long, and had six doorways—narrow arches of heavy stone without a door to any of them. Three of these arches were at the west and three at the east end of the room, and on the south were two old windows, each in a separate gable, high up from the floor, and dark with stone-work and with lead-work; and in the calmest weather these would draw the air and make a rattle. At the north side of the hall was nothing but dead wall, and fireplace, and cupboards, and the broad oak staircase. Having used the freedom to light a pipe, I sate with my face to the chimney-corner, where some wood-ashes were smouldering, after the dinner was done with; and sitting thus, I became aware of a presence of some sort over my right shoulder. At first I thought it was nothing more than the smoke from my own pipe, for I puffed rather hard, in anxiety about that little darling. But seeing surprise, and alarm perhaps, in Watkin's face, who sate opposite, I turned round, and there beheld three distinct and several pillars of a brownish-yellow light standing over against the doorways of the western end.

At first I was a little scared, and the more so because the rest of the hall was darkening with a pulse of colour gradually vanishing; and for an instant I really thought that the ghosts of the wrecked child's father and mother, and perhaps her nurse, were come to declare the truth about her, and challenge me for my hesitation. But presently I called to mind how many strange things had befallen me, both at sea and on the coast, in the way of feeling and vision too, designed, however, by the Power that sends them, more to forewarn than frighten us, and, as we get used to them, to amuse or edify.

Therefore I plucked my spirit up and approached this odd appearance, and found that no part of it was visible upon the spot where it seemed to stand. But Watkin, who was much emboldened by my dauntless carriage, called out in Welsh that he could see me walking in and out of them, like so many haystacks. Upon this I took yet further courage, having a witness so close at hand, and nothing seeming to hurt me. So what did I do but go outside, without any motion of running away, but to face the thing to its utmost; and Watkin, keeping along the wall, took good care to come after me.

Here I discovered in half a second that I had been wise as well as strong in meeting the matter valiantly; for what we had seen was but the glancing—or reflection, as they call it now—of what was being done outside. In a word, the thick and stifling heat of the day (which had gathered to a head the glaring and blazing power of the last two months of hot summer) was just beginning to burst abroad in whirlwind, hail, and thunder. All the upper heaven was covered with a spread of burning yellow; all the half-way sky was red as blood with fibres under it, and all the sides and margin looked as black as the new-tarred bends of a ship. But what threw me most astray was, that the whole was whirling, tossing upward jets of darkness, as a juggler flings his balls, yet at one time spinning round, and at the same time scowling down.

"It is a hurricane," said I, having seen some in the West Indies which began like this. Watkin knew not much of my meaning, but caught hold of my coat, and stood. And in truth it was enough to make not only a slip of a boy, but a veteran sailor, stand and fear.

Not a flash of lightning yet broke the expectation of it, nor had been a drop of rain. But to my surprise, and showing how little we know of anything, over the high land broke a sand-storm, such as they have in Africa. It had been brewing some time, most likely in the Kenfig burrows, toward the westward and the windward, although no wind was astir with us. I thought of a dance of waterspouts, such as we had twice encountered in the royal navy; once, I know, was after clearing the mouth of the Strait of Malaccas; where the other was I truly forget, having had so much to go everywhere. But this time the whirling stuff was neither water, nor smoke, nor cloud; but sand, as plain as could be. It was just like the parson's hour-glass—only going up, not coming down, and quickly instead of slowly. And of these funnels, spinning around, and coming near and nearer, there may have been perhaps a dozen, or there may have been threescore. They differed very much in size, according to the breadth of whirlwind, and the stuff it fed upon, and the hole in the air it bored; but all alike had a tawny colour, and a manner of bulking upward, and a loose uncertain edge, often lashing off in frays; and between them black clouds galloped; and sometimes two fell into one, and bodily broke downward; then a pile (as big as Newton Rock) rose in a moment anyhow. Hill or valley made no odds; sand-hill, or sand-bottom; the sand was in the place of the air, and the air itself was sand.

Many people have asked me, over and over again (because such a thing was scarcely known, except at the great storm of sand four hundred years ago, they say)—our people, ever so many times, assert their privilege to ask me (now again especially) how many of these pillars there were? I wish to tell the truth exactly, having no interest in the matter—and if I had, no other matter would it be to me; and after going into my memory deeper than ever I could have expected there would be occasion for, all I can say is this—legion was their number; because they were all coming down upon me; and how could I stop to count them?

Watkin lost his mind a little, and asked me (with his head gone under my regulation-coat) if I thought it was the judgment-day.

To this question I "replied distinctly in the negative" (as the man of the paper wrote, when I said "no" about poaching); and then I cheered young Watkin up, and told him that nothing more was wanted than to keep a weather-helm.

Before his wit could answer helm so much as to clear my meaning, the storm was on me, and broke my pipe, and filled my lungs and all my pockets, and spoiled every corner of the hat I had bought for my dear wife's funeral. I pulled back instantly (almost as quickly as boy Watkin could), and we heard the sand burst over the house, with a rattle like shot, and a roar like cannon. And being well inside the walls, we fixed our eyes on one another, in the gloom and murkiness, as much as we could do for coughing, to be sure of something.

"Where is Bardie gone?" I asked, as soon as my lungs gave speech to me: it should have been, "Where is Bunny gone?" But my head was full of the little one.

"Who can tell?" cried the boy, in Welsh, being thoroughly scared of his English. "Oh, Dyo dear, God the great only knows."

"God will guard her," I said softly, yet without pure faith in it, having seen such cruel things; but the boy's face moved me. Moreover, Bardie seemed almost too full of life for quenching; and having escaped rocks, waves, and quicksands, surely she would never be wrecked upon dry land ignobly. Nevertheless, at the mere idea of those helpless little ones out in all this raging havoc, tears came to my eyes, until the sand, of which the very house was full, crusted up and blinded them.

It was time to leave off thinking, if one meant to do any good. The whirlwinds spun and whistled round us, now on this side, now on that; and the old house creaked and rattled as the weather pulled or pushed at it. The sand was drifted in the courtyard (without any special whirlwind) three feet deep in the north-east corner; and the sky, from all sides, fell upon us, like a mountain undermined.

"Boy, go into your mother," I said; and I thank God for enabling me, else might she have been childless. "Tell your mother not to be frightened, but to get your father up, and to have the kettle boiling."

"Oh, Dyo—dear Dyo! let me come with you, after that poor little child, and after my five brothers."

"Go in, you helpless fool," I said; and he saw the set of my countenance, and left me, though but half-content.

It needed all my strength to draw the door of the house behind me, although the wind was bent no more on one way than another, but universal uproar. And down-roar too; for it fell on my head quite as much as it jerked my legs, and took me aback, and took me in front, and spun me round, and laughed at me. Then of a sudden all wind dropped, and yellow sky was over me.

What course to take (if I had the choice) in search of those poor children, was more at first than I could judge, or bring my mind to bear upon. For as sure as we live by the breath of the Lord, the blast of His anger deadens us.

Perhaps it was my instinct only, having been so long afloat, which drove me, straight as affairs permitted, toward the margin of the sea. And perhaps I had some desire to know how the sea itself would look under this strange visiting. Moreover, it may have come across me, without any thinking twice of it, that Bunny had an inborn trick of always running toward the sea, as behoved a sailor's daughter.

Anyhow, that way I took, so far as it was left to me to know the points of the compass, or the shape and manner of anything. For simple and short as the right road was, no simpleton or shortwitted man could have hit it, or come near it, in that ravenous weather. In the whirl and grim distortion of the air and the very earth, a man was walking (as you might say) in the depth of a perfect calm, with stifling heat upon him, and a piece of shadow to know himself by; and then, the next moment, there he was in a furious state of buffeting, baffled in front, and belaboured aback, and bellowed at under the swing of his arms, and the staggering failure of his poor legs.

Nevertheless, in the lull and the slack times, I did my utmost to get on, having more presence of mind perhaps than any landsman could have owned. Poor fellows they are when it comes to blow; and what could they do in a whirlwind?

As I began to think of them, and my luck in being a seaman, my courage improved to that degree that I was able quite heartily to commend myself to the power of God, whom, as a rule, I remember best when the world seems coming to an end. And I think it almost certain that this piety on my part enabled me to get on as I did.

For without any skill at all or bravery of mine, but only the calmness which fell upon me, as it used to do in the heat of battle, when I thought on my Maker, all at once I saw a way to elude a great deal of the danger. This was as simple as could be, yet never would have come home to a man unable to keep his wits about him.

Blurred and slurred as the whole sky was with twisted stuff and with yellowness, I saw that the whirling pillars of sand not only whirled but also travelled in one spiral only. They all came from the west, where lay the largest spread of sandhills, and they danced away to the north-east first, and then away to south of east, shaping a round like a ship with her helm up, preserving their spiral from left to right as all waterspouts do on the north of the Line.

So when a column of sand came nigh to suck me up, or to bury me—although it went thirty miles an hour, and I with the utmost care of my life could not have managed ten perhaps—by porting my helm without carrying sail, and so working a traverse, I kept the weather-gage of it and that made all the difference.

Of course I was stung in the face and neck as bad as a thousand musquitoes when the skirts of the whirl flapped round at me, but what was that to care about? It gave me pleasure to walk in such peril, and feel myself almost out of it by virtue of coolness and readiness. Nevertheless it gave me far greater pleasure, I can assure you, to feel hard ground beneath my feet, and stagger along the solid pebbles of the beach of Sker, where the sandstorm could not come so much.

Hereupon I do believe that, in spite of all my courage—so stout and strong in the moment of trial—all my power fell away befor the sense of safety. What could my old battered life matter to any one in the world, except myself and Bunny? However, I was so truly thankful to kind Providence for preserving it, that I cannot have given less than nine jumps, and said, "Matthew, Mark, Luke, and John," three times over, and in both ways.

This brought me back to the world again, as any power of piety always does when I dwell therein, and it drove me thereupon to trust in Providence no longer than the time was needful for me to recover breathing.

When I came to my breath and prudence, such a fright at first oppressed me, that I made a start for running into the foremost of the waves, thinking (if I thought at all) of lying down there, with my head kept up, and defying the sand to quench the sea.

Soon, however, I perceived that this was not advisable. Such a roar arose around me from the blows of hills and rocks, and the fretful eagerness of the sea to be at war again, and the deep sound of the distance—the voice of man could travel less than that of a sandpiper, and the foot of man might long to be the foot of a sandhopper. For the sea was rising fast up the verge of ground-swell, and a deep hoarse echo rolling down the shoaling of the surges. This to me was pleasant music, such as makes a man awake.

The colour of the sun and sky was just as I had once beholden near the pearl-grounds of Ceylon, where the bottom of the sea comes up with a very mournful noise, and the fish sing dirges, and no man, however clear of eye, can open the sea and the sky asunder. And by this time being able to look round a little—for the air was not so full of sand, though still very thick and dusty—I knew that we were on the brink of a kind of tornado, as they call it in the tropics,—a storm that very seldom comes into these northern latitudes, being raised by violence of heat, as I have heard a surveyor say, the air going upward rapidly, with a great hole left below it.

Now as I stood on watch, as it were, and, being in such a situation, longed for more tobacco, what came to pass was exactly this—so far as a man can be exact when his wits have long been failing him.

The heaven opened, or rather seemed to be cloven by a sword-sweep, and a solid mass of lightning fell, with a cone like a red-hot anvil. The ring of black rocks received its weight, and leaped like a boiling caldron, while the stormy waters rose into a hiss and heap of steam. Then the crash of heaven stunned me.

When I came to myself it was raining as if it had never rained before. The rage of sand and air was beaten flat beneath the rain, and the fretful lifting of the sea was hushed off into bubbles. What to do I could not tell, in spite of all experience, but rubbed the sand from both my eyes, as bad as the beard of an oyster, and could see no clear way anywhere.

Now the sky was spread and traversed with a net of crossing fires, in and out like mesh and needle, only without time to look. Some were yellow, some deep red, and some like banks of violet, and others of a pale sweet blue, like gazing through a window. They might have been very beautiful, and agreeable to consider, if they had been further off, and without that wicked crack of thunder through the roar. Worse storms I had seen, of course, in the hot world and up mountains, and perhaps thought little of them; but then there was this difference, I had always plenty of fellows with me, and it was not Sunday. Also, I then was young, and trained for cannons to be shot at me. Neither had I a boat of my own, but my dear wife was alive.

These considerations moved me to be careful of my life—a duty which increases on us after the turn of the balance; and seeing all things black behind me, and a world of storm around, knowing every hole as I did, with many commendations of myself to God for the sake of Bunny, in I went into a hole under a good solid rock, where I could watch the sea, and care for nothing but an earthquake.

CHAPTER X.

UNDER THE ROCK.

For a while the power of the lightning seemed to quench the wind almost, and one continuous roar of thunder rang around the darkness. Then, with a bellow, the wind sprang forth (like a wild bull out of a mountain), and shattered the rain and drowned the thunder, and was lord of everything. Under its weight the flat sea quivered, and the crests flew into foam, and the scourge upon the waters seemed to beat them all together. The whirlwinds now were past and done with, and a violent gale begun, and in the burst and change of movement there appeared a helpless ship.

She was bearing towards Pool Tavan, as poor Bardie's boat had done, but without the summer glory and the golden wealth of waves. All was smooth and soft and gentle, as the moonlight in a glass, when the little boat came gliding with its baby captain. All was rough and hard and furious as a fight of devils, when that ship came staggering with its load of sin and woe. And yet there had not been so much as twenty-four hours between the two.

Not one of our little coasting vessels, but a full-rigged ship she loomed, of foreign build, although at present carrying no colours. I saw at once what her business was, to bring from the West Indies sugar, rum, and suchlike freight, to Bristol, or to the Dutchmen. This was in her clearance-bill; but behind that she had other import not so clearly entered. In a word, she carried negroes from the overstocked plantations, not to be quite slaves (at least in the opinion of their masters), but to be distributed, for their own Christian benefit, at a certain sum per head, among the Bristol or Dutch merchants, or wherever it might be. And it serves them right, I always say; for the fuss that we now make about those black men must bring down the anger of the Creator, who made them black, upon us.

As the gale set to its work, and the sea arose in earnest, and the lightning drifted off into the scud of clouds, I saw, as plain as a pikestaff, that the ship must come ashore, and go to pieces very likely, before one could say "Jack Robinson." She had been on the Sker-weather sands already, and lost her rudder and some of her sternpost, as the lift of the water showed; and now there was nothing left on board her of courage or common seamanship. The truth of it was, although of course I could not know it then, that nearly all the ship's company acted as was to be expected from a lot of foreigners; that is to say, if such they were. They took to the boats in a kind of panic when first she struck among the sands in the whirlwind which began the storm. There could have been then no great sea running, only quiet rollers; and being but two miles off the shore, they hoped, no doubt, to land well enough, after leaving the stupid negroes and the helpless passengers to the will of Providence.

However, before they had rowed a mile, with the flood tide making eastward, one of the boats was struck by lightning, and the other caught in a whirl vorago (as the Spaniards call it), and not a soul ever came to land, and scarcely any bodies. Both these accidents were seen from Porthcawl Point by Sandy Macraw through a telescope: and much as he was mine enemy, I do him the justice to believe it; partly because he could look for no money from any lies in the matter, and still more because I have heard that some people said that they saw him see it.

But to come back to this poor ship: the wind, though blowing madly enough (as a summer gale is often hotter for a while than a winter one), had not time and sweep as yet to raise any very big rollers. The sea was sometimes beaten flat and then cast up in hillocks; but the mighty march of waters fetched by a tempest from the Atlantic was not come, and would not come in a veering storm like this. For it takes a gale of at least three tides, such as we never have in summer, to deliver the true buffet of the vast Atlantic.

Nevertheless the sea was nasty and exceeding vicious; and the wind more madly wild, perhaps, than when it has full time to blow; in short, the want of depth and power was made up by rage and spite. And for a ship not thoroughly sound and stanch in all her timbers it had been better, perhaps, to rise and fall upon long billows, with a chance of casting high and dry, than to be twirled round and plucked at, thrown on beam-ends, and taken aback, as this hapless craft was being, in the lash of rocky waters and the drift of gale and scud.

By this time she was close ashore, and not a man (except myself) to help or even pity her. All around her was wind and rocks, and a mad sea rushing under her. The negroes, crouching in the scuppers, or clinging to the masts and rails, or rolling over one another in their want of pluck and skill, seemed to shed their blackness on the snowy spray and curdled foam, like cuttle-fish in a lump of froth. Poor things! they are grieved to die as much, perhaps, as any white man; and my heart was overcome, in spite of all I know of them.

The ship had no canvas left, except some tatters of the foretopsail, and a piece of the main-royals; but she drifted broadside on, I daresay five or six knots an hour. She drew too much water, unluckily, to come into Pool Tavan at that time of the tide, even if the mouth had been wide enough; but crash she went on a ledge of rocks thoroughly well known to me, every shelf of which was a razor. Half a cable's length below the entrance to Pool Tavan, it had the finest steps and stairs for congers and for lobsters, whenever one could get at it in a low spring-tide; but the worst of beaks and barbs for a vessel to strike upon at half-flow, and with a violent sea, and a wind as wild as Bedlam.

With the pressure of these, she lay so much to leeward before striking (and perhaps her cargo had shifted), that the poor blackies rolled down the deck like pickling walnuts on a tray; and they had not even the chance of dying each in his own direction.

I was forced to shut my eyes; till a grey squall came, and caught her up, as if she had been a humming-top, and flung her (as we drown a kitten) into the mashing waters.

Now I hope no man who knows me would ever take me for such a fool as to dream for a moment—after all I have seen of them—that a negro is "our own flesh and blood, and a brother immortal," as the parsons begin to prate, under some dark infection. They differ from us a great deal more than an ass does from a horse; but for all that I was right down glad—as a man of loving-kindness—that such a pelt of rain came up as saved me from the discomfort—or pain, if you must have the truth—of beholding several score, no doubt, of unfortunate blacks a-drowning.

If it had pleased Providence to drown any white men with them, and to let me know it, beyond a doubt I had rushed in, though without so much as a rope to help me; and as it was, I was ready to do my very best to save them if they had only shown some readiness to be hawled ashore by a man of proper colour. But being, as negroes always are, of a most contrary nature, no doubt they preferred to drift out to sea rather than Christian burial. At any rate, none of them came near me, kindly disposed as I felt myself, and ready to tuck up my Sunday trousers at the very first sight of a woolly head. But several came ashore next tide—when it could be no comfort at all to them. And such, as I have always found, is the nature of black people.

But for me it was a sad, and, as I thought, severe, visitation to be forced on a Sabbath-day—my only holiday of the week— to meditate over a scene like this. As a truly consistent and truth-seeking Christian (especially when I go round with fish on a Monday morning among Nonconformists), it was a bitter trial for me to reflect upon those poor negroes, gone without any sense at all, except of good Christians' wickedness, to the judgment we decree for all, except ourselves and families.

But there was worse than this behind; for after waiting as long as there seemed good chance of anything coming ashore, which might go into my pocket, without risk of my pension, and would truly be mine in all honesty—and after seeing that the wreck would not break up till the tide rose higher, though all on board were swept away—suddenly it came into my head about poor Bardie and Bunny. They were worth all the niggers that ever made coal look the colour of pipeclay; and with a depth of self-reproach which I never deserved to feel, having truly done my utmost—for who could walk in such weather?—forth I set, resolved to face whatever came out of the heavens. Verily nothing could come much worse than what was come already. Rheumatics, I mean, which had struck me there, under the rock, as a snake might. Three hours ago all the world was sweat, and now all the air was shivers. Such is the climate of our parts, and many good people rail at it, who have not been under discipline. But all who have felt that gnawing anguish, or that fiery freezing, burning at once and benumbing (like a dead bone put into the live ones, with a train of powder down it)—all these will have pity for a man who had crouched beneath a rock for at least three hours, with dripping clothes, at the age of two-and-fifty.

For a hero I never set up to be, and never came across one until my old age in the navy, as hereafter to be related. And though I had served on board of one in my early years, off La Hague and Cape Grisnez, they told me she was only a woman that used to hold a lantern. Hero, however, or no hero, in spite of all discouragement and the aching of my bones, resolved I was to follow out the fate of those two children. There seemed to be faint hope, indeed, concerning the little stranger; but Bunny might be all alive and strong, as was right and natural for a child of her age and substance. But I was sore downcast about it when I looked around and saw the effect of the storm that had been over them. For the alteration of everything was nothing less than amazing.

It is out of my power to tell you how my heart went up to God, and all my spirit and soul was lifted into something purer, when of a sudden, in a scoop of sand, with the rushes overhanging, I came on those two little dears, fast asleep in innocence. A perfect nest of peace they had, as if beneath their Father's eye, and by His own hand made for them. The fury of the earth and sky was all around and over them; the deep revenge of the sea was rolling, not a hundred yards away; and here those two little dots were asleep, with their angels trying to make them dream.

Bunny, being the elder and much the stronger child, had thrown the skirt of her frock across poor little Bardie's naked shoulders; while Bardie, finding it nice and warm, had nestled her delicate head into the lap of her young nurse, and had tried (as it seemed), before dropping off, to tell her gratitude by pressing Bunny's red hands to her lips. In a word, you might go a long way and scarcely see a prettier or more moving picture, or more apt to lead a man who seldom thinks of his Maker. As for me, I became so proud of my own granddaughter's goodness, and of the little lady's trust and pure repose therein, that my heart went back at once to my dead boy Harry, and I do believe that I must have wept, if I could have stopped to look at them.

But although I was truly loath to spoil this pretty picture, the poor things must be partly wet, even in that nest of rushes, which the whirlwinds had not touched. So I awoke them very gently, and shook off the sand, while they rubbed their eyes, and gaped, and knew no more of their danger than if they had been in their own dear beds. Then, with Bardie in my arms, and Bunny trotting stoutly with her thumb spliced into my trousers, I shaped a course for Sker farmhouse, having a strong gale still abaft, but the weather slightly moderating.

CHAPTER XI.

A WRECKER WRECKED.

NEAR the gate I met Evan Thomas, the master of the house himself, at length astir, but still three-parts drunk, and—if I may say so with due compassion for the trouble then before him—in a very awkward state of mind. It happened so that the surliness of his liquor and of his nature mingled at this moment with a certain exultation, a sense of good-luck, and a strong desire to talk and be told again of it. And this is the nature of all Welshmen; directly they have any luck, they must begin to brag of it. You will find the same in me perhaps, or, at any rate, think you do, although I try to exclude it, having to deal with Englishmen, who make nothing of all the great deeds they have done until you begin to agree with them. And then, my goodness, they do come out! But the object of my writing is to make them understand us, which they never yet have done, being unlike somehow in nature, although we are much of their fathers.

Having been almost equally among both these nations, and speaking English better perhaps than my native tongue of the Cymry—of which anybody can judge who sees the manner in which I do it—it is against my wish to say what Evan Thomas looked like. His dark face, overhung with hair, and slouched with a night of drinking, was beginning to burn up, from paleness and from weariness, into a fury of plunder. Scarcely did I know the man, although I had so many recollections of evil against him. A big, strong, clumsy fellow at all times, far more ready to smite than smile, and wholly void of that pleasant humour, which among almost all my neighbours—though never yet could I find out why—creates a pleasing eagerness for my humble society as punctual as my pension-day.

But now his reeling staggering manner of coming along towards us, and the hunching of his shoulders, and the swagging of his head, and, most of all, the great gun he carried, were enough to make good quiet people who had been to church get behind a sand-hill. However, for that it was too late. I was bound to face him. Bardie dropped her eyes under my beard, and Bunny crept closer behind my leg. For my part, although the way was narrow, and the lift of the storm gave out some light, it would have moved no resentment in me if he had seen (as rich men do) unfit to see a poor man.

However, there was no such luck. He carried his loaded gun with its muzzle representing a point of view the very last I could have desired—namely, at my midships; and he carried it so that I longed to have said a little word about carefulness. But I durst not, with his coal-black eyes fixed upon me as they were, and so I pulled up suddenly. For he had given me an imperious nod, as good as ordering me to stop.

"Wreck ashore!" he cried out in Welsh, having scarce a word of English—"wreck ashore! I smell her, Dyo. Don't tell me no lies, my boy. I smelled her all the afternoon. And high time to have one."

"There is a wreck ashore," I answered, looking with some disgust at him, as a man who has been wrecked himself must do at a cruel wrecker; "but the ebb most likely will draw her off and drift her into the quicksands."

"Great God! speak not like that, my boy. The worst you are of everything. If those two children came ashore, there must have been something better." And he peered at the children as if to search for any gold upon them.

"Neither child came from that wreck. One is my granddaughter Bunny. Bunny, show yourself to black Evan." But the child shrank closer behind me. "Evan black, you know her well. And the other is a little thing I picked up on the coast last night."

"Ha, ha! you pick up children where you put them, I suppose. But take them indoors and be done with them. Cubs to come with a wreck ashore, a noble wreck ashore, I say! But come you down again, fisherman Dyo." He used the word "fisherman" with a peculiar stress, and a glance of suspicion at my pockets. "Come you down again, Dyo dear. I shall want you to help me against those thieves from Kenfig. Bring my other gun from the clock-case, and tell the boys to run down with their bando-sticks. I'll warrant we'll clear the shore between us; and then, good Dyo, honest Dyo, you shall have some—you shall, you dog. Fair-play, Dyo; fair share and share, though every stick is mine of right. Ah, Dyo, Dyo, you cunning sheep's head, you love a keg of rum, you dog."

This I knew to be true enough, but only within the bounds of both honesty and sobriety. But so much talking had made his brain, in its present condition, go round again; and while I was thinking how far it might be safe and right to come into his views, his loaded gun began wagging about in a manner so highly dangerous, that for the sake of the two poor children I was obliged to get out of his way, and, looking back from a safer distance, there I beheld him flourishing with his arms on the top of a sand-hill, and waving his hat on the top of his gun, for his sons to come over the warren.

Moxy Thomas was very kind; she never could help being so, and therefore never got any thanks. She stripped the two wet children at once, and put them in bed together to keep each other warm. But first she had them snugly simmering in a milk-pan of hot water with a little milk for the sake of their skins. Bunny was heavy and sleepy therein, and did nothing but yawn and stretch out her arms. Bardie, on the other hand, was ready to boil over with delight and liveliness, flashing about like a little dab-chick.

"Old Davy," she said, as I came to see her at her own invitation, and she sate quite over Bunny, "'Ill 'a have a ickle dop?" With the water up to her neck, she put one mite of a transparent finger to my grizzled mouth, and popped a large drop in, and laughed, until I could have worshipped her.

Now, having seen these two little dears fast asleep and warmly compassed, I began, according to Evan's orders, to ask about the boys, not having seen any sign of them. Moxy said that Watkin went out to look for his five brothers about an hour after I had left, and in spite of the rain and lightning. She had tried in vain to stop him: something was on his mind, it seemed; and when she went up to attend on his father, he took the opportunity to slip out of the kitchen.

Now Moxy having been in the house, and the house away from the worst of the storm, being moreover a woman, and therefore wholly abroad about weather, it was natural that she should not have even the least idea of the jeopardy encountered by her five great sons in the warren. Enough for her that they were not at sea. Danger from weather upon dry land was out of her comprehension.

It wanted perhaps half an hour of dusk, and had given over raining, but was blowing a good reef-topsail gale, when I started to search for the sons of Sker. Of course I said nothing to make their mother at all uneasy about them, but took from the clock-case the loaded gun (as Evan had commanded me), and set forth upon the track of young Watkin, better foot foremost. For he was likely to know best what part of the warren his five great brothers had chosen for their sport that day; and in the wet sand it was easy to follow the course the boy had taken.

The whirlwinds had ceased before he went forth, and the deluge of rain was now soaked in, through the drought so long abiding. But the wind was wailing pitifully, and the rushes swaying wearily; and the yellow baldness, here and there, of higher sand-hills, caught the light. Ragged clouds ran over all, and streamers of the sunset; and the sky was like a school let loose, with the joy of wind and rain again. It is not much of me that swears, when circumstances force me; only a piece, perhaps, of custom, and a piece of honesty. These two lead one astray sometimes; and then comes disappointment. For I had let some anger vex me at the rudeness of black Evan, and the ungodliness of his sons, which forced me thus to come abroad, when full of wet and weariness. In spite of this, I was grieved and frightened, and angry with no one but myself, when I chanced upon boy Watkin, fallen into a tuft of rushes, with his blue eyes running torrents. There he lay, like a heap of trouble, as young folk do ere they learn the world; and I put him on his legs three times, but he managed to go down again. At last I got his knees to stick; but even so he turned away, and put his head between his hands, and could not say a word to me. And by the way his shoulders went, I knew that he was sobbing. I asked him what the matter was, and what he was taking so much to heart; and, not to be too long over a trifle, at last I got this out of him:—

"Oh, good Mr Llewellyn, dear, I never shall see nothing more of my great brothers five, so long as ever I do live. And when they kicked me out of bed every Sunday morning, and spread the basins over me, it was not that they meant to harm —I do feel it, I do feel it; and perhaps my knees ran into them. Under the sands, the sands, they are; and never to kick me again no more! Of sorrow it is more than ever I can tell."

"Watty," said I, "why talk you so? Your brothers know every crick and corner of this warren, miles and miles; and could carry a sand-hill among them. They are snug enough somewhere with their game, and perhaps gone to sleep, like the little ones."

Of the babies' adventures he knew nothing, and only stared at me; so I asked him what had scared him so.

"Under the sands, the sands, they are, so sure as ever I do live. Or the rabbit-bag would not be here, and Dutch, who never, never leaves them, howling at the rabbit-bag!"

Looking further through the tussocks, I saw that it was even so. Dutch, the mongrel collie, crouched beside a bag of something, with her tail curled out of sight, and her ears laid flat and listless, and her jowl along the ground. And every now and then she gave a low but very grievous howl.

"Now, boy, don't be a fool," I said, with the desire to encourage him; "soon we shall find your brothers five, with another great sack of rabbits. They left the bitch yonder to watch the sack, while they went on for more, you see."

"It is the sack; the sack it is! And no other sack along of them. Oh, Mr Llewellyn, dear, here is the bag, and there is Dutch, and never no sign at all of them!"

At this I began to fear indeed that the matter was past

helping—that an accident and a grief had happened worse than the drowning of all the negroes, which it has ever pleased Providence (in a darkness of mood) to create for us. But my main desire was to get poor Watty away at once, lest he should encounter things too dreadful for a boy like him.

"Go home," I said, "with the bag of rabbits, and give poor Dutch her supper. Your father is down on the shore of the sea, and no doubt the boys are with him. They are gone to meet a great shipwreck, worth all the rabbits all the way from Dunraven to Giant's Grave."

"But little Dutch, it is little Dutch! They never would leave her, if wreck there was. She can fetch out of the water so good almost as any dog."

I left him to his own devices, being now tired of arguing. For by this time it was growing dark; and a heavy sea was roaring; and the wreck was sure to be breaking up, unless she had been swallowed up. And the common-sense of our village, and parish, would go very hard against me for not being on the spot to keep the adjacent parish from stealing. For Kenfig and Newton are full of each other, with a fine old ancient hatred. So we climbed over the crest of high sand, where the rushes lay weltering after the wind; and then with a plunge of long strides down hill, and plucking our feet out hastily, on the watered marge we stood, to which the sea was striving.

Among the rocks black Evan leaped, with white foam rushing under him, and sallies of the stormy tide volleying to engulf him. Strong liquor still was in his brain, and made him scorn his danger, and thereby saved him from it. One timid step, and the churning waters would have made a curd of him. The fury of his visage showed that somebody had wronged him, after whom he rushed with vengeance, and his great gun swinging.

"Sons of dogs!" he cried in Welsh, alighting on the pebbles; "may the devil feed their fathers with a melting bowl!"

"What's the rumpus now?" I asked; "what have your sons been doing?"

For he always swore at his sons as freely as at anybody's, and at himself for begetting them.

"My sons!" he cried, with a stamp of rage; "if my sons had been here, what man would have dared to do on the top of my head this thing? Where are they? I sent you for them."

"I have sought for them high and low," I answered; "here is the only one I could find."

"Watkin! What use of Watkin? A boy like a girl or a baby! I want my five tall bully-boys to help their poor father's livelihood. There's little Tom tailor gone over the sand-hills with a keg of something; and Teddy shoemaker with a spar; and I only shot between them! Cursed fool! what shall I come to, not to be able to shoot a man?"

He had fired his gun, and was vexed, no doubt, at wasting a charge so randomly; then spying his other gun on my shoulder, with the flint and the priming set, he laid his heavy hand on it. I scarce knew what to do, but feared any accident in the struggle; and after all, he was not so drunk that the law would deny him his own gun.

"Ha, ha!" with a pat of the breech, he cried; "for this I owe thee a good turn, Dyo. Thou art loaded with rocks, my darling, as the other was with cowries. Twenty to the pound of lead for any longshore robbers. I see a lot more sneaking down. Dyo, now for sport, my boy."

I saw some people, dark in the distance, under the brow of a sand-hill; and before I could speak or think, black Evan was off to run at them. I too set my feet for speed, but the strings of my legs hung backward; and Watty, who could run like a hare, seemed to lag behind me. And behind him there was little Dutch, crawling with her belly down, and her eyes turned up at us, as if we were dragging her to be hanged.

Until we heard a shout of people, through the roar of wind and sea, in front of where black Evan strode; and making towards it, we beheld, in glimmering dusk of shore and sky, something we knew nothing of.

A heavy sand-hill hung above them, with its brow come over; and long roots of rushes naked in the shrillness of the wind. Under this were men at work, as we work for lives of men; and their Sunday shirt-sleeves flashed, white like ghosts, and gone again. Up to them strode Evan black, over the marge of the wild March tides; and grounded his gun and looked at them. They for a breath gazed up at him, and seemed to think and wonder; and then, as though they had not seen him, fell again a-digging.

"What means this?" he roared at them, with his great eyes flashing fire, and his long gun levelled. But they neither left their work nor lifted head to answer him. The yellow sand came sliding down, in wedge-shaped runnels, over them, and their feet sank out of sight; but still they kept on working.

"Come away, then, Evan great; come away and seek for

wreck," I shouted, while he seemed to stand in heaviness of wonder. "This is not a place for you. Come away, my man, my boy."

Thus I spoke, in Welsh of course, and threw my whole weight on his arm, to make him come away with me. But he set his feet in sand, and spread his legs, and looked at me; and the strongest man that was ever born could not have torn him from his hold, with those eyes upon him.

"Dyo, I am out of dreaming. Dyo, I must see this wreck; only take the gun from me."

This I would have done right gladly, but he changed his mind about it, falling back to a savage mood.

"You down there, who gave you leave to come and dig my sand-hills? Answer, or have skins of lead."

Two or three of the men looked up, and wanted to say something. But the head-man from the mines, who understood the whole of them, nodded, and they held their tongues. Either they were brave men all (which never is without discipline), or else the sense of human death confused and overpowered them. Whatever they meant, they went on digging.

"Some damned sailor under there," cried Evan, losing patience; "little mustard-spoons of sand. Can't you throw it faster? Fine young fellows three of them, in the hole their own ship made, last March tide, it must have been. Let us see this new batch come. They always seem to have spent their wages before they learn to drown themselves."

He laughed and laid his gun aside, and asked me for tobacco, and, trying to be sober, sang "the rising of the lark." I, for my part, shrunk away, and my flesh crawled over me.

"Work away, my lads, work away. You are all of a mind to warm yourselves. Let me know when you have done. And all you find belongs to me. I can sit and see it out, and make a list of everything. Ear-rings gold, and foreign pieces, and the trinkets they have worn. Out with them! I know them all. Fools! what use of skulking? You are on soft stuff, I see. Have out every one of them."

So they did; and laid before him, in the order of their birth, the carcases of his five sons. Evan first, his eldest born; Thomas next, and Rees, and Hopkin, and then (with the sigh of death still in him) Jenkin, newly turned fifteen.

CHAPTER XII.

HOW TO SELL FISH.

WHAT I had seen that night upset me more than I like to dwell upon. But with all my fish on hand, I was forced to make the best of it. For a down-hearted man will turn meat, as we say, and much more, fish, to a farthing's-worth. And though my heart was sore and heavy for my ancient sweetheart Moxy, and for little Bardie in the thick of such disasters, that could be no excuse to me for wasting good fish—or at least pretty good—and losing thoroughly good money.

Here were the mullet, with less of shine than I always recommended and honestly wish them to possess; here were the prawns, with a look of paleness and almost of languishing, such as they are bound to avoid until money paid and counted; and most of all, here were lawful bass, of very great size and substance, inclined to do themselves more justice in the scales than on the dish.

I saw that this would never answer to my present high repute. Concerning questions afterwards, and people being hard upon me, out of thoughtless ignorance, that was none of my affair. The whole of that would go, of course, upon the weather and sudden changes, such as never were known before. And if good religious people would not so be satisfied with the will of Providence to have their fish as fish are made, against them I had another reason, which never fails to satisfy.

The "burning tide," as they called it (through which poor Bardie first appeared), had been heard of far inland, and with one consent pronounced to be the result of the devil improperly flipping his tail while bathing. Although the weather had been so hot, this rumour was beyond my belief; nevertheless I saw my way, if any old customer should happen, when it came to his dinner-time, to be at all discontented (which no man with a fine appetite and a wholesome nose should indulge in)—I saw my way to sell him more, upon the following basket-day, by saying what good people said, and how much I myself had seen of it.

With these reflections I roused my spirits, and resolved to let no good fish be lost, though it took all the week to sell them. For, in spite of the laws laid down in the books (for young married women, and so forth), there is scarcely any other thing upon which both men and women may be led astray so pleasantly as why to buy fish, and when to buy fish, and what fish to buy.

Therefore I started in good spirits on the Monday morning, carrying with me news enough to sell three times the weight I bore, although it was breaking my back almost. Good fish it was, and deserved all the praise that ever I could bestow on it, for keeping so well in such shocking weather; and so I sprinkled a little salt in some of the delicate places, just to store the flavour there; for cooks are so forgetful, and always put the blame on me when they fail of producing a fine fresh smell.

Also knowing, to my sorrow, how suspicious people are, and narrow-minded to a degree none would give them credit for, I was forced to do a thing which always makes me to myself seem almost uncharitable.

But I felt that I could trust nobody to have proper faith in me, especially when they might behold the eyes of the fishes retire a little, as they are very apt to do when too many cooks have looked at them. And knowing how strong the prejudice of the public is in this respect, I felt myself bound to gratify it, though at some cost of time and trouble. This method I do not mind describing (as I am now pretty clear of the trade) for the good of my brother fishermen.

When the eyes of a fish begin to fail him through long retirement from the water, you may strengthen his mode of regarding the world (and therefore the world's regard for him) by a delicate piece of handling. Keep a ray-fish always ready —it does not matter how stale he is—and on the same day on which you are going to sell your bass, or mullet, or cod, or whatever it may be, pull a few sharp spines, as clear as you can, out of this good ray. Then open the mouth of your languid fish and embolden the aspect of either eye by fetching it up from despondency with a skewer of proper length extented from one ball to the other. It is almost sure to drop out in the cooking; and even if it fails to do so, none will be the wiser, but take it for a provision of nature—as indeed it ought to be.

Now, if anybody is rude enough to gainsay your fish in the market, you have the evidence of the eyes and hands against that of the nose alone. "Why, bless me, madam," I used to say, "a lady like you, that understands fish a great deal better than I do! His eyes are coming out of his head, ma'am, to hear you say such things of him. Afloat he was at four this morning, and his eyes will speak to it." And so he was, well afloat in my tub, before I began to prepare him for a last appeal to the public. Only they must not float too long, or the scales will not be stiff enough.

Being up to a few of these things, and feeling very keenly how hard the public always tries to get upper hand of me, and would beat me down to half nothing a pound (if allowed altogether its own way), I fought very bravely the whole of that Monday to turn a few honest shillings. "Good old Davy, fine old Davy, brave old Davy!" they said I was every time I abated a halfpenny; and I called them generous gentlemen and Christian-minded ladies every time they wanted to smell my fish, which is not right before payment. What right has any man to disparage the property of another? When you have bought him, he is your own, and you have the title to canvas him; but when he is put in the scales, remember "nothing but good of the dead," if you remember anything.

As I sate by the cross roads in Bridgend on the bottom of a bucket, and with a four-legged dressing-table (hired for twopence) in front of me, who should come up but the well-known Brother Hezekiah? Truly tired I was getting, after plodding through Merthyr Mawr, Ogmore, and Ewenny, Llaleston, and Newcastle, and driven at last to the town of Bridgend. For some of my fish had a gamesome odour, when first I set off in the morning; and although the rain had cooled down the air, it was now become an unwise thing to recommend what still remained to any man of unchristian spirit, or possessing the ear of the magistrates.

Now perhaps I should not say this thing, and many may think me inclined to vaunt, and call me an old coxcomb; but if any man could sell stinking fish in the times of which I am writing—and then it was ten times harder than now, because women looked after marketing—that man I verily believe was this old Davy Llewellyn; and right he has to be proud of it. But what were left on my hands that evening were beginning to get so strong, that I feared they must go over Bridgend bridge into the river Ogmore.

The big coach with the London letters, which came then almost twice a-week, was just gone on, after stopping three hours to rest the horses and feed the people; and I had done some business with them, for London folk for the most part have a kind and pleasing ignorance. They paid me well, and I served them well with fish of a fine high flavour; but now I had some which I would not offer to such kind-hearted gentry.

Hezekiah wanted fish. I saw it by his nostrils, and I knew it for certain when he pretended not to see me or my standing. He went a good bit round the corner, as if to deal with the ironmonger. But for all that, I knew as well as if I could hear his wife beginning to rake the fire, that fish for supper was the business which had brought him across the bridge. Therefore I refused an offer which I would have jumped at before seeing Hezekiah, of twopence a-pound for the residue from an old woman who sold pickles; and I made up my mind to keep up the price, knowing the man to have ten in family, and all blessed with good appetites.

"What, Davy! Brother Davy!" he cried, being compelled to begin, because I took care not to look at him. "Has it been so ordered that I behold good brother Davy with fish upon a Monday?" His object in this was plain enough—to beat down my goods by terror of an information for Sabbath-labour.

"The Lord has been merciful to me," I answered, patting my best fish on his shoulder; "not only in sending them straight to my net, at nine o'clock this morning; but also, brother Hezekiah, in the hunger all people have for them. I would that I could have kept thee a taste; not soon wouldst thou forget it. Sweeter fish and finer fish never came out of Newton Bay"—this I said because Newton Bay is famous for high quality. "But, brother Hezekiah, thou art come too late." And I began to pack up very hastily.

"What!" cried Hezekiah, with a keen and hungrily grievous voice; "all those fish bespoken, Davy?"

"Every one of them bespoken, brother; by a man who knows a right down good bass, better almost than I do. Griffy, the 'Cat and Snuffers.'"

Now, Griffith, who kept the "Cat and Snuffers," was a very jovial man, and a bitter enemy to Hezekiah Perkins; and I knew that the latter would gladly offer a penny a-pound upon Griffy's back, to spoil him of his supper, and to make him offend his customers.

"Stop, brother Davy," cried Hezekiah, stretching out his broad fat hands, as I began to pack my fish, with the freshest smellers uppermost; "Davy dear, this is not right, nor like our ancient friendship. A rogue like Griffy to cheat you so! What had he beaten you down to, Davy?"

"Beaten me down!" I said, all in a hurry; "is it likely I would be beaten down, with their eyes coming out of their heads like that?"

"Now, dear brother Dyo, do have patience! What was he going to give you a-pound?"

"Fourpence a-pound, and ten pound of them. Three-and-fourpence for a lot like that! Ah, the times are bad indeed!"

"Dear brother Dyo, fourpence-halfpenny! Three-and-nine down, for the lot as it stands."

"Hezekiah, for what do you take me? Cut a farthing in four, when you get it. Do I look a likely man to be a rogue for fivepence?"

"No, no, Davy; don't be angry with me. Say as much as tenpence. Four-and-twopence, ready money; and no Irish coinage."

"Brother Hezekiah," said I, "a bargain struck is a bargain kept. Rob a man of his supper for tenpence!"

"Oh, Dyo, Dyo! you never would think of that man's supper, with my wife longing for fish so! Such a family as we have, and the weakness in Hepzibah's back! Five shillings for the five, Davy."

"There, there; take them along," I cried at last, with a groan from my chest: "you are bound to be the ruin of me. But what can I do with a delicate lady? Brother, surely you have been a little too hard upon me. Whatever shall I find to say to a man who never beats me down?"

"Tell that worldly 'Cat and Snuffers' that your fish were much too good—why, Davy, they seem to smell a little!"

"And small use they would be, Hezekiah, either for taste or for nourishment, unless they had the sea-smell now. Brother, all your money back, and the fish to poor Griffy, if you know not the smell of salt water yet."

"Now, don't you be so hot, old Davy. The fish are good enough, no doubt; and it may be from the skewer-wood; but they have a sort, not to say a smell, but a manner of reminding one——"

"Of the savoury stuff they feed on," said I; "and the thorough good use they make of it. A fish must eat, and so must we, and little blame to both of us."

With that he bade me "good-night," and went with alacrity

towards his supper, scornfully sneering as he passed the door of the "Cat and Snuffers." But though it was a fine thing for me, and an especial Providence, to finish off my stock so well, at a time when I would have taken gladly a shilling for the lot of it, yet I felt that circumstances were against my lingering. Even if Hezekiah, unable to enter into the vein of my fish, should find himself too fat to hurry down the steep hill after me, still there were many other people, fit for supper, and fresh for it, from the sudden coolness, whom it was my duty now to preserve from mischief; by leaving proper interval for consideration, before I might happen to be in front of their dining room windows another day.

Therefore, with a grateful sense of goodwill to all customers, I thought it better to be off. There I had been, for several hours, ready to prove anything, but never challenged by anybody; and my spirit had grown accordingly. But I never yet have found it wise to overlie success. Win it, and look at it, and be off, is the quickest way to get some more. So I scarcely even called so much as a pint at the "Cat and Snuffers," to have a laugh with Griffy; but set off for Newton, along the old road, with a good smart heel, and a fine day's business, and a light heart inside of me.

When I had passed Red-hill and Tythegston, and clearly was out upon Newton Down, where the glow-worms are most soft and sweet, it came upon me, in looking up from the glow-worms to the stars of heaven, to think and balance how far I was right in cheating Hezekiah. It had been done with the strictest justice, because his entire purpose was purely to cheat me. Whereupon Providence had stepped in and seen that I was the better man. I was not so ungrateful—let nobody suppose it—as to repine at this result. So far from that, that I rattled my money and had a good laugh, and went on again. But being used to watch the stars, as an old sailor is bound to do, I thought that Orion ought to be up, and I could not see Orion. This struck me as an unkindly thing, although, when I thought of it next day, I found that Orion was quite right, and perhaps the beer a little strong which had led me to look out for him; anyhow, it threw me back to think of Hezekiah, and make the worst of him to myself for having had the best of him.

Everybody may be sure that I never would have gone out of the way to describe my traffic with that man unless there were good reason. Nay, but I wanted to show you exactly the cast

and the colour of man he was, by setting forth his low attempt
to get my fish for nothing.

There was no man, of course, in my native village, and very
few in Bridgend perhaps, to whom I would have sold those fish,
unless they were going to sell it again. But Hezekiah Perkins,
a member and leading elder of the "Nicodemus-Christians,"
was so hard a man to cheat—except by stirring of his gall—
and so keen a cheat himself; so proud, moreover, of his wit and
praying, and truly brotherly,—that to lead him astray was the
very first thing desired by a sound Churchman.

By trade and calling he had been—before he received his
special call—no more than a common blacksmith. Now a
blacksmith is a most useful man, full of news and full of jokes,
and very often by no means drunk; this, however, was not
enough to satisfy Hezekiah. Having parts, as he always told
us—and sometimes we wished that he had no whole—culti-
vated parts, moreover, and taken up by the gentry, nothing of
a lower order came up to his merits than to call himself as
follows: "Horologist, Gunsmith, Practical Turner, Working
Goldsmith and Jeweller, Maker of all Machinery, and Engine-
man to the King and Queen."

The first time he put this over his door, all the neighbours
laughed at him, knowing (in spite of the book he had got full
of figures and shapes and crossings, which he called "Three-
gun-ometry") that his education was scarcely up to the rule of
three, without any guns. Nevertheless he got on well, having
sense enough to guide him when to talk large (in the presence
of people who love large talk, as beyond them), and when to
sing small, and hold his tongue, and nod at the proper distances,
if ever his business led him among gentry of any sense or science,
such as we sometimes hear of. Hence it was that he got the
order to keep the church-clock of Bridgend a-going by setting
the hands on twice a-day, and giving a push to the pendulum;
and so long as the clock would only go, nobody in the town
cared a tick whether it kept right time or wrong. And if people
from the country durst say anything about it, it was always
enough to ask them what their own clocks had to say.

There were not then many stable-clocks, such as are growing
upon us now, so that every horse has his own dinner-bell; only
for all those that were, Hezekiah received, I daresay, from five
to ten shillings a-month apiece in order to keep them moving.
But, bless my heart! he knew less of a clock than I, old Davy
Llewellyn, and once on a time I asked him, when he talked too

much of his "ometries"—as a sailor might do in his simpleness—I asked him to take an "observation," as I had seen a good deal of it. But all he did was to make a very profane and unpleasant one. As for this man's outward looks, he was nothing at all particular, but usually with dirt about him, and a sense of oiliness. Why he must needs set up for a saint the father of evil alone may tell; but they said that the clock that paid him best (being the worst in the neighbourhood) belonged to a Nicodemus-Christian, with a great cuckoo over it. Having never seen it, I cannot say; and the town is so full of gossip that I throw myself down on my back and listen, being wholly unable to vie with them in depth or in compass of story-telling, even when fish are a week on my hands.

CHAPTER XIII.

THE CORONER AND THE CORONET.

An officer of high repute had lately been set over us, to hold account of the mischief, and to follow evidence, and make the best he could of it when anybody chose to die without giving proper notice. He called himself "Coroner of the King;" and all the doctors, such as they were, made it a point that he must come, whenever there was a dead man or woman who had died without their help.

Now all about the storm of sand, and all about the shipwreck, was known in every part of the parish, before the church clock had contrived, in gratitude to Hezekiah, to strike the noon of Monday. Every child that went to the well knew the truth of everything; and every woman of Newton and Nottage had formed from the men her own opinion, and was ready to stand thereby, and defy all the other women.

Nevertheless some busy doctor (who had better been in the stocks) took it for a public duty to send notice and demand for the Coroner to sit upon us. The wrath of the parish (now just beginning to find some wreck, that would pay for the ropes) was so honest and so grave, that the little doctor was compelled to run and leave his furniture. And so it always ought to be with people who are meddlesome.

It came to my knowledge that this must happen, and that I

was bound to help in it, somewhere about middle-day of Tuesday; at a time when I was not quite as well as I find myself when I have no money. For, being pleased with my luck perhaps, and not content quite to smoke in the dark, and a little dry after the glow-worms, it happened (I will not pretend to say how) that I dropped into the "Jolly Sailors," to know what the people could be about, making such a great noise as they were, and keeping a quiet man out of his bed.

There I smelled a new tobacco, directly I was in the room; and somebody (pleased with my perception) gave me several pipes of it, with a thimbleful—as I became more and more agreeable—of a sort of rum-and-water. And, confining myself, as my principle is, to what the public treat me to, it is not quite out of the question that I may have been too generous. And truly full I was of grief, upon the following morning, that somebody had made me promise, in a bubbling moment, to be there again, and bring my fiddle, on the Tuesday night.

Now, since the death of my dear wife, who never put up with my fiddle (except when I was courting her), it had seemed to my feelings to be almost a levity to go fiddling. Also I knew what everybody would begin to say of me; but the landlord, foreseeing a large attendance after the Coroner's inquest, would not for a moment hear of any breach of my fiddle pledge.

Half of Newton, and perhaps all Nottage, went to Sker the following day to see the Coroner, and to give him the benefit of their opinions. And another piece of luck there was to tempt them in that direction. For the ship which had been wrecked and had disappeared for a certain time, in a most atrocious manner, was rolled about so by the tide and a shift of the wind on Monday, that a precious large piece of her stern was in sight from the shore on Tuesday morning. It lay not more than a cable's length from low-water mark, and was heaved up so that we could see as far as the starboard mizzen-chains. Part of the taffrail was carried away, and the carving gone entirely, but the transom and transom-knees stood firm; and of the ship's name done in gold I could make out in large letters TA LUCIA; and underneath, in a curve, and in smaller letters, ADOR.

Of course no one except myself could make head or tail of this; but after thinking a little while, I was pretty sure of the meaning of it—namely, that the craft was Portuguese, called the Santa Lucia, and trading from San Salvador, the capital of Brazils. And in this opinion I was confirmed by observing through my spy-glass, copper bolt-heads of a pattern such as I had seen at Lisbon, but never in any British ship. However, I resolved, for the present, to keep my opinion to myself, unless it were demanded upon good authority. For it made me feel confused in mind, and perhaps a little uneasy, when, being struck by some resemblance, I pulled from the lining of my hat a leaf of a book, upon which I copied all that could be made out of the letters, each side of the tiller of my new boat; and now I found them to be these,—UC from the starboard side, just where they would have stood in Lucia—and DOR from the further end of the line, just as in San Salvador.

The sands were all alive with people, and the rocks, and every place where anything good might have drifted. For Evan Thomas could scarcely come at a time of such affliction to assert his claims of wreck, and to belabour right and left. Therefore, for a mile or more, from where the land begins to dip, and the old stone wall, like a jagged cord, divides our parish from Kenfig, hundreds of figures might be seen, running along the grey wet sands, and reflected by their brightness. The day was going for two of the clock, and the tide growing near to the turn of ebb; and the landsprings oozing down from the beach, spread the whole of the flat sands so, with a silver overlaying, that without keen sight it was hard to tell where the shore ended and sea began. And a great part of this space was sprinkled with naked feet going pattering—boys and girls, and young women and men, who had left their shoes up high on the rocks to have better chance in the racing.

Now it is not for me to say that all or half of these good people were so brisk because they expected any fine thing for themselves. I would not even describe them as waiting in readiness for the force of fortune by the sea administered. I believe that all were most desirous of doing good, if possible. In the first case, to the poor people drowned; but if too late, then to console any disconsolate relations: failing of which, it would be hard if anybody should blame them for picking up something for themselves.

"What! you here, mother Probyn?" I cried, coming upon a most pious old woman, who led the groaning at Zoar Chapel, and being for the moment struck out of all my manners by sight of her.

"Indeed, and so I am, old Davy," she answered, without abashment, and almost too busy to notice me; "the Lord may bless my poor endeavours to rescue them poor Injuns. But I can't get on without a rake. If I had only had the sense to bring my garden-rake. There are so many little things, scarcely as big as cockle-shells; and the waves do drag them away from me. Oh, there, and there goes another! Gwenny, if I don't smack you!"

All these people, and all their doings, I left with a sort of contempt, perhaps, such as breaks out on me now and then at any very great littleness. And I knew that nothing worth wet of the knees could be found with the ebb-tide running, and ere the hold of the ship broke up.

So I went toward the great house, whose sorrows and whose desolation they took little heed of. And nothing made me feel more sad—strange as it may seem, and was—than to think of poor black Evan, thus unable to stand up and fight for his unrighteous rights.

In the great hall were six bodies, five of strong young men laid quiet, each in his several coffin; and the other of a little child in a simple dress of white, stretched upon a piece of board. Death I have seen in all his manners, since I was a cabin-boy, and I took my hat off to the bodies, as I had seen them do abroad; but when I saw the small dead child, a thrill and pang of cold went through me. I made sure of nothing else, except that it was dear Bardie. That little darling whom I loved, for her gifts direct from God, and her ways, so out of the way to all other children—it struck my heart with a power of death, that here this lively soul was dead.

When a man makes a fool of himself, anybody may laugh at him; and this does him good, perhaps, and hardens him against more trouble. But bad as I am, and sharp as I am, in other people's opinion (and proud sometimes to think of it), I could not help a good gulp of a tear, over what I believed to be the body of poor little Bardie. For that child had such nice ways, and took such upper hand of me; that, expecting to find a Captain always, especially among women——

"Old Davy, I 'ants 'a. Old Davy, 'hen is 'a coming?"

By the union-jack, it was as good as a dozen kegs of rum to me. There was no mistaking the sweetest and clearest voice ever heard outside of a flute. And presently began pit-pat of the prettiest feet ever put in a shoe, down the great oak staircase. She held on by the rails, and showed no fear at all about it, though the least slip might have killed her. Then she saw the sad black sight after she turned the corner, and wondered at the meaning of it, and her little heart stood still. As she turned to me in awe, and held out both hands quivering, I caught her up, and spread my grey beard over her young frightened eyes, and took her out of sight of all those cold and very dreadful things.

I had never been up the stairs before in that dark and ancient house; and the length, and the width, and the dreariness, and the creaking noises, frightened me; not so much for my own sake (being never required to sleep there), but for the tender little creature, full already of timid fancies, who must spend the dark nights there. And now the house, left empty of its noise, and strength, and boastfulness, had only five more ghosts to wander silent through the silent places. And this they began the very night after their bodies were in the churchyard.

The Coroner came on an old white pony, nearly four hours after the time for which his clerk had ordered us. Being used, for my part, to royal discipline, and everything done to the minute fixed, with the captain's voice like the crack of a gun, I was vexed and surprised; but expected him to give us some reason, good or bad. Instead of that he roared out to us, with his feet still in both stirrups, "Is there none of you Tallies with manners enough to come and hold a gentleman's horse? Here you, Davy Jones, you are long enough, and lazy enough; put your hand to the bridle, will you?"

This was to me, who was standing by, in the very height of innocence, having never yet seen any man appointed to sit upon dead bodies, and desiring to know how he could help them. I did for his Honour all I could, although his manner of speech was not in any way to my liking. But my rule has always been that of the royal navy, than which there is no wiser. If my equal insults me, I knock him down; if my officer does it, I knock under.

Meanwhile our people were muttering "Sassenach, Sassenach!" And from their faces it was plain that they did not like an Englishman to sit upon Cymric bodies. However, it was the old, old thing. The Welsh must do all the real work; and the English be paid for sitting upon them after they are dead.

"I never sate on a black man yet, and I won't sit on a black man now," the Coroner said, when he was sure about oats enough for his pony; "I'll not disgrace his Majesty's writ by sitting upon damned niggers."

"Glory be to God, your Honour!" Stradling Williams cried, who had come as head of the jury: clerk he was of Newton

Church, and could get no fees unless upon a Christian burial: "we thought your Honour would hardly put so great a disgrace upon us; but we knew not how the law lay."

"The law requires no Christian man," pronounced the Crowner, that all might hear, "to touch pitch, and defile himself. Both in body and soul, Master Clerk, to lower and defile himself!"

Hereupon a high hard screech, which is all we have in Wales for the brave hurrah of Englishmen, showed that all the jury were of one accord with the Coroner: and I was told by somebody that all had shaken hands, and sworn to strike work, rather than put up with misery of conscience.

"But, your Honour," said Mr Lewis, bailiff to Colonel Lougher, "if we hold no quest on the black men, how shall we certify anything about this terrible shipwreck?"

"The wreck is no concern of mine," answered the Crowner, crustily: "it is not my place to sit upon planks, but upon Christian bodies. Do you attend to your own business, and leave mine to me, sir."

The bailiff, being a nice quiet man, thought it best to say no more. But some of the people who were thronging from every direction to see his Honour, told him about the little white baby found among the bladder-weed. He listened to this, and then he said,—

"Show me this little white infant discovered among the black men. My business here is not with infants, but with five young smothered men. However, if there be an infant of another accident, and of Christian colour, I will take it as a separate case, and damn the county in the fees."

We assured his lordship, as every one now began to call him (in virtue of his swearing so, which no doubt was right in a man empowered to make other people swear), we did our best at anyrate to convince the Crowner, that over and above all black men, there verily was a little child, and, for all one could tell, a Christian child, entitled to the churchyard, and good enough for him to sit on. And so he entered the house to see it.

But if he had sworn a little before (and more than I durst set down for him), he certainly swore a great deal now, and poured upon us a bitter heat of English indignation. All of the jury were taken aback; and I as a witness felt most uneasy; until we came to understand that his Honour's wrath was justly kindled on account of some marks on the baby's clothes.

"A coronet!" he cried, stamping about; "a coronet on my young lord's pinafore, and you stupid oafs never told me!"

Nobody knew except myself (who had sailed with an earl for a captain) what the meaning of this thing was; and when the clerk of the church was asked, rather than own his ignorance, he said it was part of the arms of the crown; and the Crowner was bound like a seal by it.

This explanation satisfied all the people of the parish, except a few far-going Baptists, with whom it was a point of faith always to cavil and sneer at every "wind of doctrine" as they always called it—the scent of which could be traced, anyhow, to either the parson or the clerk, or even the gravedigger. But I was content to look on and say nothing, having fish to sell, at least twice a-week, and finding all customers orthodox, until they utter bad shillings.

CHAPTER XIV.

IN ACCORDANCE WITH THE EVIDENCE.

THERE is no need for me to follow all the Crowner's doings, or all that the juries thought and said, which was different altogether from what they meant to think and say. And he found himself bound to have two of them, with first right of inquest to the baby because of the stamp on his pinafore. And here I was, foreman of the jury, with fifteenpence for my services, and would gladly have served on the other jury after walking all that way, but was disabled for doing so, and only got ninepence for testimony. With that, however, I need not meddle, as every one knows all about it; only, to make clear all that happened, and, indeed, to clear myself, I am forced to put before you all that we did about that baby, as fully and emphatically as the state of our doings upon that occasion permitted me to remember it.

For the Coroner sate at the head of the table, in the great parlour of the house; and the dead child came in on his board, and we all regarded him carefully, especially heeding his coronet mark, and then set him by the window. A fine young boy enough to look at, about the age of our Bardie, and might have been her twin-brother, as everybody vowed he was, only his face was bolder and stronger, and his nose quite different, and altogether a brave young chap, instead of funny and delicate. All this, however, might well have come from knocking about in the sea so much.

I would have given a good half-crown to have bitten off my foolish tongue, when one of the jury-men stood up and began to address the Coroner. He spoke, unluckily, very good English, and his Honour was glad to pay heed to him. And the clerk put down nearly all he said, word for word, as might be. This meddlesome fellow (being no less than brother Hezekiah's self) nodded to me for leave to speak, which I could not deny him; and his Honour lost no time whatever to put his mouth into his rummer of punch, as now provided for all of us, and to bow (whenever his mouth was empty) to that Hezekiah. For the man had won some reputation, or rather had made it, for himself, by perpetual talking, as if he were skilled in the history and antiquities of the neighbourhood. Of these he made so rare a patchwork, heads and tails, prose, verse, and proverbs, histories, and his stories, that (as I heard from a man of real teaching and learning who met him once and kept out of his way ever after) any one trusting him might sit down in the chair of Canute at King Arthur's table. Not that I or any of my neighbours would be the worse for doing that; only the thought of it frightened us, and made us unwilling to hearken him much.

However, if there was any matter on which Hezekiah deserved to be heard, no doubt it was this upon which he was now delivering his opinions—to wit, the great inroad or invasion of the sand, for miles along our coast; of which there are very strange things to tell, and of which he had made an especial study, having a field at Candleston with a shed upon it and a rick of hay, all which disappeared in a single night, and none was ever seen afterwards. It was the only field he had, being left to him by his grandmother; and many people were disappointed that he had not slept with his cow that night. This directed his attention to the serious consideration, as he always told us at first start, being a lover of three-decked words, of the most important contemplation which could occupy the attention of any Cambrian landowner.

"Show your land," cried a wag of a tailor, with none to cross his legs upon; but we put him down, and pegged him down, till his manners should be of the pattern-book. Hezekiah went on to tell, in words too long to answer the helm of such a plain sailor as I am, how the sweep of hundreds of miles of sand had come up from the west and south-west in only two hundred and fifty years. How it had first begun to flow about the Scilly Islands, as mentioned by one Borlase, and came to the mouth of Hayle river, in Cornwall, in the early years of King Henry VIII., and after that blocked up Bude Haven, and swallowed the ploughs in the arable land. Then at Llanant it came like a cloud over the moon one winter night, and buried five-and-thirty houses with the people in them.

An Act of Parliament was passed—chapter the second of Philip and Mary—to keep it out of Glamorganshire ; and good commissioners were appointed, and a survey made along the coast, especially of Kenfig. Nevertheless the dash of sand was scarcely on their ink, when swarming, driving, darkening the air, the storm swept on their survey. At the mouths of the Tawey and Afan rivers the two sailors' chapels were buried, and then it swept up the great Roman road, a branch of the Julian way, and smothered the pillars of Gordian, and swallowed the castle of Kenfig, which stood by the side of the western road ; and still rushing eastward, took Newton village and Newton old church beneath it. And so it went on for two hundred years, coming up from the sea, no doubt, carried by the perpetual gales, which always are from the south and west—filling all the hollow places, changing all bright mossy pools into hills of yellow drought, and, like a great encampment, dwelling over miles and leagues of land. And like a camp it was in this, that it was always striking tent. Six times in the last few years had the highest peak of sand—the general's tent it might be called—been shifted miles away, perhaps, and then come back towards Ogmore ; and it was only the other day that, through some shift or swirl of wind, a windmill, with its sails entire, had been laid bare near Candleston, of which the last record was in Court-rolls of a hundred and fifty years agone.*

Now all this, though Hezekiah said it, was true enough, I do believe, having heard things much to the same purpose from my own old grandfather. The Coroner listened with more patience than we had given him credit for, although he told us that brother Perkins should have reserved his learned speech for the

---

* A clear and interesting account of this mighty sand-march may be found in a very learned paper by the Rev. H. H. Knight, B.D., formerly rector of Neath, Glamorgan ; which paper, entitled " An Account of Newton-Nottage," was reprinted at Tenby in 1853, from the 'Archæologia Cambrensis.' Considerable movements still occur, but of late years no very great advance.

second inquiry, which was to be about the deaths of the five young men; for to him it appeared that this noble infant must lay the blame of his grievous loss not on the sand but upon the sea. Hezekiah replied, with great deference, that the cause in both cases was the same, for that the movement of sand went on under the sea even more than ashore, and hence the fatal gulfing of that ship, the Andalusia, and the loss of his young lordship.

The name he had given the ship surprised me; and indeed I felt sure that it was quite wrong; and so I said immediately, without any low consideration of what might be mine own interest. But the Coroner would not hearken to me, being much impressed now with the learning and wisdom of Hezekiah Perkins. And when Hezekiah presented his card, beginning with "horologist," and ending with the "king and queen," he might have had any verdict he liked, if he himself had been upon trial.

Therefore, after calling in (for the sake of form) the two poor women who found the dead baby among the sea-weed, and had sevenpence apiece for doing so, and who cried all the while that they talked in Welsh (each having seen a dear baby like him not more than twenty years ago), we came in the most unanimous manner, under his lordship's guidance, to the following excellent verdict:—

"Found drowned on Pool Tavan rocks, a man-child, supposed to be two years old; believed to be a young nobleman, from marks on pinafore, and high bearing; but cast away by a storm of sand from the ship Andalusia of Appledore."

Now I was as certain, as sure could be, that half of this verdict must be wrong; especially as to the name of the ship, and her belonging to Appledore, which never yet owned any craft of more than 200 tons at the utmost—a snow, or a brig at the very outside. Nevertheless I was compelled to give in to the rest of them, and most of all to the Coroner. Only I said, as many who are still alive can remember, and are not afraid to speak to, and especially my good friend Mr Lewis, "The ship was not called the Andalusia; the ship was never from Appledore; neither was she of British build. As an old seaman, it is likely that I know more of the build of a ship than a lubber of a clock-maker, or rather a clock-mauler."

But here I was put down sternly; and hearing of verdicts a great deal worse, without any mischief come of them, I was even content to sign the return, and have a new pipe of bird's-eye. And a bird's-eye view this gave me of them at the second inquest wherein I had to give evidence; and was not of the jury. They wanted to cross-examine me, because I had been unpleasant, but of that they got the worst, and dropped it. But as all our jurymen declared upon their oaths that the little nobleman was drowned in a storm of sand, so they found that the five young rabbiters came to their end of smothering through a violent sea-tempest.

In the days of my youth such judgments perhaps would have tried my patience; but now I knew that nothing ever follows truth and justice. People talk of both these things, and perhaps the idea does them good.

Be that according to God's will—as we always say when deprived of our own—at any rate, I am bound to tell one little thing more about each quest. And first about the first one. Why was I so vexed and angry with my foolish tongue when Hezekiah began to speak? Only because I knew full well that it would lead to the very thing, which it was my one desire to avoid, if possible. And this—as you may guess at once, after what happened on the stairs—was the rude fetching and exposing of the dear little maid among so many common fellows; and to show her the baby-corpse. I feared that it must come to this, through my own thoughtless blabbing about her "ickle bother" in the presence of Hezekiah: and if ever man had a hollow dry heart from over-pumping of the tongue, I had it when Hezekiah came in; bearing, in a depth of fright and wonder, and contempt of him, my own delicate Bardie. I had set my back against the door, and sworn that they should not have her; but crafty Perkins had stolen out by another door while they humoured me. Now my pretty dear was awed, and hushed beyond all crying, and even could not move her feet, as children do, in a kicking way. Trying to get as far as possible from Hezekiah's nasty face—which gave me a great deal of pleasure, because she had never done the like to me, unless I were full of tobacco—she stretched away from his greasy shoulder, and then she saw old Davy. Her hands came toward me, and so did her eyes, and so did her lips, with great promise of kisses, such as her father and mother perhaps might have been mightily tempted by; but nobody now to care for them.

When Hezekiah, pretending to dandle this little lady in a jaunty way, like one of his filthy low children, was taking her towards that poor little corpse, so white in the light of the window; and when he made her look at it, and said, "Is that ickle bother, my dear?" and she all the time was shivering and turning her eyes away from it, and seeking for me to help her, I got rid of the two men who held me, nor hearkened I the Coroner, but gave Hezekiah such a grip as he felt for three months afterwards, and with Bardie on my left arm, kept my right fist ready.

Nobody cared to encounter this; for I had happened to tell the neighbourhood how the Frenchman's head came off at the time when he tried to injure me; and so I bore off the little one, till her chest began to pant and her tears ran down my beard. And then as I spoke softly to her and began to raise her fingers, and to tickle her frizzy hair, all of a sudden she flung both arms around my neck, and loved me.

"Old Davy, poor ickle Bardie not go to 'e back pithole yet?"

"No, my dear, not for ever so long. Not for eighty years at least. And then go straight to heaven!"

"Ickle bother go to 'e back pithole? Does 'a think, old Davy?"

This was more than I could tell, though inclined to think it very likely. However, before I could answer, some of the jury followed us, and behind them the Coroner himself; they insisted on putting a question to her, and so long as they did not force her again to look at that which terrified her, I had no right to prevent them. They all desired to speak at once; but the clerk of the Coroner took the lead, having as yet performed no work toward the earning of his salt or rum. An innocent old man he was, but very free from cleanliness; and the child being most particular of all ever born in that matter, turned away with her mite of a nose, in a manner indescribable.

He was much too dull to notice this; but putting back his spectacles, and stooping over her hair and ears (which was all she left outside my beard), he wanted to show his skill in babies, of which he boasted himself a grandfather. And so he began to whisper,—

"My little dear, you will be a good child—a very good child; won't you, now? I can see it in your little face. Such a pretty dear you are! And all good children always do as they are told, you know. We want you to tell us a little thing about pretty little brother. I have got a little girl at home not so old as you are, and she is so clever, you can't think. Everything she does and says; everything we tell her——"

"Take ayay 'e nasty old man. Take ayay 'e bad old man; or I never tis 'a again, old Davy."

She flashed up at me with such wrath, that I was forced to obey her; while the old man put down his goggles to stare, and all the jury laughed at him. And I was running away with her, for her little breath was hot and short; when the Coroner called out, "Stop, man; I know how to manage her." At this I was bound to pull up, and set her to look at him, as he ordered me. She sate well up in my arms, and looked, and seemed not to think very highly of him.

"Look at his Honour, my dear," said I, stroking her hair as I knew she liked; "look at his lordship, you pretty duck."

"Little child," began his Honour, "you have a duty to perform, even at this early period of your very beginning life. We are most desirous to spare your feelings, having strong reasons to believe that you are sprung from a noble family. But in our duty towards your lineage, we must require you, my little dear— we must request you, my little lady—to assist us in our endeavour to identify——"

"I can say 'dentify,' old Davy; tell 'e silly old man to say 'dentify' same as I does."

She spread her little open hand with such contempt at the Coroner, that even his own clerk could not keep his countenance from laughing. And his Honour, having good reason to think her a baby of high position before, was now so certain that he said, "God bless her! What a child she is! Take her away, old mariner. She is used to high society."

CHAPTER XV.

A VERDICT ON THE JURY.

As to the second inquest, I promised (as you may remember) to tell something also. But in serious truth, if I saw a chance to escape it, without skulking watch, I would liefer be anywhere else almost—except in a French prison.

After recording with much satisfaction our verdict upon Bardie's brother—which nearly all of us were certain that the little boy must be—the Coroner bade his second jury to view the bodies of the five young men. These were in the great dark hall, set as in a place of honour, and poor young Watkin left to mind them; and very pale and ill he looked.

"If you please, sir, they are all stretched out, and I am not afraid of them;" he said to me, as I went to console him: "father cannot look at them; but mother and I are not afraid. They are placed according to their ages, face after face, and foot after foot. And I am sure they never meant it, sir, when they used to kick me out of bed: and oftentimes I deserved it."

I thought much less of those five great corpses than of the gentle and loving boy who had girt up his heart to conquer fear, and who tried to think evil of himself for the comforting of his brethren's souls.

But he nearly broke down when the jurymen came; and I begged them to spare him the pain and trial of going before the Coroner to identify the bodies, which I could do, as well as any one; and to this they all agreed.

When we returned to the long oak parlour, we found that the dignity of the house was maintained in a way which astonished us. There had been some little refreshment before, especially for his Honour; but now all these things were cleared away, and the table was spread with a noble sight of glasses, and bottles, and silver implements, fit for the mess of an admiral. Neither were these meant for show alone, inasmuch as to make them useful, there was water cold and water hot, also lemons, and sugar, and nutmeg, and a great black George of ale, a row of pipes, and a jar of tobacco, also a middling keg of Hollands, and an anker of old rum. At first we could hardly believe our eyes, knowing how poor and desolate, both of food and furniture, that old grange had always been. But presently one of us happened to guess, and Hezekiah confirmed it, that the lord of the manor had taken compassion upon his afflicted tenant, and had furnished these things in a handsome manner, from his own great house some five miles distant. But in spite of the custom of the country, I was for keeping away from it all, upon so sad an occasion. And one or two more were for holding aloof, although they cast sheep's-eyes at it.

However, the Crowner rubbed his hands, and sate down at the top of the table, and then the foreman sate down also, and said that, being so much upset, he was half inclined to take a glass of something weak. He was recommended, if he felt like that, whatever he did, not to take it weak, but to think of his wife and family; for who could say what such a turn might lead to, if neglected? And this reflection had such weight, that instead of mixing for himself, he allowed a friend to mix for him.

The Crowner said, "Now, gentlemen, in the presence of such fearful trouble and heavy blows from Providence, no man has any right to give the rein to his own feelings. It is his duty, as a man, to control his sad emotions; and his duty, as a family-man, to attend to his constitution." With these words he lit a pipe, and poured himself a glass of Hollands, looking sadly upward, so that the measure quite escaped him. "Gentlemen of the jury," he continued with such authority, that the jury were almost ready to think that they must have begun to be gentlemen—till they looked at one another; "gentlemen of the jury, life is short, and trouble long. I have sate upon hundreds of poor people who destroyed themselves by nothing else than want of self-preservation. I have made it my duty officially to discourage such shortcomings. Mr Foreman, be good enough to send the lemons this way; and when ready for business, say so."

Crowner Bowles was now as pleasant as he had been grumpy in the morning; and finding him so, we did our best to keep him in that humour. Neither was it long before he expressed himself in terms which were an honour alike to his heart and head. For he told us, in so many words—though I was not of the jury now, nevertheless I held on to them, and having been foreman just now, could not be, for a matter of form, when it came to glasses, cold-shouldered,—worthy Crowner Bowles, I say, before he had stirred many slices of lemon, told us all, in so many words—and the more, the more we were pleased with them—that for a thoroughly honest, intelligent, and hard-working jury, commend him henceforth and as long as he held his Majesty's sign-manual, to a jury made of Newton parish and of Kenfig burgesses!

We drank his health with bumpers round, every man upon his legs, and then three cheers for his lordship; until his clerk, who was rather sober, put his thumb up, and said "Stop." And from the way he went on jerking with his narrow shoulders, we saw that he would recall our thoughts to the hall that had no door to it. Then following his looks, we saw the distance of the silence.

This took us all aback so much, that we had in the witnesses —of whom I the head man was there already—and for fear of their being nervous, and so confusing testimony, gave them a cordial after swearing. Everybody knew exactly what each one of them had to say. But it would have been very hard, and might have done them an injury, not to let them say it.

The Coroner, having found no need to charge (except his rummer), left his men for a little while to deliberate their verdict."

"Visitation of God, of course it must be," Stradling Williams began to say; "visitation of Almighty God."

Some of the jury took the pipes out of their mouths and nodded at him, while they blew a ring of smoke; and others nodded without that trouble; and all seemed going pleasantly. When suddenly a little fellow, whose name was Simon Edwards, a brother of the primitive Christians, or at least of their minister, being made pugnacious by ardent spirits, rose, and holding the arm of his chair, thus delivered his sentiments; speaking, of course, in his native tongue.

"Head-man, and brothers of the jury, I-I-I do altogether refuse and deny the goodness of that judgment. The only judgment I will certify is in the lining of my hat,—'Judgment of Almighty God, for rabbiting on the Sabbath-day.' Hezekiah Perkins, I call upon thee, as a brother Christian, and a consistent member, to stand on the side of the Lord with me."

His power of standing on any side was by this time, however, exhausted; and falling into his chair he turned pale, and shrunk to the very back of it. For over against him stood Evan Thomas, whom none of us had seen till then. It was a sight that sobered us, and made the blood fly from our cheeks, and forced us to set down the glass.

The face of black Evan was ashy grey, and his heavy square shoulders slouching forward, and his hands hung by his side. Only his deep eyes shone without moving; and Simon backed further and further away, without any power to gaze elsewhere. Then Evan Thomas turned from him, without any word, or so much as a sigh, and looked at us all; and no man had power to meet the cold quietness of his regard. And not having thought much about his troubles, we had nothing at all to say to him.

After waiting for us to begin, and finding no one ready, he spake a few words to us all in Welsh, and the tone of his voice seemed different.

"Noble gentlemen, I am proud that my poor hospitality pleases you. Make the most of the time God gives; for six of you have seen the white horse." With these words he bowed his head, and left us shuddering in the midst of all the heat of cordials. For it is known that men, when prostrate by a crushing act of God, have the power to foresee the death of other men that feel no pity for them. And to see the white horse on the night of new moon, even through closed eyelids, and without sense of vision, is the surest sign of all sure signs of death within the twelvemonth. Therefore all the jury sate glowering at one another, each man ready to make oath that Evan's eyes were not on him.

Now there are things beyond our knowledge, or right of explanation, in which I have a pure true faith—for instance, the "Flying Dutchman," whom I had twice beheld already, and whom no man may three times see, and then survive the twelvemonth; in him, of course, I had true faith—for what can be clearer than eyesight? Many things, too, which brave seamen have beheld, and can declare; but as for landsmen's superstitions, I scarcely cared to laugh at them. However, strange enough it is, all black Evan said came true. Simon Edwards first went off, by falling into Newton Wayn, after keeping it up too late at chapel. And after him the other five, all within the twelvemonth; some in their beds, and some abroad, but all gone to their last account. And heartily glad I was for my part (as one after other they dropped off thus), not to have served on that second jury; and heartily sorry I was also that brother Hezekiah had not taken the luck to behold the white horse.

Plain enough it will be now, to any one who knows our parts, that after what Evan Thomas said, and the way in which he withdrew from us, the only desire the jury had was to gratify him with their verdict, and to hasten home, ere the dark should fall, and no man to walk by himself on the road. Accordingly, without more tobacco, though some took another glass for strength, they returned the following verdict:—

"We find that these five young and excellent men"—here came their names, with a Mister to each—"were lost on their way to a place of worship, by means of a violent storm of the sea. And the jury cannot separate without offering their heartfelt pity"—the Crowner's clerk changed it to 'sympathy'—"to their bereaved and affectionate parents. God save the King!"

After this, they all went home; and it took good legs to keep up with them along "Priest Lane," in some of the darker places, and especially where a white cow came, and looked over a gate for the milking-time. I could not help laughing, although myself not wholly free from uneasiness; and I grieved that my joints were not as nimble as those of Simon Edwards.

But while we frightened one another, like so many children, each perceiving something which was worse to those who perceived it not, Hezekiah carried on as if we were a set of fools, and nothing ever could frighten him. To me, who was the bravest of them, this was very irksome; but it happened that I knew brother Perkins's pet belief. His wife had lived at Longlands once, a lonely house between Nottage and Newton, on the rise of a little hill. And they say that on one night of the year, all the funerals that must pass from Nottage to Newton in the twelvemonth, go by in succession there, with all the mourners after them, and the very hymns that they will sing passing softly on the wind.

So as we were just by Longlands in the early beat of the stars, I managed to be at Perkins's side. Then suddenly, as a bat went by, I caught the arm of Hezekiah, and drew back, and shivered.

"Name of God, Davy! what's the matter?"

"Can't you see them, you blind-eye? There they go! there they go! All the coffins with palls to them. And the names upon the head-plates:—Evan, and Thomas, and Hopkin, and Rees, and Jenkin, with only four bearers! And the psalm they sing is the thirty-fourth."

"So it is! I can see them all. The Lord have mercy upon my soul! Oh Davy, Davy! don't leave me here."

He could not walk another step, but staggered against the wall and groaned, and hid his face inside his hat. We got him to Newton with much ado; but as for going to Bridgend that night, he found that our church-clock must be seen to, the very first thing in the morning.

CHAPTER XVI.

TRUTH LIES SOMETIMES IN A WELL.

The following morning it happened so that I did not get up over early; not, I assure you, from any undue enjoyment of the grand Crowner's quests; but partly because the tide for fishing would not suit till the afternoon, and partly because I had worked both hard and long at the "Jolly Sailors:" and this in fulfilment of a pledge from which there was no escaping, when I promised on the night before to grease and tune my violin, and display the true practice of hornpipe. Rash enough this promise was, on account of my dear wife's memory, and the things bad people would say of it. And but for the sad uneasiness created by black Evan's prophecy, and the need of lively company to prevent my seeing white horses, the fear of the parish might have prevailed with me over all fear of the landlord. Hence I began rather shyly; but when my first tune had been received with hearty applause from all the room, how could I allow myself to be clapped on the back, and then be lazy?

Now Bunny was tugging and clamouring for her bit of breakfast, almost before I was wide-awake, when the latch of my cottage-door was lifted, and in walked Hezekiah. Almost any other man would have been more welcome; for though he had not spoken of it on the day before, he was sure to annoy me, sooner or later, about the fish he had forced me to sell him. When such a matter is over and done with, surely no man, in common-sense, has a right to reopen the question. The time to find fault with a fish, in all conscience, is before you have bought him. Having once done that, he is now your own; and to blame him is to find fault with the mercy which gave you the money to buy him. A foolish thing as well; because you are running down your own property, and spoiling your relish for him. Conduct like this is below contempt; even more ungraceful and ungracious than that of a man who spreads abroad the faults of his own wife.

Hezekiah, however, on this occasion, was not quite so bad as that. His errand, according to his lights, was of a friendly nature; for he pried all round my little room with an extremely sagacious leer, and then gazed at me with a dark cock of his eye, and glanced askance at Bunny, and managed to wink, like the Commodore's ship beginning to light poop-lanterns.

"Speak out, like a man," I said; "is your wife confined with a prophecy, or what is the matter with you?"

"Hepzibah, the prophetess, is well; and her prophecies are abiding the fulness of their fulfilment. I would speak with you on a very secret and important matter, concerning also her revealings."

"Then I will send the child away. Here, Bunny, run and ask mother Jones——"

"That will not do; I will not speak here. Walls are thin, and walls have ears. Come down to the well with me."

"But the well is a lump of walls," I answered, "and children almost always near it."

"There are no children. I have been down. The well is dry, and the children know it. No better place can be for speaking."

Looking down across the churchyard, I perceived that he was right; and so I left Bunny to dwell on her breakfast, and went with Hezekiah. Among the sand-hills there was no one; for fright had fallen on everybody, since the sands began to walk, as the general folk now declared of them. And nobody looked at a sand-hill now with any other feeling than towards his grave and tombstone.

Even my heart was a little heavy, in spite of all scientific points, when I straddled over the stone that led into the sandy passage. After me came Hezekiah, groping with his grimy hands, and calling out for me to stop, until he could have hold of me. However, I left him to follow the darkness, in the wake of his own ideas.

A better place for secret talk, in a parish full of echoes, scarcely could be found, perhaps, except the old "Red House" on the shore. So I waited for Perkins to unfold, as soon as we stood on the bottom step, with three or four yards of quicksand, but no dip for a pitcher below us. The children knew that the well was dry, and some of them perhaps were gone to try to learn their letters.

What then was my disappointment, as it gradually came out, that so far from telling me a secret, Hezekiah's object was to deprive me of my own! However, if I say what happened, nobody can grumble.

In the first place, he manœuvred much to get the weather-gage of me, by setting me so that the light that slanted down the grey slope should gather itself upon my honest countenance. I for my part, as a man unwarned how far it might become a duty to avoid excess of accuracy, took the liberty to prefer a less conspicuous position; not that I had any lies to tell, but might be glad to hear some. Therefore, I stuck to a pleasant seat upon a very nice sandy slab, where the light so shot and wavered, that a badly inquisitive man might seek in vain for a flush or a flickering of the most delicate light of all—that which is cast by the heart or mind of man into the face of man.

Upon the whole, it could scarcely be said, at least as concerned Hezekiah, that truth was to be found, just now, at the bottom of this well.

"Dear brother Dyo," he gently began, with the most brotherly voice and manner; "it has pleased the Lord, who does all things aright, to send me to you for counsel now, as well as for comfort, beloved Dyo."

"All that I have is at your service," I answered very heartily; looking for something about his wife, and always enjoying a thing of that kind among those righteous fellows; and we heard that Hepzibah had taken up, under word of the Lord, with the Shakers.*

"Brother David, I have wrestled hard in the night-season, about that which has come to pass. My wife——"

"To be sure," I said.

"My wife, who was certified seven times as a vessel for the Spirit——"

"To be sure—they always are; and then they gad about so——"

"Brother, you understand me not; or desire to think evil. Hepzibah, since her last confinement, is a vessel for the Spirit to the square of what she was. Seven times seven is forty-nine, and requires no certificate. But these are carnal calculations."

All this took me beyond my depth, and I answered him rather crustily; and my word ended with both those letters which, as I learned from my Catechism, belong to us by baptism.

"Unholy David, shun evil words. Pray without ceasing, but swear not at all. In a vision of the night, Hepzibah hath seen terrible things of thee."

"Why, you never went home last night, Hezekiah. How can you tell what your wife dreamed?"

"I said not when it came to pass. And how could I speak of it yesterday before that loose assembly?"

"Well, well, out with it! What was this wonderful vision?"

"Hepzibah, the prophetess, being in a trance, and deeply

---

* These fine fellows are talked of now as if we had found a novelty. They came through South Wales on a "starring" tour thirty years agone, and they seemed to be on their last legs then. Under the moon is there anything new?

inspired of the Lord, beheld the following vision: A long lonely sea was spread before her, shining in the moonlight smoothly, and in places strewed with gold. A man was standing on a low black rock, casting a line, and drawing great fish out almost every time he cast. Then there arose from out the water a dear little child all dressed in white, carrying with both hands her cradle, and just like our little maiden, Martha——"

"Like your dirty Martha indeed!" I was at the very point of saying, but snapped my lips, and saved myself.

"This small damsel approached the fisherman, and presented her cradle to him, with a very trustful smile. Then he said, 'Is it gold?' And she said, 'No, it is only a white lily.' Upon which he shouted, 'Be off with you!' And the child fell into a desolate hole, and groped about vainly for her cradle. Then all the light faded out of the sea, and the waves and the rocks began moaning, and the fisherman fell on his knees, and sought in vain for the cradle. And while he was moaning, came Satan himself, bearing the cradle red-hot and crackling; and he seized the poor man by his blue woollen smock, and laid him in the cradle, and rocked it, till his shrieks awoke Hepzibah. And Hepzibah is certain that you are the man."

To hear all this in that sudden manner quite took my breath away for a minute, so that I fell back and knocked my head, purely innocent as I was. But presently I began to hope that the prophetess might be wrong this time; and the more so because that vile trance of hers might have come from excessive enjoyment of those good fish of mine. And it grew upon me more and more, the more I disliked her prediction about me, that if she had such inspiration, scarcely would she have sent Hezekiah to buy her supper from my four-legged table. Therefore I spoke without much loss of courage.

"Brother Hezekiah, there is something wrong with Hepzibah. Send her, I pray you, to Dr Ap-Yollup before she prophesies anything more. No blue woollen smock have I worn this summer, but a canvas jacket only, and more often a striped jersey. It is Sandy Macraw she has seen in her dream, with the devil both roasting and rocking him. Glory be to the Lord for it!"

"Glory be to Him, Dyo, whichever of you two it was! I hope that it may have been Sandy. But Hepzibah is always accurate, even among fishermen."

"Even fishermen," I answered (being a little touched with

wrath), "know the folk that understood them, and the folk that cannot. Even fishermen have their right, especially when reduced to it, not to be blasphemed in that way, even by a prophetess."

"Dyo, you are hot again. What makes you go on so? A friend's advice is such a thing, that I nearly always take it; unless I find big obstacles. Dyo, now be advised by me."

"That depends on how I like it," was the best thing I could say.

"David Llewellyn, the only chance to save thy sinful soul is this. Open thine heart to the chosen one, to the favoured of the Lord. Confess to Hepzibah the things that befell thee, and how the tempter prevailed with thee. Especially bring forth, my brother, the accursed thing thou hast hid in thy tent, the wedge of gold, and the shekels of silver, and the Babylonish garment. Thou hast stolen, and dissembled also; and put it even among thine own stuff. Cast it from thee, deliver it up, lay it before the ark of the Lord, and Hepzibah shall fall down and pray, lest thou be consumed and burnt with fire, like the son of Carmi the son of Zabdi, and covered over with a great heap of stones, even such as this is."

My wrath at this foul accusation, and daring attempt to frighten me, was kindled so that I could not speak; and if this had happened in the open air, I should have been certain to knock him down. However, I began to think, for Perkins was a litigious fellow; and however strict a man's conduct is, he does not want his affairs all exposed. Therefore I kept my knit knuckles at home, but justly felt strong indignation. Perkins thought he had terrified me, for perhaps in that bad light I looked pale; and so he began to triumph upon me, which needs, as everybody knows, a better man than Hezekiah.

"Come, come, brother Dyo," he said, in a voice quite different from the Chapel-Scriptural style he had used; "you see, we know all about it. Two dear children come ashore, one dead, and the other not dead. You contrive to receive them both, with your accustomed poaching skill. For everybody says that you are always to be found everywhere, except in your chapel, on Sabbath-day. Now, David, what do our good people, having families of their own, find upon these children? Not so much as a chain, or locket, or even a gold pin. I am a jeweller, and I know that children of high position always have some trinket on them, when their mothers love them. A child with a coronet, and no gold! David, this is wrong of wrong. And worse than this, you conceal the truth, even from me your ancient friend. There must be a great deal to be made, either from those who would hold them in trust, or from those in whose way they stood. For the family died out, very likely, in all male inheritance. Think what we might make of it, by acting under my direction. And you shall have half of it all, old Davy, by relieving your mind, and behaving in a sensible and religious manner."

This came home to my sense of experience more than all Hepzibah's divine predictions or productions. At the same time I saw that Hezekiah was all abroad in the dark, and groping right and left after the bodily truth. And what call had he to cry shares with me, because he had more reputation, and a higher conceit of himself, of course? But it crossed my mind that this nasty fellow, being perhaps in front of me in some little tricks of machinery, might be useful afterwards in getting at the real truth, which often kept me awake at night. Only I was quite resolved not to encourage roguery, by letting him into partnership. Perceiving my depth of consideration—for it suited my purpose to hear him out, and learn how much he suspected—it was natural that he should try again to impress me yet further by boasting.

"Dyo, I have been at a Latin school for as much as three months together. My father gave me a rare education, and I made the most of it. None of your ignorance for me! I am up to the moods and the tenses, the accidents and the proselytes. The present I know, and the future I know; the Peter-perfection, and the hay-roost——"

"I call that stuff gibberish. Talk plain English if you can."

"Understand you then so much as this? I speak in a carnal manner now. I speak as a fool unto a fool. I am up to snuff, good Dyo; I can tell the time of day."

"Then you are a devilish deal cleverer than any of your clocks are. But now thou speakest no parables, brother. Now I know what thou meanest. Thou art up for robbing somebody; and if I would shun Satan's clutches, I must come and help thee."

"Dyo, this is inconsistent, nor can I call it brotherly. We wish to do good, both you and I, and to raise a little money for works of love; you, no doubt, with a good end in view, to console you for much tribulation; and I with a single eye to the advancement of the cause which I have at heart, to save many brands from the burning. Then, Dyo, why not act together? Why not help one another, dear brother; thou with the good-luck, and I with the brains?"

He laid his hand on my shoulder kindly, with a yearning of his bowels towards me, such as true Nonconformists feel at the scent of any money. I found myself also a little moved, not being certain how far it was wise to throw him altogether over.

But suddenly, by what means I know not, except the will of Providence, there arose before me that foul wrong which the Nicodemus-Christian had committed against me some three years back. I had forborne to speak of it till now, wishing to give the man fair-play.

"Hezekiah, do you remember," I asked, with much solemnity—"do you remember your twentieth wedding-day?"

"Davy, my brother, how many times—never mind talking about that now."

"You had a large company coming, and to whom did you give a special order to catch you a turbot at tenpence a-pound?"

"Nay, nay, my dear friend Dyo; shall I never get that thing out of your stupid head?"

"You had known me for twenty years at least as the very best fisherman on the coast, and a man that could be relied upon. Yet you must go and give that order, not to a man of good Welsh blood—with ten Welshmen coming to dinner, mind—not to a man that was bred and born within five miles of your dirty house—not to a man that knew every cranny and crinkle of sand where the turbots lie; but to a tag-rag Scotchman! It was spoken of upon every pebble from Briton Ferry to Aberthaw. David Llewellyn put under the feet of a fellow like Sandy Macraw—a beggarly, interloping, freckled, bitter weed of a Scotchman!"

"Well, Davy, I have apologised. How many times more must I do it? It was not that I doubted your skill. You tell us of that so often, that none of us ever question it. It was simply because—I feared just then to come near your excellent and lamented——"

"No excuses, no excuses, Mr Perkins, if you please! You only make the matter worse. As if a man's wife could come into the question, when it comes to business! Yours may, because you don't know how to manage her; but mine——"

"Well, now she is gone, Dyo; and very good she was to you. And in your heart, you know it."

Whether he said this roguishly, or from the feeling which all of us have when it comes to one another, I declare I knew not then, and I know not even now. For I did not feel so sharply up to look to mine own interest, with these recollections over me. I waited for him to begin again, but he seemed to stick back in the corner. And in spite of all that turbot business, at the moment I could not help holding out my hand to him.

He took it, and shook it, with as much emotion as if he had truly been fond of my wife; and I felt that nothing more must be said concerning that order to Sandy Macraw. It seemed to be very good reason also, for getting out of that interview; for I might say things to be sorry for, if I allowed myself to go on any more with my heart so open. Therefore I called in my usual briskness, "Lo, the water is rising! The children must be at the mouth of the well. What will the good wife prophesy if she sees thee coming up the stairs with thy two feet soaking wet, Master Hezekiah?"

CHAPTER XVII.

FOR A LITTLE CHANGE OF AIR.

On the very next day, I received such a visit as never had come to my house before. For while I was trimming my hooks, and wondering how to get out of all this trouble with my conscience sound and my pocket improved; suddenly I heard a voice not to be found anywhere.

"I 'ants to yalk, I tell 'a, Yatkin. Put me down derekkerly. I 'ants to see old Davy."

"And old Davy wants to see you, you beauty," I cried, as she jumped like a little wild kid, and took all my house with a glance, and then me.

"Does 'a know, I yikes this house, and I yikes 'a, and I yikes Yatkin, and ickle Bunny, and evelybody?"

She pointed all round for everybody, with all ten fingers spread everyway. Then Watkin came after her, like her slave, with a foolish grin on his countenance, in spite of the undertaking business.

"If you please, sir, Mr Llewellyn," he said, "we was forced to bring her over; she have been crying so dreadful, and shivering about the black pit-hole so. And when the black things came into the house, she was going clean out of her little mind.

ever so many times almost. No use it was at all to tell her ever so much a-yard they was. 'I don't yike back, and I 'on't have back. Yite I yikes, and boo I yikes; and my dear papa be so very angy, when I tells him all about it.' She went on like that, and she did so cry, mother said she must change the air a bit."

All the time he was telling me this, she watched him with her head on one side and her lips kept ready in the most comic manner, as much as to say, "Now you tell any stories at my expense, and you may look out." But Watkin was truth itself, and she nodded, and said "Ness," at the end of his speech.

"And, if you please, sir, Mr Llewellyn, whatever is a 'belung,' sir? All the way she have been asking for 'belung, belung, belung.' And I cannot tell for the life of me whatever is 'belung.'"

"Boy, never ask what is unbecoming," I replied, in a manner which made him blush, according to my intention. For the word might be English for all I knew, and have something of high life in it. However, I found, by-and-by, that it meant what she was able to call "Ummibella," when promoted a year in the dictionary.

But now anybody should only have seen her, who wanted a little rousing up. My cottage, of course, is not much to boast of, compared with castles, and so on; nevertheless there is something about it pleasant and good, like its owner. You might see ever so many houses, and think them larger, and grander, and so on, with more opportunity for sitting down, and less for knocking your head perhaps; and after all you would come back to mine. Not for the sake of the meat in the cupboard—because I seldom had any, and far inferior men had more; but because—well, it does not matter. I never could make you understand, unless you came to see it.

Only I felt that I had found a wonderful creature to make me out, and enter almost into my own views (of which the world is not capable) every time I took this child up and down the staircase. She would have jumps, and she made me talk in a manner that quite surprised myself; and such a fine feeling grew up between us, that it was a happy thing for the whole of us, not to have Bunny in the way just then. Mother Jones was giving her apple-party; as she always did when the red streaks came upon her " Early Margarets." But I always think the White Juneating is a far superior apple: and I have a tree of it. My little garden is nothing grand, any more than the rest of my premises, or even myself, if it comes to that; still you might go for a long day's walk, and find very few indeed to beat it, unless you were contradictory. For ten doors at least, both west and east, this was admitted silently; as was proved by their sending to me for a cabbage, an artichoke, or an onion, or anything choice for a Sunday dinner. It may suit these very people now to shake their heads and to run me down, but they should not forget what I did for them, when it comes to pronouncing fair judgment.

Poor Bardie appeared as full of bright spirit, and as brave as ever, and when she tumbled from jumping two steps, what did she do but climb back and jump three, which even Bunny was afraid to do. But I soon perceived that this was only a sort of a flash in the pan, as it were. The happy change from the gloom of Sker House, from the silent corners and creaking stairs, and long-faced people keeping watch, and howling every now and then—also the sight of me again (whom she looked upon as her chief protector), and the general air of tidiness belonging to my dwelling—these things called forth all at once the play and joyful spring of her nature. But when she began to get tired of this, and to long for a little coaxing, even the stupidest gaffer could see that she was not the child she had been. Her little face seemed pinched and pale, and prematurely grave and odd; while in the grey eyes tears shone ready at any echo of thought to fall. Also her forehead, broad and white, which marked her so from common children, looked as if too much of puzzling and of wondering had been done there. Even the gloss of her rich brown poll was faded, with none to care for it; while the dainty feet and hands, so sensitive as to a speck of dirt, were enough to bring the tears of pity into a careful mother's eyes.

"Gardy la! 'Ook 'e see, 'hot degustin' naily pailies! And poor Bardie nuffin to kean 'em with!"

While I was setting this grief to rest (for which she kissed me beautifully), many thoughts came through my mind about this little creature. She and I were of one accord, upon so many important points; and when she differed from me, perhaps she was in the right almost: which is a thing that I never knew happen in a whole village of grown-up people. And by the time I had brushed her hair and tied up the bows of her frock afresh, and when she began to dance again, and to play every kind of trick with me, I said to myself, "I must have this child. Whatever may come of it, I will risk—when the price of butcher's-meat comes down."

This I said in real earnest; but the price of butcher's-meat went up, and I never have known it come down again.

While I was thinking, our Bunny came in, full of apples, raw and roasted, and of the things the children said. But at the very first sight of Bardie, everything else was gone from her. All the other children were fit only to make dirt-pies of. This confirmed and held me steadfast in the opinions which I had formed without any female assistance.

In spite of all her own concerns (of which she was full enough, goodness knows), Bunny came up, and pulled at her, by reason of something down her back, which wanted putting to rights a little—a plait, or a tuck, or some manner of gear; only I thought it a clever thing, and the little one approved of it. And then, our Bunny being in her best, these children took notice of one another, to settle which of them was nearer to the proper style of clothes. And each admired the other for anything which she had not got herself.

"Come, you baby-chits," said I, being pleased at their womanly ways, so early; "all of us want some food, I think. Can we eat our dresses?" The children, of course, understood me not; nevertheless, what I said was sense.

And if, to satisfy womankind—for which I have deepest regard and respect—I am forced to enter into questions higher than reason of men can climb—of washing, and ironing, and quilling, and gaufreing, and setting up, and styles of transparent reefing, and all our other endeavours to fetch this child up to her station—the best thing I can do will be to have mother Jones in to write it for me; if only she can be forced to spell.

However, that is beyond all hope; and even I find it hard sometimes to be sure of the royal manner. Only I go by the Bible always, for every word that I can find; being taught (ever since I could read at all) that his Majesty, James I., confirmed it.

Now this is not all the thing which I wanted to put before you clearly; because I grow like a tombstone often, only fit to make you laugh, when I stand on my right to be serious. My great desire is to tell you what I did, and how I did it, as to the managing of these children, even for a day or two, so as to keep them from crying, or scorching, or spoiling their clothes, or getting wet, or having too much victuals or too little. Of course I consulted that good mother Jones five or six times every day; and she never was weary of giving advice, though she said every time that it must be the last. And a lucky thing it was for me in all this responsibility to have turned enough of money, through skilful catch and sale of fish, to allow of my staying at home a little, and not only washing and mending of clothes, but treating the whole of the household to the delicacies of the season. However, it is not my habit to think myself anything wonderful; that I leave to the rest of the world: and no doubt any good and clever man might have done a great part of what I did. Only if anything should befall us, out of the reach of a sailor's skill and the depth of Bunny's experience, mother Jones promised to come straight in, the very moment I knocked at the wall; and her husband slept with such musical sound that none could be lonely in any house near, and so did all of her ten children who could crack a lollipop.

Upon the whole, we passed so smoothly over the first evening, with the two children as hard at play as if they were paid fifty pounds for it, that having some twenty-five shillings in hand after payment of all creditors, and only ten weeks to my pension-day, with my boat unknown to anybody, and a very good prospect of fish running up from the Mumbles at the next full moon, I set the little one on my lap, after a good bout of laughing at her very queer ins and outs—for all things seem to be all alive with, as well as to, her.

"Will you stay with me, my dear?" I said, as bold as King George and the Dragon; "would you like to live with old Davy and Bunny, and have ever so many frocks washed, soon as ever he can buy them?" For nothing satisfied her better than to see her one gown washed. She laid her head on one side a little, so that I felt it hot to my bosom, being excused of my waistcoat; and I knew that she had overworked herself.

"Ness," she said, after thinking a bit. "Ness, I live with 'a, old Davy, till my dear mama come for me. Does 'e know, old Davy, 'hot I thinks?"

"No, my pretty; I only know that you are always thinking." And so she was; no doubt of it.

"I tell 'a, old Davy, 'hot I thinks. No—I can't tell 'a; only sompfin. 'Et me go for more pay with Bunny."

"No, my dear, just stop a minute. Bunny has got no breath left in her; she is such a great fat Bunny. What you mean to say is, that you don't know how papa and mama could eve. think of leaving you such a long, long time away."

She shook her curly pate as if each frizzle were a puzzle; and her sweet white forehead seemed a mainsail full of memory; and then gay presence was in her eyes, and all the play which I had stopped broke upon her mind again.

"Tinker, tailor, soldier, sailor," she began, with her beautiful fingers crawling, like white carnelian compasses, up the well-made buttons of my new smock-guernsey; for though I had begged my hot waistcoat off, I never was lax of dress in her presence as I would be in Bunny's—or, in short, with anybody except this little lady. I myself taught her that "tinker, tailor," and had a right to have it done to me. And she finished it off with such emphasis upon button No. 7, which happened to be the last of them, "gentleman, ploughboy, fief," looking straight into my eyes, and both of us laughing at the fine idea that I could possibly be called a thief! But fearing to grow perhaps foolish about her, as she did these charming things to me, I carried her up to bed with Bunny, and sung them both away to sleep with a melancholy dirge of sea.

Into whatever state of life it may please God to call me—though I fear there cannot be many more at this age of writing—it always will be, as it always has been, my first principle and practice to do my very utmost (which is far less than it was, since the doctor stopped my hornpipes) to be pleasant and good company. And it is this leading motive which has kept me from describing—as I might have done, to make you tingle and be angry afterwards—the state of Sker House, and of Evan Thomas, and Moxy his wife, and all their friends, about those five poor rabbiters. Also other darkish matters, such as the plight of those obstinate black men when they came ashore at last, three together, and sometimes four, as if they had fought in the water. And, after all, what luck they had in obtaining proper obsequies, inasmuch as, by order of Crowner Bowles, a great hole in the sand was dug in a little sheltered valley, and kept open till it was fairly thought that the sea must have finished with them; and then, after being carefully searched for anything of value, they were rolled in all together and kept down with stones, like the parish mangle, and covered with a handsome mound of sand. And not only this, but in spite of expense and the murmuring of the vestry, a board well tarred (to show their colour) was set up in the midst of it, and their number "35" chalked up; and so they were stopped of their mischief awhile, after shamefully robbing their poor importer.

But if this was conducted handsomely, how much more so

were the funerals of the five young white men! The sense of the neighbourhood, and the stir, and the presence of the Coroner (who stopped a whole week for sea air and freshness, after seeing so many good things come in, and perceiving so many ways home that night, that he made up his mind to none of them); also the feeling (which no one expressed, but all would have been disappointed of) that honest black Evan, after knocking so many men down in both parishes and the extra-parochial manor, was designed, by this downright blow from above, to repent and to entertain every one; and most of all, the fact that five of a highly respectable family were to be buried at once, to the saving of four future funerals, all of which must have been fine ones,—these universal sympathies compelled the house and the people therein to exert themselves to the uttermost.

Enough that it gave satisfaction, not universal, but general; and even that last is a hard thing to do in such great outbursts of sympathy. Though Moudlin church is more handy for Sker, and the noble Portreeve of Kenfig stood upon his right to it, still there were stronger reasons why old Newton should have the preference. And Sker being outside either parish, Crowner Bowles, on receipt of a guinea, swore down the Portreeve to his very vamps. For Moxy Thomas was a Newton woman, and loved every scrape of a shoe there; and her uncle, the clerk, would have ended his days if the fees had gone over to Kenfig. Our parson, as well, was a very fine man, and a match for the whole of the service; while the little fellow at Moudlin always coughed at a word of three syllables.

There was one woman in our village who was always right. She had been disappointed, three times over, in her early and middle days; and the effect of this on her character was so lasting and so wholesome, that she never spoke without knowing something. When from this capital female I heard that our churchyard had won the victory, and when I foresaw the demented condition of glory impending upon our village (not only from five magnificent palls, each with its proper attendance of black, and each with fine hymns and good howling, but yet more than that from the hot strength of triumph achieved over vaunting Kenfig), then it came into my mind to steal away with Bardie.

A stern and sad sacrifice of myself, I assured myself that it was, and would be; for few even of our oldest men could enjoy a funeral more than I did, with its sad reflections and junketings. And I might have been head-man of all that day, entitled not only to drop the mould, but to make the speech afterwards at the Inn.

But I abandoned all these rights, and braved once more the opinions of neighbours (which any man may do once too often); and when the advance of sound came towards us, borne upon the western wind from the end of Newton Wayn, slowly hanging through the air, as if the air loved death of man—the solemn singing of the people who must go that way themselves, and told it in their melody; and when the Clevice rock rung softly with the tolling bell, as well as with the rolling dirges, we slipped away at the back of it—that is to say, pretty Bardie and I. For Bunny was purer of Newton birth than to leave such a sight without tearing away. And desiring some little to hear all about it, I left her with three very good young women, smelling strongly of southernwood, who were beginning to weep already, and promised to tell me the whole of it.

As we left this dismal business, Bardie danced along beside me, like an ostrich-feather blown at. In among the sand-hills soon I got her, where she could see nothing, and the thatch of rushes deadened every pulse of the funeral bell. And then a strange idea took me, all things being strange just now, that it might prove a rich wise thing to go for a quiet cruise with Bardie. In that boat, and on the waves, she might remember things recovered by the chance of semblance. Therefore, knowing that all living creatures five miles either way of us were sure to be in Newton churchyard nearly all the afternoon, and then in the public-houses, I scrupled not to launch my boat and go to sea with the little one. For if we steered a proper course no funeral could see us. And so I shipped her gingerly. The glory of her mind was such that overboard she must have jumped, except for my Sunday neck-tie with a half-hitch knot around her. And the more I rowed the more she laughed, and looked at the sun with her eyes screwed up, and at the water with all wide open. "'Hare is 'a going, old Davy?" she said, slipping from under my Sunday splice, and coming to me wonderfully, and laying her tiny hands on mine, which beat me always, as she had found out; " is 'a going to my dear papa, and mama, and ickle bother?"

"No, my pretty, you must wait for them to come. We are going to catch some fish, and salt them, that they may keep with a very fine smell, till your dear papa brings your mama and all the family with him; and then what a supper we will have!"

"'Ill 'a," she said; "and poor Bardie too?"

But the distance of the supper-time was a very sad disappointment to her, and her bright eyes filled with haze. And then she said "Ness" very quietly, because she was growing to understand that she could not have her own way now. I lay on my oars and watched her carefully, while she was shaking her head and wondering, with her little white shoulders above the thwart, and her innocent and intelligent eyes full of the spreading sky and sea. It was not often one had the chance, through the ever-flitting change, to learn the calm and true expression of that poor young creature's face. Even now I could not tell, except that her playful eyes were lonely, and her tender lips were trembling, and a heartful of simple love could find no outlet, and lost itself. These little things, when thinking thus, or having thought flow through them, never ought to be disturbed, because their brains are tender. The unknown stream will soon run out, and then they are fit again for play, which is the proper work of man. We open the world, and we close the world, with nothing more than this; and while our manhood is too grand (for a score and a half of years, perhaps), to take things but in earnest, the justice of our birth is on us,—we are fortune's plaything.

CHAPTER XVIII.

PUBLIC APPROBATION.

IF that child had no luck herself (except, of course, in meeting me), at any rate she never failed to bring me wondrous fortune. The air was smooth, and sweet, and soft, the sky had not a wrinkle, and the fickle sea was smiling, proud of pleasant manners. Directly I began to fish at the western tail of the Tuskar, scarcely a fish forebore me. Whiting-pollacks run in shoals, and a shoal I had of them; and the way I split and dried them made us long for breakfast-time. And Bardie did enjoy them so.

The more I dwelled with that little child, the more I grew wrapped up in her. Her nature was so odd and loving, and her ways so pretty. Many men forego their goodness, so that they forget the nature of a little darling child. Otherwise, perhaps, we might not, if we kept our hearts aright, so despise the days of loving, and the time of holiness. Now this baby almost shamed me, and I might say Bunny too, when, having undressed her, and put the coarse rough night-gown on her, which came from Sker with the funerals, my grandchild called me from up-stairs, to meet some great emergency.

"Granny, come up with the stick dreckly moment, granny dear! Missy 'ont go into bed. Such a bad wicked child she is."

I ran up-stairs, and there was Bunny all on fire with noble wrath, and there stood Bardie sadly scraping the worm-eaten floor with her small white toes.

"I'se not a yicked shild," she said, "I'se a vae good gal, I is; I 'ont go to bed till I say my payers to 'Mighty God, as my dear mama make me. She be very angy with 'a, Bunny, 'hen she knows it."

Hereupon I gave Bunny a nice little smack, and had a great mind to let her taste the stick which she had invoked so eagerly. However, she roared enough without it, because her feelings were deeply hurt. Bardie also cried for company, or, perhaps, at my serious aspect, until I put her down on her knees and bade her say her prayers, and have done with it. At the same time it struck me how stupid I was not to have asked about this before, inasmuch as even a child's religion may reveal some of its history.

She knelt as prettily as could be, with her head thrown back, and her tiny palms laid together upon her breast, and thus she said her simple prayer.

"Pay God bless dear papa, and mama, and ickle bother. Gentle Jesus, meek and mild, 'ook upon a ickle shild, and make me a good gal. Amen."

Then she got up and kissed poor Bunny, and was put into bed as good as gold, and slept like a little dormouse till morning.

Take it altogether now, we had a happy time of it. Every woman in Newton praised me for my kindness to the child; and even the men who had too many could not stand against Bardie's smile. They made up, indeed, some scandalous story, as might have been expected, about my relationship to the baby, and her sudden appearance so shortly after my poor wife's death. However, by knocking three men down, I produced a more active growth of charity in our neighbourhood.

And very soon a thing came to pass, such as I never could

have expected, and of a nature to lift me (even more than the free use of my pole) for a period of at least six months, above the reach of libel, from any one below the rank of a justice of the peace. This happened just as follows:—One night the children were snug in bed, and finding the evenings long, because the days were shortening in so fast—which seemed to astonish everybody—it came into my head to go no more than outside my own door, and into the "Jolly Sailors." For the autumn seemed to be coming on, and I like to express my opinions upon that point in society; never being sure where I may be before ever another autumn. Moreover, the landlord was not a man to be neglected with impunity. He never liked his customers to stay too long away from him, any more than our parson did; and pleasant as he was when pleased, and generous in the way of credit to people with any furniture, nothing was more sure to vex him, than for a man without excuse, to pretend to get on without him.

Now when I came into the room, where our little sober proceedings are—a narrow room, and dark enough, yet full of much good feeling, also with hard wooden chairs worn soft by generations of sitting—a sudden stir arose among the excellent people present. They turned and looked at me, as if they had never enjoyed that privilege, or, at any rate, had failed to make proper use of it before. And ere my modesty was certain whether this were for good or harm, they raised such a clapping with hands and feet, and a clinking of glasses in a line with it, that I felt myself worthy of some great renown. I stood there and bowed, and made my best leg, and took off my hat in acknowledgment. Observing this, they were all delighted, as if I had done them a real honour; and up they arose with one accord, and gave me three cheers, with an Englishman setting the proper tune for it.

I found myself so overcome all at once with my own fame and celebrity, that I called for a glass of hot rum-and-water, with the nipple of a lemon in it, and sugar the size of a nutmeg. My order was taken with a speed and deference hitherto quite unknown to me; and better than that, seven men opened purses, and challenged the right to pay for it. Entering into so rare a chance of getting on quite gratis, and knowing that such views are quick to depart, I called for six oz. of tobacco, with the Bristol stamp (a red crown) upon it. Scarce had I tested the draught of a pipe—which I had to do sometimes for half an hour, with all to blow out, and no drawing in—

when the tobacco was at my elbow, served with a saucer, and a curtsey. "Well," thought I, "this is real glory." And I longed to know how I had earned it.

It was not likely, with all those people gazing so respectfully, that I would deign to ask them coarsely, what the deuce could have made them do it. I had always felt myself unworthy of obscure position, and had dreamed, for many years, of having my merits perceived at last. And to ask the reason would have been indeed a degradation, although there was not a fibre of me but quivered to know all about it. Herein, however, I overshot the mark, as I found out afterwards; for my careless manner made people say that I must have written the whole myself—a thing so very far below me, that I scorn to answer it. But here it is: and then you can judge from the coarse style, and the three-decked words, whether it be work of mine.

Felix Farley's Bristol Journal, Saturday, July 24, 1782.—"*Shipwreck and loss of all hands—Heroism of a British tar.*—We hear of a sad catastrophe from the coast of Glamorganshire. The season of great heat and drought, from which our readers must have suffered, broke up, as they may kindly remember, with an almost unprecedented gale of wind and thunder, on Sunday, the 11th day of this month. In the height of the tempest a large ship was descried, cast by the fury of the elements upon a notorious reef of rocks, at a little place called Sker, about twenty miles to the east of Swansea. Serious apprehensions were entertained by the spectators for the safety of the crew, which appeared to consist of black men. Their fears were too truly verified, for in less than an hour the ill-fated bark succumbed to her cruel adversaries. No adult male of either colour appears to have reached the shore alive, although a celebrated fisherman, and heroic pensioner of our royal navy, whose name is David Llewellyn, and who traces his lineage from the royal bard of that patronymic, performed prodigies of valour, and proved himself utterly regardless of his own respectable and blameless life, by plunging repeatedly into the boiling surges, and battling with the raging elements, in the vain hope of extricating the sufferers from a watery grave. With the modesty which appears to be, under some inscrutable law of nature, inseparable from courage of the highest order, this heroic tar desires to remain in obscurity. This we could not reconcile with our sense of duty; and if any lover of our black brethren finds himself moved by this narration, we shall be happy to take charge of any remittance marked 'D. L.' It grieves us to add that none escaped except an intelligent young female, who clung to the neck of Llewellyn. She states that the ship was the Andalusia, and had sailed from Appledore, which is, we believe, in Devonshire. The respected Coroner Bowles held an inquest, which afforded universal satisfaction."

Deeply surprised as I was to find how accurately, upon the whole, this paper had got the story of it—for not much less than half was true—it was at first a puzzle to me how they could have learned so much about myself, and the valiant manner in which I intended to behave, but found no opportunity. Until I remembered that a man, possessing a very bad hat, had requested the honour of introducing himself to me, in my own house, and had begged me by all means to consider myself at home, and to allow him to send for refreshment, which I would not hear of twice, but gave him what I thought up to his mark, according to manners and appearance. And very likely he made a mistake between my description of what I was ready, as well as desirous, to carry out, and what I bodily did go through, ay, and more, to the back of it. However, I liked this account very much, and resolved to encourage yet more warmly the next man who came to me with a bad hat. What, then, was my disgust at perceiving, at the very foot of that fine description, a tissue of stuff like the following!

"*Another account* [from a highly-esteemed correspondent].—The great invasion of sand, which has for so many generations spread such wide devastation, and occasioned such grievous loss to landowners on the western coast of Glamorganshire, made another great stride in the storm of Sabbath-day, July 11. A vessel of considerable burthen, named the Andalusia, and laden with negroes, most carefully shipped for conversion among the good merchants of Bristol, appears to have been swallowed up by the sand; and our black fellow-creatures disappeared. It is to be feared, from this visitation of an ever-benign Providence, that few of them had been converted, and that the burden of their sins disabled them from swimming. If one had been snatched as a brand from the burning, gladly would we have recorded it, and sent him forward prayerfully for sustenance on his way to the Lord. But the only eyewitness (whose word must never be relied upon when mammon enters into the conflict), a worn-out but well-meaning sailor, who fattens upon the revenue of an overburdened country—this man ran away so fast that he saw hardly anything. The Lord, however, knoweth His own in the days of visitation. A little child came ashore alive, and a dead child bearing a coronet. Many people have supposed that the pusillanimous sailor aforesaid knows much more than he will tell. It is not for us to enter into that part of the question. Duty, however, compels us to say, that any one desiring to have a proper comprehension of this heavy but righteous judgment—for He doeth all things well—cannot do better than apply to the well-known horologist of Bridgend, Hezekiah Perkins, also to the royal family."

The above yarn may simply be described as a gallow's-rope spun by Jack Ketch himself from all the lies of all the scoundrels he has ever hanged, added to all that his own vile heart can invent, with the devil to help him. The cold-blooded, creeping, and crawling manner in which I myself was alluded to—although without the manliness even to set my name down—as well as the low hypocrisy of the loathsome white-livered syntax of it, made me,—well, I will say no more—the filthiness reeks without my stirring, and, indeed, no honest man should touch it; only, if Hezekiah Perkins had chanced to sneak into the room just then, his wife might have prophesied shrouds and weeds.

For who else was capable of such lies, slimed with so much sanctimony, like cellar slugs, or bilge-hole rats, rolling in Angelica, while all their entrails are of brimstone, such as Satan would scorn to vomit? A bitter pain went up my right arm, for the weakness of my heart, when that miscreant gave me insult, and I never knocked him down the well. And over and over again I have found it a thorough mistake to be always forgiving. However, to have done with reflections which must suggest themselves to any one situated like me—if, indeed, any one ever was—after containing myself, on account of the people who surrounded me, better than could have been hoped for, I spoke, because they expected it.

"Truly, my dear friends, I am thankful for your goodwill towards me. Also to the unknown writer, who has certainly made too much of my poor unaided efforts. I did my best; it was but little: and who dreams of being praised for it? Again, I am thankful to this other writer, who has overlooked me altogether. For the sake of poor Sandy Macraw, we must thank him that he kindly forbore to make public the name"

You should have seen the faces of all the folk around the table when I gave them this surprise.

"Why," said one, "we thought for sure that it was you he was meaning, Dyo dear. And in our hearts we were angry to him, for such falsehoods large and black. Indeed and indeed, true enough it may be of a man outlandish such as Sandy Macraw is."

"Let us not hasten to judge," I replied; "Sandy is brave enough, I daresay, and he can take his own part well. I will not believe that he ran away; very likely he never was there at all. If he was, he deserves high praise for taking some little care of himself. I should not have been so stiff this night, if I had only had the common-sense to follow his example."

All our people began to rejoice; and yet they required, as all of us do, something more than strongest proof.

"What reason is to show then, Dyo, that this man of letters meant not you, but Sandy Macraw, to run away so?"

"Hopkin, read it aloud," I said; "neither do I know, nor care, what the writer's meaning was. Only I thought there was something spoken about his Majesty's revenue. Is it I, or is it Sandy, that belongs to the revenue?"

This entirely settled it. All our people took it up, and neglected not to tell one another. So that in less than three days' time, my name was spread far and wide for the praise, and the Scotchman's for the condemnation. I desired it not, as my friends well knew; but what use to beat to windward, against the breath of the whole of the world? Therefore I was not so obstinate as to set my opinion against the rest; but left it to Mr Macraw to rebut, if he could, his pusillanimity.

As for Hezekiah Perkins, all his low creations fell upon the head from which they sprang. I spoke to our rector about his endeavour to harm a respectable Newton man—for you might call Macraw that by comparison, though he lived at Porthcawl, and was not respectable—and everybody was struck with my kindness in using such handsome terms of a rival. The result was that Perkins lost our church-clock, which paid him as well as a many two others, having been presented to the parish, and therefore not likely to go without pushing. For our rector was a peppery man, except when in the pulpit, and what he said to Hezekiah was exactly this.

"What, Perkins! another great bill again! 'To repair of church-clock, seven-and-sixpence; to ten miles' travelling, at threepence per mile,'—and so on, and so on! Why, you never came further than my brother the Colonel's, the last three times you have charged for. Allow me to ask you a little question—to whom did you go for the keys of the church?"

"As if I should want any keys of the church! There is no church-lock in the county that I cannot open, as soon as whistle."

"Indeed! So you pick our lock. Do you ever open a church-door honestly, for the purpose of worshipping the Lord? I have kept my eye upon you, sir, because I hear that you have been reviling my parishioners. And I happen to know that you never either opened the lock of our church or picked it, for the last three times you have charged for. But one thing you have picked for many years, and that is the pocket of my rate-payers. Be off, sir—be off with your trumpery bill! We will have a good churchman to do our clock—a thoroughly honest seaman, and a regular church-goer."

"Do you mean that big thief, Davy Llewellyn? Well, well, do as you please. But I will thank you to pay my bill first."

"Thank me when you get it, sir. You may fall down on your canting knees, and thank the Lord for one thing."

"What am I to thank the Lord for? For allowing you to cheat me thus?"

"For giving me self-command enough not to knock you down, sir." With that the rector came so nigh him, that brother Perkins withdrew in haste; for the parson had done that sort of thing to people who ill-used him; and the sense of the parish was always with him. Hence the management of the church-clock passed entirely into my hands, and I kept it almost always going, at less than half Hezekiah's price; and this reunited me to the Church (from which my poor wife perhaps had led me astray some little), by a monthly arrangement which reflected equal credit on either party.

And even this was not the whole of the blessings that now rolled down upon me, for the sake, no doubt, of little Bardie, as with the ark in the Bible. For this fine Felix Farley was the only great author of news at that time prevalent among us. It is true that there was another journal nearer to us, at Hereford, and a highly good one, but for a very clear reason it failed to have command of the public-houses. For the customers liked both their pipes and their papers to be of the same origin, and go together kindly. And Hereford sent out no tobacco; while Bristol was more famous for the best Virginian birdseye, than even for rum, or intelligence.

Therefore, as everybody gifted with the gift of reading came to the public-houses gradually, and to compare interpretation over those two narratives, both of which stirred our county up, my humble name was in their mouths as freely and approvingly as the sealing-wax end of their pipe stems. Unanimous consent accrued (when all had said the same thing over, fifty times in different manners, and with fine-drawn argument) that after all, and upon the whole, David Llewellyn was an honour to county and to country.

After that, for at least a fortnight, no more dogs were set at me. When I showed myself over a gentleman's gate, in the hope of selling fish to him, it used to be always, "At him, Pincher!" "Into his legs, Growler, boy!" so that I was compelled to carry my conger-rod to save me. Now, however, and for a season till my fame grew stale, I never lifted the latch of a gate without hearing grateful utterance, "Towser, down, you son of a gun! Yelp and Vick, hold your stupid tongues, will you?" The value of my legs was largely understood by gentlemen. As for the ladies and the housemaids, if conceit were in my nature, what a run it would have had! Always and always the same am I, and above even women's opinions. But I know no other man whose head would not have been turned with a day of it. For my rap at the door was scarcely given (louder, perhaps, than it used to be) before every maid in the house was out, and the lady looking through the blinds. I used to dance on the step, and beat my arms on my breast, with my basket down between my legs, and tremble almost for a second rap; and then it was, "Like your imperence!" "None of your stinking stuff!" and so on. But now they ran down beautifully, and looked up under their eyelids at me, and left me to show them what I liked, and never beat down a halfpenny, and even accepted my own weight. Such is the grand effect of glory; and I might have kissed every one of them, and many even of the good plain cooks, if I could have reconciled it with my sense of greatness.

CHAPTER XIX.

A CRAFT BEYOND THE LAW

COLONEL LOUGHER, of Candleston Court, was one of the finest and noblest men it was ever my luck to come across. He never would hear a word against me, any more than I would against him; and no sooner did I see him upon the Bench than I ceased to care what the evidence was. If they failed to prove their falsehoods (as nearly always came to pass), he dismissed them with a stern reprimand for taking away my character; and if they seemed to establish anything by low devices against me, what did he say? Why, no more than this: "David, if what they say be true, you appear to have forgotten yourself in a very unusual manner. You have promised me always to improve; and I thought that you were doing it. This seems to be a trifling charge—however, I must convict you. The penalty is one shilling, and the costs fifteen."

"May it please your worship," I always used to answer, "is an honest man to lose his good name, and pay those who have none for stealing it?"

Having seen a good deal of the world, he always felt the force of this, but found it difficult to say so with prejudiced men observing him. Only I knew that my fine and costs would be slipped into my hand by-and-by, with a glimpse of the Candleston livery.

This was no more than fair between us; for not more than seven generations had passed since Griffith Llewellyn, of my true stock, had been the proper and only bard to the great Lord Lougher of Coity, whence descended our good Colonel. There had been some little mistake about the departure of the title, no doubt through extremes of honesty, but no lord in the county came of better blood than Colonel Lougher. To such a man it was a hopeless thing for the bitterest enemy—if he had one—to impute one white hair's breadth of departure from the truth. A thoroughly noble man to look at, and a noble man to hearken to, because he knew not his own kindness, but was kind to every one. Now this good man had no child at all, as generally happens to very good men, for fear of mankind improving much. And the great king of Israel, David, from whom our family has a tradition—yet without any Jewish blood in us—he says (if I am not mistaken) that it is a sure mark of the ungodly to have children at their desire, and to leave the rest of their substance to ungodly infants.

Not to be all alone, the Colonel, after the death of his excellent wife, persuaded his only sister, the Lady Bluett, widow of Lord Bluett, to set up with him at Candleston. And this she was not very loath to do, because her eldest son, the present Lord Bluett, was of a wild and sporting turn, and no sooner became of age but that he wanted no mother over him. Therefore she left him for a while to his own devices, hoping every month to hear of his suddenly repenting.

Now this was a lady fit to look at. You might travel all day among people that kept drawing-rooms, and greenhouses, and the new safe of music, well named from its colour "grand pæony," and you might go up and down Bridgend, even on a fair-day, yet nobody would you set eyes on fit to be looked at as a lady on the day that you saw Lady Bluett.

It was not that she pretended anything; that made all the difference. Only she felt such a thorough knowledge that she was no more than we might have been, except for a width of accidents. And nothing ever parted her from any one with good in him. For instance, the first time she saw me again (after thirty years, perhaps, from the season of her beauty-charm, when I had chanced to win all the prizes in the sports given at Candleston Court, for the manhood of now Colonel Lougher), not only did she at once recognise me, in spite of all my battering, but she held out her beautiful hand, and said, "How are you, Mr Llewellyn?" Nobody had ever called me "Mr Llewellyn" much till then; but, by good luck, a washer-woman heard it and repeated it; and since that day there are not many people (leaving out clods and low enemies) with the face to accost me otherwise.

However, this is not to the purpose, any more than it is worthy of me. How can it matter what people call me when I am clear of my fish-basket? as, indeed, I always feel at the moment of unstrapping. No longer any reputation to require my fist ready. I have done my utmost, and I have received the money.

These are the fine perceptions which preserve a man of my position from the effects of calumny. And, next to myself, the principal guardian of my honour was this noble Colonel Lougher. Moreover, a fine little chap there was, Lady Bluett's younger son, Honourable Rodney Bluett by name; for his father had served under Admiral Rodney, and been very friendly with him, and brought him to church as a godfather. This young Rodney Bluett was about ten years old at that time, and the main delight of his life was this, to come fishing with old Davy. The wondrous yarns I used to spin had such an effect on his little brain, that his prospects on dry land, and love of his mother, and certain inheritance from the Colonel, were helpless to keep him from longing always to see the things which I had seen. With his large blue eyes upon me, and his flaxen hair tied back, and his sleeves tucked up for paddling, hour by hour he would listen, when the weather was too rough to do much more than look at it. Or if we went out in a boat (as we did when he could pay for hiring, and when his mother was out of the way), many and many a time I found him, when he should have been quick with the bait, dwelling upon the fine ideas which my tales had bred in him. I took no trouble in telling them, neither did I spare the truth when it would come in clumsily (like a lubber who cannot touch his hat), but they all smelled good and true, because they had that character.

However, he must bide his time, as every one of us has to do, before I make too much of him. And just at the period now in hand he was down in my black books for never coming near me. It may have been that he had orders not to be so much with me, and very likely that was wise; for neither his mother nor his uncle could bear the idea of his going to sea, but meant to make a red herring of him, as we call those poor land-soldiers. Being so used to his pretty company, and his admiration, also helping him as I did to spend his pocket-money, I missed him more than I could have believed; neither could I help sorrowing at this great loss of opportunity; for many an honest shilling might have been turned ere winter by the hire of my boat to him when he came out with me fishing. I had prepared a scale of charges, very little over Captain Bob's, to whom he used to pay 4d. an hour, when I let him come after the whiting with me. And now, for no more than 6d. an hour, he should have my very superior boat, and keep her head by my directions, for he understood a rudder, and bait my hooks, and stow my fish, and enjoy (as all boys should) the idea of being useful.

For, as concerns that little barkie, I had by this time secured myself from any further uneasiness, or troublesome need of concealment, by a bold and spirited facing of facts, which deserve the congratulation of all honest fishermen. The boat.

like her little captain, was at first all white—as I may have said—but now, before her appearance in public, I painted her gunwale and strakes bright blue, even down to her water-mark; and then, without meddling with her name, or rather that of the ship she belonged to, I retraced very lightly, but so that any one could read it, the name of the port from which she hailed, and which (as I felt certain now, from what I had seen on the poor wrecked ship) must have been San Salvador; and the three last letters were so plain, that I scarcely had to touch them.

Now this being done, and an old worn painter shipped instead of the new one, which seemed to have been chopped off with an axe, I borrowed a boat and stood off to sea from Porthcawl Point, where they beach them, having my tackle and bait on board, as if for an evening off the Tuskar, where turbot and whiting-pollack are. Here I fished until dusk of the night, and as long as the people ashore could see me; but as soon as all was dark and quiet, I just pulled into Newton Bay, and landed opposite the old " Red house," where my new boat lay in ordinary, snug as could be, and all out of sight. For the ruins of this old " Red house" had such a repute for being haunted, ever since a dreadful murder cast a ban around it, that even I never wished to stop longer than need be there at night; and once or twice I heard a noise that went to the marrow of my back; of which, however, I will say no more, until it comes to the proper place. Enough that no man, woman, or child, for twenty miles round, except myself, had a conscience clear enough to go in there after dark, and scarcely even by daylight. My little craft was so light and handy, that, with the aid of the rollers ready, I led her down over the beach myself, and presently towed her out to sea, with the water as smooth as a duck-pond, and the tide of the neap very silent. The weather was such as I could not doubt, being now so full of experience. Therefore, I had no fear to lie in a very dangerous berth indeed, when any cockle of a sea gets up, or even strong tides are running. This was the west-end fork of the Tuskar, making what we call " callipers;" for the back of the Tuskar dries at half-ebb, and a wonderful ridge stops the run of the tide, not only for weeds but for fish as well. Here with my anchor down, I slept, as only a virtuous man can sleep.

In the grey of the morning, I was up, ere the waning moon was done with, and found the very thing to suit me going on delightfully. The heavy dew of autumn, rising from the land by perspiration, spread a cloud along the shore. A little mist was also crawling on the water here and there; and having slept with a watch-coat and tarpaulin over me, I shook myself up, without an ache, and like a good bee at the gate of the hive, was brisk for making honey.

Hence I pulled away from land, with the heavy boat towing the light one, and even Sandy Macraw unable to lay his gimlet eye on me. And thus I rowed, until quite certain of being over three miles from land. Then with the broad sun rising nobly, and for a moment bowing, till the white fog opened avenues, I spread upon my pole a shirt which mother Jones had washed for me. It was the time when Sandy Macraw was bound to be up to his business; and I had always made a point of seeing that he did it. To have a low fellow of itchy character, and no royal breed about him, thrust by a feeble and reckless government into the berth that by nature was mine, and to find him not content with this, but even in his hours of duty poaching, both day and night, after my fish; and when I desired to argue with him, holding his tongue to irritate me,— satisfaction there could be none for it; the only alleviation left me was to rout up this man right early, and allow him no chance of napping.

Therefore, I challenged him with my shirt, thus early in the morning, because he was bound to be watching the world, if he acted up to his nasty business, such as no seaman would deign to; and after a quarter of an hour perhaps, very likely it was his wife that answered. At any rate there was a signal up, and through my spy-glass I saw that people wanted to launch a boat, but failed. Therefore I made a great waving of shirt, as much as to say, "extreme emergency; have the courage to try again." Expecting something good from this, they laid their shoulders, and worked their legs, and presently the boat was bowing on the gently-fluted sea.

Now it was not that I wanted help, for I could have managed it all well enough; but I wanted witnesses. For never can I bear to seem to set at nought legality. And these men were sure, upon half-a-crown, to place the facts before the public in an honest manner. So I let them row away for the very lives of them, as if the salvage of the nation hung upon their thumbs and elbows; only I dowsed my shirt as soon as I found them getting eager. And I thought that they might as well hail me first, and slope off disappointment.

"Hoy there! Boat ahoy! What, old Davy Llewellyn!"

What man had a right to call me "old"? There I was as fresh as ever. And I felt it the more that the man who did it was grey on the cheeks with a very large family, and himself that vile old Sandy! Nevertheless I preserved good manners.

"Ship your starboard oars, you lubbers. Do you want to run me down? What the devil brings you here, at this time of the morning?" Hereupon these worthy fellows dropped their oars, from wonder; until I showed them their mistake, and begged them to sheer off a little. For if I had accepted rope, such as they wished to throw me, they might have put in adverse claims, and made me pay for my own boat!

"When a poor man has been at work all night," said I, to break off their officiousness; "while all you lazy galley-rakers were abed and snoring, can't he put his shirt to dry, without you wanting to plunder him?"

To temper off what might appear a little rude, though wholesome, I now permitted them to see a stoneware gallon full of beer, or at least I had only had two pints out. Finding this to be the case, and being hot with rowing so rapidly to my rescue, they were well content to have some beer, and drop all further claims. And as I never can bear to be mean, I gave them the two and sixpence also.

Sandy Macraw took all this money; and I only hope that he shared it duly; and then, as he never seemed at all to understand my contempt of him, he spoke in that dry drawl of his, which he always droned to drive me into very dreadful words, and then to keep his distance.

"I am heartily glad, ma mon, to see the loock ye have encoontered. Never shall ye say agin that I have the advantage of ye. The boit stud me in mickle siller; but ye have grappit a boit for nort."

I cannot write down his outlandish manner of pronouncing English; nor will I say much more about it; because he concealed his jealousy so, that I had no enjoyment of it, except when I reasoned with myself. And I need have expected nothing better from such a self-controlling rogue. But when we came to Porthcawl Point—where some shelter is from wind, and two public-houses, and one private—the whole affair was so straightforward, and the distance of my boat from shore, at time of capture, so established and so witnessed, that no steward of any manor durst even cast sheep's-eyes at her. A paper was drawn up and signed; and the two public-houses, at my expense, christened her "Old Davy." And indeed, for a little spell, I had enough to do with people, who came at all hours of the day, to drink the health of my boat and me; many of whom seemed to fail to remember really who was the one to pay. And being still in cash a little, and so generous always, I found a whole basket of whiting, and three large congers, and a lobster, disappear against chalk-marks, whereof I had no warning, and far worse, no flavour. But what I used to laugh at was, that when we explained to one another how the law lay on this question, and how the craft became legally mine, as a derelict from the Andalusia, drifting at more than a league from land,—all our folk being short and shallow in the English language, took up the word, and called my boat, all over the parish, my "RELICT;" as if, in spite of the Creator's wisdom, I were dead and my wife alive!

CHAPTER XX.

CONFIDENTIAL INTERCOURSE.

But everybody must be tired of all this trouble about that boat. It shows what a state of things we live in, and what a meddlesome lot we are, that a good man cannot receive a gift straight into his hands from Providence, which never before rewarded him, though he said his prayers every night almost, and did his very best to cheat nobody; it proves, at least to my mind, something very rotten somewhere, when a man of blameless character must prove his right to what he finds. However, I had proved my right, and cut in Colonel Lougher's woods a larger pole than usual, because the law would guarantee me, if at all assaulted.

And truly, after all my care to be on the right side of it, such a vile attack of law was now impending on me, that with all my study of it, and perpetual attempts to jam its helm up almost into the very eye of reason, my sails very nearly failed to draw, and left me shivering in the wind. But first for what comes foremost.

At that particular moment all things seemed to be most satisfactory. Here was my property duly secured and most useful to me, here was a run of fish up from the Mumbles of a very superior character, here was my own reputation spread by the vigilance of the public press, so that I charged three farthings a-pound more than Sandy Mac did, and here was my cottage once more all alive with the mirth of our Bunny and Bardie. To see them playing at hide-and-seek with two chairs and a table; or "French and English," which I taught them; or "come and visit my grandmother;" or making a cat of the kettle-holder, with a pair of ears and a tail to it; or giving a noble dinner party with cockles and oyster-shells, and buttons, and apple-peel chopped finely; or, what was even a grander thing, eating their own dinners prettily, with their dolls beside them,—scarcely any one would have believed that these little ones had no mothers.

And yet they did not altogether seem to be forgetful, or to view the world as if there were no serious side to it. Very grave discourse was sometimes held between their bouts of play, and subjects of great depth and wonder introduced by doll's clothes. For instance :—

"Hasn't 'a got no mama, poor Bunny, to thread 'e needle?"

"No, my dear," I answered, for my grandchild looked stupid about it; "poor Bunny's mother is gone to heaven."

"My mama not gone to heaven. My mama come demorrow-day. I'se almost tired of yaiting, old Davy, but she sure to come demorrow-day."

But as the brave little creature spoke, I saw that "the dust was in her eyes." This was her own expression always, to escape the reproach of crying, when her lonely heart was working with its misty troubles, and sent the tears into her eyes, before the tongue could tell of them. "Demorrow-day, demorrow-day," all her loss was to be recovered always on "demorrow-day."

Not even so much as a doll had been saved from the total wreck of her fortunes; and when I beheld her wistful eyes set one day upon Bunny's doll—although only fit for hospital, having one arm and one leg and no nose, besides her neck being broken—I set to at once and sharpened my knife upon a piece of sandstone. Then I sought out a piece of abele, laid by from the figure-head of a wrecked Dutchman, and in earnest I fell to, and shaped such a carving of a doll as never was seen before or since. Of course the little pet came, and stood, and watched every chip as I sliced it along, with sighs of deep expectancy, and a laugh when I got to the tail of it; and of course she picked up every one, not only as neatest of the neat, but also accounting them sacred offsets of the mysterious doll unborn. I could not get her to go to bed; and it was as good as a guinea to me to see the dancing in her eyes, and the spring of her body returning.

"'E can make a boofely doll, old Davy; but 'e doesn't know the yay to dess a doll."

"You are quite wrong there," said I, perceiving that I should go up, or down, according to my assertion; and it made her open her eyes to see me cut out, with about five snips, a pair of drawers quite good enough for any decent woman. And she went to bed hugging the doll in that state, and praying to have her improved to-morrow.

At breakfast-time mother Jones dropped in, for she loved a good salt-herring, and to lay down the law for the day almost; as if I knew scarce anything. And I always let her have her talk, and listened to it gravely; and clever women, as a rule, should not be denied of this attention; for if they are, it sours them. While she was sucking the last of the tail, and telling me excellent scandal, my little lady marched in straight, having finished her breakfast long ago, and bearing her new doll pompously. The fly-away colour in her cheeks, which always made her beautiful, and the sparkle of her gleeful eyes, were come again with pleasure, and so was the lovely pink of her lips, and the proper aspect of her nose. Also she walked with such motherly rank, throwing her legs with a female jerk — it is enough for me to say that any newly-married woman would have kissed her all round the room.

Now, mother Jones, having ten fine children (five male and five female) going about with clothes up to their forks, need not have done what she did, I think, and made me so bashful in my own house. For no sooner did she see this doll, than she cried, "Oh, my!" and covered up her face. The little maid looked up at me in great wonder, as if I were leading her astray; and I felt so angry with Mrs Jones, after all the things I had seen abroad, and even in English churches, that I would not trust myself to speak. However, to pay her out for that, I begged her to cure the mischief herself, which she could not well decline; and some of the green blind still remaining, Dolly became a most handsome sight, with a crackle in front and a sweeping behind, so that our clerk, a good natured man, was invited to christen her; and "Patty Green" was the name he gave: and Bunny's doll was nobody. Such a baby-like thing might seem almost below my dignity, and that of all the rest of us; only this child had the power to lead us, as by a special enchantment, back to our own childhood. Moreover, it was needful for me to go through with this doll's birth (still more so with her dress, of course, having her a female), because through her I learned a great deal more of Bardie's history than ever our Bunny could extract.

Everybody who has no patience with the ways of childhood, may be vexed, and must be vexed, with our shipwrecked maid for knowing many things, but not the right; but I think she was to blame, only for her innocence. In her tiny brain was moving some uncertain sense of wrong; whether done by herself, or to her, was beyond her infant groping. If she could have made her mind up, in its little milky shell, that the evil had befallen, without harm on her part, doubtless she had done her best to let us know the whole of it. Her best, of course, would be but little, looking at her age and so on; and perhaps from some harsh word or frown, stamped into the tender flux of infantile memory, a heavy dread both darkened and repressed much recollection. Hence, if one tried to examine her, in order to find out who she was, she would shake her head, and say, "No! sompfin;" as she always did when puzzled or unable to pronounce a word. The only chance of learning even any little things she knew, was to leave her to her own way, and not interrupt her conversation with wooden or crockery playmates. All of these she endowed with life, having such power of life herself, and she reckoned them up for good behaviour, or for bad, as the case might be. And often was I touched at heart, after a day of bitter fighting with a world that wronged me, by hearing her in baby-prattle tell her playthings of their unkindness to a little thing with none to love her.

But when I had finished Patty's face up to complete expression, with two black buttons for her eyes, and a cowry for her mouth, and a nose of coral, also a glorious head of hair of crinkled sea-weed growing out of a shell (toothed like an ivory comb almost), the ecstasy of the child was such, that I obtained, as well as deserved, some valuable information.

"Patty Geen, 'e's been aye good," I heard her say in my window-place, one morning after breakfast; "and 'e is the most boofely doll ever seen, and I tell 'a sompfin; only 'e musn't tell anybody, till my dear mama comes. Nat wasn't ickle bother, Patty."

"How do you know, Miss?" Patty inquired by means of my voice in the distance, and a little art I had learned abroad of throwing it into corners.

"I tell 'a, Patty, I tell 'a. I 'ouldn't tell 'e nasty man, but I tell old Davy some day. Ickle bother not like nat at all. Ickle bother not so big enough, and only two ickle teeth in front, and his hair all gone ayay it is, but mama say soon come back again."

"And what is little brother's name?" said Patty, in a whisper; "and what is your name and papa's?"

"Oh, 'e silly Patty Geen! As if 'e didn't know I'se Bardie, ever since I was anytin. And papa, is papa, he is. Patty, I'se kite ashamed of 'a. 'E's such a silly ickle fin!"

"Well, I know I am not very clever, Miss. But tell me some more things you remember."

"I tell 'a, if 'e stop kiet. 'I 'ish 'a many happy turns of the day, Miss Bardie. Many happy turns of the day to 'a!' And poor Bardie get off her stool, and say what her dear papa tell. 'Gentleyums and yadies, I'se aye much obiged to 'a.' And then have boofely appledies, and carbies, and a ickle dop of good yiney-piney. Does 'e know 'hot that means, poor Patty?"

"No, my dear; how should I know?"

"'E mustn't call me 'my dear,' I tell 'a. 'E must know 'a's pace in yife. Why, 'e's only a doll, Patty, and Bardie's a young yady, and a 'streamly 'cocious gal I is, and the gentleyums all say so. Ickle bother can't say nuffin, without me to sow him the yay of it. But Bardie say almost anyfin; anyfin, when I yikes to ty. Bardie say 'Pomyoleanian dog!'"

This cost her a long breath, and a great effort; but Patty expressed intense amazement at such power of diction, and begged to know something more about that extraordinary animal.

"Pomyoleanian dog is yite, yite all over 'sept his collar, and his collar's boo. And he's got hair that long, Patty, ever so much longer than yours. And he yun yound and yound, he does. Oh, I do so yant my Pomyoleanian dog!"

Patty waited for two great tears to run quietly down two little cheeks; and then she expressed some contempt of the dog, and a strong desire to hear some more about the happy turns of the day.

"Don't 'e be jealous, now, Patty, I tell 'a. 'E ickle yite dog can eat, but 'e can't. And happy turns of the day is yen a geat big gal is two years old with a ickle bother. And he can't say nuffin, 'cos he grow too strong enough, and 'e young yady must repy; and ayebody yooks at 'a, and yaffs, and put 'e gasses up, and say, "Hot a 'cocious ickle fin!' And my dear papa say, "Hot a good gal!' and mama come and tiss 'a all over a'most, and then 'e all have some more puddeny-pie!"

Overcome with that last memory, she could go no further; and being unable to give her pies, I felt myself bound to abandon any more inquiries. For that child scarcely ever roared, so as to obtain relief; but seemed with a kind of self-control—such as unlucky people form, however early in their lives—to take her troubles inwardly, and to be full to the very lip of them, without the power of spilling. This, though a comfort to other people, is far worse for themselves, I fear. And I knew that she did love pastry rarely; for one day, after a fine pair of soles, I said to the two children, "Now, put your little hands together, and thank God for a good dinner." Bunny did this in a grateful manner, but Bardie said, "No, I 'ont, old Davy; I'll thank God when I gets puddeny-pie."

Upon the whole, I concluded thus, that the little creature was after all (and as might have been expected with any other child almost) too young, in the third year of her age, to maintain any clear ideas of place, or time, or names, or doings, or anything that might establish from her own words only, whence she came or who she was. However, I now knew quite enough, if the right people ever came to seek for her, to "'dentify" her, as she expressed it to that stupid Coroner.

Moxy Thomas came to fetch her back to Sker, in a few days' time. I was now resolved to keep her, and she resolved to stay with me—and doubtless I had first right to her. But when I saw poor Moxy's face, and called to mind her desolation, and when she kissed my fishy hand to let her have this comfort, after all the Lord had taken from her, I could not find it in my heart to stand to my own interest. It came across me too that Bardie scarcely throve on so much fish; and we never had any butcher's meat, or meat of any kind at all, unless I took shares in a pig, after saving up money for Christmas, or contrived to defend myself against the hares that would run at me so, when I happened to come through a gate at night.

So with a clearly-pronounced brave roar, having more music than Bunny's in it, and enough to wash a great deal of "dust" out of her woefully lingering eyes, away she went in Moxy's arms, with Patty Green in her own looking likely to get wet through. And Bunny stuck her thumbs into my legs, which she had a knack of doing, especially after sucking them; so thus we stood, at our cottage door, looking after Bardie; and I took off my hat, and she spread her hand out, in the intervals of woe; and little thought either of us, I daresay, of the many troubles in store for us both.

Only before that grievous parting, she had done a little thing which certainly did amaze me. And if anybody knows the like, I shall be glad to hear of it. I had a snug and tidy locker very near the fireplace, wherein I kept some little trifles; such as Bunny had an eye for, but was gradually broken into distant admiration. One morning I came suddenly in from looking to my night-lines, and a pretty scene I saw. The door of my cupboard was wide open, and there stood little Bardie giving a finishing lick to her fingers. Bunny also in the corner, with her black eyes staring, as if at the end of the world itself. However, her pinafore was full.

No sooner did my grandchild see me, than she rushed away with shrieks, casting down all stolen goods in agony of conscience. I expected Bardie to do the same; but to my great wonderment up she walked and faced me.

"Must I beat poor Patty Geen?" The tears were in her eyes at having to propose so sad a thing. And she stroked the doll, to comfort her.

"Beat poor Patty!" said I, in amazement. "Why, what harm has Patty done?"

"Nare she have been, all 'e time, stealing 'a soogar, old Davy!" And she looked at me as if she had done a good turn by the information. I scarcely knew what to do, I declare; for her doll was so truly alive to her, that she might and perhaps did believe it. However, I shut her in my little bedroom, until her heart was almost broken; and then I tried to reason with her, on the subject of telling lies; but she could not understand what they were; until I said what I was forced to do, when I went among bad people.

That evening, after she was gone, and while I was very dull about it, finding poor Bunny so slow and stupid, and nothing to keep me wide awake—there I was bound to be wide awake, more than at Petty Sessions even, when mine enemies throng against me. For almost before I had smoked two pipes, or made up my mind what to do with myself, finding a hollow inside of me, the great posting-coach from Bridgend came up, with the sun setting bright on its varnish, and at my very door it stopped. Next to the driver sat a constable who was always unjust to me; and from the inside came out first Justice Anthony Stew of Pen Coed, as odious and as meddlesome a justice of the peace as ever signed a warrant; and after him came a tall elderly gentleman, on whom I had never set eyes before, but I felt that he must be a magistrate.

CHAPTER XXI.

CROSS-EXAMINATION.

THOSE justices of the peace, although appointed by his Majesty, have never been a comfort to me, saving only Colonel Lougher. They never seem to understand me, or to make out my desires, or to take me at my word, as much as I take them at theirs. My desire has always been to live in a painfully loyal manner, to put up with petty insults from customers who know no better, leaving them to self-reflection, and if possible to repentance, while I go my peaceful way, nor let them hear their money jingle, or even spend it in their sight. To be pleased and trustful also with the folk who trust in me, and rather to abandon much, and give back twopence in a shilling, than cause any purchaser self-reproach for having sworn falsely before the bench,—now, if all this would not do, to keep me out of the session-books, can any man point out a clearer proof of the vicious administration of what they call "justice" around our parts? And when any trumpery case was got up, on purpose to worry and plague me, the only chance left me, of any fair-play, was to throw up my day's work, and wear out my shoes in trudging to Candleston Court, to implore that good Colonel Lougher to happen to sit on the bench that day.

When those two gentlemen alighted from that rickety old coach, and ordered that very low constable to pace to and fro at the door of my house, boldly I came out to meet them, having injured no man, nor done harm of any sort that I could think of, lately. Stew came first, a man of no lineage, but pushed on by impudence; "Anthony Stew can look you through," an English poacher said of him; and this he tried always to do with me, and thoroughly welcome he was to succeed.

I will not say that my inner movements may not have been uneasy, in spite of all my rectitude; however, I showed their two worships inside, in the very best style of the quarter-deck such as I had gathered from that coroneted captain, my proud connection with whom, perhaps, I may have spoken of ere this, or at any rate ought to have done so, for I had the honour of swabbing his pumps for him almost every morning; and he was kind enough to call me "Davy."

Every Briton, in his own house, is bound to do his utmost; so I touched my grey forelock, and made two good bows, and set a chair for each of them, happening to have no more just now, though with plenty of money to buy them. Self-controlled as I always am, many things had tried me, of late, almost to the verge of patience; such imputations as fall most tenderly on a sorrowful widower; and my pure admiration of Bardie, and certainty of her lofty birth, had made me the more despise such foulness. So it came to pass that two scandalous men were given over by the doctors (for the pole I had cut was a trifle too thick), nevertheless they recovered bravely, and showed no more gratitude towards God, than to take out warrants against me! But their low devices were frustrated by the charge being taken before Colonel Lougher. And what did that excellent magistrate do? He felt himself compelled to do something. Therefore he fined me a shilling per head for the two heads broken, with 10s. costs (which he paid, as usual), and gave me a very severe reprimand.

"Llewellyn," he said, "the time is come for you to leave off this course of action. I do not wonder that you felt provoked; but you must seek for satisfaction in the legal channels. Suppose these men had possessed thin heads, why you might have been guilty of murder! Make out his commitment to Cardiff Gaol, in default of immediate payment."

All this was good, and sustained one's faith in the efficacy of British law; and trusting that nothing might now be amiss in the minds of these two magistrates, I fetched the block of sycamore, whereupon my fish were in the habit of having their fins and tails chopped off; and there I sate down, and presented myself both ready and respectful. On the other hand, my visitors looked very grave and silent; whether it were to prolong my doubts, or as having doubts of their own, perhaps.

"Your worships," I began at last, in fear of growing timorous, with any longer waiting—"your worships must have driven far."

"To see you, Llewellyn." Squire Stew said, with a nasty snap, hoping the more to frighten me.

"Not only a pleasure to me, your worships, but a very great honour to my poor house. What will your worships be pleased to eat? Butcher's meat I would have had, if only I had known of it. But one thing I can truly say, my cottage has the best of fish."

"That I can believe," said Stew; "because you sell all the worst to me. Another such a trick, Llewellyn, and I have you in the stocks."

This astonished me so much—for his fish had never died over four days—that nothing but my countenance could express my feelings.

"I crave your pardon, Justice Stew," said the tall grey gentleman with the velvet coat, as he rose in a manner that overawed me, for he stood a good foot over Anthony Stew, and a couple of inches over me; "may we not enter upon the matter which has led us to this place?"

"Certainly, Sir Philip, certainly," Stew replied, with a style which proved that Sir Philip must be of no small position; "all I meant, Sir Philip, was just to let you see the sort of fellow we have to deal with."

"My integrity is well known," I answered, turning from him to the gentleman; "not only in this parish, but for miles and miles round. It is not my habit to praise myself; and in truth I find no necessity. Even a famous newspaper, so far away as Bristol, the celebrated 'Felix Farley's Journal'——"

"Just so," said the elder gentleman; "it is that which has brought us here; although, as I fear, on a hopeless errand."

With these words he leaned away, as if he had been long accustomed to be disappointed. To me it was no small relief to find their business peaceable, and that neither a hare which had rushed at me like a lion through a gate by moonlight, nor a stupid covey of partridges (nineteen in number, which gave me no peace while excluded from my dripping-pan), nor even a pheasant cock whose crowing was of the most insulting tone,—that none of these had been complaining to the bench emboldened me, and renewed my sense of reason. But I felt that Justice Stew could not be trusted for a moment to take this point in a proper light. Therefore I kept my wits in the chains, taking soundings of them both.

"Now, Llewellyn, no nonsense, mind!" began Squire Stew, with his face like a hatchet, and scollops over his eyebrows: "what we are come for is very simple, and need not unsettle your conscience, as you have allowed it to do, I fear. Keep your aspect of innocent wonder for the next time you are brought before me. I only wish your fish were as bright and slippery as you are."

"May I humbly ask what matter it pleases your worship to be thinking of?"

"Oh, of course you cannot imagine, Davy. But let that pass, as you were acquitted, by virtue of your innocent face, in the teeth of all the evidence. If you had only dropped your eyes, instead of wondering so much—but never mind, stare as you may, some day we shall be sure to have you."

Now, I will put it to anybody whether this was not too bad, in my own house, and with the Bench seated on my own best chairs! However, knowing what a man he was, and how people do attribute to me things I never dreamed of, and what little chance a poor man has if he takes to contradiction, all I did was to look my feelings, which were truly virtuous. Nor were they lost upon Sir Philip.

"You will forgive me, good sir, I hope," he said to Squire Anthony; "but unless we are come with any charge against this—Mr Llewellyn, it is hardly fair to reopen any awkward questions of which he has been acquitted. In his own house, moreover, and when he has offered kind hospitality to us—in a word, I will say no more."

Here he stopped, for fear perhaps of vexing the other magistrate; and I touched my grizzled curl and said, "Sir, I thank you for a gentleman." This was the way to get on with me, instead of driving and bullying; for a gentleman or a lady can lead me to any extremes of truth; but not a lawyer, much less a justice. And Anthony Stew had no faith in truth, unless she came out to his own corkscrew.

"British tar," he exclaimed, with his nasty sneer; "now for some more of your heroism! You look as if you were up for doing something very glorious. I have seen that colour in your cheeks when you sold me a sewin that shone in the dark. A glorious exploit; wasn't it now?"

"That it was, your worship, to such a customer as you."

While Anthony Stew was digesting this, which seemed a puzzle to him, the tall grey gentleman, feeling but little interest in my commerce, again desired to hurry matters. "Forgive me again, I beseech you, good sir; but ere long it will be dark. and as yet we have learned nothing."

"Leave it all to me, Sir Philip; your wisest plan is to leave it to me. I know all the people around these parts, and especially this fine fellow. I have made a sort of study of him, because I consider him what I may call a thoroughly typical character."

"I am not a typical character," I answered, over-hastily, for I found out afterwards what he meant. "I never tipple; but when I drink, my rule is to go through with it."

Squire Stew laughed loud at my mistake, as if he had been a great scholar himself; and even Sir Philip smiled a little in his sweet and lofty manner. No doubt but I was vexed for a moment, scenting (though I could not see) error on my own part. But now I might defy them both, ever to write such a book as this. For vanity has always been so foreign to my nature, that I am sure to do my best, and, after all, think nothing of it, so long as people praise me. And now, in spite of all rude speeches, if Sir Philip had only come without that Squire Anthony, not a thing of all that happened would I have retained from him. It is hopeless for people to say that my boat crippled speech on my part. Tush! I would have pulled her plug out on the tail of the Tuskar rather than one moment stand against the light for Bardie.

Squire Stew asked me all sorts of questions having no more substance in them than the blowing-hole at the end of an egg, or the bladder of a skate-fish. All of these I answered boldly, finding his foot outside my shoes. And so he came back again, as they do after trying foolish excursions, to the very point he started with.

"Am I to understand, my good fellow, that the ship, which at least you allow to be wrecked, may have been or might have been something like a foreigner?"

"Therein lies the point whereon your worship cannot follow me, any more than could the Coroner. Neither he, nor his clerk, nor the rest of the jury, would listen to common-sense about it. That ship no more came from Appledore than a whale was hatched from a herring's egg."

"I knew it; I knew it," broke in Sir Philip. "They have only small coasters at Appledore. I said that the newspaper must be wrong. However, for the sake of my two poor sons, I am bound to leave no clue unfollowed. There is nothing more to be done, Mr Stew, except to express my many and great obligations for your kindness." Herewith he made a most stately bow, and gave even me a corner of it.

"Stay, Sir Philip; one moment more. This fellow is such a crafty file. Certain I am that he never would look so unnaturally frank and candid unless he were in his most slippery mood. You know the old proverb, I daresay, 'Put a Taffy on his mettle, he'll boil Old Nick in his own fish-kettle.' Dyo, where did your boat come from?"

This question he put in a very sudden, and I might well say vicious, manner, darting a glance at me like the snake's tongues in the island of Das Cobras. I felt such contempt that I turned my back, and gave him a view of the "boofely buckens" admired so much by Bardie.

"Well done!" he cried. "Your resources, Dyo, are an infinite credit to you. And, do you know, when I see your back, I can almost place some faith in you. It is broad and flat and sturdy, Dyo. Ah! many a fine hare has swung there head downwards. Nevertheless, we must see this boat."

Nothing irritates me more than what low Englishmen call "chaff." I like to be pleasant and jocular upon other people; but I don't like that sort of thing tried upon me when I am not in the humour for it. Therefore I answered crustily,

"Your worship is welcome to see my boat, and go to sea in her if you please, with the plug out of her bottom. Under Porthcawl Point she lies; and all the people there know all about her. Only, I will beg your worship to excuse my presence, lest you should have low suspicions that I came to twist their testimony."

"Well said, David! well said, my fine fellow! Almost I begin to believe thee, in spite of all experience. Now, Sir Philip."

"Your pardon, good sir; I follow you into the carriage."

So off they set to examine my boat; and I hoped to see no more of them, for one thing was certain—to wit, that their coachman never would face the sand-hills, and no road ever is, or ever can be, to Porthcawl; so that these two worthy gentlemen needs must exert their noble legs for at least one-half of the distance. And knowing that Squire Stew's soles were soft, I thought it a blessing for him to improve the only soft part about him.

CHAPTER XXII.

ANOTHER DISAPPOINTMENT.

HIGHLY pleased with these reflections, what did I do but take a pipe, and sit like a lord at my own doorway, having sent poor Bunny with a smack to bed, because she had shown curiosity: for this leading vice of the female race cannot be too soon discouraged. But now I began to fear almost that it would be growing too dark very soon for me to see what became of the carriage returning with those two worships. Moreover, I felt that I had no right to let them go so easily, without even knowing Sir Philip's surname, or what might be the especial craze which had led them to honour me so. And sundry other considerations slowly prevailed over me; until it would have gone sore with my mind, to be kept in the dark concerning them. So, when heavy dusk of autumn drove in over the notch of sandhills from the far-away of sea, and the green of grass was gone, and you hardly could tell a boy from a girl among the children playing, unless you knew their mothers; I rejoicing in their pleasures, quite forgot the justices. For all our children have a way of letting out their liveliness, such as makes old people feel a longing to be in with them. Not like Bardie, of course; but still a satisfactory feeling. And the better my tobacco grew, the sweeter were my memories.

Before I had courted my wife and my sweethearts (a dozen and a-half perhaps, or at the outside say two dozen) anything more than twice a-piece, in the gentle cud of memory; and with very quiet sighs indeed, for echoes of great thumping ones; and just as I wondered what execution a beautiful child, with magnificent legs, would do when I lay in the churchyard—all of a heap I was fetched out of dreaming into common-sense again. There was the great yellow coach at the corner of the old grey wall that stopped the sand; and all the village children left their "hide-and-seek" to whisper. Having fallen into a different mood from that of curiosity, and longing only for peace just now, or tender styles of going, back went I into my own cottage, hoping to hear them smack whip and away. Even my hand was on the bolt—for a bolt I had now on account of the cats, who understand every manner of latch, wherever any fish be—and perhaps it is a pity that I did not shoot it.

But there came three heavy knocks; and I scarcely had time to unbutton my coat, in proof of their great intrusion, before I was forced to show my face, and beg to know their business.

"Now, Dyo, Dyo," said that damned Stew [saving your presence, I can't call him else]; "this is a little too bad of you! Retiring ere dusk! Aha! aha! And how many hours after midnight will you keep your hornpipes up, among the 'jolly sailors!' Great Davy, I admire you."

I saw that it was not in his power to enter into my state of mind: nor could I find any wit in his jokes, supposing them to be meant for such.

"Well, what did your worships think of Porthcawl?" I asked, after setting the chairs again, while I bustled about for my tinder-box: "did you happen to come across the man whose evil deeds are always being saddled upon me?"

"We found a respectable worthy Scotchman, whose name is Alexander Macraw; and who told us more in about five minutes than we got out of you in an hour or more. He has given us stronger reason to hope that we may be on the right track at last to explain a most painful mystery, and relieve Sir Philip from the most cruel suspense and anxiety."

At these words of Squire Anthony, the tall grey gentleman with the velvet coat bowed, and would fain have spoken, but feared perhaps that his voice would tremble.

"Macraw thinks it highly probable," Justice Stew continued, "that the ship, though doubtless a foreigner, may have touched on the opposite coast for supplies, after a long ocean voyage: and though Sir Philip has seen your boat, and considers it quite a stranger, that proves nothing either way, as the boat of course would belong to the ship. But one very simple and speedy way there is of settling the question. You thought proper to conceal the fact that the Coroner had committed to your charge as foreman of the jury—and a precious jury it must have been—so as to preserve near the spot, in case of any inquiry, the dress of the poor child washed ashore. This will save us the journey to Sker, which in the dusk would be dangerous. David Llewellyn, produce that dress, under my authority."

"That I will, your worship, with the greatest pleasure. I am sure I would have told you all about it, if I had only thought of it."

"Ahem!" was all Squire Stew's reply, for a horribly suspicious man hates such downright honesty. But without taking further notice of him, I went to my locker of old black oak, and thence I brought that upper garment something like a pinafore, the sight of which had produced so strong an effect upon the Coroner. It was made of the very finest linen, and perhaps had been meant for the child to wear in lieu of a frock in some hot climate. As I brought this carefully up to the table, Squire Stew cried, "Light another candle," just as if I kept the village shop! This I might have done at one time, if it had only happened to me, at the proper period, to marry the niece of the man that lived next door to the chapel, where they dried the tea-leaves. She took a serious liking to me, with my navy trousers on; but I was fool enough to find fault with a little kink in her starboard eye. I could have carried on such a trade, with my knowledge of what people are, and description of foreign climates—however, it was not to be, and I had to buy my candles.

As soon as we made a fine strong light, both the gentlemen came nigh, and Sir Philip, who had said so little, even now forbore to speak. I held the poor dress, tattered by much beating on the points of rocks; and as I unrolled it slowly, he withdrew his long white hands, lest we should remark their quivering.

"You are not such fools as I thought," said Stew; "it is a coronet beyond doubt. I can trace the lines and crossings, though the threads are frayed a little. And here in the corner, a moneygrum—ah! you never saw that, you stupes—do you know the mark, sir?"

"I do not," Sir Philip answered, and seemed unable to fetch more words; and then like a strong man turned away, to hide all disappointment. Even Anthony Stew had the manners to feel that here was a sorrow beyond his depth, and he covered his sense of it, like a gentleman, by some petty talk with me. And it made me almost respect him to find that he dropped all his banter, as out of season.

But presently the tall grey gentleman recovered from his loss of hope, and with a fine brave face regarded us. And his voice was firm and very sweet.

"It is not right for me to cause you pain by my anxieties; and I fear that you will condemn me for dwelling upon them overmuch. But you, Mr Stew, already know, and you my friend have a right to know, after your kind and ready help, that it is not only the piteous loss of two little innocent children, very dear ones both of them, but also the loss of fair repute to an honourable family, and the cruel suspicion cast upon a fine brave fellow, who would scorn, sir, who would scorn, for the wealth of all this kingdom, to hurt the hair of a baby's head."

Here Sir Philip's voice was choked with indignation more than sorrow, and he sate down quickly, and waved his hand, as much as to say, "I am an old fool, I had much better not pretend to talk." And much as I longed to know all about it, of course it was not my place to ask.

"Exactly, my dear sir, exactly," Squire Anthony went on, for the sake of saying something; "I understand you, my dear sir, and feel for you, and respect you greatly for your manly fortitude under this sad calamity. Trust in Providence, my dear sir; as indeed I need not tell you."

"I will do my best; but this is now the seventh disappointment we have had. It would have been a heavy blow, of course, to have found the poor little fellow dead. But even that, with the recovery of the other, would have been better than this dark mystery, and, above all, would have freed the living from these maddening suspicions. But as it is, we must try to bear it, and to say, 'God's will be done.' But I am thinking too much about ourselves. Mr Stew, I am very ungrateful not to think more of your convenience. You must be longing to be at home."

"At your service, Sir Philip—quite at your service. My time is entirely my own."

This was simply a bit of brag; and I saw that he was beginning to fidget; for, bold as his worship was on the bench, we knew that he was but a coward at board, where Mrs Stew ruled with a rod of iron: and now it was long past dinner-time, even in the finest houses.

"One thing more, then, before we go," answered Sir Philip, rising; "according to the newspaper, and as I hear, one young maiden was really saved from that disastrous shipwreck. I wish we could have gone on to see her; but I must return to-morrow morning, having left many anxious hearts behind. And to cross the sands in the dark, they say, is utterly impossible."

"Not at all, Sir Philip," said I, very firmly, for I honestly wished to go through with it; "although the sand is very deep, there is no fear at all, if one knows the track. It is only the cowardice of these people ever since the sand-storm. I would answer to take you in the darkest night, if only I had ever learned to drive." But Anthony Stew broke in with a smile,

"It would grieve me to sit behind you, Dyo, and I trow that Sir Philip would never behold Appledore again. There is nothing these sailors will not attempt."

Although I could sit the bow-thwart of a cart very well, with a boy to drive me, and had often advised the hand at the tiller, and sometimes as much as held the whip, all this, to my diffidence, seemed too little to warrant me in navigating a craft that carried two horses.

Sir Philip looked at me, and perhaps he thought that I had not the cut of a coachman. However, all he said was this:

"In spite of your kindness, Mr Stew, and your offer, my good sir"—this was to me, with much dignity—"I perceive that we must not think of it. And of what use could it be except to add new troubles to old ones? Sir, I have trespassed too much on your kindness; in a minute I will follow you." Anthony Stew, being thus addressed, was only too glad to skip into the carriage. "By, by, Dyo," he cried; "mend your ways, if you can, my man. I think you have told fewer lies than usual; knock off one every time of speaking, and in ten years you will speak the truth."

Of this low rubbish I took no heed any more than any one would who knows me, especially as I beheld Sir Philip signalling with his purse to me, so that Stew might not be privy to it. Entering into the spirit of this, I had some pleasant memories of gentlemanly actions done by the superior classes towards me, but longer agone than I could have desired. And now being out of the habit of it, I showed some natural reluctance to begin again, unless it were really worth my while. Sir Philip understood my feelings, and I rose in his esteem, so that half-guineas went back to his pocket, and guineas took the place of them.

"Mr Llewellyn, I know," he said, "that you have served your country well; and it grieves me to think that on my account you have met with some harsh words to-day."

"If your worship only knew how little a thing of that sort moves me when I think of the great injustice. But I suppose it must be expected by a poor man such as I am. Justice Stew is spoiled by having so many rogues to deal with. I always make allowance for him; and of course I know that he likes to play with the lofty character I bear. If I had his house and his rich estate—but it does not matter—after all, what are we?"

"Ah, you may well say that, Llewellyn. Two months ago I could not have believed—but who are we to find fault with the doings of our Maker? All will be right if we trust in Him, although it is devilish hard to do. But that poor maid at that wretched place—what is to become of her?"

"She has me to look after her, your worship, and she shall not starve while I have a penny."

"Bravely said, Llewellyn! My son is a sailor, and I understand them. I know that I can trust you fully to take charge of a trifle for her."

"I love the maid," I answered truly; "I would sooner rob myself than her."

"Of course you would, after saving her life. I have not time to say much to you, only take this trifle for the benefit of that poor thing."

From a red leathern bag he took out ten guineas, and hastily plunged them into my hand, not wishing Stew to have knowledge of it. But I was desirous that everybody should have the chance to be witness of it, and so I held my hand quite open. And just at that moment our Bunny snored.

"What! have you children yourself, Llewellyn? I thought that you were an old bachelor."

"An ancient widower, your worship, with a little grandchild; and how to keep her to the mark, with father none and mother none, quite takes me off my head sometimes. Let me light your honour to your carriage."

"Not for a moment, if you please; I wish I had known all this before. Mr Stew never told me a word of this."

"It would have been strange if he had," said I; "he is always so bitter against me, because he can never prove anything."

"Then, Llewellyn, you must oblige me. Spend this trifle on clothes and things for that little snorer."

He gave me a little crisp affair, feeling like a child's caul dried, and I thought it was no more than that. However I touched my brow and thanked him as he went to the carriage-steps; and after consulting all the village, I found it a stanch pledge from the Government for no less than five pounds sterling.

CHAPTER XXIII.

INTO GOOD SOCIETY.

IN spite of all that poor landsmen say about equinoctial gales and so on, we often have the loveliest weather of all the year in September. If this sets in, it lasts sometimes for three weeks or a month together. Then the sky is bright and fair, with a firm and tranquil blue, not so deep of tint or gentle as the blue of springtide, but more truly staid and placid, and far more trustworthy. The sun, both when he rises over the rounded hills behind the cliffs, and when he sinks into the level of the width of waters, shines with ripe and quiet lustre, to complete a year of labour. As the eastern in the morning, so at sunset the western heaven glows with an even flush of light through the entire depth pervading, and unbroken by any cloud. Then at dusk the dew fog wavers in white stripes over the meadow-land, or in winding combes benighted pillows down, and leaves its impress a sparkling path for the sun's return. To my mind no other part of the year is pleasanter than this end of harvest, with golden stubble, and orchards gleaming, and the hedgerows turning red. Then fish are in season, and fruit is wholesome, and the smell of sweet brewing is rich on the air.

This beautiful weather it was that tempted Colonel Lougher and Lady Bluett to take a trip for the day to Sker. The distance from Candleston Court must be at least two good leagues of sandy road, or rather of sand without any road, for a great part of the journey. Therefore, instead of their heavy coach, they took a light two-wheeled car, and a steady-going pony, which was very much wiser of them. Also, which was wiser still, they had a good basket of provisions, intending to make a long sea-side day, and expecting a lively appetite. I saw them pass through Newton as I chanced to be mending my nets by the well; and I touched my hat to the Colonel of course, and took it off to the lady. The Colonel was driving himself, so as not to be cumbered with any servant; and happening to see such a basket of food, I felt pretty sure there would be some over, for the quality never eat like us. Then it came into my memory that they could not bear Evan Thomas, and it struck me all of a sudden that it might be well worth my while to happen to meet them upon their return, before they passed any poor houses, as well as to happen to be swinging an empty basket conspicuously. It was a provident thought of mine, and turned out as well as its foresight deserved.

They passed a very pleasant day at Sker (as I was told that evening), pushing about among rocks and stones, and routing out this, that, and the other, of shells and sea-weed and starfish, and all the rest of the rubbish, such as amuses great gentry, because they have nothing to do for their living. And though money is nothing to them, they always seem to reckon what they find by money-value. Not Colonel Lougher, of course, I mean, and even less Lady Bluett. I only speak of some grand people who come raking along our beach. And of all of these there was nobody with the greediness Anthony Stew had. A crab that had died in changing his shell would hardly come amiss to him. Let that pass—who cares about him? I wish to speak of better people. The Colonel, though he could not keep ill-will against any one on earth, did not choose to be indebted to Sker-grange for even so much as a bite of hay for his pony. Partly, perhaps, that he might not appear to play false to his own tenantry; for the Nottage farmers, who held of the Colonel, were always at feud with Evan Thomas. Therefore he baited the pony himself, after easing off some of the tackle, and moored him to an ancient post in a little sheltered hollow. Their rations also he left in the car, for even if any one did come by, none would ever think of touching this good magistrate's property.

Quite early in the afternoon, their appetites grew very brisk by reason of the crisp sea-breeze and sparkling freshness of the waves. Accordingly, after consultation, they agreed that the time was come to see what Crumpy, their honest old butler, had put into the basket. The Colonel held his sister's hand to help her up rough places, and breasting a little crest of rushes, they broke upon a pretty sight, which made them both say "hush," and wonder.

In a hollow place of sand, spread with dry white bones, skates' pouches, blades of cuttle-fish, sea-snail shells, and all the other things that storm and sea drive into and out of the sands, a very tiny maid was sitting, holding audience all alone. She seemed to have no sense at all of loneliness or of earthly trouble in the importance of the moment and the gravity of play. Before her sat three little dolls, arranged according to their rank, cleverly posted in chairs of sand. The one in the middle was "Patty Green," the other two strange imitations fashioned by young Watkin's knife. Each was urging her claim to shells, which the mistress was dispensing fairly, and with good advice to each, then laughing at herself and them, and trying to teach them a nursery-song, which broke down from forgetfulness. And all the while her quick bright face, and the crisp grain of her attitudes, and the jerk of her thick short curls, were enough to make any one say, "What a queer little soul!" Therefore it is not to be surprised at that Colonel Lougher could not make her out, or that while he was feeling about for his eyeglass of best crystal, his sister was (as behoves a female) rasher to express opinion. For she had lost a little girl, and sometimes grieved about it still.

"What a queer little, dear little thing, Henry! I never saw such a child. Where can she have dropped from? Did you see any carriage come after us? It is useless to tell me that she can belong to any of the people about here. Look at her forehead, and look at her manners, and how she touches everything! Now did you see that? What a wonderful child! Every movement is grace and delicacy. Oh, you pretty darling!"

Her ladyship could wait no longer for the Colonel's opinion (which he was inclined to think of ere he should come out with it), and she ran down the sand-hill almost faster than became her dignity. But if she had been surprised before, how was she astonished now at Bardie's reception of her?

"Don'e tush. Knee tushy paw, see voo pay. All 'e dollies is yae good; just going to dinny, and 'e mustn't 'poil their appeties."

And the little atom arose and moved Lady Bluett's skirt out of her magic circle. And then, having saved her children, she stood scarcely up to the lady's knee, and looked at her as much as to ask, "Are you of the quality?" And being well satisfied on that point, she made what the lady declared to be the most elegant curtsy she ever had seen.

Meanwhile the Colonel was coming up, in a dignified manner, and leisurely, perceiving no cause to rush through rushes, and knowing that his sister was often too quick. This had happened several times in the matter of beggars and people on crutches, and skin-collectors, and suchlike, who cannot always be kept out of the way of ladies; and his worship the Colonel had been compelled to endeavour to put a stop to it. Therefore (as the best man in the world cannot in reason be expected to be in a moment abreast with the sallies of even the best womankind, but likes to see to the bottom of it) the Colonel came up crustily.

"Eleanor, can you not see that the child does not wish for your interference? Her brothers and sisters are sure to be here from Kenfig most likely, or at any rate some of her relations, and busy perhaps with our basket."

"No," said the child, looking up at him, "I'se got no 'lations now; all gone ayae; but all come back de-morrow day."

"Why, Henry, what are we thinking of? This must be the poor little girl that was wrecked. And I wanted you so to come down and see her; but you refused on account of her being under the care of Farmer Thomas."

"No, my dear, not exactly that, but on account of the trouble in the house I did not like to appear to meddle."

"Whatever your reason was," answered the lady, "no doubt you were quite right; but now I must know more of this poor little thing. Come and have some dinner with us, my darling; I am sure you must be hungry. Don't be afraid of the Colonel. He loves little children when they are good."

But poor Bardie hung down her head and was shy, which never happened to her with me or any of the common people; she seemed to know, as if by instinct, that she was now in the company of her equals. Lady Bluett, however, was used to children, and very soon set her quite at ease by inviting her dolls, and coaxing them and listening to their histories, and all the other little turns that unlock the hearts of innocence. So it came to pass that the castaway dined in good society for the first time since her great misfortune. Here she behaved so prettily, and I might say elegantly, that Colonel Lougher (who was of all men the most thoroughly just and upright) felt himself bound to confess his error in taking her for a Kenfig nobody. Now, as it happened to be his birthday, the lady had ordered Mr Crumpy, the butler, to get a bottle of the choicest wine, and put it into the hamper without saying anything to the Colonel, so that she might drink his health, and persuade him to do himself the like good turn. Having done this, she gave the child a drop in the bottom of her own wine-glass, which the little one tossed off most fluently, and with a sigh of contentment said—

"I'se not had a dop of that yiney-piney ever since—sompfin."

"Why, what wine do you call it, my little dear?" the

Colonel asked, being much amused with her air of understanding it.

"Doesn't 'a know?" she replied, with some pity; "nat's hot I calls a dop of good Sam Paine."

"Give her some more," said the Colonel; "upon my word she deserves it. Eleanor, you were right about her; she is a wonderful little thing."

All the afternoon they kept her with them, being more and more delighted with her as she began to explain her opinions; and Watty, who came to look after her, was sent home with a shilling in his pocket. And some of the above I learned from him, and some from Mr Crumpy (who was a very great friend of mine), and a part from little Bardie, and the rest even from her good ladyship, except what trifles I add myself, being gifted with power of seeing things that happen in my absence.

This power has been in my family for upwards of a thousand years, coming out and forming great bards sometimes, and at other times great story-tellers. Therefore let no one find any fault or doubt any single thing I tell them concerning some people who happen just now to be five or six shelves in the world above me, for I have seen a great deal of the very highest society when I cleaned my Earl's pumps and epaulettes, and waited upon him at breakfast; and I know well how those great people talk, not from observation only, but by aid of my own fellow-feeling for them, which, perhaps, owes its power of insight not to my own sagacity only, but to my ancestors' lofty positions, as poets to royal families. Now although I may have mentioned this to the man of the Press—whose hat appeared to have undergone Press experience—I have otherwise kept it quite out of sight, because every writer should hold himself entirely round the corner, and discover his hand, but not his face, to as many as kindly encourage him. Of late, however, it has been said—not by people of our own parish, who have seen and heard me at the well and elsewhere, but by persons with no more right than power to form opinions—that I cannot fail of breaking down when I come to describe great people. To these my answer is quite conclusive. From my long connection with royalty, lasting over a thousand years, I need not hesitate to describe the Prince of Wales himself; and inasmuch as His Royal Highness is not of pure ancient British descent, I verily doubt whether he could manage to better my humble style to my liking.

Enough of that. I felt doubts at beginning, but I find

myself stronger as I get on. You may rely upon me now to leave the question to your own intelligence. The proof of the pudding is in the eating; and if any one fears that I cannot cook it, I only beg him to wait and see.

Lady Bluett was taken so much with my Bardie, and the Colonel the same—though he tried at first to keep it under—that nothing except their own warm kindness stopped them from making off with her. The lady had vowed that she would do so, for it would be so much for the little soul's good; and of course, so far as legality went, the Chief-Justice of the neighbourhood had more right to her than a common rough farmer. But Watty came down, being sent by Moxy, after he went home with that shilling, and must needs make show of it. He came down shyly, from habit of nature, to the black eyebrows of the tide, where the Colonel and Bardie were holding grand play, with the top of the spring running up to them. She was flying at the wink of every wave, and trying to push him back into it; and he was laughing with all his heart at her spry ways and audacity, and the quickness of her smiles and frowns, and the whole of her nature one whirl of play, till he thought nothing more of his coat-tails.

"What do you want here, boy?" the Colonel asked, being not best pleased that a man of his standing should be caught in the middle of such antics.

Watkin opened his great blue eyes, and opened his mouth as well, but could not get steerage-way on his tongue, being a boy of great reverence.

"Little fellow, what are you come for?" with these words he smiled on the boy, and was vexed with himself for frightening him.

"Oh sir, oh sir, if you please, sir, mother says as Miss Delushy must come home to bed, sir."

"'E go ayay now, 'e bad Yatkin! I 'ants more pay with my dear Colonel Yucca."

"I am not at all sure," said the Colonel, laughing, "that I shall not put her into my car, and drive away with her, Watkin."

"You may go home, my good boy, and tell your mother that we have taken this poor little dear to Candleston." This, of course, was Lady Bluett.

You should have seen Watkin's face, they told me, when I came to hear of it. Betwixt his terror of giving offence, and his ignorance how to express his meaning, and the sorrow he felt on his mother's account, and perhaps his own pain also, not a word had he to say, but made a grope after the baby's hands. Then the little child ran up to him, and flung both arms around his leg, and showed the stanchness of her breed. Could any one, even of six years old, better enter into it?

"I yoves Yatkin. Yatkin is aye good and kind. And I yoves poor Moky. I 'ont go ayay till my dear papa and my dear mamma comes for me."

Lady Bluett, being quick and soft, could not keep her tears from starting; and the Colonel said, "It must be so. We might have done a great wrong, my dear. Consider all"—and here he whispered out of Watkin's hearing, and the lady nodded sadly, having known what trouble is. But the last words he spoke bravely, "God has sent her for a comfort where He saw that it was needed. We must not give way to a passing fancy against a deep affliction; only we will keep our eyes upon this little orphan darling."

CHAPTER XXIV.

SOUND INVESTMENTS.

The spring-tides led me to Sker the next day, and being full early for the ebb, I went in to see what the Colonel had done. For if he should happen to take up the child, she would pass out of my hands altogether, which might of course be a serious injury, as well as a very great hardship. For of Moxy's claim I had little fear if it came to a question of title, inasmuch as I had made her sign a document prepared and copied by myself, clearly declaring my prior right in virtue of rescue and providential ordinance. But as against Colonel Lougher I durst not think of asserting my claims, even if the law were with me; and not only so; but I felt all along that the matter was not one for money to heal, but a question of the deepest feelings.

And now the way in which Moxy came out, while Bardie was making much of me (who always saw everything first, of course), and the style of her meddling in between us, led me to know that a man has no chance to be up to the tricks of a female. For the dialogue going on between us was of the very simplest nature, as you may judge by the following:—

"Hy'se 'a been so long, old Davy, afore 'a come to see poor Bardie?"

"Because, my pretty dear, I have been forced to work, all day long almost."

"Hasn't 'a had no time to pay?"

"No, my dear, not a moment to play. Work, work, work! Money, money, money! Till old Davy is quite worn out."

I may have put horns to the truth in this. But at any rate not very long ones. And the child began to ponder it.

"I tell 'a, old Davy, 'hot to do. Susan say to me one day, kite yell, I amember, ickle Bardie made of money! Does 'a sink so?"

"I think you are made of gold, you beauty; and of diamonds, and the Revelations."

"Aye yell! Then I tell 'a hot to do. Take poor Bardie to markiss, old Davy; and 'o get a great big money for her."

She must have seen some famous market; for acting everything as she did (by means of working face, arms, and legs), she put herself up like a fowl in a basket, and spread herself, making the most of her breast, and limping her neck as the dead chickens do. Before I could begin to laugh, Moxy was upon us.

"Dyo! Why for you come again? Never you used to come like this. Put down Delushy, directly moment. No fish she is for you to catch. When you might have had her, here you left her through the face of everything. And now, because great Evan's staff is cloven, by the will of God, who takes not advantage of him? I thought you would have known better, Dyo. And this little one, that he dotes upon——"

"It is enough," I answered, with a dignity which is natural to me, when females wound my feelings; "Madame Thomas, it is enough. I will quit your premises." With these words I turned away, and never looked over my shoulder even, though the little one screamed after me; until I felt Watty hard under my stern, and like a kedge-anchor dragging. Therefore, I let them apologise; till my desire was to forgive them. And after they brought forth proper things, I denied all evil will, and did my best to accomplish it.

Mrs Thomas returning slowly to her ancient style with me, as I relaxed my dignity, said that now the little maid was getting more at home with them. Mr Thomas, after what had happened in the neighbourhood—this was the death of her five sons—felt naturally low of spirit; and it was good for him to have a lively child around him. He did not seem quite what he was. And nothing brought him to himself so much as to watch this shadow of life; although she was still afraid of him.

Every word of this was clear to me. It meant ten times what it expressed. Because our common people have a "height of kindness," some would say, and some a "depth of superstition," such as leads them delicately to slope off their meaning. But in my blunt and sailor fashion, I said that black Evan must, I feared, be growing rather shaky. I had better have kept this opinion quiet; for Moxy bestowed on me such a gaze of pity mingled with contempt, that knowing what sort of a man he had been, I felt all abroad about everything. All I could say to myself was this, that the only woman of superior mind I ever had the luck to come across, and carefully keep clear of, had taken good care not to have a husband, supposing there had been the occasion. And I think I made mention of her before; because she had been thrice disappointed; and all she said was true almost.

However, Sker-house might say just what it pleased, while I had my written document, and "Delushy" herself (as they stupidly called her by corruption of Andalusia) was not inclined to abandon me. And now she made them as jealous as could be, for she clung to me fast with one hand, while she spread the beautiful tiny fingers of the other to Moxy, as much as to say, "Interrupt me not; I have such a lot of things to tell old Davy."

And so she had without any mistake; and the vast importance of each matter lost nothing for want of emphasis. Patty Green had passed through a multitude of most surprising adventures, some of them even transcending her larceny of my sugar. Watty had covered himself with glory, and above all little "Dutch," the sheep-dog, was now become a most benevolent and protecting power.

"'Hots 'a think, old Davy? Patty Geen been yecked, she has."

"'Yecked!' I don't know what that is, my dear."

"Ness, I said, 'yecked,' old Davy; yecked down nare, same as Bardie was."

It was clear that she now had taken up with the story which everybody told; and she seemed rather proud of having been wrecked.

"And Patty," she went on, quite out of breath; "Patty

poiled all her boofely cothes : such a mess 'e never see a'most!
And poor Patty go to 'e back pit-hole, till 'e boofely Dush yun
all into 'e yater."

"Oh, and Dutch pulled her out again, did she?"

"Ness, and her head come kite out of her neck. But Yatty
put 'e guepot on, and make it much better than ever a'most."

"Now, Delushy, what a child you are!" cried Mrs Thomas,
proudly; "you never told Mr Llewellyn that you ran into the
sea yourself, to save your doll; and drownded you must have
been, but for our Watkin."

"Bardie 'poil her cothes," she said, looking rather shy about
it: "Bardie's cothes not boofely now, not same as they used
to be."

But if she regretted her change of apparel, she had ceased by
this time, Moxy said, to fret much for her father and mother.
For Watkin, or some one, had inspired her with a most comforting idea—to wit, that her parents had placed her there for
the purpose of growing faster; and that when she had done
her best to meet their wishes in this respect, they would suddenly come to express their pride and pleasure at her magnitude. Little brother also would appear in state, and so would
Susan, and find it needful to ascend the dairy-stool to measure
her. As at present her curly head was scarcely up to the mark
of that stool, the duty of making a timely start in this grand
business of growing became at once self-evident. To be "a
geat big gal" was her chief ambition; inasmuch as "'hen I'se
a geat big gal, mama and papa be so peased, and say, 'hot a
good gal 'e is, Bardie, to do as I tell 'a!"

Often when her heart was heavy in the loneliness of that
house, and the loss of all she loved, and with dirty things
around her, the smile would come back to her thoughtful eyes,
and she would open her mouth again for the coarse but wholesome food, which was to make a "big gal" of her. Believing
herself now well embarked toward this desired magnitude, she
had long been making ready for the joy it would secure. "'E
come and see, old Davy. I sow 'a sompfin," she whispered to
me, when she thought the others were not looking, so I gave
a wink to Moxy Thomas, whose misbehaviour I had overlooked, and humouring the child I let her lead me to her sacred
spot.

This was in an unused passage, with the end door nailed to
jambs, and black oak-panelling along it, and a floor of lias
stone. None in the house durst enter it except this little

creature; at least unless there were three or four to hearten one another, and a strong sun shining. The Abbot's Walk was its proper name; because a certain Abbot of Neath, who had made too much stir among the monks, received (as we say) his quietus there during a winter excursion; and in spite of all the masses said, could not keep his soul at rest. Therefore his soul came up and down; and that is worse than a dozen spirits; for the soul can groan, but the spirit is silent.

Into this dark lonely passage I was led by a little body, too newly inhabited by spirit to be at all afraid of it. And she came to a cupboard door, and tugged, and made a face as usual, when the button was hard to move. But as for allowing me to help her,—not a bit of it, if you please. With many grunts and jerks of breath, at last she fetched it outward, having made me promise first not to touch, however grand and tempting might be the scene disclosed to me.

What do you think was there collected, and arranged in such a system that no bee could equal it? Why, every bit of everything that every one who loved her (which amounts to everybody) ever had bestowed upon her, for her own sweet use and pleasure, since ashore she came to us. Not a lollipop was sucked, not a bit of "taffy" tasted, not a plaything had been used, but just enough to prove it; all were set in portions four, two of which were double-sized of what the other two were. Nearly half these things had come, I am almost sure, from Newton; and among the choicest treasures which were stored in scollop shells, I descried one of my own buttons which I had honestly given her, because two eyelets had run together; item, a bowl of an unsmoked pipe (which had snapped in my hand one evening); item, as sure as I am alive, every bit of the sugar which the Dolly had taken from out my locker.

Times there are when a hardy man, at sense of things (however childish), which have left their fibre in him, finds himself, or loses self, in a sudden softness. So it almost was with me (though the bait on my hooks all the time was drying), and for no better reason than the hopeless hopes of a very young child. I knew what all her storehouse meant before she began to tell me. And her excitement while she told me scarcely left her breath to speak.

"'Nat for papa, with 'e kean pipe to 'moke, and 'nat for mamma with 'e boofely bucken for her coke, and 'nat for my dear ickle bother, because it just fit in between his teeth, and 'nis with 'e 'ooking-gass for Susan, because she do her hair all day yong."

She held up the little bit of tin, and mimicked Susan's self-adornment, making such a comic face, and looking so conceited, that I felt as if I should know her Susan, anywhere in a hundred of women, if only she should turn up so. And I began to smile a little; and she took it up tenfold.

"'E make me yaff so, I do decare, 'e silly old Davy; I doesn't know 'hat to do a'most. But 'e mustn't tell anybody."

This I promised, and so went a-fishing, wondering what in the world would become of the queerest fish I had ever caught, as well as the highest-flavoured one. It now seemed a toss-up whether or not something or other might turn up, in the course of one's life, about her. At any rate she was doing well, with her very bright spirits to help her, and even Black Evan, so broken down as not to be hard upon any one. And as things fell out to take me from her, without any warning, upon the whole it was for the best to find the last sight comfortable.

And a man of my power must not always be poking after babies, even the best that were ever born. Tush, what says King David, who was a great-grandfather of mine; less distant than Llewellyn Harper, but as much respected; in spite of his trying to contribute Jewish blood to the lot of us in some of his rasher moments? But ancestor though we acknowledge him (when our neighbourhood has a revival), I will not be carried away by his fame to copy, so much as to hearken him. The autumn now grew fast upon us, and the beach was shifting; and neither room nor time remained for preaching under the sandhills, even if any one could be found with courage to sit under them. And as the nights turned cold and damp, everybody grumbled much; which was just and right enough, in balance of their former grumbling at the summer drought and heat. And it was mainly this desire not to be behind my neighbours in the comfort and the company of grumbling and exchanging grumbles, which involved me in a course of action highly lowering to my rank and position in society, but without which I could never have been enabled to tell this story. And yet before entering on that subject, everybody will want to know how I discharged my important and even arduous duties as trustee through Sir Philip's munificence for both those little children. In the first place, I felt that my position was strictly confidential, and that it would be a breach of trust to disclose to any person (especially in a loquacious village) a matter so purely of private discretion. Three parties there were to be considered, and only three, whatever point of view one chose to take of it. The first of these was Sir Philip, the second the two children, and the third of course myself. To the first my duty was gratitude (which I felt and emitted abundantly), to the second both zeal and integrity; and for myself there was one course only (to which I am naturally addicted), namely, a lofty self-denial. This duty to myself I discharged at once, by forming a stern resolution not to charge either of those children so much as a single farthing for taking care of her property until she was twenty-one years of age. Then as regards the second point, I displayed my zeal immediately, by falling upon Bunny soon after daylight, and giving her a small-tooth-combing to begin with, till the skin of her hair was as bright as a prawn; after which, without any heed whatever of roars, or even kicks, I took a piece of holy-stone, and after a rinsing of soda upon her, I cleaned down her planking to such a degree that our admiral might have inspected her. She was clean enough for a captain's daughter before, and dandy-trimmed more than need have been for a little craft built to be only a coaster. But now when her yelling had done her good, and her Sunday frock was shipped, and her black hair spanked with a rose-coloured ribbon, and the smiles flowed into her face again with the sense of all this smartness, Sir Philip himself would have thought her consistent with the owner of five pounds sterling.

And as touching the money itself, and the honesty rightly expected from me, although the sum now in my hands was larger than it ever yet had pleased the Lord to send me, for out and out my own, nevertheless there was no such thing as leading me astray about it. And this was the more to my credit, because that power of evil, who has more eyes than all the angels put together, or, at any rate, keeps them wider open, he came aft, seeing how the wind was, and planted his hoof within half a plank of the tiller of my conscience. But I heaved him overboard at once, and laid my course with this cargo of gold, exactly as if it were shipper's freight, under bond and covenant. Although, in downright common-sense, having Bunny for my grandchild, I also possessed beyond any doubt whatever belonged to Bunny; just as the owner of a boat owns the oars and rudder also. And the same held true, as most people would think, concerning Bardie's property; for if I had not saved her life, how could she have owned any?

So far, however, from dealing thus, I not only kept all their money for them, but invested it in the manner which seemed to be most for their interest. To this intent I procured a book for three halfpence (paid out of mine own pocket), wherein I declared a partnership, and established a fishing association, under the name, style, and description of "Bardie, Bunny, Llewellyn, and Co." To this firm I contributed not only my industry and skill, but also nets, tackle, rods and poles, hooks and corks, and two kettles for bait, and a gridiron fit to land and cook with; also several well-proven pipes, and a perfectly sound tobacco-box. Every one of these items, and many others, I entered in the ledger of partnership; and Mother Jones, being strange to much writing, recorded her mark at the bottom of it (one stroke with one hand and one with the other), believing it to be my testament, with an Amen coming after it.

But knowing what the tricks of fortune are, and creditors so unreasonable, I thought it much better to keep my boat outside of the association. If the firm liked, they might hire it, and have credit until distribution-day, which I fixed for the first day of every three months. My partners had nothing to provide, except just an anchor, a mast, and a lug-sail, a new net or two, because mine were wearing, and one or two other trifles perhaps, scarcely worth describing. For after all, who could be hard upon them, when all they contributed to the firm was fifteen pounds and ten shillings?

It was now in the power of both my partners to advance towards fortune; to permit very little delay before they insisted on trebling their capital; and so reinvest it in the firm; and hence at the age of twenty-one, be fit to marry magistrates. And I made every preparation to carry their shares of the profits over. Nevertheless, things do not always follow the line of the very best and soundest calculations. The fish that were running up from the Mumbles, fast enough to wear their fins out, all of a sudden left off altogether, as if they had heard of the association. Not even a twopenny glass of grog did I ever take out of our capital, nor a night of the week did I lie a-bed, when the lines required attendance. However, when fish are entirely absent, the very best fishermen in the world cannot manage to create them; and therefore our partnership saw the wisdom of declaring no dividends for the first quarter.

CHAPTER XXV.

A LONG GOOD-BYE.

It is an irksome task for a man who has always stood upon his position, and justified the universal esteem and respect of the neighbourhood, to have to recount his own falling off, and loss of proper station, without being able to render for it any cause or reason, except indeed his own great folly, with fortune too ready to second it. However, as every downfall has a slope which leads towards it, so in my case small downhills led treacherously to the precipice. In the first place, the dog-fish and the sting-rays (which alone came into the nets of our new association) set me swearing very hard; which, of course, was a trifling thing, and must have befallen St Peter himself, whose character I can well understand. But what was wrong in me was this, that after it went on for a fortnight, and not even a conger turned up, I became proud of my swearing with practice, instead of praying to be forgiven, which I always feel done to me, if desired. For my power of words began to please me—which was a bait of the devil, no doubt—as every tide I felt more and more that married life had not deprived me of my gift of language; or, at any rate, that widowership had restored my vigour promptly.

After this, being a little exhausted, for two days and two nights I smoked pipes. Not in any mood soever unfit for a Christian; quite the contrary, and quite ready to submit to any discipline; being ordered also to lay by, and expect a sign from heaven. And at this time came several preachers; although I had very little for them, and was grieved to disappoint their remembrance of the ham that my wife used to keep in cut. And in so many words I said that now I was bound to the Church by a contract of a shilling a-week, and if they waited long enough, they might hear the clock strike— something. This, combined with a crab whose substance had relapsed to water, and the sign of nothing in my locker except a pint of peppermint, induced these excellent pastors to go; and if they shook off (as they declared) the dirt of their feet at me, it must have been much to their benefit. This trifle, however, heaped up my grievance, although I thought scorn to think of it; and on the back of it there came another wrong far more serious. Tidings, to wit, of a wretched warrant being likely to issue against me from that low tyrant Anthony Stew, on a thoroughly lying information by one of his own gamekeepers. It was true enough that I went through his wood, with a couple of sailors from Porthcawl; by no means with any desire to harm, but to see if his game was healthy. Few things occur that exalt the mind more than natural history; and if a man dare not go into a wood, how can he be expected to improve his knowledge? The other men perhaps employed their means to obtain a more intimate acquaintance with the structure and methods of various creatures, going on two legs, or going on four; but as for myself, not so much as a gun did any one see in my hands that day.

At first I thought of standing it out on the strength of all my glory; but knowing what testimony is, when it gets into the mouths of gamekeepers, and feeling my honour concerned, to say nothing of the other fellows (who were off to sea), also cherishing much experience of the way Stew handled me, upon the whole I had half a mind to let the neighbourhood and the county learn to feel the want of me.

Also what Joe Jenkins said perhaps had some effect on me. This was a young fellow of great zeal, newly appointed to Zoar Chapel, instead of the steady Nathaniel Edwards, who had been caught sheep-stealing; and inasmuch as the chapel stood at the western end of the village, next door to the "Welcome to Town, my Lads," all the maids of Newton ran mightily to his doctrine. For he happened to be a smart young fellow, and it was largely put abroad that an uncle of his had a butter-shop, without any children, and bringing in four pounds a-week at Chepstow.

There is scarcely a day of my life on which I do not receive a lesson: and the difference betwixt me and a fool is that I receive, and he scorns it. And a finer lesson I have rarely had than for letting Joe Jenkins into my well-conducted cottage, for no better reason than that the "Welcome to Town" was out of beer. I ought to have known much better, of course, with a fellow too young to shave himself, and myself a good hearty despiser of schism, and above all having such a fine connection with the Church of England. But that fellow had such a tongue—they said it must have come out of the butter. I gave him a glass of my choicest rum, when all he deserved was a larruping. And I nearly lost the church clock through it.

When I heard of this serious consequence, I began to call to mind, too late, what the chaplain of the Spitfire—32-gun razy—always used to say to us; and a finer fellow to stand to his guns, whenever it came to close quarters, I never saw before or since. "Go down, parson, go down," we said; "sir, this is no place for your cloth." "Sneaking schismatics may skulk," he answered, with the powder-mop in his hand; for we had impressed a Methody, who bolted below at exceeding long range; "but if my cloth is out of its place, I'll fight the devil naked." This won over to the side of the Church every man of our crew that was gifted with any perception of reasoning.

However, I never shall get on if I tell all the fine things I have seen. Only I must set forth how I came to disgrace myself so deeply that I could not hope for years and years to enjoy the luxury of despising so much as a lighterman again. The folk of our parish could hardly believe it; and were it to be done in any way consistent with my story, I would not put it on paper now. But here it is. Make the worst of it. You will find me redeem it afterwards. The famous David Llewellyn, of His Majesty's Royal Navy, took a berth in a trading-schooner, called the "Rose of Devon!"

After such a fall as this, if I happened to speak below my mark, or not describe the gentry well, everybody must excuse me: for I went so low in my own esteem, that I could not have knocked even Anthony Stew's under-keeper down! I was making notes, here and there, already, concerning the matters at Sker House, and the delicate sayings of Bardie, not with any view to a story perfect and clear as this is, but for my own satisfaction in case of anything worth going on with. And but for this forethought, you could not have learned both her sayings and doings so bright as above. And now being taken away from it, I tried to find some one with wit enough to carry it on in my absence. In a populous neighbourhood this might have been; but the only man near us who had the conceit to try to carry it on a bit, fell into such a condition of mind that his own wife did not know him. But in spite of the open state of his head, he held on very stoutly, trying to keep himself up to the mark with ale, and even Hollands; until it pleased God that his second child should fall into the chicken-pox; and then all the neighbours spoke up so much—on account of his being a tailor—that it came to one thing or the other. Either he must give up his trade, and let his apprentice have it—to think of which was worse than gall and wormwood to his wife—or else he must give up all meddling with pen and ink and the patterns of chicken-pox. How could he hesitate, when he knew that the very worst tailor can make in a day as much as the best writer can in a month?

Upon the whole I was pleased with this; for I never could bear that rogue of a snip, any more than he could put up with me for making my own clothes and Bunny's. I challenged him once on a buttonhole, for I was his master without a thimble. And for this ninth part of a man to think of taking up my pen!

The name of our schooner, or rather ketch—for she was no more than that (to tell truth), though I wished her to be called a "schooner"—was, as I said, the "Rose of Devon," and the name of her captain was "Fuzzy." Not a bad man, I do believe, but one who almost drove me wicked, because I never could make him out. A tender and compassionate interest in the affairs of everybody, whom it pleases Providence that we should even hear of, has been (since our ancestors baffled the Flood, without consulting Noah) one of the most distinct and noblest national traits of Welshmen. Pious also; for if the Lord had not meant us to inquire, He never would have sent us all those fellow-creatures to arouse unallayed disquietude. But this man "Fuzzy," as every one called him, although his true name was "Bethel Jose," seemed to be sent from Devonshire for the mere purpose of distracting us. Concerning the other two "stone-captains" (as we call those skippers who come for limestone, and steal it from Colonel Lougher's rocks), we knew as much as would keep us going whenever their names were mentioned; but as to Fuzzy, though this was the third year of his trading over, there was not a woman in Newton who knew whether he had a wife or not! And the public eagerness over this subject grew as the question deepened; until there were seven of our best young women ready to marry him, at risk of bigamy, to find out the matter and to make it known.

Therefore, of course, he rose more and more in public esteem, voyage after voyage; and I became jealous, perhaps, of his fame, and resolved to expose its hollow basis, as compared with that of mine. Accordingly, when it came to pass that my glory, though still in its prime, was imperilled by that Irish Stew's proceedings—for he must have been Irish by origin—having my choice (as a matter of course) among the three stone captains, I chose that very hard stone to crack; and every one all through the village rejoiced, though bitterly grieved to lose me, and dreading the price there would be for fish, with that extortionate Sandy Macraw left alone to create a monopoly. There was not a man in all Newton that feared to lay half-a-crown to a sixpence that I brought back the whole of old Fuzzy's concerns: but the women, having tried Skipper Jose with everything they could think of, and not understanding the odds of betting, were ready to lay a crooked sixpence on Fuzzy, whenever they had one.

To begin with, he caught me on the hop; at a moment of rumours and serious warnings, and thoroughly pure indignation on my part. At the moment, I said (and he made me sign) that I was prepared to ship with him. After which he held me fast, and frightened me with the land-crabs, and gave me no chance to get out of his jaws. I tried to make him laugh with some of the many jokes and stories, which everybody knows of mine, and likes them for long acquaintance' sake. However, not one of them moved him so much as to fetch one squirt of tobacco-juice. This alone enabled him to take a strong lead over me. Every time that he was bound to laugh, according to human nature, and yet had neither a wag in his nose, nor a pucker upon his countenance, nor even so much as a gleam in his eye, so many times I felt in my heart that this man was the wise man, and that laughter is a folly. And I had to bottle down the laughs (which always rise inside of me, whenever my joke has the cream on it) until I could find some other fellow fit to understand me; because I knew that my jokes were good.

When I found no means of backing out from that degrading contract, my very first thought was to do strict justice to our association, and atone for the loss of my services to it. Therefore, in case of anything undesirable befalling me—in short, if I should be ordered aloft with no leave to come down again—there I made my will, and left my property to establish credit, for a new start among them. Chairs and tables, knives and forks, iron spoons, brought into the family by my wife's grandfather, several pairs of duds of my own, and sundry poles, as before described, also nets to a good extent—though some had gone under usury—bait-kettles, I forget how many, and even my character in a silk-bag; item, a great many sundry things of almost equal value; the whole of which I bravely put into my will, and left them. And knowing that the proper thing is to subscribe a codicil, therein I placed a set of delf, and after that my blessing. Eighteenpence I was compelled to pay for this pious document to a man who had been turned out of the law because he charged too little. And a better shilling-and-sixpence worth of sense, with heads and tails to it, his lordship the Bishop of Llandaff will own that he never set seal upon; unless I make another one. Only I felt it just to leave my boat entire to Bardie.

Having done my duty thus, I found a bracing strength upon me to go through with everything. No man should know how much I felt my violent degradation from being captain of a gun, to have to tread mercantile boards! Things have changed since then so much, through the parsimony of Government, that our very best sailors now tail off into the Merchant service. But it was not so, when I was young; and even when I was turned of fifty, we despised the traders. Even the largest of their vessels, of four or as much as five hundred tons, we royal tars regarded always as so many dust-bins with three of the clothes-props hoisted. And now, as I looked in the glass, I beheld no more than the mate of a fifty-ton ketch, for a thirty-mile voyage out of Newton bay!

However, I had lived long enough then to be taught one simple thing. Whatever happens, one may descry (merely by using manly aspect) dawning glimpses of that light which the will of God intended to be joy for all of us; but so scattered now and vapoured by our own misdoings, still it will come home some time, and then we call it "comfort."

Accordingly, though so deeply fallen in my own regard, I did not find that people thought so very much the less of me. Nay, some of them even drove me wild, by talking of my "rise in life," as if I had been a pure nobody! But on the whole we learned my value, when I was going away from us. For all the village was stirred up with desire to see the last of me. My well-known narratives at the well would be missed all through the autumn; and those who had dared to call them "lies," were the foremost to feel the lack of them. Especially the children cried "Old Davy going to be drownded! No more stories at the well!" Until I vowed to be back almost before they could fill their pitchers.

These things having proved to me, in spite of inordinate modesty, that I had a certain value, I made the very best of it; and let everybody know how much I wished to say "Goodbye" to them, although so short of money. From "Felix

Farley" I had received no less than seven-and-tenpence—for saving the drowned black people—under initials "D. L." at the office; accruing to a great extent from domestic female servants. Some of these craved my candid opinion as to accepting the humble addresses of coloured gentlemen in good livery, and whether it made so much difference. And now I thought that Newton might have a mark of esteem prepared for me.

But though they failed to think of that—purely from want of experience—everything else was done that could be done for a man who had no money, by his neighbours who had less; and sixpence never entered twice into the thoughts of any one. Richard Matthews, the pilot, promised to mind the church-clock for me, without even handling my salary. As for Bunny, glorification is the shortest word I know. A young man, who had never paid his bill, put her into two-inch ribbon from the Baptist preacher's shop. Also a pair of shoes upon her, which had right and left to them, although not marked by nature. And upon the front of her bosom, lace that made me think of smuggling; and such as that young man never could have expected to get booked to him, if he had felt himself to be more than a month converted.

Moreover, instead of Mother Jones (who was very well in her way, to be sure), the foremost folk in all the village, and even Master Charles Morgan himself, carpenter and church-warden, were beginning to vie, one with the other, in desire to entertain her, without any word of her five-pound note. In short, many kind things were said and done; enough to make any unbashful man desire to represent them. But I, for my part, was quite overcome, and delivered my speech with such power of doubt concerning my own worthiness, that they had to send back to the inn three times, before they could properly say "Good-bye."

CHAPTER XXVI.

BRAUNTON BURROWS.

THE weather was still as fair as could be, with a light wind from the east-north-east; and as our course lay west by south, and the ebb was running, we slipped along at the rate of six or seven knots an hour, though heavily-laden with the Colonel's rocks; and after rounding Porthcawl Point we came abreast of the old Sker House a little after sunset. Skipper Jose would never have ventured inside the Sker-weathers, only that I held the tiller, and knew every vein of sand and rock. And I kept so close in shore, because one of the things that vexed me most in all this sudden departure, was to run away without proper ceremony from Bardie. She was certain to feel it much, and too young to perceive the necessity; and fried pudding had been promised her at my table come the very next Sunday.

The windows of the old grey mansion gleamed in the fading western light, but we descried no smoke or movement, neither any life or variance, only a dreary pile of loneliness in the middle of yellow sands. Then I rigged out my perspective glass, and levelled it on the cuddy chimney—for the ketch was a half-decker—to spy if the little one might so chance to be making her solitary play, as she was used to do all day, and most of all ere bedtime. And if she should so happen, I knew how wild her delight would be to discover a vessel so near the shore; because whenever a sail went by, even at two or three leagues of distance, there was no containing her. Out she would rush with her face on fire, and curly hair all jogging, and up would go two little hands, spread to the sky and the vast wide sea. " Mammy dear, I 'ants 'a so. Dear papa, I has yaited so yong. Ickle bother, such a lot of things Bardie's got to tell 'a." And thus she would run on the brink of the waves with hope and sadness fluctuating on her unformed countenance, until the sail became a speck. However, now I saw no token of this little rover, unless it were some washed clothes flapping on the rushen tufts to dry; and Jose called me back to my spell at the helm before I had finished gazing. And in less than half an hour the landmark of the ancient house was fading in the dew-fog.

Our ship's company amounted to no less than four, all hands told—viz., Captain Bethel Jose, *alias* Fuzzy; Isaac Hutchings, the mate; my humble self (who found it my duty to supersede Ikey and appoint myself); and a boy of general incapacity, and of the name of "Bang."

Making fine weather as we did, and with myself at the helm all night, and taking command (as my skill required), we slanted across Channel very sweetly; and when the grey of morning broke, Lundy Isle was on our lee-bow. Hereupon I gave the helm to old Ike, for beyond this was unknown to me, and

Providence had never led me over Barnstaple bar as yet. So I tumbled in, and turned up no more until we were close on the bar itself, about ten o'clock of the forenoon. This is a thoroughly dangerous place, a meeting of treacherous winds and waters, in amongst uncertain shoaling, and would be worse than our Sker-weathers if it lay open to south-west gales. We waited for the tide, and then slipped over very cleverly, with Hartland Point on our starboard beam; and presently we found ourselves in a fine broad open water, with plenty of grey stretch going along it, and green hills tufting away from it. Everything looked so mild and handsome, that I wondered whether these men of Devonshire might not be such fools for bragging after all, when tested.

Because, when I found no means to escape this degrading voyage to Devonshire, I had said to myself that at any rate it would enable me to peg down those people for the future. Not that they boasted, so to speak, but that they held their tongues at our boasts; as much as to say, "You may talk if you please; it does you good; and our land is such that we never need contradict you."

But now when I saw these ins and outs, and ups and downs, and cornering places, and the wrinkles of the valleys, and the cheeks of the very rocks, set with green as bright and lively (after a burning summer) as our own country can show in May, I began to think—though I would not say it, through patriotic unwillingness—that the people who lived in such land as this could well afford to hold their tongues, and hearken our talk with pleasure. Captain Fuzzy said no word, to show that he was home again; neither did he care to ask my opinion about the look of it. And old Ike treating me likewise, though he ought to have known much better, there I found myself compelled by my natural desire to know all about my fellow-creatures, to carry on what must have been a most highly flattering patronage towards the boy who did our slop-work, and whose name was "Bang," because everybody banged him.

This boy, forgetting the respect which is due to the mate of a ship of commerce—for I now assumed that position legally, over the head of old Ikey, who acknowledged my rank when announced to him—this ignorant boy had the insolence to give me a clumsy nudge, and inquire—

"Du 'e knaw thiccy peart over yanner? Them down-plasses, and them zandy backs?"

"My boy," I replied, "I have not the honour of knowing

anything about them. Very likely you think a good deal of them."

"Whai, thee must be a born vule. Them be Braunton Burrusses!"

"Be them indeed? Take this, my boy, for such valuable information." And I gave him a cuff of an earnest nature, such as he rarely obtained, perhaps, and well calculated to be of timely service to him. He howled a good bit, and attempted to kick; whereupon I raised him from his natural level, and made his head acquainted with the nature of the foremast, preserving my temper quite admirably, but bearing in mind the great importance of impressing discipline at an early age. And I reaped a well-deserved reward in his life-long gratitude and respect.

While Bang went below to complete his weeping, and to find some plaster, I began to take accurate observation of these Braunton Burrows, of which I had often heard before from the Devonshire men, who frequent our coast for the purpose of stealing coal or limestone. An up-and-down sort of a place it appeared, as I made it out with my spyglass; and I could not perceive that it beat our sands, as those good people declared of it. Only I noticed that these sand-hills were of a different hue from ours. Not so bare and yellow-faced, not so swept by western winds, neither with their tops thrown up like the peak of a new volcano. Rushes, spurge, and goose-foot grasses, and the rib-leafed iris, and in hollow places cat's-mint, loose-strife, and low eye-bright—these and a thousand other plants seemed to hold the flaky surface so as not to fly like ours. Ike broke silence, which to him was worse than breaking his own windows, and said that all for leagues around was full of giants and great spectres. Moreover, that all of it long had been found an unkid and unholy place, bad for a man to walk in, and swarming with great creatures, striped the contrary way to all good-luck, and having eight legs every side, and a great horn crawling after them. And their food all night was known to be travellers' skulls and sailors' bones. Having seen a good deal of land-crabs, I scarcely dared to deny the story, and yet I could hardly make it out. Therefore, without giving vent to opinions of things which might turn out otherwise, I levelled my spyglass again at the region of which I had heard such a strange account. And suddenly here I beheld a man of no common appearance, wandering in and out the hollows, as if he never meant to stop; a tall man with a long grey beard, and wearing a cocked-hat like a colonel. There was something about him that startled me, and drew my whole attention. Therefore, with my perspective glass not long ago cleaned, and set ship-shape by a man who understood the bearings—after that rogue of a Hezekiah had done his best to spoil it—with this honest magnifier (the only one that tells no lies) I carefully followed up and down the figure, some three cables'-lengths away, of this strange walker among the sand-hills. We were in smooth water now, gliding gently up the river, with the mainsail paying over just enough for steerage-way; and so I got my level truly, and could follow every step.

It was a fine old-fashioned man, tall and very upright, with a broad ribbon upon his breast, and something of metal shining; and his Hessian boots flashed now and then as he passed along with a stately stride. His beard was like a streak of silver, and his forehead broad and white; but all the rest of his face was dark, as if from foreign service. His dress seemed to be of a rich black velvet, very choice and costly, and a long sword hung at his side, although so many gentlemen now have ceased to carry even a rapier. I like to see them carry their swords—it shows that they can command themselves; but what touched me most with feeling was his manner of going on. He seemed to be searching, ever searching, up the hills and down the hollows, through the troughs and on the breastlands, in the shadow and the sunlight, seeking for some precious loss.

After watching this figure some little time, it was natural that I should grow desirous to know something more about him; especially as I obtained an idea, in spite of the distance and different dress, that I had seen some one like this gentleman not such a very long time ago. But I could not recall to my mind who it was that was hovering on the skirts of it; therefore I looked around for help. Ike Hutchings, my undermate, was at the tiller, but I durst not lend him my glass, because he knew not one end from the other; so I shouted aloud for Captain Jose, and begged him to take a good look, and tell me everything that he knew or thought. He just set his eye, and then shut up the glass, and handed it to me without a word and walked off, as if I were nobody! This vexed me, so that I holloaed out: "Are all of you gone downright mad on this side of the Channel? Can't a man ask a civil question, and get a civil answer?"

"When he axeth what consarneth him," was the only answer Captain Fuzzy vouchsafed me over his shoulder.

I could not find it worth my while to quarrel with this ignorant man for the sake of a foolish word or two, considering how morose he was, and kept the keys of everything. For the moment, I could not help regretting my wholesome chastisement of the boy Bang; for he would have told me at least all he knew, if I could have taught him to take a good look. And as for Ike, when I went and tried him, whether it was that he failed of my meaning, or that he chose to pretend to do so (on account of my having deposed him), or that he truly knew nothing at all—at any rate, I got nothing from him. This was, indeed, a heavy trial. It is acknowleged that we have such hearts, and strength of goodwill to the universe, and power of entering into things, that not a Welshman of us is there but yearns to know all that can be said about every one he has ever seen, or heard, or even thought of. And this kind will, instead of being at all repressed by discouragement, increases tenfold in proportion as others manifest any unkind desire to keep themselves out of the way of it. My certy, no low curiosity is this, but lofty sympathy.

My grandfather nine generations back, Yorath the celebrated bard, begins perhaps his most immortal ode to a gentleman who had given him a quart of beer with this noble moral precept: "Lift up your eyes to the castle gates and behold on how small a hinge they move! The iron is an inch and a quarter thick, the gates are an hundred and fifty feet wide!" And though the gates of my history are not quite so wide as that, they often move on a hinge even less than an inch and a quarter in thickness; though I must not be too sure, of course, as to the substance of Bang's head. However, allow even two inches for it, and it seems but a very trifling matter to tell as it did upon great adventures. The boy was as sound as a boy need be in a couple of hours afterwards, except that he had, or pretended to have, a kind of a buzzing in one ear; and I found him so grateful for my correction, that I could not bear to urge his head with inquiries for the moment.

To Captain Fuzzy I said no more. If he could not see the advantage of attending to his own business, but must needs go out of his way to administer public reproof to me, I could only be sorry for him. To Ikey, however, I put some questions of a general tendency; but from his barbarous broken English —if this jargon could be called English at all—the only thing I could gather was, that none but true Devonshire folk had a right to ask about Devonshire families. This might be true to a certain extent, though I never have seen such a law laid down. The answer, however, is perfectly simple. If these people carry on in a manner that cannot fail to draw public attention, they attack us at once on our tenderest point, and tenfold so if they are our betters; for what man of common-sense could admit the idea of anybody setting up to be nobody? Therefore I felt myself quite ready to give a week's pay and victuals, in that state of life to which God alone could have seen fit to call me —as mate of that Devonshire ketch, or hoy, or tub, or whatever it might be—four shillings and a bag of suet-dumplings, twice a-day, I would have given, to understand upon the spot all about that elderly gentleman.

It helped me very little, indeed, that I kept on saying to myself, "This matters not; 'tis a few hours only. The moment we get to Barnstaple, I shall find some women;—the women can never help telling everything, and for the most part ten times that. Only contradict them bravely, and they have no silence left." However, it helped me not a little when Captain Fuzzy, with a duck of his head, tumbled up from the cuddy, brimful, as we saw, of the dinner-time. A man of my experience, who has lived for six weeks on the horns of sea-snails, which the officers found too hard for them, that time we were wrecked in the Palamede—what can a man of this kind feel when a trumpery coaster dares to pipe all hands to dinner?

However, it so happened for the moment that what I felt was appetite: and Fuzzy, who was a first-rate cook, and knew seasoning without counting, had brought an iron ladle up, so as to save his words, and yet to give us some idea. Soup it was of a sort, that set us thinking of all the meat under it. I blew upon it, and tasted a drop, and found that other people's business would keep till at least after dinner. In the midst of dinner we came to the meeting of two fine rivers, called Tawe and Torridge, and with the tide still making strong we slanted up the former. The channel was given to twists and turns, but the fine open valley made up for it, and the wealth of land on either side, sloping with green meadows gently, and winding in and out with trees. Here were cattle, as red as chesnuts, running about with tails like spankers, such as I never saw before; but Ikey gave me to understand that the colour of the earth was the cause of it, and that if I lived long upon corned beef made of them (whose quality no other land could create), I should be turned to that hue myself. At this I laughed, as a sailor's yarn; but after regarding him steadfastly, and then gazing again at the bullocks, I thought there might be some truth in it.

One thing I will say of these sons of Devon: rough they may be, and short of grain, and fond of their own opinions, and not well up in points of law—which is our very nature—queer, moreover, in thought and word, and obstinate as hedgehogs,—yet they show, and truly have, a kind desire to feed one well. Money they have no great love of spending round the corner, neither will they go surety freely for any man who is free to run; but "vittels," as they call them, "vittels!"—before you have been in a house two minutes out come these, and eat you must! Happily, upon this point I was able to afford them large and increasing satisfaction, having rarely enjoyed so fine a means of pleasing myself and others also. For the things are good, and the people too; and it takes a bad man to gainsay either.

CHAPTER XXVII.

A FINE SPECTACLE.

WE brought the Rose of Devon to her moorings on the south side of the river, about two miles short of Barnstaple, where a little bend and creek is, and a place for barges, and "Deadman's Pill" was the name of it. What could a dead man want with a pill, was the very first thing I asked them; but they said that was no concern of theirs; there were pills up and down the river for miles, as well as a town called Pill-town. The cleverest man that I came across said that it must be by reason of piles driven in where the corners were to prevent the washing, and he showed me some piles, or their stumps, to prove it, and defied all further argument. For the time I was beaten, until of a sudden, and too late to let him know, I saw like a stupid that it must be no other than our own word "Pwll," which differs much from an English "pool," because it may be either dry or wet, so long as it lies in a hollow. And with that I fell a-thinking of poor Bardie and Pwll Tavan. To be quit of remorse, and to see the world, I accepted old Ikey's invitation to Barnstaple fair for the very next day. We could not begin to discharge our limestone, as even that obstinate Fuzzy confessed, upon a sacred day like that. Fuzzy him self had a mind for going, as we half suspected, although he held his tongue about it; and my under-mate told me to let him alone, and see what would come of it.

The town is a pleasant and pretty one, and has always been famous for thinking itself more noble than any other; also the fair was a fine thing to see, full of people, and full of noise, and most outrageous dialect; everybody in fine broad humour, and no fighting worth even looking at. This disappointed me; for in Wales we consider the off-day market a poor one, unless at least some of the women pull caps. I tried, however, not to miss it, having seen in foreign countries people meeting peaceably. Of this I could have had no intention to complain to poor Ikey Hutchings. However, he took it as if I had, and offered to find me a man from Bratton, or himself, to have a square with me, and stake half-a-crown upon it. He must have found early cause for repentance, if I had taken him at his word; but every one would have cried shame upon me against such a poor little fellow. And so we pushed on, and the people pushed us.

After a little more of this, and Ikey bragging all the time, though I saw nothing very wonderful, we turned the corner of a narrow street, and opened into a broader one. Here there seemed to be no bullocks, such as had made us keep springs on our cables, but a very amazing lot of horses, trotting about, and parading, and rushing, most of them with their tails uphoisted, as if by discharging tackle. Among them stood men, making much of their virtues, and sinking their faults (if they had any), and cracking a whip every now and then, with a style of applause toward them.

Now I have a natural love of the horse, though I never served long on board of one; and I regularly feel, at sight of them, a desire to mount the rigging. Many a time I have reasoned to my own conviction and my neighbours', that a man who can stand on the mizzen-top-gallant yard in a heavy gale of wind, must find it a ridiculously easy thing to hold on by a horse with the tackle to help him, and very likely a dead calm all round. Nevertheless, somehow or other, the result seems always otherwise.

I had just hailed a man with a colt to show off, and commodore's pendants all over his tail, and was keeping clear of his counter to catch the rise of the wave for boarding him, when a hush came over all hands as if the street had been raked with chain-shot. And on both sides of the street all people fell back and backed their horses, so that all the roadway stood as clear as if the fair had turned into a Sunday morning.

Up the centre, and heeding the people no more than they would two rows of trees, came two grave gentlemen, daintily walking arm in arm, and dressed in black. They had broad-flapped hats, long coats of broadcloth, black silk tunics, and buckled breeches, and black polished boots reaching up to the buckles.

Meanwhile all the people stood huddled together upon the pitched stones on either side, touching their hats, and scarce whispering, and even the showing off of the horses went into the side-streets.

After all the bowing and legging that I had beheld in the Royal Navy, the double file, the noble salutes, the manning of the sides and yards, the drums, the oars all upon the catch, and all the other glorious things that fit us to thrash the Frenchmen so, there was nothing else left for me to suppose but that here were two mighty admirals, gone into mourning very likely for the loss of the Royal George, or come on the sly perhaps to enjoy the rollicking of the fair, and sinking the uniform for variety. How could I tell, and least of all would I think of interfering with the pleasure of my betters; therefore I stopped in my throat the cheer (which naturally seemed to rise the moment I took my hat off), for fear of letting the common people know that I understood their Honours. But after looking again so long as one might without being inquisitive, I saw that neither of these great men could walk the deck in a rolling sea.

I had been so bold in the thick of the horses, that Ikey had found it too much for him always to keep close to me; but now, as the nearest horse must have drifted the length of two jolly-boats away, this little sailor came up and spoke.

"Can 'e show the laikes of they two, in Taffy-land, old Taffy now?"

"Plenty, I should hope," said I (though proud in the end to say "not one"); "but what a fuss you make! Who are they?"

"As if thee didn't know!" cried Ikey, staring with indignation at me.

"How should I know when I never clapped eyes on either of them till this moment?"

"Thou hast crossed the water for something then, Davy. Them be the two Passons!"

"Two Passons!" I could not say it exactly as he sounded it. "I never heard of two Passons."

"'A wants to draive me mad, 'a dooth," said Ikey, in self-commune: "Did 'e never hear tell of Passon Chowne, and Passon Jack, man alive now?"

It was hopeless to try any more with him, for I could not ding into his stupid head the possibility of such ignorance. He could only believe that I feigned it for the purpose of driving him out of his senses, or making little of his native land. So I felt that the best thing I could do was to look at these two great gentlemen accurately and impartially, and thus form my own opinion. Hence there was prospect of further pleasure, in coming to know more about them.

Verily they were goodly men, so far as the outer frame goes; the one for size, and strength, and stature—and the other for face, form, and quickness. I felt as surely as men do feel, who have dealt much among other men, that I was gazing upon two faces not of the common order. And they walked as if they knew themselves to be ever so far from the average. Not so much with pride, or conceit, or any sort of arrogance, but with a manner of going distinct from the going of fellow-creatures. Whether this may have been so, because they were both going straight to the devil, is a question that never crossed my mind, until I knew more about them. For our parsons in Wales, take them all in all, can hardly be called gentlemen; except, of course, our own, who was Colonel Lougher's brother, also the one at Merthyr Mawr, and St Brides, and one or two other places where they were customers of mine; but most of the rest were small farmers' sons, or shopkeepers' boys, and so on. These may do very well for a parish, or even a congregation that never sees a gentleman (except when they are summoned—and not always then); however, this sort will not do for a man who has served, ay, and been in battle, under two baronets and an earl.

Therefore I looked with some misgiving at these two great parsons; but it did not take me long to perceive that each of them was of good birth at least, whatever his manners afterwards,—men who must feel themselves out of their rank when buttoned into a pulpit for reasoning with Devonshire ploughtail Bobs, if indeed they ever did so; and as for their flocks, they kept dogs enough at any rate to look after them. For they both kept hounds; and both served their Churches in true hunting fashion—that is to say, with a steeplechase, taking the country at full gallop over hedges and ditches, and stabling the horse in the vestry. All this I did not know as yet, or I

L

must have thought even more than I did concerning those two gentlemen. The taller of the two was as fair and ruddy, and as free of countenance as a June rose in the sunshine; a man of commanding build and figure, but with no other command about him, and least of all, that of his own self. The other it was that took my gaze, and held it, having caught mine eyes, until I forgot myself, and dropped them under some superior strength. For the time, I knew not how I felt, or what it was that vanquished me; only that my spirit owned this man's to be its master. Whether from excess of goodness, or from depth of desperate evil, at the time I knew not.

It was the most wondrous unfathomable face that ever fellow-man fixed gaze upon; lost to mankindliness, lost to mercy, lost to all memory of God. As handsome a face as need be seen, with a very strong forehead and coal-black eyes, a straight white nose, and a sharp-cut mouth, and the chin like a marble sculpture. Disdain was the first thing it gave one to think of; and after that, cold relentless humour; and after that, anything dark and bad.

Meanwhile this was a very handsome man, as women reckon beauty; and his age not over forty, perhaps; also of good average stature, active and elegant form, and so on. Neither years nor cubits make much odds to a man of that sort; and the ladies pronounce him perfect.

When these two were gone by, I was able to gaze again at the taller one. Truly a goodly man he was, though spared from being a good one. He seemed to stand over me, like Sir Philip; although I was measured for six feet and one inch, before I got into rheumatic ways. And as for size and compass, my parents never could give me food to fetch out my girth, as this parson's was. He looked a good yard and a half round the chest, and his arms were like oak-saplings. However, he proved to be a man void of some pride and some evil desires, unless anybody bore hard on him; and as for reading the collects, or lessons, or even the burial service, I was told that no man in the British realm was fit to say "Amen" to him. This had something to do with the size of his chest, and perhaps might have helped to increase it. His sermons also were done in a style that women would come many miles to enjoy; beginning very soft and sweet, so as to melt the milder ones; and then of a sudden roaring greatly with all the contents of enormous lungs, so as to ring all round the sides of the strongest weaker vessels. And as for the men, what could they think, when the preacher could drub any six of them?

This was "Parson Jack," if you please, his surname being "Rambone," as I need not say, unless I write for unborn generations. His business in Boutport Street that day was to see if any man would challenge him. He had held the belt seven years, they said, for wrestling, as well as for bruising; the condition whereof was to walk the street both at Barnstaple fair and at Bodmin revels, and watch whether any man laid foot across him.

This he did purely as a layman might. But the boxing and bruising were part of his office, so that he hung up his cassock always for a challenge to make rent in it. There had been some talk of a Cornishman interfering about the wrestling; and bad people hoped that he might so attempt, and never know the way home again; but as for the fighting, the cassock might hang till the beard of Parson Jack was grey, before any one made a hole in it. Also the Cornish wrestler found, after looking at Parson Jack, that the wisest plan before him was to challenge the other Cornishmen, and leave the belt in Devonshire.

All this I found out at a little gathering which was held round the corner, in Bear Street, to reflect upon the business done at the fair, and compare opinions. And although I had never beheld till then any of our good company, neither expected to see them again, there were no two opinions about my being the most agreeable man in the room. I showed them how to make punch to begin with, as had been done by his Royal Highness, with me to declare proportions; and as many of the farmers had turned some money, they bade me think twice about no ingredient that would figure on the bill, even half-a-crown.

By right of superior knowledge, and also as principal guest of the evening, I became voted the chairman, upon the clear understanding that I would do them the honour of paying nothing; and therein I found not a man that would think of evading his duty towards the chair. I entreated them all to be frank, and regard me as if I were born in Barnstaple, which they might look upon as being done otherwise, as the mere turn of a shaving; for my father had been there twice, and my mother more than once thought of trying it. Everybody saw the force of this; and after a very fine supper we grew as genial as could be. And leading them all with a delicate knowledge of the ins and outs of these natives (many of which I had learned at the fair), and especially by encouraging their bent for contradiction, I heard a good deal of the leading people in the town or out of it. I listened, of course, to a very great deal, which might be of use to me or might not; but my object was, when I could gather in their many-elbowed stories, to be thoroughly up to the mark on three points.

First, about Fuzzy, and most important. Who was he? What was he? Where did he live? Had he got a wife? And if so, why? And if not, more especially, why again? Also, how much money had he, and what in the world did he do with it; and could he have, under the rose, any reason for keeping our women so distant? Particularly, I had orders to know whether he was considered handsome by the Devonshire women. For our women could not make up their minds, and feared to give way to the high opinion engendered by his contempt of them. Only they liked his general hairiness, if it could be warranted not to come off.

Upon this point I learned nothing at all. No man even knew Bethel Jose, or, at any rate, none would own to it, perhaps because Ikey was there to hearken; so I left that until I should get with the women. My next matter was about Braunton Burrows, and the gentleman of high rank who wandered up and down without telling us why. And I might hereupon have won some knowledge, and was beginning to do so, when a square stout man came in and said "Hush!" and I would gladly have thrown a jug at him. Nevertheless, I did learn something which I mean to tell next to directly.

But as concerned the third question before me (and to myself the most itching of any), satisfaction, to at least half-measure, was by proper skill and fortune brought within my reach almost. And this I must set down at leisure, soberly thinking over it.

CHAPTER XXVIII.

SOMETHING ABOUT HIM.

It was of course not Parson Rambone but the Parson Chowne who aroused my desire of knowledge so strongly. And even here I was met at first by failure and disappointment. The men would only shake their hands and say "Ah, he is a queer one!" or, "Well, well, we can't expect all folk to be alike, you know;" or even some of the ruder spirits, "You had better go yourself and ask him"—a most absurd suggestion, for never yet had I seen a man less fit to encourage impertinence. Far more ready would I have been to displease even his great comrade, the Reverend John Rambone; and no one who saw them together could doubt which of the two was the master. My true course was clearly to bide my time, and, as chairman, to enhance the goodwill and geniality of the evening. And this I was ready enough to do—ay, and in the vein for it—bearing in mind the wisdom of enjoying to the utmost such favourable circumstances, to be on the free boot, and well received in a place entirely new to me, where I found myself so much ahead of everybody in matter of mind, and some of them glad to acknowledge it; also where no customer could be waiting to reproach me, nor even a justice of the peace well versed in my countenance; moreover, blessed as I was with a sense of pity for these natives, and a largeness of goodwill to them, such a chance had never crossed me since the day my wife did.

Ikey and I had a good laugh also at that surly Bethel Jose, who had shown himself so much above the fair in mind, yet was there in body. None but Bang, the boy, had been left for captain and crew of the Rose of Devon, and before it was dark we had found Bang shooting, at four shots a-penny, for cocoanut slices, with ginger-beer poured over them.

Now fortune stood my friend that night, for before we began to find ourselves in a condition at all uproarious, I managed to loosen the tongues of these natives by means of some excellent stories. Recalling the fame of my grandfather (that long David Llewellyn, who made on his harp three unconquered ballads, and won the first prize at all the Eisteddfods held during his life for Englynion), I could not accept it as my business to play second fiddle. Therefore, being in a happy mood, I was enabled to recount such stories as made these Devonshire folk open their mouths like a man at a great rock-oyster, while their experience was in contention with faith and perhaps good manners. And as their nature is obstinate and most unwilling to be outdone, they found themselves driven down at last to tell the most wonderful things they knew, or else to be almost nobodies. And putting aside what their grandfathers might have seen or heard or even done—which is a mistake to dwell upon—all their stories worth curve of the ear were of Parson Chowne, and no other.

For this man was a man, as we say. No other man must have a will that stood across the path of his. If he heard of any one unwilling to give way to him, he would not go to bed until he had taken that arrogance out of him. Many people, and even some of ten times his own fortune, had done their best, one after the other, not to be beaten by him. All of them found that they could not do it, and that their only chance of comfort was to knock under to Parson Chowne. And even after that had been done, he was not always satisfied, but let them know from time to time their folly in offending him. And most of all, he made a point (as was natural perhaps) of keeping the Lord Bishop of the country under him. Some of these had done their best (before they understood him) to make his habits hold themselves within some stretch of discipline; or, if that could not be hoped, at any rate to keep silent. When he heard of these ideas he was not a little pleased, because he descried a rare chance of sport, and he followed it up with their lordships. The law he knew to its lowest tittle, and while he broke it every day himself, woe to any man who dared to break it against him. And gradually these bishops came (one after the other growing a little alive to what the parsons were) not so much to let him alone as to desire his acquaintance—out of school, if so I may put it, in my ignorance of the bench of bishops. For well as I know a fish called "the Pope," and also a pear said to be "Bishop's thumb," not to mention a grass called "Timothy," it has not been my luck thus far to rise above the bench of magistrates.

"Let be" is the wisest thing one can say; and so everybody said of him, so soon as ever it was acknowledged that he could never be put down. And thus he might have done well enough if he would have been content with this. Only it never was his nature to be content with anything, which is the only true way to get on; if any one cares for that sort of thing, who knows mankind's great randomness. Because the one who shoves and swears without being too particular, has the best chance to hoist himself upon the backs of the humble. By dint of this, and to keep him quiet, Parson Chowne himself, they said, might have been bishop if so he had chosen. For this he had some fine qualifications, for his very choicest pleasure was found in tormenting his fellow-parsons: and a man of so bold a mind he was, that he believed in nothing except himself

Even his own servants never knew how to come nigh him. One at the stables would touch his hat, and he would kick him for reply; then another would come without ceremony, and he knocked him down to learn it. Also in the house, the maidens had the same account to give. However much they might think of themselves, and adorn themselves to that estimate, he never was known to do so much as to chuck any one of them under the chin, as they had been at all other places much in the habit of feeling; neither did he make a joke to excuse himself for omitting it. As to that, they would scorn themselves ever to think of permitting it, being young women of high respect, and quite aware how to conduct themselves. But they might have liked to stop him, and they got no chance of doing it.

All this small-talk almost vexed me more than the content it gave. Every now and then I could see the man in these little corner views, but they did not show me round him so as to get his girth and substance. "Think of the devil," is an old saying; and while I thought of him, in he walked.

At the very first glimpse of him, all those people who had been talking so freely about him shrank away, and said, "Servant, sir!" and looked so foolish more than usual, that he read them with one eye. He had his riding-clothes on now, and it made him look still sharper.

"Talking of me, good people, eh? I hope the subject pleases you. Open your ranks, if you please, and show me whether my groom is behind you." He cracked a great hunting-whip as he spoke, and it seemed a poor prospect for the groom, wherever he might be loitering.

"Plaize your honour, your honour's groom have not been here all day a'most; and if her coom'th, us 'ont keep un."

"In that resolution you are wise. What! you here, Welshman? I marked you to-day. You will come to me by noon to-morrow. Here is for your charges."

He threw on the table two crown-pieces, and was gone before I knew what answer I was bound to make to him. The men, recovering from his presence, ran to the window to watch him as far as the flaring lights of the fair, now spluttering low, displayed him. Without being able to see so much as I strongly desired to see of him, I could not help admiring now his look, and his manner, and strong steady gait, and the general style of his outward man. His free way of going along made clear the excellence of his clothing; and he swung his right elbow, as I was told, from his constant desire to lash a horse. He was the devil himself to ride, so everybody said of him; and Parson Chowne's horse was now become a by-word for any one thoroughly thrashed. And yet no other man must ever dare to touch his horses. If any one did, no deadlier outrage could be put upon him.

Hearing these things from fourteen customers able to express their thoughts, I was sorry when the corner turned upon Parson Chowne, so walking in the light of long deal tables, set with finely-guttering candles, and with goods not quite sold out. And he left upon my memory a vision of a great commander, having a hat of controlling movements, and a riding-coat so shaped that a horse appeared to be under it; and lower down, buff leathern breeches, and boots well over the hinge of his legs, and silver heels, and silver spurs, and nothing to obscure him. No topcoat or outer style of means to fend the weather, because he could keep it in order always.

"I wish I was like him, then," said I; "and what does he mean by insulting me? I know a hundred bigger fellows. Am I at his beck and call?"

"I warr'n thou wilt be, zoon enough," answered, with a heavy grin, a lout of a fellow, who had shown no more sense than to leave the room at the very crash and crown of one of my best stories; "hast heered what Passon have now a dooed?" He was come in primed with some rubbishing tale, and wanted the room to make much of him. Nevertheless, the men of perception had not done with me yet.

"Wuttever be un? wuttever be un? Spak up, Oasler Jan!" cried some of the altogether younger men, who never know good work from bad, but seek some new astonishment. Goodness knows how hard it was, and how wholly undeserved, for me to withdraw and let them talk, only because their news was newer, and about a favourite man to talk of. However, I pressed down my feelings, not being certain about my bill, if I offended any one. For mercy's sake I spare their brogue, and tell their story decently. And Ostler John's tale was as follows, so far as I could make it out, by means of good luck, and by watching his face.

A certain justice of the peace, whose name was Captain Vellacott, a gentleman of spirit, who lived in one of the parishes belonging to this Parson Chowne (who happened to have two churches), this gentleman had contrived to give, as almost every one managed to do, deadly offence to Parson Chowne. It was expected that the Parson would be content to have him down and horsewhip him (as his manner was), and burn his house down afterwards. But the people who thought this were too hasty, and understood not his reverence. Whether from dislike of sitting upon the bench with him afterwards, or whether because Mrs Vellacott also had dared to shake hands with her gauntlet on, or because the baby cried when offered up to kiss the Parson—at any rate, Captain Vellacott must have more than a simple chastisement. The Captain being a quick sharp man, who said a hot word and forgot it, laughed at every one who told him to see to himself; and so on. "The Parson," said he, "is a man of his cloth; so am I of mine; and I will not insult him by expecting insult." So it came to pass that he made the mistake of measuring another man by his own measure. After a few months this gentleman felt that the Parson had quite forgiven him, no evil having befallen him yet, except that his rickyard had twice been fired, and his wife insulted by the naked people whom Chowne maintained upon Nympton Moor. And so, when they met in the fair this day, the Captain bowed to the Parson, and meant to go on and see to his business. But the other would not have it so. He offered his hand most cordially, and asked how Mrs Vellacott was, and all the five children, according to ages, using the Christian name of each. Captain Vellacott was so pleased by the kindness of his memory, and the nobility shown in dropping whatever had been between them, that what did he do but invite Master Chowne to dine with him up at the Fortescue Arms Hotel, and see a young horse he had bought in the fair, giving his own for it and five guineas; for he was not a rich man at all, and was come to make a moderate bargain.

Everything might have gone on well, and perhaps the Parson really meant to forgive him at the moment for having dared, in the bygone matter, to have a will of his own almost. But, as bad luck would have it, this very horse that the Captain had bought turned out to be one which the Parson had eye upon ever since last year's hunting season. However, not to paint the devil too black, it was confessed that he offered Vellacott five pounds for his bargain. This ought to have satisfied any man who knew what Parson Chowne was, and that fifty times five pounds would be saved by keeping out of his black books. Nevertheless the Captain stuck to his bargain and ruined himself.

The two gentlemen parted very good friends, shaking hands warmly, and having their joke, and hoping to dine again soon together; for Parson Chowne could beat all the world at after-dinner stories; and the Captain was the best man to laugh anywhere round the neighbourhood. And so he started rather early, on purpose to show his new horse to his wife.

But the ostler, who was a very old codger, and had seen a little of Parson's ways, shook his head after the Captain's shilling, and spat upon it to prevent bad luck, and laid it on the shelf where he kept his blacking. He was too clever to say one word; but every one remembered how he had behaved, and the sigh he gave—when he reminded them.

It may have been half an hour afterwards, or it may have been an hour and a half (so much these people differed), when Captain Vellacott on a hurdle came to Surgeon Cutcliffe's door, and the horse was led to Farrier Gould, who sent him to the mayor for opinions, and his worship sent him on to Pilch of the knacker's yard. Poor Justice Vellacott's collar bone was snapped in two places, and his left thigh broken, also three of his ribs stoven in, and a good deal of breakage abroad in his head. However, they hoped that he might come round; and being a Devonshire man, he did, as I found out afterwards.

This tale, which Ostler John delivered at ten times the length of the above, caused a very great stir and excitement and comparison of opinions. And when these wiseacres had almost exhausted their powers of wonder, I desired to know, in the name of goodness, why the poor Parson must be saddled with every man who fell off his horse. In the first place, he must have been far away from the scene of the misfortune, inasmuch as no more than an hour ago he was seeking his groom amongst us. And, again, what could be more likely than that Captain Vellacott might have taken, with a view to good luck for his purchase, a bottle or two of wine beyond what otherwise would have contented him? And even if not—why, a horse might fall, much more a man (who has only two legs), without anybody having designed it.

This reasoning of mine made no impression, because everybody's opinion was set. "Passon Chowne had adooed it;" they scratched their heads and went into side questions, but on the main point all agreed—"'twor ayther the Passon or the devil himzell."

CHAPTER XXIX.

A VISIT TO A PARSON.

My opinion of Devonshire now grew fast that most of the people are mad there. Honest, respectable, very kind-hearted, shrewd at a bargain, yet trustful, simple, manly, and outspoken, nevertheless they must be mad to keep Parson Chowne among them. But here, as in one or two other matters, I found myself wrong ere I finished with it. If a man visits a strange country, he ought to take time to think about it, and not judge the natives by first appearance, however superior he may be. This I felt even then, and tried my very best to act up to it: nevertheless it came back on me always that in the large county of Devon there were only two sound people; Parson Chowne for the one—and, of course, for the other, Davy Llewellyn.

So I resolved to see this thing out, especially as (when I came to think) nothing could be clearer than that the Parson himself had descried and taken me (with his wonderful quickness) for the only intelligent man to be found. How he knew me to be a Welshman, I could not tell then, and am not sure now. It must have been because I looked so superior to the rest of them. I gazed at the two crown-pieces, when I came to be active again the next day; and finding them both very good, I determined to keep them, and go to see after some more. But if I thought to have got the right side of the bargain, so far as the money went, I reckoned amiss considerably; for I found that the Parson lived so far away, that I could not walk thither and back again without being footsore for a week; and Captain Fuzzy would not allow it, especially as he had bound me to help in discharging cargo. And being quite ignorant as to the road, to hire a horse would not avail me, even supposing I could stay on board of him, which was against all experience. And by the time I had hired a cart to take me to Nympton on the Moors, as well as a hand to pilot her, behold I was on the wrong side of my two crowns, without any allowance for rations. They told me that everybody always charged double price for going up to the Parson's, and even so did not care for the job much. Because, though it was possible to come back safe, there was a poor chance of doing so without some damage to man or beast, and perhaps to the vehicle also.

Hereupon I had a great mind not to go; but being assured upon all sides that this would be a most dangerous thing, as well as supported, perhaps, by my native resolution and habits of inquiry, I nailed my colours to the mast, and mounted the cart by the larboard slings. It was a long and tiresome journey, quite up into a wilderness; and, for the latter part of it, the track could not have been found, except by means of a rough stone flung down here and there. But the driver told me that Parson Chowne took the whole of it three times a-week at a gallop, not being able to live without more harm than this lonely place afforded. Finding this fellow more ahead of his wits than most of those Devonshire yokels are, I beguiled the long journey by letting him talk, and now and then putting a question to him. He was full, of course, like all the town, of poor Captain Vellacott's misadventure, and the terrible spell put upon his new horse, which had seemed in the morning so quiet and docile. This he pretended at first to explain as the result of a compact formed some years back between his reverence and the devil. For Parson Chowne had thoroughly startled and robbed the latter of all self-esteem, until he had given in, and contracted to be at his beck and call (like a good servant) until it should come to the settlement. And poor Parson Jack was to be thrown in, though not such a very bad man sometimes; it being thoroughly understood, though not expressed between them, that Parson Chowne was to lead him on, step by step, with his own pilgrimage.

All this I listened to very quietly, scarce knowing what to say about it. However, I asked the driver, as a man having intimate knowledge of horses, whether he really did believe that they (like the swine of the Gadarenes) were laid open to infection from even a man with seven devils in him; and the more so as these had been never cast out, according to all that appeared of him. At this he cracked his whip and thought, not being much at theology; and not having met, it may be, until now, a man so thoroughly versed in it. I gave him his time to consider it out; but the trouble seemed only to grow on him, until he laid down his whip and said, not being able to do any more, "Horses is horses, and pigs is pigs, every bit the same as men be men. If the Lord made 'em both, the devil had the right to take 'em both."

This was so sound in point of reasoning, as well as of what we do hear in church, that never another word could I say, being taken in my own shallowness. And this is the only thing that can happen to a fellow too fond of objections. However, the driver, perceiving now that he had been too much for me, was pleased with me, and became disposed to make it up by a freedom of further information. If I were to put this in his own words, who could make head or tail of it? And indeed I could not stoop my pen to write such outlandish language. He said that his cousin was the very same knacker who had slaughtered that poor horse last night, to put it out of misery. Having an order from the mayor, "Putt thiss here hannimall to deth," he did it, and thought no more about it, until he got up in the morning. Then, as no boiling was yet on hand, he went to look at this fine young horse, whose time had been so hastened. And the brains being always so valuable for mixing with fresh—but I will not tell for the sake of honour—it was natural that he should look at the head of this poor creature. Finding the eyes in a strange condition, he examined them carefully, and, lifting the lids and probing round, in each he found a berry. My coachman said that his cousin now took these two berries which he had thus discovered out of a new horn-box, in which he had placed them for certainty, and asked him to make out what they were. The knacker, for his part, believed that they came from a creeping plant called the "Bitter-sweet nightshade," or sometimes the "Lady's necklace." But his cousin, my coachman, thought otherwise. He had wandered a good deal about in the fields before he married his young woman; and there he had seen, in autumnal days, the very same things as had killed the poor horse. A red thing that sticks in a cloven pod, much harder than berries of nightshade, and likely to keep in its poison until the moisture and warmth should dissolve its skin. I knew what he meant after thinking a while, because when a child I had gathered them. It is the seed of a nasty flag, which some call the "Roast-beef plant," and others the "Stinking Iris." These poisonous things in the eyes of a horse, cleverly pushed in under the lids, heating and melting, according as the heating and working of muscles crushed them; then shooting their red fire over the agonised tissues of eyeballs,—what horse would not have gone mad with it?

Also finding so rare a chance of a Devonshire man who was not dumb, I took opportunity of going into the matter of that fine old gentleman, whose strange and unreasonable habit of seeking among those Braunton Burrows (as if for somebody buried there) had almost broken my rest ever since, till I stumbled on yet greater wonders. Coachman, however, knew nothing about it, or else was not going to tell too much, and took a sudden turn of beginning to think that I asked too many questions, without even an inn to stand treat at. And perhaps he found out, with the jerks of the cart, that I had a very small phial of rum, not enough for two people to think of.

He may have been bidding for that, with his news; if so, he made a great mistake. Not that I ever grudge anything; only that there was not half enough for myself under the trying circumstances, and the man should have shown better manners than ever to cast even half an eye on it.

At last we were forced, on the brow of a hill, to come to a mooring in a fine old ditch, not having even a wall, or a tree, or a rick of peat to shelter us. And half a mile away round the corner might be found (as the driver said) the rectory house of Parson Chowne. Neither horse nor man would budge so much as a yard more in that direction, and it took a great deal to make them promise to wait there till two of the clock for me. But I had sense enough to pay nothing until they should carry me home again. Still I could not feel quite sure how far their courage would hold out in a lonely place, and so unkid.

And even with all that I feel within me of royal blood from royal bards—which must be the highest form of it—I did not feel myself so wholly comfortable and relishing as my duty is towards dinner-time. Nevertheless I plucked up courage, and went round the corner. Here I found a sort of a road with fir-trees on each side of it, all blown one way by strong storms, and unable to get back again. The road lay not in a hollow exactly, but in a shallow trough of the hills, which these fir-trees were meant to fill up, if the wind would allow them occasion. And going between them I felt the want of the pole I had left behind me. And if I had happened to own a gold watch, or anything fit to breed enemies, the knowledge of my price would have kept me from such temptation of Providence.

A tremendous roaring of dogs broke upon me the moment I got the first glimpse of the house; and this obliged me to go on carefully, because of that race I have had too much, and never found them mannersome. One huge fellow rushed up to me, and disturbed my mind to so great a degree that I was unable to take heed of anything about the place except his savage eyes and highly alarming expression and manner. For he kept on showing his horrible tusks, and growling a deep growl broken with snarls, and sidling to and fro, so as to get the better chance of a dash at me; and I durst not take my eyes from his, or his fangs would have been in my throat at a spring. I called him every endearing name that I could lay my tongue to, and lavished upon him such admiration as might have melted the sternest heart; but he placed no faith in a word of it, and nothing except my determined gaze kept him at bay for a moment. Therefore I felt for my sailor's knife, which luckily hung by a string from my belt; and if he had leaped at me he would have had it, as sure as my name is Llewellyn; and few men, I think, would find fault with me for doing my best to defend myself. However, one man did, for a stern voice cried—

"Shut your knife, you scoundrel! Poor Sammy, did the villain threaten you?"

Sammy crouched, and fawned, and whimpered, and went on his belly to lick his master, while I wiped the perspiration of my fright beneath my hat.

"This is a nice way to begin," said Chowne, after giving his dog a kick, "to come here and draw a knife on my very best dog. Go down on your knees, sir, and beg Sammy's pardon."

"May it please your reverence," I replied, in spite of his eyes, which lay fiercer upon me than even those of the dog had done, "I would have cut his throat; and I will, if he dares to touch me."

"That would grieve me, my good Welshman, because I should then let loose the pack, and we might have to bury you. However, no more of this trifle. Go in to my housekeeper, and recover your nerves a little, and in half an hour come to my study."

I touched my hat and obeyed his order, following the track which he pointed out, but keeping still ready for action if any more dogs should bear down on me. However, I met no creature worse than a very morose old woman, who merely grunted in reply to the very best flourish I could contrive, and led me into a long low kitchen. Dinner-time for the common people being now at maturity, I expected to see all the servants of course, and to smell something decent and gratifying. However, there was no such luck, only, without even asking my taste, she gave me a small jug of sour ale, and the bottom of a loaf, and a bit of Dutch cheese. Of course this was good enough for me; and having an appetite after the ride, I felt truly grateful. However, I could not help feeling also that in the cupboard just over my elbow there lay a fillet of fine spiced beef, to which I have always been partial. And after the perils I had encountered, the least she could do was to offer it down. Anywhere else I might have taken the liberty of suggesting this, but in that house I durst not, further than to ask very delicately—

"Madam, it is early for great people; but has his reverence been pleased to dine?"

"Did he give you leave to ask, sir?"

"No, I cannot say that he did. I meant no offence; but only——"

"I mean no offence; but only, you must be a stranger to think of asking a question in this house without his leave."

Nothing could have been said to me more thoroughly grievous and oppressive. And she offered no line or opening for me to begin again, as cross women generally do, by not being satisfied with their sting. So I made the best of my bread-and-cheese, and thought that Sker House was a paradise compared to Nympton Rectory.

"It is time for you now to go to my master," she broke in with her cold harsh voice, before I had scraped all the rind of my cheese, and when I was looking for more sour beer.

"Very well," I replied; "there is no temptation of any sort, madam, to linger here."

She smiled, for the first time, a very tart smile, even worse than the flavour of that shrewd ale, but without its weakness. And then she pointed up some steps, and along a stone passage, and said, exactly as if she took me for no more than a common tramp—

"At the end of that passage turn to the left, and knock at the third door round the corner. You dare not lay hands on anything. My master will know it if you do."

This was a little too much for me, after all the insults I had now put up with. I turned and gazed full on her strange square face, and into the depth of her narrow black eyes, with a glimpse of the window showing them.

"Your master!" I said. "Your son, you mean! And much there is to choose between you!"

She did not betray any signs of surprise at this hap-hazard shot of mine, but coldly answered my gaze, and said—

"You are very insolent. Let me give you a warning. You seem to be a powerful man: in the hands of my master you would be a babe, although you are so much larger. And were I to tell him what you have said, there would not be a sound piece of skin on you. Now, let me hear no more of you."

"With the greatest pleasure, madam. I am sure I can't understand whatever could bring me here."

"But I can;" she answered, more to her own thoughts than to mine, as she shut the door quite on my heels, and left me to my own devices. I felt almost as much amiss as if I were in an evil dream of being chased through caves of rock by some of my very best customers, all bearing red-hot toasting forks, and pelting me with my own good fish. It is the very worst dream I have, and it never comes after a common supper; which proves how clear my conscience is. And even now I might have escaped, because there were side passages; and for a minute I stood in doubt, until there came into my mind the tales of the pack of hounds he kept, and two or three people torn to pieces, and nobody daring to interfere. Also, I wanted to see him again, for he beat everybody I had ever seen; and I longed to be able to describe him to a civilised audience at the "Jolly Sailors." Therefore I knocked at the door of his room, approaching it very carefully, and thanking the Lord for His last great mercy in having put my knife into my head.

"You may come in," was the answer I got at last; and so in I went; and a queerer room I never did go into. But wonderful as the room was surely, and leaving on memory a shade of half-seen wonders afterwards, for the time I had no power to look at anything but the man.

People may laugh (and they always do until they gain experience) at the idea of one man binding other men prisoners to his will. For all their laughing, there stands the truth; and the men who resist such influence best are those who do not laugh at it. I have seen too much of the tricks of the world to believe in anything supernatural; but the granting of this power is most strictly within nature's scope; and somebody must have it. One man has the gift of love, that everybody loves him; another has the gift of hate, that nobody comes near him; the third, and far the rarest gift, combines the two others (one more, one less), and adds to them both the gift of fear. I felt, as I tried to meet his gaze and found my eyes quiver away from it, that the further I kept from this man's sight, the better it would be for me.

He sat in a high-backed chair, and pointed to a three-legged stool, as much as to say, "You may even sit down." This I did, and waited for him.

"Your name is David Llewellyn," he said, caring no more

to look at me; "you came from the coast of Glamorgan, three days ago, in the Rose of Devon schooner."

"Ketch, your reverence, if you please. The difference is in the mizzen-mast."

"Well, Jack Ketch, if you like, sir. No more interrupting me. Now you will answer a few questions; and if you tell me one word of falsehood——"

He did not finish his sentence, but he frightened me far more than if he had. I promised to do my best to tell the truth, so far as lies in me.

"Do you know what child that was that came ashore drowned upon your coast, when the coroner made such a fool of himself?"

"And the jury as well, your reverence. About the child I know nothing at all."

"Describe that child to the best of your power: for you are not altogether a fool."

I told him what the poor babe was like, so far as I could remember it. But something holy and harmless kept me from saying one word about Bardie. And to the last day of my life I shall rejoice that I so behaved. He saw that I was speaking truth; but he showed no signs of joy or sorrow, until I ventured to put in—

"May I ask why your reverence wishes to know, and what you think of this matter, and how——"

"Certainly you may ask, Llewellyn; it is a woman's and a Welshman's privilege; but certainly you shall have no reply. What inquiry has been made along your coast about this affair?"

I longed to answer him in my humour, even as he had answered me. With any one else I could have done it, but I durst not so with him. Therefore I told him all the truth, to the utmost of my knowledge,—making no secret of Hezekiah, and his low curiosity; also the man of the press with the hat; and then I could not quite leave out the visit of Anthony Stew and Sir Philip.

This more than anything else aroused Parson Chowne's attention. For the papers he cared not a damn, he said; for two of them lived by abusing him; but as he swore not (except that once), it appeared to me that he did care. However, he pressed me most close and hard about Anthony Stew and Sir Philip.

When he had got from me all that I knew—except that he

never once hit upon Bardie (the heart and the jewel of everything), he asked me without any warning—

"Do you know who that Sir Philip is?"

"No, your reverence; I have not even heard so much as his surname, although, no doubt, I shall find out."

"You fool! Is that all the wit you have? Three days in and out of Barnstaple! It is Sir Philip Bampfylde of Narnton Court, close by you."

"There is no Narnton Court, that I know of, your reverence, anywhere round our neighbourhood. There is Candleston Court, and Court Isa, and Court——"

"Tush, I mean near where your ship is lying. And that is chiefly what I want with you. I know men well; and I know that you are a man that will do anything for money."

My breath was taken away at this: so far was it from my true character. I like money well enough in its way; but as for a single disgraceful action——

"Your reverence never made such a mistake. For coming up here I have even paid more than you were pleased to give me. If that is your point I will go straight back. Do anything, indeed, for money!"

"Pooh! This is excellent indignation. What man is there but will do so? I mean, of course, anything you consider to be right and virtuous."

"Anything which is undeniably right, and upright, and virtuous. Ah! now your reverence understands me. Such has always been my character."

"In your own opinion. Well, self-respect is a real blessing: I will not ask you to forego it. Your business will be of a nature congenial as well as interesting to you. Your ship lies just in the right position for the service I require; and as she is known to have come from Wales, no Revenue-men will trouble you. You will have to keep watch, both day and night, upon Sir Philip and Narnton Court."

"Nothing in the nature of spying, your reverence, or sneaking after servants, or underhand work——"

"Nothing at all of that sort. You have nothing to do but to use your eyes upon the river-front of the building, especially the landing-place. You will come and tell me as soon as ever you see any kind of boat or vessel either come to or leave the landing-place. Also, if any man with a trumpet hails either boat or vessel. In short, any kind of communication betwixt

Narnton Court and the river. You need not take any trouble, except when the tide is up the river."

"Am I to do this against Sir Philip, who has been so kind and good to me? If so, I will hear no more of it."

"Not so; it is for Sir Philip's good. He is in danger, and very obstinate. He stupidly meddles with politics. My object is to save him."

"I see what your reverence means," I answered, being greatly relieved by this; for then (and even to this day, I believe) many of the ancient families were not content with his gracious Majesty, but hankered after ungracious Stuarts, mainly because they could not get them. "I will do my best to oblige you, sir." I finished, and made a bow to him.

"To obey me, you mean. Of course you will. But remember one thing—you are not to dare to ask a single word about this family, or even mention Sir Philip's name to anybody except myself. I have good reason for this order. If you break it I shall know it, and turn you to stone immediately. You are aware that I possess that power."

"Please your reverence, I have heard so; and I would gladly see it done—not to myself as yet, but rather to that old woman in the kitchen. It could not make much difference to her."

"Keep your position, sir," he answered, in a tone which frightened me; it was not violent, but so deep. "And now for your scale of wages. Of course, being opposite that old house, you would watch it without any orders. The only trouble I give you is this—when the tide runs up after dark, and smooth water lets vessels over the bar, you will have to loosen your boat or dingy, punt, or whatever you call her, and pull across the river, and lie in a shaded corner which you will find below Narnton Court, and commanding a view of it. Have you firearms? Then take this. The stock is hollow, and contains six charges. You can shoot; I am sure of that. I know a poacher by his eyelids."

He gave me a heavy two-barrelled pistol, long enough for a gun almost, and meant to be fired from the shoulder. Then pressing a spring in the stock, he laid bare a chamber containing some ammunition, as well as a couple of spare flints. He was going to teach me how to load it, till I told him that I had been captain of cannon, and perhaps the best shot in the royal navy.

"Then don't shoot yourself," he said, "as most of the old sailors have reason to do. But now you will earn your living well, what with your wages on board the schooner and the crown a-week I shall give you."

"A crown a-week, your reverence!" My countenance must have fallen sadly; for I looked to a guinea a-week at least. "And to have to stay out of my bed like that!"

"It is a large sum, I know, Llewellyn. But you must do your best to earn it, by diligence and alacrity. I could have sent one of my fine naked fellows, and of course not have paid him anything. But the fools near the towns are so fidgety now that they stare at these honest Adamites, and talk of them—which would defeat my purpose. Be off with you! I must go and see them. Nothing else refreshes me after talking so long to a fellow like you. Here are two guineas for you—one in advance for your first month's wage; the other you will keep until I have done with you, and then return it to me."

"A month, your honour!" I cried in dismay. "I never could stop in this country a month. Why, a week of it would be enough to drive me out of my mind almost."

"You will stay as long as I please, Llewellyn. That second guinea, which you pouched so promptly, is to enable you to come to me, by day or by night, on the very moment you see anything worth reporting. You are afraid of the dogs? Yes, all rogues are. Here, take this whistle. They are trained to obey it—they will crouch and fawn to you when you blow it."

He gave me a few more minute instructions, and then showed me out by a little side-door; and all the way back such a weight was upon me, and continual presence of strange black eyes, and dread of some hovering danger, that I answered the driver to never a word, nor cared for any of his wondrous stories about the naked people (whose huts we beheld in a valley below us); nay, not even—though truly needing it, and to my own great amazement—could I manage a drop of my pittance of rum. So the driver got it after all, or at least whatever remained of it, while I wished myself back at Old Newton Nottage, and seemed to be wrapped in an evil dream. Both horse and driver, however, found themselves not only thankful, but light-hearted, at getting away from Nympton Moor. Jack even sang a song when five miles off, and in his clumsy way rallied me. But finding this useless, he said that it was no more than he had expected; because it was known that it always befell every man who forgot his baptism, and got into dealings with Parson Chowne.

CHAPTER XXX.

ON DUTY.

THERE are many people who cannot enter into my meaning altogether. This I have felt so often that now I may have given utterance to it once or possibly twice before. If so, you will find me consistent wholly, and quite prepared to abide by it. In all substantial things I am clearer than the noon-day sun itself; and, to the very utmost farthing, righteous and unimpeachable. Money I look at, now and then, when it comes across me; and I like it well enough for the sake of the things it goes for. But as for committing an action below the honour of my family and ancestors (who never tuned their harps for less than a mark a-night), also, and best of all, my own conscience—a power that thumps all night like a ghost if I have not strictly humoured it,—for me to talk of such things seems almost to degrade the whole of them.

Therefore, if any one dreams, in his folly, that I would play the spy upon that great house over the river, I have no more to say, except that he is not worthy to read my tale. I regard him with contempt, and loathe him for his vile insinuations. Such a man is only fit to take the place of a spy himself, and earn perhaps something worth talking of, if his interest let him talk of it. For taking friendly observation of Narnton Court, for its inmates' sake, I was to have just five shillings a-week!

It became my duty now to attend to the getting out of the limestone; and I fetched it up with a swing that shook every leaf of the Rose of Devon. Fuzzy attempted to govern me; but I let him know that I would not have it, and never knocked under to any man. And if Parson Chowne had come alongside, I would have said the same to him.

Nevertheless, as an honest man, I took good care to earn my money, though less than the value of one good sewin, or at any rate of a fine turbot, each week. No craft of any sort went up or down that blessed river without my laying perspective on her, if there chanced to be light enough; or if she slipped along after dark—which is not worth while to do, on account of the shoals and windings—there was I, in our little dingy, not so far off as they might imagine. And I could answer for it, even with disdainful Chowne looking down through me, that nothing larger than a row-boat could have made for Narnton Court. But I have not said much of the river as yet; and who can understand me?

This river bends in graceful courtesies to the sweet land it is leaving, and the hills that hold its birth. Also with a vein of terror at the unknown sea before it, back it comes, when you grieve to think that it must have said "good-bye" for ever. Such a lovely winding river, with so many wilful ways, silvery shallows, and deep, rich shadows, where the trees come down to drink; also, beautiful bright-green meadows, sloping to have a taste of it, and the pleaches of bright sand offered to satisfy the tide, and the dark points jutting out on purpose to protect it! Many rivers have I seen, nobler, grander, more determined, yet among them all not one that took and led my heart so.

Had I been born on its banks, or among the hills that gaze down over it, what a song I would have made to it!—although the Bardic inspiration seems to have dropped out of my generation, yet will it return with fourfold vigour, probably in Bunny's children, if she ever has any, that is to say, of the proper gender; for the thumb of a woman is weak on the harp. And Bunny's only aspiration is for ribbons and lollipops, which must be beaten out of her.

However, my principal business now was not to admire this river, but watch it; and sometimes I found it uncommonly cold, and would gladly have had quite an ugly river, if less attractive to white frosts. And what with the clearing of our cargo, and the grumbling afterwards, and the waiting for sailing-orders and never getting any, and the setting-in of a sudden gale (which, but for me, must have capsized us when her hold was empty), as well as some more delays which now I cannot stop to think of—the middle of October found us still made fast, by stem and stern, in Barnstaple river, at Deadman's Pill.

Parson Chowne (who never happened to neglect a single thing that did concern his interests, any more than he ever happened to forget an injury), twice or thrice a-week he came, mounted on his coal-black mare, to know what was going on with us. I saw—for I am pretty sharp, though not pretending to vie with him, as no man might who had not dealt in a wholesale mode with the devil—I saw (though the clumsy understrappers meant me not to notice it) that Bethel Jose, our captain, was no more than a slave of the Parson's. This made clear to me quite a lump of what had seemed hopeless mysteries. Touching my poor self, to begin with, Chowne knew all about me, of course, by means of this dirty Fuzzy. Also Fuzzy's silence now, and the difficulty of working him (with any number of sheets in the wind), which had puzzled both Newton and Nottage, and the two public-houses at Porthcawl, and might have enabled him to marry even a farmer's widow with a rabbit-warren, and £350 to dispose of, and a reputation for sheep's-milk cheese, and herself not bad-looking, in spite of a beard.

I could see, and could carry home the truth, having thoroughly got to the bottom of it; and might have a chance myself to settle, if I dealt my secret well, with some of the women who had sworn to be single, until that Fuzzy provoked them so. This consideration added, more than can be now described, to my desire to get home before any one got in front of me. But Fuzzy, from day to day, pretended that the ketch was not victualled to sail, any more than she was even ballasted. She must load with hay, or with bricks, or pottery, or with something to fill her hold and pay freight, or what was to fill our bellies all the way back? And so on, and so on; until I was sure that he had some dark reason for lingering there.

Of course I had not been such a pure fool—in spite of short seasons for going from home—as to forget my desire and need to come home, after proper interval. The whole of the parish would yearn for me, and so would Ewenny and Llaleston, long ere the Christmas cod comes in; and I made a point in my promises to be back before Gunpowder Treason and Plot. As a thoroughly ancient hand at the cannon, I always led the fireworks; and the Pope having done something violent lately, they were to be very grand this year. What is a man when outside his own country—a prophet, a magistrate, even a sailor, who has kept well in with his relations? All his old friends are there, longing to praise him, when they hear of good affairs; and as to his enemies—a man of my breadth of nature has none.

This made it dreadfully grievous for me not to be getting home again; and my heart was like a sprouted onion when I thought of Bardie. Bunny would fight on, I knew, and get converted to the Church in the house of our churchwarden, and perhaps be baptised after all, which my wife never would have done to her. However, I did not care for that, because no great harm could come of it; and if the Primitives gave her ribbons, the Church would be bound to grant Honiton lace.

Thinking of all my engagements, and compacts, and serious trusteeships, and the many yearnings after me, I told Bethel

Jose, in so many words, that I was not a black man, but a white man, unable to be trampled on, and prepared (unless they could show me better) to place my matter in the hands of his worship, no less than the Mayor of Barnstaple. Fuzzy grinned, and so did Ike; and finding the mayor sitting handsomely upon the very next market-day, I laid my case before him. His worship (as keeping a grocer's shop, at which I had bought three pounds of onions, and a quarter of a pound of speckled cheese, and half an ounce of tobacco) was much inclined to do me justice; and, indeed, began to do so in a loud and powerful voice, and eager for people to hearken him. But somebody whispered something to him, containing, no doubt, the great Parson's name, and he shrank back into his hole, and discharged my summons, like a worm with lime laid on his tail.

Such things are painful; yet no man must insist upon them hardly, because our ancestors got on among far greater hardships. And it would prove us a bad low age if we turned sour about them. We are the finest fellows to fight that were ever according to Providence; we ought to be thankful for this great privilege (as I mean to show by-and-by), and I would not shake hands with any man, who, for trumpery stuff, would dare to make such a terrible force internal.

This grand soundness of my nature led me to go under orders, though acquit of legal contract, only seeking to do the right while receiving the money beforehand. Now this created a position of trust, for it involved a strong confidence in one's honour. Any man paying me beforehand places me at a disadvantage, which is hardly fair of him. I do not like to refuse him, because it would seem so ungraceful; and yet I can never be sure but that I ought to take consideration.

Not to dwell too much upon scruples which scarcely any one else might feel, and no other man can enter into, be it enough that my honour now was bound to do what was expected. But what a hardship it was, to be sure, to find myself debarred entirely from forming acquaintance, or asking questions, or going into the matter in my own style! especially now that my anxiety was quickened beyond bearing to get to the bottom of all these wonders about Sir Philip Bampfylde. What had led him to visit me? What was he seeking on Braunton Burrows —for now I knew that it must be he? Why did Parson Chowne desire to keep such watch on the visitors to Narnton Court by water, while all the world might pass into or out of the house by land? Or did the Parson keep other people watching the other side of the house, and prevent me from going near them, lest we should league together to cheat him? This last thing seemed to be very likely, and it proved to be more than that.

Revolving all this much at leisure in the quiet churn of mind, I pushed off with my little dingy from the side of the Rose of Devon, when the evening dusk was falling, somewhere at October's end. This little boat now seemed to be placed at my disposal always, although there used to be such a fuss, and turn for turn, in taking her. Now the glance of light on water, and the flowing shadows, keeping humour with the quiet play of evening breezes, here a hill and there a tree or rock to be regarded, while the strong influx of sea with white wisps traced the middle channel, and the little nooks withdrawn under gentle promontories took no heed of anything; when the moon came over these, dissipating clouds and moving sullen mists aside her track, I found it uncommonly difficult to be sure what I was up to. The full moon, lately risen, gazed directly down the river; but memory of daylight still was coming from the westward, feeble, and inclined to yield. What business was all this of mine? God makes all things to have turn; and I doubt if He ever meant mankind to be always spying into it. Ever so much better go these things without our bother; and our parson said, being a noble preacher, and fit any day for the navy, that the people who conquered the world, according to the prophet Joel—20th after Trinity—never noticed nature, never did consult the Lord of Hosts, and yet must have contented Him.

Difficult questions of this colour must be left to parsons (who beat all lawyers, out and out, in the matter of pure cleverness; because the latter never can anyhow, but the former, somehow, with the greatest ease, reconcile all difficulties). The only business I have to deal with is what I bodily see, feel, and hear, and have mind to go through with, and work out to perfect satisfaction. And this night I found more than ever broke upon my wits before, except when muzzle gapes at muzzle, and to blow or be blown up depends upon a single spark.

Because now, in my quiet manner (growing to be customary, under Parson Chowne's regard) dipping oars, I crossed the river, making slant for running tide. That man, knowing everybody who might suit his purpose, had employed me rather than old Ikey or even Fuzzy, partly because I could row so well and make no sound in doing it; while either of them, with muffled rowlocks, would splash and grunt, to be heard across river, and half-way to Barnstaple Bridge almost. As silently as an owl I skimmed across the silent river, not with the smallest desire to spy, but because the poetry of my nature came out strongly. And having this upon me still, I rowed my boat into a drooping tree, overhanging a quiet nook. Here I commanded the river-front of all that great house, Narnton Court, which stands on the north side of the water over against our Deadman's Pill. After several voyages under sundry states of light and weather, this was now approved to me as the very best point of observation. For all the long and straggling house (quite big enough for any three of the magistrates' houses on our side) could have been taken and raked (as it were) like a great ship with her stern to me, from the spot where I lay hidden. Such a length it stretched along, with little except the west end to me, and a show of front-windows dark and void; and all along the river-terrace, and the narrow spread of it, overlooking the bright water, pagan gods, or wicked things just as bad, all standing. However, that was not my business; if the gentry will forego the whole of their Christianity, they must answer for themselves, when the proper time appears. Only we would let them know that we hold aloof from any breach of their commandments.

A flight of ten wild ducks had been seen coming up the river, every now and then, as well as fourteen red-caps, and three or four good wisps of teal. Having to see to my victualling now, as well as for the sport of it, I loaded the Parson's two-foot pistol, which was as good as a gun almost, with three tobacco pipes full of powder poured into each barrel, and then a piece of an ancient hat (which Ikey had worn so long that no man could distinguish it from wadding), and upon the top of the hat three ounces of leaden pellets, and all kept tight with a good dollop of oakum. It must kill a wild duck at forty yards, or a red-cap up to fifty, if I hit the rogues in the head at all.

The tide must have been pretty nigh the flood, and the moon was rising hazily, and all the river was pale and lonely, for the brown-sailed lighters (which they call the "Tawton fleet") had long passed by, when I heard that silvery sound of swiftness cleaving solitude—the flight of a wedge of wild ducks. I knelt in the very smallest form that nature would allow of, and with one hand held a branch to keep the boat from surging. Plash they came down, after two short turns (as sudden as forked lightning), heads down for a moment, then heads up, and wings flapping, sousing, and subsiding. Quacks began, from the old drake first, and then from the rest of the company, and a racing after one another, and a rapid gambolling. Under and between them all, the river lost its smoothness, beaten into ups and downs that sloped away in ridge and furrow.

These fine fellows, as fat as butter after the barley-stubble time, carried on such joy and glory within twenty yards of me that I could not bring my gun to bear for quiet shot, so as to settle four. Like an ancient gunner, I bided my time, being up to the tricks of most of them. When their wild delight of water should begin to sate itself, what would they do? Why, gather in round the father of the family, and bob their heads together. This is the time to be sure of them, especially with two barrels fired at once, as I could easily manage. I never felt surer of birds in my life; I smelt them in the dripping-pan, and beheld myself quite basting them, but all of a sudden, up they flew, when I had got three in a line, and waited for two more to come into it, just as the muzzle was true upon them—up and away, and left me nothing except to rub my eyes and swear. I might have shot as they rose, but something told me not to do so. Therefore I crept back in my little punt, and waited. In another moment I heard the swing of stout oars pulled with time and power, such as I had not heard for years, nor since myself was stroke of it. Of course I knew that this must be a boat of the British navy, probably the captain's gig, and choice young fellows rowing her; and the tears sprang into my eyes at thought of all the times and things between, and all the heavy falls of life, since thus I clove the waters. All my heart went out towards her, and I held my breath with longing (as I looked between the branches of the dark and fluttering tree), just to let them know that here was one who understood them.

CHAPTER XXXI.

TWO LOVERS.

THE boat came round the corner swiftly of the wooded stretch of rock, within whose creek I lay concealed; and the officer in the stern-sheets cried, in the short sharp tone of custom, "Easy, stroke; hold all!" I heard him jerk the rudder-lines, as they passed within biscuit-toss of me, and with a heavy sheer he sent her, as if he knew every inch of water, to the steps of Narnton Court: not the handsome balustrade, only a landing of narrow stone-way nearer to me than the western end, and where the river-side terrace stopped. Two men sprang ashore and made the boat fast at the landing, and then some others lifted out what seemed to be a heavy chest, and placed it on the topmost step, until the officer, having landed, signed to them to bear it further to a corner of the parapet. I could see the whole of these doings, and distinguish him by his uniform, because the boat and the group of sailors were not more than fifty yards from me, and almost in the track of the moon from the place where I was hiding. In a minute or two all returned to the boat, with the exception of the officer, and I heard him give orders from the shore—

"Round the point, men! Keep close, and wait for me under the Yellow Hook I showed you."

The coxswain jumped into the stern-sheets; in a second or two they had put about, and the light gig pulling six good oars shot by me, on the first of the ebb, as swiftly almost as the wild ducks flew. Meanwhile the officer stood and gazed until they had rounded the western point, from which they had spoiled my shot so; and knowing the vigilant keenness of a British captain's eyes, I feared that he might espy my punt, which would have disgraced me dreadfully. And even without this I felt how much I would rather be far away. There could have been no man more against my taste to keep a watch upon than a captain in the royal navy, whose father might have been over me. And vigorously as I called to mind that all I was doing must be for his good, as well as for that of his relatives, I could not find that satisfaction which ought to flow from such benevolence. However, it now was too late to back out, even if my desire to know the end of this matter allowed of it

The officer stood for a minute or two, as if in brown thoughts and deep melancholy, and turned to the house once or twice, and seemed to hesitate as to approaching it. The long great house, with the broad river-front, looked all dark and desolate; not a servant, a horse, or even a dog was moving, and the only sign of life I could see was a dull light in a little window over a narrow doorway. While I was wondering at all this, and the captain standing gloomily, a little dark figure crossed the moonlight from the shadowy doorway, and the officer made a step or two, and held out his arms and received it. They seemed to stay pretty well satisfied thus, the figure being wholly female, until, with a sudden change of thought, there seemed to be some sobbing. This led the captain to try again some soft modes of persuasion, such as I could not see into, even if I would have deigned to do a thing against my grain so, because I have been in that way myself, and did not want to be looked at. However, not to be too long over what every man almost goes through (some honestly, and some anyhow, but all tending to experience), my only desire was, finding them at it, to get out of the way very quickly. For, poor as I am, there were several women of Newton, and Llaleston, and Ewenny, and even of Bridgend, our market-town, setting their caps, like springles, at me! Whereas I laboured at nothing else but to pay respect to my poor wife's memory, and never have a poor woman after her. And now all these romantic doings made me feel uneasy, and ready to be infected, so as to settle with nothing more than had been offered me thrice, and three times refused—a 7-foot-and-6-inch mangle; and (if she proved a tiger) have to work it myself perhaps!

Be that either way, these two unhappy lovers came along, while I was wondering at them, yet able to make allowance so, until they must have seen me, if they had a corner of an eye for anything less than one another. They stood on a plank that crossed the narrow creek or slot (wherein I lay, under a willow full of brown leaves), and scarcely ten yards from me. Here there was a rail across, about as big as a kidney-bean stick, whereupon they leaned, and looked into the water under them. Then they sighed, and made such sorrow (streaked somehow with happiness) that I got myself ready to leap overboard if either or both of them should jump in. However, they had more sense than that; though they went on very tenderly, and with a soft strain quite unfit to belong to a British officer. Being, from ancient though humble birth, gifted with a deal of delicacy, I pulled out two plugs of tobacco, which happened to be in my mouth just now, and I spared them both to stop my ears, though striking inwards painfully. I tried to hear nothing for ever so long; but I found myself forced to ease out the plugs, they did smart so confoundedly. And this pair wanted some one now to take a judicious view of them, for which few men, perhaps, could be found better qualified than I was. For they carried on in so high a manner, that it seemed as if they could be cured by nothing short of married life, of which I had so much experience. And the principal principle of that state is, that neither party must begin to make too much of the other side. But being now over that sort of thing, I found myself snug in a corner, and able to view them with interest and considerable candour.

"Is there no hope of it, then, after all; after all you have done and suffered, and the prayers of everybody?" This was the maiden, of course having right to the first word, and the last of it.

"There is hope enough, my darling; but nothing ever comes of it. And how can I search out this strange matter, while I am on service always?"

"Throw it up, Drake; my dear heart, for my sake, throw it up, and throw over all ambition, until you are cleared of this foul shame."

"My ambition is slender now," he answered, "and would be content with one slender lady." Here he gave her a squeeze, that threatened not only to make her slenderer, but also to make the rail need more stoutness, and me to keep ready for plunging. "Nevertheless, you know," he went on, when the plank and the rail put up with it, "I cannot think of myself for a moment, while I am thus on duty. We expect orders for America."

"So you said; and it frightens me. If that should be so, what ever, ever can become of us?"

"My own dear, you are a child; almost a child for a man like me, knocked about the world so much, and ever so unfortunate."

The rest of his speech was broken into, much to my dissatisfaction, by a soft caressing comfort, such as women's pity yields without any consideration. Only they made all sorts of foolish promises, and eternal pledges, touched up with confidence, and hope, and mutual praise, and faith, and doubt, and the other ins and outs of love.

"I won't cry any more," she said, with several sobs between it; "I ought not to be so with you, who are so strong, and good, and kind. Your honour is cruelly wronged at home: you never shall say that your own, own love wished you to peril it also abroad."

He took her quietly into his arms; and they seemed to strengthen one another. And to my eyes came old tears, or at any rate such as had come long ago. These two people stood a great time, silent, full of one another, keeping close with reverent longing, gazing yet not looking at the moonlight and the water. Then the delicate young maiden (for such her voice and outline showed her, though I could not judge her face) shivered in the curling fog which the climbing moon had brought. Hereupon the captain felt that her lungs must be attended to, as well as her lips, and her waist, and heart; and he said in a soft way, like a shawl—

"Come away, my lovely darling, from the cold, and fog, and mist. Your little cloak is damp all through; and time it is for me to go. Discipline I will have always; and I must have the same with you, until you take command of me."

"Many, many a weary year, ere I have the chance of it, Captain Drake." The young thing sighed as she spoke, though perhaps without any sense of prophecy.

"Isabel, let us not talk like that, even if we think it. The luck must turn some day, my darling; even I cannot be always on the evil side of it. How often has my father said so! And what stronger proof can I have than you? As long as you are true to me——"

They were turning away, when this bright idea, which seems to occur to lovers always, under some great law of nature, to prolong their interviews;—this compelled them to repeat pretty much the same forms, and ceremonies, assurances, pledges, and suchlike, which had passed between them scarcely more than three or four minutes ago, at the utmost. And again I looked away, because I would have had others do so to me; and there was nothing new to learn by it.

"Only one thing more, my own," said the lady, taking his arm again; "one more thing you must promise me. If you care for me at all, keep out of the way of that dreadful man."

"Why, how can I meet him at sea, my Bell? Even if he dislikes me, as you tell me perpetually, though I never gave him cause, that I know of."

"He does not dislike you, Drake Bampfylde; he hates you

with all the venomous, cold, black hatred, such as I fear to think of—oh my dear, oh my dear!"

"Now, Isabel, try not to be so foolish. I never could believe such a thing, and I never will, without clearest proof. I never could feel like that myself, even if any one wronged me deeply. And in spite of all my bad luck, Bell, I have never wronged any one. At least more than you know of."

"Then don't wrong me, my own dear love, by taking no heed of yourself. Here, there, and everywhere seems to be his nature. You may be proud of your ship and people, and of course they are proud of you. You may be ordered to Gibraltar, where they have done so gloriously, or to America, or to India. But wherever you are, you never can be out of the reach of that terrible man. His ways are so crooked, and so dark, and so dreadfully cold-blooded."

"Isabel, Isabel, now be quiet. What an imagination you have! A man in holy orders, a man of a good old family, who have been ancient friends of ours——"

"A bad old family, you mean—bad for generations. It does not matter, of course, what I say, because I am so young and stupid. But you are so frank, and good, and simple, and so very brave and careless, and I know that you will own some day—oh, it frightens me so to think of it!—that you were wrong in this matter, and your Isabel was right."

What his answer was I cannot tell, because they passed beyond my hearing upon their way towards the house. The young lady, with her long hair shining like woven gold in the moonlight, tried (so far as I could see) to persuade him to come in with her. This, however, he would not do, though grieving to refuse her; and she seemed to know the reason of it, and to cease to urge him. In and out of many things, which they seemed to have to talk of, he showed her the great chest in the dark corner; and perhaps she paid good heed to it. As to that, how can I tell, when they both were so far off, and river-fogs arising? Yet one thing I well could tell, or at any rate could have told it in the times when my blood ran fast, and my habit of life was romantic. Even though the light was foggy, and there was no time to waste, these two people seemed so to stay with a great dislike of severing.

However, they managed it at last; and growing so cold in my shoulders now, as well as my knees uncomfortable, right glad was I to hear what the maiden listened to with intense despair; that is to say, the captain's footfall, a yard further off every time of the sound. He went along the Braunton road, to find his boat where the river bends. And much as I longed to know him better, and understand why he did such things, and what he meant by hankering so after this young lady, outside his own father's house, and refusing to go inside when invited, and speaking of his own bad luck so much, and having a chest put away from the moonlight, likewise his men in the distance so far, and compelled to keep round the corner, not to mention his manner of walking, and swinging his shoulders, almost as if the world was nothing to him; although I had never been perhaps so thoroughly pushed with desire of knowledge, and all my best feelings uppermost, there was nothing for me left except to ponder, and to chew my quid, rowing softly through the lanes and lines of misty moonlight, to my little cuddy-home across the tidal river.

CHAPTER XXXII.

AMONG THE SAVAGES.

At this moment it became a very nice point to perceive what was really honest and right, and then to carry it out with all that fearless alacrity, which in such cases I find to be, as it were, constitutional to me. My high sense of honour would fain persuade me to keep in strictest secrecy that which (so far as I could judge) was not, or might not have been, intended for my eyes, or ears, or tongue. On the other hand, my still higher sense of duty to my employer (which is a most needful and practical feeling), and that power of loyalty which descends to me, and perhaps will die with me, as well as a strong, and no less ancestral, eagerness to be up to the tricks of all mysterious beings—I do not exaggerate when I say that the cutwater of my poor mind knew not which of these two hands pulled the stronger oar.

In short, being tired, and sleepy, and weary, and worn out with want of perceiving my way, although I smoked three pipes all alone (not from the smallest desire for them, but because I have routed the devil thus many and many a night I know—as the priests do with their incense; the reason of which I take to be, that having so much smoke at home, he shuns it when coming for change of air—growing dreamy thus), I said, with nobody to answer me, "I will tumble into my berth, as this dirty craft has no room for hammocks; and, between Parson and Captain, I will leave my dreams to guide me."

I played with myself, in saying this. No man ever should play with himself. It shows that he thinks too troublesomely; and soon may come, if he carries it on, almost to forget that other people are nothing, while himself is everything. And if any man comes to that state of mind, there is nothing more to hope of him.

I was not so far gone as that. Nevertheless, it served me right (for thinking such dreadful looseness) to have no broad fine road of sleep, in the depth whereof to be borne along, and lie wherever wanted; but instead of that to toss and kick, with much self-damage, and worst of all, to dream such murder that I now remember it. What it was, belongs to me, who paid for it with a loss of hair, very serious at my time of life. However, not to dwell upon that, or upon myself in any way—such being my perpetual wish, yet thwarted by great activity—let it be enough to say that Parson Chowne in my visions came and horribly stood over me.

Therefore, arising betimes, I hired a very fine horse, and, manning him bravely, laid his head east and by south, as near as might be, according to our binnacle. But though the wind was abaft the beam, and tide and all in his favour, and a brave commander upon his poop, what did he do but bouse his stem, and run out his spanker-driver, and up with his taffrail, as if I was wearing him in a thundering heavy sea. I resolved to get the upper hand of this uncalled-for mutiny; and the more so because all our crew were gazing, and at the fair I had laid down the law very strictly concerning horses. I slipped my feet out of the chains, for fear of any sudden capsize, and then I rapped him over the catheads, where his anchor ought to hang. He, however, instead of doing at all what I expected, up with his bolt-sprit and down with his quarter, as if struck by a whale under his forefoot. This was so far from true seamanship, and proved him to be so unbuilt for sailing, that I was content to disembark over his stern, and with slight concussions.

"Never say die" has always been my motto, and always will be: nailing my colours to the mast, I embarked upon another horse of less than half the tonnage of that one who would not answer helm. And this craft, being broken-backed, with a strange sound at her portholes, could not under press of sail bowl along more than four knots an hour. And we adjusted matters between us so, that when she was tired I also was sore, and therefore disembarked and towed her, until we were both fit for sea again. Therefore it must have been good meridian when I met Parson Chowne near his house.

This man was seldom inside his own house, except at his meal-times, or when asleep, but roving about uncomfortably, seeing to the veriest trifles, everywhere abusing or kicking everybody. And but for the certainty of his witchcraft (ninefold powerful, as they told me, when conferred upon a parson), and the black strength of his eyes, and the doom that had befallen all who dared to go against him, the men about the yards and stables told me—when he was miles away—that they never could have put up with him; for his wages were also below their deserts.

He came to me from the kennel of hounds, which he kept not for his own pleasure so much as for the delight of forbidding gentlemen, whenever the whim might take him so, especially if they were nobly accoutred, from earning at his expense the glory of jumping hedges and ditches. Now, as he came towards me, or rather beckoned for me to come to him, I saw that the other truly eminent parson, the Reverend John Rambone, was with him, and giving advice about the string at the back of a young dog's tongue. Although this man was his greatest friend, Master Chowne treated him no better than anybody else would fare; but signed to the mate of the hounds, or whatever those fox-hunters call their chief officer, to heed every word of what Rambone said. Because these two divines had won faith throughout all parishes and hundreds: Chowne for the doctrine of horses; and for discipline of dogs, John Rambone.

His Reverence fixed a stern gaze upon me, because I had not hurried myself—a thing which I never do except in a glorious naval action—and then he bade me follow him. This I did; and I declare even now I cannot tell whither he took me. For I seemed to have no power, in his presence, of heeding anything but himself: only I know that we passed through trees, and sate down somewhere afterwards. Wherever it was, or may have been, so far as my memory serves, I think that I held him at bay some little. For instance, I took the greatest care not to speak of the fair young lady; inasmuch as she might not have done all she did, if she had chanced to possess the knowledge of my being under the willow-tree. But Parson Chowne, without my telling, knew the whole of what was done; and what he thought of it none might guess in the shadowy shining of his eyes.

"You have done pretty well on the whole," he said, after asking many short questions; "but you must do better next time, my man. You must not allow all these delicate feelings, chivalry, resolute honesty, and little things of that sort, to interfere thus with business. These things do some credit to you, Llewellyn, and please you, and add to your happiness, which consists largely with you (as it does with all men) in conceit. But you must not allow yourself thus to coquet with these beauties of human nature. It needs a rich man to do that. Even add my five shillings to your own four, and you cannot thus go to Corinth."

I had been at Corinth twice, and found it not at all desirable; so I could not make out what his Reverence meant, except that it must be something bad; which at my time of life should not be put into the mind even by a clergyman. But what I could least put up with was, the want of encouragement I found for all my better feelings. These seemed to meet with nothing more than discouragement and disparagement, whereas I knew them to be sound, substantial, and solid; and I always felt upon going to bed what happiness they afforded me. And if the days of my youth had only passed through learned languages, Latin and Greek and Hebrew, I doubt whether even Parson Chowne could have laid his own will upon me so.

"Supposing, then, that your Reverence should make it ten," I answered; "with my own four, that would be fourteen."

"I can truly believe that it would, my man. And you may come to that, if you go on well. Now go into the house and enjoy yourself. You Welshmen are always hungry. And you may talk as freely as you like; which is your next desire. Every word you say will come back to me; and some of it may amuse me. If you have no sense you have some cunning. You will know what things to speak of. And be sure that you wait until I come back."

This was so wholly below and outside of the thing which I love to reconcile with my own constitution (having so long been respected for them, as well as rewarded by conscience), that I scarcely knew where or who I was, or what might next come over me. And to complete my uncomfortable sense of being nobody, I heard the sound of a galloping horse downhill as wild as could be, and found myself left as if all the ideas which I was prepared to suggest were nothing. However, that was not my loss, but his; so I entered the house, with considerable hope of enjoying myself, as commanded. For this purpose I have always found it, in the house of a gentleman, the height of luck to get among three young women and one old one. The elderly woman attends to the cooking, which is not understood by the young ones, or at any rate cannot be much expected; while, on the other hand, the young ones flirt in and out in a pleasant way, laying the table and showing their arms (which are of a lovely red, as good as any gravy); and then if you know how to manage them well, with a wholesome deference to the old cook, and yet an understanding—while she is basting, and as one might almost say, behind her back—a confidential feeling established that you know how she treats those young ones, and how harshly she dares to speak, if a coal comes into the dripping-pan, and in casting it out she burns her face, and abuses the whole of them for her own fault; also a little shy suggestion that they must put up with all this, because the old cook is past sweethearting time, and the parlour-maid scarcely come to it, accompanied by a wink or two, and a hint in the direction of the stables—some of the very noblest dinners that ever I made have been thus introduced. But what forgiveness could I expect, or who would listen to me, if I dared to speak in the same dinner-hour of the goodly kitchen at Candleston Court, or even at Court Ysha, and the place that served as a sort of kitchen, so far as they seemed to want one, at this Nympton Rectory? A chill came over every man, directly he went into it; and he knew that his meat would be hocks and bones, and his gravy (if any) would stand cold dead. However, I made the best of it, as my manner is with everything; and though the old stony woman sate, and seemed to make stone of every one, I kept my spirits up, and became (in spite of all her stoppage) what a man of my knowledge of mankind must be among womankind. In a word, though I do not wish to set down exactly how I managed it, in half an hour I could see, while carefully concealing it, that there was not a single young woman there without beginning to say to herself, "Should I like to be Mrs Llewellyn?" After that, I can have them always. But I know them too well, to be hasty. No prospects would suit me, at my time of life, unless they came after some cash in hand. The louts from the stables and kennels poured in, some of them very "degustin" (as my Bardie used to say), nevertheless the girls seemed to like them; and who was I, even when consulted, to pretend to say otherwise? In virtue of what I had seen, among barbarous tribes and everywhere, and all my knowledge of ceremonies, and the way they marry one another, it took me scarcely half an hour (especially among poor victuals) to have all the women watching for every word I was prepared to drop. Although this never fails to happen, yet it always pleases me; and to find it in Parson Chowne's kitchen go thus, and the stony woman herself compelled to be bitten by mustard for fear of smiling, and two or three maids quite unfit to get on without warm pats on their shoulder-blades, and the dogs quite aware that men were laughing, and that this meant luck for them if they put up their noses; it was not for me to think much of myself; and yet how could I help doing it?

In the midst of this truly social joy, and natural commune over victuals, and easing of thought to suit one another in the courtesies of digestion; and just as the slowest amongst us began to enter into some knowledge of me, in walked that great Parson Rambone, with his hands behind his back, and between them a stout hunting-crop. The maidens seemed to be taken aback, but the men were not much afraid of him.

"What a rare royster you are making! Out by the kennel I heard you. However can I write my sermons?"

"Does your Reverence write them in the kennel?" Thus the chief huntsman made inquiry, having a certain privilege.

"Clear out, clear out," said Rambone, fetching his whip toward all of us; "I am left in authority here, and I must have proper discipline. Mrs Steelyard, I am surprised at you. Girls, you must never go on like this. What will his Reverence say to me? Come along with me, thou villain Welshman, and give me a light for my pipe, if you please."

It was a sad thing to behold a man of this noble nature, having gifts of everything (whether of body, or heart, or soul), only wanting gift of mind; and for want of that alone, making wreck of all the rest. I let him lead me; while I felt how I longed to have the lead of him. But that was in stronger hands than mine.

"Come, and I'll show thee a strange sight, Taffy," he said to me very pleasantly, as soon as his pipe was kindled; "only I must have my horse, to inspire them with respect for me, as well as to keep my distance. Where is thy charger, thou valiant Taffy?"

I answered his Reverence that I would rather travel afoot, if it were not too far; neither could he persuade me, after the experience of that morning, to hoist my flag on an unknown horse, the command of which he offered me. So forth we set, the Parson on horseback, and in very high spirits, trolling songs, leaping hedges, frolicking enough to frighten one, and I on foot, rather stiff and weary, and needing a glass of grog, without any visible chance of getting it.

"Here, you despondent Taffy; take this, and brighten up a bit. It is true you are going to the gallows: but there's no room for you there just now."

I saw what he meant, as he handed me his silver hunting-flask, for they have a fashion about there of hanging bad people at cross ways, and leaving them there for the good of others, and to encourage honesty. And truly the place was chosen well; for in the hollow not far below it, might be found those savage folk, of whom I said something a good while ago. And I did not say then what I might have said; because I felt scandalised, and unwilling to press any question of doubtful doings upon thoroughly accomplished people. But now I am bound, like a hospital surgeon, to display the whole of it.

"Take hold of the tail of my horse, old Taffy," said his Reverence to me; "and I will see you clear of them. Have no fear, for they all know me."

By this time we were surrounded with fifteen or twenty strange-looking creatures, enough to frighten anybody. Many fine savages have I seen—on the shores of the Land of Fire, for instance, or on the coast of Guinea, or of the Gulf of Panama, and in fifty other places—yet none did I ever come across so outrageous as these were. They danced, and capered, and caught up stones, and made pretence to throw at us; and then, with horrible grimaces, showed their teeth and jeered at us. Scarcely any of the men had more than a piece of old sack upon him; and as for the women, the less I say, the more you will believe it. My respect for respectable women is such that I scarcely dare to irritate them, by not saying what these other women were as concerns appearance. And yet I will confine myself, as if of the female gender, to a gentle hint that these women might have looked much nicer, if only they had clothes on.

But the poor little "piccaninies," as the niggers call them

these poor little devils were far worse off than any hatch of negroes, or Maroons, or copper-colours anywhere in the breeding-grounds. Not so much from any want of tendance or clean management, which none of the others ever got; but from difference of climate, and the moisture of their native soil. These little creatures, all stark naked, seemed to be well enough off for food, of some sort or another, but to be very badly off for want of washing and covering up. And their little legs seemed to be growing crooked; the meaning of which was beyond me then; until I was told that it took its rise from the way they were forced to crook them in, to lay hold of one another's legs, for the sake of natural warmth and comfort, as the winter-time came on, when they slept in the straw all together. I believe this was so; but I never saw it.

The Reverend John Rambone took no other notice of these people than to be amused with them. He knew some two or three of the men, and spoke of them by their nicknames, such as "Browny," or "Horse-hair," or "Sandy boy;" and the little children came crawling on their bellies to him. This seemed to be their natural manner of going at an early age: and only one of all the very little children walked upright. This one came to the Parson's horse, and being still of a tottery order, laid hold of a fore-leg to fetch up his own; and having such moorage, looked up at the horse. The horse, for his part, looked down upon him, bending his neck, as if highly pleased; yet with his nostrils desiring to snort, and the whole of his springy leg quivering, but trying to keep quiet, lest the baby might be injured. This made me look at the child again, whose little foolish life was hanging upon the behaviour of a horse. The rider perceived that he could do nothing, in spite of all his great strength and skill, to prevent the horse from dashing out the baby's brains with his fore-hoof, if only he should rear or fret. And so he only soothed him. But I, being up to all these things, and full for ever of presence of mind, slipped in under the hold of the horse, as quietly as possible, and in a manner which others might call at the same time daring and dexterous, I fetched the poor little fellow out of his dangerous position.

"Well done, Taffy!" said Parson Jack; "I should never have thought you had sense enough for it. You had a narrow shave, my man."

For the horse, being frightened by so much nakedness, made a most sudden spring over my body, before I could rise with the child in my arms; and one of his after-hoofs knocked my hat off, so that I felt truly thankful not to have had a worse business of it. But I would not let any one laugh at my fright.

"A miss is as good as a mile, your Reverence. Many a cannon-ball has passed me nearer than your horse's hoof. Tush, a mere trifle! Will your Reverence give this poor little man a ride?" And with that I offered him the child upon his saddle-bow, naked, and unwashed, and kicking.

"Keep off, or you shall taste my horsewhip. Keep away with your dirty brat—and yet—oh, poor little devil! If I only had a cloth with me!"

For this parson was of tender nature, although so wild and reckless; and in his light way he was moved at the wretched plight of this small creature, and the signs of heavy stripes upon him. Not all over him, as the Parson said, being prone to exaggerate; but only extending over his back, and his hams, and other convenient places. And perhaps my jacket made them smart, for he roared every time I lifted him. And every time I set him down, he stared with a wistful kind of wonder at our clothes, and at the noble horse, as if he were trying to remember something. "Where can they have picked up this poor little beggar?" said Parson Jack, more to himself than to me: "he looks of a different breed altogether. I wonder if this is one of Stoyle's damned tricks." And all the way back he spoke never a word, but seemed to be worrying with himself. But I having set the child down on his feet, and dusted my clothes, and cleaned myself, followed the poor little creature's toddle, and examined him carefully. The rest of the children seemed to hate him, and he, to shrink out of their way almost; and yet he was the only fine and handsome child among them. For in spite of all the dirt upon it, his face was honest, and fair, and open, with large soft eyes of a dainty blue, and short thick curls of yellow hair that wanted combing sadly. And though he had rolled in muddy places, as little wild children always do, for the sake of keeping the cold out, his skin was white, where the mud had peeled, and his form lacked nothing but washing.

CHAPTER XXXIII.

IN A STATE OF NATURE.

Now all these things contributed, coming as they did so rapidly, to arouse inside me a burning and almost desperate curiosity. It was in vain that I said to myself, "these are no concerns of mine: let them manage their own affairs: the less I meddle, the better for me: I seem to be in a barbarous land, and I must expect things barbarous. And after all, what does it come to, compared with the great things I have seen, ay, and played my part in?" To reason thus, and regard it thus, and seek only to be quit of it, was a proof of the highest wisdom any man could manifest: if he could only stick to it. And this I perceived, and thus I felt, and praised myself for enforcing it so; until it became not only safe, but a bounden duty to reward my conscience by a little talk or so.

Hence I lounged into the stable-yard—for that terrible Chowne was not yet come back, neither were maids to be got at for talking, only that stony Steelyard—and there I found three or four shirt-sleeved fellows, hissing at horses, and rubbing away, to put their sleeping polish on them, before the master should return. Also three or four more were labouring in the stalls very briskly, one at a sort of holy-stoning, making patterns with brick and sand, and the others setting up the hammocks for the nags to lie in, with a lashing of twisted straw aft of their after-heels and taffrails, as the wake of a ship might be. And all of it done most ship-shape. This amused me mightily; for I never had seen such a thing before, even among wild horses, who have power to manage their own concerns. But to see them all go in so snugly, and with such a sweet, clean savour, each to his own oats or mashings, with the golden straw at foot, made me think, and forced me to it, of those wretched white barbarians (white, at least, just here and there), whom good Parson Jack —as one might almost try to call him—had led me to visit that same afternoon.

Perceiving how the wind sate, I even held back, and smoked a pipe, exactly as if I were overseer, and understood the whole of it, yet did not mean to make rash reproach. This had a fine effect upon them, especially as I chewed a straw, by no means so as to stop my pipe, but to exhibit mastery. And when I put my leg over a rail, as if I found it difficult to keep myself from horseback, the head-man came to me straightforward, and asked me when I had hunted last.

I told him that I was always hunting, week-days, and Sundays, and all the year round, because it was our fashion; and that we hunted creatures such as he never had the luck to set eyes on. And when I had told him a few more things (such as flow from experience, when mixed with imagination), a duller man than myself might see that he longed for me to sup with him. And he spoke of things that made me ready, such as tripe and onions.

However, this would never do. I felt myself strongly under orders; and but for this paramount sense of duty, never could I have done the things modestly mentioned as of yore; and those of hereafter tenfold as fine, such as no modesty dare suppress. So, when I had explained to him exactly how I stood about it, he did not refuse to fill his pipe with a bit of my choice tobacco, and to come away from all idle folk, to a place in the shelter of a rick, where he was sure to hear the hoofs of his master's horse returning. I sate with him thus, and we got on well; and as he was going to marry soon the daughter of a publican, who had as good as fifty pounds, and nothing that could be set on fire, and lived fifty miles away almost, he did not mind telling me all the truth, because he saw that I could keep it; and at his age he could not enter into the spirit of being kicked so. I told him I should like to see a man kick me! But he said that I might come to it.

This was a very superior man, and I durst not contradict him; and having arranged so to settle in life, how could he hope to tell any more lies? For I have always found all men grow pugnaciously truthful, so to put it, for a month almost before wedlock; while the women are doing the opposite. However, not to go far into that, what he told me was much as follows:—

Parson Chowne, in early life, before his mind was put into shape for anything but to please itself, had been dreadfully vexed and thwarted. Every matter had gone amiss, directly he was concerned in it; his guardians had cheated him, so had his step-mother, so had his favourite uncle, and of course so had his lawyers done. In the thick of that bitterness, what did his sweetheart do but throw him over. She took a great scare of his strange black eyes, when she found that his money was doubtful. This was instinct, no doubt, on her part, and may have been a great saving for her; but to him it was terrible loss. His faith was already astray a little; but a dear wife might have brought it back, or at any rate made him think so. And he was not of the nature which gropes after the bottom of everything, like a twisting augur. Having a prospect of good estates, he was sent to London to learn the law, after finishing at Oxford, not that he might practise it, but to introduce a new element to the county magistrates, when he should mount the bench among them. Here he got rogued, as was only natural, and a great part of his land fell from him, and therefore he took to the clerical line; and being of a stern and decided nature, he married three wives, one after the other, and thus got a good deal of property. It was said, of course, as it always is of any man thrice a widower, that he or his manner had killed his wives; a charge which should never be made without strong evidence in support of it. At any rate there had been no children; and different opinions were entertained whether this were the cause or effect of the Parson's dislike and contempt of little ones. Moreover, as women usually are of a tougher staple than men can be, Chowne's successive liberation from three wives had added greatly to his fame for witchcraft, such as first accrued from his commanding style, nocturnal habits, method of quenching other people, and collection of pots and kettles. The head-groom told me, with a knowing wink, that in his opinion the Parson was now looking after wife No. 4, for he never had known him come out so smart with silver heels and crested head-piece, and even the mark of the saddle must not show upon his breeches. This was a sure sign, he thought, that there was a young lady in the wind, possessing both money and good looks, such as Chowne was entitled to, and always had insisted on. Upon that point I could have thrown some light (if prudence had permitted it), or at least I had some shrewd suspicions, after what happened beside the river; however, I said nothing. But I asked him what in his opinion first had soured the young man Chowne against the whole of the world so sadly, as he seemed to retain it now. And he answered me that he could not tell, inasmuch as the cause which he had heard given seemed to him to be most unlikely, according to all that he saw of the man. Nevertheless I bade him tell it, being an older man than he was, and therefore more able to enter into what young folk call "inconsistencies." And so he told me that it was this. Chowne, while still a young boy, had loved, with all the force of his heart, a boy a few years younger than himself, a cousin of his own, but not with prospects such as he had. And this boy had been killed at school, and the matter hushed up comfortably among all high authorities. But Stoyle Chowne had made a vow to discover and hunt it out to the uttermost, and sooner or later to have revenge. But when his own wrongs fell upon him, doubtless he had forgotten it. I said that I did not believe he had done so, or ever would, to the uttermost.

Then I asked about Parson Jack, and heard pretty much what I expected. That he was a well-meaning man enough, although without much sense of right or wrong, until his evil star led him into Parson Chowne's society. But still he had instincts now and then, such as a horse has, of the right road; and an old woman of his church declared that he did feel his own sermons, and if let alone, and listened to, might come to act up to them. I asked whether Parson Chowne might do the like, but was told that he never preached any.

We were talking thus, and I had quite agreed to his desire of my company for supper-time, when the sound of a horse upon stony ground, tearing along at a dangerous speed, quite broke up our conference. The groom, at the sound of it, damped out his pipe, and signified to me to do the same.

"I have fired a-many of his enemies' ricks," he whispered, in his haste and fright; "but if he were to smell me a-smoking near to a rick of his own, good Lord!" and he pointed to a hay-rope, as if he saw his halter. And though he had boasted of speedy marriage, and caring no fig for Parson Chowne, he set off for the stables at a pace likely to prove injurious to his credit for consistency.

On the other hand, I, in a leisurely manner, picked myself up from the attitude natural to me when listening kindly, and calmly asserting my right to smoke, approached the track by which I knew that the rider must come into the yard; for all the dogs had no fear of me now, by virtue of the whistle which I bore. And before I had been there half a minute, the Parson dashed up with his horse all smoking, and himself in a heavy blackness of temper, such as I somehow expected of him.

"No Jack here! not a Jack to be seen. Have the kindness to look for my stable-whip. Ho, Llewellyn is it?"

"Yes, your Reverence, David Llewellyn, once of his Majesty's Royal Navy, and now of——"

"No more of that! You have played me false. I expected it from a rogue like you. Restore me that trust-guinea."

This so largely differed from what even Anthony Stew would dare to say in conversation with me (much less at times of evidence), that I lifted up my heart to heaven, as two or three preachers had ordered me; and even our parson had backed it up, with lineage at least as good and perhaps much better than Parson Chowne's, by right of Welsh blood under it: the whole of this overcame me so, that I could only say, "What guinea, sir?"

"What guinea, indeed! You would rob me, would you? Don't you know better than that, my man? Come to me in two hours' time. Stop, give me that dog's whistle!"

Taking that heed of me, and no more, he cast the reins to my friend the head-groom, who came up, looking for all the world as if never had he seen me, and wondered strangely who I could be. And this air of fright and denial always pervaded the whole household. All of which was quite against what I had been long accustomed to, wherever I deigned to go in with my news to the servants' place, or the housekeeper's room, or anywhere pointed out to me as the best for entertainment. Here, however, although the servants seemed to be plentiful enough, and the horses and the hounds to have as much as they could eat, there was not a trace of what I may call good domestic comfort. When this prevails, as it ought to do in every gentleman's household, the marks may be discovered in the eyes and the mouth of everybody. Nobody thinks of giving way to injudicious hurry when bells ring, or when shouts are heard, or horses' feet at the front door. And if on the part of the carpeted rooms any disquietude is shown, or desire to play, or feed, or ride, at times outside the convenience of the excellent company down-stairs, there is nothing more to be said, except that it cannot be done, and should never in common reason have been thought of. For all servants must enjoy their meals, and must have time to digest them with proper ease for conversation and expansion afterwards. At Candleston Court it was always so; and so it should be everywhere.

However, to return to my groom, whose cordiality revived at the moment his master turned the corner, perceiving that Chowne had some matter on hand which would not allow him to visit the stables, just for the present at any rate, he turned the black mare over to the care of an understrapper, and with a wink and a smack of his lips, gave me to know that his supper was toward. Neither were we disappointed, but found it all going on very sweetly, in a little private room used for cleaning harness. And he told me that this young cook maid, of unusual abilities, had attached herself to him very strongly, with an eye to promotion, and having no scent of his higher engagement: neither would he have been unwilling to carry out her wishes if she could only have shown a sixpence against the innkeeper's daughter's shilling. I told him that he was too romantic, and he said with a sigh that he could not help it; but all would come right in the end, no doubt.

This honest affection impressed me not a little in his favour, and in less than half an hour I found him a thoroughly worthy fellow: while he perceived, through a square-stalked rummer, that my character was congenial. I told him therefore some foreign stories, many of which were exceedingly true, and he by this time was ready to answer almost anything that I chose to ask, even though he knew nothing about it. As for the people that wore no clothes, but lived all together in the old mud-house, there need be and could be no mystery. Every one knew that his Reverence had picked them up in his early days, and been pleased with their simple appearance and dislike of cultivation. Perceiving even then how glad he might be, in after-life, to annoy his neighbours, what did he do but bring these people (then six in number, and all of them wives and husbands to one another) and persuade them to dig themselves out a house, and by deed of gift establish them on forty acres of their own land, so that, as Englishmen love to say, their house was now their castle. Not that these were perhaps English folk, but rather of a Gipsy cross, capable, however, of becoming white if a muscular man should scrub them. The groom said that nobody durst go near them, except Parson Chowne and Parson Jack, and that they seemed to get worse and worse, as they began to be persecuted by clothes-wearing people. I asked him what their manners were; and he said he believed they were good enough, so long as not interfered with; and who could blame them for maintaining that whether they wore clothes or not was entirely their own concern: also, that if outer strangers intruded, from motives of low curiosity, upon their unclad premises, it was only fair to point out to them the disadvantages of costume, by making it very hard to wash? There was some sense in this, because the main anxiety of mankind is to convert one another; and the pelting of mud is usually the beginning of such overtures. And these fine fellows having recurred (as Parson Chowne said) to a natural state, their very first desire would be to redeem all fellow-creatures from the evils of civilisation. Whereof the foremost perhaps is clothes, and the time we take in dressing—a twelfth part of their waking life, with even the wisest women, and with the unwise virgins, often not less than three-quarters; and with many men not much better.—But to come back to my savages. I asked this good groom how it came to pass that none of the sheriffs, or deputies, or even magistrates of the shire, put down this ungoodly company. He said that they had tried, but failed, according to the laws of England, on the best authority. Because these men of the ancient Adam went back to the time before the beasts had come to Adam to get their names. They brought up their children without a name, and now all names were dying out, and they agreed much better in consequence. And how could any writ, warrant, or summons, run against people without a name? It had once been tried with a "Nesho Kiss," the meaning of which was beyond me; but Parson Chowne upset that at once; and the bailiff was fit to make bricks of.

At this I shook my head and smiled; because we put up with many evils on our side of the water, but never with people so unbecoming in their manner of life and clothes. And I thought how even mild Colonel Lougher would have behaved upon such a point, and how sharp Anthony Stew would have stamped when they began to pelt him; and how I wished him there to try it!

Nevertheless I desired to know what victuals these good barbarians had; because, although like the Indian Jogis (mentioned by some great traveller) they might prove their right to go without clothes, which never were born upon them, they could not to my mind prove their power to do so well without victuals. He answered that this was a clever thing on my part to inquire about; but that I was so far wrong that these people would eat anything. His Reverence sent them every week the refuse of his garden, as well as of stable-yard and kennel, and they had a gift of finding food in everything around them. Their favourite dish—so to say, when they had never a dish among them—was what they discovered in the pasture-land; and this they divided carefully; accounting it the depth of shame, and the surest mark of civilisation, to cheat one another. But they could not expect to get this every day, in a neighbourhood of moorland; therefore, instead of grumbling, they did their best to get on without it. And Providence always sends thousands of victuals for all whose stomachs have not been ruined by thinking too much about them; or very likely through the women beginning to make them delicate. So when a man is sea-sick, he thinks of and hates almost everything.

On the other hand, these noble fellows hated nothing that could be chewed. Twenty-one sorts of toad-stool, with the insects which inhabit them; three varieties of eft, and of frogs no less than seven; also slugs six inches long, too large to have a house built; moles that live in lines of decks, like a man-of-war's-man; also rats, and brindled hedgehogs, and the grubs of hornets (which far surpass all oysters)--these, and other little things, like goat-moths, leopards, and money-grubs, kept them so alive as never to come down on the parish. Neither was there any hen-roost, rick-yard, apple-room, or dairy, on the farms around them, but in it they found nourishment. Into all this I could enter, while the groom only showed the door of it.

But while we were talking thus, I heard the stable-clock strike eight, which brought Hezekiah to my mind, and my own church-clock at Newton. It struck in such a manner, that I saw the door of my own cottage, also Bunny in bed, with her nostrils ready to twitch for snoring, and Mother Jones, with a candle, stooping to ease her by means of a drop of hot grease; and inside, by the wall, lay Bardie, sleeping (as she always slept) with a smile of high-born quietude. And what would all three say to me if ever I got back again?

Thanking this excellent groom for all his hospitality to me, and promising at his desire to keep it from his master, I took my way (as pointed out) to the room where his Reverence might be found. I feared that his temper would be black, unless he had dined as I had supped, and taken a good glass afterwards. And I could not believe what the groom had told me concerning one particular. There is a most utterly pestilent race arising, and growing up around us, whose object is to destroy old England, by forbidding a man to drink. St Paul speaks against them, and all the great prophets; and the very first thing that was done by our Lord, after answering them in the Temple, was to put them to shame with a great many firkins. Also one of the foremost parables is concerning bottles, as especially honest things (while bushels are to the contrary), and the tendency of all Scripture is such—whichever Testament you take—that no man in his wits can doubt it. And though I never read the Koran, and only have heard some verses of it, I know enough to say positively, that Mahomet began this movement to establish Antichrist.

However, my groom said that Parson Chowne, though not such a fool as to stop other people, scarcely ever took a drop himself; and his main delight was to make low beasts of the clergy who had no self-command. And two or three years ago he had played a trick on his brother parsons, such as no man would ever have tried who took his own glass in moderation and enjoyed it heartily, as Scripture even commands us to do, to promote good-fellowship and discretion. Having a power of visitation, from some faculty he enjoyed, he sent all round to demand their presence at a certain time, for dinner. All the parsons were glad enough, especially as their wives could not, in good manners, be invited, because there was now no Mrs Chowne. And they saw a rare chance to tell good stories, and get on without the little snaps which are apt to occur among ladies. Therefore they all appeared in strength, having represented it as a high duty, whatever their better halves might think. When a parson says this, his wife must knock under, or never go to church again. Being there, they were treated well, and had the good dinner they all deserved, and found their host very different from what they had been led to expect of him. He gave them as much wine as they needed, and a very good wine too. He let them tell their stories, though his own taste was quite different; and he even humoured them so as to laugh the while he was despising them. And though he could not bear tobacco, that and pipes were brought in for them.

All went smoothly until one of them, edged on by the others, called for spirits and hot water. This Master Chowne had prepared for, of course, and meant to present the things in good time; but now being gored thus in his own house, the devil entered into him. His dark face grew of a leaden colour, while he begged their pardon. Then out he went to Mother Steelyard, and told her exactly what to do. Two great jacks of brown brandy came in, and were placed upon the table, and two silver kettles upon the hobs. He begged all his guests to help themselves, showing the lemons and sugar-caddy, the bottles, and kettles, and everything: and then he left them to their own devices, while he talked with Parson Jack, who had dropped in suddenly.

Now, what shall I tell you came to pass—as a very great traveller always says—why, only that these parsons grew more drunk than despair, or even hope. Because, in the silver kettles was not water, but whisky at boiling-point, and the more they desired to weaken their brandy, the more they fortified it: until they tumbled out altogether, in every state of disorder. For this he had prepared, by placing at the foot of his long steps half-a-dozen butts of liquid from the cleaning of his drains, meant to be spread on the fields next day. And into the whole of this they fell, and he bolted the doors upon them.

This made a stir in the clerical circles, when it came to be talked about; but upon reference to the bishop, he thought they had better say nothing about it, only be more considerate. And on the whole it redounded greatly to the credit of Parson Chowne.

CHAPTER XXXIV

WAITING AND LEARNING.

WHAT this great man now said to me had better not be set down perhaps; because it proved him incapable of forming due estimate of my character. Enough that he caused me some alarm and considerable annoyance by his supercilious vein, and assumption of evil motives. Whereas you could not find anywhere purer or loftier reasons, and I might say, more poetical ones, than those which had led me to abstain from speaking of the fair young lady. However, as this Chowne had learned all about her, from some skulking landsman, whom he maintained as a spy at the back of the premises, it was certain that I could in no way harm her, by earning a trifle of money in front, in a thoroughly open and disciplined way. And it might even lie in my power thereby to defeat the devices of enemies, and rescue this beautiful young female from any one who would dare to think of presuming to injure her.

I found my breast and heart aglow with all the fine feeling of younger days, the moment the above occurred to me; and it would not have cost me two blows to knock down any man who misunderstood me. However, his Reverence did not afford me any chance for this exercise; but seemed to allow me the benefit which such ideas afford a man; and promised to give me three half-crowns, instead of five shillings a week, as before.

He allowed me a hay-loft to sleep in that night, after taking good care that I had not even a flint to strike a light with. For, cordially as he did enjoy the firing of an enemy's barns or stacks, his Reverence never could bear the idea of so much as a spark coming near his own. And the following morning I saddled my horse, with a good chain undergirding, and taking turn and turn about, got home to the Rose of Devon.

And here I found very unjust work, Fuzzy gone, and Ike not to be found, and the ketch laid up for the winter. Only Bang, the boy, was left, and the purpose of his remaining was to bear me a wicked message. Namely, that I had been so much away, both in the boat and on horseback, that the captain would not be bound to me, except to get home again, how I might. And if this could not be brought about, and I chose to take care of the ketch for the winter, two shillings a-week was what I might draw, also the wood on the wharf, so long as it would last for firing; and any fish I could catch with lines; and any birds I could shoot on the river, with a stone of rock-powder that was in the hold.

Bang was ashamed to deliver this message; and I cannot describe to you my wrath, as slowly I wrung it out of him. His head went into his neck almost, for fear of my taking it by the handles, which nature had provided in his two ears, and letting him learn (as done once before) that the mast had harder knots in it. But I always scorn injustice; and Bang was not to be blamed for this. So I treated him kindly; as I might wish a boy of my own to be treated by a man of large experience. And I let him go home to his mother's house, which was said to be somewhere within a league, and then I went to see what manners had been shown in the pickling-tub.

Here I found precious little indeed, and only the bottom stuff of coxcombs, tails, and nails, and over-harpings, thready bits, and tapeworm stuff, such as we pray deliverance from, unless it comes to famine. Nevertheless, in my now condition I grieved that there was not more of it. Because how could I get across to my native land again? All the small coasting-craft were laid up, as if they were china for shelfing, immediately after that gale of wind, which (but for me) must have capsized us. These fellows up the rivers never get a breath of seamanship. Sudden squalls are all they think of. Sea room, and the power of it, they would be afraid of.

At one time I thought of walking home, because none of these traders would venture it; and if I had only a guinea to start with on the road to Bristol, nothing could have stopped me. For, say what I might to myself about it, and reason however carefully, I could not reconcile with my conscience these things that detained me. The more I considered only three half-crowns, and the mere chance of wild-ducks on the river, the less I perceived how my duty lay, and the more it appeared to be movable. And why was I bound to stop here like this, when their place was to take me home again, according to stipulation? To apply to the mayor, as I knew, was useless, especially now that I owed him a bill; as for the bench of magistrates, one had already a bias against me, because I went into a wood one night to watch an eclipse of the moon, and took my telescope; which they all swore was a gun! Being disappointed with the moon's proceedings, I slammed up my telescope hastily, and at the same time puffed my pipe; and there was a fellow on watch so vile as to swear to the sound and the smoke of a gun! And this fellow proved to be a Welshman of the name of Llewellyn, and a cousin of mine within seven generations! I acquit him of knowing this fact at the time; and when in cross-examination I let him know it, and nobody else, he came back to his duty, and swore white all the black he had sworn before. Nevertheless I did not like it (though acquitted amidst universal applause) on account of the notoriety; and finding him one night upon the barge walk, and his manners irritating, I was enabled to impress him with a sense of consanguinity. And after that I might bear my telescope, and take observations throughout the coverts, whenever the pheasants did not disturb me.

This privilege, and a flight of wild-ducks, followed by a team of geese, and rumours even of two wild swans, moderated my desire to be back at home again. There no man can get a shot, except in very bitter weather, or when the golden plovers come in, unless he likes to take on himself a strong defiance of public opinion. Because Colonel Lougher is so kind, and so forbears to prosecute, that to shoot his game is no game at all, and shames almost any man afterwards. And the glory of all that night-work is, the sense of wronging somebody.

Moreover, a little thing occurred, which, in my doubt of conclusion, led me to stay a bit longer. Some people may think nothing of it, but a kind touch takes a hold on me. I have spoken of a boy, by the name of Bang, possessing many good qualities, yet calling for education. Of this I had given him some little, administered not to his head alone, but to more influential quarters; and the result was a crop of gratitude watered by humility. When he went home for the winter months, I expected to hear no more of him, having been served in that manner often by boys whom I have corrected. Therefore all who have ever observed the want of thankfulness in the young, will enter into my feelings when an ancient woman, Bang's grandmother, hailed me in a shaky voice over the side of my ketch, with Bang in the distance watching her. Between her feet was a good large basket, which with my usual fine feeling I leaped out to ease her of. But on no account would she let me touch it, until she knew more about me.

"Be you the man?" she said.

"Madam," I answered, "I be the man."

"The man as goes on so wicked to Bang, for the sake of his soul hereafter?"

"Yes, madam, I am he who clothed in the wholesome garb of severity a deep and parental affection;" for now I smelled something uncommonly good.

"Be you the chap as wolloped him?"

"That I can proudly say I am."

"Look 'e see, here, this be for 'e, then!"

With no common self-approval, I observed what she turned out; although I longed much to unpack them myself, for fear of her spoiling anything. But she put me back in a wholesale manner, and spread it all out like a market-stand. And really it was almost enough to make a market of; for she was a very wiry old woman, and Bang had helped carry, as far as the wharf, when he saw me, and fled. Especially did I admire a goose, fat with golden fat upon him, trussed, and laid on stuffing-herbs. Also, a little pig for roasting, too young to object to it, yet with his character formed enough to make his brains delicious. And as for sausages—but no more.

The goodness of these things preserved me from going off on the tramp just yet. That is the last thing a sailor should do, though gifted with an iron-tipped wooden leg. The Government drove me into it once, when my wound allowed me to be discharged; but it took more out of my self-respect than ever I have recovered. And if I do anything under the mark (which, to my knowledge, I never do), it dates from the time the King drove me to alms. However, I never do dwell upon that, unless there is something wrong down in my hold; and when that is right, I am thankful again. And none of that ever befalls me, when I get my rations regular. But who cares to hear any more about me, with all these great things coming on? You may look on me now as nobody.

Because I fell so much beneath my own idea of myself, and all that others said of me, through my nasty want of strength, when Parson Chowne came over me. It is easy enough to understand that a man, in good-nature, may knock under to another man of good-nature also; all in friendship and in fun, and for the benefit of the world. But for a man of intellect not so very far under the average—as will now be admitted of me, in spite of all inborn diffidence—as well as a man of a character formed and framed by experience, now to be boarded and violently driven under hatches, without any power to strike a blow, by a man who was never on board of a ship—at any rate to my knowledge; to think of this and yet not help it, made me chafe like a fellow in irons.

There was one thing, however, that helped to make me put up with my present position a little, and that was my hope to be truly of service to my genuine benefactor, poor Sir Philip Bampfylde. This old gentleman clearly was not going on very comfortably; and Parson Chowne had given me to understand, without any words, that the great chest landed at the end of his house, was full of arms and all other treason. These were to be smuggled in, after the Captain's departure; and the Captain would not enter the house, through fear of the servants suspecting something.

I could not reconcile this account with what I had seen the young lady do, and the Captain's mode of receiving it; but as I would not tell the Parson a word about that young lady, I could not make that objection to him. Nor did I say, though I might have done so, that I would not and could not believe for a moment that any British naval captain would employ his ship and crew for a purpose of high treason to his lawful master. That Parson Chowne should dare to think that I would swallow such stuff as that, made me angry with myself for not having contradicted him. But all this time I was very wise, and had no call to reproach myself. Seldom need any man repent for not having said more than he did; and never so needeth a Welshman.

And now, though I still took observation of Narnton Court (as in honour bound to deserve my salary), and though the

Parson still rode down, and went the round of the deck at
times when nobody could expect him; yet it was not in my
nature to be kept from asking something as to all these people.
You may frighten a man, and scare his wits, and keep him
under, and trample on him, and even beat his feelers down,
and shut him up like a jellyfish; but, after all this, if he is a
man, he will want to know the reason. For this makes half of
the difference between man and the lower animals:—the latter,
when punished, accept it as a thing that must befall them;
and so do the negroes, and all proper women: but a man
always wants to know why it must be; though it greatly
increases his trouble to ask, and still more to tell it again, if
you please.

Sir Philip Bampfylde, as every one said, was a very nice
gentleman indeed, the head of an ancient family, and the
owner of a large estate. Kind, moreover, and affable, though
perhaps a little stately, from having long held high command
and important rank in the army. Some years ago he had
attained even to the rank of general, which is the same thing
among land-forces as an admiral is with us; and he was so
proud of this position that he always wished to be so addressed, rather than by the title which had been so long in
the family. For his argument was that he had to thank good
fortune for being a baronet, whereas good conduct and perseverance alone could have made him a general. Now if these
had made him an admiral, I would always entitle him so; as
it is, I shall call him "Sir Philip," or "General," just as may
happen to come to my mind. Now this gentleman had two
sons, and no other children; the elder was Philip Bampfylde,
Esquire, and the younger Captain Drake Bampfylde, of whom I
have spoken already. Philip, the heir, had been appointed to
manage the family property, which spread for miles and miles
away; and this gave him quite enough to do, because his
father for years and years was away on foreign service. And
during this time Squire Philip married a lady of great beauty,
sent home by his father from foreign parts after rescue from
captivity. She was of very good extraction, so far as foreigners
can be, and a princess (they said) in her own right, though
without much chance of getting it. And she spoke the prettiest broken English, being very sensitive.

Well, everything thus far went purely enough, and the lady
had brought him a pair of twins, and was giving good promise
of going on, and everybody was pleased with her, and most of

all her husband, and Sir Philip was come home from governorship, but only on leave of absence, and they were trying hard to persuade him now to retire and live in peace, when who should come with his evil luck to spoil everything, but Drake Bampfylde? How it came to pass was not clearly known, at least to the folk on our side of the river, or those whom I met in Barnstaple. And I durst not ask on the further side, that is to say around Narnton Court, because the Parson's spies were there. Only the old women felt pretty sure that they had heard say, though it might be wrong, that Captain Drake Bampfylde had drowned the children, some said by accident, some said on purpose, and buried them somewhere on Braunton Burrows. And the effect of this on the foreign lady, being as she was, poor thing, might have been foreseen almost. For she fell into untimely pains, and neither herself nor her babe survived, exactly as happened to my son's wife.

This was a very sad story, I thought, but they said that the worst of it still lay behind: for poor Squire Philip had been so upset by the hurry of all these misfortunes, that nobody knew what to do with him. He always had been a most warm-hearted man, foolishly fond of his wife and children, and of a soft and retiring nature. Moreover, he looked on his younger brother, who had seen so much more of the world than himself, and was of a bolder character, not with an elder son's usual carelessness, but with a thorough admiration. And when he found him behave in this manner (according, at least, to what every one said), and all for the sake of the property, without a sharp word between them, it went to his heart, in the thick of his losses, so that he was beside himself. He let his beard grow and his hair turn white, although he was not yet forty, and he put up the shutters of his room, and kept candles around him, and little dolls. He refused to see his brother Drake, and his father Sir Philip, and everybody, except his own attendant, and the nurse of his poor children. And finding this, the Captain left the house, as if cursed out of it.

The only one who took things bravely was the ancient General. Much as he grieved at the loss of his race, and extinction, perhaps, of the family, he swore that he never would be cast down, or doubt the honour of his favourite son, until that son confessed it. This Drake Bampfylde had never done, although the case was hard against him, and scarcely any one, except his father, now stood up for him. But of the few who still held him guiltless, was one especial comforter:

Isabel Carey to wit, a young lady of very good Devonshire family, left as a ward to Sir Philip Bampfylde, and waiting for three or four years more of age, to come into large estates in South Devon.

The general people did not know this; but I happened to get ahead of them; and having a knack in my quiet way of putting two and two together, also having seen the Captain, and shaped my opinions, I would have staked my boat against a cuttle-fish that he was quite innocent. If the children were found buried—although I could never quite get at this, but only a story of a man who had seen him doing it, as I shall tell hereafter—but even supposing them deep in the sand (which I was a little inclined to do, from trusting my spy-glass so thoroughly), yet there might have been other people quite as likely to put them there as that unlucky Captain Drake.

It has been my lot to sail under a great many various captains, not only whom I have hinted at in the days when I was too young for work, but whom I mean to describe hereafter in my far greater experiences; really finding (although I have tried to convince people to the contrary) that what they have told me was perfectly true, and that I come out far stronger and better whenever my reins are tried and proved; and my loins as sound as a bell, although hereditary from King David. Let that pass. I find one fault, and it is the only one to be found with me; it is that the style of our bards will come out, and spread me abroad in their lofty allusions.

To come back to these captains. I never found one who would do such a thing as kill and slay two children, much less dig their graves in the sand, and come home to dinner afterwards. And of all the captains I had seen, Drake Bampfylde seemed as unfit as any to do a thing of that dirtiness. However, as I have not too much trust in human nature (after the way it has used me, and worst of all when in the Government), I said to myself that it was important to know at what time this Captain Bampfylde won the love of that fine Miss Carey. Because, after that, he had no temptation to put the little ones out of the way; and I quite settled it in my own mind, that if they had set up their horses together, before the young children went out of the world, Captain Drake Bampfylde was not likely to have made them go so. For that fair maiden's estates, I was told, would feed four hundred people.

No one had seen this, exactly as I did, nor could I beat it into them; and I found from one or two symptoms that it was high time for me to leave off talking. Parson Chowne came down one night, as black as a tarred thunderbolt, and though he said nothing to let me know, I felt afraid of his meaning. Also Parson Jack rode down, in his headlong careless way, and filled his pipe from my tobacco-bag, and gave me a wink, and said, "Keep your mouth shut." It was always a pleasure to me to behold him; whatever his principles may have been, and if I could have said a word to stop him from his downward road, or to make it go less sudden, goodness knows I would have done it, at the risk of three half-crowns a-week.

CHAPTER XXXV.

THE POLITE FERRYMAN.

Now, for a man of my age and knowledge, keeping an eye on his own concerns, and under the eyes of a good many women (eager to have him, because confessed superior to the neighbourhood, yet naturally doubtful how much money would be wanted), for such a man to attend to things which could not concern him in any way, without neglecting what now he had found a serious matter at his time of life—this, to my mind, proves a breadth of sympathy rarely found outside of Wales.

Entering into these things largely, and desiring to do my best, having, moreover, nought else to do except among dabs and flounders, I was led by a naturally active mind to try to turn a penny; not for my own good so much as for the use of Bunny. Therefore, having the punt at command, and a good pair of oars, and a good pair of arms, what did I do but set up a ferry, such as had never been heard of before, and never might have been dreamed of, except for my intelligence? Because we had two miles to Barnstaple Bridge, and no bridge at all to be found below us, and a good many houses here and there, on either side of the river. And I saw that they must know one another, and were longing to dine or to gossip together, except for the water between them, or the distance to walk all the way by the bridge. So being left in this desolate state, and shamefully treated by Captain Fuzzy, and Bang's grandmother now neglecting me, at a period of sadness, while smoking a pipe, Providence gave me this brilliant idea.

I never had dreamed for a moment of settling without something permanent; and not even £30 a-year would tempt me to do any despite to my late dear wife's remembrance. A year and a day at the very least was I resolved to mourn for her: still, as the time was drawing on, I desired to have some prospect. Not to settle rashly, as young people do in such affairs (which really should be important), but to begin to feel about, and put the price against the weight, and then take time to think about it. Only I had made up my mind not to look twice at the very richest and most beautiful Methodist. Enough had I had for my life of them, and the fellows that come after them: Church of England, or Church of Rome, for me this time at any rate; with preference to the latter because having no chapel in our neighbourhood.

And I worked this ferry, if you will believe me, not for the sake of the twopence both ways, half so much as because of my thoughts of the confidence that I must create. I knew for I won't say forty years, but at any rate good thirty, what women are the very moment they must needs come into a boat. The very shyest and wisest of them are at the mercy of a man right out. And I never could help believing that they come for that very reason. I know all their queerness of placing their toes, and how they fetch their figures up, and manage to hitch their petticoats, and try to suppose they are quite on a balance, and then go down plump on the nearest thwart, and pretend that they did it on purpose. Nevertheless they are very good; and we are bound to make the best of them.

When I told Parson Chowne of my ferry-boat, rather than let him find it out, which of course must have happened immediately, a quick gleam of wrath at my daring to do such a thing without consulting him moved in the depth of his great black eyes. At least I believed so, but was not sure; for I never could bear to look straight at his eyes, as I do to all other people, especially Anthony Stew, Esquire. I thought that my ferry would be forbidden; but with his usual quickness he saw that it might serve his purpose in several ways. Because it would help to keep me there, as well as account for my being there, and afford me the best chance in the world of watching the river traffic. So he changed his frown to an icy smile, such as I never could smile at, and said—

"Behold now what good-luck comes of my service! Only remember, no fares to be taken when the tide serves for you know what. And especially no gossiping."

This being settled to my content, I took a great peace of loose tarpaulin out of the hold of the Rose of Devon, and with a bucket of thick lime-whiting explained to the public in printing letters, each as large as a marlin-spike, who I was, and of what vocation, and how thoroughly trustworthy. And let any one read it, and then give opinion in common fairness, whether any man capable of being considered a spy would ever have done such a thing as this:—

"David Llewellyn, Mariner of the Royal Navy, Ferryman to King George the IIId. Each way or both ways only Twopence. Ladies put carefully over the Mud. Live Fish on hand at an hour's notice, and of the choicest Quality." This last statement was not quite so accurate as I could have desired. To oblige the public, I kept the fish too long on hand occasionally, because I never had proper notice when it might be wanted. And therefore no reasonable person ever took offence at me.

One fine day towards the frosty time, who should appear at my landing-stage on the further side of the river, just by the lime-kiln not far from the eastern end of Narnton Court—who but a beautiful young lady with her maid attending her? The tide was out, and I was crossing with a good sixpennyworth, that being all that my boat would hold, unless it were of children. And seeing her there, I put on more speed, so as not to keep her waiting. When I had carried my young women over the mud and received their twopences, I took off my hat to the fair young lady, who had kept in the background, and asked to what part I might have the honour of conveying her ladyship.

"I am not a ladyship," she answered, with a beautiful bright smile; "I am only a common lady; and I think you must be an Irishman."

This I never am pleased to hear, because those Irish are so untruthful; however, I made her another fine bow, and let her have her own way about it.

"Then, Mr Irishman," she continued; "you are so polite, we will cross the water. No, no, thank you," as I offered to carry her; "you may carry Nanette, if she thinks proper. Nanette has the greatest objection to mud; but I am not quite so particular." And she tripped with her little feet over the bank too lightly to break the green cake of the ooze.

"You sall clave me, my good man," said Nanette, who was rather a pretty French girl; "Mamselle can afford to defigure ner dress; but I can no such thing do at all."

Meanwhile the young lady was in the boat, sitting in the stern-sheets like a lieutenant, and laughing merrily at Nanette, who was making the prettiest fuss in the world, not indeed with regard to her legs, which an English girl would have considered first, but as to her frills and fripperies; and smelling my quid, she had no more sense than to call me a coachman, or something like it. However, I took little heed of her, although her figure was very good; for I knew that she could not have sixpence, and scarcely a hundred a-year would induce me to degrade myself down to a real French wife. For how could I expect my son ever to be a sailor?

Now as I pulled, and this fine young lady, who clearly knew something about a boat, nodded her head to keep time with me, and showed her white teeth as she smiled at herself, my own head was almost turned, I declare; and I must have blushed, if it could have been that twenty years of the fish-trade had left that power in me. Because this young lady was so exactly what my highest dreams of a female are, and never yet realised in my own scope. And her knowledge of a boat, and courage, and pleasant contempt of that French chit who had dared to call me a "coachman," when added to her way of looking over the water with fine feeling (such as I very often have, and must have shown it long ago), also the whole of this combined with a hat of a very fine texture indeed, such as I knew for Italian, and a feather that curled over golden pennon of hair in the wind like a Spanish ensign; and not only these things, but a face, and manner, and genuine beauty of speech, not to be found in a million of women,—after dwelling on all these things both steadily and soberly, over my last drop of grog, before I went into my berth that night, and prayed for the sins of the day to go upward, what do you think I said on the half-deck, and with all the stars observing me—"I'm damned if I'll serve Parson Chowne any more." I said it, and I swore it.

And when I came to think of it, in a practical manner, next morning, and to balance the ins and outs, and what I might come to, if thus led astray, by a man in holy orders (yet whose orders were all unholy, at any rate, such as he gave to me), and when I reflected on three half-crowns for finding me in everything, and then remembered how I had turned two guineas in a day, when poor Bardie came to me, and with a conscience as clear as a spent cuttlefish; and never a sign of my heels behind me, when squeamish customers sat down to dinner;

also good Mother Jones with sweet gossip, while my bit of flesh was grilling, and my little nip of rum, and the sound of Bunny snoring, while I smoked a pipe and praised myself; also the pleasure of doubting whether they could do without me at the " Jolly " through the wall, and the certain knowledge how the whole of the room would meet me, if I could deny myself enough to go among them;—these things made me lose myself, as in this sentence I have done, in longing to find old times and places, and old faces, once again, and some one to call me " Old Dyo."

Now who would believe that the whole of all this was wrought in my not very foolish mind, by the sight of a beautiful high-bred face, and the sound of a very sweet softening voice? Also the elegant manner in which she never asked what the passage would come to, but gave me a bright and true half-crown for herself and that frippery French girl. I must be a fool; no doubt I am, when the spirit of ancestors springs within me, spoiling all trade; as an inborn hiccough ruins the best pipe that ever was filled. For though I owed three tidy bills, I had no comfort until I drilled a little hole in that bright half-crown, and hung it with my charms and knobs and caul inside my Jersey. And thus the result became permanent, and my happiness was in my heart again, and all my self-respect leaped up as ready to fight as it ever had been, when I had shaped a firm resolve to shake off Chowne, like the devil himself.

I cannot imagine a lower thing than for any man to say— and some were even to that degree base—that I thus resolved upon calculation, and ability now to get on without him, and balance of his three half-crowns against the income of my ferry, with which I admit that his work interfered. Neither would any but a very vile man dare to cast reflections upon me, for having created by skill and eloquence a small snug trade in the way of fish, and of those birds which are sent by the Lord in a casual way, and without any ownership, for the good of us unstated folk. While I deny as unequivocally as if upon oath before magistrates, that more than fifty hares and pheasants— but there! I may go on for ever rebutting those endless charges and calumnies, which the mere force of my innocent candour seems to strike out of maliciousness. Once for all, I never poach, I never stab salmon, I never smuggle, I never steal boats, I never sell fish with any stink outside of it,—and how can I tell what it does inside, or what it may do afterwards?

I never tell lies to anybody who does not downright call for it; and you may go miles and miles, I am sure, to find a more thoroughly honourable, good-hearted, brave, and agreeable man.

Now I did not mean to say any of this, when I began about it; neither am I in the habit of deigning even to clear myself; but once beginning with an explanation, I found it the best to start clear again; because Parson Chowne, and my manner towards him (which for the life of me I could not help), also my service under him, and visit at his house, and so on, and even my liking for Parson Jack (after his sale to Satan, though managed without his privity), as well as my being had up for shooting pheasants with a telescope;—these and many other things, too small now to dwell upon, may have spread a cloud betwixt my poor self and my readers; and a cloud whose belly is a gale of wind.

It is not that I ever could do any unworthy action. It is simply that I can conceive the possibility of it seeming so to those who have never met me; and who from my over-candid account (purposely shaped dead against myself) may be at a loss to enter into the delicacies of my conduct. But you shall see by-and-by; and seeing is believing.

Now it was a lucky thing, that on the very morning after I had made my mind up so, and before it was altered much, down came Chowne in a tearing mood, with his beautiful black mare all in a lather. I was on board of the Rose of Devon, smoking my first after-breakfast pipe, and counting my cash from the ferry business of the day before—except, of course, the half-crown which lay among my charms, and strengthened me. The ketch was aground in a cradle of sand, which she had long ago scooped for herself, and which she seldom got out of now, except just to float at the top of the springs. She stood almost on an even keel, unless it were blowing heavily. Our punt (or rather I should call her mine by this time, for of course she most justly belonged to me, after all their breach of contract, and desertion of their colours)—at any rate, there she was afloat and ready for any passenger, while my notice to the public flapped below the mainboom of the ketch.

"You precious rascal," cried Chowne, from the wharf, with his horse staring at the tarpaulin, and half inclined to shy from it; "who was it crossed the river twice in your rotten ferry-boat yesterday?"

"Please your Reverence," I answered, calmly puffing at my pipe, which I knew would still more infuriate him: "will you

Reverence give me time to think? Let me see—why, let me see—there was Mother Pugsley from up the hill, and Mother Bidgood from round the corner, and Farmer Skinner, and young Joe Thorne, and Eliza Tucker from the mill, and Jenny Stribling, and Honor Jose, first cousin to our captain, and—well I think that's nearly all that I know the name of, your Reverence."

"I thought you knew me better now than to lie to me, Llewellyn. You know what I mean as well as I do."

"To be sure, to be sure, your Reverence; I beg your pardon altogether. I ought to have remembered poor old Nanny Gotobed."

The wharf was high, and our gunwale below it; he put his mare at it, clapped in the spurs, and before I could think or even wonder, he had me by the nape of the neck, with his knuckles grinding into me, and his face, now ashy white with rage, fixed on me, so that I could not move.

"Will you tell me?" he cried.

"I won't," said I: crack came his hunting-whip round my sides—crack, and wish, and crack again; then I caught up a broken spar, and struck him senseless over the tail of his horse. The mare ramped all round the half-deck mad, then leaped ashore, with her legs all bloody, and scoured away with her saddle off.

Chowne lay so long insensible, that a cold sweat broke through the heat of my wrath, to think that I had killed him. And but for his hat, I had done no less, for I struck with the strength of a maddened man, and the spar was of heavy Dantzic. I untied his neckcloth, and ran for water, and propped him up, and bathed his forehead, although my hands were trembling so that I could scarcely hold the swab. And now as I watched his pale stern face without a weak line in it even from fainting, I was amazed at having ever dared to lift hand against him. But what Royal Navyman could ever put up with horsewhip?

At last he fetched a strong breath, and opened the usual wickedness of his eyes, and knew me at once, but did not know exactly what had befallen him. I have had a good deal to do with knocking down a good many men, and know that such is their usual practice; and that if you take them promptly then, they will sometimes believe things very freely. Therefore I said, "Your Reverence has contrived to hit yourself very hard, but I hope you will soon be better again."

"Hit myself! Why, somebody hit me!" and then he went off again into a doze, from the buzzing of his head perhaps

Perceiving that he would soon come to himself, and desiring to be acquitted of any violent charge of battery, I jumped down into the hold and fetched an old boom that was lying there, and hoisted it up in the tackle-fall, so as to hang at about the right height. Moreover, I put the spar well away; and then, with a sluice of water, I fetched his Reverence back to himself again. I found him very correct this time, and beginning to look about pretty briskly, therefore I turned him away and said, "Your Reverence must not look at it—it will make your head go round again; either shut your eyes or look away, your Worship."

He seemed not to notice me, so I went on, "Your Reverence has had a narrow escape. What a mercy your head is not broken! Your Reverence went to chastise me, and lo! your horse reared and threw your Reverence against that great boom which that lubberly Jose has left there ever since we broke cargo."

"You are a liar," he said; "you struck me. To the last day of your life you shall rue it."

The voice of his throat ran cold all through me, being so low and so cold itself; and the strength of his eyes was coming back, and the bitter disdain of his countenance. The devil, who wanted him for a rare morsel in the way of cannibalism, stood at my elbow; but luckily thought it sweeter not to hurry it. The foulest man on all God's earth, who made a scoff of mercy's self, lay at my mercy for a minute, defied it, took it, and hated it. For the sake of myself, I let him go. For the sake of mankind, I should have slain him.

CHAPTER XXXVI.

UNDER FAIRER AUSPICES.

KNOWING now what I had to expect from Parson Chowne and from all his train (whether clothed or naked), and even perhaps from Parson Jack, who lay beneath his thumb so much, and who could thrash me properly; I seized the chance of a good high tide, and gave a man sixpence to help me, and warped the Rose of Devon to a berth where she could float and swing, and nobody come a-nigh her without a boat or a swimming-bout. Because I knew from so many folk what a fiend I had to deal

with, and that his first resort for vengeance (haply through his
origin) generally was to fire. They told me that when he condescended to do duty in either church—for two he had, as I may
have said—all the farmers took it for a call to have their ricks
burned. They durst not stay away from church, to save the very
lives of them, nor could they leave their wives behind, on account
of the unclothed people : all they could hope was that no offence
had come from their premises, since last service. The service
he held just as suited his mood ; sometimes three months, and
the church-door locked ; sometimes three Sundays one after
the other, man, woman, and child demanded. Whenever this
happened, the congregation knew that the parish had displeased
him, and that he wanted them all in church ; while his boy was
at the stackyards. He never deigned to preach, but made the
prayers themselves a comedy, singing them up to the clerk's
"amen," and the neigh of his mare from the vestry.

I cannot believe even half that I hear from the very best
authority ; therefore I set nothing down which may be overcoloured. But the following story I know to be true, because
seven people have told it me, and not any two very different.
Two or three bishops and archdeacons (or deacons of arches, I
know not which, at any rate high free-masons) desired to know
some little more about a man in their jurisdiction eminent to
that extent, and equally notorious. They meant no harm at
all, but just to take a little feel of him. Because he had come
to visitation, once or twice when summoned, with his huntsman and his hounds, and himself in leathern breeches. There
must have been something amiss in this, or at any rate they
thought so ; and his lordship, a bishop just appointed, made
up his mind to tackle him. He came in a coach-and-four, and
wearing all his high canonicals, and they managed somehow to
get up the hill, and appear at Nympton Rectory. Then a footman struck the door with a gold stick well embossed ; and he
struck again, and he struck again, more in dudgeon every time.

Because no man had yet been seen, nor woman on the premises ; only dogs very wild and mad, but kept away from biting. "Strike again," said his lordship, nodding under his wig,
with some courtesy ; "we must never be impatient. Jemmy,
strike again, my lad." Jemmy struck a thundering stroke, and
out came Mrs Steelyard. She looked at them all, and then she
said, with her eyes full on the Bishop's, "Are you robbers, or
are you savages ? My master in that state and you do this !"
And they all saw that she could not weep, by reason of too

much sorrow. "It is the Lord Bishop," said the footman, keeping a little away from her. "Excellent female," began his Lordship, spreading his hands in a habit learned according to his duties, "tell your master that his *Jehoshaphat wishes to see him." "Mr Jehoshaphat," she replied, "you are just in time, and no more, sir. How we have longed for a minister! You are just in time and no more, sir. Will you have the kindness to come this way, and to step as quietly as you can?" His Lordship liked not the look of this; being, however, a resolute man, he followed the stony woman up the staircase, and into a bedroom with the window-curtains three quarters drawn. And here he found a pastille burning, and a lot of medicine bottles, and a Bible on the table open, and on it a pair of spectacles. In the bed lay some one, with a face of fire heavily blotched with bungs of black, and all his body tossing with spasms and weak groaning. "What means this?" asked his Lordship, drawing considerably nearer to the door. "Only the †plague," said the stony woman; "he was took with it yesterday; doctor says he may last two hours more almost, particular if he can get anybody to take the symptoms off him. I expect to be down with it some time to-night, because I feel the tingling. But your Highness will stop and help us." "I am damned if I will," cried the Bishop, sinking both manners and dignity in the violence of alarm; and he ran down the stairs at such a pace that his apron strings burst, and he left it behind, and he jumped into the coach with his two feet foremost, and slammed up the windows, and ordered full speed. Then Parson Chowne rose, and threw off his mask, and drew back the window-curtain, and sat in his hunting-clothes, and watched with his usual bitter smile the rapid departure of his foe. And he had the Bishop's apron framed, and hung it in the parsonage hall, from a red-deer's antlers, with the name and date below. And so of that Bishop he heard no more.

Now a man who had beaten three bishops, and all the archdeacons in the country, was of course tenfold of a match for me; and when he rode down smoothly to me, as he did in a few days' time, and never touched on our little skirmish, except with a sort of playful hit (so far as his haughty mind could play), and riding another horse without a word about the mis-

---

* † Diocesan.
† There are several entries of deaths from plague in parish registers of North Devon, circa 1790. Perhaps it was what they now call "black fever," the most virulent form of typhus.

chief which his favourite mare had taken, and demanded, as a matter of justice, that having quitted his service now, I should pay back seven-and-sixpence drawn in advance for wages, I was obliged to touch my hat, as if I had never made stroke at his, or put my knee upon him. He had flogged me to such purpose that I ever must admire him; for the flick of the boatswain's lash was a tickle compared to what Chowne took out of me; and if I must tell the whole truth, I was prouder of having knocked down such a wonderful man than of all of my victories put together. But one of my weak and unreasonable views of life is this, that having thrashed a man, I feel a great power of goodwill to him, and a desire to give him quarter, and the more so the less he cries for it.

But, on the whole, I was not so young after all that was said by everybody, as to imagine for a moment that I had felt the last of him. The very highest in the land had been compelled to yield to him: as when he turned out my Lord G——'s horses from the stabling ordered at Lord G——'s inn. Would such a man accept defeat from a crazy old mariner like me? Feeling my danger, and meaning never to knock under any more, I refused, as a matter of principle, to restore so much as a halfpenny; and if I understand law at all, he was bound to give me another week's wages, in default of notice. However, I could not get it; and therefore am glad to quit such trifles.

From all experience it was known that this man never hurried vengeance. He knew that he was sure to get it; and he liked to dwell upon it, thus prolonging his enjoyment by the means of hope. He loved, as in the case of that unfortunate Captain Vellacott, to persuade his enemies that he had forgiven, or at least forgotten them, and then to surprise them, and laugh to himself at their ignorance of his nature. So I felt pretty sure that I had some time till my life would be in danger. For, of course, he knew that my ferry business, growing in profit daily, would keep me within his reach for the present, over and above the difficulty of getting across the Channel now. However, he began upon me sooner than I expected, on account, perhaps, of my low degree.

But in the meanwhile, feeling sure that I could not stand worse with him than I did—desiring, moreover, to ease my conscience, and perhaps improve my income, by an act of justice—I crossed the river to Narnton Court, and getting among the servants nicely, sent word in to Miss Isabel Carey that the old ferryman begged leave to see her upon business most particular.

For, of course (although, in the hurry of things, I may have forgotten to mention it), the lovely young lady I ferried across, and whose name I was thrashed so for not betraying, was Captain Drake's sweetheart, the ward of Sir Philip.

One of the most hateful things in Chowne was, that he never did anything in the good old-fashioned manner, unless it were use of the horsewhip. And it now rejoiced my heart almost to be shown into a fine dark room, by the side of good long passages, with a footman going before me, and showing legs of a quite superior order, and then under my instructions boldly throwing an oaken door wide, and announcing, "Mr David Llewellyn, ma'am!"

For though I had left Felix Farley behind, from a sort of romantic bashfulness, I had seen in the hall a coloured gentleman, who seemed justly popular; therefore I had just dropped a hint (not meant to go any further) concerning my risk of life and fortitude for the sake of black men. And this made the women admire me, for it turned out that this worthy negro stood high in the house, and had saved some cash. The room which I entered was large and high, with an amazing number of books in it, and smelling exceeding learned. And there in a deep window sat the young lady, with the light from the river glancing on the bright elegance of her hair. And when she rose and came towards me, I felt uncommonly proud of having been even thrashed for her sake: nor did I wonder at Captain Drake's warm manner of proceeding, or at Chowne's resolve to keep so jealous a watch over her. Over and above her beauty, which was no business of mine, of course, she had such pretty eyebrows and so sweet a way of looking, that a thrill went to my experienced heart, in spite of all experience; and women seemed a different thing from what I was accustomed to.

Therefore I left her to begin; while I made bows, and felt afraid of giving offence by gazing. She, however, put me at my ease almost directly, having such a high-bred way, so clarified and gentle, that I neither could be distant nor familiar with her. Only to be quite at ease, like, respect, and love her. And this lady was only about seventeen! It is wonderful how they learn so much.

I need not follow all I said, or even what she said to me. Without for a moment sacrificing my true sense of dignity, I gave her to understand, very mildly, that I had seen something, and had taken a vague sense of its import, when I chanced to be after wild-ducks. Also that strong attempts had been made to set me spying after her, and that I might have yielded to them, but for my own lofty sense of being a victorious veteran, and the way in which I was conquered by her extraordinary beauty.

She seemed for a moment to doubt how far I should have touched that subject; and if I had only looked up she would have rung the bell decidedly. But I bowed, and kept down my eyelashes; which were grey now, and helped me much in paying innocent compliments to every kind of woman. Even in the bar of very first-rate public-houses have I been pressed to take, and not pay for, glasses even of ancient stingo, because of the way I have paid respects, and looked through my shadows afterwards. Therefore this young lady said, "I hardly know what to do or say. Mr Llewellyn, it is a strange tale. Why should any one watch me?"

"That is more than I can say, my lady. I only know that the thing is done, and by a very wicked man indeed."

"And you have found it out, as ferryman? How clever of you, to be sure! And how honest to come and tell me! You have been a royal sailor?"

"In the Royal Navy, ma'am! Our captains are the most noble men, so brave, and glorious, and handsome! If you could only see one of them!"

"Perhaps I have," she said, under her breath, being carried away by my description, as I hoped to do to her; and then she came back through a shading of colours to herself, and looked at me, as if to say, "Have you detected me now?" I touched my lock; and by no means seemed to have dreamed a suspicion of anything.

"You are a most worthy man," she said; "and wonderfully straightforward. None but a Royal Navy sailor could have behaved so nobly. In spite of all the bribes offered you——"

"No, no, no!" I cried; "nothing to speak of! nothing to speak of! What is a guinea and a half a-week when it touches a man's integrity?"

"Three guineas a-week you shall have at once; because you have behaved so nobly, and because you have fought for your country so, and been left with nothing (I think you said), with half of your lungs quite shot away, except twopence a-day to live upon!"

"One and eightpence farthing a-week, my lady; and to be signed by a clergyman; and twenty-eight miles to walk for it."

"It vexes me so to hear such things. Don't tell me any more of it. What is the use of having money except for the people who want it? Mr Llewellyn, you must try not to be offended."

I saw that there was something coming, but looked very grave about it. A man of my rank and mark must never be at all ready, and much less eager, to lay himself under any form of trifling obligation. And thoroughly as she had won me over, I tried very hard not to be offended, while she was going to a small black desk. If she had come thence with a guinea or two, my mind was made up to do nothing more than gracefully wave it back again, and show myself hurt at such ignorance of me. But now when she came with a £5 note (such as Sir Philip seemed to keep in stock), my duty to Bardie and Bunny rose as upright as could be before my eyes, and overpowered all selfish niceties. I would not make a fuss about it, lest I might hurt her feelings, but placed it in my pocket with a bow of silent gratitude. Perhaps my face conveyed to her that it was not the money I cared for; only to do what was just and right, as any British sailor must when delicately handled. Also her confidence in me was so thoroughly sweet and delicate, that I felt the whole of my heart wrapped up in saving her from her enemies. We made no arrangements about it; but I went into her service bodily, being left to my own discretion, as seemed due to my skill and experience. I was to keep the ferry going, because of the opportunities, as well as to lull suspicion, and always at dark I was bound to be (according to my own proposal) near the river front of the house, to watch against all wicked treachery. And especially if a spy of Chowne's should come sneaking and skulking there, whether in a boat or out of it, I gladly volunteered to thrash him within an inch of his foul base life. The bad man's name never passed between us; and indeed I may say that the lady forbore from committing herself against anybody, so that I was surprised to find such wit in one so youthful.

We settled between us that my duties were to begin that very day, and my salary of course to run, also how the lady was to let me know when wanted, and I to tell her when I discovered anything suspicious. And as I had been compelled to restore the Parson's gun to his gunmaker, Miss Carey led me to a place you might almost call an armoury, and bade me choose any piece I liked, and her own maid should place it where I could find it that same evening, as though it were to shoot wild-fowl for them. But she advised me on no account to have any talk with Nanette, or any servants of the household, whether male or female, not only because of the wicked reports and cruel slanders prevailing, but also that it might not be known how I was to act in her interest. And then having ordered me a good hot dinner in the butler's pantry, as often was done for poor people, she let me go once, and then called me back, and said, "Oh, nothing;" and then called me again, and said, looking steadily out of the window, "By the by, I have quite forgotten to say that there is a boat belonging to a ship commanded by a son of Sir Philip Bampfylde, a white boat, with three oars on each side, and sometimes an officer behind them. If they should happen to come up the river, or to go ashore upon business here, you need not—I mean, you will quite understand that no harm whatever is intended to me, and therefore that you may—you see what I mean."

"To be sure, to be sure, my lady. Of course I may quit my duty so long as there is a man-of-war's boat in the river; even the boldest and worst of men would venture nothing against you then."

"Quite so," she replied, looking bravely round, with as much of pride in her bright blue eyes as of colour on her soft fresh cheeks. So I made my best bow and departed.

CHAPTER XXXVII.

TWO POOR CHILDREN.

By this time I owe it to all the kind people who have felt some pity for our Bardie and her fortunes, to put off no longer a few little things which I ought to tell them. In the first place, they must not think of me, but look upon me as nobody (treat me, in fact, as I treat myself), and never ask what I knew just now, and what I came to know afterwards. Only to trust me (as now they must) to act in all things honourably, and with no regard to self; and not only that, but with lofty feeling, and a sense of devotion towards the members of the weaker sex.

Captain Drake Bampfylde was the most unlucky of born mortals. To begin with, he was the younger son of that very fine Sir Philip, and feeling that he had far more wit and enterprise than his elder brother, while thankful to nature for these endowments, he needs must feel amiss with her for having mismanaged his time of birth. Now please to observe my form of words. I never said that he did so feel, I only say that he must have done so, unless she had made him beyond herself; which, from her love for us, she hardly ever tries to do. However, he might have put up with that mistake of the goddess that sits cross-legged,—I have heard of her, I can tell you, and a ship named after her; though to spell her name would be a travail to me, fatal perhaps at my time of life,—I mean to say, at any rate, that young Drake Bampfylde might have managed to get over the things against him, and to be a happy fellow, if he only had common luck. But Providence having gifted him with unusual advantages of body, and mind, and so forth, seemed to think its duty done, and to leave him to the devil afterwards.

This is a bad way of beginning life, especially at too young an age to be up to its philosophy; and the only thing that can save such a man is a tremendous illness, or the downright love of a first-rate woman. Thence they recover confidence, or are brought into humility, and get a bit of faith again, as well as being looked after purely, and finding a value again to fight for, after abandoning their own. Not that Drake Bampfylde ever did slip into evil courses, so far as I could hear of him, or even give way to the sense of luck, and abandon that of duty. I am only saying how things turn out, with nineteen men out of twenty. In spite of chances, he may have happened just to be the twentieth. I know for sure that he turned up well, though vexed with tribulation. Evil times began upon him, when he was nothing but a boy. He fell into a pit of trouble through his education; and ever since from time to time new grief had overtaken him. A merrier little chap, or one more glad to make the best of things, could not be found; as was said to me by the cook, and also the parlour-maid. He would do things, when he came out among the servants, beautifully; and the maids used to kiss him so that his breath was taken away with pleasing them. And then he went to school, and all the maids, and boys, and men almost, came out to see the yellow coach, and throw an old shoe after him. This, however, did not help him, as was seriously hoped; and why? Because it went heel-foremost, from the stupidity of the caster. News came, in a little time, that there was mischief upward, and that Master Drake must be fetched home, to give any kind of content again. For he was at an ancient grammar-school in a town seven miles from Exeter, where everything was done truly well to keep the boys from fighting. Only the habit and tradition was that if they must fight, fight they should until one fell down, and could not come to the scratch again. And Drake had a boy of equal spirit with his own to contend against, not however of bone and muscle to support him thoroughly. But who could grieve, or feel it half so much as young Drake Bampfylde did, when the other boy, in three days' time, died from a buzzing upon his brain? He might have got into mischief now, even though he was of far higher family than the boy who had foundered instead of striking; but chiefly for the goodwill of the school, and by reason of the boy's father having plenty of children still to feed, and consenting to accept aid therein, that little matter came to be settled among them very pleasantly. Only the course of young Drake's life was changed thereby, as follows.

The plan of his family had been to let him get plenty of learning at school, and then go to Oxford Colleges and lay in more, if agreeable; and so grow into holy orders of the Church of England, well worth the while of any man who has a good connection. But now it was seen, without thinking twice, that all the disturbers and blasphemers of the Nonconformist tribe, now arising everywhere (as in dirty Hezekiah, and that greasy Hepzibah, who dared to dream such wickedness concerning even me), every one of these rogues was sure to cast it up against a parson, in his most heavenly stroke of preaching, that he must hold his hand, for fear of killing the clerk beneath him. And so poor Drake was sent to sea; the place for all the scape-goats.

Here ill fortune dogged him still, as its manner always is, after getting taste of us. He heeded his business so closely that he tumbled into the sea itself; and one of those brindle-bellied sharks took a mouthful out of him. Nevertheless he got over that, and fell into worse trouble. To wit, in a very noble fight between his Britannic Majesty's sloop of war "Hellgoblins," carrying twelve guns and two carronades (which came after my young time), and the French corvette "Heloise," of six-and twenty heavy guns, he put himself so forward that they trained every gun upon him. Of course those fellows can never shoot anything under the height of the moon, because they never stop to think; nevertheless he

contrived to take considerable disadvantage. By a random
shot they carried off the whole of one side of his whiskers;
and the hearing of the other ear fell off, though not involved
in it. The doctors could not make it out: however, I could
thoroughly, from long acquaintance with cannon-balls. Also
he had marks of powder under his skin, that would never come
out, being of a coarse-grained sort, and something like the bits
of tea that float in rich folks' tea-cups. Happening, as he did
by nature, to be a fine, florid, and handsome man, this powder
vexed him dreadfully. Nevertheless the ladies said, loving
powder of their own, that it made him look so much nicer.

That, however, was quite a trifle, when compared to his
next misfortune. Being gazetted to a ship, and the whole
crew proud to sail under him, he left the Downs with the
wind abaft, and all hands in high spirits. There was nothing
those lads could not have done; and in less than twelve hours
they could do nothing. A terrible gale from south-west arose;
in spite of utmost seamanship they were caught in the callipers
of the Varne, and not a score left to tell of it.

These were things to try a man, and prove the stuff inside
him. However, he came out gallantly. For being set afloat
again, after swimming all night and half a day, he brought
into the Portland Roads a Crappo ship of twice his tonnage,
and three times his gunnage; and now his sailors were delighted, having hope of prize-money. That they never got, of
course (which, no doubt, was all the better for their constitutions), but their knowledge of battle led them to embark
again with him, having sense (as we always have) of luck, and
a crooked love of a man whose bad luck seems to have taken
the turn. And yet their judgment was quite amiss, and any
turn taken was all for the worse. Captain Bampfylde did a
thing, which even I, in my hotter days, would rather have
avoided. He ran a thirty-two gun frigate under the chains of
a sixty-four. He thought that they must shoot over him,
while he laid his muzzles to her water-line, and then carried
her by boarding.

Nothing could have been finer than this idea of doing it,
and with eight French ships out of nine, almost, he must have
succeeded. But once more his luck came over, like a cloud,
and darkened him. The Frenchmen had not only courage
(which they have too much of), but also what is not their
gift, with lucky people against them, self-command and steadiness. They closed their lower ports, and waited for the

Englishmen to come up. They knew that the side of their ship fell in, like the thatch of a rick, from the lower ports, ten feet above the enemy. They had their nettings ready, and a lively sea was running.

It grieves as well as misbecomes me to describe the rest of it. The Englishmen swore with all their hearts at their ladders, the sea, and everything, and their captain was cast down between the two ships, and compelled to dive tremendously; in a word it came to this, that our people either were totally shot and drowned, or spent the next Sunday in prison at Brest.

Now here was a thing for a British captain, such as the possibility of it never could be dreamed of. To have lost one ship upon a French shoal, and the other to a Frenchman! Drake Bampfylde, but for inborn courage, must have hanged himself outright. And, as it was, he could not keep from unaccustomed melancholy. And, when he came home upon exchange, it was no less than his duty to abandon pleasure now, and cheerfulness, and comfort; only to consider how he might redeem his honour.

In the thick of this great trouble came another three times worse. I know not how I could have borne it, if it had been my case, stoutly as I fight against the public's rash opinions. For this Captain was believed, and with a deal of evidence, to have committed slaughter upon his brother's children, and even to have buried them. He found it out of his power to prove that really he had not done it, nor had even entertained a wish that it might happen so. Everybody thought how much their dying must avail him; and though all had a good idea of his being upright, most of them felt that this was nothing, in such strong temptation. I have spoken of this before, and may be obliged again to speak of it; only I have rebutted always, and ever shall rebut, low ideas. Yet if truly he did kill them, was he to be blamed or praised, for giving them good burial? The testimony upon this point was no more than that of an unclad man, which must of course have been worthless; until they put him into a sack, and in that form received it. This fellow said that he was coming home towards his family, very late one Friday night; and he knew that it was Friday night because of the songs along the road of the folk from Barnstaple market. He kept himself out of their way, because they had such a heap of clothes on; and being established upon the sands, for the purpose of washing his wife and children, who never had seen water before, and had therefore become visited, he made a short cut across the sands to the hole they had all helped to scoop out, in a stiff place where some roots grew. This was his home; and not a bad one for a seaside visit. At any rate he seemed to have been as happy there as any man with a family can experience; especially when all the members need continual friction.

This fine fellow was considering how he could get on at all with that necessary practice, if the magistrates should order all his frame to be covered up; and fearing much to lose all chance of any natural action—because there was a crusade threatened—he lay down in the moonlight, and had a thoroughly fine roll in the sand. Before he had worn out this delight, and while he stopped to enjoy it more, he heard a sound, not far away, of somebody digging rapidly. Or at any rate, if it was not digging, it was something like it. The weather was wonderfully hot, so that the rushes scarcely felt even cool to his breast and legs. In that utterly lonely place (for now the road was a mile behind him, and the sands without a track, and the stars almost at midnight), there came upon him sudden fright, impossible to reason with. He had nothing to be robbed off, neither had he enemy; as for soul, he never yet had heard of any such ownership. But an unknown latitude of terror overpowered him. Nothing leads a man like fear; and this poor savage, though so naked, was a man of some sort.

Therefore, although he would far liefer have skulked off in the crannying shadows, leaving the moon to see to it, he could by no means find the power to withdraw himself like that. The sound came through the rushes, and between the moonlit hillocks so, that he was bound to follow it. Crouching through the darker seams, and setting down his toe-balls first, as naked feet alone can do, step by step he drew more near, though longing to be further off. And still he heard the heel-struck spade, and then a cast, and then the sullen sound of sand a-sliding. Then he came to a hollow place, and feared to turn the corner.

Being by this time frightened more than any words can set before us, back he stroked his shaggy hair, and in a hat of rushes laid his poor wild face for gazing. And in the depth of the hollow where the moonlight scarcely marked itself, and there seemed a softer herbage than of dry junk-rushes, but the banks combed over so as to bury the whole three fathoms deep at their very first subsiding—a man was digging a small deep grave.

On the slope of the bank, and so as to do no mischief any longer, two little bodies lay put back; not flung anyhow; but laid, as if respect was shown to them. Each had a clean white night-gown on, and lay in decorous attitude, only side by side, and ready to go into the grave together. The man who was digging looked up at them, and sighed at so much necessity; and then fell to again, and seemed desirous to have done with it.

So was the naked man who watched him, fright by this time overcreeping even his very eyeballs. He blessed himself for his harmlessness, and ill-will to discipline, all the way home to his own sand-hill; and a hundredfold when he came to know (after the dregs of fright had cleared) that he had seen laid by for coolness, by this awful gravedigger, the cocked-hat of a British Captain in the Royal Navy. This hat he had seen once before, and wondered much at the use of it, and obtained an explanation which he could not help remembering. And fitting this to his own ideas, he was as sure as sure could be, that Captain Bampfylde was the man who was burying the children.

Now when this story reached the ears of poor old Sir Philip, whether before or after his visit to our country matters not, it may be supposed what his feelings were of sorrow and indignation. He sent for this savage, who seemed beyond the rest of his tribe in intelligence, as indeed was plainly shown by his coming to bathe his family, and in spite of all the difference of rank and manner between them, questions manifold he put, but never shook his story. And then he sent to Exeter for a lawyer, thoroughly famous for turning any man inside out and putting what he pleased inside him. But even he was altogether puzzled by this man in the sack, wherein he now lived for decorum's sake, however raw it made him. And the honest fellow said that clothing tempted him so to forsake the truth, when he could not tell his own legs in it, that it sapped all principle.

That question is not for me to deal with, nor even a very much wiser man, except that my glimpses of foreign tribes have all been in favour of nudity. And the opposite practice is evidently against all the bent of our civilised women, who are perpetually rebelling, and more and more eager to open their hearts to their natural manifestation. For the heart of a woman is not like a man's, "desperately wicked;" and how can they prove this unless they show its usual style of working? Only the other day I saw——but back I must go to the heart of my tale. In a word, this fine male savage convinced every one he came into contact with (which after his bathing was permitted, if the other man bathed afterwards), that truly, surely, and with no mistake he must have seen something. What it was became naturally quite another question; and upon this head no two people could be found of one opinion. But though it proved an important point, I will not dwell too long on it.

Captain Drake's boat, to my firm belief, never came once up the river now; and I thought that my beautiful young lady seemed a little grieved at this. Every now and then she crossed, on her way to see old women, and even that old Mother Bang; and the French maid became a plague to me. She had laid herself out to obtain me, because of the softness with which I carried her; and her opposition to my quid naturally set her heart all the more upon me. I will not be false enough to say that I did not think of her sometimes, because she really did go on in a tantalising manner. And we seemed to have between us something, when her lady's back was turned. However, she ought to have known that I never mean anything by this; and if she chose to lie back like that, and put her red lips toppermost, the least thing she should have done was first to be up to our manners and customs.

CHAPTER XXXVIII.

A FINE OLD GENTLEMAN.

When I came to look round upon this state of things, and consider it, I made up my mind to tempt Providence, or rather perhaps the most opposite Power, by holding on where I was, in spite of the Parson and all his devices. This was a stupid resolve, and one on which he had fully calculated. I was getting a little perhaps fond of Nanette, though not quite so much as she fancied; feeling unable to pin my faith to a thing she had whispered into my ear; to wit, that she would thrice soon inherit one three grand money, hunder tousand, more than one great strong man could leeft. I asked her to let me come and try; and she said it was possible to be. Having a thorough acquaintance with Crappos, and the small wretched particles of their money, I did not attach much importance to this; for I like our King's face, and they have not got it; and they seem to stamp their stuff anyhow. But in spite of all prejudice, it would be well to look a little into it; particularly as this girl (whether right or wrong in thousands) had a figure not to be denied, when you came home to her.

Nevertheless I am not the man to part with myself at random; and there was a good farmer's daughter now, solid, and two-and-thirty—which is my favourite ship to sail in, handy, strong, and with guns well up—this young woman crossed the ferry, at eightpence a-day, for my sake; and I thought of retaining a lawyer to find what might be her prospects. She was by no means bad to look at, when you got accustomed; and her nature very kind, and likely to see to Bunny's clothes; also she never contradicted; which is cotton-wool to one who ever has rheumatics. But I did not wish to pay six-and-eightpence, and then be compelled to lose eightpence a-day, in order to steer clear of her. So I ferried both her and Nanette alike, and let them encounter one another, and charged no difference in their weight.

Nothing better fits a man, for dealing with the womankind, than to be well up in fish. Now I found the benefit of that knowledge where I never looked for it; and I knew the stale from the fresh—though these come alike in the pickle of matrimony—also (which is far more to the point) the soft roes from the hard roes. These you cannot change; but must persuade yourself to like whichever you happen to get of them. And that you find out afterwards.

While I was dwelling upon these trifles, and getting on well with my serious trade, working my ferry, and catching salmon so as to amaze the neighbourhood, also receiving my well-earned salary from the fair Mistress Isabel, and surprising the public-houses every night with my narratives—in a word, becoming the polar-star of both sides of the river—a thing befell me which was quite beyond all sense of reason.

Through wholesome fear of Parson Chowne, and knowledge of his fire-tricks, I kept the Rose of Devon in a berth of deep fresh water; where a bulk of sand backed up, and left a large calm pool of river. Here the dimpling water scarcely had the life to flow along—when the tide was well away; and scarcely brought a single bubble big enough to break upon us. According to the weather, so the colour of the water was. Only when you understood, it seemed to please you always.

One night I was not asleep, but getting very near it; setting in my mind afloat (as I felt the young tide flowing) thoughts or dreams, or lighter visions than the lightest dream that flits, of, about, concerning, touching, anyhow regarding, or, in any lightest side-light, gleaming, who can tell, or glancing from the chequers of the day-work. Suddenly a great explosion blew me out of my berth, and filled the whole of the cuddy with blaze and smoke. I lay on the floor half-stunned, and with only sense enough for wondering. Then Providence enabled me, on the strength of the battles I had been through, to get on my elbow, and look around. Everything seemed quite odd and stupid for a little while to me. I neither knew where I was, nor what had happened or would happen me.

It may have been half an hour, or it may have been only half a minute, before I was all alive again, and able to see to the mischief. Then I found that a very rude thing had been done, and a most unclerical action, not to be lightly excused, and wholly undeserved on my part. A good-sized kettle of gunpowder had been cast into my cuddy, possibly as a warning to me; but, to say the least, a dangerous one. My wrath overcame all fear so much, that in spite of the risk of meeting others, I rushed through the smoke and up the ladder, and seized my gun from its sling on the deck, and gazed (or rather I should say stared) in every direction around me. But whether from the darkness of the night, or the stinging and stunning turmoil in my eyes and upon my brain, I could not descry any moving shape, or any living creature. And this even added to my alarm, so that I got very little more sleep that night, I do assure you.

However, I kept my own counsel about it, even from my lady patroness, resolving to maintain a sharp look-out, and act as behoved a gallant Cymro, thrown amongst a host of savages. To this intent, I took our tiller, which was just about six feet long, and entirely useless now, and I put a bit of a bottom to it, so as to stand quite decently, and fixed a cross-tressel for shoulders, and then dressed it up so with my old fishing-suit and a castaway hat to encourage my brains, that really, though the thing was so grave, I could not help laughing at myself; in the dusk it was so like me. When the labours of the day were over, and the gleam of the water deadened, I set up this other fine Davy Llewellyn on board the ketch, now here now there, sometimes leaning over the bulwarks in contemplation of the river (which was my favourite attitude, from my natural turn for reflection), sometimes idly at work with a rope, or anything or nothing, only so as to be seen from shore, and expose to the public his whereabouts. Meanwhile I crouched in a ditch hard by, and with both barrels loaded.

You will say this was an unchristian thing, especially as I suspected strongly that my besiegers wore naked backs, and would therefore receive my discharge in full. I will not argue that point, but tell you (in common fairness to myself, and to prevent any slur of the warm affection, long subsisting between all who have cared to listen to me and my free self) that whenever I hoped for a chance at those fellows, I drew the duck-shot from the first barrel, and put a light charge of snipe-shot in, which no man could object to. The second barrel was ready, in case that the worst should come to the worst, as we say.

Now it is a proof of my bad luck, and perhaps of my having done a thing below the high Welsh nature, that Providence never vouchsafed me a single shot at any one of them. The more trouble I took, the less they came; until I could scarcely crook my fingers through the rheumatics they brought on me. Night after night, I said to myself, "If it only pleases the Lord to save me from the wiles of this anointed one, I vow to go back to my duty, and teach those other young chits of boys their work." For I had observed (though I would not tell it, except in a rheumatic twinge) that even Captain Bampfylde's men had lost the style of drawing oars through the water properly, and as I used to give the tune, five-and-twenty years agone.

It is needless to say, that after all the close actions I have conquered in, a canister of gunpowder was nothing to disturb me. But as they might do worse next time, whether in joke or earnest, I made me a hutch of stout strong oak, also cut the bulk-head out, and freed myself into the hold at once, upon any unjust disturbance. Nigh me was my double gun, heavily shotted at bed-time, and the spar which had knocked down Parson Chowne, and might have to do it again perhaps. And now I began to persuade myself into happy sleep again; for my nature is not vindictive.

One night I lay broad awake, perhaps from having shot a curlew, and eaten him, without an onion sewn inside while roasting, but he had been so hard to shoot that I was full of zeal to dine upon him, and had no onion handy. Whether it were so or not, I lay awake and thought about the strange things now come over me. To be earning money at a very noble rate indeed; to be winning the attentions of it may be ten young women (each of whom believed that never had I been in love before); and to be establishing a business which could scarcely fail of growing to a public-house with benches and glass windows looking down upon the river; and yet with all this prospect brewing, scarcely to have a moment's peace! What a lucky thing for Parson Chowne that I have no cold black blood in me! In this medley of vague thoughts (such as all men of large brain have, and even myself when the moon ordains it) a strong and good idea struck me, and one to be dwelled upon to-morrow; and if then approved, to be carried out immediately. This was no less than to beg an audience of Sir Philip Bampfylde himself, and tell him all that I ever had seen of Chowne and his devices, and place Sir Philip on his guard, and learn maybe a little of the many things that puzzled me. Of course I had thought of this before; but for several reasons had forborne to carry it any further. In the first place, it seemed such a coarse rude way of meeting plans that should be met with equal stealth and subtlety, unless a man were prepared to own himself vanquished in intelligence. Again, it would have been very difficult to obtain a private interview without some stir concerning it. Moreover, I felt a delicacy with respect to my stewardship on behalf of those two children; for a stranger might not at a glance perceive that prudence and self-denial on my part, which the worrisome frivolousness of the fish had, for the time, frustrated. However, I now perceived that a gentleman of Sir Philip's lofty bearing could not with any grace or dignity allude to his own beneficence; and as for the second difficulty, I might hope for Miss Carey's good offices, while I could no longer think to encounter Chowne with his own weapons, since he had blown me out of bed.

Accordingly I persuaded my beautiful young lady, who had plenty of sense but not much craft, and was pleased with my straightforwardness, to lead me into Sir Philip's presence in a lonely part of the grounds near the river, to the westward, and out of sight of the house; in a word, not far from the Braunton Burrows.

Here the river made a bend and came to the breast of

an ancient orchard, rich with grass and thick with trees leafless now, but thickly bearded upon every twig with moss. This was of every form and fashion, and of almost every hue. I had never seen such a freaksome piece of work outside the tropics, although in Devonshire common enough, where the soil is moist and the climate damp. Some of these trees lay down on the ground, as if they were tired of standing, and some were in sitting postures, and some half leaning over; but all alive, in spite of that, and fruitful when it suited them. And everything being neglected now, from want of the Squire's attention, heaps of rosy and golden apples lay where they had been piled to sweat, but never led to the cider-press.

Perceiving no sign of Sir Philip about, and remembering how it was now beginning to draw on for Christmas-time, I felt myself welcome to one or two of these neglected apples; for it was much if nobody of the farmers' wives who crossed the ferry could afford me a goose for Christmas in my solitary hole. And even if all should fail disgracefully of their duty towards me, I had my eye on a nice young bird of more than the average plumpness, who neglected his parents' advice every day, and came for some favourite grass of his, which only grew just on the river's verge, within thirty yards of my fusil. It would have shown low curiosity to ask if he owned an owner. From his independent manner I felt that he must be public property; and I meant to reduce him into possession right early in the morning of the Saint that was so incredulous. It is every man's duty to treat himself well at the time of the Holy Nativity; and having a knowledge of Devonshire geese, after two months on the stubbles, I could not do better than store in my boat one or two of these derelict apples.

Never do I see or taste an apple without thinking of poor Bardie. "Appledies," she always called them, and she was so fond of them, and her little white teeth made marks like a small-tooth comb in the flesh of them. I was thinking of her, and had scarcely embarked more than a bushel or so, for sauce, in a little snug locker of my own, when I had the pleasure of seeing the gentleman whom I had come all that way to see.

At my own desire, and through Miss Carey's faith in me, it had not been laid before Sir Philip that I was likely to meet him here; only she had told me when and where to come across him, so as not to be broken in upon. Now he came down the narrow winding walk, at the lower side of the orchard, a path overhanging a little brook which murmured under last summer's growth ; and I gazed at him silently for a while, through the bushes that overhung my boat. He was dressed as when I had seen him last through my telescope, at the time we came up the river ; that is to say, in black velvet, and with his long sword hanging beside him. A brave, and stately, and noble man, walking through a steady gloom of grief, and yet content to walk alone, and never speak of it.

I leaped through the bush at the river's brink, and suddenly stood before him. He set his calm cold gaze upon me, without a shadow of surprise, as if to say, "You have no business in my private grounds ; however, it is not worth speaking of." I made him a low bow with my hat off ; and he moved his own, and was passing on.

"Will your Worship look at me," I said, "and see whether you remember me?" He seemed just a little surprised, and then with his inborn courtesy complied.

"I have seen you before, but I know not where. Sir, I often need pardon now for the weakness of my memory."

In a few short words I brought to his mind that evening visit to my cottage, with Anthony Stew and the yellow carriage.

"To be sure, to be sure! I remember now," he said, with his grave and placid smile : "David Llewellyn! Both good old names, and the latter, I daresay, in your belief, both the older and the better one. I remember your hospitality, your patience, and your love of children. Is there anything I can do for you?"

"No, your Worship, nothing. I am here for your sake only ; although if I wanted, I would ask you, having found you so good and kind."

"Whence did you get that expression, my friend? The common usage is 'kind and good ;' I once knew a very little child—but I suppose it is the Welsh idiom."

"Your Worship, I can speak English thoroughly ; better even than my own language ; and all around us the scholarly people have more English than of Welsh. But to let your Worship know my cause to come so much upon you, is of things more to the purpose. I have found a bad man meaning mischief to your Worship."

"It cannot be so," he replied, withdrawing, as if I were taking a liberty ; "no doubt but you mean me well, Llewellyn, and yourself believe it. But neither I, nor any one else of all my family, now so small, can have given reason for any ill-will towards us."

It was not for me to dare to speak, while the General was reflecting thus, as if in his own mind going through every small accident of his life; even the servants he might have discharged; or the land-forces ordered for punishment, whereof to my mind they lack more than they get, and grow their backs up in a manner beyond all perception of discipline.

For my part, I could not help thinking, as I watched him carefully, how low and black must be the nature of the heart that could rejoice in such a man's unhappiness. A man who, at threescore years and five, was compelled to rack his memory (even after being long in uncontrolled authority) to find a time when he might have given cause for private enmity! If I had only enjoyed such chances, I must have had at least a score of strong enemies by this time. Being a little surprised, I looked again and again at his white eyebrows, while his eyes were on the ground; also at his lips and nostrils, which were highly dignified. And I saw, in my dry low way, one reason why he had never given offence. He was perhaps a little scant of humour and of quickness; which two things give more offence to the outer world that has them not, than the longest course of rigid business carried on without them. I have seen a man who could not crack nuts fly into a fury with one who could. And these reflections made me even yet more anxious to serve him, so grave, and calm, and simple-minded, and so patient was his face.

Nevertheless I did not desire, and would at the point of his sword have refused, a halfpenny, for the things of import which I now disclosed to him. He led me to an ancient bench, beneath a well-worn apple-tree; and sat thereon, and even signed for me to sit beside him. My knowledge of his rank would not permit me to do this; until I was compelled to argue. A gentleman more shaped and set inside his own opinions, it had never been my luck to have to deal with, now and then. There are men you cannot laugh at, though you get the best of them, unless your conscience works with such integrity as theirs does. And the sense of this, in some way unknown, may have now been over me. How I began it, or even showed my sense of manners, and of all the different rank between us, is beyond my knowledge now; and must have flowed from instinct then. Enough that I did lead Sir Philip to have thoughts, and to hearken me.

With a power not expected by myself at first beginning, while in doubt of throat and words, I contrived to set before him much that had befallen me. Though I never said a word that lay outside my knowledge, neither let a spark of heat find entrance to my mind at all, and would rather speak too little than be thought outrageous, there could be no doubt that my simple way of putting all I had to say, moved this lofty man, as if he were one of the children at the well belonging to John the Baptist. I thought of all those pretty dears (as I beheld him listening), and the way they sat around me, and their style of moving toes at any great catastrophe; whiles they kept their hands and noses under very stiff control; also the universal sigh, when my story killed any one by any means unfit to die; and their pure contempt of the things they suck, the whole while they are swallowing. Sir Philip (to whom my thoughts meant no failure of respect, but feeling of simplicity), this old gentleman let me speak as one well accustomed to lengthiness. But I did my best to keep a small helm, and yards on the creak for bracing.

"If I take you aright," he said, as I drew near the end of my story, "you have not a high opinion of that reverend gentleman, Stoyle Chowne."

"I look upon him, your Worship, as the blackest-hearted son of Belial ever sent into this world."

Sir Philip frowned, as behoved a man accustomed to authority, and only to have little words, half spoken out, before him. But at my time of life, no officer under an admiral on full pay, could have any right to damp my power of expression. However, my respect was such for the presence of this noble man, that I rose and made a leg to him.

"I am sorry to say," he answered, bowing to my bow, as all gentlemen must do; "that this is not the first time I have heard unpleasant things about poor Stoyle. He is my godson, and has been almost as one of my own children. I never can believe that he would ever do me injury. If I thought it, I should have to think amiss of almost every one."

He turned away, as if already he had said more than he meaned; and feeling how he treated me, as if of his own rank almost, I did not wonder at the tales of men who gave their lives to save him, in the bloody battle-time. Knowing the world as I do, I only sighed, and waited for him.

"You are very good," he said, without a tone of patronage, "to have thought to help me by delivering your opinions. A heavy trouble has fallen upon us, and the goodwill of the neighbourhood has many times astonished me. However, you must indulge no more in any such wild ideas. They all proceed from the evil one, and are his choicest device to lower the value of holy orders. The Reverend Stoyle Chowne descends from a very good old family, at any rate on his father's side; and he has his dignity to maintain, and his holy office to support him. On this head, I will hear no more."

The General shut his mouth and closed it, so that I could never dare to open mine again to him, concerning this one subject. And his manner stopped me so that I only made my duty. This he acknowledged in a manner which became both him and me; and then he passed through a little gate to his usual walk upon Braunton Burrows.

CHAPTER XXXIX.

NOTICE TO QUIT.

We were now come to the time of year which all good Christians celebrate by goodwill and festivities. Even I, in my humble way, had made some preparation for this holy period, by shooting Farmer Badcock's goose; which had long been in my mind. Upon plucking, he turned out even whiter and better than expectation, and the tender down clung to him, in a way that showed his texture. I hung him up in a fine through-draught, and rejoiced in the thought of him every time my head came in between his legs. Neither did he fall away when he came to roasting.

But when I had put him down, upon the Christmas morning, with intent to stick thereby, and baste him up to one o'clock, dipping bits of bread beneath him, as he might begin to drip, and winning thus foretaste of him—all my plans were overset by a merry party coming, and demanding "ferry." With my lovely goose beginning just to spread his skin a little, and hiss sweetly at the fire, up I ran, with resolution not to ferry anybody, but to cook my goose aright.

Nevertheless it might not be so. Here were three young fellows ramping of the high nobility, swearing to come aboard and stick me, if I would not ferry them. It was not that I feared of this, but that I beheld a guinea spinning in the morning sun, which compelled me to forego, and leave my poor young goose to roll around, and try to roast himself. Therefore I backed him from the fire, and laid half a pound of slow lard on his breast, and trusted his honour to keep alive.

These young joyous fellows now were awake to everything. They had begun the morning bravely with a cup of rum and lemon, then a tender grill of beef, and a quart of creamy ale, every one accordingly. And they meant to keep the day up to no less a pattern, being all of fine old birth, and bound to act accordingly. However, it had been said by some one, that they ought to go to church; and they happened to feel the strength of this, and vowed that the devil should catch the hindmost, unless they struck out for it.

Hence I came to win the pleasure of their company, that day. Their nearest church was the little, simple, quiet old church at Ashford. From my ferry I could see it; and it often made me sigh, because it looked so tranquil. Sweet green land sloped up towards it, with a trace of crooked footpaths, and the nicks of elbowed hedges, where the cows came down and stood. Also from it, looking downward through the valley of the Tawe, may be seen a spread of beauty, and of soft variety, and of largeness opening larger with the many winding waters, to the ocean unbeheld, that the sternest man must sigh, and look again and look again.

A genuine parson now was master of this queer old quiet church; a man who gave his life entire for the good of other men. In a little hut he lived, which the clerk's house overrode, just at the turning of the lane, upon the steep ascent, and where the thunder-showers flooded it. All the poor folk soon began to dwell upon his noble nature, and to feel that here was some one fit to talk of Saviours. Miles around they came to hear him, so that he was forced to stand on a stool in the porch, and speak to them. For speaking it was, and not preaching; which made all the difference.

These three gay young sparks leaped lightly into the bow of my ferry-boat, and bade me pull for my very life, unless I desired to be flung into the water then and there. A strong spring-tide was running up, and I was forced to pull the starboard oar with all my might to keep the course. My passengers were carrying on with every sort of quip and crank, and jokes, that made the boat to tilt, when suddenly a rush of water flooded their silk stockings. I thought at first that the bung was out, and told them not to be frightened; but in another breath I saw that it was a great deal worse than that. The water was rushing in through a mighty hole in the planks of the larboard bow; and in three minutes we must be swamped. "All aft, all aft in a moment!" I cried; "it is our only chance of reaching shore." The gallants were sobered at once by fright, and I bundled them into the stern-sheets, sat on the aftmost thwart myself, and for the lives of us all pulled back towards the bank we had lately quitted. By casting all the weight thus astern, I raised the leak up to the water-line, except when we plunged to the lift of the oars, and the water poured in less rapidly now, with the set of the tide on our starboard beam. However, with all this, and all my speed, and my passengers showing great presence of mind, we barely managed to touch the bank and jump out, when down she foundered.

At first I was at a loss altogether even to guess how this thing had happened; for the boat seemed perfectly sound and dry at the time of our leaving the shore. But as soon as the tide was out, and I could get at her, I perceived that a trick of entirely fiendish cunning and atrocity had been played upon me. A piece of planking a foot in length and from eight to ten inches wide had been cut out with a key-hole saw, at the time she was lying high and dry, and doubtless before daybreak. This had been then replaced most carefully with a little caulking, so that it was water-tight without strong pressure from outside; but the villain had contrived it, knowing in what state of tide I was likely next to work the ferry, so that the rush of water could not fail to beat the piece in.

It made my blood run cold to think of the stealthiness of this attempt, as well as the skill it was compassed with, for the chances were ten to one almost in favour of its drowning me, and leaving a bad name behind me too, for having drowned my passengers. And to this it must have come if so much as a single woman had been in the boat that day. For these, when in danger, always do the very worst thing possible; and the manager of this clever scheme knew of course that my freight was likely, on the Christmas morning, to be chiefly female. Luckily I had refused two boat-loads of young and attractive womankind, not from religious feeling only, but because I had to chop a trencherful of stuffing.

This affair impressed me so with a sense of awe and reverence, and a certainty that Parson Chowne must be in direct receipt of counsel from the evil one, that my mind was good to be off at once, and thank the Lord for escaping him. For let us see what must have happened but for the goodness and fatherly care of a merciful Providence over me. The boat would have sunk in the very midst of the rapid and icy river. David Llewellyn, with his accustomed fortitude, would have endeavoured to swim ashore, and yet could not have resisted the claims of three or even four young women, who doubtless would have laid hold of him, all screaming, splashing, and dragging him down. The mind refuses to contemplate such a picture any longer!

This matter could not be kept quiet, as the first attempt had been, but spread from house to house, and gained in size from each successive tongue, until the man at the foot of the bridge, who naturally detested me, whispered into every ear, that it was high time to have a care of that interloping Welshman, who had drowned six fine young noblemen, for the sake of their buckles and watches. And my courage was at so low an ebb, that when he retreated into his house, I could not even bring my mind to the power of kicking his door in. Hence that calumny, not being quenched, went the round of the neighbourhood; and I might as well haul down my sign, and the hopes of any public-house became a fading vision. And of all the fine young women who had set their hearts upon keeping it (as I described my intention to them), and who had picked up bits of Welsh, for an access to my heart in all its patriotism, there was not one worth looking at, or fit to be a landlady, who took the trouble to come near me, in the frosty weather.

When a man is forsaken by the world, he must have recourse to reason. And if only borne up thereby, and with a little cash in hand, he can wait till the world comes round again. This was my position now. I never had behaved so well in all my life before, I think; though always conscientious. But of late I had felt, as it were, in one perpetual round of bitter wrestling with the evil one. Men of a loose kind may not see that this was tenfold hard upon me, from my props being knocked away. I mean my entire trust and leaning upon the ancient Church of England, which (perhaps by repulsion from those fellows that came after our old ham, as well as our proper parson's knowledge of soles and the way to fry them) had increased upon me so, that my heart leaped up whenever I heard the swing of a bell on Sunday. Some of this perhaps was owing to my thoughts of Newton clock, and twelve shillings now due to me from my captainship thereof: but how could this loyal and ecclesiastical fervour thrive, while a man in holy orders did such unholy things to me?

The only one with faith enough, and sense enough, to stand by me now, through this bitter trial, was that beautiful young lady, whom I did admire so. And if till now I admired only, now I did adore her. Nanette did for herself with me, and all her hopes of ever being Mrs David Llewellyn, by poking up her little toes,—and I saw that they were all square almost,—and with guttural noises crying that on board my boat she would not dare. Miss Carey laughed at her, and stepped with her beautiful boots on board of me; and from that moment she might do exactly as she pleased with me.

However my ferry was knocked on the head; and all the hopes of a wife and family, and even a public-house and skittles, which I had long been building up, as well as to train our Bunny for barmaid; which must always be done quite young, to get the proper style of it, and thorough acquaintance with measures, how to make them look quite brim up when they are only three-parts full. All golden dreams will vanish thus; no life of smiling Boniface, but of gun-muzzles was before me; no casting-up of shot by pence, but ramming down on pounds of powder. Let that pass; my only wish is to conceal, in the strictest manner, little trifles about myself.

Isabel Carey was so shocked at hearing of our danger (as by me distinctly told without a word of flourish), that she made me promise strongly to give up my ferrying. This I was becoming ready, more and more every day, to do; especially as nobody ever now came down for porterage. But I told the lady how hard it was to have formed such a valuable trade, or you might say an institution; and then to lose it all, because of certain private enmities. What she said or did hereon is strictly a family question, and can in no way concern the public, since I hauled my flag down.

And now I gained more insight into my great enemy's schemes and doings, than I could have acquired while engaged so much at ferry. For time allowed me to maintain that strict watch upon Narnton Court, which was now become my duty, as well as an especial pleasure, for the following reason. I began to see most clearly that the foul outrage upon my boat must have been perpetrated by one or both of those savage fellows who were employed as spies upon this great house, from the landward side. They must have forded the river, which is not more than three feet deep in places, when the tide is out, and no floods coming down. These two cunning barbarians came of course from the Nympton rookery, but were lodging for the present in a hole they had scooped for themselves in the loneliest part of Braunton Burrows. Of course they durst not go about in a peopled and civilised neighbourhood, with such an absence of apparel as they could indulge at home. Still they were unsightly objects; and decent people gave them a wide berth, when possible. But my firm intention was to grapple with these savage scoundrels, and to prove at their expense what a civilised Welshman is, and how capable of asserting his commercial privileges. Only as they carried knives, I durst not meet them both at once; and even should I catch them singly, some care was advisable, so as take them off their guard; because I would not lower myself to the use of anything more barbarous than an honest cudgel.

However, although I watched and waited, and caught sight of them more than once, especially at night-time when they roved most freely, it was long before I found it prudent to bear down on the enemy. Not from any fear of them, but for fear of slaying them, as I might be forced to do, if they rushed with steel at me.

One night, after the turn of the days, and with mild weather now prevailing, and a sense of spring already fluttering in the valleys, I sat in a dark embrasure at the end of Narnton Court. There had been more light than usual in the windows of the great dining-room, which now was very seldom used for hospitable purposes. And now two gentlemen came forth, as if for a little air, to take a turn on the river-terrace. It did not cost me long to learn that one was good Sir Philip Bampfylde, and the other that very wicked Chowne. The latter had manifestly been telling some of his choicest stories, and held the upper hand as usual.

"General, take my arm. The flags are rough, and the night is of the darkest. You must gravel this terrace, for the sake of your guests, after your port-wine."

"Dick," said the General, with a sigh, for he was a most hospitable man, and accustomed to the army; "Dick, thou hast hardly touched my port; and I like not to have it slighted, sir."

What excuse the Parson made I did not hear, but knew already that one of his countless villanies was his rude contempt of the gift of God, as vouchsafed to Noah, and confirmed by the very first rainbow, which continues the colours thereof up to this time of writing.

Sir Philip leaned on the parapet some twenty yards to windward of me, and he sniffed the fine fresh smell of sea-weed and sea-water coming up the river with a movement of four knots an hour. And in his heart he thanked the Lord, very likely without knowing it. Then he seemed to sigh a little, and to turn to Chowne, and say—

"Dick, this is not as it should be. Look at all this place, and up and down all this length of river; every light you can see burning, is in a house that 'longs to me. And who is now to have it all? It used to make me proud; but now it makes me very humble. You are a parson; tell me, Dick, what have I done to deserve it all?"

The Rev. Richard Stoyle Chowne had not—whatever his other vices were—one grain of pious hypocrisy in all his foul composition. If he had, he might have flourished, and with his native power, must have been one of the foremost men of this, or any other age. But his pride allowed him never to let in pretence religious into the texture of his ways. A worse man need not be desired: and yet he did abhor all cant, to such a degree that he made a mock of his own church-services.

"General, I have nought to say. You have asked this question more than once. You know what my opinion is."

"I know that you have the confidence, sir, every honourable man must have, in my poor son's innocence. You support it against every one."

"Against all the world: against even you, when you allow yourself to doubt it. Tush! I would not twice think of it. However many candles burn"—this was a touch of his nasty sarcasm, which he never could deny himself — "up and down the valley, General, no son of yours, however wild, and troubled in expenditure, could ever shape or even dream of anything dishonourable."

"I hope not—I hope to God, not," Sir Philip said, with a little gasp, as if he were fearing otherwise: "Dick, you are my godson, and you have been the greatest comfort to me; because you never would believe——"

"Not another word, General. You must not dwell on this matter so. The children were fine little dears of course, very clever and very precious——"

"Oh, if you only knew the words, Dick, my little granddaughter could come out with! Scarcely anything you could think of would have been too big for her little mouth. And if she could not do it once, she never left it till she did. Where it came from I could not tell, for we are not great at languages: but it must have been of her mother's race. And the boy, though not with gifts of that sort—oh, you ought to have seen his legs, Dick—at least till he took the whooping-cough!" The stately old gentleman leaned, and dropped a tear perhaps into the river Tawe.

"General, I understand it all," said Chowne, though he never had a child, by reason of the Almighty's mercy to the next generation: "of course these pretty children were a great delight to every one. But affairs of this sort happen in all ancient families. The mere extent of land appears to open for clandestine graves——"

"That wicked devilish story, Dick! Did you tell me, or did you not, to take it as the Fiend's own lie?"

"A lie, of course, as concerns the Captain: from their want of knowledge. But concerning some one else, true enough, I fear, I fear."

Both men had by this time very nearly said their say throughout. The General seemed to be overcome, and the Parson to be growing weary of a subject often treated in discourse between them. "Before you go in the morning, Dick," said the old man, now recovering, "I wish to consult you about a matter nearly concerning young Isabel. She is a distant cousin of yours. You thoroughly understand the law, of which I have very little knowledge. Perhaps you will meet me in the book-room, for half an hour's quiet talk, before we go to breakfast."

"I cannot do it, Sir Philip. I have my own affairs to see to: I must be off when the moon is up I cannot sleep in your house, this night."

CHAPTER XL.

FORCIBLE EJECTMENT.

Those things which have been settled for us by long generations of ancestors, all of whom must have considered the subjects, one after the other painfully, and brought good minds

of ancient strength (less led away than ours are) to bear upon
what lay before them, also living in a time when money went
much further, and got a deal more change in honesty, which
was then more plentiful—to rush, I say, against the bulwarks
of our noble elders (who showed the warmth of their faith by
roasting all who disagreed with them), would be, ay and ever
will be, a proof of a rebellious, scurvy, and perpetually scabby
nature. The above fine reflection came home to me, just as
my pipe grew sweet and rich, after an excellent dinner, provided by that most thoughtful and bright young lady, the
Honourable Isabel Carey, upon a noble New Year's Day, in
the year of our Lord one thousand seven hundred and eighty-
three. Her ladyship now had begun to feel that interest in
my intelligence and unusual power of narrative, as well as that
confidence in my honour and extreme veracity, which, without
the smallest effort or pretence on my part, seem to spring by
some law of nature in every candid mind I meet.

Combining this lady's testimonials, as presented weekly,
with some honourable trifles picked up here and there along
shore, in spite of all discouragement, perhaps I congratulated
myself on having turned the corner of another year not badly.
I counted my money, to the tune of five-and-twenty level
pounds; an amount of cash beyond all experience! Yet,
instead of being dazzled, I began to see no reason for not
having fifty. Not that I ever thought of money; but for the
sake of the children. The tears came into my eyes, to think
of these poor little creatures; Bardie with all her fount of life
sanded up (as one might say) in that old Sker warren; and
Bunny with her strength of feeding weakened over rice and fowl-
food; such as old Charles Morgan kept, who had been known
to threaten to feed his family upon sawdust. A most respectable man, as well as churchwarden and undertaker; but being
bred a pure carpenter, he thought (when his money came in
fast, and great success surprised him) that Providence would
be offended at his waste of sawdust.

Now this was the man who had Bunny to keep, entirely
from his own wish of course, or the sense of the village concerning her; and many times I had been ready to laugh, and
as many times to cry almost, whenever I thought of the many
things that were likely to happen between them. To laugh,
when I thought of Churchwarden's face regarding our Bunny
at breakfast-time, and the way she would say, "I want some
more," through his narrow-shouldered children. To cry, when

I thought of my dear son's child (and as dear to me as my own almost) getting less of victuals daily, as her welcome should grow staler, and giving way to her old trick of standing on the floor with eyes shut, and with shut mouth to declare, "I won't eat, now you have starved me so;" and no one in that house with wit to understand and humour her. And then I could see her go to bed, in a violent temper anyhow: and when the wind boxed round to north, I could hear her calling, "Granny."

This very tender state of mind, and sense of domestic memories, seems to have drawn me (so far as I can, in a difficult case, remember it) towards a very ancient inn having two bow-windows. When I entered, no man could be in a stricter state of sobriety: and as if it were yesterday, I remember asking the price of everything. The people were even inclined to refuse to draw anything in the small-liquor line for a man with so little respect for trade as to walk so straight upon New Year's Day. After a little while, I made them see that this was not so much my fault as my misfortune; and when I declared my name, of course, and my character came forward, even rum-shrub out of a cask with golden hoops around it scarcely seemed to be considered good enough for me, gratis. But throughout the whole of this, I felt an anxious and burning sense of eager responsibility, coupled with a strong desire to be everywhere at once.

Right early, to the very utmost of my recollection, I tumbled into my lonely berth, after seeing my fusil primed, and praying to the Lord for guidance through another and a better year. I had clean sheets, which are my most luxurious gift of feeling; and having no room to stretch my legs, or roll, I managed space to yawn, and then went off deliciously. Now I was beginning to dream about the hole I had placed my money in —a clever contrivance of my own, and not in the cuddy at all, because the enemy might attack me there—when a terrible fit of coughing came and saved my life by waking me. The little cuddy was full of smoke—parching, blinding, choking smoke —so thick that I could scarcely see the red glare of fire behind it, through the brattice of the bulkhead.

"Good Lord," I cried, "have mercy on me! Sure enough, I am done for now. And nobody ever will know or care what the end was of old Dyo!"

I did not stop still to say all this, that you may be quite sure of; and it argues no small power of speech that I was able to say anything. For with a last desire for life, and despairing resolve to try again, I broke my knuckles against the hatch which I had made so heavy for the purpose of protecting me. To go out through my door would have been to rush into the fire itself; and what with the choking, and the thickness, and the terror of the flames violently reddening and roaring a few feet away, I felt my wits beginning to fail me, which of course was certain death. So I sate down on a three-legged stool, which was all my furniture; and for a moment the rushing smoke drew, by some draught, otherwhere; and whether I would or no, a deal of my past life came up to me. I wondered whether I might have been too hard sometimes on any one, or whether I might have forgotten to think of the Lord, upon any Sunday. And then my thoughts were elevated to the two dear children.

Now what do you think happened to me, when I thought of those two darlings, and the tears from smoke made way for the deep-born tears of a noble heart? Why simply that a flash of flame glanced upon the iron crowbar, wherewith I had opened hatch. I could not have been in pure bright possession of my Maker's gifts to me when I chanced, before going to bed, to lay that crowbar for my pillow-case. Nevertheless I had done it well: and in the stern perception of this desperate extremity, I could not help smiling at the way I had tucked up my head on the crowbar. But (though no time is lost in smiling) I had not a moment to lose even now, although with my utmost wits all awake and coughing. I prised the hatch up in half a moment, where it was stuck in the combings; and if ever a man enjoyed a draught, I did so of air that moment. Many men might have been frightened still, and not have known what to do with themselves. But I assure you, in all honour, that the whole of my mind came back quite calmly, when I was out of smothering. People may say what they like; but I know, after seeing every form of death (and you need not laugh at me very much, if I even said feeling it) —I know no anguish to be compared to the sense of being pressed under slowly; and the soul with no room to get away.

But I was under the good stars now, and able to think and to look about; and though the ketch could not last long, being of 92 tons only, I found time enough to kneel and thank my God for His mercy to me. There was no ice in the river now, and to swim ashore would have been but little, except for rheumatics afterwards. But it seemed just as well to escape even these; and having been burned out at sea before, I was better enabled to manage it. The whole of the waist of the ketch was in flames, curling and beginning now to indulge their desire of roaring; but the kindness of the Lord prevented wind from blowing. Had there been only a four-knot breeze, you would never have heard of me again; surely which would grieve you.

In this very sad state of mind, combined with a longing for thankfulness, and while I was thinking about the fire—to say the truth, very stupidly, and wondering instead of working— quite an old-fashioned affair restored me to my wits and my love of the world again. This was the strong sour sound of the air when a bullet comes through it hastily, and casting reproach upon what we breathe, for its want of a stronger activity. A man had made a shot at me, and must have been a lubber by his want of range and common-sense. Before I could think, I was all alive, and fit to enjoy myself almost, as if it were a fight with Frenchmen. The first thing I thought of was the gun lent to me by Miss Carey. To rescue this, I went down even into the cuddy which had so lately proved my very grave almost; and after this I saw no reason why I should not save my money, if the Lord so willed it. From a sense of all the mischief even now around me, I had made a clever hole in the bow-knees of the ketch (where the wood lay thickest), and so had plugged my money up, with the power to count it daily. And now in spite of flame, and roar, and heat of all the 'midships, and the spluttering of the rock-powder bags too wet to be unanimous, I made my mind up just to try to save my bit of money.

Because, although a man may be as coarse, and wicked, and vile-hearted, as even my very worst enemies are, he cannot fail of getting on, and being praised, and made the best of, if he only does his best to stick tight to his money. Therefore, having no boat within reach, and the 'midship all aflame, I made a raft of the cuddy-hatch, and warped along by the side of the ketch, and purchased my cash from its little nest; and then with a thankful heart, and nothing but a pair of breeches on, made the best of my way ashore, punting myself with a broken oar.

This desire to sacrifice me (without the trouble even taken to count what my value was) gave me such a sense of shock, and of spreading abroad everywhere, without any knowledge left of what might have become of me, and the subject liable to be dropped, if ever entered into by a Jolly Crowner, and a jury glad to please him, that for the moment I sate down upon a shelf of clay, until the wet came through my want of clothes. Suddenly this roused me up to make another trial for the sake of my well-accustomed and familiar suit of clothes, so well beloved; also even my Sunday style, more striking but less comfortable; in lack of which the world could never have gone on in our neighbourhood. Therefore I ran to my little punt, and pushed off and was just in time to save my kit, with a little singeing.

The ketch burned down to the water's edge, and then a rough tide came up and sank her, leaving me in a bitter plight, and for some time quite uncertain how to face the future. From knowledge of the Parson's style of treating similar cases, I felt it to be a most likely thing that I should be charged with firing her, robbing her, and concealing booty. And this injustice added to the bitterness of my close escape. "It is no use," I said aloud; "it is useless to contend with him. He has sold himself to Satan, and, thank God, I have no chance with him." Therefore by the time the fire had created some disturbance in the cottage bedrooms, I had got my clothing on, in a decent though hasty manner, and slipped into a little wood with my spy-glass, happily saved, and resolved to watch what happened in among the bumpkins.

These came down, and stared and gawked, and picked up bits of singed spars, and so on, and laid down the law to one another, and fought for the relics, and thought it hard that no man's body was to be found with clothes on. I saw them hunting for me, up and down the river channel, with a desperate ignorance of tide (although living so close to it), and I did not like to have my body hunted for like that. But I repressed all finer feelings, as a superior man must do, and chewed the tip of a bullock's tongue, which luckily was in my waistcoat-pocket, ready for great emergency; and which, if a man keeps going on with, he may go, like the great Elijah, forty days, and feel no hunger. At least, I have heard so, and can believe it, having seen men who told me so; but I would rather have it proved by another man's experience.

While I was looking on at these things, down came **Parson Chowne** himself, in a happy mood, and riding the black mare, now brought out of dock again. The country folk all fell away from their hope of stealing something, and laid fingers to their hats, being afraid to talk of him. He, however, did **no more than** sign to the serving-man behind him, to acknowledge compliments (which was outside his own custom), and then he put spurs to his horse and galloped right and left through the lot of them. In my anxiety to learn what this dreadful man was up to, I slipped down through the stubs of the wood, where the faggot-cutters had been at work, gliding even upon my jersey, because of the Parson's piercing eyes, and there in the ditch I found some shelter, and spied through a bushy breastwork.

"No more than I expected," he cried, "from what I have seen of the fellow; he has fired the ship, and run away with all he could lay hands on. As a Justice of the Peace, I offer ten pounds reward for David Llewellyn, brought before me, alive or dead. Is there one of you rantipoles can row? Oh, you can. Take this shilling, and be off with that big thief's ferry-boat, and leave it at Sam Tucker's shipyard, in the name of the Reverend Stoyle Chowne."

It went to my heart that none of the people to whom I had been so "good and kind"—to use pretty Bardie's phrase—now had the courage to stand up, and say that my character was most noble, and claim back my boat for me. Instead of that, they all behaved as if I had never ferried them; and the ingratitude of the young women made me long to be in Wales again. Because, you may say what you like; but the first point in our people is gratitude.

"Of course," cried Chowne, and his voice, though gently used, came down the wind like a bell; "of course, good people, you have not found the corpse of that wretched villain."

"Us would giv' un up, glad enough, if us only gat the ioock, for tan zhilling, your Raverance. Lave aloun tan poond."

When that miserable miser said a thing so low as that, my very flesh crept on my bones, and my inmost heart was sick with being made so very little of. To myself I always had a proper sense of estimation; and to be put at this low figure made me doubt of everything. However, I came to feel, after a bit, that this is one of the trials which all good men must put up with: neither would a common man find his corpse worth ten pounds sterling.

Betwixt my sense of public value (a definite sum, at any rate) and imagination of what my truly natural abilities might lead me to, if properly neglected, I found it a blessed hard thing to lie quiet until dark, and then slip out. And the more so, because my stock of food was all consumed by middle day; and before the sun went down, hunger of a great shape and size arose and raged within me. This is always difficult to discipline or to reason with; and to men of the common order it suggests great violence. To me it did nothing of that kind, but led me into a little shop, where I paid my money, and got my loaf. My flint and steel and tinder-box lay in my pocket handy. These I felt and felt again, and went into the woods and thought, and found that even want of food had failed to give me a thorough-going and consistent appetite. Because, for the first time in my life, I had shaped a strong resolve, and sworn to the Lord concerning it—to commit a downright crime, and one which I might be hanged for. Although every one who has entered into my sufferings and my dignity must perceive how right I was, and would never inform against me, I will only say that on Saturday evening Parson Chowne had fourteen ricks, and on Sunday morning he had none, and might begin to understand the feelings of the many farmers who had been treated thus by him. Right gladly would I have beheld his face (so rigid and contemptuous at other people's trouble) when he should come to contemplate his own works thus brought home to him. But I could not find a hedge thick enough to screen me from his terrible piercing eyes.

This little bit of righteous action made a stir, you may be sure, because it was so contrary to the custom of the neighbourhood. Although I went to see this fire, I took the finest care to leave no evidence behind me; and even turned my bits of toggery inside out at starting. But there was a general sense in among these people, that only a foreigner could have dared to fly in the Parson's face so. I waited long enough to catch the turn of the public feeling, and finding it set hard against me, my foremost thought was the love of home.

Keeping this in view, and being pressed almost beyond bearing now, with no certainty, moreover, as to warrants coming out, and the people looking strangely, every time they met me, I could have no peace until I saw the beautiful young lady, and to her told everything. You should have seen her eyes and cheeks, as well as the way her heart went; and the pride with which she gathered all her meaning up to speak; even after I had told her how the ricks would burn themselves.

"You dear old Davy," she said, "I never thought you had so much courage. You are the very bravest man—but stop, did you burn the whole of them?"

"Every one burned itself, your ladyship; I saw the ashes dying down, and his summer-house as well took fire, through the mischief of the wind, and all his winter stock of wood, and his tool-house, and his——"

"Any more, any more, old David?"

"Yes, your ladyship, his cow-house, after the cows were all set free, and his new cart-shed fifty feet long, also his carpenter's shop, and his cider-press."

"You are the very best man," she answered, with her beautiful eyes full upon me, "that I have seen, since I was a child. I must think what to do for you. Did you burn anything more, old Davy?"

"The fire did, your ladyship, three large barns, and a thing they call a 'linhay;' also the granary, and the meal-house, and the apple-room, and the churn-room, and only missed the dairy by a little nasty slant of wind."

"What a good thing you have done! There is scarcely any man I know, that would have shown such courage. Mr Llewellyn, is there anything in my power to do for you?"

Nothing could have pleased me more than to find this fair young lady rejoicing in this generous manner at the Parson's misadventure. And her delight in the contemplation made me almost feel repentance at the delicate forbearance of the flames from the Rectory itself. But I could not help reflecting how intense and bitter must be this young harmless creature's wrong received and dwelling in her mind, ere she could find pleasure from wild havoc and destruction.

"There is one thing you can do," I answered very humbly; "and it is my only chance to escape from misconstruction. I never thought, at my time of life, to begin life so again. But I am now a homeless man, burned out of my latest refuge, and with none to care for me. Perhaps I may be taken up to-morrow, or the next day. And with such a man against me, it must end in hanging."

"I never heard such a thing," she said: "he tries to burn you in your bed, after blowing you up, and doing his very best to drown you; and then you are to be hanged because there is a bonfire on his premises! It is impossible, Mr Llewellyn, to think twice of such a thing."

"Your ladyship may be right," I answered; "and in the case of some one else, reasoning would convince me. But if I even stop to think twice, it will lead to handcuffs; and handcuffs lead to halter."

At this she began to be frightened much, and her fright grew worse, as I described the unpleasantness of hanging; how

I had helped myself to run up nine good men at the yard-arm. And a fine thing for their souls, no doubt, to stop them from more mischief, and let them go up while the Lord might think that other men had injured them.

"Your ladyship," I began again, when I saw all her delicate colour ebbing; "it is not for a poor hunted man to dare to beg a favour."

"Oh yes, it is, it is," she cried; "that is the very time to do it. Anything in my power, David, after all you have done for me."

"Then all that I want of your ladyship is to get me rated aboard of Captain Drake Bampfylde's ship."

She coloured up so clearly that I was compelled to look away: and then she said—

"How do you know—I mean who can have told you that— but are you not too—perhaps a little——"

"Too old, your ladyship? Not a day. I am worth half-a-dozen of those young chips who have got no bones to their legs yet. And as for shooting, if his Honour wants a man to train a cannon, I can hit a marlinspike with a round-shot, at a mile and a half, as soon as I learn the windage."

For I knew by this time that Captain Bampfylde's ship, the Alcestis, was in reserve, as a feeder for the Royal Navy, to catch young hands and train them to some knowledge of sea-life, and smartness, and the styles of gunnery. And who could teach them these things better than a veteran like me?

Miss Carey smiled at my conceit, as perhaps she considered it; "Well, Davy, if you can fire a gun, as well as you can a hay-rick——"

"No more, your ladyship, I beseech you. Even walls like these have ears; and every time I see my shadow, I take it for a constable. I am sure there are two men after me——"

"Have you then two shadows?" she asked, in her peculiar pleasant way: "at any rate no one will dare to meddle with you, or any of us, I should hope, in the General's own house. Come in here. I expect, or at least I think, there is some prospect of a boat from the Alcestis coming up the river this very evening. Perhaps you have some baggage."

"No, your ladyship, not a bit. They burned me out of all of it. But I saved some money kindly, by special grace of God, at the loss of all my leg-hair."

I ought not to have said that, I knew, directly after uttering it, to a young lady who could not yet be up to things of that kind.

CHAPTER XLI.

THE RIGHT MAN IN THE RIGHT PLACE.

THE very next day, I was afloat as a seaman of the Royal Navy of the United Kingdom. None but a sailor can imagine what I felt and what I thought. Here for years I had been adrift from the very work God shaped me for, wrecked before my time by undue violence of a Frenchman. Also I had bred my son up to supply my place a little; and a very noble fellow, though he could not handle cutlash or lay gun as I had done. But he might have come to it if he ever had come to my own time of life. This however had been cut short by the will of Providence; and now I felt bound to make good for it. Only one thing grieved me, viz., to find the war declining. This went to my heart the more, because our Navy had not done according to its ancient fame, anywhere but at Gibraltar and with Admiral Rodney, in the year before I rejoined it. Off the coast of America, things I could not bear to hear; also the loss of the Royal George, the capture of the Leeward Islands, and of Minorca by the French; and even a British sloop of war taken by a French corvette. Such things moved me to the marrow, after all I had seen and done; and all our ship's company understood that I returned to the service in the hope to put a stop to it. This reclaiming of me to the thing that I was meant for took less time than I might use to bring a gun to its bearings. That beautiful Miss Carey managed everything with Captain Drake, and in less than fifty kisses they had settled my affairs. I could have no more self-respect, if I said another word.

But the King and the nation won the entire benefit of this. It came to pass that I was made a second-instructor in gunnery, with an entire new kit found me, and six-and-twopence a-week appointed, together with second right to stick a fork into the boiler. Of course I could not have won all this by favour; but showed merit. It had however been allowed me, under an agreement (just enough, yet brought about by special love of justice) that I should receive a month ashore at Newton-Nottage, in the course of the spring, whenever it might suit our cruising. My private affairs demanded this; as well as love of neighbours, and strong desire to let them know how much they ought to make of me.

How I disdained my rod and pole, and the long-shore life and the lubberly ways, when I felt once more the bounding of the open water, the spring of the buoyant timbers answering every movement gallantly, the generous vehemence of the canvas, and the noble freedom of the ocean winds around us! The rush up a liquid mountain, and the sway on the balance of the world, then the plunge into the valley, almost out of the sight of God, though we feel Him hovering over us. While the heart leaps with the hope of yet more glorious things to come —the wild delight, the rage, suspense, and majesty of battle.

Nothing vexed me now so much as to hear from private people, and even from the public sailors, that the nation wanted peace. No nation ever should want peace, until it has thoroughly thrashed the other, or is bound by wicked luck to knock under hopelessly. And neither of those things had befallen England at this period. But I have not skill enough to navigate in politics. And before we had been long at sea, we spoke a full-rigged ship from Hamburg, which had touched at Falmouth; and two German boys, in training for the British Navy, let us know that peace was signed between Great Britain, France, and Spain, as nearly as might be on Valentine's Day of the year 1783. A sad and hard thing we found to believe it, and impossible to be pleased after such practice of gunnery.

Nevertheless it was true enough, and confirmed by another ship; and now a new Ministry was in office under a man of the name of Fox, doubtless of that nature also, ready always to run to earth. Nothing more could be hoped except to put up with all degradation. A handful of barbarous fellows, wild in the woods and swamps of America, most of them sent from this home-country through their contempt of discipline, fellows of this sort had been able (mainly by skulking and shirking fight) to elude and get the better of His Britannic Majesty's forces, and pretend to set up on their own account, as if they could ever get on so. No one who sees these things as clearly as I saw them then and there, can doubt as to the call I felt to rejoin the Royal Navy.

Of course I could not dream that now there was rising in a merchant-ship captured from the Frenchmen, and fitted with two dozen guns, a British Captain such as never had been seen before, nor will ever be again; and whose skill and daring left the Frenchmen one hope only—to run ashore, and stay there.

However, not to dwell too long on the noblest and purest motives, it did not take me quite three weeks to supersede the first instructor, and to get him sent ashore, and find myself hoisted into his berth, with a rise of two-and-two per week. This gave me eight-and-fourpence, with another stripe on my right arm, and what was far more to the purpose, added greatly to the efficiency of the British Navy. Because the man was very well, or at any rate well enough, in his way and in his manners, and quite worth his wages; but to see him train a gun, and to call him First Instructor! Captain Bampfylde saw, in twenty minutes, that I could shoot this fine fellow's head off, unwilling as I was to give offence, and delicate about priming. And all the men felt at once the power of a practised hand set over them. I saw that the Navy had fallen back very much in the matter of gunnery, in the time of the twenty years, or so, since I had been Gun-captain; and it came into my head to show them many things forgotten. The force of nature carried me into this my proper position; and the more rapidly, because it happened to occur to me that here was the very man pointed out, as it were by the hand of Providence, for Parson Chowne to blow up next. Our Captain had the very utmost confidence that could be in him, and he stood on his legs with a breadth that spoke to the strength of his constitution; a man of enduring gravity. Also his weight was such that the Parson never could manage to blow him up, with any powder as yet admitted into the Royal Dockyards. I liked this man, and I let him know it; but I thought it better for him to serve his country on shore a little, after being so long afloat; if (as I put it to his conscience) he could keep from poaching, and from firing stackyards, or working dangerous ferries. He told me that he had no temptation towards what I had mentioned; but on the other hand felt inclined, after so many years at sea, to have a family of his own; and a wife, if found consistent. This I assured him I could manage; and in a few words did so; asking for nothing more on his part than entire confidence. My nature commanded this from him; and we settled to exchange our duties in a pleasant manner. I gave him introduction to the liveliest of the farmers' daughters, telling him what their names were. And being over-full of money, he paid me half-a-crown apiece, for thirteen girls to whom I gave him letters of commendation. This was far too cheap, with all of them handsomer than he had any right to; and three of them only daughters, and two with no more than grandmothers. But I love to help a fellow-sailor; and thus I got rid of him. For our Captain had the utmost faith in this poor man's discretion, and had thought, before I said it, of laying him up at Narnton Court, to keep a general look-out, because his eyes were failing. I did not dare to offer more opinion than was asked for, but it struck me that if Parson Chowne had been too clever for David Llewellyn, and made the place too hot for him, he was not likely to be outwitted by Naval Instructor Heaviside.

However, I could not see much occasion for Chowne to continue his plots any longer, or even to keep watch on the house, unless it were from jealousy of our Captain's visits. As far as any one might fathom that unfathomable Parson, he had two principal ends in view. The first was to get possession of Miss Carey and all her property, by making her Mrs Chowne, No. 4; the second, which would help him towards the first, was to keep up against poor Captain Drake the horrible charge of having killed those two children, whose burial had been seen as before related. And here I may mention what I had forgotten, through entire want of vindictive feeling—to wit, that I had, as a matter of duty, contrived to thrash very heavily both of those fellows on Braunton Burrows, who had been spying on Narnton Court, and committed such outrages against me. Without doing this, I could not have left the county conscientiously.

And now on board the Alcestis, a rattling fine frigate of 44 guns, it gave me no small pleasure to find that (although the gunnery-practice was not so good as I was accustomed to), in seamanship, and discipline, and general smartness, there was little to be reasonably complained of; especially when it was borne in mind what our special duty was, and why we were kept in commission when so many other ships were paid off, at the conclusion of the war. Up to that time the Alcestis had orders to cruise off the western coasts, not only on account of some French privateers, which had made mischief with our shipping, but also as a draft-ship for receiving and training batches of young hands, who were transferred, as occasion offered, to Halifax, or the West Indies station. And now as the need for new forces ceased, Captain Drake was beginning to expect orders for Spithead to discharge. Instead of that, however, the Admiralty had determined to employ this ship, which had done so much in the way of education, for the more thorough settlement of a question upon which they differed from the general opinion of the Navy, and especially of the Ordnance Board. This was concerning the value of a new kind of artillery invented by a clever Scotchman, and called a "Carronade," because it was cast at certain iron-works on the banks of the river Carron. This gun is now so thoroughly well known and approved, and has done so much to help us to our recent triumphs, that I need not stop to describe it, although at first it greatly puzzled me. It was so short, and light, and handy, and of such large caliber, moreover with a great chamber for the powder, such as a mortar has, that at first it quite upset me, knowing that I must appear familiar, yet not being so. However, I kept in the background, and nodded and shook my head so that every one misunderstood me differently.

That night I arose and studied it, and resolved to back it up, because only Captain Drake was in its favour, and the first-lieutenant. Heaviside was against it strongly, although he said that six months ago the Rainbow, an old 44, being refitted with nothing else but carronades of large caliber, had created such terror in a French ship of almost equal force, that she fired a broadside of honour, and then surrendered to the Rainbow. But to come back to our Alcestis, at the time I was promoted to first place in gunnery. Over and above her proper armament of long guns, eighteen and twelve pounders, she carried on the quarter-deck six 24-pounder carronades, and two of 18 in the forecastle. So that in truth she had fifty-two guns, and was a match in weight of metal for a French ship of sixty guns, as at that time fitted. Afterwards it was otherwise; and their artillery outweighed ours, as much as a true Briton outweighs them.

Now Naval Instructor Mr Llewellyn had such a busy time of it, and was found so indispensable on board the Alcestis, that I do assure you they could not spare him for even a glimpse of old Newton-Nottage, until the beginning of the month of May. But as I always find that people become loose in their sense of duty, unless girt up well with money (even as the ancients used to carry their cash in their girdles), I had taken advantage of a run ashore at Pembroke, to send our excellent Parson Lougher a letter containing a £5 note, as well as a few words about my present position, authority, and estimation. I trusted to him as a gentleman not to speak of those last matters to any untrustworthy person whatever; because there would be six months' pension falling due to me at Swansea, at the very time of writing; and which of course I meant to have; for my zeal in overlooking my wound could not replace me unwounded, I trow. But knowing our Government to be thoroughly versed in every form of stinginess and peculation (which was sure to be doubled now a Fox was in), I thought that they might even have the dishonesty to deny me my paltry pittance on account of ancient merit and great valour, upon the shabby plea that now I was on full pay again! They would have done so, I do believe, if their own clumsy and careless ways had allowed them to get scent of it. But they do things so stupidly, that a clever man need never allow them to commit roguery upon him. And by means of discreet action, I was enabled for fourteen years to draw the pension I had won so nobly, as well as the pay I was earning so grandly. However, these are trifles.

The £5 note was for Mother Jones, to help our Bunny with spring-clothes, and to lay out at her discretion for my grandchild's benefit, supposing (as I must needs suppose) that Churchwarden Morgan, in face of his promise, would refuse indignantly to accept a farthing for the child's nourishment. He disappointed me, however, by accepting four pound ten, and Mrs Jones was quite upset; for even Bunny never could have eaten that much in the time. Charles was a worthy man enough (as undertakers always are), but it was said that he could not do according to his lights, when fancy brought his wife across them. Poor Mother Jones was so put out, that she quite forgot what she was doing until she had spent the ten shillings of change in drawers for her middle children. And so poor Bunny got nothing at all; nor even did poorer Bardie. For this little dear I had begged to be bought, for the sake of her vast imagination, nothing less than a two-shilling doll, jointed both at knee and elbow, as the Dutchmen turn them out. It was to be naked (like Parson Chowne's folk), but with the girls at the well stirred up to make it more becoming. And then Mother Jones was to go to Sker, and in my name present it.

All things fail, unless a man himself goes and looks after them. And so my £5 note did; and when I was able to follow it, complaint was too late, as usual. But you should have seen the village on the day when our Captain Drake—as we delighted to call him—found himself for the first time able to carry out his old promise to me, made beneath the very eyes of his true-love, Isabel. The thought of this had long been chafing in between his sense of honour, and of duty set before him by the present Naval Board. And but for his own deeper troubles, though I did my best for ease, he must have felt discomfort. If I chose, I could give many tokens of what he thought of me, not expressed, nor even hinted; yet to my mind palpable. But as long as our Navy lasts, no man will dare to intrude on his Captain.

Be it enough, and it was enough, that his Majesty's 44-gun ship Alcestis brought up, as near as her draught allowed, to Porthcawl Point, on the 5th of May 1783. This was by no means my desire, because it went against my nature to exhibit any grandeur. And I felt in my heart the most warm desire that Master Alexander Macraw might happen to be from home that day. Nothing could have grieved me more, than for a man of that small nature to behold me stepping up in my handsome uniform, with all the oars saluting me, and the second-lieutenant in the stern-sheets crying, "Farewell, Mr David!" also officership marked upon every piece of my clothes in sight; and the dignity of my bearing not behind any one of them. But as my evil luck would have it, there was poor Sandy Mac himself, and more half-starved than ever. Such is the largeness of my nature, that I sank all memory of wrongs, and upon his touching his hat to me I gave him an order for a turbot, inasmuch as my clothes were now too good, and my time too valuable, to permit of my going fishing.

This, however, was nothing at all, compared with what awaited me among the people at the well. All Newton was assembled there to welcome and congratulate me, and most of them called me "Captain Llewellyn," and every one said I looked ten years younger in my handsome uniform. I gave myself no airs whatever—that I leave for smaller men—but entered so heartily into the shaking of hands, that if I had been a pump, the well beneath us must have gone quite dry. But all this time I was looking for Bunny, who was not among them; and presently I saw short legs of a size and strength unparalleled, except by one another, coming at a mighty pace down the yellow slope of sand, and scattering the geese on the small green patches. Mrs Morgan had kept her to smarten up, —and really she was a credit to them, so clean, and bright, and rosy-faced. At first she was shy of my grand appearance; but we very soon made that right.

s

Now I will not enlarge upon or even hint at the honour done me for having done such honour to my native place, because as yet I had done but little, except putting that coat on, to deserve it. Enough that I drew my salary for attending to the old church clock, also my pension at Swansea, and was feasted and entertained, and became for as long as could be expected the hero of the neighbourhood. And I found that Mother Jones had kept my cottage in such order, that after a day or two I was able to go to Sker for the purpose of begging the favour of a visit from Bardie.

But first, as in duty bound, of course, I paid my respects to Colonel Lougher. As luck would have it, both the worthy Colonel and Lady Bluett were gone from home; but my old friend Crumpy, their honest butler, kindly invited me in, and gave me an excellent dinner in his own pantry; because he did not consider it proper that an officer of the Royal Navy should dine with the maids in the kitchen, however unpretending might be his behaviour. And here, while we were exchanging experience over a fine old cordial, in bursts the Honourable Rodney, without so much as knocking at the door. Upon seeing me his delight was such that I could forgive him anything; and his admiration of my dress, when I stood up and made the salute to him, proved that he was born a sailor. A fine young fellow he was as need be, in his twelfth year now, and come on a mitching expedition from the great grammar-school at Cowbridge. To drink his health, both Crumpy and myself had courage for another glass; and when I began to tell sea-stories, with all the emphasis and expression flowing out of my uniform, he was so overpowered that he insisted on a horn-pipe. This, although it might be now considered under dignity, I could not refuse as a mark of respect for him, and for the service; and when I had executed, as perhaps no other man can, this loyal and inimitable dance, his feelings were carried away so strongly that he offered all the money left him by a course of schoolwork (and amounting to fourpence-halfpenny) if I would only agree to smuggle him on board our Alcestis, when she should come to fetch me.

This, of course, I could not think of, even for a hundred pounds; and much as I longed for the boy to have the play of his inclination. And in the presence of Crumpy too, who with all his goodwill to me, would be sure to give evidence badly, if his young master were carried away! And under such love and obligation to the noble Colonel, I behaved as a man should do, when having to deal with a boyish boy; that is to say, I told his guardians on the next opportunity.

But to break away at once from all these trifling matters, only one day came to pass before I went for Bardie. All along the sea-coast I was going very sadly; half in hopes, but more in fear, because I had bad news of her. What little they could tell at Newton was that Delushy was almost dead, by means of a dreadful whooping-cough, all throughout the winter, and the small caliber of her throat. And Charles Morgan had no more knowledge of my warm feeling thitherway, than to show me that he had been keeping some boards of sawn and seasoned elm, two feet six in length, and in breadth ten inches, from what he had heard about her health, and the likelihood of her measurement. When I heard this, you might knock me down, in spite of all my uniform, with a tube of macaroni. People have a foolish habit, when a man comes home again, of keeping all the bad news from him, and pushing forward all the good. If this had not been done to me, I never could have slept a wink, ere going to Sker Manor.

To me that old house always seemed even more desolate and forlorn with the summer sunshine on it, than in the fogs and storms of winter; perhaps from the bareness of the sand-hills, and the rocks, and dry-stone walls, showing more in the brightness, and when woods and banks are fairest. I looked in vain for a moving creature; there seemed to be none for miles around, except a sullen cormorant sleeping far away at sea. Only little Dutch was howling in some lonely corner slowly, as when her five young masters died.

As I approached the door in fear of being too late to say good-bye to my pretty little one, yet trying to think how well it might be for her poor young life to flutter to some guardian angel, my old enemy Black Evan stood and barred the way for me. I doubt if he knew me, at first sight; and beyond any doubt at all, I never should have known him, if I had chanced to meet him elsewhere. For I had not set eyes on his face from the day when he frightened us so at the Inquest; and in those ten months, what a change from rugged strength to decrepitude!

"You cannot see any one in this house," he said very quietly, and of course in Welsh; "every one is very busy, and in great trouble every one."

"Evan black, I feel sorrow for you. And have felt it, through all your troubles. Take the hand of a man who has come with goodwill, and to help you."

He put out his hand, and its horn was gone. I found it flabby, cold, and trembling. A year ago he had been famous for crushing everything in his palm.

"You cannot help us; neither can any man born of a woman," he answered, with his black eyes big with tears: "it is the will of the Lord to slay all whom He findeth dear to me."

"Is Delushy dead?" I asked, with a great sob rising in my throat, like wadding rammed by an untaught man.

"The little sweetheart is not yet dead; but she cannot live beyond the day. She lies panting with lips open. What food has she taken for five days?"

Any one whose nature leads him to be moved by little things, would have been distressed at seeing such a most unlucky creature finishing her tender days in that quiet childish manner, among strangers' tenderness. In her weak, defeated state, with all her clever notions gone, she lay with a piece of striped flannel round her, the lips, that used to prattle so, now gasping for another breath, and the little toes that danced so, limp, and frail, and feebly twitching. The tiny frame was too worn to cough, and could only shudder faintly, when the fit came through it. Yet I could see that the dear little eyes looked at me, and tried to say to the wandering wits that it was Old Davy; and the helpless tongue made effort to express that love of beauty, which had ever seemed to be the ruling baby passion. The crown and stripes upon my right arm were done in gold—at my own expense, for Government only allowed yellow thread. Upon these her dim eyes fastened, with a pleasure of surprise; and though she could not manage it, she tried to say, "How boofely!"

CHAPTER XLII.

THE LITTLE MAID, AND THE MIDSHIPMAN.

In this sad predicament, I looked from one to other of them, hoping for some counsel. There was Moxy, crying quite as if it were her own child almost; and there was Peggy the milking-maid, allowed to offer her opinion (having had a child, although not authorised to produce one); also myself in uniform, and Black Evan coming up softly, with a newly-discovered walk. And yet not one had a word to say except "poor little dear!" sometimes; and sometimes, "we must trust in God."

"I tell you," I cried; "that never does. And I never knew good come of it. A man's first place is to trust to himself, and to pray to the Lord to help him. Have you nothing more to say?"

"Here be all her little things," Black Evan whispered to his wife; "put them ready to go with her." His two great hands were full of little odds and ends which she had gathered in her lonely play along the beach, and on the sand-hills.

"Is that all that you can do? Watkin could do more than that. And now where is young Watkin?"

They assured me there was no more to do. They were tired of trying everything. As for Watkin, he it was who had brought the malady into the house, and now they had sent him for change of air to an uncle he had at Llynvi. Concerning Delushy, there was nothing for her to do, but to die, and to go to heaven.

"She shan't die, I tell you," I cried out strongly: "you are a set of hopeless ones. Twice have I saved her life before, when I was only a fisherman. I am a man in authority now; and please God, I am just in time to save her life, once more, my friends. Do you give her up, you stupids?"

They plainly thought that I was gone mad, by reason of my rise in life; and tenfold sure of it they were, when I called for a gown of red Pembrokeshire flannel, belonging to Moxy for ten years now. However poor Moxy herself went for it; and I took the child out of her stuffy bed, and the hot close room containing it, and bore her gently in my arms with the red flannel round her, and was shocked to find how light she was. Down the great staircase I took her, and then feeling her breath still going, and even a stir of her toes, as if the life was coming back to her, what did I do but go out of doors, into the bright May sunshine? I held her uncommon and clearly-shaped face on my bosom, to front the sunlight, and her long eyelashes lifted, and her small breast gave three sighs.

"Good-bye all of you," I cried: "she comes away with me this minute. Peggy may come, if she likes, with half a sheep on her back to-morrow."

And so she did: and I could not give her less than half-a-crown for it; because of the difference and the grace of God to darling Bardie. In my arms the whole way home, she lay like a new-born lamb almost, with her breath overcome at first, and heavily drawn, while her eyes were waking. Then as the air of the open heaven found its way to her worn-out lungs, down her quiet eyelids dropped, with a sleepy sense of happiness, and her weak lips dreamed of smiling, and her infant breast began to rise and fall quite steadily. And so she fell into a great deep sleep, and so I took her to my home, and the air of Newton saved her.

Our Bunny was very good. There could hardly have been any better child, when her victuals were not invaded. She entered into Bardie's condition, and took quite a motherly attitude towards her. And while the tiny one lay so weak, Bunny felt that the lead of mind was hers for the present, and might be established by a vigorous policy. However in this point she was wrong, or at any rate failed to work it out. In a fortnight Bardie was mistress again; and poor Bunny had to trot after her.

Now although it was very pleasant to see the thankfulness of Black Evan, when he came over every day, and brought his pockets full of things, and tried to look pleased when truthful Bardie refused downright to kiss him; pleasant also for me to be begged not only to fish, but even to shoot—perhaps because now the wrong time of year—in and over and through a place, where the mere sight of my hat had been sure to lead to a black eye under it; in despite of all these pleasures, I perceived that business must be thoroughly attended to. And taking this view I was strengthened in my own opinions, by the concurrence of every neighbour possessing a particle of sense. Not only Mother Jones—who might be hard, from so much family—but also the landlord of the Jolly quite agreed with the landlady, and even Crumpy, a man of the utmost tenderness ever known almost, and who must admire children, because he never yet had owned any—all these authorities agreed that I must take care what I was about. For my part, finding their opinions go beyond my own almost, or at any rate take a form of words different from my own, and having no assurance how it might end, I felt inclined to go back, and give fair-play to both sides of the argument.

But, as often happens when a man desires to see the right, and act strictly up to it, the whole affair was interrupted, and my attention called away by another important matter, and the duties springing out of it. And this came to pass in the following manner. It happened upon Oak-apple morning that I was down on a little sand-hill, smoking a pipe, and with both children building houses upon my pumps. These pumps had lovely buckles of the very latest regulation; and it was a pleasure to regard them when at leisure, and reflect upon their quality, as well as signification. The children, however, took this matter from another point of view; and there was scarcely anything to their little minds more delightful than to obscure my pumps with sand, and put up a tower over them. And then if I moved, down came the whole; and instead of themselves, they laughed at me. I had worked very hard in the Alcestis, and for almost a week after landing found it a most delicious thing, because so incomprehensible, to have nothing whatever to do. But long before now, I was tired of it, and yearned to put on my old slops again, and have a long day of fishing as if Bunny's life and mine hung on it. And when I gave a feast of turbot caught by that excellent Sandy Macraw (and paid for at just what he chose to charge), you would not have guessed it, but such were my feelings, that I only could make believe to eat. And Sandy himself, by special desire, took the foot of the table, and went largely into everything; but behaved uncommonly well, for him.

Now this is just the way I keep on going out of the proper track. If I could not train a gun, much straighter than I can tell a story, France would have conquered England, I believe, in spite of Nelson. It is the excess of windage, coming down to me from great bards, which prevents my shot from flying point-blank, as it ought to do. Nevertheless the village children loved my style, especially since his Majesty had embellished me. And this was why I shunned the well, and sate among the sand-hills; for really it was too hard to be expected to have in throat a new story, never heard before, every time a little pitcher came on the head of a little maid, to be filled, and then to go off again. Bardie and Bunny knew better than that, and never came for stories, till the proper time—the twilight.

Now, as I was longing much to sacrifice all dignity, and throw off gold-lace and blue-cloth, and verily go at the congers (which I did the next day, and defied the parish to think what it chose of me), I beheld a pair of horses, with a carriage after them, coming in a lively manner towards my nest of refuge.

"It is useless now," I cried aloud; "I can hope for no more peace. Everybody knows me, or believes it right to know me."

Nevertheless, on the whole, I felt pleased, when I saw that

the harness was very bright, and the running-gear knopped with silver. And my amazement was what you may enter into, when really the driver proved to be no bigger than that little Master Rodney Bluett. He had the proper coachman by his side, for fear of accidents; but to me, who had seen so much of horses now in Devonshire, it appeared a most rash thing to allow such a boy to navigate.

However, having caught me thus, he jumped out without accident, while the coachman touched his hat to me, or to his Majesty as now represented by me.

Then that noble boy—as he ought no doubt to be entitled, being the son of a nobleman, although in common parlance styled an honourable boy, which to my mind is no more than a simple contradiction—up he ran with his usual haste, expecting to find only Bunny and me. But his astonishment was worth seeing, on account of his being such a fair young chap, when suddenly he beheld poor Bardie, standing weakly on her legs not quite re-established yet, and in her shy manner of inner doctrine taking observation of him. A more free-and-easy schoolboy there could scarcely be than Rodney; and as for our Bunny, he used to toss her, until her weight overpowered him. But with this little lady looking so pale, and drawn, and delicate, he knew (as if by instinct) that he must begin very gingerly.

"Captain Llewellyn," he said; "I am come to tell you that my mind is quite made up. I mean to go to sea as soon as I can have my clothes made."

"But, young sir," I answered, with a wish to humour this fine boy, yet a desire to escape the noble Colonel's anger; "it is useless now to go to sea. There is no war. We must wait, and trust the Lord to send one."

"And how shall I be fit to manage a ship, and fight our enemies, unless I begin at once, and practise, Captain Llewellyn?"

In this there was so much truth, as well as sense of discipline, moreover such fine power of hope for another good bout at the French, that I looked at my pocket-lappets for an answer; and found none.

"I can stand a great deal," he cried; "on account of my age, and so on. But I can't stand Latin and Greek, and I cannot stand being put off always. I know what they want me to do. They want me to grow too old for the Navy! And I do believe they will manage it. I am getting twelve, every day almost, and I can pull a pair of oars, and fire a cannon nine inches long, and sail a boat, if it doesn't blow."

"For all that I can answer, sir," my words were, being proud of him; "and you know who taught you this, and that. And you know that he always did impress upon your early mind the necessity of stern discipline, and obedience to superiors. Your first duty is to your King and country, in the glorious time of war. But with a wretched peace prevailing, your duty is to the powers placed by Providence to look after you."

"I have heard that till I am sick of it," he answered rather rudely, for I seemed to myself to have put it well: "is that all you can do for me? I had better not have come at all. Look, I have five guineas here, given me yesterday, and all good ones. I will put them just in there—and my word of honour——"

"My boy, if it were fifty, five hundred, or five thousand, would an officer of the Royal Navy think of listening to them? You have hurt my sense of honour."

"I beg your pardon, Captain Llewellyn," he said, hanging down his head: "but you used not to be quite so proud. You used to like five shillings even."

"That is neither here nor there," I answered very loftily, and increasing his confusion: "five shillings honourably earned no man need be ashamed of. But what you have offered me is a bribe, for the low purpose of cheating your good uncle and dear mother. You ought to sink into the sand, sir."

He seemed pretty nearly fit to do so, for I put a stern face on, though all the time I could hardly keep from laughing most good-naturedly; when a little hand went into his, and a little face defied me. Poor sick Bardie had watched every word, and though unable to understand, she took hot sides with the weaker one.

"'E san't sink into 'e sand, I tell 'a, 'e yicked bad old Davy. 'Hot's a done to be 'colded so? I's very angy with 'a indeed, to go on so to a gentleyum."

By what instinct could she tell that this was a young gentleman? By the same, I suppose, by which he knew that she was a young lady. And each of them ready to stand up for the other immediately! It made me laugh: and yet it is a sad thing to go into.

"Now, my boy," I began for fear of losing the upper hand of them; "you are old enough to understand good sense when put before you. It is true enough that if you mean to walk the planks like a sailor, you can hardly begin too soon at the time of life you are come to. I was afloat at half your age, so far as I can remember. But I am bound to lay before you two very serious questions. You will have to meet, and never escape from, every kind of dirt, and hardship, narrowness, and half-starving—not an atom of comfort left, such as you are accustomed to. Danger I will not speak of, because it would only lead you on to it. But the other thing is this: By going to sea, you will for ever grieve and drive out of your prospects not only your good uncle, but perhaps almost your mother."

I thought I had made a most excellent speech, and Bardie looked up with admiration, to know when I meant to finish. But to my surprise, young Rodney took very little heed of it.

"That shows how much you know, old Davy! Why I was come on purpose to tell you that they are tired out at last: and that I may go to sea, if only you will appoint me a place on board of your ship Alcestis. Now do, Captain Llewellyn, do, and I will never forget it to you, if ever I become a great man."

"My dear boy, I would do it this minute if I had the power. But though they call me 'Captain' here, I am only Captain of a gun, and Instructor of Artillery. And even our Captain himself could not do it. He could only take you as a volunteer, and now there is no call for them. You must get your appointment as midshipman in the regular way from London. And the chances are fifty to one against your joining the Alcestis. That is to say, of course, unless you have some special interest."

His countenance fell to the lowest ebb, and great tears stood in his bold blue eyes; but presently the hopeful spirit of youth and brave lineage returned.

"I will write to my brother in London," he said; "he has never done me a good turn yet; perhaps he will begin this time."

Not to be too long about it, either by that or some other influence, he obtained his heart's desire, and was appointed midshipman, with orders to join the Alcestis, upon her next appearance off our coast. You should have seen the fuss he made, and his mother too, about his outfit; and even Colonel Lougher could not help being much excited. As for me, I was forced to go to and fro betwixt Newton and Candleston Court every day, and twice a-day, for the purpose of delivering judgment upon every box that came. But when Master Rodney made me toss his spelling-books and grammar at his breast, to practise parrying with his little dirk, I begged him to let me take them home, as soon as he was tired. I have them now with his little stabs in them, and they make me almost independent of the schoolmaster in writing.

Not only was I treated so that I need not have bought any food at all—except for Bardie and Bunny—but also employed at a pleasant price to deliver lessons every morning as to the names of sails and ropes and the proper style of handling them. We used to walk down to the hard sea-shore, with a couple of sharp sticks, whenever the tide allowed fair drawing-room. And the two little children enjoyed it almost as much as the rising hero did. The difficulty was to keep the village children, who paid nothing, from taking the benefit of my lecture as much as Midshipman Bluett did. And they might have done so, if they cared to do it, for I like a good large audience; but they always went into playing hopscotch, in among my ropes and yards, when all done beautifully in fine sand, and ready to begin almost—for the proper way is to have a ship spread naked first, and then hoist sail, if you want to show its meaning. I could not bear to be hard upon these young ones— and some of them good Mother Jones's own—all in a mess of activity; and I tried to think that it was all right, because money was earning anyhow. But I could not reconcile it with my sense of duty to make a game of well-paid work; therefore I kept the children out, in a manner I need not now describe, only you may rely upon it for real ingenuity; for children are worse to manage than folk who have been through having them.

CHAPTER XLIII.

A FINE PRICE FOR BARDIE.

Now our own two little darlings had behaved so beautifully, gazing at the bad works of the others from a distance only, though sadly pushed to share in them, and keeping their little garters up, when the others were hopscotching; also feeling, and pointing out, and almost exaggerating the ruin wrought by the other small ones (which they durst not come down to help), that I determined to give them both a magnificent

Sunday dinner. I would gladly have had the young midshipman down—for on Sunday he was such an ornament, as good as the best church-window!—but now our time was almost up; and though his mother would have let him come to grace my humble cottage, the Colonel insisted that he must go to take farewell of some excellent aunts, from whom he had large expectations, and who had ordered him up for the Sunday to the neighbourhood of Cardiff. However, we could get on very well with our own aristocracy only, which I was sure poor Bardie was, though without any aunts to dine her, and it only made me the more determined to have a family party fed on good fare. We envied nobody as we sate down, and the little ones put up both hands, according to some ancient teaching. For the first course, we had conger, baked; a most nourishing, excellent dish, full of jelly and things for children. And this one was stuffed, like a loaded cannon, with meat-balls, pork fat, and carraways. Bunny went at him as if she had never secured such a chance in her life before, but Bardie seemed inclined to wait for what was coming afterwards, and spent the time in watching Bunny with admiration and contempt mixed, as they are on a child's face only.

Then I brought in the dish of the day, with Bunny skipping and going about, and scorching her fingers to help me; but Bardie (having gone into her grandeur) sitting at table steadfastly, and with a resolute mind to know what it was before approval. She had the most delicate nostrils, but what I brought made her open them. Because I had the very best half of the very best ham ever cured in our parish, through a whole series of good-luck. Luck, and skill, and the will of the Lord, must all combine for a first-rate ham; and here they were met, and no mistake, both by one another and by excellent cooking afterwards. It would not become me to say any more, when it comes to my mind that the delicate gold of infant cabbage, by side of it, was also of my own planting, in a bit of black mould in a choice niche, ere Bethel Jose had tempted me. In spite of all this wonderful cheer, and the little ones going on famously, the sight of that young cabbage struck a vein of sorrow in me somewhere. To go away, and leave my house and garden for whole years perhaps, and feel that it was all behind me, in neglect and loneliness, with no one to undo the windows, or to sow a row of peas, or even dib a cabbage in, and perhaps myself to find no chance of coming back to it, and none to feel the difference! Like a knife all this went through me; so that I must look upward quite, for fear of the little ones watching me.

Those two little creatures ate with a power and a heartiness enough to make anybody rejoice in the harmless glory of feeding them. After the very first taste, they never stopped to wipe their lips, or to consider anything, but dealt with what they had won, and felt, and thoroughly entered into it. Only every now and then they could not help admiring what I take to be the surest proof of a fine ham and good cookery; that is to say, bright stripes of scarlet in between fat of a clear French white, not unlike our streaky jaspers interlaid with agate. To see that little thing, who scarce could lift a finger three weeks ago, now playing so brisk a knife and fork, filled me with gratitude and joy, so that I made up my mind to finish my dinner from the conger, and keep the rest of the ham for her.

I gave the little souls their wine—as they called it—of gooseberry-water, a good egg-cup full apiece; and away they went, like two little women, into the garden to play with it, and see who would keep it the longest. Then I put the rest of the ham in the cupboard, and returning to the conger, began to enjoy the carver's privilege of ten minutes for his own fork. But just as I had done handsomely well, and was now preparing to think about a pipe of fine Navy tobacco, and a small nip of old rum and water, suddenly my door was darkened, and there stood the very last man (save one) whom, for my comfort and calm Sabbath feeling, I could ever have wished to see.

"Peace be to this house," he began, with his hands spread out, and his eyes turned up, but his nostrils taking sniff of things: "peace be to this humble home, and the perishing flesh contained in it! Brother Davy, is it well with thee?"

"Brother Hezekiah," said I, perceiving what he was up to: "no flesh does this house contain; for that it is too humble. But in the name of the Lord, right welcome art thou to cold conger! Brother, I pray thee, arise and eat; and go forty days hence on the strength of it."

"It hath been done," replied Hezekiah, "by Divine grace and unceasing prayer. But come, old chap, I am sure you have got something better in that cupboard. Stinking fish hast thou often sold me, and lo I have striven to like it! therefore give me good meat now, and let us rejoice at thy great doings."

This speech was so full of truth that it got the upper hand of me, both by the sense of compunction and the strength of hospitality, and I could no longer deny to Perkins all that remained of poor Bardie's ham. "I have expounded the word of the Lord, I have been as Lot in your little Zoar," he cried, going on for the third help of ham; "my spirit was mighty within me, David; and Hepzibah took up the wondrous tale. Backsliding brother, where hast thou been? There is a movement and revival set afoot from my burning words and Hepzibah's prophecies such as shall make your rotten old Church——"

"Have a drop of beer," I said, for I did not like to see him shake his fist at our church-tower.

"Well, I don't mind if I do," he answered, "now I come to think of it. Everything in its season, brother. And a drop of your old rum afterwards."

I pretended not to hear this last; for though I might stand him in twopenny ale, I saw no reason for spoiling the tops of a bottle or two that I scorned to open, even when my rheumatics had leapt from my double half-ribs to my ear-drops. So, after observing that things were locked up, I ran into the Jolly, and fetched a pint of small ale, very rapidly. Not expecting me back so soon, he had made a good round, with his knife in his hand, to see what might be hoped for. Now back he came with a groan, and said that he knew not what he was fit for. When the power of the Word came upon him, he had such spasms afterwards.

I never love to be in company with a man of this sort. When my time is come for thanking God for a fine dinner, I would rather be alongside of a simple man and a stupid one, who can sit and think with me, and say no more about it. He knew my feelings, I do believe, and enjoyed them like pickles with his meat; and after finishing every morsel, even down to the mark of the saw upon the very knuck of it, up he put his tallowy thumbs with the black nails outwards, and drew a long breath, and delivered, "In the name of the Lord, Amen. And now, Brother David, rejoice a little, as behoves a Christian man, upon the blessed Sabbath-day."

"Hezekiah, I have rejoiced to behold your joy in feeding, and to minister thereto. Now, having fruition of fleshly things, take the word of the Lord, oh my brother, and expound doctrinally; though it be but a score of chapters. I will smoke, and hearken thee."

"Strong meat is not for babes, my son; and a babe art thou, old Dyo. Chaps like you must wait and watch for the times of edification. There is a time for sowing, and there is a time for reaping. Small ale is not meat for such as bear the burden of the day."

"'Kiah, the smith," I asked, very shortly, "what is it you would have of me?"

"Brother Davy, I have offered a blessing on thy flesh-pots; and good they were, though not manifold. It is comely that I should offer another blessing on thy vessels, Davy."

What could I do with such a man in my own house? Brother Hezekiah became, at my expense, most hospitable. I found no escape from my own bottle, without being rude to my visitor's glass; and yet I enjoyed not a single drop, for want of real companionship. For all my wits were up in arms, as if against Parson Chowne almost; because I knew that Master Perkins wanted to make a fool of me. So I feigned to be half-seas-over, that he might think he had done it.

"Ancient friend," he began at last, when he thought that I was ripe for it; "thou hast lifted me above the height of edification. Peradventure I say words that savour not of wisdom, beloved brother, the fault is thine: here I am, and there you are."

"How can any man having a smithy of his own go on so? An thou wert not tipsy, 'Kiah, thou couldst see the contrary. I am here, and thou art there."

"Just so. You have put it wonderfully," he answered, after thinking: "we may both say right is right, which is the end of everything. Keziah said to me, 'Go seek where he is, and how he is; because I have seen noble visions of his exaltation.' And yet, you see, exalted brother, scarce the tenth part came to her."

"She knows what she is about," said I; "she dreamed of a red-hot cradle, and the hoof of Satan rocking me. Now I see the whole of it. It was Parson Chowne, and the ferry-boat, and the ketch I was all but burned in. Perkins, tell me more, my friend. I have groaned much for neglecting the warning of the prophetess."

"How many men have groaned in vain for that same cause, old Dyo! Vainglorious males, they doubt her gift, because she is a female! Out of the mouths of babes and women—brother, I forget the passage, but it comes to that, I think. And now she hath been again in trouble."

"Concerning what, old Hezekiah? As concerning what, I pray thee?"

"Even touching the child Delushy, in the godless house of Sker. In a holy trance it hath been vouchsafed her to behold that poor kid of the flock bearing in her mouth a paper, whereupon in letters of blood was written, ' Come over, and help us.' And we have found a way to help her, with thy faithful testimony."

In his crafty sheep's-eyed manner, made of crawling piety mixed with sharp and spiteful worldliness, he began to feel my soundings towards a scheme so low and infamous, that my blood within me boiled for being forced to bear with him. He had prepared the whole plot well, and what it came to was just this: Inland there lived a wealthy smelter of the Methodist tribe, and Hezekiah was deep in his books for long supply of material. Rees ap Rees was his name, and he longed, as every year he grew older, to make up for an ancient wrong, which was coming home to him. In the early days when he was poor, and clever, and ambitious, he had ousted his elder brother from his father's hearth, and banished him. This poor fellow fled to the colonies; and for many years no token and no news came home of him. Meanwhile Rees ap Rees was growing elderly, and worn out with money, which is a frightful thing to feel. But about a year ago, a half-cast sailor had come to his house, bringing a wretched death-scrawl from this supplanted, but never yet forgotten, and only brother. There were not a dozen lines, but they told a tale that made the rich man weep and eat dry bread for days and days. His brother having been born without the art of getting on at all, was dying for want of food and comfort, having spent his last penny to keep the mouths of his two little babes at work. These poor children had lost their mother, and were losing their father now, who with his last breath almost, forgetting wrongs, as we do in death, very humbly committed them to the charge of his rich brother. And he said that his only remaining friend, captain of the Nova Scotia, had promised to deliver them safe in Bristol, to be sent for. The dying father had no strength to speak of their names, or age, or any other particulars.

Now it so happened that Rees ap Rees was dearly fond of children, as all rich childless people are, on account of being denied them: and since his wife died, he had often thought of adopting some one. But being rich, he was fidgety now; and none of the children in his neighbourhood ever blew their noses.

So here he found, as it were from heaven, two little dears coming down upon him, his next of kin and right heirs, and also enabling him to go to his parish churchyard, with a sense of duty done, although preferring to rest elsewhere, if by law allowable. You may suppose how he waited and watched; but those two little dears never came. Upon that he longed for them so much more that he offered a reward of £100 for any tidings of them, and of £200 for both or either, brought to his house in safety. Hence it will be clear enough what Hezekiah's scheme was; and half the reward was to be my own.

"All thou hast to say, good Dyo, is what thou saidest at the very time; that the ship was not called Andalusia, but to the best of thy belief was more like Nova Scotia. Also that she was bound for Bristol, and that the other baby's clothes bore no coronet, as they fancied, but the letter R. done fancifully, as might be by a freemason, such as the poor father was said to be. That garment must be destroyed of course. I have one prepared for the child Delushy, with 'Martha ap Rees' in faint writing upon it. This the old man must find out for himself, after our overlooking it. He will then believe it tenfold. And after the sight of thy uniform, Dyo—— ha! how sayest thou, old friend? A snug little sum to invest for old age. Thou knowest the old saying, 'Scurvy in the Navy; but the Navy's self more scurvy!' When thou art discharged with three halfpence a-day, one hundred pound with accumulations, say £150 then, will help to buy sulphur for thy rheumatics. Myself will give thee ten per cent for it, upon sound security."

"It sounds very well," said I, to lead him; "one hundred and fifty pounds have a fine sound."

"Not only that, my noble boy: but the hold thou wilt have on a rich young maiden, such as Martha ap Rees will be. The old fellow can't last very long: none of those smelters ever do, and he hath heart-disease as well. Little Martha will come into £20,000 or more, and every penny of it hanging upon thee, and me, my lad. Is it well devised, is it grand, my boy; is it worthy of old 'Kiah?"

"That it is," I cried; "most worthy!"

He flourished his glass in the pride of his heart, and even began to sing a song with a chorus of "Spankadilloes," forgetting whose holy day it was. Unfortunately I did the same; for my nature can never resist a song: moreover I wanted to think a little. Not from any desire to dwell for a moment on my own interest, but from the great temptation to make the fortunes of our poor castaway. But while I was nursing my left knee, with the foot giving time for another chorus (which was just beginning), I heard a tiny pipe, and turned round, and there was the little thing herself, dancing on one foot, and jerking the other in mockery of my attitude, nodding her head to keep time as well, and for her very life singing out, "Pankydillo, dillo, dillo," while Bunny peeping round the door-post, with a power of Sabbath feeling, looked as if the world were ending. It was clear that Bardie had not seen Perkins, whom she never could endure, else would she not have run in from the garden, to bear a share in our melody; and that good brother was so full of his noble scheme, and his song, and my rum, that he never noticed her baby voice; and her quick light figure was out of his sight, from the corner of his boozing. Therefore I managed to get her away, and send her for a good walk with Bunny, to look for water-cress at Bruwys Well; for I thought it wiser to keep that Perkins ignorant of her whereabouts; and Bunny could be trusted now to see to any one anywhere.

Off went the heavy one very gravely, and the light one full of antics, even in front of the cottages singing "Pankydillo" (which hit her fancy), so that I feared some disrepute, at such a thing going forth from our house upon a Sabbath evening. I tried to frown, but she made me laugh by turning round and clapping her knee, exactly as she had seen me do; and it seemed the best thing to go back out of sight, ere neighbours got the key to it. Little she guessed that the fate of her life was dancing in the balance, and that her own lightsome play had turned it, whether for good or evil.

How could I let such a spring of life, such a mischievous innocence, and thoroughly earnest devotion to play, sink and be quenched by a formal old Methodist in the iron district? Sker House was dull enough for dry bones: but there at least she had the sands, and sea, and shells, and rabbits, and wildfowl: nor any one to terrify her with religious terrors—which to the young are worst of all—unless it were a ghost or two of wicked abbots repenting. Whereas I knew what an old compunctious Methodist is, who has made some money, and devotes his last years to "the service of Jehovah." Even £20,000 could not make it up to her.

Therefore I shook Master Perkins up, for he really had been a little too free, and was going to sleep with his spectacles stuck for a corkscrew into another bottle, and I made him understand that his plan was a great deal too crooked for me, and that the sooner he went to seek Hepzibah (who was prophesying on a stool for pickling pork, down at Betsy Matthew's), and to prepare for his midnight service, with a strong Revival rising, the better chance he would have of escaping my now rapidly-growing desire to afford him total immersion (which is the only salvation of one highly respectable lot of them) in the well of John the Baptist. Hezekiah dreaded water so much that this hint was enough for him; and off he set in a tipsy shamble, to lie down on the sand-hills, ere he came face to face with the prophetess. When I had put things a little aright, and brushed up the hearth to a bit of fire (to warm the milk for the little ones), and by opening doors and windows sweetened all the place with summer flowing in and nestling round the relics of the sunset, and when the neighbours' chairs (whereon the very old men had been sitting for their Sunday evening) creaked, as if carried in and dusted for another Sunday, and there was not one child left (except a bad child by the well, whose loose mind was astray with stars, and took no heed of supper-time), then the two best children in the village, neighbourhood, or county, hand-in-hand came to my door. They were wonderfully silent, and they stole (each in her own manner) just a little glimpse at me, to feel how my temper lay; then they looked at one another, to exchange opinions on that all-important matter. They knew they had been out too late, and had frightened Granny a little perhaps, and therefore now had angered him. And in their simple way, they thought it wiser not to broach the question. I meant to scold them, but could not find it, when I beheld their pretty ways, within my power to do so. And lucky for them that I did not know, until next day, when too late to scold, what a dreadful mess their clothes were in. In that light I could only see their pretty faces glowing, and their bright eyes full of doubt, and their little bodies shrinking back. Also bundles of water-cress put forward to mitigate righteous wrath. I felt that I had been having my spree, and these small creatures had only had theirs. So I kissed them both, and gave them good supper, and blessed them into their little bed.

CHAPTER XLIV.

PROVIDES FOR EDUCATION.

HAVING before me several years of absence from home, if it should please the Lord so long to spare me, I now took measures for the welfare of those who would chiefly miss me. The little cottage was my own from many generations, and in a new will made by a clever man (no less than our new schoolmaster), I left it to Bunny, and all my effects, except my boat, and the sum of ten guineas, which two items, as honour demanded, were for Miss Delushy. But what is wealth without education? No more than a plummet without the line. Knowing this, I provided as follows.

A thoroughly fine new schoolmaster had arisen, as aforesaid, for the purpose of educating all our Newton children. Our good parson had brought him in, not because the old one, being challenged by the village tailor to spell the word "horse" without the picture, proved his command of the alphabet by accomplishing it in nine different ways, all wrong (for that was entered to his credit, when the tailor failed to do the like), but because he horsed a boy and left him there for the afternoon, having fallen asleep without thrashing him. And it shows what the public confusion of mind is, that there were not three people in all the parish who could help jumbling these stories together, because each of them had a horse in it! However the poor old man had to go, and Colonel Lougher, having nothing to do with the spelling of the children, thought it so hard on his brother's part, that he made the old man his head gardener, so as to double his wages, and enable him to sleep not half, but the whole of the afternoon.

His successor in the school had been sought out very diligently, and he could spell almost as well as Bardie could pronounce a word. But when we found that he came from a distance more than a quick man could walk in a day, and that he could not through all his forefathers (although they were quite at his finger-ends) claim so much even as intermarriage with any of our third-rate families, much less with any Llewellyns, or Hopkins, or Bevans, or even Thomases, we saw that even Parson Lougher had gone a little too far for us, and not a woman in the place would let a bedroom to that man.

However we could not bolt him out of his own schoolroom, and there he slept, contented with a pile of slates for bedstead, and of copy-books for bolster and for pillow. For a week at least he had no school, but he went to church and sang beautifully (which brought half the women over), and the children began to be such a plague, at home, before Monday morning, that eight or nine were sent back to school, as if with halters round their necks. With these he took so much kind trouble, that in three hours they learned more than the parish had learned for a generation; so much that they could not keep it down when they went home for dinner. In the afternoon there were twenty pupils, and by the end of the week three dozen. But how could they prove him to their parents qualified for a bedroom?

Upon the strength of my present position, and unrivalled experience, I found it my duty to come to the fore, and take the command of the householders. And knowing of course what a waste of time it is to reason with anybody, I seized the bull by the horns, and offered Master Roger Berkrolles the occupancy of my cottage upon most liberal conditions. "That is to say for rent per quarter, one sea-snail, and per annum one cockleshell, to preserve the title; provided nevertheless and upon this express condition that my lawful granddaughter Bunny should be fed, alimented, sufficiently nourished, clothed, clad, apparelled, and in garments found; also taught, instructed, indoctrined, educated and perfected in every branch of useful knowledge by the said Roger Berkrolles. Item, that if a certain child of tender years known as 'Delushy,' should at any time appear on the premises and demand instruction, instruction of the highest order, and three slices of bread-and-butter, should be imparted to her without charge, *de die in diem*." I objected to these "dies," as being of a nasty churchyard sound; but Master Roger convinced me soon, and must have convinced a far tougher fellow, that to put our latter end out of sight and out of mind so, is a bad example and discouragement for the young ones, whose place it is to dwell on it.

A man of far coarser tone of mind than mine would be required to describe Master Roger's sense of gratitude towards me. When I do a handsome thing, I cannot bear to tell of it, nor even to receive the praise accruing from what neighbours know. "Do it, and be done with it," in all such cases is my rule; and if Roger chose to give me an inventory of goods and chattels, he can bear me out in saying that I scorned to call a witness in to put his name to it. Business is not my strong point, and it never is with a man of largeness.

The next thing for me to see to was to get some wicked warrants quashed; which a deep ignorance of my character, and the lies of very low villains, had induced some weak or vicious magistrates to issue; so that in the sporting season (when I might have done my best), I was forced to decamp with my telescope. This has been mentioned perhaps before; but not my strong resolution to face it out, as soon as ever the sense of a strong position enabled me. No doubt they had meant to do their duty; and I forgave them altogether. There were three of them. Two names I quite forget. How can one think of such trifles at sea? But the third was one Master Anthony Stew, who had tyrannised over me dreadfully, in the times of my tribulation. Up to this man's gate I went, and rang the great bell, with my three stripes on, and a cap of fronted tapestry. Squire Anthony was about, somewhere on the premises, would my honour mind waiting while the boy went round to look for him? This maid never guessed how often she had told me my fish was bad, and what a shame it was to make them eat it up in the kitchen, or starve; and where did I hope to go to? Neither did she recollect how she had as good as made me kiss her behind the meat-screen, when my glory began to grow for saving those drowned niggers. And yet I could not be sure that she did not know it all, and hide it all, for the joy of boasting afterwards. I understand everything, except women.

When I was shown into the drawing-room, and Mrs Stew with a curtsy went out, as if afraid to trust herself in a presence so imposing, I had a great mind to take a nip at some of the rubbish upon the table. The whole of these nick-nacks could never have paid me half what this fellow had cost me in fines, expenses, costs, and so on; without a bit of evidence from any man of character. However, I only looked at them.

When that low Anthony Stew came in, he knew me (before I could speak almost); he gave a quick glance at the table, and then without another word showed me out, in spite of all my uniform, to his dirty little justice-room. With such a man, I should think it wrong to go into his ribaldry; only he said this, at last;

"Davy, thou thief, we will withdraw them, because we cannot execute them; now thou art in Royal Service. Five there are, if I remember. Does your conscience plead to more?"

"My conscience pleads to none, your Worship. Perjured scoundrels all of them. Five was the number, I do believe. Alas! what may we come to?"

"The gallows, Dyo, the gallows, thou rogue! Thou hast had some shavings. But when thy turn comes, good Dyo, I will do thee a good turn, if I can."

"Will your Worship tell me why? I never looked for anything but the flint-edge from your Worship."

"Because thou art the only rogue I never was a match for. There, go thy way now; go thy way; or I shall be asking thee to dinner."

"Nay, your Worship, God forbid! What food have I had since breakfast-time?" And so I won the last word of him.

After this provision for my good repute, and defiance of magisterial scandal on behalf of Bunny, my next act was one of pure generosity towards an ancient enemy. Poor Sandy Macraw had a very hard fight to maintain himself and his numerous and still increasing family. Sometimes they did not taste so much as a rind of bacon for months together, but lived on barley-bread and dog-fish, or such stuff as he could not sell, with oatmeal cakes for a noble treat every other Sunday. What did I do but impart to him, under document drawn by Berkrolles, that licence to fish off and on Sker Point which my courage had well established, with authority to him and covenant by him to attack and scare all poachers; the whole to be void upon my return, if so I should think proper. And not only this, but I put him in funds to replace all his tackle, by enabling him to sell his boat. For I went so far as to lease him my own, at a moderate yearly rental, upon condition that he should keep her in thorough repair and as good as new. And for the further validity (as the lease said) of this agreement, two years' rent became due at once, and was paid from the price of the other boat. My boat went twice as fast as Sandy's, and was far more handy, so that this bargain was fair and generous, and did honour to all concerned.

The next and last thing, before starting, was to provide for poor Bardie herself. For I feared that Hezekiah, or some other unprincipled fellow, might trump up a case, and get hold of her, and sell, or by other means turn into money my little pet, to the loss of my rights, and perhaps her own undoing. Resolved as I was to stop all chances of villany of that kind, I went direct to Colonel Lougher and to Lady Bluett. Here I made the cleanest breast that ever was scooped out almost.

I may declare that I kept in nothing, except about painting the boat, and one or two infinite trifles of that sort, which it would have been a downright impertinence to dwell upon. Nevertheless Colonel Lougher said that some blame might attach to me in spite of all pure intentions.

But Lady Bluett said no, no. She would not hear of it for a moment. The only thing that surprised her was Llewellyn's thorough unselfishness, and chivalrous devotion to a child who was nothing to him. She was a bewitching little dear; no one who saw her could doubt that; still it showed a very soft side to a wonderfully gallant character, when through all modesty it appeared what womanly tenderness there had been. And this proved how entirely right her opinion had been from the very first, and what a mistake the good Colonel had made, in declining to let her even argue.

"My dear Eleanor, my dear Eleanor," cried the Colonel, with his eyes wide open, and his white hand spread to her; "I am surprised to hear you say so. But we cannot go into that question now. Llewellyn begged for my opinion. Yours, my dear (as you have proved), is of course more valuable: still I thought that it was mine——"

"To be sure it was, dear Henry. Yours is what was asked for. My rule is never to interrupt you, but to listen silently."

"To be sure, Eleanor, to be sure! And we always agree in the end, my dear. But so far as I can judge at present, Llewellyn, although with the very best meaning——"

"And a display of the greatest valour. Come, Colonel, even by his own account——"

"Yes, my dear, great valour, no doubt, coupled with very sound discretion. Yet when I come to consider the whole, I really do think that your hero might have entered more fully into these particulars about the boat. Of course, he had no motive, and it was simply an error of judgment——"

"Henry, there was no error at all. What could he do when they would not even listen to him about the name of the ship? If they would not listen about a ship, is it likely they would listen about a boat? And a very small atom of a boat! The thing is too ridiculous."

Perceiving a pause, I made my bow; for the very last thing I could desire would be to sow a controversy between the gentleman and lady, whom of all the county I esteemed the most and loved the best. And I knew that if I caused dissension in a pair so well united, each would think the less of me, when they came to make it up together. Moreover, my object was attained. Their attention was drawn to the child again: the Colonel, as the nearest magistrate, was put in legal charge of her: I was now quit of all concealment: and Lady Bluett had promised to see to the poor thing's education, if ever she should need any.

This I hoped with all my heart that she would do, and quickly too. And indeed she was growing at such a pace after that long illness, also getting so wonderfully clever about almost everything, and full of remarks that might never strike a grown man till he thought of them, that the only way or chance I saw of taking the genius out of her, was to begin her education. Forgetting just now a good deal of my own, and being so full of artillery, I got Master Berkrolles to make the first start, and show her the way to the alphabet. Our Bunny now could spell "cat" and "dog," and could make a good shot at some other words, and enjoyed a laugh at children (head and shoulders over her) whenever they went amiss, and she from the master's face was sure of it. But Bardie had never been to school; for I thought it below her rank so much; and now I contrived for our great schoolmaster to come to my cottage, and there begin.

It must have made the very gravest man, ever cut from a block of wood, laugh to behold Master Roger, and her. He with his natural dignity, and well-founded sense of learning, and continual craving for a perfect form of discipline; yet unable to conceal his great wonder at her ways: she on her side taking measure of him in a shy glance or two, and letting her long eyelashes fall, and crossing her feet with one shoulder towards him, for him to begin with her. He vowed that he never had such a pupil; instead of learning, she wanted to know the reason why of everything. Why had A two legs and a girdle, while B had two stomachs and no leg at all? C was the moon, from the shape of it. It was no good to tell her that C was the cat; a cat had four legs and C had none: and as for D being a dog, she would fetch dear Dutch, if he would not believe her, and show him what a dog was like. And then perceiving how patient he was, and understanding his goodness, the poor little fatherless soul jumped up on his knee, and demanded a play with him. He did not know how to play very well, because he was an ancient bachelor; but entering into her sad luck, from knowledge of her history, he did the very best thing (as I thought) that ever had been done to her. He put her on a stool between his knees, and through the gloss of her hair he poured such very beautiful and true stories, that one could almost see her mind (like the bud of a primrose) opening. She pushed up her little hands and tossed her thick hair out of the hearing way, and then, being absorbed in some adventures like her own almost, round she turned and laid her eyes upon his furrowed yet beaming face, and her delicate elbows on his knees, and drank in every word, with sighs, and short breath, and a tear or two.

Although, from one point of view, I did not like to be superseded so, especially in my own department, as might be said, of story-telling, yet I put small feelings away, and all the jaundice of jealousy. If I were bound to go wherever Government might order me, for the safety of our native land, and with moderate pay accruing, also with a high position, and good hopes of raising it, the least I could do was to thank the Lord for sending those two poor children a man, so wise, and accomplished, and kind-hearted, bound over to look after them. And yet I would almost as lief have committed them into the hands of Mother Jones, who could scarcely vie with me. But they promised never to forget me; and the night before I went away, I carried Bardie back to Sker, and saw that Black Evan was dying.

CHAPTER XLV.

INTRODUCES A REAL HERO.

My orders were to rejoin at Pembroke on the 10th of June, where the Alcestis lay refitting, and taking in stores for an ocean-cruise. Of course I was punctual to the day, and carried with me a fine recruit, Master Rodney Bluett. I received not only minute directions from his lady-mother, but also a tidy little salary, to enable me to look after him. This was a lady of noble spirit, and ready to devote her son for the benefit of his country; because there was no fighting now, nor any war in prospect. Also Colonel Lougher came as far as the gate, where the griffins are, and patted his nephew's curly head; and said that although it was not quite as he himself could have wished it, he could trust the boy to be an honour to a loyal family, and to write home every now and then, for the sake of his poor mother. For his own sake also, I think the Colonel might have very truly said; because while he was talking so, and trying to insist on duty, as the one thing needful, I could not for a moment trust my own eyes to examine him. So we all tried to say "good-bye," as if there was nothing in it.

It was a very long "good-bye," even longer than we could by any stretch have dreamed of. Two or three years was the utmost that we then looked forward to: but I tell you simple truth, in saying that not one of us had the chance of seeing England, much less any part of Wales, for a shorter period than seven years and two months added. You may doubt me, and say, "Pooh, pooh! that was your fault;" and so on. But you would be wholly wrong; and from the Admiralty records our Captain could prove it thoroughly. And what is much clearer than all, do you think that Captain Drake Bampfylde would have been seven years, or even seven days, away, without sight of his beautiful lady, Isabel Carey, if it could have been managed otherwise?

It was a mixture of bad luck. I can explain a good deal of it, but not all the ins and outs. We were ordered here, and ordered there, and then sometimes receiving three contradictions of everything. Until we should scarcely have been surprised at receiving signal, "H.M.S. Alcestis to the moon; to wait for orders."

And if we had received that signal, I believe we should have tried it, being by this time the best-trained and finest ship's company in the world. We had ceased to be a receiving-ship, as soon as the war was over, and now were what they begin to call—though it sounds against the grain to me—an "Experimental Ship." And the Lord knows that we made experiments enough to drown, or blow up, or blow arms off, every man borne on our blessed books. They placed me at the head of it all, until the others were up to it; and a more uneasy or ticklish time I never have known, before or since. Over and over again I expected to go up to the sky almost; and you may pretty well conceive how frequent was my uneasiness. Nevertheless I still held on; and Government had to pay for it.

In four years' time the old frigate began to be knocked almost to pieces; and we made up our minds to be ordered home, and set our memories at work upon all who were likely to meet us, if still in the land of the living. While at Halifax thinking thus, and looking forward to Christmas-time among our own families, a spick and span new frigate came, of the loveliest lines we had ever seen, and standing-gear the most elegant. She took our eyes so much at once, and she sat the water so, that there was not a man of us able to think of anything else till all hands piped down. This was the Thetis, if you please, taken from the Crappos in the very last action of the war, a 46-gun frigate, but larger than an English 60-gun ship. The French shipbuilders are better than ours, but their riggers not to be compared; which is the reason perhaps why they always shoot at our rigging instead of our hulls. At any rate, having been well overhauled, and thoroughly refitted at Chatham, and rigged anew from step to truck, she presented an appearance of most tempting character.

It was a trick of the Naval Board to keep us together, and it succeeded. Those gentlemen knew what we were by this time, the very best ship's company to be found in all the service; and as there were signs already of some mischief brewing, their desire was still to keep together such a piece of discipline. My humble name had been brought forward many times with approval, but without any effect so far upon wages or position. Now, however, my Lords had found it expedient to remember me, and David Llewellyn was appointed master's mate to the Thetis, if he should think fit to join her; for the whole after our long service was a matter of volunteering.

There was not a man of us dared to leave Captain Drake Bampfylde shabbily. We turned over to the Thetis, in a body, with him; and the crew that had manned her from England took the old Alcestis home again. And junior Lieutenant Bluett, now a fine young fellow, walked the quarter-deck of the Thetis, so that you should have seen him. But first and foremost was to see our great Captain Drake; as ready as if he were always looking out for an enemy's ship from the foretop. He walked a little lame, on account of the piece the shark took out of him; nevertheless we had not a man to equal him for activity. I remember once when a violent gale caught us on the banks of Newfoundland, and the sky came down upon us black as any thunder-cloud. The wind grew on us so towards nightfall, that after taking in reef after reef, the orders were to make all snug, send down the topgallant-masts, and lie-to under close-reefed main-topsail and fore-topmast staysail. Captain Drake was himself on deck, as he always was in time of danger, and through the roar of the gale his orders came as clear as a bell almost, from the mouth of his speaking-trumpet. "Main-top men, to station! Close reef the main-topsail. Mr Bluett, clew up, clew up. There is not a moment to lose, my men. Spit to your hands and stick like pitch. What! are you afraid then, all of you?"

For the sail was lashing about like thunder, having broken from the quarter-gasket, and when the men came to the topsail-yard they durst not go upon it. Then a black squall struck them with blinding rain, and they scarce could see one another's faces, till a cheery voice came from the end of the yard, "Hold on, my lads—hold on there! You seem so skeery of this job, I will do it for you." "'Tis the devil himself!" cried old Ben Bower, captain of the main-top; "let him fly, let him fly, my lads!" "It is our Captain," said I, who was coming slowly up to see to it, myself prepared to do the job, and shame all those young fellows; "skulk below, you jelly-pots, and leave it to me and the Captain." "A cheer for the Captain, a cheer for the Captain!" they cried before I could follow them, and a score of men stood against the sky, in the black pitch of the hurricane, as if it were a review almost. For they guessed what the Captain must have done, and it made a hero of each of them. While they came slowly up the ratlins, he clomb the rigging like a cat, and before they got to the lubber's hole he was at the topmasthead, whence he slid down by the topping-lift to the very end of the mainyard. Such a thing done in a furious gale, and the sea going mountains high almost, beat even my experience of what British captains are up to. After that, if he had cried, "Make sail to"—Heligoland, with no landing to it—there was not a man of us but would have touched his hat, and said, "Ay, ay, sir!"

And now we first met Captain Nelson in command of the Boreas, a poor little frigate; we could have sunk her as easily as we outsailed her. But as senior to Captain Drake, he at once assumed command of us; although it was not in our instructions to be at his disposal. The Americans then were carrying on with the privileges of British subjects, in trading with the Leeward Islands; although they had cast off our authority in a most uncourteous, and I might say headstrong manner. Captain Nelson could never put up with the presumptuous manners of this race, and he felt bitterly how feeble had been our behaviour to them. These are people who will always lead the whole world, if they can; counting it honour to depart from and get over old ideas. And now they were doing a snug bit of roguery with the Leeward Islands, pretending to have British bottoms, while at bottom Yankees.

Nelson set his face against it; and whenever he set his face, his hand came quickly afterwards. We soon cut up that bit of smuggling, although the Governor of the Islands was himself against us. Captain Nelson's orders were to enforce the Navigation Act; and we did it thoroughly.

Ever so many times I met him, as he now came to and fro; and he took the barge-tiller out of my hand, at least a dozen times, I think. For he never could bear that another man should seem to do his work for him, any more than he could bear to see a thing done badly. Not that he found fault with my steering (which was better than his own, no doubt), but that he wanted to steer himself. And he never could sit a boat quietly, from his perpetual ups and downs, and longing to do something. He knew my name; he knew every one's name; he called me "old Dyo," continually, because the men had caught it up; and in my position, I could not perceive what right he had to do so. I had him on my lap, I won't say fifty times, but at least fifteen: for he never had sea-legs at all when a heavy sea was running: and I never thought it any honour, but cherished some hopes of a shilling, or so. As for appearance, at first sight he struck me as rather grotesque-looking than imposing, in spite of his full-laced uniform, and the broad flaps of his waistcoat. His hair, moreover, was drawn away from his forehead, and tied in a lanky tail, leaving exposed, in all its force, rather a sad face, pale and thin, and with the nose somewhat lop-sided. Also the shoulders badly shaped, and the body set up anyhow; and the whole arrangement of his frame nervous, more than muscular.

In spite of all this, any man who knows the faces of men, and their true meaning, could not fail to perceive at once that here was no common mortal. The vigour and spirit of his eyes were such that they not only seemed to be looking through whatever lay before them, but to have distinct perception of a larger distance, and eagerness to deal with it. And the whole expression of his face told of powerful impatience, and a longing for great deeds, dashed with melancholy. The entire crew of his ship, I was told, were altogether wrapped up in him, and would give their lives for him without thought; and there was not one of them but was mad with our Government for being at peace, and barring Captain Nelson from the exploits he was pining for. One of them struck at me with an oar, when I said how puny Nelson was, compared with our Drake Bampfylde, and only the strong sense of my position enabled me to put up with it. And what I said was all the time the very truest of the true; and that was why it hurt them so. We being now the finest and smartest frigate in the service, looked down upon that tub of a Boreas, and her waddle-footed crew, and her pale, pig-tailed commander, with a power of ignominy which they were not pleased with. And all the time we were at their orders, and they took care to let us know it! We would have fought them with pleasure, if the rules of the service allowed it.

Enough of that uncomfortable discontent and soreness. The hardest point is for a very great man to begin to set forth his greatness. We could not, at the moment, see why Horatio Nelson should thus sweep off with the lead so. But after he had once established what he was, and what he meant, there was no more jealousy. To this I shall come in its proper place; I am only now picking up crumbs, as it were, and chewing small jobs honourably.

But against one thing I must guard. Our Captain Drake was never for a moment jealous of Captain Nelson. It was one of the things that annoyed us most, when we looked down on the Boreas, and would gladly have had a good turn with those fellows who assumed such airs to us, to find that our beloved Captain was as full of Nelson as the worst of the Boreasses. And one of our men who went on strongly, took six dozen, and no mistake, and acknowledged how well he deserved it. That is the way to do things, and makes all of us one family.

It is time for me now to crowd all sail for Spithead, as we did at last. Seven round years and two months were gone since I had seen old Cymru, and I could fill seven thousand pages with our whole adventures. But none of them bore much on my tale, and nobody cares for my adventures, since I ceased to be young and handsome; and sometimes I almost thought (in spite of all experience) that I had better have gone into matrimony with a young woman of moderate substance. But (as is the case with those things) when I had the chance I scorned it; not being touched in the heart by any one, and so proud of freedom. Moreover, the competition for a man amongst young women may become so lively as to make him bear away large down wind. Exactly what had happened to me in the land of Devonshire.

Three quarters of my pay had been assigned to Roger Berkrolles, under my hand and signature, for the maintenance of our Bunny (so far as the rent might not provide it), and for the general management of things, and then to accumulate. So that, after all, I had not any amazing sum to draw, remembering, too, that from time to time we had our little tastes of it. Nevertheless, when added up, I really was surprised to find that the good clerks thought it worth so much quill-chop over it. And now I had been for several years on the pay of a petty officer (master's mate), and looking forward to be master, if he were good enough to drop off.

He was truly tough, and would never drop off; and I felt it the more because he was ten years my junior, and unseasoned. He drew half again as much as I did, though he knew that I had done all the work. He gave me two fingers to say good-bye, which is a loathsome trick to me; so I put out my thumb, which was difficult to him : and the next time I saw him, he lay dead in the cockpit of the Goliath.

In a word, I got so little after all my long endeavours to secure the British nation from its many enemies, that verily I must have fallen to the old resource again, and been compelled to ask for alms to help me home in 1790, as had happened to me in the year of grace 1759. We sailors always seem to be going either up or down so much, without seeming to know why. Perhaps it is a custom from our being on the waves so much. However, I was saved from doing such disgrace to the uniform and to my veteran aspect, and the hair by this time as white as snow, simply through the liberality of our Captain Bampfylde. For he made me an offer both kind and handsome, though not more perhaps than might be expected, after our sailing together so long. This was to take me home with him to Narnton Court, or the neighbourhood, according to how the land might lie, and thence to secure me a passage (which is easy enough in the summer-time) by one of the stone-boats to Newton Nottage. I felt that I might have come home in grander style than this was like to be; and yet it was better than begging my way ; and scarcely any man should hope to be landed twice in all his life, at his native village from a man-of-war. Of course, if Master Rodney Bluett had still been with us, he would have seen to my return, and been proud of it; but he had been forced to leave us, having received his appointment as 3d lieutenant to the Boadicea, 74.

Therefore I travelled with Captain Drake, and made myself useful upon the road, finding his coxswain (who came with us in a miserably menial manner) utterly useless, whenever a knowledge of life and the world was demanded. And over and over again, my assistance paid my fare, I am sure of it, whether it were by coach or post. Because the great mass of seaman appear, whenever they come on shore, to enjoy a good cheating more than anything. The reason is clear enough—to wit, that having seen no rogues so long, they are happy to pay for that pleasure now.

It was said that even the Admiralty had been playing the rogue with us, stopping our letters, and our news, to keep us altogether free from any disturbances of home. At any rate, very few of us had heard a word of England, except from such old papers as we picked up in the colonies. And now, after seven years, how could we tell what to expect, or how much to fear?

CHAPTER XLVI.

AFTER SEVEN YEARS.

FROM Exeter to Barnstaple, we crowded sail with horses' tails, and a heavy sea of mud leaping and breaking under the forefoot of our coach. Also two boys on the horses, dressed like any admirals, one with horn on his starboard thigh, and the other with jack-boots only. It was my privilege to sit up in the foretop, as might be, with Coxswain Toms in the mizentop, and the Captain down in the waist by himself. We made about six knots an hour perhaps; whenever we got jerks enough to keep up the swearing.

But the impatience of our Captain showed how very young he was, now at forty years of age, according to chronology, though nobody would believe it! Surely he might have waited well, after so long waiting; and if he could not chew a quid—which breeds a whole brood of patience—at any rate he had fine pipes, and with common-sense might have kindled them. I handed him down my flint and steel, and my hat to make a job of it; but he shut up the glass, and cried, "More sail!" in a voice that almost frightened me.

It was as dark as main-top-tree holes by the time we got to Barnstaple; but we found no less than four fine lamps of sperm-oil burning, and tallow-candles here and there, in shops of spirit and enterprise. The horses were stalled, and the baggage housed in a very fine inn, looking up the street, and then the Captain told Toms and me to bouse up our jibs, while he went out. This we were only too glad to do after so much heavy rolling upon *terra firma*, as those landsmen love to call it, in spite of all earthquakes, such as killed thirty thousand Italian people, when first I took to the sea again.

But before long, Toms and I began to feel that we had no right to abandon our commander so. Here we were in a town that hardly ever saw a royal sailor, and could not be supposed to know for a moment what his duties were, or even to take a proper pride in seeing him borne harmless. And here was our Captain gone out in the dark, with his cocked-hat on, and his gold lace shining wherever a tallow-candle hung; also with a pleasant walk as if he were full of prize-money; though the Evil One had so patched up a peace that we never clinked a half-penny.

When old Jerry Toms and my humble self had scarcely gone through three glasses, he said to me, and I said to him, that we were carrying on too coolly in a hostile town like this. And just at this moment the Navy was down in popular estimation; for such is the public urgency, whenever we are paid for, without being killed or wounded. Therefore Jerry and I were bound to steer with a small helm, and double the watch.

We beat up the enemy's quarters calmly, finding none to challenge us; and then we got tidings of our Captain out upon the Braunton road. Jerry was a man of valour, and I could not hang back to be far behind him; and we had been concerned in storming many savage villages. So we stormed this little town, carrying our hangers, and nobody denied us. But before we were half a mile entirely out of hearing, the mayor arose from his supper, and turned out the watch, and beat the drums, and bred such alarm that in one street there were three more people alive ere morning.

Meanwhile Jerry Toms and I shaped our course for the Braunton road, and hit it, and held on to it. And, because no man, in strange places, knows what the air may contain for him, Jerry sang a song, and I struck chorus; with such an effect that the cows were frightened all along the hedgerows. This put us quite on our legs again; and a more deeply sober couple could not, or at any rate need not, be seen, than that which myself and Jerry were, after two miles of walking.

In this manner, steering free, yet full of responsibility, we doubled the last point of the road, where it fetches round to Narnton Court. And here we lay to, and held council, out of the tide of the road, and in what seemed to be a lime-kiln.

The coxswain wanted to board the house, and demand our Captain out of it; we had carried all public opinion thus, and the right thing was to go on with it. But I told him very strongly (so that he put down his collar from his ears to listen) that no doubt he was right enough upon a hundred thousand subjects, yet was gone astray in this. And if we boarded a house at night, after carrying all the town by storm, what ship had we to bear us away from the mayor and his constables to-morrow?

In this dilemma, who should appear but the Captain himself, with his head bowed down, and his walk (which was usually so brisk in spite of a trifling lameness), his very walk expressing that his heart was full of sadness.

"How much longer? How much longer?" he was saying to himself, being so troubled that he did not see us in the shadow there. "My own brother to have sworn it! Will the Lord never hold His hand from scourging and from crushing me? Would that I were shot and shrouded! It is more than I can bear."

In this gloomy vein he passed us; and we looked at one another, daring not to say a word. How could a pair of petty officers think of intruding upon the troubles and private affairs of a post-captain, even though, since our ship was paid off, we could hardly be said to serve under him? "Blow me out of the mouth of a gun," cried Coxswain Toms, in a shaking voice, "if ever I was so amazed before! I would have sworn that our Skipper was not only the handsomest but the happiest man in all the service."

"Then, Jerry, I could have set you to rights. How many times have I hinted that our Skipper had something on his mind, and none of you would hearken me?"

"True for you, my lad. I remember, now you come to speak of it. But we paid no heed; because you looked so devilish knowing, and would go no further. Old Dyo, I beg your pardon now; there is good stuff in you, friend Dyo—thoroughly good stuff in you."

"I should rather think there was," I replied, perhaps a little drily, for he ought to have known it long ago: "Jerry, I could tell you things that would burst the tar of your pig-tail. Nevertheless I will abstain, being undervalued so. Ho, ship mate! Haul your wind, and hail! I am blessed if it isn't old Heaviside!"

Even in the dark, I knew by the walk that it was a seaman, and now my eyes were so accustomed to look out in all sorts of weather, that day or night made little difference to my sense of vision, which (as you may see hereafter) saved a British fleet, unless I do forget to tell of it.

"Heaviside is my name, sir. And I should like to know what yours may be."

"David Llewellyn." And so we met; and I squeezed his hand till he longed to dance; and I was ready to cut a caper from my depth of feeling.

I introduced him to Jerry Toms, according to strict formality; and both being versed in the rules of the service, neither would take precedence; but each of them hung back for the other fellow to pretend to it, if he dared. I saw exactly how they stood; and being now, as master's mate, superior officer to both, I put them at their ease, by showing that we must not be too grand. Thus being all in a happy mood, and desirous to make the best of things, we could not help letting our Captain go to dwell upon his own fortunes. Not that we failed of desire to help him, but that our own business pressed.

Gunner Heaviside led us down to a little cabin set up by himself on the very brink of Tawe high-water mark, as a place of retirement when hard pressed, and unable to hold his own in the bosom of his family. You may well be surprised—for I was more, I was downright astonished—to find that this was my old ferry-boat, set up (like a dog begging) on shores, with the poop channelled into the sand, and the sides eked out with tarpaulin. A snugger berth I never saw for a quiet man to live in: and though Heaviside scorned to tell us, and we disdained to ask him, that—as I guessed from the first—was the true meaning of it. This poor fellow had been seduced—and I felt for his temptations—(when he came fresh from salt water, and our rolling ideas of women) into rapid matrimony with that sharp Nanette. He ought to have known much better; and I ought to have given him warning; but when he had made up his mind to settle, I thought it was something solid. I gave him the names, as I may have said, of good substantial farmers' daughters, owning at least a good cow apiece from the date of their majority, also having sheets and blankets, and (as they told me many a time) picked goose feathers enough for two. And yet he must go and throw himself away upon that Nanette so!

But when I came to hear his case, and he for a moment would not admit that it was worse than usual, or that he wanted pity more than any other men do, and scarcely knew how far he ought, or dared even, to accept it; and then at the gurgling of his pipe, fancied that he heard somebody; Jerry and I squeezed hands for a moment, and were very careful not to tantalise this poor man, with our strong-set resolution. "Give a wide berth to all womankind," was what we would have said, if we could when now it was too late for him; "failing that, stand off and on, and let the inhabitants come down, and push off their boats, and victual you."

Poor Heaviside fetched a sigh enough to upset all arrangements; for Jerry and I (good widowers both) were not likely to be damped, at the proper time for jollifying, by the troubles of a man who was meant to afford us rather a subject for rejoicing. Therefore we roused him up, and said, or at least conveyed to him, that he must not be so sadly down upon his luck like this. And hearing that he had six children now, and was in fear of a seventh one, I was enabled to recollect more than twenty instances of excellent women who had managed six, and gone off at the seventh visitation.

This good news put such sudden spirit into my old shipmate, that he ceased for a long time to be afeared of all that his wife could do to him. He never said a word to show what his mind suggested to him, whether good or evil. Only he made me tell those cases of unmerited mercy (as he put it) such a number of times that I saw what comfort he was deriving. And then we challenged him to tell us what was going on with him.

He seemed rather shy of discussing himself, but said that he was in Sir Philip's service, as boatman, long-shoreman, and river-bailiff, also pork-salter (as a son of the brine), and watercress-picker to the family. In a word, he had no work whatever to do; as you may pretty safely conclude, when a man is compelled to go into a catalogue of his activities. This sense of ease overweighed him no doubt, and made the time hang heavily, after so much active service, so that Naval Instructor Heaviside moved about, and began to gossip, and having no business of his own, spent his mind upon other folks'. Now, as we began to see through him, and the monotony of a fellow who is under his wife's thumb (without the frankness to acknowledge, and enlist our sympathies for this universal burden), both Jerry and I desired to hear something a little more new than this. All things are good in their way, and devised by a finely careful Providence ; so that no man, whose wife is a plague to him, can fail of one blessed reflection—to wit, that things are ordered so for the benefit of his fellow-creatures.

Thus our noble Heaviside, not being satisfied with the state of things at home—especially after he had appealed to Nanette's strong sense of reason (which bore sway in the very first week of half the honeymoon gloriously), and after he had yielded slowly all his outworks of tobacco, coming down from plugs to pipes, and from pipes to paper things, without stink enough to pay for rolling, and so on in the downward course, till he would have been glad of dry sugar-canes, or the stems of "old-man's beard,"—this poor but very worthy fellow gallantly surrendered, and resolved to rejoice, for the rest of his time, in his neighbours' business mainly.

Herein he found great and constant change from his own sharp troubles. Everybody was glad to see him; and the wives who were the very hardest upon their own husbands, thought that he showed himself much too soft in the matter of Madame Heaviside. It was not his place, when that subject arose, to say either "yes" or "no;" but to put aside the question, as one that cannot be debated, out of the house, with dignity. Only every one liked him the more, the moment they remembered how contagious his complaint was.

Regard this question as you will (according to lack of experience), it was much for our benefit that the Naval Instructor was henpecked. He had accumulated things, such as no man can put together, whose wife allows him to have his talk. If he may lay down the law, or even suggest for consideration, he lets out half his knowledge, and forgets the other half of it. Whereas, if all his utterance is cut short at beginning, he has a good chance to get something well condensed inside him. Thus, if you find any very close-texture and terseness in my writings, the credit is due to my dear, good wife, who never let me finish a sentence. I daresay she had trouble with me; and I must be fair to her. It takes a very different man to understand a different woman; and these things will often touch us too late, and too sadly. I gave her a beautiful funeral, to my utmost farthing; and took her headstone upon credit, almost before the sexton would warrant that the earth was settled.

That night my old friend Heaviside (who has led me, from like experience, into a wholly different thing) showed some little of himself again, before our whale-oil light began to splutter and bubble too violently. Our society quite renewed his hope of getting away again; especially when I explained to him that (according to my long acquaintance with law), no one could hold him accountable for any quantity of children which a Frenchwoman might happen to have. An alien, to wit, and a foreigner, worst of all a Frenchwoman, could not expect all her froggy confinements to hold good in England. He had committed a foolish and unloyal act in buckling to with an alien enemy, and he deserved to pay out for it; but I thought (and Coxswain Toms was of the same opinion) that poor Heaviside now had suffered ever so much more than even a Frenchwoman could expect of him. And we begged him to go afloat again.

He shook his head, and said that he had not invited our opinions, but to a certain extent endeavoured to be thankful for them. Yet he suggested delicately that after being so long at sea, we might have waited for our land-legs, before we became so positive. And if we would not mind allowing him to see to his own concerns, he would gladly tell all he knew about those of other people. This appeared to me to be a perfectly fair offer; but Jerry Toms took a little offence, on account of not knowing the neighbourhood. As superior officer of the three, I insisted upon silence, especially as from old times I knew what villany might be around us. And as soon as Heavyside could descry quite clearly what tack I stood upon, he distinctly gave his pledge to be open as the day. Therefore we all filled our pipes again, and took fresh lights for them, and looked at one another, while this old chap told his story. And please to mind that he had picked up a prawn-netful of little trifles, such as I never could stoop to scoop, because he won such chances through the way the women pitied him. Only I must in ship-shape put his rambling mode of huddling things. If you please, we are now going back seven years, and more than that, to the very date of my escape from Devonshire; so as to tell you what none of us knew, until we met with Heaviside.

CHAPTER XLVII.

MISCHIEF IN A HOUSEHOLD.

It seems that no sooner did Parson Chowne discover how cleverly I had escaped him (after leaving my mark behind, in a way rather hard to put up with), than he began to cast about to win the last stroke somehow. And this, not over me alone, but over a very much greater man, who had carried me off so shamefully—that is to say, Captain Bampfylde. Heaviside was not there as yet, but with us in the Alcestis, so that he could not describe exactly the manner of Chowne's appearance. Only he heard from the people there, that never had such terror seized the house within human memory. Not that Chowne attempted any violence with any one; but that all observed his silence, and were afraid to ask him.

What was done that night between Sir Philip and the Parson, or even between the Parson and Sir Philip's heir, the Squire (whose melancholy room that Chowne had dared to force himself into), nobody seemed to be sure, although every one craved to have better knowledge. But it was certain that Isabel Carey went to her room very early that night, and would have no Nanette for her hair; and in the morning was "not fit for any one to look at," unless it were one who loved her.

Great disturbances of this sort happen (by some law of nature), often in large households. Give me the quiet cottage, where a little row, just now and then, comes to pass, and is fought out, and lapses (when its heat is over) into very nice explanations, and women's heads laid on men's shoulders, and tears that lose their way in smiles, and reproach that melts into self-reproach. However, this was not the sort of thing that any sane person could hope for in thirty miles' distance from Master Stoyle Chowne, after once displeasing him. And what do you think Parson Chowne did now, or at least I mean soon afterwards? That night he had pressed his attentions on the beautiful young lady, so that in simple self-defence she was forced to show her spirit. This aroused the power of darkness always lurking in him, so that his eyes shone, and his jaws met, and his forehead was very smooth. For he had a noble forehead; and the worse his state of mind might be, the calmer was his upper brow. After frightening poor Miss Carey, not with words, but want of them (which is a far more alarming thing, when a man encounters women), he took out his rights in the house by having an interview with Sir Philip; and no one could make any guess about what passed between them. Only it could not be kept from knowledge of the household, that Parson Chowne obtained or took admission to Squire Philip also.

Of this unhappy gentleman very little has been said, because I then knew so little. I am always the last man in the world to force myself into private things; and finding out once that I must not ask, never to ask is my rule of action, unless I know the people. However, it does not look as if Master Heaviside had been gifted with any of this rare delicacy. And thus he discovered as follows.

Squire Philip's brain was not so strong as Captain Bampfylde's. He had been very good at figures, while things went on quietly; also able to ride round and see the tenants, and deal with them, as the heir to a large estate should do. The people thought him very good: and that was about the whole of it. He never hunted, he never shot, he did not even care for fishing. A man may do without these things, if he gets repute in other ways (especially in witchcraft), but if he cannot show good cause for sticking thus inside four walls, an English neighbourhood is apt to set him down for a milksop. And tenfold thus, if he has the means to ride the best horse, and to own the best dogs, and to wear the best breeches that are to be bought.

Squire Philip must not be regarded, however, with prejudice. He had good legs, and a very good seat, and his tailor said the same of him. Also, he took no objection to the scattering of a fox, with nothing left for his brush to sweep up, and his smell made into incense; nor was the Squire, from any point of view, or of feeling, squeamish. Nevertheless he did not give satisfaction as he should have done. He meant well, but he did not outspeak it; only because to his quiet nature that appeared so needless. And the rough, rude world undervalued him, because he did not overvalue himself. This was the man who had withdrawn, after deep affliction, into a life, or a death, of his own, abandoning hope too rapidly. He had been blessed, or cursed, by nature, with a large, soft heart; and not the flint in his brains there should be for a wholesome balance. I know the men. They are not very common; and I should like to see more of them.

This Squire Philip's hair was whiter than his father's now

they said; and his way of sitting, and of walking, growing older. No wonder, when he never took a walk, or even showed himself; rather like a woman yielding, who has lost her only child. It is not my place to defend him. All our ways are not alike. To my experience he seemed bound to grieve most about his children. For a man may always renew his wife more easily than his children. But Squire Philip's view of the matter took a different starting-point. It was the loss of his wife that thus unwisely overcame him.

Accordingly he had given orders for women alone to come near him, because they reminded him of his wife, and went all around in a flat-footed way, and gave him to see that they never would ask, yet gladly would know, his sentiments. And living thus, he must have grown a little weak of mind, as all men do, with too much of a female circle round them.

What Parson Chowne said to this poor gentleman, on the night we are speaking of, was known to none except themselves and two or three maids who listened at the door, because their duty compelled them thus to protect their master. And all of these told different stories, agreeing only upon one point; but the best of them told it, as follows. Chowne expressed his surprise and concern at the change in his ancient friend's appearance, and said that it was enough to make him do what he often had threatened to do. Squire Philip then asked what he meant by this; and he answered in a deep, low voice, "Bring to justice the villain who, for the sake of his own advantage, has left my poor Philip childless: and with all the fair Isabel's property too! Greedy, greedy scoundrel!" They could not see the poor Squire's face, when these words came home to him; but they knew that he fell into a chair, and his voice so trembled that he could not shape his answer properly.

"Then you too think, as I have feared, as I have prayed, as I would die, rather than be forced to think. My only brother! And I have been so kind to him for years and years. That he was strong and rough, I know—but such a thing, such a thing as this——"

"He began to indulge his propensities for slaughter rather early—I think I have heard people say."

"Yes, yes, that boy at school. But this is a wholly different thing—what had my poor wife done to him?"

"Did you ever hear that Drake Bampfylde offered himself to the Princess, while you were away from home, and a little before you did?"

"I never heard anything of the kind. And I think that she would have told me."

"I rather think not. It would be a very delicate point for a lady. However, it may not be true."

"Chowne, it is true, from the way you say it. You know it to be true; and you never told me, because it prevents any further doubt. Now I see everything, everything now. Chowne, you are one of the best of men."

"I know that I am," said the Parson, calmly; "although it does not appear to be the public opinion. However, that will come right in the end. Now, my poor fellow, your wisest plan will be to leave yourself altogether to a thoroughly trustworthy man. Do you know where to find him?"

"Only in you, in you, my friend. My father will never come to see me, because—you know what I mean—because—I dared to think what is now proved true."

"Now, Philip, my old friend, you know what I am. A man who detests every kind of pretence. Even a little inclined perhaps to go too far the other way."

"Yes, yes; I have always known it. You differ from other men; and the great fault of your nature is bluntness."

"Philip, you have hit the mark. I could not have put it so well myself. My fine fellow, never smother yourself while you have such abilities."

"Alas! I have no abilities, Chowne. The whole of them went, when my good-luck went. And if any remained to me, how could I care to use them? After what you have told me too. My life is over, my life is dead."

All the maids agreed at this point, and would scorn to contradict, that poor Squire Philip fell down in a lump, and they must have run in with their bottles and so on, only that the door was locked. Moreover, they felt, and had the courage to whisper to one another, that they were a little timid of the Parson's witchcraft. There had been a girl in Sherwell parish who went into the Parson's service, and because she dared to have a sweetheart on the premises, she had orders for half an hour, before and after the moon rose, to fly up and down the river Yeo, from Sherwell Mill to Pilton Bridge; and her own mother had seen her. Therefore these maids only listened.

"All this shows a noble vein of softness in you, my good friend"—this was the next thing they could hear—"it is truly good and grand. What a happy thing to have a darling wife and two sweet children, for the purpose of having them slain, and then in the grandeur of soul forgiving it! This is noble, this is true love! How it sets one thinking!" This was the last that the maids could hear; for after that all was whispering. Only it was spread in every street, and road, and lane around, in about twelve hours afterwards, that a warrant from Justices Chowne and Rambone, and, with consent of Philip Bampfylde, was placed in the hands of the officers of the peace for the apprehension of Captain Drake, upon a charge of murder.

When Sir Philip heard of this outrage on himself—and tenfold worse—upon their blameless lineage, he ordered his finest horse to be saddled, and put some of his army-clothes on; not his best, for fear of vaunting, but enough to know him by. Then he rode slowly up and down the narrow streets of Barnstaple, and sent for the mayor and the town-council, who tumbled out of their shops to meet him. To these he read a copy of the warrant, obtained from the head-constable, and asked, upon what information laid, such a thing had issued. Betwixt their respect for Sir Philip Bampfylde and their awe of Parson Chowne, these poor men knew not what to say, but to try to be civil to every one. Sir Philip rode home to Narnton Court, and changed his dress, and his horse as well, and thus set off for Chowne's house.

What happened there was known to none except the two parsons and the General; but every one was amazed when Chowne, in company with Parson Jack, rode into Barnstaple at full gallop, and redemanded his warrant from the head-constable, who held it, and also caused all entries and copies thereof to be destroyed and erased, as might be; and for this he condescended to assign no reason. In that last point he was consistent with his usual character; but that he should undo his own act, was so unlike himself that no one could at first believe it. Of course people said that it was pity for Sir Philip's age and character and position, that made him relent so: but others, who knew the man better, perceived that he had only acted as from the first was his intention. He knew that the Captain could not be taken, of course, for many a month to come, and he did not mean to have him taken or put upon his trial; for he knew right well that there was no chance of getting him convicted. But by issue of that warrant he had stirred up and given shape to all the suspicions now languishing, and had enabled good honest people to lay their heads together and shake them, and the boldest of them to whisper that if a common man had done this deed, or been called in question of it, the warrant would have held its ground, until he faced an impartial jury of his fellow-countrymen. And what was far more to Chowne's purpose, he had thus contrived to spread between Sir Philip and his eldest son a deadly breach, unlikely ever to be bridged across at all, and quite sure to stand wide for healing, up to the dying hour. Because it was given to all to know that this vile warrant issued upon oath of Squire Philip and by his demanding; and the father's pride would never let him ask if this were so.

Now people tried to pass this over, as they do with unpleasant matters, and to say, "let bygones go;" yet mankind will never have things smothered thus, and put away. When a game is begun, it should be played out: when a battle is fought, let it be fought out—these are principles quite as strong in the bosoms of spectators, as in our own breasts the feeling—"let us live our lives out."

But Isabel Carey's wrath would not have any reason laid near it. Her spirit was as fine and clear almost as her lovely face was, and she would not even dream that evil may get the upper hand of us.

She said to Sir Philip, "I will not have it. I will not stay in a house where such things can be said of any one. I am very nearly eighteen years old, and I will not be made a child of. You have been wonderfully kind and good, and as dear to me as a father; but I must go away now; I must go away."

"So you shall," said poor Sir Philip; "it is the best thing that can be done. You have another guardian, more fortunate than I am; and, my dear, you shall go to him."

Then she clung to his neck, and begged and prayed him not to think of it more, only to let her stop where she was, in the home of all her happiness. But the General was worse to move than the rock of Gibraltar, whenever his honour was touched upon.

"My dear Isabel," he answered, "you are young, and I am old. You were quicker than I have been, to see what harm might come to you. That is the very thing which I am bound to save you from, my darling. I love you as if you were my own daughter; and this sad house will be, God knows, tenfold more sad without you. But it must be so, my child. You ought to be too proud to cry, when I turn you out so."

Not to dwell upon things too much—especially when grievous—Narnton Court was compelled to get on without that bright young Isabel, and the female tailors who were always coming after her, as well as the noble gallants who hankered, every now and then, for a glimpse of her beauty and property. Isabel Carey went away to her other guardian, Lord Pomeroy, at a place where a castle of powder was; and all the old people at Narnton Court determined not to think of it; while all the young folk sobbed and cried; and take it on the average, a guinea a-year was lost to them.

All this had happened for seven years now: but it was that last piece of news, no doubt, almost as much as the warrant itself, that made our Captain carry on so when we were in the lime-kiln. Because Lord Pomeroy had forbidden Isabel to write to her lover, while in this predicament. He, on the other hand, getting no letters, without knowing why or wherefore, was too proud to send any to her.

We saw the force of this at once, especially after our own correspondence (under both mark and signature) had for years been like the wind, going where it listeth. So we resolved to stop where we were, upon receipt of rations; and Heaviside told us not to be uneasy about anything. For although he durst not invite us to his own little cottage, or rather his wife Nanette's, he stood so well in the cook's good graces that he could provide for us; so he took us into the kitchen of Narnton Court, where they made us very welcome as Captain Drake's retainers, and told us all that had happened since the departure of Miss Isabel, between Narnton Court and Nympton. In the first place, Parson Chowne had been so satisfied with his mischief, that he spared himself time for another wedlock, taking as Mrs Chowne No. 4 a young lady of some wealth and beauty, but reputed such a shrew that nobody durst go near her. Before she had been Mrs Chowne a fortnight, her manners were so much improved that a child might contradict her; and within a month she had lost the power of frowning, but had learned to sigh. However, she was still alive, having a stronger constitution than any of the Parson's former wives.

Parson Jack had also married, and his wife was a good one; but Chowne (being out of other mischief) sowed such jealousies between them for his own enjoyment, that poor Master Rambone had taken to drink, and his wife was so driven that she almost did the thing she was accused of. Very seldom now did either of these two great parsons come to visit Sir Philip Bampfylde. Not that the latter entertained any ill-will towards Chowne for the matter of the warrant. For that he blamed his own son, the Squire, having received Chowne's version of it, and finding poor Philip too proud and moody to offer any explanation.

We had not been at Narnton Court more than a night, before I saw the brave General; for hearing that I was in the house, and happening now to remember my name, he summoned me into his private room, to ask about the Captain, who had started off (as I felt no doubt) for the castle of Lord Pomeroy. I found Sir Philip looking of course much older from the seven years past, but as upright and dignified, and trustful in the Lord as ever. Nevertheless he must have grown weaker, though he did his best to hide it; for at certain things I told him of his favourite son, great tears came into his eyes, and his thin lips trembled, and he was forced to turn away without finishing his sentences. Then he came back, as if ashamed of his own desire to hide no shame, and he put his flowing white hair back, and looked at me very steadily.

"Llewellyn," he said, "I trust in God. Years of trouble have taught me that. I speak to you as a friend almost, from your long acquaintance with my son, and knowledge of our story. My age will be three score years and ten, if I live (please God) till my next birthday. But I tell you, David Llewellyn, and I beg you to mark my words, I shall not die until I have seen the whole of this mystery cleared off, the honour of my name restored, and my innocent son replaced in the good opinion of mankind."

This calm brave faith of a long-harassed man in the goodness of his Maker made me look at him with admiration and with glistening eyes; for I said to myself that with such a deep knave as Chowne at the bottom of his troubles, his confidence even in the Lord was very likely to be misplaced. And yet the very next day we made an extraordinary discovery, which went no little way to prove the soundness of the old man's faith.

CHAPTER XLVIII.

A BREATHLESS DISINTERMENT.

By this time we were up to all the ins and outs of everything. A sailor has such a knowledge of knots, and the clever art of splicing, that you cannot play loose tricks, in trying on a yarn with him. Jerry Toms and I were ready, long before that day was out, to tie up our minds in a bow-line knot, and never more undo them. Jerry went even beyond my views, as was sure to be, because he knew so much less of the matter; he would have it that Parson Chowne had choked the two children without any aid, and then in hatred and mockery of the noble British uniform, had buried them deep in Braunton Burrows, wearing a cocked for a shovel hat, purely by way of outrage.

On the other hand, while I agreed with Jerry up to a certain distance, I knew more of Parson Chowne (whom he never had set eyes upon) than to listen to such rubbish. And while we agreed in the main so truly, and thoroughly praised each other's wisdom, all the people in the house made so highly much of us, that Jerry forgot the true line of reasoning, even before nine o'clock at night, and dissented from my conclusions so widely, and with so much arrogance, that it did not grieve me (after he got up) to have knocked him down like a ninepin.

However, in the morning he was all right, and being informed upon every side that the cook did it with the rolling-pin, he acknowledged the justice of it, having paid more attention to her than a married lady should admit, though parted from her husband. However, she forgave him nobly, and he did the same to her; and I, with all my knowledge of women, made avowal in the presence of the lady-housekeeper, that my only uneasiness was to be certain whether I ought to admire the more Jerry's behaviour or Mrs Cook's. And the cook had no certainty in the morning, exactly what she might have done.

This little matter made a stir far beyond its value; and having some knowledge of British nature, I proposed to the comitatus, with deference both to the cook and housekeeper, also a glance at the first housemaid, that we should right all misunderstanding by dining together comfortably, an hour before the usual time. Because, as I clearly expressed it, yet most inoffensively, our breakfast had been ruined by a piece, I might say, of misconstruction overnight between two admirable persons. And Heaviside came in just then, and put the cap on all of it, by saying that true sailors were the greatest of all sportsmen; therefore, in honour of our arrival, he had asked, and got leave from the gamekeepers, to give a great rabbiting that afternoon down on Braunton Burrows; and he hoped that Mrs Cockhanterbury, being the lady-housekeeper, would grace the scene with her presence, and let every maid come to the utmost.

Heaviside's speech, though nothing in itself, neither displaying any manner at all, was received with the hottest applause; and for some time Jerry and I had to look at one another, without any woman to notice us. We made allowance for this, of course, although we did not like it. For, after all, who was Heaviside? But we felt so sorely the ill effects of the absence of perfect harmony upon the preceding evening (when all our male members of the human race took more or less the marks of knuckles), that a sense of stiffness helped us to make no objection to anything. And tenfold thus, when we saw how the maids had made up their minds for frolicking.

These young things must have their way, as well as the nobler lot of us: for they really have not so very much less of mind than higher women have; and they feel what a woman is too well to push themselves so forward. They know their place, and they like their place, and they tempt us down into it.

Be that either way—and now unwomanly women waste their good brains upon a trifle of this kind—rabbiting was to be our sport; and no sooner was the dinner done, and ten minutes given to the maids to dress, than every dog on the premises worth his salt was whistled for. It would have amused you to see the maids, or I might say all the womankind, coming out with their best things on, and their hair done up, and all pretending never even to have seen a looking-glass.

Madame Heaviside (as she commanded all people to entitle her) was of the whole the very grandest as regards appearance. Also in manner and carrying on; but of this I have no time to speak. Enough that the former Naval Instructor thought it wiser to keep his own place, and let her flirt with the game keepers. We had dogs, and ferrets, and nets, and spades, and guns for those who were clever enough to keep from letting them off at all, and to frighten the women without any harm. There must have been five-and-twenty of us in number altogether, besides at least a score of children who ran down from Braunton village, when they saw what we were at. There was no restraint laid upon us by any presence of the gentry; for Sir Philip was not in the humour for sport, and the Squire of course kept himself to his room; and as for the Captain, we had no token of his return from South Devon yet.

Therefore we had the most wonderful fun, enjoying the wildness of the place, and the freshness of the river air, and wilfulness of the sandhills, also the hide-and-seek of the rushes, and the many ups and downs and pleasure of helping the young women in and out, also how these latter got (if they had any feet to be proud of) into rabbit-holes on purpose to be lifted out of them, and fill the rosettes of their shoes, and have them dusted by a naval man's very best pocket-handkerchief— together with a difficulty of standing on one foot while doing it, or having it done to them, and a fear of breathing too much out—after smothered rabbit at dinner-time—which made their figures look beautiful. Enough that I took my choice among them, for consideration; and jotted down the names of three, who must have some cash from their petticoats. Let nobody for a moment dream that I started with this intention. The rest of my life was to be devoted to the Royal Navy, if only a hot war should come again; of which we already felt simmerings. But I could not regard all these things, after so many years at sea, without some desire for further acquaintance with the meaning of everything. At sea we forget a great deal of their ways. When we come ashore—there they are again!

This is a very childish thing for a man like me to think of. Nevertheless I do fall back from perfect propriety sometimes; never as regards money; but when my feelings are touched by the way in which superior young women try to catch me; or when my opinion is asked conscientiously as to cordials. And this same afternoon the noble clearness of the sun and air, and the sound of merry voices glancing where all the world (unless it were soft sand) would have echoed them, and the sense of going sporting—which is half the game of it—these and other things, as well as the fatness of the rabbits' backs, and great skill not to bruise them, led the whole of us, more or less, into contemplation of Nature's beauties. We must have killed more than a hundred and fifty coneys, in one way and another, when Heaviside came up, almost at a run, to a hill where Jerry Toms and I were sitting down, to look about a bit, and to let the young women admire us.

"What's the matter?" said I, not liking to be interrupted thus.

"Matter enough," he panted out; "where is Madame? The Lord keep her away."

"Madame is gone down to the water-side," said Jerry, though I frowned at him, "together with that smart young fellow—I forget his name—underkeeper they call him."

"Hurrah, my hearties!" cried Heaviside; "that is luck, and no mistake. Now lend a hand, every lubber of you. Her pet dog Snap is in the sand; 'with the devil to pay, and no pitch hot,' if we take long to get him out again."

We knew what he meant; for several dogs of an over-zealous character had got into premature burial in the rabbit-galleries, through the stupidity of people who crowded upon the cone over them. Some had been dug out alive, and some dead, according to what their luck was. And now we were bound to dig out poor Snap, and woe to us all if we found him dead!

I took the biggest spade, as well as the entire command of all of us, and we started at quick step for the place which Heaviside pointed out to us. He told us, so far as his breath allowed, that his small brown terrier Snap had found a rabbit of tender age hiding in a tuft of rushes Snap put all speed on at once, but young bunny had the heels of him, and flipped up her tail at the mouth of a hole, with an air of defiance which provoked Snap beyond all discretion. He scarcely stopped to think before he plunged with a yelp into the hole, while another and a wiser dog came up, and shook his ears at it. For a little while they heard poor Snap working away in great ecstasy, scratching at narrow turns, and yelping when he almost got hold of fur. Heaviside stood, in his heavy way, whistling into the entrance-hole, which went down from a steep ascent with a tuft of rushes over it. But Snap was a great deal too gamesome a dog to come back—even if he heard him. Meanwhile a lot of bulky fellows, who could do no more than clap their hands, got on the brow of the burrow and stamped, and shouted to Snap to dig deeper. Then of a sudden the whole hill slided, as a hollow fire does, and cast a great part of itself into a deep gully on the north of it. And those great louts who had sent it down so, found it very hard (and never deserved) to get their clumsy legs out.

No wonder that Heaviside had made such a run to come and fetch us. For Snap must be now many feet underground, and the Naval Instructor knew what it would be to go home to Nanette without him. He stood above the slip and listened, and there was no bark of Snap; while to my mind came back strangely thoughts of the five poor sons of Sker, and of the little child dwelling in sand, forlorn and abandoned Bardie.

"Dig away, my lads, dig away!" I cried, from force of memory, and setting example to every one; "I have seen a thing like this before; it only wants quick digging." We dug and dug, and drove our pit through several decks of rabbit-berths; and still I cried "Dig on, my lads!" although they said it was hopeless. Then suddenly some one struck something hard, and cried "Halloa!" and frightened us. We crowded round, and I took the lead, and made the rest keep back from me, in right of superior discipline. And thence I heaved out a beautiful cocked-hat of a British Captain of the Royal Navy, with Snap inside of it and not quite dead!

Such a cheer and sound arose (the moment that Snap gave a little sniff), from universal excitement and joy, with Heaviside at the head of it, that I feared to be hoisted quite out of the hole, and mounted on human shoulders. This I like well enough now and then, having many a time deserved without altogether ensuing it; but I could not stop to think of any private triumph now. The whole of my heart was hot inside me, through what I was thinking of.

That poor honest fellow, who so eschewed the adornment of the outward man, and carried out pure Christianity so as to take no heed of what he wore, or whether he wore anything whatever; yet who really felt for people of a weaker cultivation, to such an extreme that he hardly ever went about by day much,—this noble man had given evidence such as no man, who had lost respect by keeping a tailor, could doubt of. In itself, it was perspicuous; and so was the witness, before he put up with a sack, in order to tender it.

The whole force of this broke upon me now; while the others were showing the hat round, or blowing into the little dog's nostrils, and with a rabbit's tail tickling him; because in a single glance I had seen that the hat was our Captain Bampfylde's. And then I thought of old Sir Philip, striding sadly along these burrows, for ever seeking something.

"Dig away, dig away, my lads. Never mind the little dog. Let the maidens see to him. Under our feet there is something now, worth a hundred thousand dogs."

All the people stood and stared, and thought that I was off my wits; and but for my uniform, not one would ever have stopped to harken me. It was useless to speak to Heaviside. The whole of his mind was exhausted by anxiety as to his wife's little dog. No sleep could he see before him for at least three lunar months, unless little Snap came round again. So I had to rely on myself alone, and Jerry Toms, and two gamekeepers.

All these were for giving up; because I can tell you it is no joke to throw out spadeful after spadeful of this heavy deceitful sand, with half of it coming back into the hole; and the place where you stand not steadfast. And the rushes were combing darkly over us, showing their ginger-coloured roots, and with tufts of jagged eyebrows threatening overwhelment. For our lives we worked away—with me (as seems to be my fate) compelled to be the master—and all the people looking down, and ready to revile us, if we could not find a stirring thing. But we did find a stirring thing, exactly as I will tell you.

For suddenly my spade struck something soft, something which returned no sound, and yet was firm enough to stop, or at any rate to clog the tool. Although it was scarcely twilight yet, and many people stood around us, a feeling not of fear so much as horror seized upon me. Because this was not like the case of digging out poor bodies smothered by accident or the will of God, but was something far more dreadful; proof, to wit, of atrocious murder done by villany of mankind upon two little helpless babes. So that I scarce could hold the spade, when a piece of white linen appeared through the sand, and then some tresses of long fair hair, and then two little hands crossed on the breast, and a set of small toes sticking upward. And close at hand lay another young body, of about the same size, or a trifle larger.

At this terrible sight, the deepest breath of awe drew through all of us, and several of the women upon the hill shrieked and dropped, and the children fled, and the men feared to come any nearer. Even my three or four fellow-diggers leaped from the hole with alacrity, leaving me all by myself to go on with this piteous disinterment. For a moment I trembled too much to do so, and leaned on my spade in the dusky grave, watching the poor little things, and loath to break with sacrilegious hands such innocent and eternal rest. "Ye pure and stainless souls," I cried, "hovering even now above us, in your guardian angel's arms, and appealing for judgment on your icy-hearted murderer, pardon me for thus invading, in the sacred cause of justice, the calm sleep of your tenements."

In this sad and solemn moment, with all the best spectators moved to tears by my deep eloquence, as well as their own rich sympathies, it struck me that the legs of one of the corpses stuck up rather strangely. I had not been taken aback, at all, by the bright preservation of hands and toes, because I knew well what the power of sand is when the air is kept far away; but it was dead against all my experience, that even a baby, eight years buried, should have that muscular power of leg. Without any further hesitation, up I caught the nearest of them, being desperate now to know what would be the end of it.

Three or four women, whose age had passed from lying in to laying out, now ran down the hill in great zealousness; but though their profession is perhaps the most needful of all yet invented by human nature, there was no exercise for it now. For behold, in the evening light, and on the brink of the grave, were laid two very handsome and large Dutch dolls, clad in their night-gowns, and looking as fresh as when they left the doll-maker's shop. The sand remained in their hair of course, and in their linen, but fell away (by reason of its dryness) from their faces, and hands, and feet, the whole of which were of fine hard wax. But the joints of their arms and legs had stiffened, from having no children to work them, also their noses had been spoiled at some stage of their obsequies; and upon the whole it seemed hard to say whether their appearance was more ludicrous or deplorable.

However, that matter was settled for them by the universal guffaw of the fellows who had been scared of their scanty wits not more than two minutes since, but all of whom now were as brave as lions to make laughter at my expense. This is a thing which I never allow, but very soon put a stop to it. And so I did now, without any hard words, but turning their thoughts discreetly.

"Come, my lads," I said, "we have done a better turn to the gentleman who feeds us, than if we had found two thousand babies, such as you ran away from. Rally round me, if you have a spark of courage in your loutish bodies. You little know how much hangs on this; while in your clumsy witless way, you are making a stupid joke of it. Mr Heaviside, I pray you, seek for me Mistress Cockhanterbury; while I knock down any rogue who shows the impudence to come near me."

Every man pulled his proud stomach in, when I spoke of the lady-housekeeper, who was a Tartar, high up on a shelf, allowing no margin for argument. She appeared in the distance, as managing-women always do when called upon; and she saw the good sense of what little I said, and she laid them all under my orders.

CHAPTER XLIX.

ONE WHO HAS INTERRED HIMSELF.

Such an effect was now produced all over all around us, that every man pressed for his neighbour's opinion, rather than offer his own, almost. This is a state of the public mind that cannot be long put up with; for half the pleasure goes out of life when a man is stinted of argument. But inasmuch as I was always ready for all comers, and would not for a moment harken any other opinion, the great bulk of conclusion ran into the grooves I laid for it.

This was neither more nor less than that Satan's own chaplain, Chowne, was at the helm of the whole of it. Some people said that I formed this opinion through an unchristian recollection of his former rudeness to me; I mean when he blew me out of bed, and tried to drown, and to burn me alive. However, the great majority saw that my nature was not of this sort, but rather inclined to reflect with pleasure upon any spirited conduct. And to tell the whole truth, upon looking back at the Parson, I admired him more than any other man I had seen, except Captain Nelson. For it is so rare to meet with a man who knows his own mind thoroughly, that if you find him add thereto a knowledge of his neighbours' minds, certain you may be that here is one entitled to lead the nation. He may be almost too great to care about putting this power in exercise, unless any grand occasion betides him; just as Parson Chowne refused to go into the bishopric; and just as Nelson was vexed at being the supervisor of smugglers. Nevertheless these men are ready, when God sees fit to appoint them.

However, to come back to these dolls, and the opening now before them. The public (although at first disappointed not to have found two real babies strangled in an experienced manner) perceived the expediency of rejoicing in the absence of any such horror. Only there were many people, of the lower order, so disgusted at this cheat, and strain upon their glands of weeping, with no blood to show for it, that they declared their firm resolve to have nothing more to do with it.

For my part, being some little aware of the way in which laurels are stolen, I kept my spade well up, and the two dolls in my arms, with their heads down, and even their feet grudged to the view of the gossipers. In the midst of an excited mob, a calm sight of the right thing to do may lead them almost anywhere. And I saw that the only proper thing was to leave everything to me. They (with that sense of fairness which exists in slow minds more than in quick ones) fell behind me, because all knew that the entire discovery was my own. Of course without Snap I could never have done it; nor yet without further accidents: still there it was; and no man even of our diffident Welsh nation, can in any fairness be expected to obscure himself.

My tendency, throughout this story, always has been to do this. But I really did begin to feel the need of abjuring this national fault, since men of a mixture of any sort, without even Celtic blood in them, over and over again had tried to make a mere nobody of me.

Hence it was, and not from any desire to advance myself, that among the inferior race, I stood upon my rights, and stuck to them. If ever there had been any drop of desire for money left in me, after perpetual purification (from seven years of getting only coppers, and finding most of them forgeries), this scene was alone sufficient to make me glad of an empty purse. For any man who has any money must long to put more to it; as the children pile their farthings, hoping how high they may go. I like to see both old and young full of schemes so noble; only they must let an ancient fellow like me keep out of them.

These superior senses glowed within me, and would not be set aside by any other rogue preceding me, when I knocked at Sir Philip's door, and claimed first right of audience. The other fellows were all put away by the serving-men, as behoved them; then I carried in everything, just as it was, and presented the whole with the utmost deference.

Sir Philip had inkling of something important, and was beginning to shake now and then; nevertheless he acknowledged my entrance with his wonted dignity; signed to the footman to refresh the sperm-oil lamps in the long dark room; and then to me to come and spread my burden on a table. Nothing could more clearly show the self-command which a good man wins by wrestling long with adversity. For rumour had reached him that I had dug up his son's cocked-hat, and his two grandchildren, all as fresh as the day itself. It is not for me (who have never been so deeply stirred in the grain of the heart by heaven's visitations) to go through and make a show of this most noble and ancient gentleman's doings, or feelings, or language even. A man of low station, like myself, would be loath to have this done to him, at many and many a time of his life; so (if I could even do it in the case of a man so far above me, and so far more deeply harrowed) instead of being proud of describing, I must only despise myself.

Enough to say that this snowy-haired, most simple yet stately gentleman, mixed the usual mixture of the things that weep and the things that laugh; which are the joint-stock of our nature, from the old Adam and the young one. What I mean—if I keep to facts—is, that he knelt on a strip of canvas laid at the end of the table, and after some trouble to place his elbows (because of the grit of the sandiness), bowed his white forehead and silvery hair, and the calm majesty of his face, over those two dollies, and over his son's very best cocked-hat, and in silence wept thanksgiving to the great Father of everything.

"David Llewellyn," he said, as he rose and approached me as if I were quite his equal; "allow me to take your hand, my friend. There are few men to whom I would sooner owe this great debt of gratitude than yourself, because you have sailed with my son so long. To you and your patience and sagacity, under the mercy of God, I owe the proof, or at any rate these tokens of my poor son's innocence. I—I thank the Lord and you——"

Here the General for the moment could not say another word.

"It is true, your Worship," I answered, "that none of your own people showed the sense or the courage to go on. But it is a Welshman's honest pride to surpass all other races in valour and ability. I am no more than the very humblest of my ancestors may have been."

"Then all of them must have been very fine fellows," Sir Philip replied, with a twinkling glance. "But now I will beg of you one more favour. Carry all these things, just as they are, to the room of my son, Mr Philip Bampfylde."

At first I was so taken aback that I could only gaze at him. And then I began to think, and to see the reason of his asking it.

"I have asked you to do a strange thing, good David; if it is an unpleasant one, say so in your blunt sailor's fashion."

"Your honour," I answered, with all the delicacy of my nature upwards; "say not another word. I will do it."

For truly to speak it, if anything had been often a grief and a care to me, it was the bitterness of thinking of that Squire Philip deeply, and not knowing anything. The General bowed to me with a kindness none could take advantage of, and signalled me to collect my burden. Then he appointed me how to go, together with a very old and long-accustomed servitor. Himself would not come near his son, for fear of triumph over him.

After a long bit of tapping, and whispering, and the mystery servants always love to make of the simplest orders, I was shown with my arms well aching (for those wooden dolls were no joke, and the Captain's hat weighed a stone at least, with all the sand in the lining) into a dark room softly strewn, and hung with ancient damask. The light of the evening was shut out, and the failure of the candles made it seem a cloudy starlight. Only in the furthest corner there was light enough to see by; and there sate, at a very old desk, a white-haired man with his hat on.

If I can say one thing truly (while I am striving at every line to tell the downright honesty), this truth is that my bones and fibres now grew cold inside of me. There was about this man, so placed, and with the dimness round him, such an air of difference from whatever we can reason with, and of far withdrawal from the ways of human nature, as must send a dismal shudder through a genial soul like mine. There he sate, and there he spent three parts of his time with his hat on, gazing at some old grey tokens of a happy period, but (so far as could be judged) hoping, fearing, doing, thinking, even dreaming—nothing! He would not allow any clock or watch, or other record of time in the chamber, he would not read or be read to, neither write or receive a letter.

There he sate, with one hand on his forehead pushing back the old dusty hat, with his white hair straggling under it and even below the gaunt shoulder-blades, his face set a little on one side, without any kind of meaning in it, unless it were long weariness, and patient waiting God's time of death.

I was told that once a-day, whenever the sun was going down over the bar, in winter or summer, in wet or dry, this unfortunate man arose, as if he knew the time by instinct without view of heaven, and drew the velvet curtain back and flung the shutter open, and for a moment stood and gazed with sorrow-worn yet tearless eyes upon the solemn hills and woods, and down the gliding of the river, following the pensive footfall of another receding day. Then with a deep sigh he retired from all chance of starlight, darkening body, mind, and soul, until another sunset.

Upon the better side of my heart, I could feel true pity for a man overwhelmed like this by fortune; while my strength of mind was vexed to see him carry on so. Therefore straight I marched up to him, when I began to recover myself, having found no better way of getting through perplexity.

As my footsteps sounded heavily in the gloomy chamber, Squire Philip turned, and gazed at first with cold displeasure, and then with strong amazement at me. I waited for him to begin, but he could not, whether from surprise or loss of readiness through such long immurement.

"May it please your Honour," I said; "the General has sent me hither to clear my Captain from the charge of burying your Honour's children."

"What—what do you mean?" was all that he could stammer forth, while his glassy eyes were roving from my face to the dolls I bore, and round the room, and then back again.

"Exactly as I say, your Honour. These are what the wild man took for your two children in Braunton Burrows; and here is the Captain's cocked-hat, which some one stole, to counterfeit him. The whole thing was a vile artifice, a delusion, cheat, and mockery."

I need not repeat how I set this before him, but only his mode of receiving it. At first he seemed wholly confused and stunned, pressing his head with both hands, and looking as if he knew not where he was. Then he began to enter slowly into what I was telling him, but without the power to see its bearing, or judge how to take it. He examined the dolls, and patted them, and added them to a whole school which he kept,

with two candles burning before them. And then he said,
"They have long been missing: I am pleased to recover them."

Then for a long time he sate in silence, and in his former attitude, quite as if his mind relapsed into its old condition: and verily I began to think that the only result of my discovery, so far as concerned poor Squire Philip, would be a small addition to his gallery of dolls. However, after a while he turned round, and cried with a piercing gaze at me—

"Mariner, whoever you are, I do not believe one word of your tale. The hat is as new and the dolls are as fresh as if they were buried yesterday. And I take that to be the truth of it. How many years have I been here? I know not. Bring me a looking-glass."

He pointed to a small mirror which stood among his precious relics. Being mounted with silver and tortoise-shell, this had been (as they told me afterwards) the favourite toy of his handsome wife. When I handed him this, he took off his hat, and shook his white hair back, and gazed earnestly, but without any sorrow, at his mournful image.

"Twenty years at least," he pronounced it, in a clear decided voice; "twenty years it must have taken to have made me what I am. Would twenty years in a dripping sand-hill leave a smart gentleman's laced hat and a poor little baby's dolls as fresh and bright as the day they were buried? Old mariner, I am sorry that you should lend yourself to such devices. But perhaps you thought it right."

This, although so much perverted, made me think of his father's goodness and kind faith in every one. And I saw that here was no place now for any sort of argument.

"Your Honour is altogether wrong," I answered, very gently: "the matter could have been, at the utmost, scarcely more than eight years ago, according to what they tell me. And if you can suppose that a man of my rank and age and service would lend himself to mean devices, there are at least thirty of your retainers, and of honest neighbours, who have seen the whole thing and can swear to its straightforwardness. And your Honour, of course, knows everything a thousand times better than I do; but of sand, and how it keeps things everlasting (so long as dry), your Honour seems, if I may say it, to have no experience."

He did not take the trouble to answer, but fell back into his old way of sitting, as if there was nothing worth argument.

People say that every man is like his father in many ways;

but the first resemblance that I perceived between Sir Philip and his elder son was, that the squire arose and bowed with courtesy as I departed.

Upon the whole, this undertaking proved a disappointment to me. And it mattered a hundredfold as much that our noble General was not only vexed, but angered more than one could hope of him. Having been treated a little amiss, I trusted that Sir Philip would contribute to my self-respect by also feeling angry. Still I did not desire more than just enough to support me, or at the utmost to overlap me, and give me the sense of acting aright by virtue of appeasing him. But on the present occasion he showed so large and cloudy a shape of anger, wholly withdrawn from my sight (as happens with the Peak of Teneriffe)—also he so clearly longed to be left alone and meditate, that I had no chance to offer him more than three opinions. All these were of genuine value at the time of offering; and must have continued so to be, if the facts had not belied them. Allowing for this adverse view, I will not even state them.

Nevertheless I had the warmest invitation to abide, and be welcome to the best that turned upon any of all the four great spits, or simmered and lifted the pot-lids suddenly for a puff of fine smell to come out in advance. To a man of less patriotic feeling this might thus have commended itself. But to my mind there was nothing visible in these hills and valleys, and their sloping towards the sea, which could make a true Welshman doubt the priority of Welshland. For with us the sun is better, and the air moves less in creases, and the sea has more of rapid gaiety in breaking. The others may have higher cliffs, or deeper valleys down them, also (if they like to think so) darker woods for robbers' nests—but our own land has a sweetness, and a gentle liking for us, and a motherly pleasure in its bosom when we do come home to it, such as no other land may claim—according to my experience.

These were my sentiments as I climbed, upon the ensuing Sunday, a lofty hill near the Ilfracombe road, commanding a view of the Bristol Channel and the Welsh coast beyond it. The day was so clear that I could follow the stretches and curves of my native shore, from the low lands of Gower away in the west through the sandy ridges of Aberavon and the grey rocks of Sker and Porthcawl, as far as the eastern cliffs of Dunraven and the fading bend of St Donat's.

The sea between us looked so calm, and softly touched with shaded lights and gentle variations, also in unruffled beauty so fostering and benevolent, that the white sailed coasters seemed to be babies fast asleep on their mother's lap.

"How long is this mere river to keep me from my people at home?" I cried; "it looks as if one could jump it almost! A child in a cockle-shell could cross it."

At these words of my own, a sudden thought, which had never occurred before, struck me so that my brain seemed to buzz.

But presently reason came to my aid; and I said, "No, no; it is out of the question; without even a thread of sail! I must not let these clods laugh at me for such a wild idea. And the name in the stern of the boat as well, downright 'Santa Lucia!' Chowne must have drowned those two poor children, and then rehearsed this farce of a burial with the Captain's hat on, to enable his man to swear truly to it. Tush, I am not in my dotage yet. I can see the force of everything."

CHAPTER L.

A BRAVE MAN RUNS AWAY.

It may be the power of honesty, or it may be strength of character coupled with a more than usual brightness of sagacity—but whatever the cause may be, the result seems always to be the same, in spite of inborn humility—to wit, that poor old Davy Llewellyn, wherever his ups and downs may throw him, always has to take the lead! This necessity, as usual, seemed to be arising now at Narnton Court—the very last place in the world where one could have desired it. Since the present grand war began (with the finest promise of lasting, because nobody knows any cause for it, so that it must be a law of nature), I have not found much occasion to dwell upon common inland incidents. These are in nature so far below all maritime proceedings, that a sailor is tempted to forget such trifles as people are doing ashore.

Even upon Holy Scripture (since the stirring times began for me henceforth to chronicle), it has not been my good-luck to be able to sit and think of anything. Nevertheless I am almost sure that it must have been an active man of the name of Nehemiah, who drew for his rations every day, one fat ox, and six choice sheep, and fowls of order various.

All of these might I have claimed, if my capacity had been equal to this great occasion. Hence it may be well supposed that the kitchen was my favourite place, whenever I deigned to enter into converse with the servants. At first the head-cook was a little shy; but I put her soon at her ease by describing (from my vast breadth of experience) the proper manner to truss and roast a man—and still better a woman. The knowledge I displayed upon a thing so far above her level, coupled with my tales of what we sailors did in consequence, led this excellent creature so to appreciate my character, and thirst for more of my narratives, that I never could come amiss, even at dishing-up time.

But here I fell into a snare, as every seaman is sure to do when he relaxes his mind too much in the charms of female society. Not concerning the cook herself—for I gave her to understand at the outset that I was not a marrying man, and she (possessing a husband somewhere) resolved not to hanker after me—but by means of a fair young maid, newly apprenticed to our head-cook, although of a loftier origin.

More than once, while telling my stories, I had obtained a little glimpse of long bright ringlets flashing and of shy young eyes just peeping through the hatch of the scullery-door, where the huckaback towel hung down from the roller. And then, on detection, there used to ensue a very quick fumbling of small red hands, as if being dried with a desperate haste in the old jack-towel; and then a short sigh, and light feet retiring.

When this had happened for three or four times, I gave my head-cook a sudden wink, and sprang through the scullery-door and caught the little red hands in the fold of the towel, and brought forth the owner, in spite of deep blushes, and even a little scream or two. Then I placed her in a chair behind the jack-chains, and continued my harrowing description of the way I was larded for roasting once; by a score of unclothed Gabooners. Also how the skewers of bar-wood thrust in to make me of a good rich colour, when I should come to table, had not that tenacity which our English wood is gifted with; so that I was enabled to shake (after praying to God for assistance) my right arm out, and then my left; and after clapping both together (to restore circulation), it came providentially into my head to lay hold of the spit and charge them. And then ensued such a scene as I could not even think of laying before young and delicate females.

This young girl, whose name was "Polly," always (at this pitch of terror) not only shivered but shuddered so, and needed support for her figure beyond the power of stays to communicate, also let such tears begin to betray themselves and then retreat, and then come out and defy the world, with a brave sob at their back almost,—that I do not exaggerate in saying how many times I had the pleasure of roasting myself for the sake of them.

However it always does turn out that pleasures of this sort are transient; and I could not have been going on with Polly more than ten days at the utmost, when I found myself in a rare scrape, to be sure. And this was the worse, because Sir Philip so strongly desired my presence now, perhaps in the vain hope of my convincing that obstinate Squire of his brother's innocence, when that brother should return.

Now I need not have spoken as yet of Miss Polly if she had been but a common servant, because in that case her peace of mind would have been of no consequence to the household. But, as it happened, she was a person of no small importance, by reason of the very lofty nature of her connections: for she was no less than genuine niece to the lady-housekeeper Mrs Cockhanterbury herself. And hence she became the innocent cause of my departure from Narnton Court, before I had time to begin my inquiries about the two poor little children.

This I had made up my mind to do, as soon as that strange idea had crossed it, while I was gazing upon the sea; and my meaning was to go through all the traces that might still be found of them, and the mode of their disappearance. It is true that this resolve was weakened by a tempest which arose that very same evening after the Channel had looked so insignificant, and which might have been expected after that appearance. Nevertheless I must have proceeded according to my intention, if my heart had not been too much for me in the matter of Polly Cockhanterbury.

Being just now in my sixtieth year, I could not prove such a coxcomb, of course, as to imagine that a pretty girl of two-and-twenty could care for me, so that no course remained open to me as an honourable man and gallant British officer who studies his own peace of mind, except to withdraw from this too tempting neighbourhood.

And in this resolution I was confirmed by Mrs Cockhanter

bury's reluctance to declare in a binding manner her intentions towards her niece. Also by finding that somehow or other the whole of the ground-floor at Narnton Court had taken it into their heads to regard me as a man of desirable substance. It is possible that in larger moments, when other people were boasting, I may have insisted a little too much upon my position as landowner in the parish of Newton Nottage. Also I may have described too warmly my patronage of the schoolmaster, and investment of cash with a view to encourage the literature of the parish. But I never could have said—what all of them deposed to—such a very strong untruth, as to convey the conclusion (even to a Devonshire state of mind), that Colonel Lougher and I divided the whole of the parish between us!

Be that as it may, there was not any maid over thirty who failed to set her cap at me, and my silver hair was quite restored to a youthful tinge of gold. Hence I was horrified at the thought that Polly might even consent to have me for the sake of my property, and upon discovering its poetical existence, lead me a perfectly wretched life, as bad as that of poor Heaviside.

So that, in spite of all attractions, and really serious business, and the important duty of awaiting the Captain's return from Pomeroy Castle, and even in spite of Jerry Toms' offer to take Polly off my hands—as if she would say a word to him!—and all the adjurations of poor Heaviside, who had defied his wife (all the time I was there to back him up), and now must have to pay out for it—what did I do but agree to doff my uniform, and work my passage on board the Majestic, a fore-and-aft-rigged limestone boat of forty-eight tons and a half? Of course she was bound on the usual business of stealing the good Colonel Lougher's rocks, but I distinctly stipulated to have nothing to do with that.

My popularity now was such, with all ranks of society, also I found myself pledged for so many stories that same evening, that I imparted to none except Sir Philip, and Polly, and Jerry Toms, and Heaviside, and one or two more, the scheme of my sudden departure. My mind was on the point of changing when I beheld sweet Polly's tears, until I felt that I must behave, at my time of life, as her father would; because she had no father.

When I brought the Majestic into shallow water off the Tuskar, every inch of which I knew, it was no small comfort to me that I could not see the shore. For years I had longed to see that shore, and dreamed of it perpetually, while tossing ten thousand miles away; and now I was glad to have it covered with the twilight fogginess. It suited me better to land at night, only because my landing would not be such as I was entitled to. And every one knows how the Navy and Army drop in public estimation, when the wars seem to be done with. Therefore I expected little; and I give you my word that I got still less.

It may have been over eleven o'clock, but at any rate nothing to call very late, just at the crest of the summer-time, when I gave three good strong raps at the door of my own cottage, knowing exactly where the knots were. I had not met a single soul to know me, or to speak my name, although the moon was a quarter old, and I found a broken spar, and bore it as I used to bear my fishing-pole.

No man who has not been long a-roving can understand all the fluttering ways of a man's heart when he comes home again. How he looks at every one of all the old houses he knows so well; at first as if he feared it for having another piece built on, or grander people inside of it. And then upon finding this fear vain, he is almost ready to beg its pardon for not having looked at it such a long time. It is not in him to say a word to, or even about, the children coming out thus to stare at him. All the children he used to know are gone to day's work long ago; and the new ones would scarcely trust him so as to suck a foreign lollipop. He knows them by their mothers; but he cannot use their names to them.

There is nothing solid dwelling for a poor man long away, except the big trees that lay hold upon the ground in earnest, and the tomb-stones keeping up his right to the parish churchyard. Along the wall of this I glanced, with joy to keep outside of it; while I struck, for the third time strongly, at not being let into mine own house.

At last a weak and faltering step sounded in my little room, and then a voice came through the latch-hole, "Man of noise, how dare you thus? you will wake up our young lady."

"Master Roger, let me in. Know you not your own landlord?"

The learned schoolmaster was so astonished that he could scarcely draw back the bolt. "Is it so? Is it so indeed? I thank the Lord for sending thee," was all he could say, while he stood there shaking both my hands to the very utmost that his slender palms could compass.

"Friend Llewellyn," he whispered at last, "I beg thy pardon heartily, for having been so rude to thee. But it is such a business to hush the young lady; and if she once wakes she talks all the night long. I fear that her mind is almost too active for a maid of her tender years."

"What young lady do you mean?" I asked; "is Bunny become a young lady now?"

"Bunny!" he cried, with no small contempt; then perceiving how rude this was to me, began casting about for apologies.

"Never mind that," I said; "only tell me who this wonderful young lady is."

"Miss Andalusia, the 'Maid of Sker,' as every one now begins to call her. There is no other young lady in the neighbourhood to my knowledge."

"Nor in the whole world for you, I should say, by the look of your eyes, Master Roger Berkrolles. Nevertheless put your coat on, my friend, and give your old landlord a bit to eat. I trow that the whole of my house does not belong even to Miss Delushy. Have I not even a granddaughter?"

"To be sure, and a very fine damsel she is, ay, and a good and comely one; though she hath no turn for erudition. What we should do without Bunny I know not. She is a most rare young housewife."

The tears sprang into my eyes at this, as I thought of her poor grandmother, and I gave Master Berkrolles' hand a squeeze which brought some into his as well.

"Let me see her," was all I said; "it is not easy to break her rest, unless she is greatly altered."

"She is not in bed; she is singing her young friend to sleep. I will call her presently."

This was rather more, however, than even my patience could endure: so I went quietly up the stairs, and pushing the door of the best room gently, there I heard a pretty voice, and saw a very pretty sight. In a little bed which seemed almost to shine with cleanliness, there lay a young girl fast asleep, but lying in such a way that none who had ever seen could doubt of her. That is to say, with one knee up, and the foot of the other leg thrown back, and showing through the bed-clothes, as if she were running a race in sleep. And yet with the back laid flat, and sinking into the pillow deeply; while a pair of little restless arms came out and strayed on the coverlet. Her full and lively red lips were parted, as if she wanted to have a snore, also her little nose well up, and the rounding of the tender cheeks untrimmed to the maiden oval. Down upon these dark lashes hung, fluttering with the pulse of sleep; while heavy clusters of curly hair, dishevelled upon the pillow, framed the gentle curve of the forehead and smiling daintiness of the whole.

Near this delicate creature sate, in a bending attitude of protection, a strong and well-made girl, with black hair, jet-black eyes, and a rosy colour spread upon a round plump face. She was smiling as she watched the effect of an old Welsh air which she had been singing—" Ar hyd y nos." To look at her size and figure, you would say that her age was fourteen at least; but I knew that she was but twelve years old, as she happened to be our Bunny.

You may suppose that this child was amazed to see her old Granny again once more, and hardly able to recognise him, except by his voice, and eyes, and manner, and a sort of way about him such as only relations have. For really, if I must tell the truth, the great roundness of the world had taken such a strong effect upon me, that I had not been able to manage one straight line towards Newton Nottage for something over six years now. Perhaps I have said that the Admiralty did not encourage our correspondence; and most of us were very well content to allow our dear friends to think of us. So that by my pay alone could my native parish argue whether I were alive or dead.

It would not become me to enter into the public rejoicing upon the morrow, after my well-accustomed face was proved to be genuine at the "Jolly." There are moments that pass our very clearest perception, and judgment, and even our strength to go through them again. And it was too early yet —except for a man from low latitudes—to call for rum-and-water. The whole of this I let them know, while capable of receiving it.

CHAPTER LI.

TRIPLE EDUCATION.

MASTER ROGER BERKROLLES had proved himself a schoolmaster of the very driest honesty. This expression, upon afterthought, I beg to use expressly. My own honesty is of a truly unusual and choice character; and I have not found, say a dozen men, fit anyhow to approach it. But there is always a sense of humour, and a view of honour, wagging in among my principles to such an extent that they never get dry, as the multiplication-table does. Master Berkrolles was a man of too much mind for joking.

Therefore, upon the very first morning after my return, and even before our breakfast-time, he poured me out such a lot of coin as I never did hope to see, himself regarding them as no more than so many shells of the sea to count. All these he had saved from my pay in a manner wholly beyond my imagination, because, though I love to make money of people, I soon let them make it of me again. And this was my instinct now; but Roger laid his thin hand on the heap most gravely, and through his spectacles watched me softly, so that I could not be wroth with him.

"Friend Llewellyn, I crave your pardon. All this money is lawfully yours; neither have I, or anybody, the right to meddle with it. But I beg you to consider what occasions may arise for some of these coins hereafter. Also, if it should please the Lord to call me away while you are at sea, what might become of the dear child Bunny, without this mammon to procure her friends? Would you have her, like poor Andalusia, dependent upon charity?"

"Hush!" I whispered; too late, however, for there stood Bardie herself, a slim, light-footed, and graceful child, about ten years old just then, I think. Her dress of slate-coloured stuff was the very plainest of the plain, and made by hands more familiar with the needle than the scissors. No ornament, or even change of colour, was she decked with, not so much as a white crimped frill for the fringes of hair to dance upon. No child that came to the well (so long as she possessed a mother) ever happened to be dressed in this denying manner. But two girls blessed with good stepmothers, having children of their own, were induced, as was known already, with dresses cut from the self-same remnant. Now, as she looked at Roger Berkrolles with a steadfast wonder, not appearing for the moment to remember me at all, a deep spring of indefinite sadness filled her dark grey eyes with tears.

"Charity!" she said at last: "if you please, sir, what is charity?"

"Charity, my dear, is kindness; the natural kindness of good people."

"Is it what begins at home, sir; as they say in the copy books?"

"Yes, my dear; but it never stops there. It is a most beautiful thing. It does good to everybody. You heard me say, my dear child, that you are dependent on charity. It is through no fault of your own, remember; but by the will of God. You need not be ashamed to depend on the kindness of good people."

Her eyes shone, for a moment, with bright gratitude towards him for reconciling her with her pride; and then being shy at my presence perhaps, she turned away, just as she used to do, and said to herself very softly—"I would rather have a home though—I would rather have a home, and a father and mother of my own, instead of beautiful charity."

Master Berkrolles told me, when she was gone, that many children of the place had no better manners than to be always shouting after her, when coming back from the sandhills, "Where's your father? Where's your mother? Where's your home, Delushy?"

This, of course, was grievous to her, and should never have been done; and I let Roger know that his business was to stop any scandal of this kind. But he declared that really the whole of his mind was taken up, and much of his body also, in maintaining rule and reason through the proper hours. After school-time it was not the place of the schoolmaster, but of the parson of the parish, or by deputy churchwardens, or failing them the clerk, and (if he were out of the way) the sexton, to impress a certain tone of duty on the young ones. Especially the sexton need not even call his wife to help, if he would but have the wit to cultivate more young thoughtfulness, by digging a grave every other day, and trusting the Lord for orders.

It was not long before Delushy learned some memory of me, partly with the aid of Bunny, partly through the ship I made

—such as no other man could turn out—partly through my uniform, and the rest of it by means of goodness only can tell what. A man who is knocked about, all over rounds, and flats, and sides of mountains, also kicked into and out of every hole and corner, and the strong and weak places of the earth, and upset after all the most by his fellow-creatures' doings, although he may have started with more principle than was good for him, comes home, in the end, to look at results far more than causes.

This was exactly mine own case. I can hardly state it more clearly. I wanted no praise from anybody; because I felt it due to me. A fellow who doubts about himself may value approbation; and such was the case with me, perhaps, while misunderstood by the magistrates. But now all the money which I had saved, under stewardship of Berkrolles, enabled all my household to stand up and challenge calumny.

There is a depth of tender feeling in the hearts of Welshmen, such as cannot anywhere else be discovered by a Welshman. Heartily we love to find man or woman of our own kin (even at the utmost nip of the calipers of pedigree) doing anything which reflects a spark of glory on us. Of this man, or woman even, we make all the very utmost, to the extremest point where truth assuages patriotism. The whole of our neighbourhood took this matter from a proper point of view, and sent me such an invitation to a public dinner, that I was obliged to show them all the corners of the road, when the stupid fellows thought it safer to conduct me home again.

Upon that festive occasion, also, Sandy Macraw took a great deal too much, so entirely in honour of me that I felt the deepest goodwill towards him before the evening was over, even going so far, it appears, as to discharge him from all back-rent for the use of my little frigate. I certainly could not remember such an excess of generosity, upon the following morning; until he pulled off his hat and showed me the following document inscribed with a pencil on the lining: "Dearest and best of friends,—After the glorious tribute paid by the generous Scotchman to the humble but warm-hearted Cambrian, the latter would be below contempt if he took a penny from him. Signed DAVID LLEWELLYN; witness Rees Hopkins, chairman, his mark."

After this, and the public manner of my execution, there was nothing to be said, except that Sandy Macraw was below contempt for turning to inferior use the flow of our finest feelings. Therefore I went, with some indignation, to resume possession of my poor boat, which might as well have been Sandy's own, during the last five years and more. However, I could not deny that the Scotchman had kept his part of the contract well, for my boat was beautifully clean and in excellent repair; in a word, as good as new almost. So I put Miss Delushy on board of her, with Bunny for the lady's-maid, and finding a strong ebb under us, I paddled away towards Sker and landed bravely at Pool Tavan.

For poor Black Evan lay now in our churchyard by the side of his five bold sons, having beheld the white horse as plainly as any of the Coroner's jury. The reason was clear enough to all who knew anything of medicine, to wit, his unwise and pernicious step in prostituting his constitution to the use of water.

If any unfortunate man is harassed with such want of self-respect, and utter distrust of Providence, as well as unpleasancy of behaviour towards all worthy neighbours, and black ingratitude to his life, as to make a vow for ever never to drink any good stuff again, that man must be pitied largely; but let no one speak harshly of him; because he must so soon be dead. And this in half the needful time, if formerly he went on too much.

Poor Moxy now, with young Watkin only, carried on this desert farm. It was said that no farmer, ever since the Abbots were turned out, could contrive to get on at Sker. One after the other failed to get a return for the money sunk into the desolate sandy soil. Black Evan's father took the place with a quarter of a bushel heaped with golden guineas of Queen Anne. And very bravely he began, but nothing ever came of it, except that he hanged himself at last, and left his son to go on with it. What chance was there now for Moxy, with no money, and one son only, and a far better heart than head?

Nevertheless she would not hear for one moment of such a thing as giving up Delushy. This little maid had a way of her own of winding herself into people's hearts, given to her by the Lord Himself, to make up for hard dealings. Moxy loved her almost as much as her own son Watkin, and was brought with the greatest trouble to consent to lose her often, for the sake of learning. Because there never could be at Sker the smallest chance of growing strongly into education. And everybody felt that Bardie was of a birth and nature such as demanded this thing highly.

However, even this public sentiment might have ended in talk alone, if Lady Bluett had not borne in mind her solemn pledge to me. Roger Berkrolles would have done his best, of course, to see to it; but his authority in the parish hung for a while upon female tongues, which forced him to be most cautious. So that I, though seven years absent, am beyond doubt entitled to the credit of this child's scholarship. I had seen the very beginning of it, as I must have said long ago, but what was that compared with all that happened in my absence? Berkrolles was a mighty scholar (knowing every book almost that ever in reason ought to have been indited or indicted), and his calm opinion was, that "he never had led into letters such a mind as Bardie's!"

She learned more in a week almost, than all the rising generation sucked in for the quarter. Not a bit of milching knowledge could he gently offer her, ere she dragged the whole of it out of his crop, like a young pigeon feeding. And sometimes she would put such questions that he could do nothing more than cover both his eyes up!

All such things are well enough for people who forget how much the body does outweigh the mind, being meant, of course, to do so, getting more food, as it does, and able to enjoy it more, by reason of less daintiness. But for my part, I have always found it human prudence to prevent the mind, or soul, or other parts invisible, from conspiracy to outgo, what I can see, and feel, and manage, and be punished for not heeding—that is to say, my body.

Now the plan arranged for Bardie was the most perfect that could be imagined, springing from the will of Providence, and therefore far superior to any human invention. Master Berkrolles told me that a human being may be supposed to consist principally of three parts—the body, which is chiefly water (this I could not bear to hear of, unless it were salt water, which he said might be the case with me); the mind, which may be formed of air, if it is formed of anything; and the soul, which is strong spirit, and for that reason keeps the longest.

Accordingly this homeless maiden's time was so divided, that her three parts were provided for, one after other, most beautifully. She made her rounds, with her little bag, from Sker to Candleston Court, and thence to Master Berkrolles at my cottage, and back again to Sker, when Moxy could not do without her. She would spend, perhaps, a fortnight at

Candleston, then a fortnight in Newton village, and after that a month at Sker, more or less, as might be, according to the weather and the chances of conveyance.

At Candleston, of course, she got the best of bodily food as well; but Lady Bluett made a point of attending especially to her soul, not in a sanctimonious way, but concerning grace, and manners, and the love of music, and the handling of a knife and fork, and all the thousand little things depending on that part of us. And here she was made a most perfect pet, and wore very beautiful clothes, and so on; but left them all behind, and went as plain as a nun to Newton, as soon as the time arrived for giving her mind its proper training.

Now when her mind was ready to burst with the piles of learning stored in it, and she could not sleep at night without being hushed by means of singing, Moxy would come from Sker to fetch her, and scold both the Master and Bunny well, for the paleness of Delushy's face, and end by begging their pardon and bearing the child away triumphantly, with Watkin to carry the bag for her.

And then for a month there was play, and sea-air, and rocks to climb over, and sandhills, and rabbits and wild-fowl to watch by the hour, and bathing throughout the summer-time, and nothing but very plain food at regular intervals of fine appetite.

So the over-active mind sank back to its due repose, and the tender cheeks recovered, with kind Nature's nursing, all the bloom the flowers have, because they think of nothing. Also the lightsome feet returned, and the native grace of movement, and the enjoyment of good runs, and laughter unrepressed but made harmonious by discipline. And then the hair came into gloss, and the eyes to depths of brightness, and all the mysteries of wisdom soon were tickled out of her.

This was the life she had been leading, now for some six years or more; and being of a happy nature, she was quite contented. In the boat I did my utmost, that day, to examine her as to all her recollections of her early history. But she seemed to dwell upon nothing now, except the most trifling incidents, such as a crab lifting up the cover one day when Old Davy was boiling him, or "Dutch" being found with a lot of small Dutches, and nobody knew where they came from. She had no recollection of any boat, or even a Coroner's inquest; and as to papa, and mama, and brother—she put her hand up to her beautiful forehead, to think, and then wondered about them.

Having cleverly brought you thus to a proper acquaintance with the present situation, I really think that you must excuse me from going into all Moxy's transports, called forth by the sight of me.

In spite of all that, I always say in depreciation of myself (ay, and often mean it too), nobody can have failed to gather that my countrymen at large, and (which matters more) my countrywomen, take a most kind view of me. And it would have been hard indeed if Moxy could not find a tear or two. And Watkin now was a fine young fellow, turned of twenty some time ago, straight as an arrow, and swift as a bird, but shy as a trout in a mountain-stream. From a humble distance he admired Miss Delushy profoundly, and was ever at her beck and call; so that of course she liked him much, but entertained a feminine contempt for such a fellow.

CHAPTER LII.

GREAT MARCH OF INTELLECT.

Now I come to larger actions, and the rise of great events, and the movements of mankind, enough to make their mother earth tremble, and take them for suicides, and even grudge her bosom for their naked burial. Often had I longed for war, not from love of slaughter, but because it is so good for us. It calls out the strength of a man from his heart, into the swing of his legs and arms, and fills him with his duty to the land that is his mother; and scatters far away small things, and shows beyond dispute God's wisdom, when He made us male and female.

The fair sex (after long peace) always want to take the lead of us, having rash faith in their quicker vigour of words and temper. But they prove their goodness always, coming down to their work at once, when the blood flows, and the bones are split into small splinters, and a man dies bravely in their arms, through doing his duty to them.

But though war is good, no doubt (till men shall be too good for it), there was not one man as yet in Great Britain, who would have gone of his own accord into the grand and endless war at this time impending. Master Roger Berkrolles told me that throughout all history (every in and out of which he knew, while pretending otherwise) never had been known such war, and destruction of God's men, as might now be looked for. He said that it was no question now of nation against nation, such as may be fought out and done with, after rapid victory; neither a piece of mere covetousness for a small advance of dominion; nor even a contest of dynasties, which might prove the tougher one. But that it was universal clash; half of mankind imbittered to a deadly pitch with the other half; and that now no peace could be, till one side was crushed under.

These things were beyond my grasp of widest comprehension, neither could I desire a war, begun about nothing, anyhow. If the Frenchmen insulted our flag, or wanted back some of their islands, or kept us from examining their customs (when imported), no true Briton could hesitate to keep his priming ready.

But at present they were only plucking up courage to affront us, being engrossed with their own looseness, and broad spread of idiocy. For they even went the length of declaring all men to be equal, the whole world common property, and the very names of the months all wrong! After this it was natural, and one might say the only sensible thing they ever did, to deny the existence of their Maker. For it could hardly be argued that the Almighty ever did lay hand to such a lot of scoundrels.

Now if these rats of the bilge-hole had chosen to cock their tales in their dirt, and devour one another, pleasure alone need have been the feeling of the human race looking down at them. But the worst of it was that real men, and women, far above them, took up their filthy tricks and antics, and their little buck-jumps, and allowed their judgment so to be taken with grimaces—even as a man who mocks a fit may fall into it—that in every country there were "sympathisers with the great and glorious march of intellect."

In Devonshire, I had heard none of all this, for none of the servants ever set eyes, or desired to do so, on "public journals." They had heard of these, but believed them to be very dangerous and wicked things; also devoid of interest, for what was the good of knowing things which anybody else might know?*

* That intelligent view still holds its own. A Devonshire farmer challenged me, the other day, to prove, "Whatt be the gude of the papper, whan any vule can rade un?"—ED*. M. of S.

And even if they had taken trouble ever to hear of the great outbreak, they would have replied (until it led to recruiting in their own parish), "Thiccy be no consarn to we."

But in our enlightened neighbourhood things were very different. There had long been down among us ever so many large-minded fellows, anxious to advance mankind, by great jumps, towards perfection. And in this they showed their wisdom (being all young bachelors) to strive to catch the golden age before they got rheumatics.

However, to men whose life has been touched with the proper grey and brown of earth, all these bright ideas seemed a baseless dance of rainbows. Man's perfection was a thing we had not found in this world; and being by divine wisdom weaned from human pride concerning it, we could be well content to wait our inevitable opportunity for seeking it in the other world. We had found this world wag slowly; sometimes better, and sometimes worse, pretty much according to the way in which it treated us. Neither had we yet perceived, in the generation newly breeched, any grand advance, but rather a very poor backsliding, from what we were at their time of life. We all like a strong fellow when we see him; and we all like a very bright child, who leaps through our misty sense of childhood. To either of these an average chap knocks under, when quite sure of it. And yet, in our parish, there was but one of the one sort, and one of the other. Bardie, of course, of the new generation; and old Davy of the elder. It vexes me to tell the truth so. But how can I help it, unless I spoil my story?

Ever so many people got a meeting in the chapel up, to sign a paper, and to say that nobody could guess the mischief done by all except themselves. They scouted the French Revolution as the direct work of the devil; and in the very next sentence vowed it the work of the seventh angel, to shatter the Church of England. They came with this rubbish for me to sign; and I signed it (and some of them also) with my well-attested toe and heel.

After such a demonstration, any man of candid mind falls back on himself, to judge if he may have been too forcible. But I could not see my way to any cross-road of repentance; and when I found what good I had done, I wished that I had kicked harder. By doing so, I might have quenched a pestilential doctrine; as every orthodox person told me, when they heard how the fellows ran. But—as my bad luck always conquers—I had but a pair of worn-out pumps on, and the only toe which a man can trust (through his own defects of discipline) happened to be in hospital now, and short of spring and flavour. Nevertheless some good was done. For Parson Lougher not only praised me, but in his generous manner provided a new pair of shoes for me, to kick harder, if again so visited. And the news of these prevented them.

But even the way these fellows had to rub themselves was not enough to stop the spreading of low opinions; for the strength of my manifestation was impressive rather than permanent. Also all the lower lot of Nonconformists and schismatics ran with their tongues out, like mad dogs, all over the country raving, snapping at every good gentleman's heels, and yelping that the seventh vial was open, and the seventh seal broken. To argue with a gale of wind would show more sense than to try discussion with such a set of ninnies; and when I asked them to reconcile their admiration of atheism with their religious fervour, one of them answered bravely that he would rather worship the Goddess of Reason than the God of the Church of England.

However, the followers of John Wesley, and all the respectable Methodists, scouted these ribalds as much as we did; and even Hezekiah had the sense to find himself going too far with them, and to repair the seventh seal, and clap it on Hepzibah's mouth. For how could he sell a clock, if time was declared by the trumpet to be no more?

Amid this universal turmoil, uproar, and upheaving, I received a letter from Captain Bampfylde, very short, and without a word of thanks for what I had done for him, but saying that he was just appointed to the Bellona, 74, carrying 6 carronades on the poop; that she was fitting now at Chatham, and in two months' time would be at Spithead, where he was to man her. He believed that the greater part of the fine ship's company of the Thetis would be only too glad to sail under him, and he was enabled to offer me the master's berth, if I saw fit. He said that he knew my efficiency, but would not have ventured to take this step but for what I had told him about my thorough acquirement of navigation under the care of a learned man. After saying that if I reported myself at Narnton Court by the end of October he would have me cared for and sent on, he concluded with these stirring words:—

"There is a great war near at hand; our country will want every man, young or old, who can fight a gun."

These last words fixed my resolve. I had not been very well treated, perhaps; at any rate, my abilities had not been recognised too highly, lest they should have to be paid for with a little handsomeness. But a man of large mind allows for this, feeling that the world, of course, would gladly have him at half-price. But when it came to talking of the proper style to fight a gun, how could I give way to any small considerations?

Fuzzy and Ike were stealing rock at this particular period in a new ketch called the Devil (wholly in honour of Parson Chowne); and through these worthy fellows, and Bang (now the most trustworthy of all), I sent a letter to Narnton Court, accepting the mastership of his Majesty's ship of the line, Bellona.

Now everybody in earnest began to call me "Captain Llewellyn"—not at my own instigation, but in spite of all done to the contrary. The master of a ship must be the captain, they argued, obstinately; and my well-known modesty had the blame of all that I urged against it. But I need not say any more about it; because the war has gone on so long, and so many seamen have now been killed, that the nation has been stirred up to learn almost a little about us.

While I was dwelling on all these subjects, who should appear but Miss Delushy, newly delivered from Candleston Court, on her round of high education? And to my amazement, who but Lieutenant Bluett delivered her? I had not even heard that he was come home; so much does a man, when he rises in life, fail in proper wakefulness! But now he leaped down from the forecastle, and with a grave and most excellent courtesy, and his bright uniform very rich and noble, and his face outdoing it, forth he led this little lady, who was clad in simple grey. She descended quite as if it was the proper thing to do; and then she turned and kissed the tips of her fingers to him gracefully. And she was not yet eleven years old! How can we be amazed at any revolutions after this?

"Bardie!" I cried, with some indignation, as if she were growing beyond my control; and she stood on the spring of her toes exactly as she had done when two years old, and offered her bright lips for a kiss, to prove that she was not arrogant. None but a surly bear could refuse her; still my feelings were deeply hurt, that other people should take advantage of my being from home so much, to wean the affections of this darling from her own old Davy, and perhaps to set up a claim for her.

Berkrolles knew what my rights were; and finding him such

a quiet man, I gave it to him thoroughly well, before I went to bed that night. I let him know that his staying there depended wholly upon myself; not only as his landlord, but as holding such a position now in Newton, and Nottage, and miles around, that the lifting of my finger would leave him without a scholar or a crust. Also I wished him to know that he must not, as a wretched landsman, take any liberties with me, because I had allowed him gratis to impart to me the vagueness of what he called "Mathematics," in the question of navigation. Of that queer science I made out some; but the rest went from me, through the clearness of my brain (which let things pass through it); otherwise I would have paid him gladly, if he had earned it. But he said (or I may myself have said, to suggest some sense to him) that my brain was now too full of experience for experiments. And of all the knowledge put into me by this good man carefully, and I may say laboriously, I could not call to mind a letter, figure, stroke, or even sign, when I led the British fleet into action, at the battle of the Nile. Nevertheless, it may all have been there, steadily underlying all, coming through great moments, like a quiet perspiration.

But if I could not take much learning, here was some one else who could; and there could be no finer sight for lovers of education than to watch old Mr Berkrolles and his pupil entering into the very pith of everything. I could not perceive any cause for excitement, in a dull matter of this sort; nevertheless they seemed to manage to get stirred up about it. For when they came to any depth of mystery for fathoming, it was beautiful to behold the long white hair and the short brown curls dancing together over it. That good old Roger was so clever in every style of teaching, that he often feigned not to know a thing of the simplest order to him; so that his pupil might work it out, and have a bit of triumph over him. He knew that nothing puts such speed into little folk and their steps—be they of mind or body—as to run a race with grown-up people, whether nurse or tutor.

But in spite of all these brilliant beams of knowledge now shed over her, our poor Bardie was held fast in an awkward cleft of conscience. I may not have fully contrived to show that this little creature was as quick of conscience as myself almost; although, of course, in a smaller way, and without proper sense of proportions. But there was enough of it left to make her sigh very heavily, lest she might have gone too far in one way or the other. Her meaning had been, from her earliest years, to marry, or be married. She had promised me through my grey whiskers often (with two years to teach her her own mind), never, as long as she lived, to accept any one but old Davy. We had settled it ever so many times, while she sate upon my shoulder; and she smacked me every now and then, to prove that she meant matrimony. Now, when I called to her mind all this, she said that I was an old stupid, and she meant to do just what she liked; though admitting that everybody wanted her. And after a little thought she told me, crossing her legs (in the true old style), and laying down her lashes, that her uncertainty lay between Master Roger and Mr Bluett. She had promised them both, she did believe, without proper time to think of it; and could she marry them both, because the one was so young and the other so old? I laid before her that the proper middle age of matrimony could not be attained in this way; though in the present upside-down of the world it might come to be thought of. And then she ran away and danced (exactly as she used to do), and came back with her merry laugh to argue the point again with me.

Before I set off for Narnton Court, on my way to join the Bellona, Lieutenant Bluett engaged my boat and my services, both with oar and net, for a day's whole pleasure off shore and on. I asked how many he meant to take, for the craft was a very light one; but he answered, "As many as ever he chose, for he hoped that two officers of the Royal Navy knew better than to swamp a boat in a dead calm such as this was." My self-respect derived such comfort from his outspoken and gallant way of calling me a brother officer (as well as from the most delicate air of ignorance which he displayed when I took up a two-guinea piece which happened to have come through my roof at this moment perhaps, or at any rate somehow to be lying in an old tobacco-box on my table), that I declared my boat and self at his command entirely.

We had a very pleasant party, and not so many as to endanger us, if the ladies showed good sense. Colonel Lougher and Lady Bluett, also the lieutenant, of course, and a young lady staying at Candleston Court, and doing her utmost to entrap the youthful sailor—her name has quite escaped me—also Delushy, and myself. These were all, or would have been all, if Master Rodney had not chanced, as we marched away from my cottage, with two men carrying hampers, to espy, in the corner of the old well, a face so sad, and eyes so black, that they pierced his happy and genial heart.

"I'll give it to you, you sly minx," I cried, "for an impudent, brazen trick like this. What orders did I give you, Miss? A master of a ship of the line, and not master of his own grandchild!"

The young lieutenant laughed so that the rushes on the sand-hills shook, for he saw in a moment all the meaning of this most outrageous trick. Bunny, forgetting her grade in life, had been crying, ever since she awoke, at receiving no invitation to this great festivity. She had even shown ill-will and jealousy towards Bardie, and a want of proper submission to her inevitable rank in the world. I perceived that these vile emotions grew entirely from the demagogic spirit of the period, which must be taken in hand at once. Wherefore I boxed her ears with vigour, and locked her into an empty cupboard, there to wait for our return, with a junk of bread and a cheese-rind. However, she made her way out, as her father had done with the prison of Dunkirk; and here she was in spite of all manners, good faith, and discipline.

"Let her come; she deserves to come; she shall come," Master Rodney cried; and as all the others said the same, I was forced to give in to it; and upon the whole I was proud perhaps of our Bunny's resolution. Neither did it turn out ill, but rather a good luck for us, because the young lady who wooed the lieutenant proved her entire unfitness for a maritime alliance, by wanting, before we had long been afloat, although the sea was as smooth as a duck-pond, some one to attend upon her.

Every one knows what the Tuskar Rock is, and the caves under Southern Down; neither am I at all of a nature to dwell upon eating and drinking. And though all these were of lofty order, and I made a fire of wreck-wood (just to broil some collops of a sewin, who came from the water into it, through a revival of my old skill; and to do a few oysters in their shells, with their gravy sputtering, to let us know when they were done, and to call for a bit of butter), no small considerations, or most grateful memories of flavour could have whispered to me twice, thus to try my mouth with waterings over such a cookery. But I have two reasons for enlarging on this happy day; and these two would be four at once, if any one contradicted them.

My chief reason is that poor dear Bardie first obtained a

pure knowledge of her desolate state upon that occasion;—at least so far as we can guess what works inside the little chips of skulls that we call babyish. Everybody had spoiled her so (being taken with her lovingness, and real newness of going on, and power to look into things, together with such a turn for play as never can be satiated in a world like ours; not to mention heaps of things which you must see to understand), let me not overdo it now, in saying that this little dear had taken such good education, through my liberal management, as to long to know a little more about herself, if possible.

This is a very legitimate wish, and deserving of more encouragement than most of us care to give to it; because so many of us are not the waifs and strays, and salvage only, but the dead shipwrecks of ourselves; content with the bottom of the great deep, only if no shallow fellows shall come diving down for us.

Having the joy of sun and sea, and the gratitude for a most lovely dinner, such as none could take from me, I happened to lie on my oars and think, while all my passengers roved on the rock. They were astray upon bladder-weed, pop-weed, dellusk, oar-weed, ribbons, frills, kelp, wrack, or five-tails—anything you like to call them, without falling over them. My orders were to stand off and on, till the gentry had amused themselves. Only I must look alive; for the Tuskar rock would be two fathoms under water, in about four hours, at a mile and a half from the nearest land.

The sunset wanted not so much as a glance of sea to answer it, but lay hovering quietly, and fading beneath the dark brows of the cliffs; which do sometimes glorify, and sometimes so discourage it. The meaning of the weather and the arrangement of the sky and sea, was not to make a show for once, but to let the sunset gently glide into the twilight, and the twilight take its time for melting into starlight. This I never thus have watched except in our old island.

There was not a wave to be seen or felt, only the glassy heave of the tide lifted my boat every now and then, or lapped among the wrinkles of the rocks, and spread their fringes. Not a sound was in the air, and on the water nothing, except the little tinkling softness of the drops that feathered off from my suspended oar-blades.

Floating round a corner thus, I came upon a sight as gently sad as sky and sea were. A little maid was leaning on a shelf of stone with her hair dishevelled as the kelp it mingled with.

Her plain brown hat was cast aside, and her clasped hands hid her face, while her slender feet hung down, and scarcely cared to paddle in the water that embraced them. Now and then a quiet sob, in harmony with the evening tide, showed that the storm of grief was over, but the calm of deep sorrow abiding.

"What is the matter, my pretty dear?" I asked, after landing, and coaxing her. "Tell old Davy; Captain David will see the whole of it put to rights."

"It cannot be put to yights," she answered, being even now unable to pronounce the *r* aright, although it was rather a lisp than any clear sound that supplied its place; "it never can be put to yights: when the other children had fathers and mothers, God left me outside of them; and the young lady says that I must not aspiya ever to marry a gentleman. I am ony fit for Watkin, or Tommy-Toms, or nobody! Old Dyo, why did I never have a father or a mother?"

"My dear, you had plenty of both," I replied; "but they were shipwrecked, and so were you. Only before the storm came on, you were put into this boat somehow, nobody living can tell how, and the boat came safe, though the ship was wrecked."

"This boat!" she cried, spreading out her hands to touch it upon either side—for by this time I had shipped her—"was it this boat saved me?"

"Yes, you beauty of the world. Now tell me what that wicked girl had the impudence to say to you."

This I need not here set down. Enough that it flowed from jealousy, jealousy of the lowest order, caused by the way in which Lieutenant Rodney played with Bardie. This of course interfered with the lady's chances of spreading nets for him, so that soon she lost her temper, fell upon Delushy, and upbraided her for being no more than an utterly unknown castaway.

CHAPTER LIII.

BEATING UP FOR THE NAVY.

My other reason for setting down some short account of that evening was to give you a little peace, and sense of gratitude to the Lord, for our many quiet sunsets, and the tranquillity of our shores. It really seems as if no other land was blest as ours is, with quiet orderly folk inside it, and good rulers over it, and around it not too much of sun or moon, or anything, unless it may be, now and then, a little bit of cloudiness. And this love of our country seems ever to be strongest, whether at departing for the wars with turbulent nations, or upon returning home, as soon as we have conquered them. But now for a long time, I shall have very little peace to dwell upon.

At Narnton Court I found no solace for my warmth of feeling. Polly had been sent out of the way, on purpose, because I was coming; which was a most unhandsome thing on the part of Mrs Cockhanterbury. For the very expectation which had buoyed me up at a flattish period, and induced me to do without three quids of cross-cut negrohead, was my simple and humble looking forward to my Polly. I knew that I was a fool, of course; but still I could not help it; and I had got on so well among young women always, that I found it very hard to miss the only chance I cared for. I feared that my age was beginning to tell; for often, since I had been ashore, my rheumatics had come back again. Neither was that my only grief and source of trouble at this time; but many other matters quite as grave combined against me. Heaviside was not there to talk, and make me hug my singleness; nor even Jerry Toms, nor the cook, who used to let me teach her. It was not that all these had left the place for any mischief. In an ancient household such a loss is not allowable. All meant to come back again, when it suited their opportunities, and each perceived that the house was sure to go to the dogs in the absence of themselves and one another. Heaviside had found Nanette (in spite of my best prognostics) overget her seventh occasion of producing small Crappos, and his natural disappointment with her led to such words that he shouldered his bundle and made off for Spithead, in company with Jerry, who was compelled to forsake his creditors. And as for the cook, I did hear, though unable to believe it, that she was in trouble about a young fellow scarcely worthy to turn her jack.

In other respects I found that nothing of much importance had occurred since I was there in the summer-time. Sir Philip continued to trust in the Lord, and the Squire to watch the sunsets; neither had the latter been persuaded to absolve his brother. The Captain had been at home one or two days, inquiring into my discovery of the buried dolls. He did not attach so much importance to this matter as his father had done, but said that it made a mysterious question even more mysterious. And failing, as a blunt sailor would, to make either head or tail of it, and being disgusted with his brother for refusing to see him, he vowed to remain in the house no longer, but set off for Pomeroy Castle again, where he had formed a close friendship with the eldest son of the owner. His lady-love, the fair Isabel, was not living there now, but might very easily be met with; for on coming of age three years ago, she had taken possession of her domain, "Carey Park," a magnificent place adjoining the Pomeroy property. It was said that the Earl had done his best to catch the young heiress for his son, and therefore had made a pretext of the old charge against the Captain, for the purpose of putting a stop to communication with him. But his son, Lord Mohun, upon finding how the young lady's heart was settled, withdrew his suit (like a man of honour), and all the more promptly, perhaps, because he had made up his mind to another lady before Miss Carey came to them.

It was said that the Captain might now have persuaded the beautiful heiress to marry him, and finish their long affection, if he could have thoroughly made up his mind that honour would bear him out in it. For her confidence was so perfect in him, that she left it to his own judgment, herself perhaps longing to put an end to their wearisome uncertainty. Sir Philip heard of it, and came down, to implore them thus to settle themselves. And Captain Bampfylde was so hard set by the nature of the case, that he might have been enticed away from what his conscience told him. This was that the solemn oath which he had taken in the church, with Isabel beside him, to purge himself of all foul charges (ere he made another guilty, if himself were guilty), could not thus be laid aside without a loss of honour. Sir Philip would be the last man in the world to counsel dishonest actions; but being an old man, and reluctant that his race should all expire, he looked upon that sacrament as no more than a piece of sacrilege, or a hasty pledge of which the Lord would never take advantage.

Nobody knows what might have happened with Captain Bampfylde so beset, and longing to think that he ought to act as everybody told him: but he begged for a night to think over it; and in the morning he received his appointment to the Bellona. Even Sir Philip could not deny that the hand

and the will of the Almighty must herein be recognised. And there was a chance of a brush with Spain, about the Nootka Sound, just then; and if anything makes a sailor's fortune, it is a fight with these fine old Dons. A Frenchman is sure to be captured, but not half so sure as a Spaniard; and the hidalgoes do turn out good gold, with good manners behind it. Many ships have I boarded, but with brightest alacrity always a good fat old Spaniard.

Therefore the Captain brushed away any little weakness, and set out for Spithead bravely, in a bachelor condition. And after trying to collect what news there was at Narnton, and finding that I must not think of meeting my dear Polly, I quietly drew my travelling-money, and set forth to join him.

Only every one will reproach me, and have right to do so, if I fail to tell the latest tidings of that Parson Chowne. People seemed to like this man, because they never could make him out, and nearly all the world is pleased to hear of the rest being vanquished. It seems that a wholly new bishop arose, by reason of the other dying, and this gentleman swore on the Bible to have things in order. When he heard of Chowne, and his high defiance of all former bishops, he said, "Fie, fie! this must not be; I will very soon put this to rights." To follow up this resolution he appointed Tiverton, and the old church of St Peter, for Chowne to bring his young people up to a noble confirmation; also for a visitation of the clergy all around; such as they have now and then, to stop the spread of king's evil.

His holiness the Bishop was surprised to receive this answer: "My dear Lord,—My meet is at Calverly on the day you speak of. We always find a fox hard by; and if he should make for Stoodleigh coverts, I may come down the Bolham road in time to meet your Lordship. At any rate, I shall dine at 'The Angel,' somewhere between three and five o'clock, and hope to find you there, and have a pleasant evening with you.—Yours very truly, R. S. CHOWNE.

"*P.S.*—If you bring your two Archdeacons, we will have a rubber: but I never go beyond guinea points."

The whole of this was written with Cumberland lead, on the back of a paper, showing how to treat hounds in distemper; and the Bishop was displeased about it, and declined his society; especially as he had invitation to the good Tidcombe Rectory. And there he was treated so hospitably by a very handsome family, that he put up his glass of a noble wine, and saw the sun set through it, and vowed that his Magna Charta, or Habeas Corpus, or Writ of Error—I never can remember which—but at any rate that his royal orders should fall out of his apron-pocket, if he failed to execute them.

In this state of mind he received a letter from Parson Chowne himself, full of respect, and most cleverly turned, as well as describing the Parson's grief at being unable to bring to his holiness any one fit to lay hands upon. The standard set before them had been (before laying on of hands) to say the Lord's Prayer backwards; and there was not one of them up to it. This angered the Bishop to such a degree, that he ordered out his heavy coach with the six long-tailed black horses, and the coachman with cocked-hat and flowing wig, and four great footmen shouldering blunderbusses; himself sate inside with his crosier and mitre, and lawn sleeves, and all the rest of it. Now this was just the very thing the refractory Parson expected; therefore he rode round overnight and bade every farmer in the neighbourhood send all his hands with pickaxes and shovels, by four o'clock the next morning: also he gathered all his own men there, as well as the unclad folk who were entirely at his orders. Then he sent for Parson Jack, as being the strongest man about there, and imparted his intention to him, and placed him over the workmen.

Early in the afternoon the Bishop's state-carriage was descried moving up the Tiverton highroad, with a noble and imposing aspect. Before he arrived at the cross-road leading off to Nympton Rectory, his Lordship was surprised to see a great collection of people standing on a hill above the road, and all saluting him with the deepest respect. "Not so bad after all," he exclaimed; "brother Chowne has brought his men into good order, which is the noblest use of the Church. Ah! they don't see a bishop every day, and they know when a thing is worth looking at, for their faces are black with astonishment. Holloa, Bob! what's that?"

"Up with the glass, your Lordship," the coachman shouted back; "or it will be all over with you. We are in a damned slough, and no mistake."

And so they were. His Lordship had no time to slam the windows up, before the coach lay wallowing in a bog of nighty blackness. In it poured, and filled the coach, and nearly smothered his Lordship, who was dragged out at last with the greatest trouble, as black as if he were dipped in pitch. For the Parson had done a most shameful thing, and too bad for even him to think of. He had taken up his private road, and dug out the ground some six feet deep, and then (by means of carts and barrows) transferred to it the contents of a quagmire, which lay handy, and spread the surface again with road-dirt, so that it looked as sound as a rock. Having seen with a telescope from his window the grand success of his engineering, he sent down a groom in smart livery, to present his compliments to the traveller who had happened to lose his way, and fall into a moor-hole, and was there anything he could do to mitigate that misfortune? But the Bishop sputtered out through his chattering teeth that he hoped to hear no more of him, and that none but a Devonshire man was fit to oversee Devonshire parsons. And this made the fifth bishop conquered by Chowne.

To return to our noble selves—that is to say, to the better people dealt with in our history. At the close of this year 1790, to wit, upon Christmas-day of that excellent year of grace, no less than three of us dined together (of course, with a good many others also) in the Captain's cabin of the Bellona, 74-gun ship of the British Navy, carrying also six carronades. These three were, Captain Drake Bampfylde, of course, the Honourable Rodney Bluett, now our second lieutenant, and the Master of the ship, whose name was something like "David Llewellyn." This latter was now remarkable for the dignity of his appearance and the gravity of his deportment; and although he was only ranked after the youngest of the lieutenants, and just before chits of reefers (called by some people "midshipmen"), and though upon any but festive occasions you might not have spied him at the Captain's table, you could scarcely have found any officer more satisfied with his position and more capable of maintaining it.

We were cruising off the south coast of Ireland, under orders to search all ships that might be likely to carry arms; but as a frigate would have done for that service, as well as, or better than, a 74, we knew that our true commission was to shake together and fall into discipline, and bring other seamen into the same, if we could get any to join us. Having a light wind and plenty of sea-room, we resolved to enjoy ourselves that day; and a very delightful party it was, especially after I was called on to spin a few of the many true yarns which make me such a general favourite.

After filling our glasses and drinking the health of his Majesty, and of the Navy at large, and especially of our

Captain, we began to talk of the state of affairs and the time at which the war might be expected to declare itself. That it must come to a great war with France, not even a fool could doubt, although he might desire to doubt it, ever since the destruction of the Bastile in July 1789. And throughout all the year and a half since that, a wild and desperate multitude had done nothing but abolish all the safeguards of their country, and every restraint upon the vilest rabble. Our wisest plan was to begin at once, before this cruel monster should learn the use of its fangs and the strength of its spring; but, as usual, Great Britain was too slow to seize the cudgel, which might haply have saved a million lives. However, we were preparing quietly for the inevitable conflict, as even our presence that day in the cabin of the Bellona might indicate.

"Master, we are sadly short of hands," said Captain Bampfylde, addressing me; "I shall have a poor report to make, unless we do something. Do you think that we could get on without you, if I sent you on a cruise for a week or so?"

"I think you might, sir." I answered humbly; "if it does not come on to blow, and if you keep well away from land. I have trained Mr Sebright with so much skill, that you may always rely upon him, except in any difficulty."

Nobly I spoke; and the Captain's reply was not very far behind me. "If we carried 750 men," he exclaimed, with generous candour, "we could not hope to have more than one Master David Llewellyn; so diffident, so truthful, so entirely free from jealousy. Gentlemen, is it not so?"

All the officers assented with a pleasant smile to me, and then to one another, so that I hardly knew what to say, except that I could not deserve it.

"Our tender the Sealark is to meet us in the Cove of Cork on New Year's Day," continued Captain Bampfylde; "and after shipping all our stores, she will be for a fortnight at my disposal. Now you know as well as I do, that our complement for war-time is 650 men and boys, and that our present strength is more than 200 short of that. War may be declared any day almost, and a pretty figure we should cut against a French liner of 80 guns. Therefore, unless the Sealark should bring us a very large draft, which I do not expect, my resolve is to man and victual her, for a fortnight's cruise, under some one who is a good hand at recruiting. Would you like the berth, Master Llewellyn?"

"Sir, I know not anything which I should like better."

Our Captain perceived that the junior lieutenants looked rather glum at being so passed over, from Master Rodney downwards; and though he had the perfect right to appoint any officer he pleased, he knew the true wisdom of shunning offence, by giving some good reason. Therefore he went on again:—

"There is not one of us, I daresay, who would not enjoy this little change. But I think that Llewellyn is our man, simply for this reason. The part to be beaten up first is the Welsh coast, from St David's Head to Penarth. I have heard of many good seamen there, and especially at Llanelly. I think that none of our officers can speak Welsh, except Master David. Even you, Bluett, though coming from Wales, are not up to the lingo."

This settled it in the best-natured manner; and all congratulated me, and wished me good speed in getting hold of old salts, if possible, or else fresh young ones. Not to be too long about it, somewhere about Epiphany Day in the year 1791, I stretched away for the coast of Wales, being in command of the Sealark, a rattling cutter of 100 tons, with two 6-pound bow-chasers, and a score of picked men under me. I have no time now to describe emotions, even of the loftiest order, such as patriotism, modesty, generosity, self-abasement, and many others which I indulged in, when I cast anchor off Porthcawl, and they thought that I meant to bombard them. I ordered a boat ashore at once, to reassure the natives, when I had given a waft of my flag, and fired a gun to salute it. But being now in such a position, and the parish to its utmost corners raving on the subject, ashore I durst not trust myself; because without rupture of ancient ties, and a low impression left behind, I could not have got aboard sober again. And after that, could I knock down any of my crew for being tipsy? Nevertheless, I had Bardie, and Bunny, and Mother Jones with her children, and Master Berkrolles, and Charles Morgan, and Betsy Matthews, and Moxy Thomas, all brought in a boat to visit me, besides a few others who came without leave. They all seemed to be very well and happy, and I entertained them beautifully.

That same afternoon we made a hit enough to encourage anybody. We impressed not only my foe the tailor, but also Hezekiah! That is to say, it was not quite what might be called impressment; because, with no war raging yet, we could not resort to violence : but we made them both so entirely drunk, that we were compelled, for their own sake, to weigh anchor while having their bodies on board. I had a stern fellow of noble mind to back me up at all hazard, and seeing what a sneak Hezekiah was, he gave him six dozen out of hand, with my official sanction. The Horologist to the Royal Family took his allotment worse than almost any man I ever saw; however, for old acquaintance' sake, I would not have him salted. In spite of this, the effect was such that it brought him round to the English Church, and cured him of all French doctrine. And as he gradually began to lose fat, and to dwell upon gunnery, we found his oiliness most useful to prevent corrosion.

Having worked this coast to our utmost power, and gathered a good deal of human stuff (some useful and some useless), pretty near threescore in all, and put upon short rations, we thought that we might as well finish our job by slanting across to Devonshire. Because for the most part, you there may find more body but less mind than ours, which is the proper state of things for the substance of our Navy. Therefore we drafted off to Cork all our noble Welshmen, and made sail for Devonshire.

Now, before telling what we did, I really must guard against any nasty misconstruction. Whatever had been done to me on the part of Parson Chowne, was by this time so wholly gone out of my heart, and mind, and everything any man can feel with, that nothing was further from my intention than to stir at all in that matter again. I knew that in spite of all the deference paid me now on every side (and too much for my comfort), Chowne would turn me inside out, ten thousand times worse than Stew could. This I like to see done, when anything wrong can be found inside a man. But a thoroughly honest fellow should stick on his honesty, and refuse it.

So when Providence, in a dream, laid before me the great mercy, and I might say miracle, of impressing the naked people, and bringing them under our good chaplain, to be trained from the error of their ways and live, I felt a sort of delicacy as to trespassing thus upon Parson Chowne's old freehold.

These naked folk belonged to him, and though he did not cultivate them as another man might have done, it was not difficult to believe that he found fine qualities in them. And to take them from under his very nose, might seem like a narrow vexation. However, times there are when duty overrides all delicacy ; the Bellona was still short of her number by a hundred hands or more: and with this reflection I cast away all further hesitation.

We left the Sealark off Heddon's Mouth, a wild and desolate part of the coast, for my object was to pounce unawares on the Parson's savage colony. For what we were going to do was not altogether lawful just at present, although it very soon would be. My force consisted of no less than fifteen jolly well-seasoned tars, all thoroughly armed, all up for a spree, and ready to do any mortal thing at a word or a signal from me. If we could only surprise the wild men, I had no fear as to our retreat, because the feeling of the country would be strongly in our favour, as the abaters of a nuisance long pronounced unbearable.

For five or it may have been six leagues we marched across the moors as straight as possible by compass, except when a quagmire or a ridge of rugged stone prevented us. We forded several beautiful streams of the brightest crystal water, so full of trout that I longed to have a turn at my old calling; and we came in view of Nympton steeple just as the sun was setting. I remembered the lie of the land quite well, ever since that night when the fire happened; so I halted my men in a little wood, and left them to eat their suppers, while I slung my spy-glass and proceeded to reconnoitre the enemy. Lying flat upon the crest of a hummocky ridge of moorland, I brought my glass to bear through the heather first upon the great Parson's house, which stood on a hill to the left of me, and then on the barbarous settlement. The Rectory looked as snug and quiet as the house of the very best man could be; with a deal more of comfort than most of these contrive to gather around them.

The dens of the tribe that objected to raiment were quite out of sight from his windows; nor were they allowed to present themselves to Mrs Chowne, unless she had done anything to vex him. Shaping my glass upon these wretches, I saw that they were in high festival. Of course I could not tell the reason, but it turned out afterwards that the Parson's hounds were off their feed through a sudden attack of distemper, and therefore a cartload of carrion had been taken down to the settlement. It was lucky that I knew it not, for I doubt whether we should have dared to invade their burrows at such a period.

However, I thought that nothing could be more suitable for our enterprise. Of course they would all overgorge themselves, and then their habit of drinking water, which alone would establish their barbarism, was sure to throw them into deep untroubled sleep till sunrise. As soon as one could strike a line from the pointers to the Pole-star (which is a crooked one, by the by), and as soon as it was dark enough for a man to count the Pleiads, I called my men with a long low whistle, and advanced in double file. The savages lay as deeply sleeping as if their consciences were perfect, whereas they could have had none at all. We entered their principal cuddy, or shanty, or shieling, or wigwam, or what you will (for it was none of these exactly, but a mixture of them all), and to our surprise not one awoke, or was civilised enough to snore. Higgledy-piggledy they lay in troughs scooped out of the side of the hill, or made by themselves, of clay and straw (called "cob," I believe, in Devonshire), with some rotten thatch above them, and the sides of their den made of brushwood. Some of the elders had sheepskins over them, but the greater part trusted to one another for warmth, and to their hairiness.

All this we saw by a blue-light which I ordered to be kindled —for at first it was as dark as pitch—and a stranger or a sadder sight has rarely been seen in England. Poor creatures! they were all so cowed by the brilliant light and the armed men standing in their filthy hovel, that they offered no resistance, but stared at us in a piteous manner, as if we were come to kill them. Escape was impossible, save for the children, and most of them thought (as we found out afterwards) that Chowne was tired of them and had ordered their destruction.

"Choose all the males from ten years to thirty," I shouted to my men, who were almost as scared as the savages: "don't touch the females, or I'll cut you down. Set another blue-light burning: we don't want any cripples."

Not to be too long with it, I only found three men worth impressing; the others were so badly built, or even actually deformed, and of appearance so repulsive that we could not bear to think of turning them into messmates.

"Now for the boys!" I cried; "we want boys even more than men almost;" but I found that all the children save one had slipped through the sailors' legs adroitly while we were dealing with the men. We could not have caught them in the dark; and more than this, the best-sized of them had popped, like snakes, into burrow-holes, or like a fox into his earth.

But the one who stood his ground, and faced us, was a noble-looking boy, in spite of dirt and nakedness, with long thick tangles of golden hair, and a forehead like a man's almost. He looked up at me in a bold steady manner, wholly unlike their savage stare, and it struck me that here was the little fellow whom I had saved eight or nine years ago from the horse of Parson Jack. But though he appeared to be twelve years old, I could not make out what he said, except "Yes, yes;" and "me come with oo." Such was his state of education!

I hoisted him on a strong man's back, for the long march had made me feel my years, and perceiving no call to molest the residue, or injure their home—such as it was—we simply handcuffed the three best fellows, and borrowed three pig-whips of their own (made right down ingeniously) so as to drive them to Heddon's Mouth. We durst not halt for a rest until there were three leagues between us and Nympton Moor; then hurrying on at the break of day, we found the Sealark at anchor; and she sent us a boat, at our signal.

Scarcely were we on board of the boat, and pushing off with our capture, when the clash of a horse's hoofs upon rock rang through the murmuring of the waves. We turned and gazed with one accord, for the boat lay broadside on to shore, through the kicking of the naked men when they felt salt water under them, and our quitting good stroke to attend to them. At furious speed a horseman dashed out of the craggy glen, and leaped the pool where the brook is barred up and vanishes. Down the shingle, and shelves of wrack, he drove his horse into the sea, until there was no firmness under him. He almost laid hold of our boat—not quite; for I struck with an oar at the horse, and scared him, shouting to all of my crew to pull.

Finding himself just a little too late, Chowne gave a turn to his horse's head, and the lather and foam of the spirited animal made a white curdle in the calm blue sea. The horse sprang gladly up the shingle crest—for the shore is very steep there—and he shook himself and scattered brine; and there were three other horses behind him. On one of these sate Parson Jack, and two huntsmen on the other twain, and the faces of these were as red as fire with hurry and indignation.

Only Chowne's wicked face was white, and settled with calm fury; and his style of address to us, just as if we were nothing but dogs of his kennel.

"Ho, you scoundrels!" he shouted out, "hold oars, and let me parley you."

At this I made a signal to my crew to slack from rowing;

and I stood up in the boat, and said, "What can we do for your Reverence?"

"Nothing for me, rogues; but much for yourselves. I will give you five pounds for that child in the stern. I want him for knife-cleaning."

"Would your Worship think fifty too much for him? We put him at fifty, your Worship."

"Fifty, you robbers! Well, then, fifty. Ten times his value to any one. But I have a fancy for him."

"Would your Worship mind saying five hundred down? Look at his hair: he is worth it." For we had washed him in the brook; and his hair in drying was full of gold.

"Who are you?" he shouted, controlling himself, as his habit was, when outbreak became useless. For the dignity of my demeanour, and the nobility of my uniform, also the snowiness of my hair, combined to defeat the unerring quickness of his rapid and yet cold eyes. And so I replied with an elegant bow—

"Your Reverence, it so happens that my name is 'Old Davy Llewellyn.'"

CHAPTER LIV.

TAMING OF THE SAVAGES.

AFTER a most successful cruise, we returned to our Bellona, and were received as behoves success, with ever so many rounds of cheers. It was true that we had sent before us, and now brought in, an awkward lot; but it is beautiful to see how in a large ship's company, and under a good commander, mere coaster fellows become true seamen, and even land-lubbers learn how to walk. Captain Drake Bampfylde did me the honour of asking my advice, as soon as his own opinion was settled; and I said no more than "Bay of Biscay," which was his own opinion. Here the very utmost of a noble sea awaited us, and none of our landsmen had any heart for fat, or even for lean stuff. We let them go on for a day, perpetually groaning, and after that we provided for each a gallon of salt water, and gave it them through the ship's trumpet, until they entirely ceased from noise.

These prudent measures brought them into such a wholesome

state of mind, that really a child might lead them, as by one of the prophets mentioned, when I read my Bible. All of our new hands, I mean, except Hezekiah, and the three wild men.

Unfortunate Master Perkins could not enter into the spirit of our exertions for his benefit; because his mind was unsettled with knowing the hardship both of his back and front. For his back was covered with raw places sitting amiss to the fit of his clothes, while the forward part of his body became too hollow to yield him comfort. But, strange to say, his wrath was kindled not against us for these misfortunes, but against his wife Hepzibah, because she had not predicted them. And for the greater part of a week, the poor fellow lay in a perfect craze upon the orlop-deck, while the ship was rolling heavily. Nothing could persuade him but that he was the prophet Jonah in the belly of the whale, and he took the stowage of our cables for the whale's intestines. You could hear him even from the main deck screaming at the top of his voice, " Wallow not, O whale! O whale! Lord, Thy servant repenteth, only let not this whale wallow so." So that in spite of all his tricks, hypocrisy, pride, and gluttony, I could not help taking compassion upon him, and having a hammock rigged tenderly for him, so that his empty and helpless body fell into a deep sleep as long as the prophet himself could have had it. For I never could show myself at Bridgend, if through my means Hezekiah found the sea his churchyard. On the other hand, the three wild men took their visitation from a wholly different point of view. They had never heard either of God or the devil, and could not believe themselves even worth the interference of either Power. For they did not believe that their souls were immortal (as I suppose they must have been), nor were they even aware of possessing anything more than a body a-piece. My own idea of treatment was, that to bring them into self-respect, we should flog the whole three very soundly, and handsomely pickle them afterwards; nor could I see any finer method of curing them of their hairiness. But Captain Bampfylde, who showed the strangest interest in these savages, would on no account have them flogged until they gave occasion. He said that their ideas of justice might be thrown into a crooked line, if the cat-and-nine-tails were promiscuously administered. Whereas I knew that the only way to make a man dwell upon justice is to give him a taste of the opposite. He values the right after this, because he thinks there is none of it left upon earth.

So for the present these three "Jack Cannibals," as our tars entitled them, sate apart and messed apart — and a precious mess it was of it. They soon got over the "Marly Mary," as the Crappos call it; and we taught them how to chew tobacco, which they did, and swallowed it. Only their fear of the waves was such that they could not look over the side of the ship, or even out of a porthole. After a few days we fell in with pelting showers of hail and sleet, with a bitter gale from the north-north-west. I saw the beauty of this occasion to show mankind their need of clothes; therefore I roused up these three poor fellows, and had them thrown into a salting-tub full of ice-cold water. This made their teeth chatter bravely, and then we started them up the rigging, with a taste of rope's end after them. They ran up the ratlines faster than even our very best hands could follow them, because of the power still left in their feet, through never having owned a shoemaker; but in the maintop they pulled up, and the wind went shivering through them.

Meanwhile I was sedately mounting (as my rank required now) with a very old pilot's coat, well worn out, hanging over my left arm.

"Here, Jack!" I cried to the biggest one; "take this, and throw it over you, to keep your poor bones warm."

The sheaves of the blocks were white with snow (which they always seem to be first to take), and so were the cleats and the weather side of topmast and top-gallant-mast. When you see this, you may make up your mind to have every rope frosted ere morning. Therefore Jack Cannibal looked at the coat, and around it, as a monkey does.

"Put it on," I cried; "poor fellow! put it on to cover you."

He nodded and laughed, as if I were making some joke which he ought to understand, and then he threw the warm coat round his body (now quite blue from cold), but without any perception of sleeves, or skirts, or anything else, except, as it were, like a bit of thatching. And after that he helped us to civilise the rest; so that in course of time we had them in decency far superior to the average show of Scotchmen. And in about the same course of time, Cannibal Jack, I do assure you, became a very good seaman, and a wonderfully honest fellow, without any lies in him. And yet he said things better than the finest lies that could be told, all coming out of his oddness, and his manner of taking tameness. And if a roaring sound of laughter came to the ears of an officer (such as never could be allowed in the discipline of war time), the officer always lifted lip, to have a smile accordingly, and said to himself, "I should like to know what Cannibal Jack has said to them."

The two other naked ones, Dick and Joe—as we christened them out of a bucket of tar, without meaning any harm to them—never could be entirely cured of their hereditary shortcomings. We taught them at last to wear clothes, by keeping a sharp leather strap always handy, against which their only protection was a good watch coat, or a piece of sailcloth; so that after a great deal of pleasantry, we set the ship tailor to work for them. But no possible amount of strap, nor even cat-and-nine-tails administered by our boatswain's mate (a most noble hand at wielding it), could prevail upon them to abandon their desire for the property of their messmates. They even had the arrogance, as their English grew more fluent, to attempt to reason it out with us.

"Father David," said Cannibal Dick, for they had agreed that now I was their patron, even as Chowne had been; "you take the Crappo ship, the enemy you call it, and then you leave them all their goods, not touch one of anything, and hand back the ship to him."

"Dick, none but a savage would talk such rubbish. We keep the ship, and all it holds, and put the men in prison."

"There for you now, there for you! And you beat us because we take not a great ship, but some little thing lying about in a ship, from our enemies."

"Will you never see things aright, Dick? We are not your enemies, we are your friends; and to steal things from us is robbery."

"You call it friends to steal us from our place, and people, and warm dry sands, and put us on this strange great wetness, where no mushrooms grow, and all we try to eat goes into it. And then you beat us, and drive us up trees such as we never saw before, and force us to hide in these dreadful things!"

Here he pointed to his breeches with a gaze of such hopeless misery, that I felt it would be an unkind thing to press him with further argument. However, the boy was enough to make up for a far worse lot than these were. We soaped him most powerfully, to begin with, even up to the skin of his eyelids, and he made no more objection than a Christian child might have offered. And after we had scraped him dry with the rough side of a spencer, he came out bright, I do assure you, and was such a model figure that we said to one another that he had some right to go naked. For his skin was now as fair and soft as the opening out of a water-lily, while his golden curls spread out, like flowers of the frogbit. Also his shoulders so nicely turned, and the slope of his sides so clever, with arms and legs of such elegant mould, being thick and thin in the proper places, and as straight as a well-grown parsnip; then, again, his ankles clear, and feet of a character never beheld after any shoemaking.

Our common fellows made so much of this superior little chap, that I was compelled to interfere, and show my resolution: and this required to be done with some small sense of how to do it; otherwise the boy might take the turn of sour grapes with them, and be bullied even more than he had been petted thitherto. Moreover, all the other boys in the ship were longing to fight with him, which (as he was the smallest of all, and not brought up in a Christian manner) would have afforded him no fair play for his nice short nose, or his soft blue eyes. The little dear was as brave as a lion, and ready to fight any one of them; and he used to stand up to my elbow, suing for permission. And now he began to talk so well, that it was very hard upon him not to be allowed to fight a bit; according to the natural issue of all honest converse. However, I would not be persuaded, loving his pretty face as I did; and I fear that he had unhappy times, through the wickedness of the other boys. Having a stronger sense of mistake than afforded me any happiness—in the thick of my rank and comforts—I could not find any ease until everything, looked at anyhow, and from all bearings contemplated, lay before our Captain. He thought, enough to look wise; and then, he said that really I was fit to see to such little things myself. He had heard of a small boy covered over with a great deal of yellow hair; this should have been fetched off long ago; and what was the barber kept for? Thus it always does befall me, to be thrown back, without guidance, on my own resources. And even Lieutenant Bluett, with whom I next went to hold counsel, was more inclined to stretch and gape, after a heavy spell on deck, than to bring his mind to bear upon this child's adventures.

"Send the poor little beggar in," he said, "and let me look at him, if I can keep my eyes open. Llewellyn, you always did love savages."

"Lieutenant, you would not like me to account you in the number."

"Davy, you might fairly do it, when I come off deck, like this. Send him in, ere I snooze, old fellow."

This I did; and when the boy entered, shyly putting one hand to his forelocks (as I had instructed him), a beam of the newly-risen sun broke in through a bull's eye, and made a golden frame for him. In the middle of this he looked so innocent and so comely, and at the same time so well bred, that Master Rodney's sleepy eyes fell open with wonder at him. This was my doing, of course, entirely. "Soap and discipline" is my signal to the next generation; and nothing else can counteract all the heresies around us. Therefore this little boy's cheeks were brighter than any rose, from towelling; and his beautiful eyes without speck of dirt; and the top of his head as sweet and curly as a feathering hyacinth.

When I perceive that I have had the luck to make an impression my rule is to say nothing at all, but appear to be unaware of it. This rule is founded on common-sense; and it took me so long to find it out, that it ought to be worth something. Otherwise, what offence one gives! And not only that, but consider how seldom the man who succeeds deserves it. Any modest man, like me, upon any moderate success, is bound to examine himself, and feel less confidence than he used to have. His success is enough to prove, according to the ways of the world, that he never can have deserved it.

This remembrance led me now to abstain from even patting "Harry" (as we had named this little fellow) on his golden head at all, lest I should manifest undue pride in a creature of my creation. For such he was, beyond all mistake; and it would have given me pleasure to back him for a crown against any boy in our fleet, or any three in the whole French navy; taking age, of course, and size, into consideration.

"What a fine little fellow!" said Rodney Bluett; "why, he ought to be a midshipman. I had no idea your savages could turn out such young ones. I must see what I can do for him, Davy. Only I can't think of anything now."

Perceiving that I was likely to do more harm than good by pressing the matter just then, I took little Harry away with me, and found him quite full of the young lieutenant's brave appearance and kindly smile. In a word, they were pleased with one another so heartily, and so lastingly, that it was the luckiest day, perhaps, of poor little Harry's unlucky career, when I first commended him to the notice of the Honourable Rodney.

For this latter was now not only a general favourite in the ship, but also a great power; being our second luff, and twice as active as our first was. He took the boy under his special care, and taught him all sorts of ennobling things—how to read, and write, and spell, and clean boots, and wait at breakfast. So that I felt many qualms sometimes, quite apart from all narrow methods of regarding anything, and springing from the simple fear that the child might be spoiled for his station in life, and fail to become a good seaman.

CHAPTER LV.

UPON FOREIGN SERVICE.

At length, when all sailors' hearts were sick with vain hopes of some enterprise, France did a truly bold thing by declaring war against Great Britain. Those people before this had given occasion for the strongest scandal, by taking their King and Queen in a dastardly manner, and cutting their heads off. Indignation and hot hatred ran throughout England and Wales, at the news; but our Government did no more than politely request that the London agent of these cut-throats should withdraw.

Nevertheless I cannot be wrong—as my pension comes from Government—in saying that to my mind the British Government, at this noble crisis, behaved in a most forbearing, prudent, Christian, generous, glorious, and magnanimous manner. They waited for war to be proclaimed by France, before they accepted it. And then they proved themselves as wholly unready as they ought to be. What finer state of feeling can be shown by any country?

It must have been either the end of February, or the early part of March, in the year of grace 1793, when we heard of this grand and momentous affair. And I remember the date by this, that the onions were sprouted, and we were compelled to make shift with shallots. For calling at Falmouth to victual a little, we sent three boats ashore, and I of course was in command of one. And though we spread abroad and ransacked all the Cornish gardeners' hoards, and gave them a taste of boat-hooks, because they had no proper things, not an onion could we find, except with a crooked thumb to it. Nor were the young ones yet fit to pull; and this fixes the date to a week or so.

And now we found that the whole of us were to be turned over, while the Bellona was refitting, to the 74-gun ship Defence, with orders for the West Indies at once—as was generally believed—to protect our shipping and commerce there.

For although the war had been so very long looked forward to, our Government was not ready yet, but had to send squadrons right and left, to see to our foreign interests; while Portsmouth, Chatham, and even London, had very few ships to defend them. Our charity never begins at home; as poor Bardie's did in her copy-book. However, it chanced to turn out all right, because the other side was quite as much abroad as we were.

Some of our men were inclined to grumble, at having barely a spree ashore, when they longed for a turn at home again. But the Admiralty settled that, by not paying their back-wages; which is the surest way of all for keeping a fellow well up to his work. His temptation for running is gone, because he has no cash to run with; neither do his people want him while in that condition. This he knows well, and it makes him think; and nine times out of ten he resolves to double what is due to him, and really pocket it when again due, and almost be admired by his own wife.

Therefore most part of us tumbled over from the Bellona into the Defence, after some liberty ashore—which, for a godly man like me, was nothing more than a trial. Captain Drake Bampfylde worked harder than even Parson Chowne's horses were said to do; and as for me—— but I will not say, for it now becomes unbecoming. Enough that the Defence cleared outward of the No-man buoy, the very day three weeks from the date of the Bellona standing inwards. We had the wind at E.N.E., as it always is in spring-time.

Now it may seem out of place, and even very rude on my part; but I could not altogether help a strong desire to know how our Captain this time managed in the matter of the female sex. I had my own feelings towards poor young Polly, and a hankering to let her see me (which, however, must not now be gratified on either side), and of course a man feels, when this is the case, that another man must be like him. However, the rules of the service forbade me to put any questions on private affairs to an officer thus set over me; and as for observing him, that was below me, even if time had availed for it. Heaviside also had shown such ill feeling and even downright ingratitude towards me, simply because my position and rank had compelled me to teach him his distance, which he was somehow too stupid to learn (especially since his rash elevation, and appointment as our chief boatswain, which made it the more incumbent upon me to preserve a firm attitude); this fellow, I say, was so utterly wanting in that deference which the Master of a line-of-battle ship not only has a right to expect, but is even bound to exact, that I could not now approach him with inquiries about our Captain. And this became tenfold more painful, as soon as I saw that he knew something.

What French sailors could have a chance with a fleet under Sir John Jervis? I cannot tell how many islands we took, for we could not stop to count them. We caught just the tail of the hurricane of the 12th and 13th of August, which ever will be remembered as the most terrible ever known. None of us had the luck to see the pine bulkhead blown through the palm-tree, or the whole of a sugar-estate set down on the other side of the mountain; but a sailor asks credit for his stories, because he has given it: and otherwise no tales can go on.

I need not dwell on our victories here, except for the sake of Harry Savage, as we had dubbed the poor Nympton boy, for want of legitimate surname. In one little skirmish ashore somewhere, I think in San Domingo, this little fellow, by genuine courage and unusual nimbleness, saved the life of his friend and protector, our Lieutenant Bluett. For while the lieutenant was engaged, sword to sword, with one vile republican, another of yet more rampant nature made at him, as it were flankwise, and must have given him a bitter stab, if Harry had not with a sudden jump grappled the rogue by the leg so tightly, that down he came on his face with a curse, so far as their language enables them. And we were so enraged, I assure you, at the duplicity of this fellow, that we borrowed a dirk from a little middy, and gave it to Harry to stick him with. But this our young savage refused to do, and turned quite pale at the thought of it, so that we placed that Equality man at the mercy of the French Royalists, who were acting with us at that period: and these made very short work with him, as justice demanded with a ringleader of pestilential principles.

Also, in a manner which true modesty forbids to dwell upon

—because neither of us had clothes on—I saved the life, before very long, of our new boatswain Heaviside. This worthy fellow was swimming along in his usual independent style, after kicking his good wife's shackles off, when I—having taken the inside of him, as his superior officer—discovered a shark of unusual size desirous to swallow our boatswain. That this should never come to pass was my resolve immediately, although I could not quite see how to be in time to stop it. For Heaviside, with his usual conceit, and desire to show himself off, was floating on his back, with arms laid square, and beard on breast, and legs spread out like rolling-pins. And the shark at twenty knots an hour split the blue water towards him.

Any man but myself would have given him over, or left all the rest to help him, especially after his utterly republican want of deference. To me, however, such want of sympathy was almost impossible, so that I swam with all speed to Heaviside, where he lay floating grandly.

"Look there!" I shouted; "all up with you, Ben, unless you capitulate." And with these words, I pointed out the fin of the shark advancing. Royal sharks we always called them, being the largest sharks in the world, in and around Port Royal. Heaviside had his fat legs foremost, and the royal shark stopped to look at them.

"Will you or will you not?" I asked, while preserving with some difficulty a proper position behind him—for even a royal shark could have wanted nothing more after Heaviside.

"Oh, Davy, Davy, I will," he answered; "only, only save me."

The look which he gave was now enough to make me sink small questions, especially as the poor fellow managed, being a first-rate swimmer, to offer me almost foremost to the jaws of the shark just opening. Therefore, as this latter creature rolled on his side to make at us, what did I do but a thing which none except a great fisherman could have done? To wit, I plucked from its strings the boatswain's heavy periwig (which had often vexed me, on account of its pretension), and clapping it on a piece of sugar-cane, which lay floating handy, down the wide jaws of the shark I thrust it, to improve his appetite.

Faithless people may doubt my word, when solemnly I declare to them that this great monster of the waters coughed and sneezed like a Christian. And we found him rolling dead the next morning, with this obstruction in his throat. Thus by much caution and presence of mind, I saved our boatswain not only from the jaws of a shark, but from a far more fatal error, arrogance and downright contumacy, which had made him refuse to touch his hat to his superior officer. Now I need not have mentioned this little affair, except that it bears upon my story, inasmuch as it reconciled Master and boatswain, and enabled them both to work together for the benefit of their Captain. Among poor Heaviside's many weak qualities, one of the most conspicuous was a resolute curiosity. This compelled him to open a great part of the breadth of his nature to the legitimate, or otherwise, affairs of his fellow-creatures.

And being an orthodox champion of wedlock (from the moment he left his wife and children, without any power to draw on him), he helped all the rest of the world in this way, as a host recommends his hot pickles.

Therefore he had been chosen, by very bad taste upon somebody's part, and an utter forgetfulness of me, to be up at our Captain's snap of a wedding, and to say "Amen" to it. What could be worse than a huddle of this kind, and a broad scattering afterwards? If they had only invited me, both sense and honesty would have been there; as well as a man not to be upset by things, however female.

That was their own concern, of course; and it misbecame me to think of it; and I saw, upon further consideration, that my sturdy honesty might not quite have suited them. For women are able, with the help of men, to work themselves up to anything. You may call them the shot and men the powder; or you may take quite another view, and regard them as the powder, with a superior man at the touchhole. Anyhow, off they go; and who shall ask the reason?

For from what Heaviside told me, it seems that the Captain and his fair Isabel, before our present cruise began, had resolved that no one should ever be able legally to sever them. But one special term of the compact was that the outer world should have no acquaintance with things that happened between them. In other words, that they should leave their excellent friends and relatives all in the dark about this matter, as well as save the poor Captain's oath, by quitting each other immediately. It is to the utmost extent beyond my own experience to deny, that this is the wisest of all

arrangements (if there can be anything wise) after the deed of
wedlock; for what can equal severance in the saving of dis-
agreement? However, they had not the wisdom as yet to
look at it in this light, and the one wept and the other sighed,
when they parted at the churchyard gate; for the Defence
must sail at 1 P.M. The lady had been content to come and
dwell in a very dirty village of the name of Gosport, so that
the licence might be forthcoming from proper people when
paid for. Because, of course, in her own county, nothing
could have been done without ten thousand people to talk of
it. And thus they were spliced, without hoisting flag; for
ever spliced, both in soul and in law (which takes the lead of
the other one), and yet in body severed always, till there
should come fair repute.

A common man of my rank in life, and having no more
than common-sense, must often find himself all abroad with
wonder about his superiors. They seem to look at things as
if everything and every person were looking back at them
again, instead of trusting to the Lord to oversee the whole of
it. If I had been of the proper age, and a lovely rich maid in
love with me, would I have stopped even twice to think what
the world might say about us? Heaviside's opinion was that
the lady wished to hide nothing whatever, but proclaim before
all people where and when, and whom she wedded, and how
proud she was of him. But the Captain, in his kind regard
and tenderness for her feelings, durst not expose her to the
pain and sense of wrong which might ensue upon his name
coming forward thus, with the county thinking as it did, and
himself not there to vindicate. And of course he knew with
what vigour and skill vile Parson Chowne would set to at
once to blacken his character, and to make his bride a most
unhappy one. Therefore Sir Philip Bampfylde and the
ancient Earl of Pomeroy were the only persons present of their
rank and kindred; and both of these confessed the wisdom of
the Captain's arguments.

Now on the 30th of April 1794, at about the hour of sun-
down, our anchor was scarcely beginning to bite in Cawsand
Bay, when the barge of the old Port-Admiral was alongside of
us. We had long been foregathering what we would do as
soon as we got ashore again; but now we could only shake
heads and fear that the whole would be disappointment. And
thus it proved, and even worse for many of our company, inasmuch as our orders were to make sail at once for St Helens.

and there to join the Channel fleet under Admiral Lord Howe. Therefore we carried on again with a gale from south-west to favour us, and on the first of May we brought up in the midst of a large society.

CHAPTER LVI.

EXILES OF SOCIETY.

A FINER sight was never seen than we had now around us; for all the convoy was come together, as well as the British fleet empowered to protect them. I stood in our foretop and counted 152 large sail, nearly 50 of which were men-of-war, and all the rest goodly merchantmen. A sight like this not only strengthens a Briton's faith in Providence, but puts him into a quiet pride concerning his King and country.

We had scarcely swung to our moorings ere we had signal from the Admiral, "Not a man to be allowed ashore. Water and victual all night, and be ready to weigh again at daybreak." Of course we did so, though a hard thing upon us; and new hands desired to grumble, until Captain Bampfylde rigged the gratings. Heaviside now was known to have such a swing of arm, with a flick to it, never being satisfied with his mate's administration, that never a man of patriotic sentiments encroached on him. We all determined to sail once more, and let the French see what our nature was (although they might hope to find it spoiled, by our being away from home so much); especially when we heard that they had 350 sail or more of merchantmen coming home, all very rich, and fattened up for capture. What we wanted, therefore, was to see our own good traders free from any chance of piracy, and at the same time to stop those French from wicked importations. If in both points we might succeed, and give battle afterwards, our gratitude to the Lord would almost equal our own glory. And we heard that the mob in Paris would starve, failing of all this American fleet.

On the 2d of May the wind fetched back to its proper place at that time of year, north-north-east, with snow-clouds always ready to endorse it; and thus we slipped from our moorings and went quietly down Channel. Concerning the rest, we have no cause to plead for man's indulgence. The Lord continued to baffle us, and would not give us any help to close quarters with the enemy. We fought three days of rolling battle, ending on the 1st of June, after two days of fog interrupting, and not a breath of sleep four nights. Every one says that we fought very well, having everything so much against us, and the French fleet far superior, carrying also a representative of the human race, large and fat and fluent, of the name of John Bone Andrews, who wrote a noble account of this action, although before it began his feelings led him to seek security in a hole far below the water-line.

But one of the strangest things ever seen, and thoroughly worth considering, was the behaviour of our two savages under heavy fire. Two, I say, although we had three, because Cannibal Jack behaved most steadily, and like a thorough Christian. But the two others most strongly proved their want of civilisation and gross ignorance of war, inasmuch as no sooner did they see the opening of bloodshed round them, than mad they became—as mad, I assure you, as any March hares, the brace of them. In the thick of our combat with the Towerful, up and down the deck these fellows danced in the most conspicuous places, as if inviting every shot, and cracking their knuckles and jabbering. I was for lashing them to the mainmast, but Captain Bampfylde would not allow it; he said that their spirited conduct might encourage and cheer the rest of us. And indeed it was strange to see how the shot flew around without striking them.

Now these poor fellows showed so much attachment and strong confidence towards me, that when we cast anchor in Plymouth Sound (being detached for refitment there, together with eight other ships of the line), I took it entirely upon myself to see them safe home, and to answer for them. Our ship had been knocked about so much, that she needed a thorough good overhauling, and many of us had a month's leave of absence, while carpenters, caulkers, and riggers were working. And these three savages outwent all of us in longing to see their homes again. So it struck me that I might both satisfy them and also gratify myself a little, by taking them under my escort as far as their native mud-holes, and then for a week perhaps enjoying good young Polly's society. Captain Bampfylde not only agreed to this, but said that he should not care twopence if he never saw two of their number again. He meant, of course, Dick and Joe, whose habits of larceny never could be thrashed out; whereas Cannibal Jack was now become as honest a hand as myself almost, and a valuable foretopman. Having pledged my word to bring this one back safe, and the others as well (if they chose to come), I set forth afoot for a cruise across Devon, than which, in the summer, with plenty of money, what can be more delightful? I would gladly have taken young Harry Savage, now a fine lad of fifteen years, so far as one might guess it; but Jack declared that he must not come, for some reason not to be told to me.

Now it was the flush of summer, very nearly twelve years from the time I first began with. Sunny hedges spread their overlap of roses over us, while the glad leaves danced in time with light and shade to foster them. Every bank of every lane was held at home with flowers, nourished by some flitting rill that made a tinkle for them. And through every gate almost, whenever there was a man to look, the spread of feathered grasses ran, like water with the wind on it.

Even a sailor may see such things, and his heart rejoice and be glad in them, and his perilous life for a while have rest without any thought of anything. Be that so, neither Dick nor Joe ever made glance at anything except the hen-roosts near the road, or the haunt of a young rabbit in the hedge, or the nesting of a partridge. I kept the poor fellows from doing harm, by precept and example too; yet we had a roast fowl every night, except when it was a boiled one. And finding myself in my sixty-fourth year, what could I do but put up with it?

It must be threescore miles, I think, even according to the shortest cut, from Plymouth to Nympton-on-the-Moors, and we wandered out of the way, of course, especially after guinea-fowls, which are most deluding creatures, but roast even better than their eggs boil. Also, we got into cherry orchards of a very noble breed; so that we spent a whole day and two nights, without any power to say farewell. And though the farmer's wife put up both hands to us at the window, she sent out the maid to say that we need not be frightened, if we were real sailors. After giving this girl a kiss (to let her know what our profession was), I sent in word that here was the Master of his Majesty's ship Defence, which had defended the British Empire, in the late great victory. That night they made all of us drunk, except me.

Upon these sweet little incidents I must venture to dwell no longer, while having so much of my yarn in the slack, and none but myself to tauten it. Enough that we came in about ten days to the genuine naked colony, without any meaning of surprise, but now as great ambassadors. And the least that we all expected was a true outburst of wild welcoming. Cannibal Jack had announced his intention to convert his relatives, while Dick and Joe only shook their heads, and seemed to doubt the advantage of it. But we need not have thought of the matter twice, for, strange to say, not one of the savages would for a moment acknowledge us. All the barbarous tribe stood aloof and scowled at their old members with utter abhorrence and contempt, as if at some vast degeneracy. Even Jack's wife, or the woman who might in humanity have been called so, stood moping and mowing at him afar, as if his clothes made a sheep of him, while he with amazement regarded her as if she were only a chimpanzee. Whereupon all of them set up a yell, and rushed with such pelting of mud at us, that we thought ourselves lucky to make our escape without any further mischief.

After hauling out of action in this most inglorious manner, we brought up to refit and revictual at the nearest public-house, a lonely hut where four roads met, and the sign hung from an ancient gibbet. Here we were treated very kindly, and for very little money, so that I was quite astonished after all our feeding. And I happened to say to the landlady that I was surprised to find honesty within a league of Parson Chowne.

"Oh, sir, do you know that dreadful man?" she answered, with her apron up; "or would you like to see him, sir?"

"Madam," said I, with that bow of mine which takes the women captive, "I should like to see him wonderfully; only without his seeing me."

"Of course, of course. All people say that, because of the evil eye he hath. This house doth belong to him. He be coming for the rent again at two o'clock, and he never faileth. Every farthing will be ready now, through your honour's generosity; and if so be you steps in here, when you hear me give three knuckles at the door, you may see him and welcome for nothing; only you must not speak for ever so."

The landlady showed me a little cellar, opening from our sitting-room, and having a narrow half-boarded hatchway bearing upon her sanded parlour, where she designed to receive the Parson. And then she was half afraid lest I might make a noise and so betray her. But almost before I had time to assure her of my perfect secrecy, the dash of horse's hoofs was heard, and the sound of a man's voice shouting.

"Well done!" said I to myself; "good Parson, years have not decreased thee."

His strong step rang on the lime-ash floor, and his silver spurs made a jingle, and lo, there he stood in the sanded parlour, as noble a Chowne as ever. There was not the sign of a spot of weakness or relenting about him; on his shaven face no bloom of greyness, nor in his coal-black hair one streak. As vigorous, springy, and strenuous seemed he, as when he leaped on board and thrashed me, nearly twelve years agone, as I do believe.

"Woman, where is my money?" he cried, with the old pale frown overcoming him; "twice I have given you time. You know what I always do thereafter."

"Yes, sir, I know what your Reverence doth. Your Reverence never calleth law, but taketh horsewhip to the mans of us."

"Your memory is correct," he answered; "my usual course is to that effect. I have brought my heaviest whip this time, for your husband has shown arrogance. Can you show cause why he should not have it?"

"Yes, your Reverence, here it is. And God knows how we have scraped for it."

With the glow of triumph which a man's face hardly ever shows, but a woman's cannot be denied of, she spread before him all his rent upon an ancient tray, and every piece of it was copper. Thirty-six shillings she had to pay, and twenty-four times thirty-six was there for his Reverence to count. The hostess looked at him, with a chuckle brewing now under her apron strings, and ready to rise to her ample breast, and thence to her mouth, if expedient. But she mistook her customer.

"Woman," said Chowne, in his deep low voice, which had no anger in it; "I am tired of signing warrants."

"Warrants, your Worship! For what, if you please?"

"Warrants for thieves who are foisting sham Irish halfpennies on the public. I see no less than seven of them in this sterling stuff of yours. Three months at the treadmill now for yourself and your husband. Say no more. You have tried a trick. Tiverton jail for you both to-morrow."

And there, if you wanted either of them, you must go to find them, only two days afterward, according to what I was told of it. No Welsh gentleman would have dreamed of behaving to his tenants thus, for trying a little joke with him; but Chowne had no sense of any joke, unless himself began it.

Our three cannibals had been trembling at the sound of the Parson's voice, believing that he would drive them back, and feeling that they had no power to withstand his orders. But luckily we had made such a smoke—all our savages having taken to the use of tobacco gloriously—that when the Parson put his head in, as he must do everywhere, he drew it back in double-quick time, for he hated the weed as Old Nick does. And then after calling his groom as a witness to the Irish coinage, he made him tie the whole of the rent-money in his pocket-handkerchief, and off he set at a good round gallop to make out the warrant. You may depend upon it that we four were very soon off as well, and in the opposite direction, after subscribing a guinea among us to comfort the poor woman, who was sobbing her heart out at her mistake, and at the prospect (as seemed to me) of being confined, in more senses than one, within the walls of a prison. For some time I found myself much at a loss about harbouring my convoy; for though I could trust Jack Wildman—as I now began to call him—anywhere and with anything, this was not the case with the other two, who could never be kept from picking up small things that took their fancy. We were shaping a course for Narnton Court, where I intended to sling my own hammock, and Jack's as well, if agreeable; but I durst not offer to introduce Dick and Joe, for the cause aforesaid. Moreover, they had not yet acquired the manners of good society, which were no little insisted upon in Sir Philip Bampfylde's kitchen. Therefore I thought myself very clever, when a settlement of this question suddenly occurred to me.

This was no less than to settle them both under my old ferry-boat, if still to be found as two years back, shored up and turned into a residence. Their rations might be sent down to them, and what happier home could they wish for, with the finest air in the world around them, as well as beautiful scenery? And if it should happen to leak a little (as seems only natural), what a blessed reflection for a man of due sentiments towards the Lord, that this water is dropping from heaven upon him, instead of rushing up to swallow him into that outrageous sea!

Accordingly so we contrived this affair. Mr Jack Wildman was introduced, under my skilful naval tactics, into the most accomplished circle on the quarter-deck of our head-cook. And he looked so very gently wild, and blushed in his clothes so beautifully, that there was not a maiden all over the place but longed to glance, unbeknown, at him. So that it seemed a most lucky thing that Polly was down with the small-pox, at a place called Muddiford; wherein she had an uncle. Meanwhile Cannibals Dick and Joe lived in the boat, as happily as if they had been born in it, and devoted their time to the slaying and cooking of Sir Philip's hares and rabbits. It was in vain that the gamekeepers did their best to catch them. Dick and Joe could catch hares, as they boasted to me, almost under the watchers' noses; so noble was the result of uniting civilised cunning with savage ingenuity.

I can well believe that no other man, either of my rank or age, would have ventured on the step which now I did resolve upon. This was no less than to pay a visit to my poor little Polly, and risk all probabilities of being disfigured by smallpox. For several times it had crossed my mind, that although she was among relatives, they were not like a father or mother to her, and perhaps she might be but poorly tended, and even in need of money perhaps. For her very own aunt, our Mrs Cockhanterbury, would not go nigh her, and almost shuddered when her name was mentioned. Now it seemed to be only fair and honest to let Sir Philip know my intention, so that he might (if he should see fit) forbid me to return to his mansion, bringing the risk of infection. But the General only shook his head, and smiled at that idea. "If it be the will of God, we shall have it, of course," he said; "and people run into it all the more by being over-timorous. And I have often thought it sinful to mistrust the Lord so. However, you had better keep smoking a pipe, and not stay more than five minutes; and perhaps you might just as well change your clothes before you come back, and sink the others to air for a week in the river." I was grieved to see him so entirely place his faith in Providence, for that kind of feeling (when thus overdone) ends in what we call "fatalism," such as the very Turks have. So that I was pleased when he called me back, and said, "Take a swim yourself, Llewellyn. I hear that you can swim five miles. Don't attempt that, but swim two, if you like. Swim back to us from Barnstaple bridge, and I will have a boat to meet you, with a wholesome wardrobe."

Thus was the whole of it arranged, and carried out most cleverly. I took poor Polly a bunch of grapes, from one of the Narnton vineries, as well as a number of nice little things, such as only a sailor can think of. And truly I went not a day too soon, for I found her in that weak condition, after the fury of the plague is past, when every bit of strengthening stuff that can be thought of, or fancied by, the feeble one may turn the scale, and one cheering glance or one smiling word is as good as a beam of the morning. Then after a long walk, I made my swim, and a change of clothes, exactly as the General had commanded me.

In a fortnight afterwards where was I? Why, under the boat, in a burning madness, without a soul to come nigh me, except Jack Wildman and Sir Philip. These two, with the most noble courage, visited me through my sad attack of small-pox, as I was told thereafter, although at the time I knew no one. And at a distance around the boat, a ring of brushwood was kept burning, day and night, to clear the air, and warn the unwary from entering. Everybody gave me up for a living Christian any more, and my coffin was ordered at a handsome figure (as a death upon Narnton premises), ay, and made also, like that of the greatest man that I ever did meet with. Not only this, but two Nonconformist preachers found out (as they always do) that in a weak period of my life, when dissatisfied with my pension, I had been washed away by my poor wife into the scuppers of Dissent. Therefore they prepared two sermons on this judgment of the Lord, and called me a scapegoat; while goodness knows what care they took never to lay hands on me.

CHAPTER LVII.

MANY WEAK MOMENTS.

NOTHING less than steadfast faith, and an ancient British constitution, can have enabled me to survive this highly-dappled period. It was not in my body only, or legs, or parts I think nothing of, but in my brain that I felt it most, when I had the sense to feel it. And having a brain which has no right to claim exemption from proper work, because of being under average, I happened to take a long time to recover from so many spots striking inwards. An empty-headed man might have laughed at the little drills into his brain-pan; but with me (as with a good bee-hive early in October) there could not be the prick of a brad-awl but went into honey. And so my brain was in a buzz for at least a twelvemonth afterwards.

Therefore I now must tell what happened, rather as it is told to me, than as myself remember it. Only you must not expect such truth, as I always give, while competent.

After the master of the ship Defence had proved so unable to defend himself, General Sir Philip Bampfylde, with his large and quiet mind forbidding all intrusion, opened out a little of his goodness to Jack Wildman. There are men of the highest station, and of noble intellect, who do this, and cannot help it, when they meet a fellow-man with something in him like them. There is no vanity in it, nor even desire to conciliate; only a little touch of something understood between them. And now being brought so together perhaps by their common kindliness, and with the door of death wide open, as it were, before them, the well-born and highly-nurtured baronet, and the lowly, neglected, and ignorant savage, found (perhaps all the more clearly from contrast) something harmonious in each other. At any rate they had a good deal of talk by the side of the lonely river, where even the lighters kept aloof, and hugged to the utmost the opposite shore. And the General, finding much amusement in poor Jack's queer simplicity, and strange remarks upon men and things, would often relax without losing any of his accustomed dignity. So while they were speaking of death one day, Jack looked at Sir Philip with an air of deep compassion and feeling, and told him with tearful eyes how heartily he was grieved at one thing. Being pressed as to what it was, he answered that it was Sir Philip's wealth.

"Because," said he, "I am sad when I think that you must go to hell, sir."

"I go to hell!" Sir Philip exclaimed, with a good deal of rather unpleasant surprise; "why should I do that, Jack? I never thought that you entertained so bad an opinion of me."

"Your Honour," said Jack, having picked up some of my correct expressions, "it is not me; it is God Almighty. I was told afore ever I learned to read, or ever heard of reading, how it was. And so it is in the Bible now. Poor men go to heaven, rich men go to hell. It must be so to be fair for both."

The General had too much sense to attempt to prove the opposite, and would have thought no more about it, if Jack had dropped the subject. But to do this at the proper moment requires great civilisation; while on the other hand Jack sought comfort, needless to men of refinement.

"Your Honour must go there," he said, with a nod of his head which was meant to settle it; "but there is one of your race, or family"—or whatever word of that sort he employed, for he scarce could have come to any knowledge of things hereditary—"who will go to heaven."

"Many are gone there already—too many," answered Sir Philip, devoutly; "but tell me whom you mean, Jack. Do you mean my son the Captain?"

"Him! no, no. I know better than that. It is plain where he must go to."

"Your Captain! you disloyal fellow. Why, you ought to be lashed to the triangles. But who is it you are thinking of?"

"I know, I know," said Jack, nodding his head; and no more could Sir Philip get out of him. And whenever he tried to begin again, Jack Wildman was more than a match for him, by feigning not to understand, or by some other of the many tricks which nature supplies, for self-defence, to the savage against the civilised. If I had been well, I must have shelled this poor Jack's meaning out of him; whereas, on the other hand, but for my illness he might never have spoken. So it came to pass that he was sent, entirely at Sir Philip's cost, and with a handsome gratuity, to rejoin our Captain in Plymouth Sound, and to carry back Cannibals Dick and Joe, who had scoured away at great speed upon hearing of my sudden misfortune.

Now I will tell you a very strange thing, and quite out of my experience: even after small-pox, which enlarged and filled me with charity, as well as what I had scarcely room for—increase of humility. This is, that though Captain Bampfylde had some little spare time at Plymouth, he had such command of himself that he never went near his beloved Isabel. Nothing could have so checked a man of heartiness and bravery, except the strongest power of honour, and a long time of chastisement. There was a lovely young woman, and here a fine though middle-aged man, her husband; they loved one another with heart and soul, and they never met, but through a telescope! It may have been right, or it may have been wrong—I should have thought it wrong, perhaps, if the case had been my own —but they pledged their honour and kept it. Drake Bampfylde (like his father) had a strength of trust in Providence. But this trust has no landed security, now that the Lord has found the world so clever, that He need not interfere with it.

The 74-gun ship Defence was known to be the fastest sailer in the British Navy; not from her build alone, or balance, but from my careful trim of her sails, and knowledge of how to handle her. Hours and hours I spent aloft, among lifts, and braces, and clue-garnets, marking the draw of every sail, and righting all useless bellying. So that I could now have warranted her the first of our Navy to break the line, if rigged according to my directions, and with me for her master. However (while I lay docked like this, careened I might say, and unlikely ever to carry a keel again), the Defence, without my knowledge even, being new-masted, sailed to join the Channel Fleet, with Heaviside acting as her master; and as might have been expected, fell to leeward one knot in three. And even worse than this befell her; for in the second of those two miserable actions, under Hotham in the year 1795, when even Nelson could do nothing, the Defence having now another captain as well as a stupid master, actually backed her mizzen-topsail, in the rear of the enemy, when the signal was to fill and stand on. However, as even that famous ship the Agamemnon did nothing that day, through getting no opportunity, we must forgive poor Heaviside, especially as he was not captain. But the one who ground his teeth the hardest, and could forgive nobody, was the Honourable Rodney Bluett, now first lieutenant of the Defence. By this time every one must desire to know why Captain Bampfylde was not there, as he might have been, and might have made himself famous, but for his usual ill-fortune. This had carried him to the East Indies, before the Defence had finished refitting; and there, with none of his old hands near him, he commanded a line-of-battle ship, under Commodore Rainier; and after some hard work, and very fine fighting, drove the brave Dutchmen out of the castle of Trincomalee, in August 1795, which we came to hear of afterwards.

Thus it was that everybody seemed to be scattered everywhere. None of us happened to hold together, except those three poor savages; and they, by a sort of instinct, managed to get over accidents. For they stuck, with that fidelity which is lost by education, to Rodney Bluett, as soon as ever poor Father Davy failed them. But this is a melancholy subject, and must soon be done with.

Let me, then, not dwell upon this visitation of the Lord for a moment longer than the claims of nation and of kin combine to make it needful. Nor did it seem to matter much for a long time what became of me. The very first thing I remember, after months of wandering, has something to do with the hush of waves, and the soft breath of heaven spread over me. Also kind young voices seemed to be murmuring around me, with a dear regard and love, and sense of pretty watchfulness; and the sound of my native tongue as soft as the wool of a nest to my bosom.

Because I was lying in a hammock, slung, by Colonel Lougher's orders, betwixt the very same mooring-posts (at about half-tide in Newton Bay) which truly enabled the sons of Devon to make such a safe job of stealing his rocks. Not only the Colonel, but Lady Bluett, who generally led his judgment, felt by this time the pleasure of owing true gratitude to somebody. My fatherly care of the young lieutenant had turned him out so nobly.

It misbecomes me to speak of this; and it misbecame me to speak at all, with the sea-breeze flowing over me, the first words of knowledge that I had spoken for how long I know not. Nothing can be too high, or too low, for human nature at both ends; but I ought to have known better than to do the thing I did.

"Give me a pipe," was all I said; and then I turned away, and cared not whether I got my pipe, or whether the rising tide extinguished me.

"Here is your pipe, sir," came in a beautiful voice from down below me; "and we have the tinder ready. Bunny, let me do it now."

That pipe must have saved my life. Everybody said so. It came and went in curls of comfort through the hollow dying places of my head, that had not even blood enough to call for it; and then it never left my soul uneasy about anything. Hammock and all must have gone afloat, with the rapid rise of the spring, except for Colonel Lougher's foresight.

Who was it that watched me so, and would have waited by my side, until the waves were over her? Who was it that kept on listening, to let me know, while I could not speak? Who was it that gave a little bit of a sigh, every now and then, and then breathed hard to smother it? Who was it, or who could it be, in the whole wide world, but Bardie?

Not only this, but when I began to be up to real sense again, the kindness of every one around me made me fit for nothing.

In the weakness of expecting all to take advantage of me (as is done in health and spirits), all the weakness I could find was in my friends and neighbours always labouring to encourage me. This to my mind proves almost the wrongness of expecting people to be worse than we are.

That winter was the most severe, all over Western Europe, known for five-and-fifty years. I well remember the dreadful winter A.D. 1740, when the Severn was frozen with a yard of ice, and the whole of the Bristol Channel blocked with icebergs like great hay-ricks. Twelve people were frozen to death in our parish, and seven were killed through the ice on the sea. The winter of 1795 was nothing to be compared to that; nevertheless it was very furious, and killed more than we could spare of our very oldest inhabitants.

And but for the extraordinary kindness of Colonel Lougher, that winter must have killed not only me in my weak and worn-out condition, but also the poor maid of Sker, if left to encounter the cold in that iceberg. For, truly speaking, the poor old house was nothing else through that winter. The snow in swirling sheets of storm first wrapped it up to the window-sills; and then in a single night overleaped gables, roofs, and chimney-tops. Moxy and Watkin passed a month of bitter cold and darkness, but were lucky enough to have some sheep, who kept them warm outside, and warmed their insides afterwards. And after that the thaw came. But all this time there was nobody in my little cottage at Newton, but poor Roger Berkrolles, and how he kept soul and body together is known to none save himself and Heaven. For Colonel Lougher and Lady Bluett, at the very beginning of the frost, sent down my old friend, Crumpy the butler, to report upon my condition, and to give his candid opinion what was the best thing to do with me. After that long struggle now (thanks to a fine constitution and the death of the only doctor anywhere on our side of Bridgend), I had begun to look up a little and to know the time of day. Crumpy felt my pulse, and nodded, and then prescribed the only medicine which his own experience in life had ever verified. Port wine, he said, was the only thing to put me on my legs again. And this he laid before the Colonel with such absence of all doubt, that on the very same afternoon a low and slow carriage was sent for me, and I found myself laid in a very snug room, with the firelight dancing in the reflection of the key of the wine-cellar. Also here was Bardie flitting, light as a gnat in spring-time, and Bunny to be had whenever anybody wanted her. Only her scantling and her tonnage unfitted her for frigate-service.

What had a poor old fellow like me—as in weak moments I called myself—ever done, or even suffered, to deserve to find the world an Inn of good Samaritans? I felt that it was all of pure unreasonable kindness; the very thing which a man of spirit cannot bear to put up with. I have felt this often, when our Parson discoursed about our gracious Lord, and all the things He did for us. A man of proper self-respect would like to have had a voice in it.

This, however (as Hezekiah told us in the cockpit, after we had pickled him), might be safely attributed to the force of unregeneracy; while a man who is down in luck, and constitution also, trusts to any stout mortal for a loan of orthodoxy. And so did I to our Rector Lougher, brother of the Colonel, a gentleman who had bought my fish, and felt my spiritual needs. To him I listened (for well he read), especially a psalm to which I could for ever listen, full of noble navigation, deeper even than our soundings in the Bay of Biscay.

Every night we used to wonder where Lieutenant Bluett was, knowing as we did from my descriptions (when the hob was hot) what it is to be at sea with all the rigging freezing. When the blocks are clogged with ice, and make mysterious groanings, and the shrouds have grown a beard as cold as their own name is, and the deck begins to slip; and all the watch with ropes to handle, spit upon their palms, and strike them (dancing with their toes the while) one man to another man's, hoping to see sparks come out. So it is, I can assure you, who have never been at sea, when the barbs of icy spray by a freezing wind are driven, like a volley of langrel-shot raking the ship from stem to stern, shrivelling blue cheeks and red noses, shattering quids from the chattering teeth. Many a time in these bitter nights, with the roar of east wind through the fir-trees, and the rattle of doors in the snow-drift, I felt ashamed of my cozy berth, and could not hug my comfort, from thinking of my ancient messmates turned to huddled icicles.

But all was ordained for the best, no doubt: for supposing that I had been at sea through the year 1795, or even 1796, what single general action was there worthy of my presence? It might have been otherwise with me there, and in a leading position. However, even of this I cannot by any means be certain, for seamen quite as brave and skilful were afloat at that very time. However, beyond a few frigate actions, and matters far away from home, at the Cape, or in the East Indies, I did not hear of anything that I need have longed much to partake in. So that I did not repent of accepting a harbour-appointment at Plymouth, which (upon my partial recovery) was obtained for me by Sir Philip Bampfylde, an old friend of the Port-Admiral there.

For that good Sir Philip was a little uneasy, after shipping me off last autumn, lest he might have behaved with any want of gratitude towards me. Of course he had done nothing of the kind; for in truth I had raved for my country so—as I came to learn long afterwards—that when all the risk of infection was over, the doctor from Barnstaple said that my only chance of recovering reason lay in the air of my native land. But at any rate this kind baronet thought himself bound to come and look after me, in the spring of the year when the buds were awake, and the iron was gone from the soul of the earth. He had often promised that fine old tyrant Anthony Stew to revisit him; so now he resolved to kill two birds with one stone, as the saying is.

I had returned to my cottage now, but being still very frail and stupid, in spite of port wine every day, I could not keep the tears from starting, when this good and great landowner bent his silver head beneath my humble lintel, and forbade me in his calm majestic manner to think for a moment of dousing my pipe. And even Justice Stew, who of course took good care to come after him, did not use an uncivil word, when he saw what Sir Philip thought of me.

"Sir," said the General to the Squire, after shaking hands most kindly with me, "this is a man whom I truly respect. There seems to be but one opinion about him. I call him a noble specimen of your fellow-countrymen."

"Yes, to be sure," answered Anthony Stew: "but my noble fellow-countrymen say that I am an Irishman."

"No doubt whatever about that, your Worship," was the proper thing for me to reply; but the condition of my head forbade me almost to shake it. If it had pleased the Lord to give me only a dozen holes and scars—which could not matter at my time of life—there would not by any means have arisen, as all the old women of Newton said, this sad pressure on the brain-pan, and difficulty of coping even with a man of Anthony Stew's kind. But, alas! instead of opening out, the subtle plague struck inwards, leaving not a sign outside, but a delicate transparency.

This visit from Sir Philip did not end without a queer affair, whereof I had no notice then, being set down by all the village as only fit to poke about among the sand-hills, and then to die. But no one could take the church-clock from me, till the bell should be tolling for me; and as a matter of duty I drew some long arrears of salary.

It seems that Sir Philip drove down one day from Pen Coed to look after me, and having done this with his usual kindness, spread word through the children (who throughout our lane abounded) that really none of his money remained for any more sticks of peppermint. It was high time for them to think, he said, after ever so much education, of earning from sevenpence to tenpence a-week, for the good of the babies they carried. All the children gathered round him at this fine idea, really not believing quite that the purse of such a gentleman could have nothing more to say. And the girls bearing babes were concave in the back, while the boys in the same predicament stuck out clumsily where their spines were setting.

"Drive me away," said Sir Philip to the groom; "drive me straight away anywhere: these Welsh children are so clever, I shall have no chance with them."

"Indeed, your Honour, they is," said the groom with a grin, as behoved a Welshman. "Would your Honour like to go down by the sea, and see our beautiful water-rocks, and our old annshent places?"

"To be sure," said Sir Philip; "the very thing. We have four hours' time to dinner yet; and I fear I have worn out poor Llewellyn. Now follow the coast-line if you are sure that your master would like it, Lewis, with this young horse, and our weight behind."

"Your Honour, nothing ever comes amiss to this young horse here. 'Tis tire I should like to see him, for a change, as we do say. And master do always tell me keep salt-water on his legs whenever."

"Right!" cried Sir Philip, who loved the spree, being as full of spirits still, when the air took his trouble out of him, as the young horse in the shafts was.

So they drove away over the sands towards Sker, which it is easy enough to do with a good strong horse and a light car behind him. And by this time the neighbourhood had quite forgotten all its dread of sand-storms. In about half an hour they found themselves in a pretty place of grass and furze known as the Lock's Common, which faces the sea over some low cliffs, and at the western end coves down to it. This is some half a mile from Sker House, and a ragged dry wall makes the parish boundary, severing it from Sker-land.

"Drive on," cried Sir Philip; "I enjoy all this: I call this really beautiful, and this fine sward reminds me of Devonshire. But they ought to plant some trees here."

The driver replied that there was some danger in driving through Sker warren, unless one knew the ground thoroughly, on account of the number of rabbit-holes; and the baronet, with that true regard which a gentleman feels for the horse of a friend, cancelled his order immediately. "But," he continued, "I am so thirsty that I scarcely know what to do. My friend Llewellyn's hospitality is so overpowering. The taste of rum is almost unknown to me; but I could not refuse when he pressed me so. It has made me confoundedly thirsty, Lewis."

"Your honour," said Lewis, "just round that corner, in a little break of the rocks, there is one of the finest springs in Glamorgan, 'Ffynnon Wen' we call it, the water does be sparkling so."

The groom, having no cup to fetch the water, stood by the horse in the little pant or combe; while old Sir Philip went down to the shore, to drink as our first forefather drank, and Gideon's men in the Bible. Whether he lapped or dipped, I know not (probably the latter, at his time of life), anyhow he assuaged his thirst—which rum of my quality could not have caused in a really sound constitution, after taking no more than a thimbleful—and then for a moment he sate on a rock, soothed by the purling water, to rest and to look around him. The place has no great beauty, as of a seaside spring in Devonshire, but more of cheer and life about it than their ferny grottoes. The bright water breaks from an elbow of rock, in many veins all uniting, and without any cliff above them; and then, after rushing a very few yards through set stone and loose shingle, loses its self-will upon the soft sand, and spreads a way over a hundred yards of vague wetness and shallow shining.

The mild sun of April was glancing on this, and the tide just advancing to see to it, when the shadow of a slim figure fell on the stones before Sir Philip. So quietly had she slipped along, and appeared from the rocks so suddenly, that neither old man nor young maiden thought of the other until their eyes met.

"What, why, who?" cried the General, with something as

much like a start as good conscience and long service had left in him: "who are you? Who are you, my dear?"

For his eyes were fixed on a fair young damsel of some fifteen summers, standing upright, with a pad on her head, and on the pad a red pitcher. Over her shoulders, and down to her waist, fell dark-brown curls abundantly, full of gleaming gold where the sun stole through the rocks to dwell in them. Her dress was nothing but blue Welsh flannel, gathered at the waist and tucked in front, and her beautifully tinted legs and azure-veined feet shone under it.

"Who are you, my pretty creature?" Sir Philip Bampfylde asked again, while she opened her grey eyes wide at him.

"Y Ferch o'r Seer, Syr," she answered shyly, and with the strong guttural tone which she knew was unpleasant to English ears. For it was her sensitive point that she could not tell any one who she was; and her pride (which was manifold) always led her to draw back from questions.

On the other hand the old man's gaze of strong surprise and deep interest faded into mere admiration at the sound of our fine language.

"Fair young Cambrian, I have asked you rudely, and you are displeased with me. Lift your curls, my little dear, and let me see your face a while. I remember one just like it. There, you are put out again! So it was with the one I mean when anything happened hastily."

The beautiful girl flung back her hair, and knelt to stoop her pitcher in the gurgling runnel; and then she looked at his silver locks, and was sorry for her impatience.

"Sir, I beg you to forgive me, if I have been rude to you. I am the maid from the old house yonder. I am often sent for this water, because it sparkles much more than our own does. If you please, I must go home, sir."

She filled the red pitcher, and tucked the blue skirt, as girls alone can manage it; and Sir Philip Bampfylde sighed at thinking of his age and loneliness, while with an old-fashioned gentleman's grace he lifted the pitcher and asked no more upon whose head he laid it.

CHAPTER LVIII.

MORE HASTE, LESS SPEED.

To do what is thoroughly becoming and graceful is my main desire. That any man should praise himself, and insist upon his own exploits and services to his native land, or even should let people guess at his valour, by any manner of side-wind,— such a course would simply deprive me of the only thing a poor battered sailor has left to support him against his pension; I mean of course humble, but nevertheless well-grounded, self-respect.

This delicacy alone forbids me even to allude to that urgent and universal call for my very humble services which launched me on the briny waves once more, and in time for a share in the glorious battle fought off Cape St Vincent. Upon that great St Valentine's Day of 1797 I was Master of the Excellent, under Captain Collingwood; and every boy in the parish knows how we captured the Saint Isidore, and really took the Saint Nicholas, though other people got the credit, and nearly took a four-decked ship of 130 guns, whose name was the Saint Miss Trinder, and who managed to sneak away, when by all rights we had got her.

However, let us be content with things beyond contradiction; the foremost of which is, that no ship ever was carried into action in a more masterly style than the Excellent upon that occasion. And the weight of this falls on the Master, far more than the Captain, I do assure you. So highly were my skill and coolness commended in the despatches, that if I could have borne to be reduced below inferior men, I might have died a real Captain in the British Navy. For (as happened to the now Captain Bowen, when Master of the Queen Charlotte) I was offered a lieutenant's commission, and doubted about accepting it. Had I been twenty years younger, of course, I must have jumped at the offer; but at my time of life, and with all my knowledge, it would have been too painful to be ordered about by some young dancer; therefore I declined; at the same time thinking it fair to suggest, for the sake of the many true Britons now dependent upon me, that a small pecuniary remittance would meet with my consideration. That faculty of mine, however, was not called to the encounter: I never heard more about it, and had to be satisfied with glory.

But if a man is undervalued often, and puts up with it, he generally finds that fortune treats him with respect in other more serious aspects. For instance, what would have happened if Providence had ordained to send me into either of those sad mutinies which disgraced our fleets so terribly? That deep respect for authority which (like the yolk of a nest-egg) lies calmly inside me, waiting to be sate upon; as well as my inborn sense of Nature's resistless determination to end by turning me into a gentleman (indications of which must have long ago been perceived by every reader), not to mention any common sense of duty in the abstract and wages in the pocket,—these considerations must have led me to lay a pistol to the head of almost every man I could find.

However, from such a course of action grace and mercy preserved me: and perhaps it was quite as well. For I am not sure that I could have stopped any one of the four mutinies entirely; although I can answer for it, that never would bad manners take the lead in any ship, while I was Master. It is the shilly-shallying that produces all the mischief. If all our Captains had behaved like Captain Peard and his first lieutenant, in the St George off Cadiz, at the first spread of disaffection, it is my opinion that a great disgrace and danger would have been crushed in the bud. But what could be expected when our Government showed the like weakness? Twice they went hankering after peace, and even sent ambassadors! Who can ram shot home with pleasure while things of this kind are encouraged? To fight it out is the true Christianity, ordered by the Church itself.

And this we did, and are doing still, as Roger Berkrolles prophesied; and the only regret I have about it is, that a stiffness in my knees enables the other boarders to take a mean advantage of their youth, and jump into the chains or port-holes of a ship (when by my tactics conquered), so as to get a false lead of me. However, no small consolation was to be gained by reflecting how much more prize-money would accrue to me than to any of these forward fellows, so that one might with an unmoved leg contemplate their precipitancy.

Even a sorer grievance was the breaking up and dispersion of our noble and gallant ship's company, so long accustomed to one another and to sharp discipline in the Defence. Where was Captain Bampfylde? Where was Lieutenant Rodney Bluett? What was become of our three fine savages? Even Heaviside and Hezekiah were in my thoughts continually, and out of my knowledge entirely. As to the latter worthy gunsmith, "Artillerist to the King and Queen, and all the Royal Family," I can only at present say that when I had been last at home, and before my acceptance of that brief appointment in the Plymouth dockyard—in short, when first I recovered strength, after that long illness, to cope with the walk both to and fro—I found occasion to go to Bridgend, with my uniform on for the sake of the town. I had not turned the corner of the bridge a good half-hour, before that important fact was known from the riverbank to the churchyard. And Griffith of the "Cat and Snuffers," set up such a Welsh hurrah [as good as the screech of a wild-cat trapped] that it went up the hill to Newcastle. In a word, Hepzibah heard of me, and ran down the hill, like a roaring lion, demanding her Hezekiah!

What ensued is painful to me even now to speak of. For though my conscience was refitting, and ready to knock about again, after carrying too much sail, I could not find it in my heart to give the mother of a rapid family nothing but lies to feed upon. Many men of noble nature dwell upon nothing but conscience; as if that were the one true compass for a man to steer by—whereas I never did find a man—outside my own Sunday clothes,—whose conscience would not back him up in whatever he had a mind for.

My own had always worked like a power plainly exposed to every one; thereby gaining strength and revolving as fast as a mountain windmill, when the corn is falling away to chaff. This, however, was not required in the present instance; for Hepzibah (like a good woman) fell from one extreme into the opposite. From bitter reviling to praise and gratitude was but a turn of the tongue to her; especially when I happened to whisper into the ear of Griffith that the whole of my stipend for Newton Church clock would now, according to my views of justice, be handed to Hezekiah's wife, inasmuch as the worthy gunsmith had rejoined the Church of England. And I said what a dreadful blow this would be to all the Nicodemites, when the gun-officer returned with money enough to build a chapel: however, I felt that it served them right, because they had lately begun to sneer at his good wife's wonderful prophecies.

In a word, I had promised to find Hezekiah; and, both while in harbour and now when afloat, I tried to get tidings not only of him, but also of the Newton tailor, and Heaviside, and the three wild men, as well as young Harry Savage, Lieutenant Bluett, and Captain Bampfylde. For all of these being at sea and in war-time, who could say what had befallen them? Whereas I knew all about most of our people now living ashore in the middle of peace. However, of course one must expect old shipmates to be parted; and with all the vast force now afloat under the British flag, it would almost be a wonder if any of us should haul our wind within hailing distance of the others during our cruise in this world.

Nevertheless it did so happen, as I plainly will set forth, so far as I remember. Through the rest of the year '97 and the early part of the following year I was knocking about off and on near the Straits, being appointed to another ship while the Excellent was refitting, and afterwards to the Goliath, a fine 74, under Captain Foley.

In the month of May 1798, all our Mediterranean fleet, except three ships of the line, lay blockading Cadiz. Our Admiral, the Earl St Vincent, formerly Sir John Jervis, had orders also to watch Toulon, where a great fleet was assembling. And our information was so scant and contradictory, that our Admiral sent but three ships of the line and a frigate or two to see what those crafty Frenchmen might be up to. But this searching squadron had a commander whose name was Horatio Nelson.

This was not by any means the man to let frog-eaters do exactly as they pleased with us. "I believe in the King of England; I have faith in discipline; I abhor all Frenchmen worse than the very devil." Such was his creed; and at any moment he would give his life for it. It is something for a man to know what he means, and be able to put it clearly; and this alone fetches to his side more than half of the arguers who cannot make their minds up. But it is a much rarer gift, and not often combined with the other, for a man to enter into, and be able to follow up, ways and turns, and ins and outs, of the natures of all other men. If this is done by practised subtlety, it arouses hatred, and can get no further. But if it be a gift of nature exercised unwittingly, and with kind love of manliness, all who are worth bringing over are brought over by it.

If it were not hence, I know not whence it was that Nelson had such power over every man of us. To know what he meant, to pronounce it, and to perceive what others meant, these three powers enabled him to make all the rest mean what he did. At any rate such is my opinion; although I would not fly in the face of better scholars than myself, who declared that here was witchcraft. What else could account for the manner in which all Nelson's equals in rank at once acknowledged him as the foremost, and felt no jealousy towards him? Even Admiral Earl St Vincent, great commander as he was, is said to have often deferred to the judgment of the younger officer. As for the men, they all looked upon it as worth a gold watch to sail under him.

Therefore we officers of the in-shore squadron, under Captain Troubridge, could scarcely keep our crews from the most tremendous and uproarious cheers when we got orders to make sail for the Mediterranean, and place ourselves under the command of Nelson. We could not allow any cheering, because the Dons ashore were not to know a word about our departure, lest they should inform the Crappos, under whose orders they now were acting. And a British cheer has such a ring over the waters of the sea, and leaps from wave to wave so, that I have heard it a league away when roused up well to windward. So our fine fellows had leave to cheer to their hearts' content when we got our offing; and partly under my conduct (for I led the way in the Goliath), nine seventy-fours got away to sea in the night of the 24th of May, and nine liners from England replaced them, without a single Jack Spaniard ever suspecting any movement. Every one knows what a time we had of it, after joining our Admiral; how we dashed away helter-skelter, from one end of the world to the other almost, in a thorough wild-goose chase, because the Board of Admiralty, with their usual management, sent thirteen ships of the line especially on a searching scurry without one frigate to scout for them! We were obliged to sail, of course, within signalling distance of each other, and so that line of battle might be formed without delay, upon appearance of the enemy. For we now had a man whose signal was "Go at 'em when you see 'em." Also, as always comes to pass when the sons of Beelzebub are abroad, a thick haze lay both day and night upon the face of the water. So that, while sailing in close order, upon the night of the shortest day, we are said to have crossed the wake of the Frenchmen, almost ere it grew white again, without even sniffing their roasted frogs. Possibly this is true, in spite of all the great Nelson's vigilance; for I went to my hammock quite early that night, having suffered much from a hollow eye-tooth ever since I lost sight of poor Polly.

Admiral Nelson made no mistake. He had in the highest degree what is called in human nature "genius," and in dogs and horses "instinct." That is to say, he knew how to sniff out the road to almost anything. Trusting to this tenfold (when he found that our Government would not hear of it, but was nearly certain of a mighty landing upon Ireland), off he set for Egypt, carrying on with every blessed sail that would or even would not draw. We came to that coast at a racing speed, and you should have seen his vexation when there was no French ship in the roadstead. "I have made a false cast, Troubridge," he cried; "I shall write to be superseded. My want of judgment may prove fatal to my King and country."

For our Government had sent him word, through the Earl St Vincent, that the great expedition from Toulon would sail for England or Ireland; and he at his peril had taken upon him to reject such nonsense. But now (as happens by Nature's justice to all very sanguine men) he was ready to smite the breast that had suggested pure truth to him. Thus being baffled we made all sail, and after a chase of six hundred leagues, and continually beating to windward, were forced to bear up on St Swithin's Day and make for the coast of Sicily. And it shows the value of good old hands, and thoroughly sound experience, that I, the oldest man perhaps in the fleet, could alone guide the fleet into Syracuse. Here our fierce excitement bubbled while we took in water.

CHAPTER LIX.

IN A ROCKY BOWER.

I NEVER hear of a man's impatience without sagely reflecting upon the rapid flight of time, when age draws on, and business thickens, and all the glory of this world must soon be left behind us. From the date of my great catch of fish and landing of Bardie at Pool Tavan, to the day of my guiding the British fleet betwixt the shoals of Syracuse, more than sixteen years had passed, and scarce left time to count them.

Therefore it was but a natural thing that the two little maidens with whom I began should now be grown up, and creating a stir in the minds of young men of the neighbourhood. Early in this present month of July, that north-west breeze, which was baffling our fleet off the coast of Anatolia, was playing among the rocks of Sker with the curls and skirts and ribbons of these two fair young damsels.

Or rather with the ribbons of one, for Bunny alone wore streamers, wherein her heart delighted; while the maid of Sker was dressed as plainly as if she had been her servant. Not that her inborn love of brightness ever had abandoned her, but that her vanities were put down quite arrogantly by Master Berkrolles whenever she came back from Candleston; and but for her lessons in music there—which were beyond Roger's compass—he would have raised his voice against her visits to the good Colonel.

For the old man's heart was entirely fixed upon the graceful maiden, and his chief anxiety was to keep her out of the way of harm. He knew that the Colonel loved nothing better (as behoved his lineage) than true and free hospitality; and he feared that the simple and nameless girl might set her affections on some grand guest, who would scorn her derelict origin.

Now she led Bunny into a cave, or rather a snug little cove of rock, which she always called her cradle, and where she had spent many lonely hours, in singing pure Welsh melodies of the sweetest sadness, feeling a love of the desert places from her own desertion. Then down she sate in her chair of stone, with limpets and barnacles studding it; while Bunny in the established manner bounced down on a pebble and gazed at her.

My son's daughter was a solid girl, very well built as our family is, and raking most handsomely fore and aft. Her fine black eyes, and abiding colour, and the modesty inherited from her grandfather, and some reflection perhaps of his fame, made her a favourite everywhere. And any grandfather might well have been proud to see how she carried her dress off.

The younger maid sate right above her, quite as if Nature had ordered it so; and drew her skirt of home-spun camlet over her dainty feet, because the place was wet and chilly. And anybody looking must have said that she was born to grace. The clear outlines of oval face and delicate strength of forehead were moulded as by Nature only can such dainty work be done. Gentle pride and quiet moods of lonely meditation had deepened and subdued the radiance of the large grey eyes, and changed the dancing mirth of childhood into soft intelligence. And it must have been a fine affair, with the sunshine glancing on the breezy sea, to take a look at the lights and shadows of so clear a countenance.

Bunny, like a frigate riding, doused her head and all her outworks forward of the bends; and then hung fluttering and doubtful, just as if she had missed stays.

"It is not your engagement, my dear Bunny," began Delushy, as if she were ten years the senior officer; "you must not suppose for a moment that I object to your engagement. It is time, of course, for you to think, among so many suitors, of some one to put up with, especially after what you told me about having toothache. And Watkin is thoroughly good and kind, and able to read quite respectably. But what I blame you for is this, that you have not been straightforward, Bunny. Why have you kept me in the dark about this one of your many 'sweetheartings,' as you always call them?"

"And for sure, miss, then I never did no such thing; unless it was that I thought you was wanting him."

"I! You surely cannot have thought it! I want Watkin Thomas!"

"Well, miss, you need not fly out like that. All the girls in Newton was after him. And if it wasn't you as wanted him, it might be him as wanted you, which comes to the same thing always."

"I don't quite think that it does, dear Bunny, though you may have made it do so. Now look up and kiss me, dear: you know that I love you very much, though I have a way of saying things. And then I am longing to beg pardon when I have vexed any one. It comes of my 'noble birth,' I suppose, which the girls of Newton laugh about. How I wish that I were but the child of the poorest good man in the parish! But now I am tired of thinking of it. What good ever comes of it? And what can one poor atom matter?"

"You are not a poor atom; you are the best, and the cleverest, and most learnedest, and most beautifullest lady as ever was seen in the whole of the land."

After or rather in the middle of which words, our Bunny, with her usual vigour and true national ardour, leaped into the arms of Delushy, so that they had a good cry together. "You will wait, of course, for your Granny to come, before you settle anything."

"Will I, indeed?" cried that wicked Bunny, and lucky for her that I was not there: "I shall do nothing of the sort. If he chooses to be always away at sea, conquering the French for ever, and never coming home when he can help it, he must make up his mind to be surprised when he happens to come home again. For sure then, that is right enough."

"Well, it does seem almost reasonable," answered the young lady: "and I think sometimes that we have no right to expect so much as that of things. It is not what they often do; and so they lose the habit of it."

"I do not quite understand," said Bunny.

"And I don't half understand," said Bardie:—"but—oh my dear, what shall I do? He is coming this way, I am sure. And I would not have you know anything of it—and of course you must feel that it is all nonsense. And I did not mean any harm about 'courting;' only you ought to be out of the way, and yet at the same time in it."

Our Bunny was such a slow-witted girl, and at the same time so particular (inheriting slowness from her good mother, and conscience from third generation), that really she could make no hand at meeting such a crisis. For now she began to perceive gold-lace, which alone discomfits the woman-race, and sets their minds going upon what they love. And so she did very little else but stare.

"I did think you would have helped me, Bunny," Delushy cried, with aggrievement. "I wanted to hear your own affairs, of course; but I would not have brought you here——"

"Young ladies, well met!" cried as solid a voice as the chops of the Channel had ever tautened: "I knew that you were here, and so I came down to look after you."

"Sure then, sir, and I do think that it is very kind of you. We was just awanting looking after. Oh what a fish I do see in that pool! Please only you now both to keep back. I shall be back again, now just, sir." With these words away flew Bunny, as if her life were set on it.

"What a fine creature, to be sure!" said Commander Bluett, thoughtfully; "she reminds me so much of her grandfather. There is something so strongly alike between them, in their reckless outspoken honour, as well as in the turn of the nose they have."

"Let us follow, and admire her a little more," cried Delushy: "she deserves it, as you say; and perhaps—well perhaps she likes it."

Young Rodney looked at her a little while, and then at the ground a little while; because he was a stupid fellow as concerns young women. He thought this one such a perfect wonder, as may well be said of all of them. Then those two fenced about a little, out of shot of each other's eyes.

There was no doubt between them as to the meaning of each other. But they both seemed to think it wise to have a little bit of vexing before doing any more. And thus they looked at one another as if there was nothing between them. And all the time, how they were longing!

"I must have yes or no:" for Rodney could not outlast the young lady: "yes or no; you know what I mean. I am almost always at sea; and to-morrow I start to join Nelson. With him there is no play-work. I hope to satisfy him, though I know what he is to satisfy. But I hope to do it."

"Of course you will," Delushy answered. "You seem to give great satisfaction; almost everywhere, I am sure."

"Do I give it, you proud creature, where I long to give it most?"

"How can I pretend to say, without being told in what latitude even—as I think your expression is—this amiable desire lies?"

"As if you did not know, Delushy!"

"As if I did know, Captain Bluett! And another thing—I am not to be called 'Delushy,' much, in that way."

"Very well, then; much in another way. Delushy, Delushy, delicious Delushy, what makes you so unkind to me? To-morrow I go away, and perhaps we shall never meet again, Delushy: and then how you would reproach yourself. Don't you think you would now?"

"When never and then come together—yes. I suppose all sailors talk so."

"If I cannot even talk to please you, there is nothing more to say. I think that the bards have turned your head with their harpings, and their fiddle-strings, and ballads (in very bad Welsh, no doubt) about 'the charming maid of Sker;' and so on. When you are old enough to know better, and the young conceit wears out of you, you may be sorry, Miss Andalusia, for your wonderful cleverness."

He made her a bow with his handsome hat, and her warm young heart was chilled by it. Surely he ought to have shaken hands. She tried to keep her own meaning at home, and bid him farewell with a curtsy, while he tried not to look back again; but fortune or nature was too much for them, and their eyes met wistfully.

These things are out of my line so much, that I cannot pretend to say now for a moment what these very young people did; and everybody else having done the same, with more or less unwisdom, according to constitution, may admire the power of charity which restrains me from describing them. My favourite writer of Scripture is St Paul, who was afraid of nobody, and who spent his time in making sails when the thorn in the flesh permitted him. And this great writer describes the quick manners of maidens far better than I can. Wherefore I keep myself up aloft until they have had a good spell of it.

"I have no opinion, now. What can you expect of me? Rodney, I must stop and think for nearly a quarter of a century before I have an opinion."

"Then stay, just so; and let me admire you, till I have to swim with you."

"Rodney, you are reckless. Here comes the tide; and you know I have got my very best Candleston side-lace boots on!"

"Then come out of this rocky bower, which suits your fate so, darling; and let us talk most sensibly."

"By all means; if you think we can. There, you need not touch me, Rodney;—I can get out very well indeed. I know these rocks better than you do perhaps. Now sit on this rock where old David first hooked me, as I have heard that old chatterbox tell fifty times, as if he had done some great great thing."

"He did indeed a grand grand thing. No wonder that he is proud of it. And he has so much to be proud of that you may take it for your highest compliment. Perhaps there is no other man in the service—or I might say in all the civilised world——" But it hurts me to tell what this excellent officer said or even thought of me. He was such a first-rate judge by this time that I must leave his opinion blank.

Over the sea they began to look, in a discontented quietude; as the manner of young mortals is before they begin to know better, and with great ideas moving them. Bunny, with the very kindest discretion, had run away entirely, and might now be seen at the far end of the sands, and springing up the rocks, on her way to Newton. So those two sate side by side, with their hearts full of one another, and their minds made up to face the world together, whatever might come of it. For as yet they could see nothing clearly through the warm haze of loving, being wrapped up in an atmosphere which generally leads to a hurricane. But to them, for a few short minutes, earth and sea and sky were all one universal heaven.

"It will not do," cried the maid of Sker, suddenly awaking with a short deep sigh, and drawing back her delicate hand from the broad palm of young Rodney: "it will never, never do. We must both be mad to think of it."

"Who could fail to be mad," he answered, "if you set the example?"

"Now, don't be so dreadfully stupid, Rodney. What I say is most serious. Of course you know the world better than I do, as you told me yesterday, after sailing a dozen times round it. But I am thinking of other things. Not of what the world will say, but of what I myself must feel. And the first of these things is that I cannot be cruelly ungrateful. It would be the deepest ingratitude to the Colonel if I went on with it."

"Went on with it! What a way to speak! As if you could be off with it when you pleased! And my good uncle loves you like his own daughter; and so does my mother. Now what can you mean?"

"As if you did not know indeed! Now, Rodney, do talk sensibly. I ought to know, if any one does, what your uncle and your mother are. And I know that they would rather see your death in the Gazette than your marriage with an unknown, nameless nobody like me, sir."

"Well, off course, we must take the chance of that," said Captain Bluett, carelessly. "The Colonel is the best soul in the world, and my dear mother a most excellent creature, whenever she listens to reason. But as to my asking their permission—it is the last thing I should dream of. I am old enough to know my own mind, and to get my own living, I should hope, as well as that of my family. And if I am only in time with Nelson, of course we shall do wonders."

For a minute or two the poor young maid had not a word to say to him. She longed to throw her arms around him, when he spoke so proudly, and to indulge her own pride in him, as against all the world beside. But having been brought up in so much trouble, she had learned to check herself. So that she did nothing more than wait for him to go on again. And this he did with sparkling eyes and the confidence of a young British tar.

"There is another thing, my beauty, which they are bound to consider, as well as all the prize-money I shall earn. And that is, that they have nobody except themselves to thank for it. They must have known what was sure to happen, if they chose to have you there whenever I was home from sea. And my mother is so clever too—to my mind it is plain enough that they meant me to do what I have done."

"And pray what is that?"

"As if you did not know! Come now, you must pay the penalty of asking for a compliment. Talk about breeding and good birth, and that stuff! Why, look at your hands and then look at mine. Put your fingers between mine—both hands, both hands—that's the way. Now just feel my great clumsy things, and then see how lovely yours are—as clear as wax-tapers, and just touched with rose, and every nail with a fairy gift, and pointed like an almond. A 'nameless nobody' indeed! What nameless nobody ever had such nails? By way of contrast examine mine."

"Oh but you bite yours shockingly, Rodney. I am sure that you do, though I never saw you. You must be cured of that dreadful trick."

"That shall be your first job, Delushy, when you are Mrs Rodney. Now for another great sign of birth. Do you see any peak to my upper lip?"

"No, I can't say I do. But how foolish you are! I ought to be crying, and you make me laugh."

"Then just let me show you the peak to yours. Honour bright—and no mean advantages—that is to say if I can help it. Oh, here's that blessed Moxy coming! May the Frenchmen rob her henroost! Now just one promise, darling, darling; just one little promise. To-morrow I go to most desperate battles, and lucky to come home with one arm and one leg. Therefore, promise a solemn promise to have no one in the world but me."

"I think," said the maid, with her lips to his ear, in the true old coaxing fashion. "that I may very well promise that. But I will promise another thing too. And that is, not to have even you, until your dear mother and good uncle come to me and ask me. And that can never never be."

CHAPTER LX.

NELSON AND THE NILE.

The first day of August in the year of our Lord 1798 is a day to be long remembered by every Briton with a piece of constitution in him. For on that day our glorious navy, under the immortal Nelson, administered to the Frenchmen, under Admiral Brewer, as pure and perfect a lathering as is to be found in all history. This I never should venture to put upon my own authority (especially after the prominent part assigned therein by Providence to a humble individual who came from Newton-Nottage), for with history I have no patience at all, because it always contradicts the very things I have seen and known: but I am bound to believe a man of such high principles and deep reading as Master Roger Berkrolles. And he tells me that I have helped to produce the greatest of all great victories.

Be that one way or the other, I can tell you every word concerning how we managed it; and you need not for one moment think me capable of prejudice. Quite the contrary, I assure you. There could not have been in the British fleet any man more determined to do justice to all Crappos, than a thoroughly ancient navigator, now master of the Goliath.

We knew exactly what to do, every Captain, every Master, every quarter-master; even the powder-monkeys had their proper work laid out for them. The spirit of Nelson ran through us all; and our hearts caught fire from his heart. From the moment of our first glimpse at the Frenchmen spread out in that tempting manner, beautifully moored and riding in a long line head and stern, every old seaman among us began to count on his fingers prize-money. They thought that we would not fight that night, for the sun was low when we found them; and with their perpetual conceit, they were hard at work taking water in. I shall never forget how beautiful these ships looked, and how peaceful. A French ship always sits the water with an elegant quickness, like a Frenchwoman at the looking-glass. And though we brought the evening breeze in very briskly with us, there was hardly swell enough in the bay to make them play their hawsers. Many fine things have I seen, and therefore know pretty well how to look at them, which a man never can do upon the first or even the second occasion. But it was worth any man's while to live to the age of threescore years and eight, with a sound mind in a sound body, and eyes almost as good as ever, if there were nothing for it more than to see what I saw at this moment. Six-and-twenty ships of the line, thirteen bearing the tricolor, and riding cleared for action, the other thirteen with the red cross flying, the cross of St George on the ground of white, and tossing the blue water from their stems under pressure of canvass. Onward rushed our British ships, as if every one of them was alive, and driven out of all patience by the wicked escapes of the enemy. Twelve hundred leagues of chase had they cost us, ingratitude towards God every night, and love of the devil at morning, with dread of our country for ever prevailing, and mistrust of our own good selves. And now at last we had got them tight; and mean we did to keep them. Captain Foley came up to me as I stood on the ratlines to hear the report of the men in the starboard fore-chains; and his fine open face was clouded. "Master," he said, "how much more of this? Damn your soundings. Can't you see that the Zealous is drawing ahead of us? Hood has nobody in the chains. If you can't take the ship into action, I will. Stand by there to set top-gallant-sails."

These had been taken in, scarce five minutes agone, as prudence demanded, for none of us had any chart of the bay; and even I knew little about it, except that there was a great shoal of rock betwixt Aboukir island and the van ship of the enemy. And but for my warning, we might have followed the two French brigs appointed to decoy us in that direction. Now, having filled top-gallant-sails, we rapidly headed our rival the Zealous, in spite of all that she could do; and we had the honour of receiving the first shot of the enemy. For now we were rushing in, stem on, having formed line of battle, towards the van of the anchored Frenchmen.

Now as to what followed, and the brilliant idea which occurred to somebody to turn the enemy's line and take them on the larboard or inner side (on which they were quite unprepared for attack), no two authorities are quite agreed, simply because they all are wrong. Some attribute this grand manœuvre to our great Admiral Nelson, others to Captain Hood of the Zealous, and others to our Captain Foley. This latter is nearest the mark; but from whom did Captain Foley obtain the hint? Modesty forbids me to say what Welshman it was who devised this noble and most decisive stratagem, while patriotic duty compels me to say that it was a Welshman, and more than that a Glamorganshire man, born in a favoured part of the quiet village of N— N—. Enough, unless I add that internal evidence will convince any unprejudiced person that none but an ancient fisherman, and thorough-going longshore-man, could by any possibility have smelled out his way so cleverly.

Our great Admiral saw, with his usual insight into Frenchmen, that if they remained at anchor we were sure to man their capstans. For Crappos fight well enough with a rush, but unsteadily when at a standstill, and worst of all when taken by surprise and outmanœuvred. And the manner in which the British fleet advanced was enough to strike them cold by its majesty and its awfulness. For in perfect silence we were gliding over the dark-blue sea, with the stately height of the white sails shining, and the sky behind us full of solemn yellow sunset. Even we, so sure of conquest, and so nerved with stern delight, could not gaze on the things around us, and the work before us, without for a moment wondering whether the Lord in heaven looked down at us.

At any rate we obeyed to the letter the orders both of our Admiral and of a man scarcely less remarkable. "Let not the sun go down on your wrath," are the very words of St Paul, I believe; and we never fired a shot until there was no sun left to look at it. I stood by the men at the wheel myself, and laid my own hand to it: for it was a matter of very fine steerage, to run in ahead of the French line, ware soundings, and then bear up on their larboard bow, to deliver a thorough good raking broadside. I remember looking over my left shoulder after we bore up our helm a-weather, while crossing the bows of the Carrier (as the foremost enemy's ship was called), and there was the last limb of the sun like the hoof of a horse disappearing. And my own head nearly went with it, as the wind of a round-shot knocked me over. "Bear up, bear up, lads," cried Captain Foley, "our time has come at last, my boys! Well done Llewellyn! A finer sample of conning and steerage was never seen. Let go the best bower. Pass the word. Ready at quarters all of you. Now she bears clear fore and aft. Damn their eyes, let them have it."

Out rang the whole of our larboard battery, almost like a single gun; a finer thing was never seen; and before the ring passed into a roar, the yell of Frenchmen came through the smoke. Masts and spars flew right and left with the bones of men among them, and the sea began to hiss and heave, and the ships to reel and tremble, and the roar of a mad volcano rose, and nothing kept either shape or tenor, except the faces of brave men.

Every ship in our fleet was prepared to anchor by the stern, so as to spring our broadsides aright; but the anchor of the Goliath did not bite so soon as it should have done, so that we ran past the Carrier, and brought up on the larboard quarter of the second French 74, with a frigate and a brig of war to employ a few of our starboard guns. By this time the rapid darkness fell, and we fought by the light of our own guns. And now the skill of our Admiral and his great ideas were manifest, for every French ship had two English upon it, and some of them even three at a time. In a word, we began with the head of their line, and crushed it, and so on joint by joint, ere even the centre and much more the tail could fetch their way up to take part in it. Our antagonist was the first that struck, being the second of the Frenchman's line, and by name the Conquerant. But she found in Captain Foley and David Llewellyn an ant a little too clever to conquer. We were a good deal knocked about, with most of our main rigging shot away, and all our masts heavily wounded. Nevertheless we drew ahead, to double upon the third French ship, of the wonderful name of Sparticipate.

From this ship I received a shot, which, but for the mercy of the Lord, must have made a perfect end of me. That my end may be perfect has long been my wish, and the tenor of my life leads up to it. Nevertheless, who am I to deny that I was not ready for the final finish at that very moment? And now, at this time of writing, I find myself ready to wait a bit longer. What I mean was a chain-shot sailing along, rather slowly as they always do; and yet so fast that I could not either duck or jump at sight of it, although there was light enough now for anything, with the French Admiral on fire. Happening to be well satisfied with my state of mind at that moment (not from congratulation, so much as from my inside conscience), I now was beginning to fill a pipe, and to dwell upon further manoeuvres. For one of the foremost points of all, after thoroughly drubbing the enemy, is to keep a fine self-control, and be ready to go on with it.

No sooner had I filled this pipe, and taken a piece of wadding to light it, which was burning handy (in spite of all my orders), than away went a piece of me; and down went I, as dead as a Dutch herring. At least so everybody thought, who had time to think about it; and "the Master's dead" ran along the deck, so far as time was to tell of it. I must have lain numb for an hour, I doubt, with the roar of the guns, and the shaking of bulk-heads, like a shiver, jarring me, and a pool of blood curdling into me, and another poor fellow cast into the scuppers and clutching at me in his groaning, when the heavens took fire in one red blaze, and a thundering roar, that might rouse the dead, drowned all the rolling battle-din. I saw the white looks of our crew all aghast, and their bodies scared out of death's manufacture, by this triumph of mortality; and the elbows of big fellows holding the linstock fell quivering back to their shaken ribs. For the whole sky was blotched with the corpses of men, like the stones of a crater cast upwards; and the sheet of the fire behind them showed their knees and their bellies, and streaming hair. Then with a hiss, like electric hail, from a mile's height, all came down again, corpses first (being softer things), and timbers next, and then the great spars that had streaked the sky like rockets.

The violence of this matter so attracted my attention that I was enabled to rally my wits, and lean on one elbow and look at it. And I do assure you that anybody who happened to be out of sight of it, lost a finer chance than ever he can have another prospect of. For a hundred-and-twenty-gun ship had blown up, with an Admiral and Rear-Admiral, not to mention a Commodore, and at least 700 complement. And when the concussion was over, there fell the silence of death upon all men. Not a gun was fired, nor an order given, except to man the boats in hopes of saving some poor fellows.

CHAPTER LXI.

A SAVAGE DEED.

NEVERTHELESS our Britons were forced to renew the battle afterwards; because those Frenchmen had not the manners to surrender as they should have done. And they even compelled us to batter their ships so seriously and sadly, that when we took possession some were scarcely worth the trouble. To make us blow up their poor Admiral was a distressing thing to begin with; but when that was done, to go on with the battle was as bad as the dog in the manger. What good could it do them to rob a poor British sailor of half his prize-money? And such conduct becomes at least twice as ungenerous when they actually have wounded him!

My wound was sore, and so was I, on the following day, I can tell you; for not being now such a very young man, I found it a precious hard thing to renew the power of blood that was gone from me. And after the terrible scene that awoke me from the first trance of carnage, I was thrown by the mercy of Providence into pure insensibility. This I am bound to declare; because the public might otherwise think itself wronged, and perhaps even vote me down as of no value, for failing to give them the end of this battle so brilliantly as the beginning. I defy my old rival, the Newton tailor (although a much younger man perhaps than myself, and with my help a pretty good seaman), to take up the tucks of this battle as well as I have done,—though not well done. Even if a tailor can come up and fight (which he did, for the honour of Cambria), none of his customers can expect any more than French-chalk flourishes when a piece of description is down in his books. However, let him cut his cloth. He is still at sea, or else under it; and if he ever does come home, and sit down to his shop-board—as his wife says he is sure to do—his very first order shall be for a church-going coat, with a doubled-up sleeve to it.

For the Frenchmen took my left arm away in a thoroughly lubberly manner. If they had done it with a good cross-cut, like my old wound of forty years' standing, I would at once have set it down to the credit of their nation. But when I came to dwell over the subject (as for weeks my duty was), more and more clear to me it became, that instead of honour they had now incurred a lasting national disgrace. The fellows who charged that gun had been afraid of the recoil of it. Half a charge of powder makes the vilest fracture to deal with—however, there I was by the heels, and now for nobler people. Only while my wound is green you must not be too hard on me.

The Goliath was ordered to chase down the bay, on the morning after the battle, together with the Theseus and a frigate called the Leader. This frigate was commanded by the Honourable Rodney Bluett, now a post-captain, and who had done wonders in the height of last night's combat. He had brought up in the most brazen-faced manner, without any sense of his metal, close below the starboard bow of the great three-decker Orient and the quarter of the Franklin, and thence he fired away at both, while all their shot flew over him. And this was afterwards said to have been the cleverest thing done by all of us, except the fine helm and calm handling of H.M. ship Goliath.

The two ships, in chase of which we were despatched, ran ashore and surrendered, as I was told afterwards (for of course I was down in my berth at the time, with the surgeon looking after me); and thus out of thirteen French sail of the line, we took or destroyed eleven. And as we bore up after taking possession, the Leader ran under our counter and hailed us, "Have you a Justice of the Peace on board?" Our Captain replied that he was himself a member of the quorum, but could not attend to such business now as making of wills and so on. Hereupon Captain Bluett came forward, and with a polite wave of his hat called out that Captain Foley would lay him under a special obligation, as well as clear the honour of a gallant naval officer, by coming on board of the Leader, to receive the deposition of a dying man. In ten minutes' time our good skipper stood in the cockpit of the Leader, while Captain Bluett wrote down the confession of a desperately-wounded seaman, who was clearing his conscience of perilous wrong before he should face his Creator. The poor fellow sate on a pallet propped up by the bulkhead and a pillow; that is to say, if a man can sit who has no legs left him. A round shot had caught him in the tuck of both thighs, and the surgeon could now do no more for him. Indeed he was only enabled to speak, or to gasp out his last syllables, by gulps of raw brandy which he was taking, with great draughts of water between them. On the other side of his dying bed stood Cannibals Dick and Joe, howling, and nodding their heads from time to time, whenever he lifted his glazing eyes to them for confirmation. For it was my honest and highly-respected friend, the poor Jack Wildman, who now lay in this sad condition, upon the very brink of another world. And I cannot do better than give his own words, as put into shape by two clear-witted men, Captains Foley and Rodney Bluett. Only for the reader's sake I omit a great deal of groaning.

"*This is the solemn and dying delivery* of me, known as 'Jack Wildman,' A.B. seaman of H.M. frigate Leader, now off the coast of Egypt, and dying through a hurt in battle with the Frenchmen. I cannot tell my name, or age, or where I was born, or anything about myself; and it does not matter, as I have nothing to leave behind me. Dick and Joe are to have my clothes, and my pay if there is any; and the woman that used to be my wife is to have my medals for good behaviour in the three battles I have partaken of. My money would be no good to her, because they never use it; but the women are fond of ornaments.

"I was one of a race of naked people, living in holes of the earth at a place we did not know the name of. I now know that it was Nympton in Devonshire, which is in England, they tell me. No one had any right to come near us, except the great man who had given us land, and defended us from all enemies.

"His name was Parson Chouane, I believe, but I do not know how to spell it. He never told us of a thing like God; but I heard of it every day in the navy whenever my betters were angry. Also I learned to read wonderful writings; but I can speak the truth all the same.

"Ever since I began to be put into clothes, and taught to kill other people, I have longed to tell of an evil thing which happened once among us. How long ago I cannot tell, for we never count time as you do, but it must have been many years back, for I had no hair on my body except my head. We had a man then who took lead among us, so far as there was any lead; and I think that he thought himself my father, because he gave me the most victuals. At any rate we had no other man to come near him in any cunningness. Our master Chouane came down sometimes, and took a pride in watching him, and liked him so much that he laughed at him, which he never did to the rest of us.

"This man, my father as I may call him, took me all over the great brown moors one night in some very hot weather. In the morning we came to a great heap of houses, and hid in a copse till the evening. At dusk we set out again, and came to a great and rich house by the side of a river. The lower portholes seemed full of lights, and on the flat place in front of them a band of music—such as now I love—was playing, and people were dancing. I had never heard such a thing before; and my father had all he could do to keep me in the black trees out of sight of them. And among the thick of the going about we saw our master Chouane in his hunting-dress.

"This must have been what great people call a 'masked ball,' I am sure of it; since I saw one, when, in the Bellona, there were many women somewhere. But at the end of the great light place, looking out over the water, there was a quiet shady place for tired people to rest a bit. When the whole of the music was crashing like a battle, and people going round like great flies in a web, my father led me down by the riverside, and sent me up some dark narrow steps, and pointed to two little babies. The whole of the business was all about these, and the festival was to make much of them. The nurse for a moment had set them upright, while she just spoke to a young sailor-man; and crawling, as all of us can, I brought down these two babies to my father; and one was heavy, and the other light.

"My father had scarcely got hold of them, and the nurse had not yet missed them, when on the dark shore by the riverside, perhaps five fathoms under the gaiety, Parson Chouane came up to my father, and whispered, and gave orders. I know not what they said, for I had no sense of tongues then, nor desired it; for we knew what we wanted by signs, and sounds, and saved a world of trouble so. Only I thought that our master was angry at having the girl-child brought away. He wanted only the boy perhaps, who was sleepy and knew nothing. But the girl-child shook her hand at him, and said, 'E bad man, Bardie knows 'a.'

"I—every one of us—was amazed—so very small—— Oh, sir, I can tell you no more, I think."

"Indeed then, but you must, my friend," cried Captain Foley, with spirit enough to set a dead man talking; "finish this story, you thief of the world, before you cheat the hangman. Two lovely childer stolen away from a first-rate family to give a ball of that kind — and devil a bit you repent of it!"

Poor dying Jack looked up at him, and then at the place where his legs should have been, and he seemed ashamed for the want of them. Then he played with the sheet for a twitch or two, as if proud of his arms still remaining; and checked back the agony tempting him now to bite it with his great white teeth.

"Ask the rest of us, Captain," he said; "Joe, you know it; Dick, you know it; now that I am telling you. The boy was brought up with us, and you call him Harry Savage. I knew the great house when I saw it again. And I longed to tell the good old man there; but for the sake of our people. Chouane would have destroyed them all. I was tempted after they pelted me so, and the old man was so good to me; but something always stopped me, and I wanted poor Harry to go to Heaven—— Oh, a little drink of water!"

Captain Foley was partly inclined to take a great deal of poor Jack's confession for no more than the raving of a light-headed man; but Rodney Bluett conjured him to take down every word of it. And when this young officer spoke of his former chief and well-known friend, now Commodore Sir Drake Bampfylde (being knighted for service in India), and how all his life he had lain under a cloud by reason of this very matter, not another word did our Captain need from him, but took up his pen again.

"I ought to have told," said the dying man slowly; "only I could not bring myself. But now you will know, you will all know now. My father is dead; but Dick and Joe can swear that the boy is the baby. He had beautiful clothes on, they shone in the boat; but the girl-child had on no more than a smock, that they might see her dancing. Our master did not stay with us a minute, but pushed us all into a boat on the tide, cut the rope, and was back with the dancers. My father had learned just enough of a boat to keep her straight in the tide-way, and I had to lie down over the babies, to keep their white clothes from notice. We went so fast that I was quite scared, having never been afloat before, so there must have been a strong ebb under us. And the boat, which was white, must have been a very light one, for she heeled with every motion. At last we came to a great broad water, which perhaps was the river's mouth, with the sea beyond it. My father got frightened perhaps; and I know that I had been frightened long ago. By a turn of the eddy, we scrambled ashore, and carried the boy-baby with us; but the boat broke away with a lurch as we jumped, for we had not the sense to bring out the rope. In half a minute she was off to sea, and the girl-baby lay fast asleep in her stern. And now after such a long voyage in the dark, we were scared so that we both ran for our lives, and were safe before daybreak at Nympton.

"My father before we got home stripped off the little boy's clothes, and buried them in a black moor-hole full of slime, with a great white stone in the midst of it. And the child himself was turned over naked to herd with the other children (for none of our women look after them), and nobody knew or cared to know who he was, or whence he came, except my poor father, and our master—and I myself, many years afterwards. But now I know well, and I cannot have quiet to die, without telling somebody. The boy-baby I was compelled to steal was Sir Philip Bampfylde's grandson, and the baby-girl his granddaughter. I never heard what became of her. She must have been drowned, or starved, most likely. But as for the boy, he kept up his life; and the man who took us most in hand, of the name of 'Father David,' gave the names to all of us, and the little one 'Harry Savage,' now serving on board of the Vanguard. I know nothing of the buried images found by Father David. My father had nothing to do with that. It may have been another of Chouane's plans. I know no more of anything. There, let me die; I have told all I know. I can write my nickname. I never had any other—*Jack Wildman.*"

At the end of this followed the proper things, and the forms the law is made of, with first of all the sign-manual of our noble Captain Foley, who must have been an Irishman, to lead us into the battle of the Nile, while in the commission of the Peace. And after him Captain Bluett signed, and two or three warrant-officers gifted with a writing elbow; and then a pair of bare-bone crosses, meaning Cannibals Dick and Joe, who could not speak, and much less write, in the depth of their emotions.

CHAPTER LXII.

A RASH YOUNG CAPTAIN.

Now if I had been sewn up well in a hammock, and cast overboard (as the surgeon advised), who, I should like to know, would have been left capable of going to the bottom of these strange proceedings? Hezekiah was alive, of course, and prepared to swear to anything, especially after a round-shot must have killed him, but for his greasiness. And clever enough no doubt he was, and suspicious, and busy-minded, and expecting to have all Wales under his thumb, because he was somewhere about on the skirts of the great battle I led them into. But granting him skill, and that narrow knowledge of the world which I call "cunning;" granting him also a restless desire to get to the bottom of everything, and a sniffing sense like a turnspit-dog's, of the shank-end bone he is roasting,—none the more for all that could we grant him the downright power, now loudly called for, to put two and two together.

Happily for all parties, poor Hezekiah was not required to make any further fool of himself. The stump of my arm was in a fine condition when ordered home with the prizes; and as soon as I felt the old Bay of Biscay, over I knocked the doctor. He fitted me with a hook after this, in consistence with an old fisherman; and now I have such a whole boxful of tools to screw on, that they beat any hand I ever had in the world—if my neighbours would only not borrow them.

Tush—I am railing at myself again! Always running down, and holding up myself to ridicule, out of pure contrariety, just because every one else overvalues me. There are better men in the world than myself; there are wiser; there are braver;—I will not be argued down about it—there are some (I am sure) as honest, in their way; and a few almost as truthful. However, I never yet did come across any other man half so modest. This I am forced to allude to now, in departure from my usual practice, because this quality and nothing else had prevented me from dwelling upon, and far more from following up, some shrewd thoughts which had occurred to me, loosely, I own, and in a random manner,—still they had occurred to me once or twice, and had been dismissed. Why so? Simply because I trusted other men's judgment, and public impression, instead of my own superior instinct, and knowledge of weather and tideways.

How bitterly it repented me now of this ill-founded diffidence, when, as we lay in the Chops of the Channel about the end of October, with a nasty head-wind baffling us, Captain Rodney Bluett came on board of us from the Leader! He asked if the doctor could report the Master as strong enough to support an interview; whereupon our worthy bone-joiner laughed, and showed him into me where I sate at the latter end of a fine aitch-bone of beef. And then Captain Rodney produced his papers, and told me the whole of his story. I was deeply moved by Jack Wildman's death, though edified much by the manner of it, and some of his last observations. For a naked heathen to turn so soon into a trousered Christian, and still more a good fore-top-man, was an evidence of unusual grace, even under such doctrine as mine was. Captain Bluett spoke much of this, although his religious convictions were not by any means so intense as mine, while my sinews were under treatment; but even with only one arm and a quarter I seemed to be better fitted to handle events than this young Captain was. His ability was of no common order, as he had proved by running his frigate under the very chains of the thundering big Frenchman, so that they could not be down on him. And yet he could not see half the bearings of Jack Wildman's evidence. We had a long talk, with some hot rum-and-water, for the evenings already were chilly; and my natural candour carried me almost into too much of it. And the Honourable Rodney gazed with a flush of colour at me, when I gave him my opinions like a raking broadside.

"You may be right," he said; "you were always so wonderful at a long shot, Llewellyn. But really it does seem impossible."

"Captain," I answered; "how many things seem so, yet come to pass continually!"

"I cannot gainsay you, Llewellyn, after all my experience of the world. I would give my life to find it true. But how are we to establish it?"

"Leave me alone for that, Captain Bluett; if it can be done it shall be done. The idea is entirely my own, remember. It had never occurred to you, had it?"

"Certainly not," he replied, with his usual downright honesty; "my reason for coming to you with that poor fellow's dying testimony was chiefly to cheer you up with the proofs of our old Captain's innocence, and to show you the turn of luck for young Harry, who has long been so shamefully treated. And now I have another thing to tell you about him; that is if you have not heard it."

"No, I have heard nothing at all. I did not even know what had become of him, until you read Jack's confession. With Nelson, on board the Vanguard!"

"That was my doing," said the Honourable Rodney. "I recommended him to volunteer, and he was accepted immediately, with the character I gave him. But it is his own doing, and proud I am of it, that he is now junior lieutenant of Admiral Lord Nelson's own ship the Vanguard. Just before Nelson received his wound, and while powder was being handed up, there came a shell hissing among them, and hung with a sputtering fuse in the coil of a cable, and the men fell down to escape it. But young Harry with wonderful quickness leaped (as he did, to save me in San Domingo), and sent the fuse over the side with a dash. Then Nelson came up, for the firing was hot, and of course he must be in the thick of it, and he saw in a moment what Harry had done, and he took down his name for promotion, being just what himself would have loved to do. It will have to be confirmed, of course; but of that there can be no question, after all that we have done; and when it turns out who he is."

"I am heartily glad of it, Captain," I cried; "the boy was worthy of any rank. Worth goes a little way; birth a long way. But all these things have to be lawfully proven."

"Oh, you old village-lawyer; as we used to call you, at Old Newton. And you deserved it, you rogue, you did. You may have lost your left hand; but your right has not lost its cunning." He spoke in the purest play and jest; and with mutual esteem we parted. Only I stipulated for a good talk with him about our measures, when I should have determined them; or at the latest on reaching port.

The boldest counsel is often the best, and naturally recommends itself to a man of warlike character. My first opinion, especially during the indignant period, was that nothing could be wiser, or more spirited, or more striking, than to march straight up to Parson Chowne and confront him with all this evidence, taken down by a magistrate, and dare him to deny it; and then hale him off to prison, and (if the law permitted) hang him. That this was too good for him, every one who has read my words must acknowledge; the best thing, moreover, that could befall him; for his body was good, though his soul was bad; and he might have some hopes to redeem the latter at the expense of the former. And if he had not, through life, looked forward to hanging as his latter end and salvation, it is quite impossible to account for the licence he allowed himself.

However, on second thoughts I perceived that the really weighty concern before us, and what we were bound to think first of, was to restore such a fine old family to its health and happiness. To reinstate, before he died, that noble and most kind-hearted man, full of religious feeling also, and of confidence that the Lord having made a good man would look after him—which is the very spirit of King David, when his self-respect returns—in a word, to replace in the world's esteem, and (what matters far more) in true family love, that fine and pure old gentleman, the much-troubled Sir Philip Bampfylde,—this, I say, was the very first duty of a fellow nursed by a general and a baronet through the small-pox; while it was also a feat well worthy of the master of a line-of-battle ship, which was not last in the battle of the Nile. And scarcely second even to this was the duty and joy of restoring to their proper rank in life two horribly injured and innocent creatures, one of whom was our own Bardie. Therefore, upon the whole, it seemed best to go to work very warily.

So it came to pass that I followed my usual practice of wholly forgetting myself; and receiving from the Honourable Rodney Bluett that most important document, I sewed it up in the watered silk-bag with my caul and other muniments, and set out for Narnton Court, where I found both Polly, and the cook, and the other comforts. But nothing would do for our Captain Rodney—all young men are so inconsiderate—except to be off at racing speed for Candleston Court, and his sweetheart Delushy, and the excellent Colonel's old port wine. And as he was so brisk, I will take him first, with your good leave, if ever words of mine can keep up with him. But of course you will understand that I tell what came to my knowledge afterwards.

With all the speed of men and horses, young Rodney Bluett made off for home, and when he got there his luck was such as to find Delushy in the house. It happened to be her visiting time, according to the old arrangement, and this crafty sailor found it out from the fine old woman at the lodge. So what did he do but discharge his carriage, and leave all his kit with her, and go on, with the spright foot of a mariner, to the ancient house which he knew so well. Then this tall and bold young Captain entered by the butler's door, the trick of which was well known to him, and in a room out of the lobby he stood, without his own mother knowing it. It was the fall of autumnal night, when everything is so rich and mellow, when the waning daylight ebbs, like a great spring-tide exhausted, into the quickening flow of star-light. And the plates were being cleared away after a snug dinner-party.

The good Colonel sat at the head of his table, after the ladies' withdrawal, with that modest and graceful kindliness, which is the sure mark of true blood. Around him were a few choice old friends, such as only good men have; friends, who would scout the evidence of their own eyes against him. According to our fine old fashion, these were drinking healths all round, not with undue love of rare port, so much as with truth and sincerity.

Rodney made a sign to Crumpy (who had been shaking him by both hands, until the tears prevented him), just to please to keep all quiet touching his arrival: and to let him have a slice or two of the haunch of venison put to grill, if there was any left of it, and give it him all on a plate : together with a twelve-pound loaf of farmhouse bread, such as is not to be had outside of Great Britain. This was done in about five minutes (for even Mrs Cook respected Crumpy); and being served up, with a quart of ale, in Crumpy's own head privacy, it had such a good effect that the Captain was ready to face anybody.

Old Crumpy was a most crafty old fellow—which was one reason why I liked him, as a contrast to my frankness—and he managed it all, and kept such a look-out, that no one suspected him of any more than an honoured old chum in his stronghold. Captain Bluett also knew exactly what his bearings were, and from a loftier point of view than would ever occur to Crumpy. A man who had carried a 50-gun ship right under the lower port-holes of a 120-gun enemy, and without any orders to that effect, and only from want of some easier business, he (I think) may be trusted to get on in almost anything.

This was the very thing—I do believe—occurring to the mind of somebody sitting, as nearly as might be now, upon a very beautiful sofa. The loveliest work that you can imagine lay between her fingers; and she was doing her very best to carry it on consistently. But on her lap lay a London paper, full of the highest authority; and there any young eyes might discover a regular pit-pat of tears.

"My dear, my dear," said Lady Bluett, being not so very much better herself, although improved by spectacles; "it is a dreadful, dreadful thing to think of those poor Frenchmen killed, so many at a time, and all in their sins. I do hope they had time to think, ever so little, of their latter end. It makes me feel quite ill to think of such a dreadful carnage, and to know that my own son was foremost in it. Do you think, my dear, that your delicate throat would be any worse in the morning, if you were to read it once more to me? The people in the papers are so clever; and there was something I did not quite catch about poor Rodney's recklessness. How like his dear father, to be sure! I see him in every word of it."

"Auntie, the first time I read it was best. The second and third time, I cried worse and worse; and the fourth time, you know what you said of me. And I know that I deserved it, Auntie, for having such foolish weak eyes like that. You know what I told you about Captain Rodney, and begged you to let me come here no more. And you know what you said—that it was a child's fancy; and if it were not, it should take its course. The Colonel was wiser. Oh, Auntie, Auntie! why don't you always harken him!"

"For a very good reason, my dear child—he always proves wrong in the end; and I don't. I have the very highest and purest respect for my dear brother's judgment. Every one knows what his mind is, and every one values his judgment. And no stranger, of course, can enter into him, his views, and his largeness, and intellect; as I do, when I agree with him. There, you have made me quite warm, my dear; I am so compelled to vindicate him."

"I am so sorry—I did not mean—you know what I am, Auntie."

"My dear, I know what you are, and therefore it is that I love you so. Now go and wash your pretty eyes, and read that again to me, and to the Colonel. Many mothers would be proud perhaps. I feel no pride whatever, because my son could not help doing it."

There was something else this excellent lady's son could not help doing. He caught the beautiful maid of Sker in her pure white dress in a nook of the passage, and with tears of pride for him rolling from her dark grey eyes, and he could not help —but all lovers, I trow, know how much to expect of him.

"Thank you, Rodney," Delushy cried; "to a certain extent, I am grateful. But, if you please, no more of it. And you need not suppose that I was crying about, about,—about anything."

"Of course not, you darling. How long have I lived, not to know that girls cry about nothing? nine times out of ten at least. Pearly tears, now prove your substance."

"Rodney, will you let me alone? I am not a French decker of 500 guns, for you to do just what you like with. And I don't believe any one knows you are here. Yes, yes, yes! Ever so many darlings, if you like—and 'with my whole heart I do love you,' as darling Moxy says. But one thing, this moment, I insist upon—no, not in your ear, nor yet through your hair, you conceited curly creature; but at the distance of a yard I pronounce that you shall come to your mother."

"Oh, what a shame!" And with that unfilial view of the subject, he rendered himself, after all those mortal perils, into the arms of his mother. With her usual quickness Delushy fled, but came back to the drawing-room very sedately, and with a rose-coloured change of dress, in about half an hour afterwards.

"How do you do, Captain Rodney Bluett?"

"Madam, I hope that I see you well."

Lady Bluett was amazed at the coolness of them, and in her heart disappointed; although she was trying to argue it down, and to say to herself, "How wise of them!" She knew how the Colonel loved this young maid, yet never could bear to think of his nephew taking to wife a mere waif of the sea. The lady had faith in herself that she might in the end overcome this prejudice. But of course if the young ones had ceased to care for it, she could only say that young people were not of the stuff that young people used to be.

While she revolved these things in her tender, warm, and motherly bosom, the gentlemen came from the dining-room, to pay their compliments to the ladies, and to have their tea and all that, according to the recent style of it. They bowed very decently, as they came in, not being topers by any means: and the lady of the house arose and curtsied to them most gracefully. Then Rodney, who had found occasion ere this to salute Colonel Lougher and his visitors, led forward the maid, and presented her to them, with a very excellent naval bow.

"My dear uncle, and friends of the family," he began, while she trembled a little, and looked at him with astonishment; "allow me the favour of presenting to you a lady who will do me the honour of becoming my wife, very shortly, I hope."

The Colonel drew back with a frown on his face. Lady Bluett on the other hand ran up.

"What is the meaning of this?" she cried. "And not a word of it to your own mother! Oh, Andalusia, how shocking of you!"

"I think, sir," said the Colonel, looking straight at the youth, "that you might have chosen a better moment to defy your uncle, than in the presence of his oldest friends. It is not like a gentleman, sir. It cuts me to the heart to say such a thing to the son of my own sister. But, sir, it is not like a gentleman."

The old friends nodded to one another, in approval of this sentiment; and turned to withdraw from a family scene.

"Wait, if you please," cried Rodney Bluett. "Colonel Lougher, I should deserve your reproach, if I had done anything of the kind. My intention is not to defy you, sir; but to please you and gratify you, my dear uncle, as your lifelong kindness to me and to this young lady deserves. And I have chosen to do it before old friends, that your pleasure may be increased by their congratulations. Instead of being ashamed, sir, of the origin of your future niece—or you my dear mother of your daughter, you may well be proud of it. She belongs to one of the oldest families in the West of England. She is the grandchild of Sir Philip Bampfylde of Narnton Court, near Barnstaple. And I think I have heard my mother speak of him as an old friend of my father."

"To be sure, to be sure!" exclaimed Lady Bluett, ere the Colonel could recover himself: "the Bluetts are an old west-country family; but the Bampfyldes even older. Come to me, my pretty darling. There, don't cry so; or if you must, come in here, and I will help you. Rodney, my dear, you have delighted us, and you have done it most cleverly. But excuse my saying that an officer in the army would have known a little better what ladies are, than to have thrown them into this excitement, even in the presence of valued friends. Come here, my precious. The gentlemen will excuse us for a little while."

"Let me kiss Colonel Lougher first," whispered Delushy; all frightened, crying, and quivering as she was, she could not forget her gratitude. So she bowed her white forehead, and drooped her dark lashes under the old man's benevolent gaze.

"Sit down, my dear friends," said Colonel Lougher, as soon as the ladies had left the room. "My good nephew's tactics have been rather blunt, and of the Aboukir order. However, he may be quite right if this matter requires at once to be spread abroad. At any rate, my dear boy, I owe you an apology. Rodney, I beg your pardon for the very harsh terms I used to you."

With these words he stood up, and bowed to his nephew; who did the same to him in silence, and then they shook hands warmly. After which the young Captain told his story, to which they all listened intently—five being justices of the shire, and one the lord-lieutenant—all accustomed to examine evidence.

"It seems very likely," said Colonel Lougher, as they waited for his opinion. "That David Llewellyn is a most shrewd fellow. But he ought to have said more about the boat. There is one thing, however, to be done at once—to collect confirmative evidence."

"There is another thing to be done at once," cried Rodney Bluett, warmly—"to pull Chowne's nose. And despite his cloth, I will do it roundly."

"My young friend," said the Lord-Lieutenant; "prove it first. And then, I think, there are some people who would pardon you."

CHAPTER LXIII.

POLLY AT HOME.

LEST any one should be surprised that Sir Philip Bampfylde could have paid two visits to this delightful neighbourhood, without calling on our leading gentleman, and his own fellow-officer, Colonel Lougher—in which case the questions concerning Delushy would have been sifted long ago—I had better say at once what it was that stopped him. When the General thought it just worth while, though his hopes were faint about it, to inquire into the twisted story of the wreck on our coast, as given by the celebrated Felix Farley; the first authority he applied to was Coroner Bowles, who had held the inquest. Coroner Bowles told him all he knew (half of which was wrong, of course, by means of Hezekiah) and gave him a letter to Anthony Stew, as the most active and penetrating magistrate of the neighbourhood. Nothing could have been more unlucky. Not only did Stew baffle my desire to be more candid than the day itself, by his official brow-beating, and the antipathy between us—not only did Stew, like an over-sharp fellow, trust one of the biggest rogues unhung—in his unregenerate dissenting days, and before we gave him six dozen, which certainly proved his salvation—(I am sorry to say such things of my present good neighbour, 'Kiah; but here he is now, and subscribes to it) Hezekiah Perkins, whose view of the shipwreck, and learned disquisition on sand, misled the poor Coroner and all of the Jury, except myself, so blindly, that we drowned the five young men, and smothered the baby —not only did Stew, I say, get thus far in bewilderment of the subject, but he utterly ruined all chance of clearing it, by keeping Sir Philip from Candleston Court!

If you ask me how, I can only say, in common fairness to

Anthony Stew (who is lately gone, poor fellow, to be cross-examined by somebody sharper even than himself—one to whom I would never afford material for unpleasant questions, by speaking amiss of a man in his power—especially when so needless), in a word, to treat Stew as I hope myself to be treated by survivors, I admit that he may not have wished to keep Sir Philip away from the Colonel. But the former having once accepted Stew's keen hospitality, and tried to eat fish (which I might have bettered, had I known of his being there), felt, with his usual delicacy, that he ought not to visit a man at feud with the host whose salt—and very little else—he was then enjoying. For Mrs Stew was more bitter of course than even her husband against Colonel Lougher, and roundly abused him the very first evening of Sir Philip's stay with them. So that the worthy General passed the gates of the excellent Colonel, half-a-dozen times perhaps, without once passing through them.

Enough about that; and I need only say, before returning to my own important and perhaps sagacious inquiries in Devonshire, that the news, so hastily blurted out by Captain Rodney Bluett, caused many glad hearts in our parish and neighbourhood; but nevertheless two sad ones. Of these one belonged to Roger Berkrolles, and the other to Moxy Thomas. The child had so won upon both these, not only by her misfortunes and the way in which she bore them, but by her loving disposition, bright manner, and docility, that it seemed very hard to lose her so, even though it were for her own good. Upon this latter point Master Berkrolles, when I came to see him, held an opinion, the folly of which surprised me, from a man of such reading and history. In real earnest he laid down that it might be a very bad thing for the maid, and make against her happiness, to come of a sudden into high position, importance, and even money. Such sentiments are to be found, I believe, in the weaker parts of the Bible, such as are called the New Testament, which nobody can compare to the works of my ancestor, King David; and which, if you put aside Saint Paul, and Saint Peter (who cut the man's ear off, and rejected quite rightly the table-cloth), exhibit to my mind nobody of a patriotic spirit.

As for Moxy, she would not have been a woman if she had doubted about the value of high position, coin of the realm, and rich raiment. Nevertheless she cried bitterly that this child, as good as her own to her, and given her to make up for them, and now so clever to see to things, and to light the fire, and show her the way Lady Bluett put her dress on, should be taken away in a heap as it were, just as if the great folk had minded her. She blamed our poor Bunny for stealing the heart of young Watkin, who might have had the maid (according to his mother's fancy) with money enough to restock the farm, now things had proved so handsome. As if everybody did not know that Bardie would never think twice of Watkin; while his mother, hearing of the ships I had taken (as all over the parish reported), had put poor Watkin on bread and water, until he fell in love with Bunny! However, now she cried very severely, and in a great measure she meant it.

Leaving all Newton, and Nottage, and Sker, and even Bridgend to consider these matters, with a pleasing divergence of facts and conclusions, I find it my duty, however repugnant, to speak once more of my humble self. In adversity, my native dignity and the true grandeur of Cambria have always united, against my own feelings, to make me almost self-confident, or at any rate able to maintain my position, and knock under to nobody. But in prosperity, all this drops; extreme affability, and my native longing to give pleasure, mark my deportment towards all the world; and I almost never commit an assault.

In this fine and desirable frame of mind I arrived at Narnton Court once more, sooner perhaps than Captain Bluett, having so much further to go, burst in on his friends at Candleston; although I have given his story precedence, not only on account of his higher rank, but because of the hurry he was in. On the other hand, my part seemed to be of a nice and delicate character—to find out all that I could without making any noise in the neighbourhood, to risk no chance, if it might be helped, of exciting Sir Philip Bampfylde, and, above all things, no possibility of arousing Chowne, till the proper time. For his craft was so great that he might destroy every link of evidence, if he once knew that we were in chase of him; even as he could out-fox a fox.

When things of importance take their hinge, a good deal, upon feminine evidence, the first thing a wise man always does is to seek female instinct, if he sees his way to guide it. And to have the helm of a woman, nothing is so certain as a sort of a promise of marriage. A man need not go too very far, and must be awake about pen and ink, and witnesses, and so on; but if he knows how to do it, and has lost an arm in battle, but preserved an unusually fine white beard, and has had another wife before, who was known to make too little of him, the fault is his own if he cannot manage half-a-dozen spinsters.

My reputation had outrun me—as it used to do, sometimes too often—for in the despatches my name came after scarcely more than fifty, though it should have been one of the foremost five; however, my wound was handsomely chronicled, and with a touch of my own description, such as is really heartfelt. Of course it was not quite cured yet, and I felt very shy about it; and the very last thing I desired was for the women to come bothering. Tush! I have no patience with them; they make such a fuss of a trifle.

But being bound upon such an errand, and anxious to conciliate them so far as self-respect allowed, and knowing that if I denied myself to them, the movement would be much greater, I let them have peeps, and perceive at the same time that I really did want a new set of shirts. Half-a-dozen of damsels began at once to take my measure: and the result will last my lifetime.

But, amid all this glorification, whenever I thought of settling, there was one pretty face that I longed to see, and to my mind it beat the whole of them. What was become of my pretty Polly, the lover of my truthful tales, and did she still remember a brave, though not young officer in the Navy, who had saved her from the jaws of death, by catching small-pox from her? These questions were answered just in time, and in the right manner also, by the appearance of Polly herself, outblushing the rose at sight of me, and without a spot on her face, except from the very smart veil she was wearing. For she was no longer a servant now, but free and independent, and therefore entitled to take the veil, and she showed her high spirit by doing this, to the deep indignation of all our maid-servants. And still more indignant were these young women, when Polly demeaned herself, as they declared, with a perfectly shameless and brazen-faced manner of carrying on towards the noble old tar. They did not allow for the poor thing's gratitude to the only one who came nigh her in her despairing hour and saved her life thereby, nor yet for her sorrow and tender feeling at the dire consequence to him; and it was not in their power, perhaps, to sympathise with the shock she felt at my maimed and war-beaten appearance. However, I carried the whole of it off in a bantering manner, as usual.

Still there was one resolution I came to, after long puzzling in what way to cope with the almost fatal difficulty of having to trust a woman. So I said to myself, that if this must be done, I might make it serve two purposes—first for discovery of what I sought, and then for a test of the value of a female, about whom I had serious feelings. These were in no way affected by some news I picked up from Nanette, or, as she now called herself, "The widow Heaviside." Not that my old friend had left this world, but that he gave a wide berth to the part containing his beloved partner. She, with a Frenchwoman's wit and sagacity, saw the advantage of remaining in the neighbourhood of her wrongs; and here with the pity now felt for her, and the help she received from Sir Philip himself, and her own skill in getting up women's fal lals, she maintained her seven children cleverly.

After shedding some natural tears for the admired but fugitive Heaviside, she came round, of course, to her neighbours' affairs; and though she had not been at Narnton Court at the time when the children were stolen, she helped me no little by telling me where to find one who knew all that was known of it. This was a farmer's wife now at Burrington (as I found out afterwards), a village some few leagues up the Tawe, and her name was Mrs Shapland.

"From her my friend the Captain shall decouver the everything of this horrible affair," said Nanette, who now spoke fine English. "She was the—what you call—the bonne, the guard of the leetle infants. I know not where she leeves, some barbarous name. I do forget—but she have one cousin, a jolly girl, of the leetle name—pray how can you make such thing of 'Mary?'"

"What! do you mean Polly?" I asked; "that is what we make of Mary. And what Polly is it then, Madame?"

"Yes, Paullee, the Paullee which have that horrible pest that makes holes in the faces. 'Verole' we call it. The Paullee that was in the great mansion, until she have the money left, the niece of the proud woman of manage. You shall with great facility find that Paullee." Of course I could, for she had told me where I might call upon her, which I did that very same afternoon.

And a pretty and very snug cottage it was, just a furlong, or so, above the fine old village of Braunton, with four or five beautiful meadows around it, and a bright pebbly brook at the turn of the lane. The cottage itself, even now in November, was hung all over with China roses, and honeysuckle in its second bloom, which it often shows in Devonshire. And up at the window, that shook off the thatch, and looked wide-awake as a dog's house, a face, more bright than the roses, came, and went away, and came again, to put a good face upon being caught.

Hereupon I dismissed the boys, who, with several rounds of cheers, had escorted me through Braunton; and with genuine thankfulness I gazed at the quiet and pleasing prospect. So charming now in the fall of the leaf, what would it be in the spring-time, with the meadows all breaking anew into green, and the trees all ready for their leaves again? Also these bright red Devonshire cows, all belonging to Polly, and even now streaming milkily—a firkin apiece was the least to expect of them, in the merry May month. A very deep feeling of real peace, and the pleasure of small things fell on me; for a man of so many years, and one arm, might almost plead to himself some right to shed his experience over the earth, when his blood had been curdling on so many seas.

The very same thought was in Polly's eyes when she ran down and opened the door for me. The whole of this property was her own; or would be, at least, when her old grandmother would allow herself to be buried. That old woman now was ninety-five, if the parsons had minded the register; and a woman more fully resolved to live on I never had the luck to meet with. And the worst of it was, that her consent to Polly's marriage was needful, under the ancient cow-keeper's will, with all of the meadows so described, that nobody could get out of them. Hereupon, somehow, I managed to see that a very bold stroke was needed. And I took it, and won the old lady over, by downright defiance. I told her that she was a great deal too young to have any right to an opinion; and when she should come to my time of life, she would find me ready to hearken her. She said that no doubt it was bred from the wars for sailors to talk so bravely; but that I ought to know better—with a fie, and a sigh, and a fie again. To none of this would I give ear, but began to rebuke all the young generations, holding to ridicule those very points upon which they especially plume themselves, until this most excellent woman began to count all her cows on her fingers.

"Her can't have them. No, her shan't have they," she cried, with a power which proved that she saw them dropping into my jaws almost; "her han't a got 'em yet; and why should her have 'em?"

Into this very fine feeling and sense of possession I entered so amiably, that amid much laughter and many blushes on the part of Polly (who pretended to treat the whole thing as a joke), the old lady put on her silver goggles, and set down her name to a memorandum, prepared on the spur of the moment by me. Whereupon I quite made my mind up to go bravely in for it, and recompense Polly for all her faith, and gratitude, and frugality, if she should prove herself capable of keeping counsel also.

To this intent I expressed myself as elegantly as could be, having led Polly out to the wooden bridge, that nobody else might hear me. For that fine old woman became so deaf, all of a sudden, that I had no faith in any more of her organs, and desired to be at safe distance from her, as well as to learn something more of the cows. Nor did I miss the chance; for all of them having been milked by Polly, came up to know what I had to say to her, and their smell was beautiful. So I gave them a bit of salt out of my pocket, such as I always carry when ashore, and offered them some tobacco; and they put out their broad yellow lips for the one, and snorted and sneezed at the other. When these valuable cows were gone to have a little more grazing, I just made Polly aware of the chance that appeared to be open before us. In short, I laid clearly before her the whole of my recent grand discovery, proving distinctly that with nothing more than a little proper management, I possessed therein at least an equivalent for her snug meadow homestead, and all the milch-cows, and the trout-stream. Only she must not forget one thing, namely, that the whole of this value would vanish, if a single word of this story were breathed any further off than our own two selves, until the time was ripe for it. Of course I had not been quite such a fool as to give Nanette the smallest inkling of any motive on my part beyond that pure curiosity, with which she could so well sympathise. Also it had been settled between Captain Bluett and myself, that a fortnight was to be allowed me for hunting up all the evidence, before he should cross the Channel; unless I took it on myself to fetch him.

Polly opened her blue eyes to such a size at all I told her, that I became quite uneasy lest she should open her mouth in proportion. For if my discovery once took wind before its entire completion, there would be at least fifty jealous fellows thrusting their oars into my own rowlocks, and robbing me of my own private enterprise. Also Miss Polly gave way to a feeling of anger and indignation, which certainly might be to some extent natural, but was, to say the least of it, in a far greater measure indiscreet, and even perilous.

"Oh the villain! oh the cruel villain!" she exclaimed, in a voice that quite alarmed me, considering how near the footpath was; "and a minister of the Gospel too! Oh the poor little babes, one adrift on the sea, and the other among them naked savages! What a mercy as they didn't eat him! And to blame the whole of it on a nice, harmless, kind-spoken, handsome gentleman, like our Captain! Oh, let me get hold of him!"

"That, my dear Polly, we never shall do, if you raise your voice in this way. Now come away from these trees with the ivy, and let us speak very quietly."

This dear creature did (as nearly as could be expected) what I told her; so that I really need not repent of my noble faith in the female race. This encouraged me; from its tendency to abolish prejudice, and to let the weaker vessels show that there is such a thing as a cork to them. Men are apt to judge too much by experience on this subject; when they ought to know that experience never does apply to women, any more than reason does.

Nevertheless my Polly saw the way in and out of a lot of things, which to me were difficult. Especially as to the manner of handling her cousin, Mrs Shapland, a very good woman in her way, but a ticklish one to deal with. And all the credit for all the truth we get out of Mrs Shapland belongs not to me (any more than herself), but goes down in a lump to poor Polly.

To pass this lightly—as now behoves me—just let me tell what Susan Shapland said, when I worked it out of her. Any man can get the truth out of a woman, if he knows the way; I mean, of course, so far as she has been able to receive it. To expect more than this is unreasonable; and to get that much is wonderful. However, Polly and I, between us, did get a good deal of it.

Of course, we did not let this good woman even guess what we wanted with her; only we borrowed a farmer's cart from Bang, my old boy, who was now set up in a farm on his grandmother's ashes; and his horse was not to be found fault with, if a man did his duty in lashing him. This I was ready to understand, when pointed out by Polly; and he never hoisted his tail but what I raked him under his counter.

So after a long hill, commanding miles and miles of the

course of the river, we fetched up in the court-yard of Farmer Shapland, and found his wife a brisk sharp woman, quite ready to tell her story. But what she did first, and for us, at this moment, was to rouse up the fire with a great dry fagot, crackling and sparkling merrily. For the mist of November was now beginning to crawl up the wavering valley, and the fading light from the west struck coldly on the winding river.

In such a case, and after a drive of many miles and much scenery, any man loves to see pots and pans goaded briskly to bubbling and sputtering, or even to help in the business himself, so far as the cook will put up with it. And then if a foolish good woman allows him (as pride sometimes induces her) to lift up a pot-lid when trembling with flavour, or give a shake to the frying-pan in the ecstasy of crackling, or even to blow on the iron spoon, and then draw in his breath with a drop of it—what can he want with any scenery out of the window, or outside his waistcoat?

Such was my case, I declare to you, in that hospitable house with these good people of Burrington; nor could we fall to any other business, until this was done with; then after dark we drew round the fire, with a black-jack of grand old ale, and our pipes, to hear Mrs Shapland's story.

CHAPTER LXIV.

SUSAN QUITE ACQUITS HERSELF.

It really does seem as wise a plan as any I am acquainted with, to let this good woman act according to the constitution of her sex,—that is to say, to say her say, and never be contradicted. We contradicted her once or twice to reconcile her to herself; but all that came of it was to make her contradict perhaps herself, but certainly us, ten times as much. She did her best to explain her meaning; and we really ought to enter more into their disabilities. Therefore let her tell her story, as nearly in her own words, poor thing, as my sense of the English language can in any style agree with.

"I was nurse at Narnton Court, ever so many years ago—when my name was Susan Moggeridge,—Charley, you cannot deny it, you know; and all of us must be content to grow old, it is foolish to look at things otherwise. Twelve and six, that makes eighteen; now, Captain Wells, you know it do; and, Charley, can you say otherwise? Then it must have been eighteen years agone, when I was took on for under-nurse, because the Princess was expecting, the same as the butler told me. And it came to pass on a Sunday night, with two miles away from the doctor. Orders had been given; but they foreigners always do belie them. Too soon always, or too late; and these two little dears was too soon, by reason of the wonderful child the eldest one was prepared for. A maid she was, and the other a boy; two real beauties both of them; as fair as could be, with little clear dots under their skin, in corner places, because of their mother the Princess. But nothing as any one would observe, except for a beauty to both of them. The boy was the biggest, though the girl came first; and first was her nature in everything, except, of course, in fatness, and by reason of always dancing. Not six months old was that child before she could dance on the kitchen table with only one hand to hold her up, and a pleasure it was to look at her. And laugh with her little funny face, and nod her head, she would, as if she saw to the bottom of everything. And when she were scarce turned the twelvemonth, she could run, like— oh, just like anything, and roll over and over on the grass with her 'Pomyolianian dog,' as she called him, and there wasn't a word in the language as ever come amiss to her, but for the r's or the y's in it. Words such as I could lay no tongue to, she would take and pronounce right off, and then laugh at herself and everybody. And the way she used to put her hands out, laying down the law to all of us—we didn't want a showman in the house so long as we had Miss Bertha, or 'Bardie,' as she called herself, though christened after her mother. Everybody, the poor little mite, she expected everybody to know her name and all about her; and nothing put her in such a passion as to pretend not to know who she was. 'I'se Bardie,' she used to cry out, with her little hands spread, and her bright eyes flashing; 'I'se Bardie, I tell 'a; and evelybody knows it.' Oh yes, and she never could say 'th'—but 'niss' and 'nat,' for this and that. And how angry she used to be, to be sure, if anybody mocked her, as we used to do for the fun of it. But even there, she was up to us, for she began to talk French, for revenge upon us, having taken the trick from her mother.

"Likewise the boy was a different child altogether in many

ways. He scarcely could learn to speak at all, because he was a very fine child indeed, and quiet, and fat, and easy. He would lie by for hours on a velvet cushion, and watch his little sister having her perpetual round of play. Dolls, and horses, and Noah's arks, and all the things that were alive to her, and she talking to them whiles the hour,—he took no more notice than just to stroke them, and say, 'Boo, boo!' or 'Poor, poor!' which was nearly all that he could say. Not that he was to blame, of course, nor would any one having sense think of it, especially after he took the pink fever, and it struck to his head, and they cut his hair off. Beautiful curls as was ever seen, and some of them in my drawer up-stairs now, with the colour of gold streaking over them. Philip his name was, of course, from Sir Philip, and being the heir to the title; but his clever sister she always called him 'little brother,' as if he was just born almost, when he weighed pretty nearly two of her.

"Sir Philip, the good old gentleman, was away in foreign parts, they said, or commanding some of the colonies, up to the time when these two twins were close upon two years old, or so. I remember quite well when he came home with his luggage marked 'General Bampfylde;' and we said it was disrespectful of the Government to call him so, when his true name was 'Sir Philip.' He had never seen his grandchildren till now, and what a fuss he made with them! But they had scarcely time to know him before they were sadly murdered; or worse, perhaps, for all that any one knows to the contrary. Because Sir Philip's younger son, Captain Drake Bampfylde, came from the seas and America, just at this time. No one expected him, of course, from among such distant places; and he had not been home for three years at least, and how noble he did look, until we saw how his shirts were cobbled! And every one all about the place said that his little finger was worth the whole of the Squire's body. Because the Squire, his elder brother, and the heir of Sir Philip, was of a nature, not to say —but I cannot make it clear to you. No one could say a word against him; only he were not, what you may call it,—not as we Devonshire people are,—not with a smile and kind look of the eye, the same as Captain Drake was.

"This poor Captain Drake—poor or bad, I scarce know which to put it, after all I have heard of him—anyhow his mind was set upon a little chit of a thing, not more than fifteen at this time. Her name was Isabel Carey, and her father had been a nobleman, and when he departed this life he ordered her off to Narnton Court. So she did at an early age; and being so beautiful as some thought, she was desperate with the Captain. They used to go walking all up in the woods, or down on the river in a boat, until it was too bad of them. The Captain, I daresay, meant no harm, and perhaps he did none; but still there are sure to be talkative people who want to give their opinions. If Charley had carried on so with me, whatever should I have thought of myself?

"Well, there was everybody saying very fine things to everybody, gay doings likewise, and great feasts, and singing, and dancing, and all the rest. And the Captain hired a pleasure-boat, by name the 'Wild Duck of Appledore;' and I never shall forget the day when he took a whole pack of us for a sail out over Barnstaple bar and back. I was forced to go, because he needs must take the children; and several even old people were sick, but no one a quarter so bad as me. And it came into my mind in that state, that he was longing, as well as welcome, to cast us all into the raging sea. However, the Lord preserved us. This little ship had one mast, as they call it, and he kept her generally in a little bend just above the salmon-weir, so as to see the men draw the pool, and himself to shoot the wild-fowl, from a covered place there is; and by reason of being so long at sea, he could not sleep comfortable at the Court, but must needs make his bed in this pleasuring-ship, and to it he used to go to and fro in a little white boat as belonged to it.

"All this time the weather was so hot we could scarcely bear our clothes on, and were ready to envy them scandalous savages belonging to the famous Parson Chowne, who went about with no clothes on. There was one of these known to be down on the burrows a-bathing of his wife and family, if a decent woman may name them so. Well, the whole of these gay goings on, to celebrate the return of Sir Philip, and of Captain Drake, and all that they owed to the Lord for His goodness, was to finish up with a great dinner to all the tenants on the property; and then on the children's birthday, a feasting of all the gentry around; and a dance with all sorts of outlandish dresses and masks on, in the evening. For the fashion of this was come down from London, and there had been a party of this sort over to Lord Bassett's; and the neighbourhood was wild with it. And after this everything was to be quiet, because my Lady the Princess Bertha was again beginning to expect almost.

"And now, Captain Wells, you would hardly believe what a blow there was sent, by the will of the Lord, upon all of this riot and revelry. There was many of us having pious disposals, as well as religious bringings-up, whose stomachs really was turned by the worldliness as was around us. Young ladies of the very best families, instead of turning their minds to the Lord, turning of themselves about, with young men laying hold of them, as if there was nothing more to be said than 'Kiss me quick!' and, 'I'll do it again!' But there was a judgment coming. They might lay the blame on me, if they like. There is folk as knows better.

"That very night it was so hot, with the sun coming up from the river, that even the great hall the dance was to be in, was only fit to lie down in. So that Captain Drake, in his man-of-war voice, shouted (and I think I can hear him now), 'Ladies and gentlemen, I propose that we have our dance out on the terrace.' This was the open made-up flat between the house and the river, and the Captain's offer was caught up at, directly the gentlefolk seen the moon.

"Here they were going on ever so long; and the more of twirling round they had, and of making heel and toe, and crossing arms and even frontesses, the more they seemed to like it; also the music up and down almost as bad as they was; so that what with the harlequin dresses, and masquerading, and mummeries, scarcely any one could have the head to be sure of any one else almost. I could not help looking at them, although my place was to heed the children only, and keep them out of mischief, and take them to bed at the proper time. But Captain Drake, who was here, there, and elsewhere, making himself agreeable, up he comes to me with a bottle, and he says, 'Mary, have some.' 'My name is not Mary, but Susan, sir, and much at your service,' I answered; so that he poured me a great glassful, and said that it was Sam—something. I was not so rude as to give him denial, but made him a curtsy, and drank it, for it was not so strong as my father's cider; no, nor so good to my liking. And for any to say that it got in my head, shows a very spiteful woman. The Captain went on to the other maids, as were looking on for the life of them, all being out-of-doors, you must mind, and longing to have their turn at it. But I held myself above them always, and went back to my children.

"These were in a little bower made up for the occasion, with boughs of trees, and twisted wood, and moss from the forest to lie upon. Master Philip was tired and heavy, and working his eyes with the backs of his hands, and yawning, and falling away almost. But that little Bertha was as wide-awake as a lark on her nest in the morning. Everywhere she was looking about for somebody to encourage her to have 'more play,' as she always called for; and 'more play' continually. That child was so full of life, it was 'more play' all day long with her! And even now, in the fiery heat and thorough down thirst of the weather, nothing was further from her mind than to go to bed without a gambol for it. She had nothing on but her little shift, or under-frock I should call it, made by myself, when the hot weather came, from a new jemmyset of the Princess, and cut out by my lady to fit her for the sake of the coolness. Her grand white upper frock, trimmed with lace, had been taken off by her papa, I believe, when the visitors would have her dance on the table, and make speeches to them; the poor little soul was so quick and so hot.

"Well, I do declare to you, Captain Wells, and Charley, Polly likewise, which will believe me, though the men may not, it was not more than a minute or so much, perhaps I should say not half a minute, as I happened to turn round to pass a compliment with a young man as seemed struck with me the Sunday before in church-time; a sailor he were, and had come with the Captain, and was his mate of the pleasure-boat. A right down handsome young man he was—no call for you to be jealous, Charley. Beneath the salt waves he do lie. Well, I turned back my head in about five seconds, and both of the babes was gone out of my sight! At first I were not frightened much. I took it for one of Miss Bertha's tricks, to make off with her little brother. So strong she was on her legs, though light, that many a time she would lift him up by his middle and carry him half round the room, and then both of them break out laughing. 'I'll whip you, you see if I don't,' I cried, as I ran round the corner to seek for them; though whip them I never did, poor dears, any more than their own mother did. I ran all about, for five minutes at least, around and among the branches stuck in to make the bower, and every moment I made up my mind for Miss Bardie to pop out on me. But pop out she never did, nor will, until the day of judgment.

"When I began to see something more than an innocent baby trick in it, and to think (I daresay) of these two babies' value, with all the land they were born to, the first thing I did was to call out 'Jack!' such being all sailors' names, of course. But Jack was gone out of all hearing; and most folk said it was Jack that took them! To the contrary I could swear; but who would listen to me when the lie went out that I was quite tipsy?

"Of the rest I cannot speak clearly, because my heart flew right up into my brain, directly moment the people came round shouting at me for the children. And of these the very worst was Parson Chowne. If it had been his own only children—such as he says he is too good to have—he scarcely could have been more rampagious, not to use worse words of him. The first thing that every one ran to, of course, was the parapetch and the river, and a great cry was made for Captain Drake Bampfylde, from his knowledge of the waterways. But, though all the evening foremost in conducting everything, now there was no sign to be had of him, or of who had seen him last. And it must have been an hour ere ever he come, and then of course it was too late.

"I was so beside myself all that night that I cannot tell how the time went by. I remember looking over the parapetch at a place where the water is always deep, and seeing the fishermen from the salmon-weir dragging their nets for the poor mites of bodies. And my blood seemed to curdle inside me almost, every time they came out with a stone or a log. Nothing was found from that night to this day, and nothing will ever be found of it. I was discharged, and a great many others; not the first time in this world, I believe, when the bottom of the whole was witchcraft. Here, Charley, put something hot in my glass; the evenings are getting so dark; and I never can see the moon and the water, like that, and the trees, without remembering. Now ask me no more, if you please, good people."

When Mrs Shapland had finished this tale, and was taking some well-earned refreshment, Polly and I looked at one another, as much as to say, "That settles it." Nor did we press her with any more questions until her mind had recovered its tone by frying some slices of ham cut thin, and half-a-dozen new-laid eggs for us. Then, I approached her with no small praise, which she deserved, and appeared (so far as I could judge) to desire, perhaps; and with a little skill on my part, she was soon warmed up again, having tasted egg-flip, to be sure of it.

"Yes, Captain Wells, you can see through the whole of it. Sailors can understand a river, when nobody else knows anything. The Captain came forward as soon as he could, and he says, 'You fools, what are you about? An hour ago the tide was running five knots an hour where you be dragging! If the poor children fell over, they must be down river-bar by this time." And off he set out on a galloping horse, to scurry the sand-hills somehow. And scurry was now the whole of it. Sir Philip came forth, and that poor Squire Philip; and a thousand pounds was as freely talked of as if it was halfpence. And every one was to be put in prison; especially me, if you please, as blameless as the unborn babe was! And that very night the Princess were taken, and died the next day, upsetting everything, ever so much worse than ever. For poor Squire Philip fell into a trance, so to say, out of sheer vexation. He cried out that the hand of the Lord was upon him, and too heavy for him to bear — particular from his own brother. And after that not an inch would he budge to make inquiry or anything, but shut himself up in his dead wife's rooms, and there he have moped from that day to this, in a living grave, as you may call it."

In reply to my question what reasons the Squire, or any one else, might have for charging the Captain with so vile a deed, this excellent woman set them forth pretty much to the following purport. First, it was the Captain himself who proposed the dancing on the terrace. Second, it was his own man who drew her attention away from the children, after a goblet of wine had been administered by the master. Third, it was his own boat which was missing, and never heard of afterwards. Fourth, the Captain himself disappeared from the party at the very time that the children were stolen, and refused to say whither, or why, he was gone. That active and shrewd man Parson Chowne no sooner heard of the loss than he raised a cry for the Captain all over the terrace, to come and command the fishermen; and though as a friend of the family Chowne would never express an opinion, he could not undo that sad shake of the head which he gave when no Captain could be found. Fifth, a man with a Captain's hat was seen burying two small bodies that night, in the depth of Braunton Wilderness; though nothing was heard of it till the next week, through the savageness of the witness; and by that time the fierce storm on the Sunday had changed the whole face of the burrows, so that to find the spot was impossible. Sixth, it was now recalled to mind that Drake Bampfylde had killed a poor schoolfellow in his young days, for which the Lord had most righteously sent a shark in pursuit of him. It was likely enough that he would go on killing children upon occasion.

Seventh reason, and perhaps worth all the rest—only think what a motive he had for it. No one else could gain sixpence by it; Drake Bampfylde would gain everything — the succession to the title and estates, and the immediate right to aspire to the hand of the beautiful heiress, Miss Carey, who was known to favour him.

An elderly woman, who had been in the workhouse, and throve upon that experience, said that the Captain would never have done it; for he might have to do the like thing again, every time the poor Princess should happen to be confined almost. But who could listen to this poor creature, while the result lay there before them?

Thus the common people reasoned; but our Susan attached no weight to any except the last argument. As for one, she knew quite well that the young seaman sauntered there quite by chance, and quite by chance she spoke to him: and as for wine, she could take a quart of her father's cider, and feel it less than she could describe to any one; and as for a rummer of that stuff she had, it was quite below contempt to her. And concerning the Captain just being away, and declining to say where he was, like a gentleman; none but ignorant folk could pretend not to know what that meant. Of course he was gone, between the dances, for a little cool walk in the firwoods, together with his Isabel; and to expose her name to the public, with their nasty way of regarding things, was utterly out of the question to a real British officer! And to finish it, Mrs Shapland said that she was almost what you might call a young woman even now; at any rate with ten times the sense any of the young ones were up to. And ten years of her life she would give, if Charley would allow of her, to know what became of them two little dears, and to punish the villain that wronged them.

Hereupon my warmth of heart got the better of my prudence. My wise and pure intention was to get out of this good woman all I could; but impart to her nothing more than was needful, just to keep her talking. Experience shows us that this need be very little indeed, if anything, in a female dialogue. But now I was brought to such a pitch of tenderness by this time, with my heart in a rapid pulse of descriptions, and the egg-flip going round sturdily, also Polly looking at me in a most beseeching way, that I could not keep my own counsel even, but was compelled to increase their comfort by declaring every thing.

CHAPTER LXV.

SO DOES POOR OLD DAVY.

Hereupon, you may well suppose that the grass must no longer grow under my feet. With one man, and positively two women, in this very same county, having possession of my secret, how long could I hope to work this latter to any good purpose? Luckily Burrington lay at a very great distance from Nympton on the Moors, and with no road from one to the other; so that if Mr and Mrs Shapland should fail of keeping their promised tightness, at least two Barnstaple market-days must pass before Nympton heard anything. And but for this consideration, even their style of treatment would not have made me so confiding.

On the following morn, while looking forth at pigs, and calves, and cocks, and ducks, I perceived that the crash must come speedily, and resolved to be downright smart with it. So after making a brisk little breakfast, upon the two wings and two legs of a goose, grilled with a trifle of stuffing, there was but one question I asked before leaving many warm tears behind me.

"Good Mistress Shapland, would you know that jemmyset of the child, if you saw it?"

"Captain Wells, I am not quite a natural. My own stitching done with a club-head, all of it, and of a three-lined thread as my uncle's, and nobody else had, to Barnstaple. Likewise the mark of the Princess done, a mannygram, as they call it."

The weather was dull, and the time of year as stormy as any I know of: nevertheless it was quite fine now, and taking upon myself to risk five guineas out of my savings, Ilfracombe was the place I sought, and found it with some difficulty. Thus might Barnstaple bar be avoided, and all the tumbling of inshore waters; and thus with no more than a pilot-yawl did I cross that dangerous channel, at the most dangerous time of the year almost. Nothing less than my Royal clothes and manifest high rank in the Navy could have induced this fine old pilot to make sail for the opposite coast in the month of November, when violent gales are so common with us. But I showed him two alternatives, three golden guineas on the one hand, impressment on the other; for a press-gang was in the neighbourhood now, and I told him that I was its captain, and that we laughed at all certificates. And not being sure that this man and his son might not combine to throw me overboard, steal my money, and run back to port, I took care to let them perceive my entry of their names and my own as well in the register of the coast-guard. However they proved very honest fellows, and we anchored under Porthcawl point soon after dark that evening.

Having proved to the pilot that he was quite safe here, unless it should come on to blow from south-east, of which there was no symptom, and leaving him under the care of Sandy, who at my expense stood treat to him, I made off for Candleston, not even stopping for a chat with Roger Berkrolles. The Colonel, of course, as well as his sister Lady Bluett, and Rodney, were delighted with what I had to tell them, while the maid herself listened with her face concealed to the tale of her own misfortune. Once or twice she whispered to herself, "Oh my poor poor father!" and when I had ended she rose from the sofa where Lady Bluett's arm was around her, and went to the Colonel and said, "How soon will you take me to my father!"

"My darling Bertha," said the Colonel, embracing her, as if she had been his daughter, "we will start to-morrow, if Llewellyn thinks the weather quite settled, and the boat quite safe. He knows so much about boats, you see. It would take us a week to go round by land. But we won't start at all, if you cry, my dear!"

I did not altogether like the tone of the Colonel's allusion to me; still less was I pleased when he interrupted Lady Bluett's congratulations, thanks, and fervent praises of my skill, perseverance, and trustiness in discovering all this villany.

"Humph!" said the Colonel; "I am not quite sure that this villany would have succeeded so long, unless a certain small boat had proved so adapted for fishing purposes."

"Why, Henry!" cried his sister; "how very unlike you! What an unworthy insinuation! After all Mr Llewellyn has done; it is positively ungrateful. And he spoke of that boat in this very room, as I can perfectly well remember, not—oh not—I am sure any more than a very few years ago, my dear."

"Exactly," said the Colonel; "too few years ago. If he had spoken of that at the time, as distinctly as he did afterwards, when the heat of inquiry was over, and when Sir Philip himself had abandoned it, I do not see how all this confusion, between the loss of a foreign ship and the casting away of a British boat, could have arisen, or at any rate could have failed to be cleared away. Llewellyn, you know that I do not judge hastily. Sir, I condemn your conduct."

"Oh, Colonel, how dreadful of you! Mr Llewellyn, go and look at the weather, while I prove to the Colonel his great mistake. You did speak of the boat at the very inquest, in the most noble and positive manner; and nobody would believe you, as you your very self told me. What more could any man do? We are none of us safe, if we do our very best, and have it turned against us."

My conscience all this time was beating, so that I could hear it. This is a gift very good men have, and I have made a point of never failing to cultivate it. In this trying moment, with even a man so kind and blameless suddenly possessed, no doubt, by an evil spirit against me, stanch as rock my conscience stood, and to my support it rose, creditably for both of us.

"Colonel Lougher," my answer was, "you will regret this attack on the honour of a British officer. One, moreover, whose great-grandfather harped in your Honour's family. Captain Bluett understands the build of a boat as well as I do. He shall look at that boat to-morrow morning, and if he declares her to be English-built, you may set me down, with all my stripes and medals, for a rogue, sir. But if he confirms my surety of her being a foreigner, nothing but difference of rank will excuse you, Colonel Lougher, from being responsible to me."

My spirit was up, as you may see; and the honour of the British Navy forced me to speak strongly: although my affection for the man was such that sooner than offend him, I would have my other arm shot away.

"Llewellyn," said the Colonel, with his fine old smile spreading very pleasantly upon his noble countenance; "you are of the peppery order which your old Welsh blood produces. Think no more of my words for the present. And if my nephew agrees with you in pronouncing the boat a foreigner, I will give you full satisfaction by asking your pardon, Llewellyn. It was enough to mislead any man."

Not to dwell upon this mistake committed by so good a man, but which got abroad somehow—though my old friend Crumpy, I am sure, could never have been listening at the door—be it enough in this hurry to say, that on the next morning I was en-

2 F

abled to certify the weather. A smartish breeze from the north-north-west, with the sea rather dancing than running, took poor Bardie to her native coast, from which the hot tide had borne her. Before we set sail, I had been to Sker in Colonel Lougher's two-wheeled gig, and obtained from good Moxy the child's jemmyset from the old oak chest it was stored in.

And now I did a thing which must for ever acquit me of all blame so wrongfully cast upon me. That is to say, I fetched out the old boat, which Sandy Macraw had got covered up; and releasing him in the most generous manner from years and years of backrent, what did I do but hitch her on to the stern of the pilot-yawl, for to tow? Not only this, but I managed that Rodney should sail on board as he: skipper, and for his crew should have somebody who had crossed the channel before in that same poor and worthless boat, sixteen years agone, I do declare! And they did carry on a bit, now and then, when our sprit-sail hid them from our view. For the day was bright, and the sea was smooth.

The Colonel and I were on board of the yawl, enjoying perfect harmony. For Captain Rodney of course had confirmed my opinion as to the build of the boat, and his uncle desired to beg my pardon, which the largeness of my nature quite refused to hear of. If a man admits that he has wronged me, satisfied I am at once, and do not even point out always, that I never could have done the like to him.

Colonel Lougher had often been at sea, in the time of his active service, and he seemed to enjoy this trip across channel, and knew all the names of the sails and spars. But falling in as we did with no less than three or four small craft on our voyage, he asked me how Delushy's boat could possibly have been adrift for a whole night and day on the channel, without any ship even sighting her. I told him that this was as simple as could be, during that state of the weather. A burning haze, or steam from the land, lay all that time on the water; and the lower part thereof was white, while the upper spread was yellow. Also the sea itself was white from the long-continued calmness, so that a white boat scarcely would show at half a mile of distance. And even if it did, what sailors were likely to keep a smart look-out in such roasting weather? Men talk of the heat ashore sometimes; but I know that for downright smiting, blinding, and overwhelming sun-power, there is nothing ashore to compare with a ship.

Also I told the Colonel, now that his faith in me was re-established, gliding over the water thus, I was enabled to make plain to him things which if he had been ashore might have lain perhaps a little beyond his understanding. I showed him the set of the tides by tossing corks from his bottles overboard, and begging him to take a glass of my perspective to watch them. And he took such interest in this, and evinced so much sagacity, that in order to carry on my reasoning with any perspicacity, cork after cork I was forced to draw, to establish my veracity.

Because he would argue it out that a boat, unmanned and even unmasted, never could have crossed the channel as Bardie's boat must needs have done. I answered that I might have thought so also, and had done so for years and years, till there came the fact to the contrary; of which I was pretty well satisfied now; and when the boat was produced and sworn to, who would not be satisfied? Also I begged to remind him how strongly the tide ran in our channel, and that even in common weather the ebb of the spring out of Barnstaple river might safely be put at four knots an hour, till Hartland point was doubled. Here, about two in the morning, the flood would catch the little wanderer, and run her up channel some ten or twelve miles, with the night-wind on the starboard-beam driving her also northward. When this was exhausted, the ebb would take her into Swansea Bay almost, being so light a boat as she was, with a southern breeze prevailing. And then the next flood might well bring her to Sker,—exactly the thing that had come to pass. Moreover I thought, as I told the Colonel (although of course with diffidence), from long acquaintance with tropical waters and the power of the sun upon them, I thought it by no means unlikely that the intense heat of the weather, then for more than six weeks prevailing, might have had some strong effect on the set and the speed of the currents.

However, no more of arguments. What good can they do, when the thing is there, and no reasoning can alter it? Even Parson Chowne might argue, and no doubt would with himself (although too proud with other people), that all he did was right, and himself as good a man as need be.

We ran across channel in some six hours, having a nice breeze abaft the beam, and about the middle of the afternoon we landed at Ilfracombe cleverly. This is a little place lying in a hole, and with great rocks all around it, fair enough to look at, but more easy to fall down than to get up them. And even the Barnstaple road is so steep that the first hill takes nearly two hours of climbing. Therefore, in spite of all eager spirits, we found ourselves forced to stay there that night, for no one would horse us onwards, so late at this November season.

Perhaps, however, it was worth while to lose a few hours for the sake of seeing Delushy's joy in her native land. This, like a newly-opened spring, arose, and could not contain itself. As soon as her foot touched the shore, I began to look forward to a bout of it. For I understand young women now, very well, though the middle-aged are beyond me. These latter I hope to be up to, if ever I live to the age of fourscore years, as my constitution promises. And if the Lord should be pleased to promote me to the ripe and honest century (as was done to my great-grandfather), then I shall understand old women also, though perhaps without teeth to express it.

However this was a pretty thing, and it touched me very softly. None but those who have roamed as I have understand the heart-ache. For my native land I had it, ever and continually, and in the roar of battle I was borne up by discharging it. And so I could enter into our poor Bardie, going about with the tears in her eyes. For she would not allow me to rest at the inn, as I was fain to do in the society of some ancient fishermen, and to leave the gentlefolk to their own manner of getting through the evening.

"Come out," she cried, "old Davy; you are the only one that knows the way about this lovely place."

Of course I had no choice but to obey Sir Philip's own grand-daughter, although I could not help grumbling; and thus we began to explore a lane as crooked as a cork-screw, and with ferns like palm-trees feathering. In among them little trickling rills of water tinkled, or were hushed sometimes by moss, and it looked as if no frost could enter through the leafy screen above.

"What a country to be born in! What a country to belong to!" exclaimed the maid continually, sipping from each crystal runnel, and stroking the ferns with reverence. "Uncle Henry, don't you think now that it is enough to make one happy to belong to such a land?"

"Well, my dear," said her Uncle Henry, as she had been ordered to call the Colonel, "I think it would still more conduce to happiness for some of the land to belong to you. Ah, Llewellyn, I see, is of my opinion."

So I was, and still more so next day, when, having surmounted that terrible hill, we travelled down rich dairy valleys on our road to Barnstaple. Here we halted for refreshment, and to let Delushy rest and beautify herself, although we could see no need of that. And now she began to get so frightened that I was quite vexed with her: her first duty was to do me credit; and how could she manage it, if her eyes were red? The Colonel also began to provoke me, for when I wanted to give the maid a stiff glass of grog to steady her, he had no more sense than to countermand it, and order a glass of cold water!

As soon as we came to Narnton Court, we found a very smart coach in the yard, that quite put to shame our hired chaise, although the good Colonel had taken four horses, so as to land us in moderate style. Of course it was proper that I, who alone could claim Sir Philip's acquaintance, as well as the merit of the whole affair, should have the pleasure of introducing his new grandchild to him; so that I begged all the rest to withdraw, and the only names that we sent in, were Captain Llewellyn and "Miss Delushy." Therefore we were wrong, no doubt, in feeling first a little grievance, then a large-minded impatience, and finally a strong desire—ay, and not the desire alone—to swear, before we got out of it. I speak of myself and Captain Bluett, two good honest sailors, accustomed to declare their meaning since the war enabled them. But Colonel Lougher (who might be said, from his want of active service, to belong to a past generation), as well as Delushy, who was scarcely come into any generation yet,—these two really set an example, good, though hard, to follow.

CHAPTER LXVI.

THE MAID AT LAST IS "DENTIFIED."

However, as too often happens, we blamed a good man without cause. A good man rarely deserves much blame; whereas a bad man cannot have too much—whether he has earned it or otherwise—to restrain him from deserving more. The reason why Sir Philip Bampfylde kept us so long waiting, proved to be a sound and valid one; namely, that he was engaged in earnest and important converse with his daughter-in-law, Lady Bampfylde, now wife (if you will please to remember) to Commodore Sir Drake Bampfylde, although by birth entitled the

Honourable Isabel Carey, the one that had been so good to me when I was a ferryman; of superior order, certainly; but still, no more than a ferryman!

Since my rise in the world began, I have found out one satisfactory thing—that a man gets on by merit. How long did I despair of this, and smoke pipes, and think over it; seeing many of my friends advancing, by what I call roguery! And but for the war (which proves the hearts and reins of men, as my ancestor says), I might still have been high and dry, being too honest for the fish-trade. However, true merit will tell in the end, if a man contrives to live long enough.

So when the beautiful lady came out through the room where I sate waiting, as I touched my venerable forelock to her (as humbly as if for a sixpenny piece), a brave man's honest pride wrought weakness in my eyes, as I gazed at her. I loved her husband; and I loved her; and I thought of the bitter luck between them, which had kept them separate. Partly, of course, the glory of England, and duty of a proud man's birth; partly also bad luck of course, and a style of giving in to it; but ten times more than these, the tricks that lower our fellow-creatures.

This noble and stately lady did not at first sight recognise me; but when I had told her in very few words who I was, and what I had done, and how long I had sailed with her husband, and how highly he respected me, her eyes brightened into the old sweet smile, although they bore traces of weeping.

"My name is not 'Lady Carey,'" she said, for I was calling her thus on purpose, not knowing how she was taking wedlock, and being of opinion that an "honourable miss" ought always to be called a lady. "My name is 'Lady Bampfylde;' and I like it, if you please: although I remember, Mr Llewellyn, what your views are of matrimony. You used to declare them only too plainly, whenever we crossed your ferry, for the purpose, as I used to think, of driving poor Nanette to despair of you."

"And a lucky thing for me, your ladyship, to have acted so consistently. But his Honour the Commodore, of course, holds the opposite opinion."

"It is hard to guess the opinions of a commodore always on service. Sir Drake, as I daresay you have heard, can scarcely bear to come home now."

I saw that she was vexed by something, and also vexed with herself, perhaps, for having even hinted it. For she turned her beautiful face away, and without a word would have left me. But with my usual quickness of step, I ran into the lobby-place, and back in a moment with our Delushy, clinging like a woodbine to a post. At such moments, I never speak, until women begin with questions. It saves so much time to let them begin; because they are sure to insist on it. Meanwhile Delushy was making the prettiest curtsy that presence of mind permitted.

"You lovely dear, why, who are you?" cried Lady Bampfylde, with a start, that made me dread hysterics.

"I do not know, Madam," answered Delushy, with the whole of her mind so well in hand, by reason of years of suffering; "but many people believe me to be the Bertha Bampfylde that was lost, nearly twenty years agone."

"What! The baby! The baby—at least one of the babies —that my husband—David Llewellyn, this is very cruel of you."

And that was all the thanks I got! While, what could I have done otherwise? In five minutes more, she would have been off in her grand coach with six horses, after offending Sir Philip so much, that he could not have borne to look after her; although, of course, he was now coming out like a gentleman to a visitor. Seeing such a pay-night coming, and a large confusion, I begged Colonel Lougher and Captain Bluett to keep for a little while out of it. And nothing could more truly prove how thoroughly these were gentlemen, than that they withdrew to a niche of the under-butler's pantry, wherein they could hear no word of it.

It was now my place to stand forward bravely, and to put things clearly; without any further loss of reason, and even without considering how these delicate ladies might contrive to take my meaning nicely. To spare good ladies from any emotion, is one of the main things of my life; although they show such a want of gratitude, when I have done my utmost.

But as for frightening Sir Philip, of course, I had no scruple about that; because of his confidence in the Lord. Therefore, abandoning Lady Bampfylde to the care of her maid, who was running up from the servants' hall to look after her, I fixed my hook (screwed on for the purpose) firmly into Delushy's sleeve, that she might not faint, or run away, or do anything else unreasonable, and I led her up the long hall to meet Sir Philip, as he came down the steps at the upper end thereof.

The old General looked rather haggard and feeble, as if the power of his life were lowered by perpetual patience. But something had happened to vex him, no doubt, in his interview with Lady Bampfylde, so that he walked with more than his usual stateliness and dignity. He had never beheld me as a one-armed man, nor yet in my present uniform, for I took particular care to avoid him during the day or two spent at his house before I went to Burrington, so for a moment he did not know me, but gazed with surprise at the lovely figure which I was sustaining so clumsily.

"Sir Philip Bampfylde, allow me," I said, stretching forth my right hand to him, "to repay you for some of the countless benefits you have heaped upon me, by presenting you with your long-lost grand-daughter—and your grandson to come afterwards."

"It cannot be ; it cannot be," was all he could say, although for so many years he had shown his faith that it must be. His fine old countenance turned as white as the silver hair that crowned it, and then as red as it could have been in the hopeful blush of boyhood. And the pure and perfect delicacy of high birth quickened with sorrow prevented him from examining Delushy, as he longed to do.

"Speak up, child, speak up," said I, giving her a haul with my hook, as when first I landed her; "can't you tell your dear Grandfather how glad you are to see him?"

"That I will with all my heart," the maiden answered bashfully, yet lifting her eyes to the old man's face with pride as well as reverence; "as soon as I perceive that you, sir, wish to hear me say it."

"You will not think me rude—I am scarcely strong enough for this—it has come on me so suddenly. And it must be quite as bad for you. Lead the young lady to a chair, Llewellyn. Or, stay; I beg your pardon. It will perhaps be better to call our kind and worthy housekeeper."

Sir Philip perceived a thing which had escaped me, though brought to my notice beforehand by our good Colonel Lougher; that is to say, how hard it would be upon the feelings of this young girl, to have her "identity" (as Crowner Bowles entitled it) discussed in her own presence. Therefore she was led away by that regular busybody the housekeeper, Mrs Cockhanterbury; while I begged leave to introduce Colonel Lougher and Captain Bluett to Sir Philip Bampfylde. And then when all had made their bows and all due salutations, I was called upon to show my documents and explain the evidence so carefully gathered by me.

It is as much above my power, as beyond my purpose, to tell how that ancient and noble gentleman, after so much worry from the long neglect of Providence, took (as if he had never deserved it) this goodness of the Lord to him. Of course, in my class of life, we cannot be always dwelling on children; whose nature is provoking always, and in nothing more so than that they will come when not wanted; yet are not forthcoming with the folk who can afford them. Nevertheless, I think that if the Lord had allowed any thief of a fellow (much more one of His own ministers) to steal two grandchildren of mine, and make a savage of one baby, and of the other a castaway, the whole of my piety would have been very hard pushed to produce any gratitude. Sir Philip, however, did appear most truly desirous to thank God for this great mercy vouchsafed to him; even before he had thoroughly gone through the ins and outs of the evidence. For he begged us to excuse him, while he should go to see to our comfort; and two fine bottles of wine (white and red) appeared, and began to disappear, under my hatches mainly, before our noble host came back to set us a good example. And when he came he had quite forgotten to dust the knees of some fine kerseymere, and the shins of black silk stockings.

Deep sense of religion is quite in its place when a man has had one arm shot off, still more so if both arms are gone, and after a leg, indispensable. Nevertheless it must not be intruded upon any one; no, not even by the chaplain, till the doctor shakes his head. Knowing also that Colonel Lougher had a tendency towards it (enough to stop the decanters if he should get upon that subject with the arguments it sticks fast in), I was delighted to see Delushy slipping into the room as if she had known the place for a century. The General clearly had managed to visit her during the time of his absence from us; what passed between them matters not, except that he must have acknowledged her. For now she went up to him and kissed him; rather timidly, perhaps, but still she touched his forehead. Then he arose and stood very upright, as if he had never begun to stoop, and passing his arm round her delicate waist, both her hands he took in his. And as they faced us, we were struck with the likeness between blooming youth and worn but yet majestic age.

"Gentlemen," he said, "or rather I should call you kind good friends, you have brought me not only a grandchild, but the very one I would have chosen if the whole world gave me choice. By-and-by you shall see her stand by the picture of my dear and long-lamented wife. That, I think, will convince you that we want no further evidence. For me, these thumb-nails are enough. Bertha, show your thumb-nails."

She laughed her usual merry laugh (although she had been crying so) while she spread her dainty hands, exactly as she used to spread them, when she was only two years old, with me alone to look at her.

"Here it is, sir," cried the General, overlooking me, in the rush of his sentiments towards the Colonel: "here is the true Bampfylde mark. Even the Bassets have it not, nor the Traceys, nor the St Albyns. Will you oblige me by observing that these two thumb-nails have a most undoubted right and left to them? Bertha, do try to keep still for a moment."

"Well, I declare," said the Colonel, calmly taking out his eye-glass; "yes, I declare you are right, my good sir. Here is a most evident right and left—Andalusia, do stand still—not only in the half-moons at the base, but in the vein, and what I may call the radiants of the pinkness. I cannot express my meaning, but—my darling, come and kiss me."

This Delushy did at once, as for years she used to do; and not being certain even now whether she ought to forsake the Colonel for a General, though proved to be a very fine and newly-turned up Grandfather. None of us had thought of her, and the many shifts of female wind, coming to pass perhaps inside her little brain and heart so. Wherefore this poor David, who desires always to be the last, but by force of nature is compelled for ever to take the lead—I it was who got her off to bed, that we might talk of her.

CHAPTER LXVII.

DOG EATS DOG.

To a man, whose time of life begins to be a subject of some consideration to him, when the few years still in hope can be counted on a hand, and may not need a finger; and with the tide of this world ebbing to the inevitable sea—to him there is scarcely any sweet and gentle pastime more delightful than to sit on a bank of ancient moss, beside a tidal river, and watch the decreasing waters, and prove his own eternity by casting a pebble into them.

Hence it was that Sir Philip Bampfylde, on the very morning after I gave him back his grandchild, sate gazing into the ebb of the Tawe, some fifty yards below the spot, whence Jack Wildman's father carried off so wickedly that helpless pair of children. Here it was my privilege to come up to Sir Philip, and spread before him my humble reasons for having preferred the kitchen last night to the dining-room and the drawing-room. It was consistent with my nature; and he, though wishing otherwise, agreed not to be offended.

Then I asked him how the young lady (whose health every one of us had honoured, all over the kitchen-table) had contrived to pass the night, and whether she had seen her father yet. He said she had slept pretty well considering, but that as concerned her father, they had not thought it wise to let her see him, until the doctor came. There was no telling how it might act upon Squire Philip's constitution, after so many years of misery, cobwebs, and desolation. For Providence had not gifted him with a mind so strong as his father's was, and the sudden break in on the death of the mind has been known, in such a case, to lead to bodily decease. But few things vexed the General more than that wretched lie of Chowne's, and slander upon a loyal family while in service of the Crown. What Captain Drake had landed from the boat was not an arm-chest, but a chest of plate and linen, belonging to his brother, which he would no longer borrow, while the Squire so cruelly dealt with him.

Then I asked Sir Philip whether the ancient builder over at Appledore had been sent for to depose to the boat; for we had brought that little craft on the top of our coach from Ilfracombe. The General said that I might see him even now examining her, if I would only take the trouble to look round the corner; but he himself was so well convinced, without any further testimony, that he did not even care to hear what the old man had to say of it, any more than he cared for the jemmyset. This, however, is not my manner of regarding questions. Not from any private fountains of conviction, and so on, but out of the mouths of many witnesses shall a thing be established. Therefore I hastened round the corner, to sift this ancient boatwright.

As surly a fellow as ever lived, and from his repugnance to my uniform, one who had made more money, I doubt, by the smuggler's keg than the shipwright's adze. Entering into his nature at sight, I took the upper hand of him, as my rank insisted on.

"Hark ye now, master ship-carpenter, where was this little craft put together, according to your opinion?"

Either this fellow was deaf as a post, or else he meant to insult me, for he took no more notice of me than he did of the pigs that were snuffling at beech-nuts down by the side of the landing-place. I am not the right man to put up with insolence; therefore I screwed my hammer-head into the socket below my muscles, and therewith dealt him a tap on his hat, just to show what might come afterwards.

Receiving this administration, and seeing that more was very likely from the same source to be available, what did this rogue do but endeavour to show the best side of his manners. Wherefore, to let him have his say, here is his opinion.

"This here boat be the same as I built, year as my wife were took with quinzy, and were called home by the Lord. I built her for Wild-duck of Appledore, a little dandy-rigged craft as used to be hired by Cap'en Bampfylde. To this here boat I can swear, although some big rogue have been at work, painting her, as knew not how to paint; and a lubber, no doubt, every now and then patching her up, or repairing of her. The name in her stern have been painted up from 'Wild-duck, Appledore,' into 'Santa Lucia, Salvador;' three or four letters are my own, the rest are the work of some pirate. She be no more foreign-build than I be. But a sailor accustomed to foreign parts would be sure to reckon so, reason why I served my time with a builder over to Port-au-Prince. And I should like to see the man anywhere round these here parts, as can tuck in the bends as I does."

Leaving this conceited fellow to his narrow unpleasantness, I turned my head, and there beheld Captain Bluett harkening.

"Come," he cried out, in his hearty manner, "what a cook's boiling of fools we are! Here we are chewing a long-chewed quid, while the devil that brewed this gale of wind may fly far away, and grin at us. Llewellyn, do you mean to allow——"

"Hush," I said softly, for that low shipwright showed his eyes coming up under his cap. And I saw that he was that particular villain, after his scurrilous words about me, who would sell his soul to that wretch of a Chowne for half-a-crown a-week almost. Therefore I led our young Captain Bluett well away out of this fellow's hearing

"Davy," said he, "we all know your courage, your readiness, and your resources. Still you appear to be under a spell—and you know you are superstitious about this cunning and cowardly blackguard, who frightens the whole of this country, as he never could frighten Glamorganshire."

"I have no fear of him, sir," I said; "I will go with you to confront him."

"Why, your teeth are ready to chatter, Llewellyn; and your lips are blue! You who stood like a mile-stone, they tell me, at the helm of the Goliath, or like a clock going steadily tick, before we fired a shot, and with both shell and shot through your grey whiskers——"

"But, Captain, a minister of the Lord——"

"Master, a minister of the devil—once for all, to-day I go to horse-whip him, if he is young enough; or to pull his nose if he is old enough, and Old Harry be with him in choice of the two? Zounds, sir, is it a thing to laugh at?"

Rodney Bluett was well known to every one who served under him for the mildness of his language, and the want of oaths he had; and so, of course, for his self-control, and the power of his heart when it did break forth. Everybody loved him because he never cursed any one at a venture, and kept himself very close to facts, however hard driven by circumstances; so that I was now amazed to hear this young man spoil my pipe with violent emotions.

"Have you consulted Sir Philip?" I asked. "It is his place to take up the question."

"What question? There is no question. The thing is proved. My duty is plain. Sir Philip is too old to see to it. The Squire is a spooney. The Commodore is not here yet. I have spoken to his wife, who is a very sweet and wise lady; and she agrees with me that it will save the family a world of scandal; and perhaps failure of the law, for me to take the law into my own hands, and thrash this blackguard within an inch of his life."

"To be sure, and save her husband from the risk of tackling a desperate man. It is most wise on her part. But I beg you, my dear sir, for the sake of your dear uncle and your good mother, keep clear of this quarrel. You know not the man you have to deal with. Even if you can thrash him, which is no easy business, he will shoot you afterwards. He is the deadest shot in the county."

"Hurrah!" cried Rodney, tossing up his hat; "that entirely

settles it. Come along, old fellow, and show us the way: and not a word to any one."

Now this may seem a very mad resolve for a man of my sense to give into. But whether I turned myself this way or that, I could see no chance of bettering it. If I refused to go, young Rodney (as I could see by the set of his mouth) would go alone, and perhaps get killed, and then how could any of the family ever look at me again? On the other hand, if I should go to the Colonel, or to the General, for opinion, and to beg them to stop it, my interference—nine chances to one—would only end in giving offence among the superior orders. Add to this my real desire to square it out with Chowne himself, after all his persecution, and you may be able to forgive me for getting upon horseback, after many years of forbearance, and with my sugar-nippers screwed on, to lay hold by the forestay, if she should make bad weather. Also, I felt it my duty to take a double-barrelled pistol, heavily loaded and well primed.

Captain Rodney forged ahead so on a real hunting-craft, that my dappled grey, being warranted not to lurch me overboard, could not keep in line whatever sail I made upon her. My chief rule in life is not to hurry. What good ever comes of it? People only abuse you, and your breath is too short to answer them. Moreover, I felt an uneasy creaking in my bends from dousing forward, and then easing backward, as a man must do who knows how to ride. The Captain was wroth with me, out of all reason; but as he could not find the way to Nympton Moors without me, I was enabled to take my leisure, having the surety of overgetting him when the next cross-road came. Therefore it was late afternoon when we turned into the black fir-grove which led up to the house of Chowne, and Rodney Bluett clutched the big whip in his hand severely. For we had asked at the little inn of which I spoke a long time ago, whether the Parson was now at home.

"Ay, that 'un be," said the man with a grin, for we did not see the landlady; "but ye best way not to go nigh 'un."

Already I seemed not to feel as I hoped, in the earlier stage of the journey. My thoughts had been very upright for a while, and spirited, and delighted; but now I began to look at things from a different point of view almost. It is not man's business to worry his head about righting of wrongs in this world, unless they are done to himself; and if so, revenge is its name, and an ugly one. Long life leads one to forgive, when to carry it on would be troublesome.

Through the drip of dying leaves, the chill of dull November now began to darken over us as we turned the corner of Chowne's own road, and faced his lonely mansion. The house had a heavy and sullen look, according to my ideas, not receiving light and pleasure of the sun when possible. Heavy fir-trees overhung it, never parting with their weight; and the sunset (when there was any) could not pierce the holm-oaks.

"What a gloomy and devilish place!" cried Rodney Bluett, beginning to tremble from some unknown influence. "Upon my soul, if I lived here, I should be hatching plots myself. Or is it the nature of the man that has made the place so horrible?"

"Let us go back," said I; "come back, my good sir, I conjure you. Such a man should be left to God, to punish in His own good time."

"Hark!" cried Rodney, pulling up, and listening through the gloomy wood; "that was a woman's scream, I am sure. Is he murdering some more little ones?"

We listened, and heard a loud piercing shriek, that made our hair stand on end almost, so mad was it, and so unearthly; and then two more of yet wilder agony; and after that a long low wailing.

"On, on!" cried Rodney Bluett; "you know these paths, gallop on, Davy."

"You go first," I answered; "your horse is fresher; I am coming—to be sure I am—do you think I am frightened?"

"Well, I don't know," he replied; "but I am not ashamed to own that I am."

Clapping spurs to his horse, he dashed on; and thoroughly miserable as I felt, there was nothing for me but to follow him.

In the name of the Lord, what a sight we came on, where the drive sweeps round at the corner of the house! Under a dark tree of some sort, and on a garden bench, we discovered the figures of two women. Or rather, one sate on the bench; the other lay stretched on the ground, with her head cast recklessly back on the ledge, her hair spread in masses over it, and both hands pressed on her eyes and ears, to shut out sight and hearing. Her lips were open, and through her white teeth came wails of anguish, that would have been shrieks, if nature had not failed her.

But the elder woman sate upright, in scorn of all such weakness, with her gaunt figure drawn like a cable taut, no sign of a tear on her shrunken cheeks, and the whole of her face as numb and cold as an iced figurehead in the Arctic seas. Yet no one, with knowledge of the human race, could doubt which of these two suffered most.

We reined up our horses, and gazed in terror, for neither of them noticed us; and then we heard, from inside the house, sounds that made our flesh creep. Barking, howling, snapping of teeth, baying as of a human bloodhound, frothy splutterings of fury, and then smothered yelling.

"Her have a gat 'un now," cried a clown, running round the end of the house, as if he were enjoying it. "Reckon our passon wun't baite much moore, after Passon Jack be atop of 'un."

"Oh sir, oh sir, oh for God's sake, sir," cried the poor lady who had lain on the ground, rushing up to us, and kneeling, and trying to get hold of us; "you must have come to stop it, sir. Only one hour—allow him one hour, dear, dear sirs, for repentance. He has not been a good man, I know, but I am his own wife, good kind sirs—and if he could only have a little time, if it were only half an hour—he might, he might——"

Here a sound of throttling came through a broken window-pane, and down she fell insensible.

"What does it mean?" cried Rodney Bluett; "is it murder, madness, or suicide? Follow me, Davy. Here I go, anyhow, into the thick of it."

He dashed through the window; and I with more caution, cocking my pistol, followed him, while I heard the clown shouting after us—

"Danged vules both of 'e. Bide outside, bide outside, I tell 'e."

Oh that we had remained outside! I have been through a great deal of horrible sights, enough to harden any man, and cure him of womanly squeamishness. Yet never did I behold, or dream of, anything so awful as the scene that lay before me. People were longing to look at it now, but none (save ourselves) durst enter.

It was Chowne's own dining-room, all in the dark, except where a lamp had been brought in by a trembling footman, who ran away, knowing that he brought this light for his master to be strangled by. And in the corner now lay his master, smothered under a feather-bed; yet with his vicious head fetched out in the last rabid struggle to bite. There was the black hair, black face, and black tongue, shown by the frothy wainscot, or between it and the ticking. On the featherbed lay exhausted, and with his mighty frame convulsed, so that a child might master him, Parson Jack Rambone, the strongest man, whose strength (like all other powers) had laid a horrible duty upon him. Sobbing with all his great heart he lay, yet afraid to take his weight off, and sweating at every pore with labour, peril of his life, and agony.

"Oh Dick, Dick," he said, quite softly, and between his pantings; "how many larks have we had together, and for me to have to do this to you! I am sure you knew me, before you died. I think you know me now, Dick. Oh, for God's sake, shut your eyes! Darling Dick, are you dead, are you dead? You are the very cleverest fellow ever I came across of. You can do it, if you like. Oh, dear Dick, Dick, my boy, do shut your eyes!"

We stood looking at them, with no power to go up to them; all experience failed us as to what was the proper thing to do, till I saw that Chowne's face ought to have a napkin over it. None had been laid for dinner; but I knew where butlers keep them.

When I had done this, Parson Jack (who could not escape from the great black eyes) arose, and said, "I thank you, sir." He staggered so that we had to support him; but not a word could we say to him. "I am bitten in two places, if not more," he rather gasped than said to us, as he laid bare his enormous arms. "I care not much. I will follow my friend. Or if the Lord should please to spare me, henceforth I am an altered man. And yet, for the sake of my family, will you heat the kitchen poker?"

CHAPTER LXVIII.

THE OLD PITCHER AT THE WELL AGAIN.

It helps a thoughtless man on his road towards a better kingdom, to get a glimpse, every now and then, of such visitations of the Lord. When I was a little boy, nothing did me so much good in almost all the Bible, as to hear my father read the way in which Herod was eaten of worms. And now in mature years, I received quite a serious turn by the death of this Parson Chowne of ignominious canine madness. And still more, when I came to know by what condign parental justice this visitation smote him.

For while the women were busy up-stairs by candle-light, and with some weeping, it fell to Parson Rambone's lot to lay the truth before us. This great man took at once to Captain Rodney Bluett, as if he had known him for years; nor did he fail to remember me, and in his distress to seek some comfort from my simple wisdom. So having packed all the country boobies, constables, doctors, and so on, out of the house, we barred the door, made a bright fire in the kitchen, and sat down in front of it, while a nice cook began to toss up some sweetbreads, and eggs and ham-collops, and so on, for our really now highly necessary sustenance.

You may remember the time I met with a very nice fellow (then Chowne's head-groom), who gave me a capital supper of tripe elegantly stewed by a young cook-maid, himself lamenting the stress (laid upon him by circumstances) not to make his wife of her. He told me then with a sigh of affection between his knife and fork, that social duties compelled him instead to marry a publican's daughter, with fifty pounds down on the nail, he believed, if it was a penny. Nevertheless he felt confident that all would be ordered aright in the end. Now Providence had not allowed such a case of faith to pass unrewarded. He married the publican's daughter, got her money, and paid the last sad duties to her, out of the pocket of his father-in-law, in a Christian-minded manner. And then back he came to Nympton Rectory, and wedded that same cook-maid, who now was turning our ham so cleverly with the egg-slice. Thus we could speak before them both, without the least constraint; and indeed he helped us much by his knowledge of the affairs of the family. Also two Justices of the Peace, who had signed the warrant for poor Chowne's end, upon the report of the doctors, but could find no one of strength and courage to carry it out, except Parson Jack; these sate with us to get their supper, before the long cold ride over the moors. And there sate Parson Jack himself, with his thick hands trembling, hopeless of eating a morsel, but dreading to be left alone for a moment.

"What a difference it will make in all this neighbourhood, to be sure!" So said one of their worships.

"Ay, that it will," answered his brother magistrate. "Since Tom Faggus died, there has not been such a man to be found, nowhere round these here parts."

"No, nor Tom Faggus himself," said the other: "a noble highwayman he were; but for mind, not fit to hold a candle to our lamented friend now lying up there in the counterpane."

Parson Jack shuddered, and shook his great limbs, and feigned to have done so on purpose; and then in defiance collected himself, and laid his iron hand on the table, watching every great muscle, to see how long he could keep it from trembling. Then I arose and grasped his hand—for nobody else understood him at all—and he let me take it with reluctance, wonder, and then deep gratitude. He had been saying to himself—as I knew, though his lips never moved; and his face was set, in scorn of all our moralising—within himself he had been thinking, "I am Jack Ketch; I am worse; I am Cain. I have murdered my own dear brother."

And I, who had seen him brand his bitten arm with the red hot poker, laying the glowing iron on, until the blood hissed out at it, I alone could gage the strength of heart that now enabled him to answer my grasp with his poor scorched arm, and to show his great tears, and check them.

Enough of this, I cannot stand these melancholy subjects. A man of irreproachable life, with a tendency towards gaiety, never must allow his feelings to play ducks and drakes with him. If the justice of the Almighty fell upon Chowne—as I said it would—let Chowne die, and let us hope that his soul was not past praying for. It is not my place to be wretched, because the biggest villain I ever knew showed his wit by dying of a disease which gave him power to snap at the very devil, when in the fulness of time he should come thirsting to lay hold of him. And but for my purpose of proving how purely justice does come home to us, well contented would I be to say no more about him. Why had he been such a villain through life? Because he was an impostor. Why did he die of rabid madness, under the clutch of his own best friend? Because he lashed his favourite hound to fly at the throat of his own grandfather.

Not only does it confirm one's faith in the honesty of breeding, but it enables me to acquit all the Chownes of Devonshire —and a fine and wholesome race they are—of ever having produced such a scamp, in true course of legitimacy; also enables me not to point out, so much as to leave all my readers to think of, the humble yet undeniable traces of old Davy's sagacity.

What had I said to Mrs Steelyard, when she overbore me so, upon an empty stomach? "Madam," I said, "your son, you mean!" And it proved to be one of my famous hits, at a range beyond that of other men. When great stirs happen, truth comes out ; as an earthquake starts the weasels.

Everybody knows what fine old age those wandering gypsies come to. The two most killing cares we have, are money, and reputation. Here behold gypsy wisdom! The disregard of the latter of the two does away with the plague of the former. They take what they want ; while we clumsy fellows toil for the cash as the only way to get the good estimation. Hence it was that Chowne's grandfather came about stealing as lively as ever, at the age of ninety. A wiry and leathery man he was, and had once been a famous conjurer. And now in his old age he came to sleep in his grandson's barn, and to live on his grandson's ducks, potatoes, and pigeons. This was last harvest-time, just as Chowne was enjoying his bit of cub-hunting.

Turning in from his sport one day, in a very sulky humour, with the hounds he was educating, the Parson caught his grandfather withdrawing in a quiet manner from a snug little hen-roost. Not knowing who it was (for his mother had never explained a thing to him, not even that she was his mother), he thought it below his dignity to ride after this old fellow. But at his heels stalked a tall young hound, who had vexed him all day by surliness, and was now whipped in for punishment.

"At him—'loo boy!" he called out ; "Hike forrard, catch him by the leg, boy!" But the hound only showed his teeth and snarled ; so that Chowne let out his long lash at him. In a moment the dog sprang at his master who was riding a low cob-horse, and bit him in the thigh and the horse in the shoulder, and then skulked off to his kennel. The hound was shot, and the horse shared his fate in less than six weeks afterwards ; and as for the Parson, we know too well what they were forced to do with him.

In her first horror, that stony woman, even Mrs Steelyard, when her son came ravening at her, could not keep her secret. "It is the judgment of God," she cried ; "after all there is a God. He set the dogs at his grandfather, and now he would bite his own mother!"

How she had managed to place him in the stead of the real Chowne heir, I never heard, or at least no clear account of it ; for she was not (as we know already) one who would answer questions. Let him rest, whoever he was. His end was bad enough, even for him.

Enough of this fright—for it was a fright even to me, I assure you—let us come back to the innocent people injured so long by his villany.

To begin with Parson Jack. Never in all his life had he taken a stroke towards his own salvation, until by that horrible job he earned repentance, fear, and conscience. And not only this (for none of these would have stood him in any service, with Chowne still at his elbow), but that the face,—which had drawn him for years, like a loadstone of hell, to destruction,—now ever present in its terror, till his prayers got rid of it, shone in the dark like the face of a scarecrow, if ever he durst think of wickedness. His wife found the benefit of this change, and so did his growing family, and so did the people who flocked to his church, in the pleasure of being afraid of him. In the roads, he might bite; but in his surplice, he was bound to behave himself, or at least, he must bite the church-warden first. Yet no one would have him to sprinkle a child, until a whole year was over. And then he restored himself, under a hint from a man beyond him in intellect; he made everybody allow that the poker had entirely cured him, by preaching from the bottom of his chest, with a glass of water upon the cushion, a sermon that stirred every heart, with the text, "Is thy servant a dog, that he should do this thing?"

I quit him with sorrow; because I found him a man of true feeling, and good tobacco. We got on together so warmly that expense alone divided us. He would have had me for parish-clerk, if I could have seen my way to it.

What prevails with a man like me, foremost first of everything? Why, love of the blessed native land—which every good Welshman will love me for. I may have done a thing, now and then, below our native dignity, except to those who can enter into all the things we look at. It is not our nature altogether, to go for less than our value. We know that we are of the oldest blood to be found in this ancient island, and we ask nothing more than to be treated as the superior race should be.

In the presence of such great ideas, who cares what becomes of me? I really feel that my marriage to Polly, and prolongation of a fine old breed, scarcely ought to be spoken of. A man who has described the battle of the Nile need not dwell on matrimony.

Hurried speech does not become me on any other subject.

Everybody has the right to know, and everybody does know, how the whole of North Devon was filled with joy, talk, and disputation, as to Commodore Bampfylde and the brightness of his acquittal. They drew him from Barnstaple in a chaise, with only two springs broken, men having taken the horses out, and done their best at collar-work. He would have gladly jumped out and kicked them, but for the feeling of their goodwill.

Nothing would have detracted from this, and the feasts that were felt to be due upon it, if Squire Philip had only known how not to die at a time when nobody was seasonably called on to think of death. But when he learned the shame inflicted by himself on his ancient race, through trusting Chowne, and misbelieving his brother out of the self-same womb; and, above all, when he learned that Chowne was the bastard of a gypsy, he cast himself into his brother's arms, fetched one long sigh, and departed to a better world with his hat on.

This was the best thing that he could do, if he had chosen the time aright; and it saved a world of trouble. Sir Philip felt it a good bit, of course; and so did Sir Drake Bampfylde. Nevertheless, if a living man withdraws into a shell so calmly, what can he expect more lively than his undertakers?

This was good, and left room for Harry, or rather young Philip Bampfylde, to step into the proper shoes, and have practice how to walk in them. Yet he was so caught with love of service, and of the Navy, and so mad about Nelson, that the General could not help himself; but let him go to sea again.

Nelson is afloat just now. The Crappos and the Dons appear to have made up their minds against us; and the former have the insolence to threaten a great invasion. If I only had two arms, I would leave my Polly to howl about me. As it is, they have turned me into a herring! Colonel Lougher has raised a regiment, and I am first drill-sergeant!

Our dear Maid of Sker would also give her beautiful son, only six months old, Bampfylde Lougher Bluett, to go to the wars, and to fight the French; if any one could only show her the way to do without him. He cocks up his toes, in a manner which proves that his feet are meant for ratlines.

How the war is raging! I run to and fro, upon hearing of Felix Farley's Journal, and am only fit to talk of it. Sir Philip comes down, with his best tobacco, whenever he stops at Candleston. And a craft has been built for me on purpose, by the old fellow at Appledore, and her name it is the "Maid of Sker"—to dance across the Channel, whenever a one-armed man can navigate. Colonel Lougher, and even Lady Bluett, have such trust in me, that they cross if their dear Delushy seems to pine too much for her husband. And the Maid herself has brought her son, as proud as if he came out of a wreck, to exhibit him to Moxy, and Roger, and Bunny, and Stradling the clerk—in a word, to all the parish, and the extra-parochial district.

Now I hope that nobody will ask me any more questions concerning any one, male or female. If I cannot speak well of a person—my rule is to be silent.

Hezekiah found his knavery altogether useless. He scraped himself home at last; and built a bellows-organ at Bridgend, with a 74-gun crash to it. His reputation is therefore up—especially since he rejoined the Church—in all churches that can afford him. Yet he will not always own that I was his salvation. Hepzibah prophesies nothing, except that Polly's little son, "David Llewellyn," will do something wonderful, to keep the ancient name up.

It may be so. And I think that he will. But his father never did it. How many chances have I missed! How many times might I have advanced to stern respectability! Yet some folk will like me better, and I like myself no less, for not having feigned to be more than I am—a poor frail fellow.

The children still come down to the well, with three of our Bunny's foremost; they get between my knees, and open blue or brown eyes up at me. In spite of Roger Berkrolles nodding to instil more manners, some of the prettiest stroke my white beard, coaxing for a story. Then they push forward little Davy, thinking that I spoil him so, because of his decided genius giving such promise of bard-hood—already it would do you good to hear him on the Jew's harp. Nevertheless I answer firmly, nine times out of ten at least—

"Little dears," is all I say, "Captain Davy is getting old. It is hard to tell a tale, but easy to find fault with it. You tell me that my left arm will grow quite as long as my right one, if I only will shake it about, and keep a hollow sleeve on. My pets, when I get another arm, I will tell you another story."

THE END.

www.ingramcontent.com/pod-product-compliance
Lightning Source LLC
Chambersburg PA
CBHW022057300426
44117CB00007B/496